Stiglitz and Walsh

PRINCIPLES OF MICROECONOMICS
Fourth Edition

The Most Modern Text for Principles of Microeconomics

Accessible and Student-friendly

Two of the most innovative researchers and educators in the field of economics, Joseph Stiglitz and Carl Walsh have written the most relevant, student-friendly Principles of Microeconomics text available. How? By giving students a text that is . . .

- Teeming with **applications and examples** from the New Economy, an economy in which students are active participants.

- **Accessible and interesting** in every paragraph.

- Always focused on the **five key fundamentals**: trade-offs, incentives, exchange, information, and distribution.

- Filled with thorough coverage of fascinating, can't-miss topics, such as Behavioral Economics, Basic Finance, Strategic Behavior, and Technological Innovation.

Accurate and Contemporary

Stiglitz and Walsh have also written the most satisfying text for instructors. How? By giving them a text that more accurately reflects their exciting and innovative field, while never losing sight of the importance of student readability and satisfaction, a text that . . .

- Contains substantial coverage of Behavioral Economics.

- Presents the most complete and accessible section on Imperfect Markets available.

- Thoroughly treats Imperfect Information within Imperfect Markets.

- Includes a full chapter on basic Game Theory/Strategic Behavior.

- Treats innovation and technological change seriously.

- Consistently emphasizes the importance of capital markets and finance.

Modern Organization and Approach

Stiglitz/Walsh has long been recognized for bringing a modern perspective to the Principles of Microeconomics course. The Fourth Edition continues that practice. Here are just a few of the key characteristics of the text that reflect its modern, realistic, and relevant approach:

Stiglitz/Walsh presents Perfect Markets in a complete unit early in the text.

Long sections on Behavioral Economics are found in Chapter 5, The Consumption Decision, and Chapter 9, Capital Markets.

Students are exposed to basic finance concepts in Chapter 9, Capital Markets.

Then, the crucially important subject of Imperfect Markets is pulled together in a full and complete section, which includes unique chapters on Imperfect Information in the product and labor markets.

The fundamentals of Game Theory are introduced in Chapter 14, Strategic Behavior.

Topics like the protection of intellectual property, which today's students confront regularly, are treated in Chapter 20, Technological Change.

Contents in Brief

Riveting Boxes That Highlight the New Economy Being Created by the Internet and Information Revolution

From Google, to eBay, StubHub, Napster, and online poker, the manifestations of the New Economy are changing the way we live, travel, spend our leisure time, shop, and work. Though the fundamentals of economics remain constant, how those fundamentals are utilized is changing, at an ever-quickening pace. Stiglitz/Walsh Fourth Edition recognizes this fact.

e-Insight
FINANCING THE NEW ECONOMY

We have seen how the capital market links households who save with firms that invest, so that saving equals investment at the equilibrium interest rate. But how do firms actually get their hands on household saving? The answer is that financial intermediaries such as banks and investment companies perform the function of transferring funds between households and firms. Their job is to make sure that the households' money is well invested, so that the households can get it back with a return.

Banks are perhaps the most important financial intermediary. In the nineteenth century, banks mainly lent money to firms to help finance their inventories. The inventories were held as collateral—that is, if the borrower defaulted on the loan, the lender could seize the inventories. Gradually, banks expanded their lending activities—for instance, to finance houses and commercial real estate, in such cases holding the buildings as collateral. The past decade's revolution in information technology has presented special problems to these traditional forms of finance. Today firms invest heavily in software and new ideas. If the idea does not pan out, the firm may

go bankrupt, but there is no collateral: there is little value that the creditor can seize.

In the United States, financial markets have adapted, and there now is a new form of financial institution—venture capital firms. Typically, the funds are provided by either wealthy private investors or institutions, such as universities, seeking high returns. The venture capital firms have developed expertise in assessing new ideas in the new economy—the most successful of the venture capital firms have an impressive record of picking winners. But they offer more than capital; they typically also give managerial assistance and take an active role in oversight. After providing the initial capital that enables a firm to get established, the firm supported by the venture capital firms typically "goes public"—that is, it sells at least some of its shares on the market. It is at this point that venture capitalists reap their gains.

While the first venture capital firms concentrated on Silicon Valley (the area surrounding Stanford University where much of the early development of computers occurred), more recently they have expanded their focus to other areas of the country and other sectors.

Table 9.1
YEARS OF SCHOOLING BY AGE

Age group (in 2003)	% with less than a high school degree	% with a high school degree but no bachelor's degree	% with at least a bachelor's degree
25–34	13	57	30
35–44	12	59	29
45–54	11	59	30
55–64	15	58	27
65–74	25	56	19
75 and older	33	52	15

SOURCE: Statistical Abstract of the United States, 2004
(www.census.gov/prod/2004pubs/04statab/educ.pdf).

EDUCATION AND HUMAN CAPITAL 205

Internet Connection
ECONOMIC DEFINITIONS

Keeping straight the terms *average cost, marginal cost, variable cost, diminishing returns,* and *economics of scale* can be difficult. Investopedia provides an online dictionary of economic terms at www.investopedia.com/dictionary/. Another useful source of economic definitions is the classroom page maintained by the Short Run (www.theshortrun.com/main.html).

Wrap-Up

THE FIRM'S COSTS: KEY IDEAS

1. Profits are equal to total revenues minus total costs.
2. Marginal cost is the extra cost of producing one more unit of output. Marginal cost normally increases at higher levels of output as diminishing returns set in.
3. Average fixed costs decline as output increases, but average variable costs eventually rise. As a result, the average total cost curve is typically U-shaped.
4. The long-run average cost curve traces out the lower boundaries of the short-run average cost curve.
5. Returns to scale: There are economies of scale if doubling all inputs more than doubles output, and when there are economies of scale, the long-run average total cost curve slopes downward. There are diseconomies of scale if doubling all inputs less than doubles output, and when there are diseconomies of scale, the long-run average total cost curve slopes upward. There are constant returns to scale if doubling all inputs doubles output; in that case, the long-run average total cost curve is flat.

Relationships between the cost curves

1. The marginal cost at output level Q is the slope of the total cost curve at output level Q.
2. The average cost curve is falling when the marginal cost is less than the average cost; the average cost curve is rising when the marginal cost is greater than the average cost. Consequently, the marginal cost curve always intersects the average cost curve at the point where average costs are at their minimum.

Production with Many Factors

The basic principles of the case with only two factors—one fixed, one variable—apply also to firms producing many products with many different inputs. The only fundamental difference is that the presence of many factors makes it possible to

146 CHAPTER 6 THE FIRM'S COST

---

by the firm: the company can try to make the workplace more attractive; it can try to make it safer; it can even try to lower the stress level of its employees. Such changes may affect the workers' level of performance. In choosing how to organize the workplace, firms consider the impact of their decisions both on productivity and on how much they will have to pay to recruit workers.

Today, much of the compensation a worker receives takes the form not of direct cash but of **fringe benefits**; these include health insurance, retirement pay, and life insurance. In recent years, fringe benefits have constituted an increasing share of total compensation.

Employers' reliance on fringe benefits rather than simply paying a straight salary to workers is largely explained by the tax code. If employees are paid income and then purchase health insurance on their own, they must pay income tax on the money. But if the company buys the insurance for them, the fringe benefit is not counted as income. From the firm's perspective, it costs less to provide workers with health insurance than to raise their wages enough to enable employees to buy the insurance themselves. In addition, many employers use fringe benefits as an incentive for employees to stay with the company. For example, firms often require that the employee remain with the company for a period of several years before becoming eligible for the company pension plan. Such benefits show that employers are not eager to lose their long-term employees, and would rather offer some added benefits than go through the cost and trouble of hiring and training new workers. But why—other than for tax reasons—they should rely so heavily on rewarding their workers through better fringe benefits rather than through cash bonuses remains unclear.

e-Insight
LABOR MARKETS AND THE INTERNET

One of the main *imperfections* in the labor market is that searching for a new job is costly. Information is imperfect and is expensive to acquire. Help-wanted ads play an important role in making the labor market work, but individuals in one city often cannot easily obtain current newspapers from other cities that might have job opportunities.

Employment agencies and government employment services have helped make the labor market work better. But the Internet promises a revolution in labor markets—or at least a vast improvement. Almost without cost, individuals can see the help-wanted ads in newspapers in other cities. Employers can post free help-wanted ads and can provide far more complete descriptions both of the job and of the characteristics of the employees that they seek. Eighty percent of the world's largest 500 firms use Web sites for job recruitment, as do more than 90 percent of American firms. Existing employment agencies (including government-provided services) have used the Internet to extend their scope, and new firms have been created. Much of the information relevant both to the employer and to the employee will still be obtained by face-to-face contact, during an interview, and this process will remain costly. Still, by lowering search costs, the Internet holds out the promise of enormously increasing the efficiency of labor markets.

MOTIVATING WORKERS 369

Internet Connection boxes provide useful links to Web resources and home pages.

e-Insight boxes apply economic principles to new developments in information technology and the Internet.

Additional Pedagogy to Heighten Student Interest

Thinking Like an Economist boxes reinforce the core ideas emphasized throughout the book: Trade-offs, Incentives, Exchange, Information, and Distribution.

Case in Point vignettes highlight real-world applications in each chapter.

Stiglitz/Walsh uses techniques designed to assist retention . . .

Fundamentals of . . . sections distill the essence of particularly important and tricky topics.

Wrap-Ups provide a short summary of the key points presented in the section.

Five Core Ideas are emphasized throughout the book.

Emphasis throughout the text on the five core ideas in Economics:

Trade-offs
Incentives
Exchange
Information
Distribution

---

goods also have the property of *nonexcludability*—that is, it costs a great deal to exclude any individual from enjoying the benefits of a public good. The standard example of a public good is national defense. Once the United States is protected from attack, it costs nothing extra to protect each new baby from foreign invasion. Furthermore, it would be virtually impossible to exclude a newborn from the benefits of this protection.

Imperfect competition, imperfect information, externalities, and public goods all represent cases in which the market does not produce economic efficiency. Economists refer to these problems as **market failures** and have studied them closely. The market "fails" not by ceasing to exist but by failing to produce efficient outcomes. Government *may* be able to correct such a market failure and improve economic efficiency. But before considering government policies to correct these failures, we first need to understand clearly how it is that market outcomes may be inefficient.

Though it describes an oversimplified world, the basic competitive model continues to provide important and powerful insights. For that reason, most economists use it as the starting point for building a richer, more complete model of the modern economy. This richer model is the focus of Part Three. In the next several chapters, we will examine how adding the complications of imperfect competition, imperfect information, externalities, and public goods to the basic model increases the ability of economics to explain our economy.

Fundamentals of Imperfect Markets 1

IMPERFECT MARKETS LEAD TO MARKET FAILURES

When the market is perfectly competitive, consumers and firms have perfect information, and there are no externalities (positive or negative) and no public goods, market outcomes will be efficient. When these conditions do not hold, markets are inefficient and there can be a role for government policies that lead to more efficient outcomes.

Imperfect Competition and Market Structure

When economists look at markets, they look first at the **market structure**—that is, how the market is organized. The market structure that formed the basis of the competitive model of Part Two is called **perfect competition**. For example, there are so many wheat farmers (producers) that no individual farmer can realistically hope to move the price of wheat from that produced by the law of supply and demand.

Frequently, however, competition is not "perfect" but limited. Economists group markets in which competition is limited into three broad categories. In the most extreme case, there is no competition: a single firm supplies the entire market. This

---

People, consciously or not, think about th... their decisions. Economists, however, bring t... tunity costs and sunk costs, marginal analys... enable economists to think systematically ab...

This kind of marginal analysis has come t... in policy discussions. For instance, the key is... tions and safety standards is not whether th... how tight they should be. Higher standard... marginal. From an economic standpoint, justification of higher standards hinges on whether the marginal benefits outweigh the marginal costs. Consider, for instance, auto safety. For the past three decades, the government has taken an active role in ensuring auto safety. It sets standards that all automobiles must meet. For example, an automobile must be able to withstand a side collision of a particular velocity. One of the most difficult problems the government faces is deciding what those standards should be. It recently considered tightening standards for withstanding side collisions on trucks. The government calculated that the higher standards would result on average in 79 fewer deaths per year. It calculated that meeting the higher standards would increase the cost of each vehicle by $81. (In addition, the heavier trucks would use more fuel.) In deciding whether to impose the higher standard, it used marginal analysis. It looked at the *additional* lives saved and at the *additional* costs.

Wrap-Up

BASIC STEPS OF RATIONAL CHOICE

Identify the opportunity sets.
Define the trade-offs.
Calculate the costs correctly, ignoring sunk costs, taking into account opportunity costs and marginal costs.

...decision making in the United States reflects... is appropriate and necessary for economic... believe that certain interventions by government are desirable. Like the appropriate balance between public and private sectors, the appropriate balance between concerns about equality (often referred to as *equity concerns*) and efficiency is a central issue of modern economies. As elsewhere, trade-offs must be made.

Wrap-Up

FIVE CORE IDEAS

1. *Trade-offs*: resources are scarce, so trade-offs are a basic fact of life.
2. *Incentives*: in making choices, decision makers respond to incentives.
3. *Exchange*: people benefit from voluntary exchange, and in market economies, market exchanges lead to the efficient use of resources.
4. *Information*: the structure that markets take and how well they can function depend critically on the information available to decision makers.
5. *Distribution*: markets determine how the goods and services produced by the economy are allocated to members of society.

The Three Major Markets

The market economy revolves around exchange between individuals (or households) who buy goods and services from firms and firms, which take *inputs*, the various materials of production, and produce *outputs*, the goods and services that they sell. In thinking about a market economy, economists focus their attention on three broad categories of markets in which individuals and firms interact. The markets in which firms sell their outputs to households are referred to collectively as the **product market**. Many firms also sell goods to other firms; the output of the first firm becomes the input of the second. These transactions too are said to occur in the product market.

On the input side, firms need (besides the materials they buy in the product market) some combination of labor and machinery to produce their output. They purchase the services of workers in the **labor market**. They raise funds to buy inputs in the **capital market**. Traditionally, economists also have highlighted the importance of a third input, land, but in modern industrial economies land is of secondary importance. For most purposes, it suffices to focus attention on the three major markets—product, labor, and capital—and this text will follow that pattern.

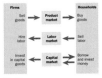

Figure 1.1
THE THREE MARKETS
To economists, people wear different hats. They are usually consumers in the product market, workers in the labor market, and borrowers or lenders in the capital market.

An Unmatched Media Package

Norton's innovative multimedia package provides everything instructors and students need to teach and learn essential economic concepts. Features include SmartWork (our new online homework management system), a Student Web site designed for quick review, and ready-to-go solutions for WebCT, BlackBoard, and in-class multimedia presentations.

NEW! SMARTWORK: NORTON'S INNOVATIVE HOMEWORK MANAGEMENT SYSTEM

SmartWork has three main advantages:

1. *SmartWork allows professors to assign smarter homework—*questions and exercises that go beyond multiple-choice. For every chapter, the instructor will be provided with 3 ready-made assignments. (You can either use these as-is or customize them.) The 3 types of ready-made assignments are

   - **Graphing Tutorials.** These graphs allow the student to move lines, curves, and points and to see the implications instantly and dramatically.

   - **Audio Graphs.** These slide shows allow the student to experience the material in a unique way. The student is taken through a lesson and sees economic equations worked out and graphs manipulated while hearing an audio presentation of the lesson.

   - **Conceptual Quizzes.** These quizzes pair questions with thought-provoking feedback. This feature asks students to reconsider their answer after they respond to a question.

2. *SmartWork gives students smarter feedback.* SmartWork's interactive feedback gives students just the help they need, right when they need it.

3. SmartWork provides professors with a smarter way to customize assignments, write their own assignments, and track student progress.

FREE STUDENT WEB SITE

All students have instant access to the powerful review materials on the Stiglitz and Walsh student Web site. Features include:

1 **Practice Quizzes with NEW! Diagnostic Feedback.** These multiple-choice review questions, when completed, give the student feedback as to which sections of the chapter they quizzed poorly on and should re-read.

2 **Chapter Reviews**—each Web chapter opens with a brief summary of the major points covered in the book chapter.

3 **Glossary**—taken from the book's glossary

4 **NEW! Economics Newsfeed**—updated daily and often hourly with new articles, this feature gives the student examples of how the concepts taught in this course are applied in the real world.

e-BOOK AVAILABLE FROM NORTONeBOOKS.COM

An affordable and convenient alternative to the print textbook, *Principles of Microeconomics*, Fourth Edition, is also available as an e-book. The Norton e-book format retains the content of the print book and replicates actual book pages for a pleasant reading experience.

Principles of

MICROECONOMICS

FOURTH EDITION

Joseph E. Stiglitz

COLUMBIA UNIVERSITY

Carl E. Walsh

UNIVERSITY OF CALIFORNIA, SANTA CRUZ

Principles of

MICROECONOMICS

FOURTH EDITION

W. W. NORTON & COMPANY
NEW YORK · LONDON

W. W. Norton & Company has been independent since its founding in 1923, when William Warder Norton and Mary D. Herter Norton first published lectures delivered at the People's Institute, the adult education division of New York City's Cooper Union. The Nortons soon expanded their program beyond the Institute, publishing books by celebrated academics from America and abroad. By mid-century, the two major pillars of Norton's publishing program—trade books and college texts—were firmly established. In the 1950s, the Norton family transferred control of the company to its employees, and today—with a staff of four hundred and a comparable number of trade, college, and professional titles published each year—W. W. Norton & Company stands as the largest and oldest publishing house owned wholly by its employees.

Manufacturing by R.R. Donnelley
Book design by Rubina Yeh
Editor: Jack Repcheck
Director of Manufacturing—College: Roy Tedoff
Manuscript editor: Alice Falk
Project editor: Lory A. Frenkel
Editorial assistants: Sarah Solomon, Mik Awake

Library of Congress Cataloging-in-Publication Data

ISBN 0-393-92623-0 (pbk.)

W. W. Norton & Company, Inc., 500 Fifth Avenue, New York, N. Y. 10110
www.wwnorton.com
W. W. Norton & Company Ltd., Castle House, 75/76 Wells Street, London W1T 3QT

1 2 3 4 5 6 7 8 9 0

ABOUT THE AUTHORS

Joseph E. Stiglitz is professor of economics, business, and international and public affairs at Columbia University. Before joining the Columbia faculty, he held appointments at Yale, Oxford, Princeton, and Stanford. Internationally recognized as one of the leading economists of his generation, Professor Stiglitz has made important contributions to virtually all of the major subfields of economics, in particular the economics of information, one of the key topics highlighted in this text. He was a co-recipient of the Nobel Prize in Economic Science in 2001, and earlier in his career received the American Economic Association's John Bates Clark Medal, which is given every two years to the most outstanding economist under the age of forty. Professor Stiglitz is the author and editor of hundreds of scholarly articles and books, including the best-selling undergraduate textbook *Economics of the Public Sector* (Norton) and, with Anthony Atkinson, the classic graduate textbook *Lectures in Public Economics.* He is the author of two influential popular books as well: *Globalization and Its Discontents* and *The Roaring Nineties.* In addition, he was the founding editor of the *Journal of Economic Perspectives.* Professor Stiglitz has also played a prominent role at the highest levels of economic policy making. He was a member and chairman of President Clinton's Council of Economic Advisers and later served as Senior Vice President and Chief Economist of the World Bank.

Carl E. Walsh is professor of economics at the University of California, Santa Cruz, where he teaches principles of economics. He previously held faculty appointments at Princeton and the University of Auckland, New Zealand, and has been a visiting professor at Stanford. He is widely known for his research in monetary economics and is the author of a leading graduate text, *Monetary Theory and Policy* (MIT Press). Before joining the Santa Cruz faculty, Professor Walsh was senior economist at the Federal Reserve Bank of San Francisco, where he continues to serve as a visiting scholar. He has also been a visiting scholar at the Federal Reserve Banks of Kansas City, Philadelphia, and at the Board of Governors. He has taught courses in monetary economics to the research department and staff economists at the central banks of Hong Kong, Norway, Portugal, Spain, and the United Kingdom, and at the International Monetary Fund. He is a past member of the board of editors of the *American Economic Review* and is currently an associate editor of the *Journal of Money, Credit, and Banking* and the *Journal of Economics and Business.* He is also on the editorial board of the *Journal of Macroeconomics.*

CONTENTS IN BRIEF

CONTENTS

CHAPTER 4 USING DEMAND AND SUPPLY 77

PART 3 IMPERFECT MARKETS 237

CHAPTER 11 INTRODUCTION TO IMPERFECT MARKETS 239

PREFACE

The study of economics has always been fascinating, yet it is difficult to remember a more exciting or important time in the discipline. Think of today's major economic issues—the huge American trade and budget deficits, global warming, the debate between proponents of conservation and energy exploration, ensuring adequate health care, ending global poverty, reforming Social Security, outsourcing, rethinking the nature of competition and regulation in the Internet age, and copyright protection in a digital, "downloadable" world. The list goes on and on. To understand these issues, the core insights of economics are invaluable.

Exciting new theoretical advances are allowing economists to understand better how individuals, families, and businesses make decisions about what to buy, what to sell, how much to save, and how to invest their savings. These advances affect the way governments design policies to protect the environment, to promote educational opportunities, and to deal with the changes in our economy brought about by technological innovations and the increasingly global economic marketplace in which we all participate.

There has never been a time when the need to be informed about economic issues has been more acute. Nor is it any less critical for students to acquire the tools that will enable them to think critically about the economic decisions they face in their personal lives and the issues they must decide on as engaged citizens. Even something as basic to the study of economics as the concept of trade-offs helps provide students with a tool that can inform the way they think about issues at the personal, local, state, national, and even global levels. Whereas the Principles of Economics course used to always be popular among business students, now most students realize that *everyone* should be conversant with the fundamentals of economics. We have written our book, and revised it for the Fourth Edition, keeping this concept of the politically engaged student in mind.

Preparing the Fourth Edition of this textbook has provided us with the opportunity to make several fundamental improvements over the previous edition. We still emphasize the five core concepts of modern economics, which are the importance of **trade-offs, incentives, exchange, information,** and **distribution.** Yet economic research is continuously yielding new, interesting, and important insights, and we believe that these exciting new developments should be conveyed to students in introductory courses. While the textbook has always offered the most integrated coverage of information economics, in this new edition we introduce students to new research in behavioral economics. We have also made several changes to the organization of the book that will give instructors increased flexibility in structuring their courses.

Mission Statement for the Fourth Edition

Our text has always strived for two goals: One, to be transparently accessible and interesting, dare we say a "good read," for the student reader; and two, to not shy away from teaching students the latest exciting insights of the discipline, to teach them the substance of economics as a field of study. Many books seem to take the stance that students cannot "handle" the new topics—we believe that it is just a matter of explaining the ideas simply and clearly.

To achieve these goals, the four main objectives of the previous editions continued to guide us. These objectives are to provide students with a clear presentation of the basic competitive model; to present macroeconomics in its modern form, consistent with the way active researchers and economists in policy-making institutions analyze the economy; to structure the textbook in ways that are conducive to good teaching and to student learning; and to ensure that the textbook reflects the contemporary scene, stressing the core insights economics provides for understanding the ever-changing economy.

Changes to the Fourth Edition—Microeconomics

The hallmark of this textbook, its emphasis on information, imperfect markets, innovation, and technology, remains in the new edition. New material on behavioral economics has been incorporated into the chapters on consumer choice and capital markets.

KEY CHANGES FOR THE FOURTH EDITION:

For the Fourth Edition, we worked hard to streamline the text. Chapters in earlier editions that many students found too long or too dense have been significantly restructured. In some cases, material has been divided into separate chapters, making the chapters shorter and more focused.

Important changes to *Principles of Microeconomics* include:

- Shortening the introductory section, Part 1, to provide a greater focus on the core concepts of economics.

- Splitting the material on the labor and capital markets under perfect competition into two separate chapters. This helps make the presentation more student-friendly and gives instructors increased flexibility in deciding what material to include in their courses.

- Reorganizing Part 3 to provide a more cohesive discussion of imperfect markets and public policy issues. Because strategic behavior is at the heart of the economist's approach to imperfect competition, the chapter on strategic behavior has been moved into Part 3 (Chapter 14).

 Reorganizing Part 4, now titled Issues in Public Policy, around the theme of public policy, rather than simply including a set of "topics." Part 4 includes chapters on the public sector (Chapter 17), environmental policy (Chapter 18), and international trade and trade policy (Chapter 19).

In making these changes, we have continued to be motivated by the desire to write a modern, student-friendly textbook that reflects the way economists approach their subject today.

The Organization of the Text

The text is organized to work for both the student and the instructor. For students, we utilize the five core concepts of trade-offs, incentives, exchange, information, and distribution throughout the text. These concepts anchor the wide range of topics we cover, linking them all to a core set of basic principles to which students can always refer. We also provide a firm grounding in basic concepts first, but we do not stop there. We ensure that students are able to understand both the tremendous insights offered by the basic economic model of competitive markets and its limitations. This prepares students to understand the lessons offered by modern economics for studying imperfect competition, information, growth, and economic fluctuations. We show how these modern insights help one understand economic phenomena that classical economics cannot. By exposing students to modern economics—from the economics of information and innovation to behavioral economics—the text helps them obtain a sense of the richness of the discipline and its value for understanding the world around them.

The text is designed to offer solid coverage of traditional topics, combined with a flexible structure that allows it to be tailored to fit with the individual needs of the instructor. The basic material of competitive markets is presented first. Then, the section dealing with imperfect markets begins with an overview chapter that allows students to gain insight into the basic institutions and key issues that are addressed in detail in subsequent chapters. This structure also allows an instructor who does not wish to devote too much time to a topic such as imperfect information to give students a sense of its importance and the lessons economists have learned about it. Finally, the topics chapters offer additional flexibility for the instructor in fine-tuning the readings from the text to the context of his or her course.

Learning Tools

We have developed a clutch of Learning Tools that will help our student readers relate to the principles being described and better retain the information.

1 RIVETING BOXES THAT HIGHLIGHT THE NEW ECONOMY BEING CREATED BY THE INTERNET AND INFORMATION REVOLUTION

From Google, to eBay, Expedia, StubHub, Napster, and online poker, the manifestations of the New Economy are changing the way we live, work, shop, travel, and spend our leisure time. Though the fundamentals of economics will not change, how those fundamentals are utilized is changing, at an ever-quickening pace. Stiglitz/Walsh Fourth Edition recognizes this fact.

e-INSIGHT boxes apply economic principles to new developments in information technology and the Internet.

INTERNET CONNECTION boxes provide useful links to Web resources and home pages.

2 ADDITIONAL TOOLS TO HEIGHTEN STUDENT UNDERSTANDING

THINKING LIKE AN ECONOMIST boxes reinforce the core ideas emphasized throughout the book: Trade-offs, Incentives, Exchange, Information, and Distribution.

CASE IN POINT vignettes highlight real-world applications in each chapter.

INTERNATIONAL PERSPECTIVE boxes present applications to international issues.

FUNDAMENTALS OF . . . sections distill the essence of particularly important and tricky topics.

WRAP-UPS provide a short summary of the key points presented in a section.

PRINCIPLES OF MICROECONOMICS, FOURTH EDITION e-BOOK

Same Great Content, Half the Price   The e-book version of *Principles of Microeconomics,* Fourth Edition, offers the full content of the print version, at half the price.

A variety of features make the e-book a powerful tool for study and review.

- **Zoomable images** allow students to get a closer look at the figures and photographs.

- **Clear text**, designed specifically for screen use, makes reading easy.

- A **search function** facilitates study and review.

- A **print function** permits individual pages to be printed as needed.

- **Sticky notes** allow students to add their own notes to the text.

Online and cross-platform software works on both Macs and PCs and allows students to access the e-book from home, school, or anywhere with an Internet connection. Visit NortonEbooks.com for more information.

Ancillary Package

An assortment of valuable supplements are available to students and teachers who use the textbook.

SmartWork Homework Management System   Developed in coordination with Science Technologies, SmartWork is an innovative online homework management system. SmartWork requires active learning from students and provides smart, interactive feedback. Instructors can choose from three types of ready-made assignments:

- *Interactive Graphing Exercises* allow students to manipulate points, lines, and curves, see the implications instantly, and then answer questions about them.

- *Audio Graphs* guide students step-by-step through a slide show presenting core concepts. On screen, students see economic equations worked out and graphs manipulated while hearing an audio presentation of the lesson.

- *Conceptual Quizzes* pair questions with thought-provoking feedback. Students are asked to reconsider their answers after they respond to each question.

With SmartWork's intuitive interface, instructors can also customize Norton's ready-made assignments or write their own exercises with remarkable ease. Access to SmartWork is free to all students who purchase a new textbook or e-book.

Student Web Site   This free companion Web site offers students powerful review materials. Practice quizzes feature diagnostic feedback indicating which sections of the chapter the student should review. The student Web site also provides chapter reviews, a glossary, and a daily economics newsfeed.

NORTON MEDIA LIBRARY

This instructor's CD-ROM includes PowerPoint lecture slides (corresponding to the lecture modules in the *Instructor's Manual*) as well as all the graphs and tables from the book. New **lecture-launcher audiovisual slide shows** provide brief segments on each chapter's material as it relates to imperfect markets or the new economy.

NORTON RESOURCE LIBARY

(WWNORTON.COM/NRL)

The Norton Resource Library provides comprehensive instructor resources in one centralized online location. In the library, instructors can download ready-to-use, one-stop solutions for online courses, such as WebCT e-packs and BlackBoard course cartridges, or can tailor these premade course packs to suit their own needs. The library's exceptional resources include PowerPoint lecture slides, graphs and tables from the book, and a computerized test-item file.

TRANSPARENCIES

A set of color transparencies is available to qualified adopters.

STUDY GUIDE

BY LAWRENCE W. MARTIN, *MICHIGAN STATE UNIVERSITY*
0-393-92826-8 • PAPER

This innovative study guide reinforces the key concepts of each chapter through reviews, practice exams, and problem sets designed to help students apply what they've learned. "Doing Economics" sections are structured around a series of "Tool Kits" in which students learn a problem-solving technique through its step-by-step application. Each "Tool Kit" is followed by worked examples and practice problems that apply the relevant technique.

INSTRUCTOR'S MANUAL

BY GERALD McINTYRE, *OCCIDENTAL COLLEGE*
0-393-92805-5 • PAPER

For each chapter of the textbook, the *Instructor's Manual* contains lecture advice, lecture modules, lecture applications, problem sets, and solutions. The extensive lecture modules can be used with a set of PowerPoint slides prepared by Gerald McIntyre. These lecture notes are far more extensive than what other publishers offer and will be extremely valuable to the first-time instructor.

TEST-ITEM FILE

BY DAVID GILLETTE, *TRUMAN STATE UNIVERSITY*
0-393-92840-3 • PAPER

The Fourth Edition *Test-Item File* includes over 4,000 questions, a 15 percent increase over the previous edition. In addition, each chapter includes a subset of questions covering the boxed inserts (such as e-Insights) that professors can use in their exams, thereby encouraging students to read these discussions.

Acknowledgments

The book's first three editions were improved immeasurable by the input of numerous reviewers. In particular, we thank Robert T. Averitt, Smith College; Mohsen Bahmani-Oskoose, University of Wisconsin, Milwaukee; Richard Barret, University of Montana; H. Scott Bierman, Carleton College; John Payne Bigelow, University of Missouri; Howard Bodenhorn, Lafayette College; Bruce R. Bolnick, Northeastern University; Adhip Chaudhuri, Georgetown University; Michael D. Curley, Kennesaw State College; John Devereus, University of Miami; Stephen Erfle, Dickinson College; Rudy Fichtenbaum, Wright State University; Kevin Forbes, Catholic University; K. K. Fung, Memphis State; Christopher Georges, Hamilton College; Ronald D. Gilbert, Texas Tech University; Robert E. Graf, Jr., United States Military Academy; Glenn W. Harrison, University of South Carolina; Marc Hayford, Loyola University; Yutaka Horiba, Tulane University; Charles How, University of Colorado; Sheng Cheng Hu, Purdue University; Glenn Hubbard, Columbia University; Nancy Jianakopolos, Colorado State University; Allen C, Kelley, Duke University; Lori Kletzer, University of California, Santa Cruz; Michael M. Knetter, Dartmouth College; Kevin Lang, Boston University; William Lastrapes, University of Georgia; John Leahy, Boston University; Eric Leeper, Indiana University; Colin Linsley, St. John Fisher College, Stefan Lutz, Purdue University, Mark J. Machina, University of California, San Diego; Burton G. Malkiel, Princeton University; Lawrence Martin, Michigan State University; Thomas Mayer, University of California, Davis; Craig J. McCann, University of South Carolina; Henry N. McCarl, University of Alabama, Birmingham; John McDermott, University of South Carolina; Marshall H. Medoff, University of California, Irvine; Peter Mieszkowski, Rice University; Myra Moore, University of Georgia; W. Douglas Morgan, University of California, Santa Barbara; John S. Murphy, Canisius College; Michael Nelson, University of Akron; William Nielson, Texas A & M University; Neil B. Niman, University of New Hampshire; David H. Papell, University of Houston; Douglas Pearce, North Carolina State University; Jerrold Peterson, University of Minnesota, Duluth; James E. Price, Syracuse University; Daniel M. Raff, Harvard Business School; Christina D. Romer, University of California, Berkeley; Richard Rosenberg, Pennsylvania State University; Rosemary Rossiter, Ohio University; David F. Ruccio, University of Notre Dame; Christopher J. Ruhm, Boston University; Suzanna A. Scotchmer, University of California, Berkeley; Richard Selden, University of Virginia; Andrei Shleifer, Harvard University; Nirvikar Singh, University of California, Santa Cruz; John L. Solow, University of Iowa; George Spiva, University of Tennessee, Mark Sproul, University of California, Los Angeles; Frank P. Stafford, University of Michigan; Raghu Sundaram, University of Rochester; Hal R. Varian, University of California, Berkeley; Franklin V. Walker, State University of New York at Albany; James M. Walker, Indiana University; Andrew Weiss, Boston University; Mark Wohar, University of Nebraska, Omaha; and Gilbert R. Yochum, Old Dominion University.

Many additional reviewers provided suggestions that help guide us in preparing the Fourth Edition. Our thanks to John Nader, Grand Valley State University;

Timothy A. Duy, University of Oregon; Richard Fox, Madonna University; Dale Cloninger, University of Houston, Clear Lake; Gavin Wright, Stanford University; Richard Stahnke, Hamilton College; Maristella Botticini, Boston University; Chris Niggle, University of Redlands; Santanu Roy, Southern Methodist University; Roger White, Franklin and Marshall College; Geoffrey Carliner, Boston University; Robert L. Pennington, University of Central Florida; Roger A. McCain, Drexel University; Nancy A. Jianakoplos, Colorado State University; Sudeshna C. Bandyopadhyay, West Virginia University; Jennifer Thacher, University of New Mexico; Alan Gummerson, Florida International University; Nejat Anbarci, Florida International University; Samuel Allen, University of California, Davis; Robert G. Bise, Orange Coast College; Sarah L. Stafford, College of William and Mary; Catherine Krause, University of New Mexico; Ariel Belasen, Binghamton University; Alina Luca, Drexel University; S. Abu Turab Rizvi, University of Vermont; Nivedita Mukherji, Oakland University; Faik A. Koray, Louisiana State University; Mehdi Haririan, Bloomsburg University; F. G. Hank Hilton, Loyola College; Michael Margolis, Oberlin College; Joseph K. Cavanaugh, Wright State University; Lisa Gundersen, Iowa State University; Eva Toth Szalvai, Bowling Green State University; Maya Federman, Pitzer College; Annie Fang Yang, University of Minnesota, Twin Cities; Molly Espey, Clemson University; Nora Underwood, University of California, Davis; Mary Schranz, University of Wisconsin, Madison; Scott Cunningham, University of Georgia; Ehsan Ahmed, James Madison University; Lee van Scyoc, University of Wisconsin, Oshkosh; Parker Wheatley, Carleton College; Daniel Rubenson, Southern Oregon University; Elliott Parker, University of Nevada, Reno; Peter Murrell, University of Maryland; Abdulhamid Sukar, Cameron University; Philip S. Heap, James Madison University; Erik D. Craft, University of Richmond; Sharmila King, University of the Pacific; Linus Yamane, Pitzer College; Cathleen Leue, University of Oregon; Daniel Monchuk, University of Southern Mississippi; Rik W. Hafer, Southern Illinois University, Edwardsville; and Ben Young, University of Missouri, Kansas City.

A particular note of appreciation is due Mary Schranz, University of Wisconsin, Madison, who provided detailed, thoughtful, and extremely helpful comments on draft chapters of the macroeconomics material. Her insights significantly improved the end product.

The major changes in the Fourth Edition and the improvements they represent are due in no small measure to the constant encouragement, advice, and enthusiasm of our editor, Jack Repcheck. Jack provided the perfect blend of critical feedback and positive reinforcement to encourage us at each stage of the process to strive toward our goals of accessibility and modernity, and to incorporate the latest insights from the forefront of economics in a manner that is accessible to students getting their first introduction to the field.

A special note of thanks continues to be owed Judy Walsh. Judy's knowledge of economics and her willingness to discuss ideas, make suggestions, and offer examples and encouragement have all contributed greatly to the improvements made to the Fourth Edition.

Alternative Course Outline

In the Fourth Edition, we have further improved the flexibility of the book, allowing it to be easily adapted to courses of varying length and objectives. **Part 4, Issues in Public Policy,** contains chapters that can be covered at the end of a course, time permitting, or integrated with the core discussion of microeconomics. Alternatively, instructors can selectively choose from among these topics and include them in a more traditional organized course. The following outlines, which represent only a small subset of those that might be devised, reflect the flexibility the Fourth Edition offers.

OUTLINE FOR A ONE-SEMESTER COURSE IN MICROECONOMICS

CHAPTER	TITLE
1	Modern Economics
2	Thinking Like an Economist
3	Demand, Supply, and Price
4	Using Demand and Supply
5	The Consumption Decision
6	The Firm's Costs
7	The Competitive Firm
8	Labor Markets
9	Capital Markets
10	The Efficiency of Competitive Markets
11	Introduction to Imperfect Markets
12	Monopoly, Monopolistic Competition, and Oligopoly
13	Government Policies Toward Competition
14	Strategic Behavior
15	Imperfect Information in the Product Market
16	Imperfections in the Labor Market

Plus any of the optional chapters comprising Part 4

17	The Public Sector
18	Environmental Economics
19	International Trade and Trade Policy
20	Technological Change
21	A Student's Guide to Investing

OUTLINE FOR A SHORT COURSE IN MICROECONOMICS

Part 1

INTRODUCTION

Learning Goals

In this chapter, you will learn

1 What economics is, and what the key concepts that define core ideas in economics are

2 What markets are, and which are the principal markets that make up the economy

3 Why economics is called a science, and why it is that economists often disagree

Chapter 1

MODERN ECONOMICS

The past decade has seen tremendous changes in the world economy. Many of these changes are linked to new technological advances that have transformed what the global economy produces, the ways in which many goods and services are produced, where they are produced, and how goods and services are transferred from the firms that produce them to the households, governments, and other firms that buy them. New technologies are transforming everything, from how airlines sell tickets to how automobiles are produced, from how we buy books to how we communicate with one another.

Like the industrial revolution of the eighteenth and nineteenth centuries that transformed first Britain and then other countries from agricultural to manufacturing-based economies, the information revolution of the late twentieth and early twenty-first centuries promises to transform almost all aspects of our daily lives. In 1999, in recognition of the growing importance of new, high-tech firms, Microsoft and Intel—the producer of the Windows computer operating system and the major producer of the microprocessors at the heart of personal computers, respectively—were added to the Dow-Jones Industrial Average, the most widely followed index of prices on U.S. stock markets. Though the booming stock market of the late 1990s that was driven in part by enthusiasm for new technologies came to an end in 2000, innovation continues to be a critical force in the economy.

But the old economy is still alive and kicking. Four of the five largest United States corporations in *Fortune* magazine's top 500 list for 2003 were traditional industrial firms—General Motors, Exxon, Ford, and General Electric. IBM at number 8 and Verizon Communications at number 10 were the only information or "tech" firms in the top 10. Hewlett-Packard was number 14 and Dell Computers was 36, but Microsoft managed to make it no higher than number 47.

So the old economy and the new economy coexist side by side. But it is not just the emergence of new software and Internet companies that represents the effects of new technologies. The way all firms do business is being changed, and their customers are being affected too. Assembly lines now rely on robots aided and controlled by computers. Car repair shops with grease-stained floors have been replaced by clean, quiet garages where computers diagnose a car's problems. The way we buy things is also changing. Whether an individual purchases a car, book, or CD over the Web; books a hotel or plane reservation; or even applies to a college through the Internet, the relationship between people and firms is evolving. New technologies are changing the way courses are taught, too—textbooks like this one have Web sites that provide students with help, with interactive exercises, and with links to news, policy debates, and the latest economic information. The address of the home page for this text is www.wwnorton.com/stiglitzwalsh4.

With such far-reaching changes, what insights and understanding does the study of economics have to offer? After all, the field usually looks to Adam Smith, an eighteenth-century Scottish professor of moral philosophy, as its founder. Smith published his most famous book, *The Wealth of Nations,* in 1776, a time when today's industrial economies were still overwhelmingly agriculture-based. It might seem unlikely that a theory developed to understand the factors that determine the price of wheat would have much to say about today's modern economy.

But, in fact, study of economics continues to provide a critical understanding of today's global economy. As Carl Shapiro and Hal Varian of the University of California, Berkeley, put it, "Technology changes. Economic laws do not."[1] The way we produce things, what we produce, and how goods are exchanged have altered tremendously since Smith wrote. Yet the same fundamental laws of economics that explained agricultural prices in the eighteenth century can help us understand how economies function in the twenty-first century The foundation laid by Adam Smith and built upon by generations of economists has yielded insights that will continue to offer guidance to anyone wishing to make sense of the modern economy.

Over the past two hundred years, economists have refined and expanded our understanding of economic behavior. By incorporating the role of information and technological change, they are now able to explain much more than was possible just twenty years ago, offering new insights into topics that range from why car dealers build fancy showrooms to how the factors important for encouraging the production of new ideas differ from those that encourage the production of new cars.

But what are these insights? What do economists study? And what can we learn from looking at things from the perspective of economics? How can economics help us understand why we need to worry about the extinction of salmon but not of sheep, why auto manufacturers advertise but wheat farmers don't, why countries that rely on uncoordinated markets have done better than countries that rely on government planners, and why letting a single firm dominate an industry is bad?

The headlines from some recent news stories involving the computer industry and the Internet illustrate some of the key issues that a study of economics can help illuminate.

- **"Bill to Curb Online Piracy Is Challenged as Too Broad,"** *New York Times,* June 24, 2004. A bill recently introduced in the U.S. Senate aims to restrict

---

[1]Carl Shapiro and Hal R. Varian, *Information Rules: A Strategic Guide to the Network Economy* (Boston: Harvard Business School Press, 1999), p. 2.

the illegal online sharing of music and other files. This proposed legislation represents just the latest development in the running battle between the companies that own the rights to the music and consumers who want to freely share music files. After all, it doesn't cost the music company any more to have a file shared by a thousand people than it does to have it shared by two. So why, many ask, should they have to pay for music files? The advent of digital music has made it possible for listeners to exchange copies indistinguishable from the originals. But if the producers of the music cannot earn a profit, they have less incentive to seek out and record new artists. Property rights—in this case, the legal right of the music company to charge for the use of its property—play an important role in market economics, and disputes over property rights aren't new. But the new information technologies have made trading this property much easier and raised new questions. As we will see, economics can tell us a great deal about the issues involved in these disputes.

- **"Internet Drug Trade Proves Bitter Pill for Canada,"** *Financial Times,* April 21, 2004. The Internet has changed the nature of the market for goods such as prescription drugs. Buyers in Florida can as easily have their prescriptions filled by a pharmacy based in California, or Canada, as by one in Florida. But why has this led to shortages of some popular prescription drugs in Canada? What will be the likely consequences for drug prices in Canada and the United States?

- **"Intel Cancels 2 Chip Projects,"** *San Jose Mercury News,* May 8, 2004. After spending as much as $2 billion on a new line of computer chips called the Itanium, Intel pulled the plug on the project. As the company decided whether to go ahead with the project, was the money already invested a factor? Firms are always concerned about costs, but economics gives critical insights that help us understand which costs are important and whether some costs, such as the $2 billion Intel had already sunk into the Itanium project, aren't.

- **"Ebay Bids and Buys Baazee,"** *The Economic Times,* June 23, 2004. According to a story on economictimes.indiatimes.com, the online auction company eBay purchased Baazee.com, an Indian online shopping company, for $50 million. The purchase extends eBay's network throughout Asia, adding to its current ventures in Hong Kong, Singapore, and China. By linking online buyers and sellers globally, eBay will enable a consumer in Sioux City, Iowa, to trade with someone in Bangalore, India.

- **"Oracle's Bid for PeopleSoft to Be Tested in Court,"** *New York Times,* June 7, 2004. In early 2004, the software giant Oracle announced that it was making a hostile bid to buy PeopleSoft, another software company. The U.S. Justice Department initially filed a lawsuit to block this takeover, arguing that it would reduce competition in the market for business software. Oracle was eventually allowed to take over PeopleSoft, but why does the government try to ensure that there is competition? What are the advantages of competition? What tools does the government use to promote competition?

- **"FASB Holds Meeting on Expensing Stock Options,"** *San Jose Mercury News,* June 24, 2004. Many tech companies, particularly those located in California's Silicon Valley, have used stock options to reward their employees.

ebay's purchase has extended consumers buys.

Internet Connection

TRACKING THE DIGITAL ECONOMY

Since 1998, the U.S. Department of Commerce has issued an annual report on the digital economy. You can find the latest report at www.esa.doc.gov/reports.cfm.

This mechanism grants the employee the opportunity to purchase shares in the company at a set price. If the company does well and its shares go up in value, the employee can sell the stock for a profit—a prospect that creates an incentive to work hard and help the company succeed. The Federal Accounting Standards Board (FASB) proposed new accounting rules requiring firms that offer stock options to report these as an expense, thereby reducing the firm's reported profits. The FASB argues that to do so would present investors with a more accurate picture of the firm's profits, enabling investors to make better decisions about buying stock in the company.

News headlines frequently focus on economic issues, and these six point to some of the key topics that economists study: the role of incentives and information, globalization and exchange, competition and government regulation, costs and business decisions. The study of economics will give you new insights into the news stories you see in the paper, it will give you insights into the world of business, and it will help you understand the world of economics you participate in every day.

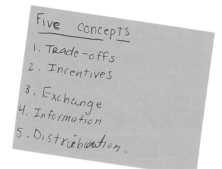

Five concepts
1. Trade-offs
2. Incentives
3. Exchange
4. Information
5. Distribution.

What Is Economics?

Headlines can illustrate many of the important issues with which economics deals, but now a definition of our subject is in order. *Economics* studies how individuals, firms, government, and other organizations within our society make *choices,* and how these choices determine society's use of its resources. Why did consumers choose to buy small, energy-efficient cars in the 1970s and large sports utility vehicles in the 1990s? What determines how many individuals work in health care industries and how many work in the computer industry? Why did the income gap between rich and poor rise in the 1980s? To understand how choices are made and how these choices affect the use of society's resources, we must examine five concepts that play an important role: trade-offs, incentives, exchange, information, and distribution.

1. Choice involves **trade-offs**—deciding to spend more on one thing leaves less to spend on something else; devoting more time to studying economics leaves less time to study physics.

2. In making choices, individuals respond to **incentives.** If the price of Zen MP3 players falls relative to the price of iPods, there is a greater incentive to buy a Zen. If the salaries for engineers rise relative to the salaries of people with an MBA, there is an increased incentive to choose to study for an engineering degree rather than a business degree.
3. When we **exchange** with others, our range of choices becomes larger.
4. Making intelligent choices requires that we have, and utilize, **information.**
5. Finally, the choices we make—about how much education to get, what occupation to enter, and what goods and service to buy—determine the **distribution** of wealth and income in our society.

These five concepts define the core ideas that are critical to understanding economics. They also guide the way economists think about issues and problems. Learning to "think like an economist" means learning how to discover the trade-offs and incentives faced, the implications of exchange, the role of information, and the consequences for distribution. These key concepts are emphasized throughout the text in "Thinking Like an Economist" boxes.

TRADE-OFFS

Each of us is constantly making choices—students decide to study at the library rather than in the dorm, to have pizza rather than sushi, to go to college rather than work full-time. Societies, too, make choices—to preserve open spaces rather than provide more housing, to produce computers and import televisions rather than produce televisions and import computers, to cut taxes rather than increase government expenditures. In some cases, individuals or governments explicitly make these choices. You decided to study economics rather than some other subject. The government decides each year whether to cut taxes or to increase spending. In other cases, however, the choices were the result of the uncoordinated actions of millions of individuals. Neither the government nor any one individual decided that the United States would import cars from Japan and export wheat to India. But in each case, choice involves trade-offs—to get more of one thing involves having less of something else. We are forced to make trade-offs because of **scarcity.**

Scarcity figures prominently in economics; choices matter because resources are scarce. For most of us, our limited income forces us to make choices. We cannot afford everything we might want. Spending more on rent leaves less available for clothes and entertainment. Getting a sunroof on a new car may mean forgoing leather seats to stay within a fixed budget. Limited income is not the only reason we are forced to make trade-offs. Time is also a scarce resource, and even the wealthiest individual must decide what expensive toy to play with each day. When we take time into account, we realize scarcity is a fact of life for everyone.

One of the most important points on which economists agree concerns the critical role of scarcity. We can summarize this point as follows: *There is no free lunch. Having more of one thing requires giving up something else. Scarcity means that* trade-offs *are a basic fact of life.*

Scare resources
• Limited income
• time

INCENTIVES

It is one thing to say we all face trade-offs in the choices we make. It is quite another to understand how individuals and firms make choices and how those choices might change as economic circumstances change. If new technologies are developed, will firms decide to increase or decrease the amount of labor they employ? If the price of gasoline rises, will individuals decide to buy different types of automobiles?

When faced with a choice, people evaluate the pros and cons of the different options. In deciding what to eat for dinner tonight, you and your roommates might weigh the advantages and disadvantages of having a frozen pizza again over going out for sushi. Similarly, a firm evaluates the pros and cons of its alternatives in terms of the effects different choices will have on its profits. For example, a retail chain deciding on the location for a new store must weigh the relative advantages of different locations. One location might have more foot traffic but also higher rent. Another location might be less desirable but have lower rent.

When decision makers systematically weigh the pros and cons of the alternatives they face, we can predict how they will respond to changing economic conditions. Higher gas prices raise the cost of driving, but the cost of driving a fuel-efficient car rises less than the cost of driving a sports utility vehicle. Therefore, households weighing a car purchase have a greater incentive to choose the fuel-efficient car. If a firm starts selling more of its goods through the Internet, it will rely less on foot traffic into its retail store. This shift reduces its incentive to pay a high rent for a good location.

Economists analyze choices by focusing on incentives. In an economic context, incentives are benefits (including reduced costs) that motivate a decision maker in favor of a particular choice. Many things can affect incentives, but among the most important are *prices*. If the price of gasoline rises, people have a greater incentive to drive less. If the price of MP3 players falls, people have a greater incentive to buy one. When the price of a good rises, firms are induced to produce more of that good, in order to increase their profits. If a resource used in production, such as labor or equipment, becomes more expensive, firms have an incentive to find new methods of production that economize on that resource. Incentives also are affected by the return people expect to earn from different activities. If the income of college graduates rises relative to that of people with only a high school diploma, people have a greater incentive to attend college.

When economists study the behavior of people or firms, they look at the incentives being faced. Sometimes these incentives are straightforward. Increasing the number of courses required to major in biology reduces the incentive to pick that major. In other circumstances, they may not be so obvious. For example, building safer cars may create incentives to drive faster. Identifying the incentives, and disincentives, to take different actions is one of the first things economists do when they want to understand the choices individuals or firms make.

Decision makers respond to incentives; for understanding choices, incentives matter.

Trade-offs and Incentives in Practice: Online Music Sharing Since 1999, when Napster introduced the first file-sharing program that allowed users to swap music files over the Internet, the practice has been embroiled in controversy. On one side is the music industry, which views the sharing of music files as an illegal activity, and on the other side are the companies producing the software that allows file sharing and the millions of music lovers who do not want to pay for music. The debates now also encompass the movie industry, as digitized movies can be shared as easily as music files. The legal battle between MGM and Grokster, a distributor of peer-to-peer file-sharing software, reached the United States Supreme Court in 2005.

Incentives are at the heart of the case against file sharing. Record companies make money by selling CDs. They, or the artists who create the music, hold copyrights that give them the right to charge others for its use. Copyrighted material, which includes books like this text as well as music, cannot be distributed or sold without the permission of the copyright holder. In that way, the holder of the copyright—the book publisher, author, artist, composer, or record company—is able to limit access to the material and charge a fee for its use. When music could only be copied by physically duplicating a tape recording or burning a CD, it was costly to make illegal copies. While people might burn a CD to use in the car or give to a friend, this type of sharing was relatively minor, and something the music industry tolerated.

The advent of digital music changed the situation dramatically. Now, a music file can be shared with millions of other listeners. In 1999, Napster introduced a file-sharing service that focused exclusively on music. In the process, Napster helped to popularize the MP3 format; by February 2001 the service had over 26 million users worldwide. Napster also quickly attracted the attention of the record companies, who sued Napster for distributing copyrighted music without paying royalties to the copyright holders. In 2001, Napster settled the lawsuit, agreeing to pay $26 million to the music copyright holders. Faced with paying this huge fee, Napster declared bankruptcy in 2002. It has recently converted itself to a subscription service for downloading music legally.

Thinking Like an Economist

INCENTIVES AND THE PRICE OF AOL

Today, most online services such as AOL charge their customers a fixed monthly fee for Internet access. In the earlier days of the Internet, the access charge was commonly based on how many minutes the member was connected to the Internet. In 1997, AOL announced that it would change its pricing policy and move to a flat monthly fee with unlimited minutes of connect time. AOL's servers were quickly overwhelmed and members found it almost impossible to log on. Why? Because charges were no longer based on the number of minutes a member was logged on, many customers never logged off. Once connected, they simply left AOL running, tying up its modem capacity. When members had to pay on a per-minute basis, they had an incentive to log off when the service was not being used. The flat fee left no incentive to economize on connect time. Thinking about incentives would have shown AOL that it needed to greatly increase its modem capacity *before* announcing the new pricing plan.

Napster's place has been taken by services such as Grokster and Morpheus that offer peer-to-peer (p2p) file sharing. In their legal battles with the music industry, these services have argued that they should not be held liable simply becuse their products might be used to duplicate copyrighted materials illegally. However, in July 2005, the U.S. Supreme Court ruled that the services could be found liable because they knowingly promoted products that were designed to infringe on the rights of copyright holders and did nothing to disourage this illegal activity.

So how does all this relate to the concept of incentives? First, free music clearly creates an incentive for music lovers to download songs rather than pay for them by buying a CD. This is at the heart of the music industry's opposition to p2p file sharing. Second, if record companies cannot charge for their music because it can be downloaded for free, they have less of an incentive to record new music. According to the record industry, by reducing the incentive to produce new music, file sharing will ultimately reduce the opportunities for new musicians to record with major record labels.

While the effects of free, online file sharing on incentives are clear, the magnitude of those effects is open to debate. The music industry points to a decline in CD sales, from 942.5 million CDs in 2000 to 766.9 in 2004, as evidence that the availability of free downloads has hurt their business. However, critics of the music industry argue that this decline in sales is simply a reflection of the economic slowdown and rise in unemployment that began in 2001. Some studies have argued that the availability of free music downloads might actually increase CD sales. Listening to music online can actually increase interest in new music and individuals who are able to listen to music online before buying an album may actually be more likely to purchase CDs. A study by economists at the University of North Carolina and the Harvard Business School was unable to find any effect of online access to music on subsequent CD sales.

Whatever the ultimate outcome of this battle might be, incentives are essential to understanding the issues. The incentive to avoid paying for music provided by low-cost or free access reduces the incentive of record companies to discover, record, and promote new musical talents.

EXCHANGE

Somehow, decisions that are made—by individuals, households, firms, and government as they face trade-offs and respond to incentives—together determine how the economy's limited resources, including its land, labor, machines, oil, and other natural resources, are used. The key to understanding how this happens lies in the role of *voluntary* exchange in *markets*.

Long before the rise of modern industrial societies, the benefits of exchange were well understood. Coastal societies with access to fishing resources, for example, would trade some of their fish to inland societies in return for meat and furs. The coastal group sought meat and furs that were worth more to them than the fish they gave up; the inland group likewise exchanged meat and furs for fish. Both groups benefited from voluntary exchange.

Today's consumers shop at both traditional markets and online markets such as eBay.com.

AUCTION SITES

An auction is one form of market that used to require potential buyers to be physically present in a single location. Now, auctions are held over the Internet and can involve participants from around the world. Some sites, such as eBay (www.ebay.com), offer just about everything for sale. Other sites specialize. For instance, Heritage Coins (www.heritagecoins. com) provides an auction site for rare coins. Even the U.S. government has gotten into the act. The U.S. Treasury does not actually auction items online, but it uses the Web to publicize the locations at which confiscated property will be auctioned (www.treas.gov/auctions/customs).

In modern societies, millions of exchanges take place. Few individuals produce any of the goods and services they themselves want to consume. Instead, teachers, police officers, lawyers, and construction workers sell their labor services to a school district, a city, a client, or a homebuilder and then exchange the income they earn for all the various goods and services they wish to consume that are produced by others. An important insight in economics is the recognition that *both* parties in a voluntary exchange gain. Whether it takes place between two individuals, between an individual and a firm, or between residents of two different countries, exchange can improve the well-being of both parties.

Economists describe any situation in which exchange takes place as a *market*. For thousands of years, societies have established physical locations such as village markets or periodic trading fairs where people have brought their products, haggled over terms of exchange, and reaped the benefits of trade. The economic concept of markets covers any situation in which exchange takes place, though this exchange may not necessarily resemble a traditional village market or a modern stock exchange. In department stores and shopping malls, customers rarely haggle over the price. When manufacturers purchase the materials they need for production, they give in exchange money, not other goods. Most goods, from cameras to clothes, are not sold directly from producers to consumers. Instead they are sold from producers to distributors, from distributors to retailers, and from retailers to consumers. All of these transactions are embraced by the concept of markets and a **market economy.**

In a market economy like that of the United States, most exchanges take place through markets, and these exchanges are guided by the prices of the goods and services involved. The goods and services that are scarcer, or require more resources for their production, come at a higher price. Automobiles are more expensive than paper cups; lawyers charge more than janitors. As a result, markets enable consumers and firms to make choices that reflect scarcity, and therefore lead to efficient uses of resources.

Market economies thus rely primarily on market exchanges to resolve the most basic economic questions: What and how much is produced? How is it produced? For whom is it produced? And who makes the economic decisions? Individuals and firms make the decisions. Individuals make decisions that reflect their own desires as they respond to the incentives they face. Firms make decisions that maximize their profits, and to do so they strive to produce the goods that consumers want at the lowest possible cost. This process determines what is produced, how it is produced, and for whom. As firms compete in the quest for profits, consumers benefit, both from the kinds of goods produced and from the prices at which they are supplied. On the whole, markets ensure that society's resources are used efficiently.

In some areas, however, markets lead to outcomes that society may find inadequate. There may be too much pollution, too much inequality, and too little concern about education, health, and safety. When the market is not perceived to be working well, people often turn to government. An economy such as in the United States is often called a *mixed economy*—one that relies primarily but not exclusively on the free interaction of producers and consumers to determine what is produced, how, and for whom. In some areas, the government makes the decisions, in others it imposes regulations that affect the incentives firms and households face; and in many areas, both the *private sector* (households and businesses) and the *public sector* (local, state, and federal governments) are involved (education is a good example).

Governments play a critical role in all market economies. For example, governments provide the legal structure within which private firms and individuals operate. No one would open a store if others could simply steal things off the shelf with impunity; the store owner needs to know there is a legal system that he can use to prosecute theft. No bank would lend money to a family to buy a home if it could not legally require the family to repay the loan. Governments also regulate businesses in many ways. There are regulations to ensure firms do not discriminate by race or sex, do not mislead consumers, and are careful about the safety of their workers. In some industries, such as education and mail service, the government is a major supplier of services. In other industries, such as the defense industry, government is the major purchaser. The government also supplies goods and services that the private sector does not, such as the national defense, roads, and currency. Government programs provide for the elderly through Social Security (which pays income to retired individuals) and Medicare (which funds the medical needs of the aged). The government helps those who have suffered economic dislocation, through unemployment insurance for those temporarily unemployed and disability insurance for those who are no longer able to work. The government also provides a safety net of support for the poor, particularly children, through various welfare programs.

One can easily imagine the government controlling the economy more directly. In countries where decision making is centralized and concentrated in the government, government bureaucrats might decide what and how much a factory should produce and set the wages that should be paid. At least until recently, governments in countries such as the former Soviet Union and China attempted to control practically all major decisions regarding resource allocation. Even in Europe, not long ago many governments ran oil companies, coal mines, and the telephone system. Increasingly, however, governments have sold these enterprises to the private sector, a process called *privatization*.

Market economies in which individuals and firms make the decisions about what to produce and how much to pay have proven adept at developing new technologies and products. It is hard to imagine government bureaucrats developing MP3 players or iMacs in neon colors. Markets also generally ensure that resources are used efficiently.

Exchange in markets is a key to understanding how resources are allocated, what is produced, and who earns what.

INFORMATION

Making informed choices requires information. After all, it is hard to weigh the costs and benefits of alternative choices if you do not know what they are! A firm that is contemplating the purchase of a new software system needs to know not only the costs of the various alternatives but also the capabilities and limitations of each. Information is, in many ways, like other goods and services. Firms and individuals are willing to purchase information, and specialized institutions develop to sell it. In many areas, separate organizations are designed solely to provide information to consumers. *Consumer Reports* is a prime example. The Internet also now serves as a major source of independent information for buyers. But there are some fundamental ways in which information differs from other goods. A car seller will let you test-drive a vehicle, but a seller of information cannot let you see the information before you buy. Once you have seen the information, you have no incentive to pay for it. Another way information differs from other goods is that unlike a can of soda or a bagel, information can be freely shared. When I tell you something, it does not subtract from what I know (though it may subtract from the profits I might earn from that information).

In some key areas of the economy, the role of information is so critical that it affects the nature of the market. In the used-car market, buyers and sellers negotiating over the price of a vehicle may have quite different information about its quality. The seller may have better information about the quality of the car but also has an incentive to misrepresent its condition, since better-quality cars command higher prices. As a result, the buyer will be reluctant to trust claims that the car is in perfect shape.

When consumers lack adequate information to make informed choices, governments frequently intervene to require that firms provide information. In the United States, we are all familiar with the mandatory nutritional information placed on food products. The Securities and Exchange Commission (SEC) that oversees American stock markets compels firms to meet certain reporting requirements before their stock can be listed on exchanges such as the New York Stock Exchange. Such reporting helps ensure that private investors have reliable information on which to base their investment decisions. Often, however, these regulations do not work adequately, as the Enron scandal in 2001 clearly illustrates. The oil trading company Enron had cooked its books to overstate its profitability in its mandated reports. One outcome of Enron's subsequent financial collapse was the introduction of new regulations designed to improve the reliability of the information that companies must provide to the public. Governments also regulate the safety of products. In the United States, the Food and Drug Administration (FDA) must approve new pharmaceuticals before they can be sold. The need for such oversight was driven home in 2005 when the drug manufacturer Merck had to pull its pain relief drug Vioxx off the market after studies suggested it increased the risk of heart attacks and strokes. Critics of the FDA argued that the agency is not adequately monitoring the safety of drugs once they are approved, and proposals have been made to establish a new government review board whose job it will be to decide when new information warrants removing a drug from the market.

Even in the absence of regulation, firms have incentives to signal to buyers that their products are of high quality. One way they do this is to offer guarantees that a producer of low-quality goods could not afford to offer.

Imperfect information also can interfere with incentives. Employers want to create incentives for employees to work hard. One way to do this is to base pay on a measure of how productive each worker is. Often, however, it is difficult to measure a worker's productivity. Under such conditions, it is difficult to link pay to performance. For example, a major debate in the United States concerns tying teacher salaries to performance. Because it is hard to measure teaching performance, the pay of most teachers is based primarily on how long they have been teaching.

Information, or its absence, plays a key role in determining the shape of markets and the ability of private markets to ensure that the economy's scarce resources are used efficiently.

DISTRIBUTION

The market economy determines not only what goods are produced and how they are produced but also for whom they are produced. Many people find unacceptable the way the market distributes goods among households. "While recognizing the efficacy of capitalism to produce wealth, there remains considerable unease among some segments about the way markets distribute that wealth and about the effects of raw competition on society."[2] Like bidders at an auction, what market participants are willing and able to pay depends on their income. Incomes differ markedly across occupations. Some groups of individuals—including those without skills that are valued by the market—may receive such a low income that they cannot feed and educate their children without outside assistance. Government provides the assistance by taking steps to increase income equality.

Steps that soften the distributional impact of markets may blunt economic incentives. While welfare payments provide an important safety net for the poor, the taxation required to finance them may discourage people from working and saving. If the government takes one out of every two or three dollars that an individual earns, that individual may not be inclined to work as much. And if the government takes one out of every two or three dollars a person earns from interest on savings, the person may decide to spend more and save less. Thus, efforts by the government to redistribute income may come at the cost of reduced economic efficiency.

[2]Alan Greenspan, speech at the Federal Reserve Bank of Kansas City Jackson-Hole Conference, August 25, 2000.

The primary reliance on private decision making in the United States reflects economists' beliefs that this reliance is appropriate and necessary for economic efficiency. However, economists also believe that certain interventions by government are desirable. Like the appropriate balance between public and private sectors, the appropriate balance between concerns about equality (often referred to as *equity concerns)* and efficiency is a central issue of modern economies. As elsewhere, trade-offs must be made.

FIVE CORE IDEAS

1. *Trade-offs:* resources are scarce, so trade-offs are a basic fact of life.
2. *Incentives:* in making choices, decision makers respond to incentives.
3. *Exchange:* people benefit from voluntary exchange, and in market economies, market exchanges lead to the efficient use of resources.
4. *Information:* the structure that markets take and how well they can function depend critically on the information available to decision makers.
5. *Distribution:* markets determine how the goods and services produced by the economy are allocated to members of society.

The Three Major Markets

The market economy revolves around exchange between individuals (or households) who buy goods and services from firms, and firms, which take *inputs,* the various materials of production, and produce *outputs,* the goods and services that they sell. In thinking about a market economy, economists focus their attention on three broad categories of markets in which individuals and firms interact. The markets in which firms sell their outputs to households are referred to collectively as the **product market.** Many firms also sell goods to other firms; the output of the first firm becomes the input of the second. These transactions too are said to occur in the product market.

On the input side, firms need (besides the materials they buy in the product market) some combination of labor and machinery to produce their output. They purchase the services of workers in the labor market. They raise funds to buy inputs in the **capital market.** Traditionally, economists also have highlighted the importance of a third input, land, but in modern industrial economies land is of secondary importance. For most purposes, it suffices to focus attention on the three major markets—product, labor, and capital—and this text will follow that pattern.

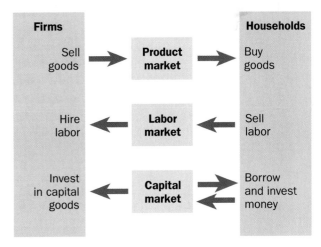

Figure 1.1

THE THREE MARKETS

To economists, people wear different hats. They are usually consumers in the product market, workers in the labor market, and borrowers or lenders in the capital market.

As Figure 1.1 shows, individuals participate in all three markets. When individuals buy goods and services, they act as *consumers* in the product market. When people act as *workers,* economists say they "sell their labor services" in the labor market. When people buy shares of stock in a firm, deposit money in a savings account, or lend money to a business, they are participating in the capital market as *investors.*

KEEPING TRACK OF TRICKY TERMS

Terms in economics often are similar to terms in ordinary usage, but they can have special meanings. The terms *markets* and *capital* illustrate this problem.

Though the term *market* is used to conjure up an image of a busy *marketplace,* there is no formal marketplace for most goods and services. There are buyers and sellers, and economists analyze the outcomes *as if* there were a single marketplace in which all transactions occur. For example, economists analyze the "market for books," even though the buyers and sellers in the market for books interact in thousands of individual bookstores and online selling locations.

Moreover, economists often talk about the "market for labor" as if all workers were identical. But workers differ in countless ways. In some cases, these differences are important. We might then talk about the "market for skilled workers" or the "market for computer engineers." In other cases—such as when we are talking about the overall state of the economy and focusing on the overall unemployment rate (the proportion of workers who are looking for jobs but cannot find them)—these differences can be ignored.

When newspapers refer to the *capital market,* they mean the bond traders and stockbrokers and the companies they work for on Wall Street and in other financial districts. When economists use the term *capital market,* they have in mind a broader concept that includes all the institutions concerned with raising funds (and, as we will see later, sharing and insuring risk), including banks and insurance companies.

The term *capital* is used in still another way—to refer to the machines and buildings used in production. To distinguish this particular usage, in this book we refer to machines and buildings as **capital goods.** The term *capital markets* thus refers to the markets in which funds are raised, borrowed, and lent. *Capital goods markets* refers to the markets in which capital goods are bought and sold.

Wrap-Up

THE THREE MAJOR MARKETS

1. *The product market:* the markets in which firms sell the goods they produce.
2. *The labor market:* the market in which households sell labor services and firms buy labor services.
3. *The capital market:* the market in which funds are borrowed and lent.

Microeconomics and Macroeconomics: The Two Branches of Economics

Economists have developed two different ways to look at the economy. The detailed study of the decisions of firms and households, and of prices and production in specific industries, is called **microeconomics.** Microeconomics (*micro* is derived from the Greek word meaning "small") focuses on the behavior of the units—the firms, households, and individuals—that make up the economy. It is concerned with how the individual units make decisions and what affects those decisions.

By contrast, **macroeconomics** (*macro* is derived from the Greek word meaning "large") looks at the behavior of the economy as a whole, in particular the behavior of such aggregate measures as the overall rates of unemployment, inflation, and economic growth and the balance of trade. The aggregate numbers do not tell us what any one firm or household is doing. They tell us what is happening in total, or on average. In a dynamic economy, there are always some industries expanding and others contracting. For instance, the economic expansion of the late 1990s saw rapid growth in Internet-related industries, while oil firms in Texas contracted. But there are times when overall growth in an economy slows and times when the level of economic activity actually declines, not just in an isolated industry but seemingly across all or almost all industries.

In macroeconomics, we also look at the behavior of the general level of prices, interest rates, and exchange rates. Why do prices of almost all goods and services seem to rise at rapid rates during some periods, while at other times they remain stable? Why do interest rates fluctuate? And what determines the value of the dollar relative to other currencies?

In approaching these questions, it is important to remember that the behavior of the economy as a whole is dependent on the decisions made by the millions of households and firms in the economy, as well as the decisions made by the government. Micro and macro perspectives are simply two ways of looking at the same thing. Microeconomics is the bottom-up view of the economy; macroeconomics is the top-down view.

THE BRANCHES OF ECONOMICS

Microeconomics: focuses on the decisions of households and firms and the detailed study of prices and production in specific industries.

Macroeconomics: focuses on the behavior of the economy as a whole and the behavior of aggregate variables such as overall employment, output, economic growth, the price level, and inflation.

The Science of Economics

Economics is a *social science*. It studies the social problem of choice from a scientific viewpoint, which means that it is built on a systematic exploration of the problem of choice. This systematic exploration involves both the formulation of theories and the examination of data.

A **theory** consists of a set of assumptions (or hypotheses) and conclusions derived from those assumptions. Theories are logical exercises: *if* the assumptions are correct, *then* the results follow. If all college graduates have a better chance of getting jobs and Ellen is a college graduate, then Ellen has a better chance of getting a job than a nongraduate. Economists make predictions with their theories. They might use their theory to predict what would happen if a tax is increased or if imports of foreign cars are limited. The predictions of a theory are of the form "If a tax is increased and if the market is competitive, then output will decrease and prices will increase."

In developing their theories, economists use *models*. To understand how models are used in economics, consider a modern car manufacturer trying to design a new automobile. It is extremely expensive to construct a new car. Rather than creating a separate, fully developed car for every conception of what engineers or designers would like the new car to be, the company uses models. The designers might use a plastic model to study the general shape of the vehicle and to assess reactions to the car's aesthetics. The engineers might use a computer model to study air resistance, from which they can calculate fuel consumption.

Just as engineers construct different models to study particular features of a car, economists construct different models of the economy—in words or equations—to depict particular features of the economy. An economic model might describe a general relationship ("When incomes rise, the number of cars purchased increases"), describe a quantitative relationship ("When incomes rise by 10 percent, the number of cars purchased rises, on average, by 12 percent"), or make a general prediction ("An increase in the tax on gasoline will decrease the demand for cars").

DISCOVERING AND INTERPRETING RELATIONSHIPS

A *variable* is any item that can be measured and that changes. Prices, wages, interest rates, and quantities bought and sold are variables. What interests economists is the connection between variables. When economists see what appears to be a systematic relationship among variables, they ask, Could it have arisen by chance or is there indeed a relationship? This is the question of **correlation.**

Economists use statistical tests to measure and test correlations. Consider the problem of deciding whether a coin is biased. If you flip the coin 10 times and get 6 heads and 4 tails, is the coin a fair one? Or is it weighted toward heads? Statistical tests will show that the result of 6 heads and 4 tails easily could have happened by chance, so the evidence does not prove that the coin is weighted. It also does not prove that the coin is *not* weighted. The evidence is not strong enough for either conclusion. But if you flip the coin 100 times and get 80 heads, statistical tests will tell you that the possibility of this happening by blind chance with a fair coin is extremely small. The evidence supports the assertion that the coin is weighted.

A similar logic can be used on correlations among economic variables. People with more education tend to earn higher wages. Is the connection merely chance? Statistical tests support the existence of a systematic relationship between education and wages.

CAUSATION AND CORRELATION

Economists want to accomplish more than just asserting that different variables are indeed correlated. They would like to conclude that changes in one variable *cause* the changes in another variable. This distinction between correlation and **causation** is important. If one variable "causes" the other, then changing the first variable necessarily will change the other. If the relationship is just a correlation, this may not be true.

During the 1970s, imports of Japanese cars into the United States increased while sales of U.S.-produced cars decreased. The two variables were negatively correlated. But did increased Japanese car sales *cause* the decrease in sales of American-made cars? Perhaps both were responding to a common factor that was the true cause of both the rise in Japanese car sales and the decline in sales of American cars. In fact, that is what was happening—the huge increase in oil prices after 1973 caused consumers to shift their purchases away from gas-guzzling American cars and toward more fuel-efficient Japanese cars.

Why Economists Disagree

Economists are frequently called on to make judgments on matters of public policy. Should the government cut taxes? How should Social Security be reformed? Should Internet commerce be taxed? In these public policy discussions, economists often disagree. These disagreements arise for two reasons. First, economists can differ in their views on the consequences of a proposed policy. Second, they can differ in how they evaluate those consequences.

When economists describe the economy and construct models that predict how the economy will be affected by different policies, they are engaged in what is called **positive economics.** When they evaluate alternative policies, weighing the various benefits and costs, they are engaged in **normative economics.**

Consider the positive and normative aspects of a proposal to restrict imports of textiles produced in developing countries. Positive economics would describe the consequences: the increased prices American consumers would have to pay for clothes, the increased sales of American textiles, the increased employment and profits of U.S. textile manufacturers, and the reduced employment among textile workers in developing countries. Economists might disagree over the consequences of restricting imports because they disagree over the magnitude of the effects, perhaps agreeing that prices to consumers would rise but disagreeing over the size of that rise.

In the end, though, the policy question is, *Should there be restraints on textile imports?* This is a normative question. Normative economics would weigh these various effects—the losses to consumers, the gains to U.S. textile workers, the increased profits—to reach an overall judgment. Normative economics develops frameworks within which these complicated judgments can be systematically made. Good normative economics also tries to be explicit about precisely which values or objectives it is incorporating. It tries to couch its statements in the form "If these are your values, then this is the best policy."

Economists, like members of any other profession, often have different values. Two economists might agree that a particular tax change would increase saving but would benefit the wealthy more than the poor. However, they might reach different conclusions about the desirability of that tax change. One might oppose it because it increases income inequality; the other might support it because it promotes saving. They differ in the values they place on the effects of the policy change, so they reach different conclusions even when they agree on the positive analysis of the proposed policy.

While economists may often seem to differ greatly among themselves, in fact they agree more than they disagree. When they do disagree, economists try to be clear about the source of their disagreement: (1) to what extent does it arise out of differences in models, (2) to what extent does it arise out of differences in estimates of quantitative relationships, and (3) to what extent does it arise out of differences in values? Clarifying the source of and reasons for disagreement can be a very productive way of learning more about an issue.

Review and Practice

SUMMARY

1. Economics is the study of how individuals, firms, and governments within our society make choices. Choices, and therefore trade-offs are unavoidable because desired goods, services, and resources are inevitably scarce.
2. Economists study how individuals, firms, and governments within our society make choices by focusing on incentives. People respond to changes in incentives by altering the decisions they make.
3. Exchange occurs in markets. Voluntary exchange can benefit both parties.
4. Making choices requires information. Limited or imperfect information can interfere with incentives and affect the ability of the private market to ensure an efficient use of society's scarce resources.
5. The incomes people receive are determined by the market economy. Concerns over the equitable distribution of wealth and income in the economy lead to government programs that increase income equality.
6. The United States has a mixed economy, one in which there is a mix of public and private decision making. The economy relies primarily on the private interaction of individuals and firms to determine how resources are allocated, but government plays a large role as well. A central question for any mixed economy is the balance between the private and public sectors.
7. The term *market* is used to describe any situation where exchange takes place. In the U.S. market economy, individuals, firms, and government interact in product markets, labor markets, and capital markets.
8. The two major branches of economics are microeconomics and macroeconomics. Microeconomics focuses on the behavior of the firms, households, and individuals that make up the economy. Macroeconomics focuses on the behavior of the economy as a whole.
9. Economists use models to study how the economy works and to make predictions about what will happen if something is changed. A model can be expressed in words or equations and is designed to mirror the essential characteristics of the particular phenomena under study.
10. A correlation exists when two variables tend to change together in a predictable way. However, the simple existence of a correlation does not prove that one factor causes the other to change. Additional outside factors may be influencing both.
11. Positive economics is the study of how the economy works. Disagreements in positive economics center on the appropriate model of the economy or market and the quantitative magnitudes characterizing the models.
12. Normative economics deals with the desirability of various actions. Disagreements in normative economics center on differences in the values placed on the various costs and benefits of different actions.

KEY TERMS

trade-offs
incentives
exchange
information
distribution
scarcity
market economy
product market
labor market
capital market
capital goods
microeconomics
macroeconomics
theory
correlation
causation
positive economics
normative economics

REVIEW QUESTIONS

1. Why are trade-offs unavoidable? Why are incentives important in understanding choices?
2. After a voluntary exchange, why are both parties better off?
3. As a commodity, how does information differ from standard goods? How do information imperfections affect markets?

4. Why might there be a trade-off between equity and efficiency?
5. What is a mixed economy? Describe some of the roles government might play, or not play, in a mixed economy.
6. Name the three main economic markets, and describe how an individual might participate in each one as a buyer or a seller.
7. Give two examples of economic issues that are primarily microeconomic and two examples that are primarily macroeconomic. What is the general difference between microeconomics and macroeconomics?
8. What is a model? Why do economists use models?
9. Give two examples of variables that you would expect to be positively correlated. For each example, explain whether a causal relationship exists between the two variables.

PROBLEMS

1. How does each of the following affect the incentive to go to college?
   (a) An increase in tuition costs
   (b) A fall in the interest rate on student loans
   (c) A rise in wages for unskilled jobs
   (d) An increase in incomes of college graduates
2. Characterize the following events as microeconomic, macroeconomic, or both.
   (a) Unemployment increases this month.
   (b) A drug company invents and begins to market a new medicine.
   (c) A bank lends money to a large company but turns down a small business.
   (d) Interest rates decline for all borrowers.
   (e) A union negotiates for higher pay and better health insurance.
   (f) The price of oil increases.
3. Characterize the following events as part of the labor market, the capital market, or the product market.
   (a) An investor tries to decide which company to invest in.
   (b) With practice, the workers on an assembly line become more efficient.
   (c) The opening up of economies in eastern Europe offers new markets for American products.
   (d) A big company that is losing money decides to offer its workers special incentives to retire early, hoping to reduce its costs.
   (e) A consumer roams around a shopping mall looking for birthday gifts.
   (f) The federal government uses a surplus to pay off some of its debt.
4. The back of a bag of cat litter claims, "Cats that use cat litter live three years longer than cats that don't." Do you think that cat litter actually causes an increased life expectancy for cats, or can you think of some other factors to explain this correlation? What evidence might you collect to test your explanation?
5. Life expectancy in Sweden is almost eighty years; life expectancy in India is close to sixty years. Does this prove that if an Indian moved to Sweden, he would live longer? That is, does this prove that living in Sweden causes an increase in life expectancy, or can you think of some other factors to explain these facts? What evidence might you collect to test your explanation?
6. During 2004, some economists argued that the Federal Reserve should undertake policies to slow the economic expansion in the United States in order to ensure low inflation. Other economists opposed such policies, arguing that the dangers of inflation were exaggerated and attempts by the Federal Reserve to slow the economy would lead to higher unemployment. Is this a disagreement about positive economics, or about normative economics? Explain.

Learning goals

In this chapter, you will learn

1 What economists mean by the "basic competitive model"

2 The role played by incentives, property rights, prices, and the profit motive in a market economy

3 About alternatives to the market system for allocating resources

4 About some of the basic tools that economists use to study how people make choices

Chapter 2

THINKING LIKE AN ECONOMIST

Economists have a distinctive way of thinking about issues, and the best way to learn economics is to understand how to think like an economist. Thinking like an economist involves focusing on trade-offs, incentives, exchange, information, and distribution—the five key concepts introduced in Chapter 1—and more. Economists focus on the choices individuals and business make when they are faced with scarcity. These choices can involve a decision to eat at home rather than to go to a restaurant, to go to college rather than take a job right out of high school, to locate a plant overseas rather than in the United States, or any of a thousand other alternatives. The choices made by individuals and business involve trade-offs and are affected by the incentives they face, the opportunities for exchange that are available, the information at hand, and the initial distribution of wealth. To understand choices, economists start with a simple model of how individuals and firms interact with one another in markets to carry out exchanges. This simple model is introduced in this chapter and developed further in Part Two.

The Basic Competitive Model

Every day, millions of people take part in thousands of exchanges in hundreds of different markets. Somehow, out of all these exchanges, computers are produced and end up in student dorm rooms, food is grown and ends up on the dinner tables of households, and electricity is delivered to millions of homes and offices at a flick of a switch. In an economy like that of the United States, markets play a critical role in ensuring that workers find jobs, things get produced, and firms sell their products. Exchange and the role of markets are important, but what makes them work? How can you be sure that your local grocery store will have bread in the morning or that your favorite café will have milk and espresso for your morning latte? And how can you be sure that the grocery store won't charge you $20 for that loaf of bread or that your espresso won't cost $10?

The answer can be given in one word—**competition.** When firms compete with one another for customers, they will offer customers the desired products at the lowest possible price. Consumers also compete with one another. Only a limited number of goods are available, and they come at a price. Consumers who are willing to pay that price can enjoy the goods, but others are left empty-handed. This picture of competitive markets, which economists call the **basic competitive model,** provides the point of departure for studying the economy. It consists of three parts: assumptions about how consumers behave, assumptions about how firms behave, and assumptions about the markets in which these consumers and firms interact. Consumers are assumed to be *rational,* firms are assumed to be *profit maximizing,* and the markets in which they interact are assumed to be highly *competitive.* The model ignores the government, because we first need to see how an economy without a government might function before we can understand the role of the government.

RATIONAL CONSUMERS AND PROFIT-MAXIMIZING FIRMS

Scarcity, which we encountered in Chapter 1, implies that individuals and firms face trade-offs and must make choices. Underlying much of economic analysis is the basic assumption of **rational choice:** that is, people weigh the costs and benefits of each possibility whenever they must make a choice. This assumption, in turn, is based on the expectation that individuals and firms will act consistently, with a reasonably well-defined notion of what they like and what their objectives are, and with a reasonable understanding of how to attain those objectives.

In the case of individuals, the rationality assumption is taken to mean that they make choices and decisions in pursuit of their own *self-interest.* Of course, different people will have different goals and desires. Sarah may want to drive a Porsche, own a yacht, and have a large house; to attain those objectives, she knows she needs to work long hours and sacrifice time with her family. Andrew is willing to accept a lower income in return for longer vacations and more leisure time throughout the year.

Economists make no judgment about whether Sarah's preferences are "better" or "worse" than Andrew's. They do not even spend much time asking why different individuals have different views on these matters, or why tastes change over time. These are important issues, but they are more the province of psychology and sociology. Economists are concerned with the consequences of these different preferences. What decisions can they expect Sarah and Andrew to make when each is rationally pursuing her or his respective interests?

In the case of firms, the rationality assumption is taken to mean that firms operate to maximize their profits.

COMPETITIVE MARKETS

To complete the model, economists make assumptions about the places where self-interested consumers and profit-maximizing firms meet: markets. Economists begin by focusing on the case of many buyers and sellers, all buying and selling the same thing. Picture a crowded farmers' market with everyone buying and selling just one good. Let's say we are in Florida, and the booths are full of oranges.

Each of the farmers would like to raise her prices. That way, if she can still sell her oranges, her profits go up. Yet with a large number of sellers, each is forced to charge close to the same price, since any farmer who charged much more would lose business to the farmer next door. Profit-maximizing firms are in the same position. In an extreme case, if a firm charged any more than the going price, it would lose *all* its sales. Economists label this case **perfect competition.** In perfect competition, each firm is a **price taker,** which simply means that it has no influence on the market price. The firm takes the market price as given because it cannot raise its price without losing all sales, and at the market price it can sell as much as it wishes. Even a decision to sell ten times as much would have a negligible effect on the total quantity marketed or on the price prevailing in the market. Markets for agricultural goods would be, in the absence of government intervention, perfectly competitive. There are so many wheat farmers, for instance, that each farmer believes he can grow and sell as much wheat as he wishes without affecting the price of wheat.

e-Insight

MARKETS, EXCHANGE, AND E-COMMERCE

In traditional societies, markets are places where people get together to exchange goods. They are active, bustling places, full of life. In the modern economy, goods and services are being exchanged *as if* there were a well-defined marketplace. The Internet has created a new kind of marketplace where people all over the world can exchange goods and services without ever getting together.

In traditional economies, prices for similar goods in different marketplaces could differ markedly. Traders would buy goods in a marketplace where they were cheap and then transport them to where the price was higher, making a handsome profit in doing so. These merchants helped make markets work better. Much of their high income could be thought of as a return on their information—on knowing where to buy cheap and sell dear. And by moving goods from places where they were valued less to places where they were valued more, the traders performed an important social function.

The Internet has enabled all of this to be done far more efficiently, at lower cost, with more complete information. Markets all over the world can be joined instantaneously, creating a global marketplace. Now any buyer (not just a merchant) can find the place where the good is selling at the lowest price, and any seller can find the place where the good is selling at the highest price.

Some have worried that the role of the middleman, of merchants, will disappear. But there is more to trade than just information about price. Many goods differ in a variety of dimensions, such as quality and durability. E-markets work best for well-defined goods, for which these issues are not relevant—goods such as wheat or steel, or products like this textbook.

(Later in the book, we will encounter markets with limited or no competition, like monopolies, in which firms can raise prices without losing all their sales.)

On the other side of our farmers' market are rational individuals, each of whom would like to pay as little as possible for oranges. But no consumer can pay less than the going price, because the seller sees another buyer in the crowd who *will* pay it. Thus, the consumers also have to compete against each other for the limited number of oranges in the market, and as a result each takes the market price as given.

While a farmers' market provides one illustration of what economists mean by a market, most markets do not take this form. Today buyers and sellers are more likely to interact over the Internet than at a farmers' market. But the same basic principles apply. When there are lots of buyers and sellers, each will take the price as given in deciding how much to buy or sell.

EFFICIENCY AND DISTRIBUTION IN THE BASIC COMPETITIVE MODEL

The basic competitive model, assuming it accurately represents actual markets, has one very strong implication: the economy will be efficient. Scarce resources will not be wasted. It will not be possible to produce more of one good without producing less of another, and it will not be possible to make any person better off without making someone else worse off. These results are obtained in the absence of any government activity.

Competitive markets also determine the distribution of goods—who gets to consume how much of the goods that are available. High levels of competition for the services of an individual with a rare and valuable skill will result in a very high income for that individual. On the other hand, competition among suppliers of unskilled labor may result in these workers earning very low wages, so low that even long workdays fail to win them a decent standard of living. This disparity raises the question of the fairness of competitive distribution. Though efficiency is a desirable property of any economic system, fairness is a separate issue that must be considered. Later in this book we will discuss how economists and policymakers approach the inequalities that inevitably emerge from the workings of the competitive market.

THE BASIC COMPETITIVE MODEL AS A BENCHMARK

Virtually all economists recognize that the competitive model is not a *perfect* representation of actual economies, but most economists still use it as a convenient benchmark—as we will throughout this book. After all, as you learned in Chapter 1, an economic *model* is never a complete and accurate description—it is not meant to be—but instead is designed to highlight critical aspects of the economy that provide insight and help us understand particular features of it. We will point out important differences between the predictions of the basic competitive model and observed outcomes, and in Part Three, we will show how this model can be extended to offer new insights into markets and situations that the basic competitive model cannot fully address. Differences between the predictions of the basic competitive model and observed outcomes can help guide us to other models that provide a better understanding of particular markets and circumstances. While the basic competitive model may not provide a *perfect* description of some markets, most economists believe that it gives us tremendous insights into a wide range of economic issues; for that reason, it is the foundation on which economists build.

Incentives and Information: Prices, Property Rights, and Profits

For market economies to work efficiently, firms and individuals must be informed and have incentives to act on available information. Indeed, incentives can be viewed as at the heart of economics. Without incentives, why would individuals go to work in the morning? Who would undertake the risks of bringing out new products? Who would put aside savings for a rainy day? There is an old expression about the importance of having someone "mind the store." But without incentives, why would anyone bother?

Market economies provide information and incentives through *prices, profits,* and *property rights*. Prices provide information about the relative scarcity of different goods. The **price system** ensures that goods go to those individuals and firms that are most willing and able to pay for them. Prices convey information to consumers about scarcity, and consumers respond by adjusting their consumption. Similarly, prices convey information to firms about how individuals value different goods.

The desire for profits motivates firms to respond to the information provided by prices. By most efficiently producing what consumers want, in ways that least use scarce resources, they increase their profits. Similarly, rational individuals' pursuit of self-interest induces them to respond to prices: they buy goods that are more expensive—in a sense, relatively more scarce—only if those goods provide commensurately greater benefits. If a good such as oil becomes scarcer, its price rises. In order to make rational decisions about how much heating oil to use, consumers do not need to know why the price of oil has risen. Perhaps a particularly cold winter has increased demand. Or perhaps troubles in the Middle East have decreased supply. In either case, the higher price signals consumers to reduce their purchases of oil products. If the price of home heating oil rises, that increase signals oil refineries to produce more heating oil. Prices provide the information that individuals and firms need to make rational decisions.

For the profit motive to be effective, there must be **private property,** with its attendant **property rights.** Under a system of private property, firms and individuals are able to own and use (or sell if they choose) factories, land, and buildings. Without private property, firms would not have an incentive to invest in new factories or new technologies, hire employees, produce goods and services that consumers want to buy, and earn profits. Even if the profits to be earned from building a new factory are huge, no firm will begin construction without the confidence that the factory cannot just be taken away. Firms need to be able to keep at least some of their profits to use as they see fit. Similarly, households need to be able to keep at least some of the return on their investments. (The return on their investment is simply what they receive back in excess of what they invested.) Property rights include both the right of the owner to use property as she sees fit and the right to sell it.

These two attributes of property rights give individuals the incentive to use property under their control efficiently. The owner of a piece of land tries to figure out the most profitable use of the land—for example, whether to build a store or a restaurant. If he makes a mistake and opens a restaurant when he should have opened a store, he bears the consequences: the loss in income. The profits he earns if he makes the right decisions—and the losses he bears if he makes the wrong ones—give him an incentive to think carefully about the decision and do the requisite research. The owner of a store tries to make sure that her customers get the kind of merchandise and the quality of service they want. She has an incentive to establish a good reputation, which will enable her to do more business and earn more profits.

The store owner will also want to maintain her property—not just the land but also the store—because doing so will enable her to get a better price when the time comes to sell her business to someone else. Similarly, the owner of a house has an incentive to maintain *his* property, so that he can sell it for more when he wishes to move. Again, the profit motive combines with private property to provide incentives.

HOW THE PROFIT MOTIVE DRIVES THE MARKET SYSTEM

In market economies, incentives are supplied to individuals and firms by prices, profits, and property rights.

INCENTIVES VERSUS EQUALITY

While incentives are at the heart of market economies, they come with a cost: inequality. Any system of incentives must tie compensation to performance. Whether through variations in luck or ability, the performances of individuals will differ. In many cases, the reason for high performance is unclear. The successful salesperson may point to his superior skill and effort, while his colleague may view him as lucky.

If pay is tied to performance, inequalities are inevitable. And the more closely compensation is tied to performance, the greater the inequality. The fact that greater incentives lead to greater resulting inequality is called the *incentive-equality trade-off*. If society provides greater incentives, total income is likely to be higher, but the gap between incomes will also probably be greater.

Society thus faces a basic question: How much would incentives be diminished by an increase in tax rates to finance a better welfare system and thus reduce inequality? And what would be the results of those reduced incentives?

WHEN PROPERTY RIGHTS FAIL

Prices, profits, and property rights are the three essential ingredients of market economies. Their importance is underscored by those cases in which property rights and prices are interfered with. Each example below highlights a general point. Whenever society fails to define the owner of its resources and does not allow the highest bidder to use them, inefficiencies result. Resources will be wasted or not used in the most productive way.

Ill-Defined Property Rights: The Grand Banks Fish are a valuable resource. Not long ago, the area between Newfoundland and Maine, called the Grand Banks, was teeming with fish. Not surprisingly, it was also teeming with fishermen, who saw scooping out the fish from the sea as an easy livelihood. Since there were no property rights, everyone tried to catch as many fish as they could. A self-interested fisherman would rationally reason that if he did not catch the fish, someone else would. The result was a tragedy: the Grand Banks was so badly overfished that commercial fishing became unprofitable.

Overfishing is just one example of what is called the **tragedy of the commons.** In the 1830s, an Oxford University economist named William Forster Lloyd explained why the commons—the pasture land in England that was not privately owned—was overgrazed. Because this land was freely available to all, each herder had an incentive to increase the size of his herd. As a result, the commons was overused until it was too damaged to support any grazing. When property rights are difficult to define, the tragedy of the commons is often addressed through international agreements. For example, Canada and the United States now have a treaty limiting the amount of fish that their fisherman can take from the Grand Banks, and in 1979 the Northwest Atlantic Fisheries Organization (NAFO) was established to manage fish stocks.

Restricted Property Rights In California, the government allocates water rights among various groups. Because water is scarce in California, these rights are very valuable. But they come with a restriction: they are not transferable. Water rights allow farmers to purchase water at much lower rates than the price charged to nonfarm households. What thirsty urban consumers would be willing to pay for additional water exceeds the profits from many of the crops the water is being used to grow. If water rights were transferable, farmers would have a strong incentive to sell them to California cities. Farmers could then switch away from water-intensive crops such as rice to crops that need less water. By selling their water rights, the farmers would be better off—the value of the water exceeds the value of the crops they are growing; urban residents would also be better off, because lower-price water would be available to them. A restriction on property rights—in this case, the restriction on the farmers' ability to sell—has led to inefficiencies.

Entitlements as Property Rights Property rights do not always entail full ownership or control. A *legal entitlement,* such as the right to occupy an apartment for life at a rent that is controlled, common in some large cities, is viewed by economists as a property right. Individuals do not own and thus cannot sell the apartment, but under normal circumstances they cannot be evicted.

These partial and restricted property rights result in many inefficiencies. Because someone in a rent-controlled apartment cannot (legally) sell the right to live in her apartment, as she gets older she may have limited incentives to maintain its condition, let alone improve it.

Incentives, prices, profits, and property rights are central features of any economy, and highlight an important area of consensus among economists: *Providing appropriate incentives is a fundamental economic problem. In modern market economies, profits provide incentives for firms to produce the goods individuals want, and wages provide incentives for individuals to work. Property rights also provide people with important incentives, not only to invest and to save but also to put their assets to the best possible use.*

Alternatives to the Price System

The price system is only one way of allocating resources, and a comparison with other systems will help clarify the advantages of markets. When individuals get less of a good than they would like at the terms being offered, the good is said to be *rationed.* Different **rationing systems** are different ways of deciding who gets society's scarce resources.

Rationing by Queues Rather than supplying goods to those willing and able to pay the most for them, a society could give them instead to those most willing to wait in line. This system is called *rationing by queues,* after the British term for lines. Tickets are often allocated by queues, whether they are for movies, sporting events, or rock concerts. A price is set, and it will not change no matter how many people line up to buy at that price. (The high price that scalpers can get for hot tickets is a good indication of how much more than the ticket price (*some*) people would be willing to pay.[1])

Rationing by queues is thought by many to be a more desirable way of supplying medical services than the price system. Why, it is argued, should the rich—who are most able to pay for medical services—be the ones to get better or more medical care? Using this reasoning, Britain provides free medical care to everyone on its soil. To see a doctor there, all you have to do is wait in line. Rationing medicine by queues turns the allocation problem around: since the value of time for low-wage workers is lower, they are more willing to wait, and therefore they get a disproportionate share of (government-supplied) medical services.

In general, rationing by queues is an inefficient way of distributing resources, because the time spent in line is a wasted resource. There are usually ways of achieving the same goal within a price system that can make everyone better off. To return to the medical example, if some individuals were allowed to pay for doctors' services instead of waiting in line, more doctors could be hired with the proceeds, and the lines for those unable or unwilling to pay could actually be reduced.

Rationing by Lotteries *Lotteries* allocate goods by a random process, such as picking a name from a hat. University dormitory rooms are usually assigned by lottery. So are seats in popular courses; when more students want to enroll in a section of a principles of economics course than the size of the section allows, there may be a lottery to determine admission. Like queue systems, lotteries are thought to be fair because everyone has an equal chance. However, they are also inefficient, because the scarce resources do not go to the individual or firm who is willing and able to pay (and therefore values them) the most.

Rationing by Coupons Most governments in wartime use *coupon rationing.* People are allowed so many gallons of gasoline, so many pounds of sugar, and so much flour each month. To get the good, consumers must pay the market price *and* produce a coupon.

Coupon systems take two forms, depending on whether coupons are tradable or not. Coupons that are not tradable give rise to the same inefficiency that occurs with most of the other nonprice systems—goods do not in general go to the individuals who are willing and able to pay the most. Moreover, the inability to legally trade coupons creates strong incentives for the establishment of a *black market,* an illegal market in which the goods or the coupons for goods are traded.

---

[1]So why are concert tickets rationed by queues rather than by price? The musicians and concert promoters could increase their profits by raising the ticket price, but consider the situation of a popular musician who is concerned with both concert income and income from CD sales. Allocating tickets by queue favors those with the most free time and helps ensure that tickets go to the musician's core fans—particularly those who are younger, who have less money to spend. These fans may be the most likely to buy CDs, and CD sales depend heavily on word-of-mouth advertising. So by ensuring that her core fans are not priced out of concerts, a musician may actually end up increasing her profits.

Opportunity Sets and Trade-offs

Market economic systems leave to individuals and firms the question of what to consume and what to produce. How are these decisions made?

For a rational individual or firm, the first step in the economic analysis of any choice is to identify what is possible—what economists call the **opportunity set,** which is simply the group of available options. If you want a sandwich and have only tuna fish and cheese in the refrigerator, then your opportunity set consists of a tuna fish sandwich, a cheese sandwich, a tuna and cheese sandwich, or no sandwich. A ham sandwich is out of the question. Defining the limitations facing an individual or firm is a critical step in any analysis of choice. You can spend time yearning after the ham sandwich, or anything else outside the opportunity set, but when it comes to making decisions, only what is within the opportunity set is relevant.

So the first step in analyzing choice is to identify what is within the opportunity set.

BUDGET AND TIME CONSTRAINTS

Constraints limit choice and define the opportunity set. In most economic situations, the constraints that limit a person's choices—that is, those constraints that actually are relevant—are time and money. Opportunity sets whose constraints are imposed by money are referred to as **budget constraints;** opportunity sets whose constraints are prescribed by time are called **time constraints.** A billionaire may feel his choices are limited not by money but by time, while the limits for an unemployed worker are set by lack of money rather than lack of time.

The budget constraint defines a typical opportunity set. Consider the budget constraint of Michelle, who has decided to spend $120 on either CDs or DVDs. A CD costs $10, a DVD $20. So Michelle can buy 12 CDs *or* 6 DVDs; or 8 CDs and 2 DVDs; or 4 CDs and 4 DVDs. The various possibilities are set forth in Table 2.1. They are also depicted graphically in Figure 2.1.[2] Along the vertical axis, we measure the number of CDs purchased, and along the horizontal axis, we measure the number of DVDs. The line marked B_1B_2 is Michelle's budget constraint. The extreme cases, in which Michelle buys only DVDs or only CDs, are represented by the points B_1 and B_2, respectively. The dots between these two points, along the budget constraint, represent the other possible combinations. The cost of each combination of CDs and DVDs must add up to $120. If Michelle decides to buy more DVDs, she will have to settle for fewer CDs. The point actually chosen by Michelle is labeled E, where she purchases 6 CDs (for $60) and 3 DVDs (for $60).

Michelle's budget constraint is the line that defines the outer limits of her opportunity set. But the whole opportunity set is larger. It also includes all points below the budget constraint—in the figure, the shaded area. The budget constraint shows the maximum number of DVDs Michelle can buy for each number of CDs purchased, and vice versa. Michelle is always happiest when she chooses a point on her budget constraint rather than below it. To see why, compare the points E and D. At point E,

---

TABLE 2.1

MICHELLE'S OPPORTUNITY SET

DVDs	CDs
6	0
5	2
4	4
3	6
2	8
1	10
0	12

---

[2]See the chapter appendix for help in reading graphs. Economists have found graphs to be extremely useful and they will be employed throughout this book. It is important that you learn to read and understand them.

she has more of both goods than at point *D*. She would be even happier at point *F,* where she has still more DVDs and CDs, but that point, by definition, is unattainable.

Figure 2.2 depicts a time constraint. The most common time constraint simply says that the sum of what an individual spends her time on each day—including sleep—must add up to 24 hours. The figure plots the hours spent watching television on the horizontal axis and the hours spent on all other activities on the vertical axis. People—no matter how rich or poor—have only 24 hours a day to spend on different activities. The time constraint is quite similar to the budget constraint. A person cannot spend more than 24 hours or fewer than zero hours a day watching TV. The more time she spends watching television, the less time she has available for all other activities. If she wants to watch more TV, she must make a trade-off and reduce her time spent in some other activity.

THE PRODUCTION POSSIBILITIES CURVE

Business firms and whole societies face constraints. They too must make choices limited to opportunity sets. The amount of goods a firm or society can produce, given a fixed amount of land, labor, and other inputs, is referred to as its **production possibilities.**

A commonly used example considers a society in which all economic production is divided into two categories, military spending and civilian spending. Of course, each of these two kinds of spending has many different elements, but for the moment, we'll focus only on the two broad categories. For the sake of simplicity, Figure 2.3 refers to military spending as "guns" and civilian spending as "butter." The production of guns is given along the vertical axis, the production of butter along the horizontal. The possible combinations of military and civilian spending—of guns and butter—is the opportunity set. Table 2.2 sets out some of the possible combinations—which 90 million guns and 40 million tons of butter, or 40 million guns and 90 million tons of butter. These possibilities are depicted in the figure. In production decisions, the boundary of the opportunity set—the maximum amount of guns that can be produced for each amount of butter and vice versa—is called the **production possibilities curve.**

When we compare the individual's opportunity set and that of society, we notice one major difference. The individual's budget constraint is a straight line, while the production possibilities curve bows outward. There is a good reason for this. An individual typically faces fixed *trade-offs:* if Michelle spends $20 more on DVDs (that is, she buys one more DVD), she has $20 less to spend on CDs (she can buy two fewer CDs).

In contrast, the trade-offs faced by society are not fixed. If a society produces only a few guns, it will use those resources—the workers and machines—that are best equipped for gun making. But as society tries to produce more and more guns, doing so becomes more difficult; it will increasingly depend on resources that are less good at producing guns.

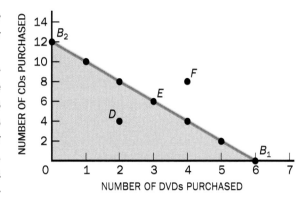

Figure 2.1

MICHELLE'S BUDGET CONSTRAINT

The budget constraint identifies the limits of Michelle's opportunity set between CDs and DVDs. Points B_1 and B_2 are extreme options, where she chooses all of one or the other. Her actual choice corresponds to point *E*. Choices from the shaded area are possible but less attractive than choices actually on the budget constraint.

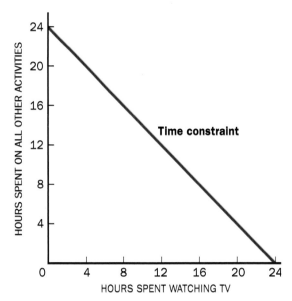

Figure 2.2

AN OPPORTUNITY SET FOR WATCHING TV AND OTHER ACTIVITIES

This opportunity set is limited by a time constraint, which shows the trade-off a person faces between spending time watching television and spending it on other activities.

TABLE 2.2

PRODUCTION POSSIBILITIES FOR THE ECONOMY

Guns (millions)	Butter (millions of tons)
100	0
90	40
70	70
40	90
0	100

It will be drawing these resources out of the production of other goods, in this case, butter. Thus, when the economy increases its production of guns from 40 million a year (point *A*) to 70 million (*B*), butter production falls by 20 million tons, from 90 million tons to 70 million tons. But if production of guns is increased further, to 90 million (*C*), an increase of only 20 million, butter production has to decrease by 30 million tons, to only 40 million tons. For each increase in the number of guns, the reduction in the number of tons of butter produced gets larger. That is why the production possibilities curve is curved.

In another example, assume that a firm owns land that can be used for growing wheat but not corn, and land that can grow corn but not wheat. In this case, the only way to increase wheat production is to move workers from the cornfields to the wheat fields. As more and more workers are put into the wheat fields, production of wheat goes up, but each successive worker increases production less. The first workers might pick the largest and most destructive weeds. Additional workers lead to better weeding, and better weeding leads to higher output. But the additional weeds removed are smaller and less destructive, so output is increased by a correspondingly smaller amount. This is an example of the general principle of **diminishing returns.** Adding successive units of any input such as fertilizer, labor, or machines to a fixed amount of other inputs—seeds or land—increases the output, or amount produced, but by less and less.

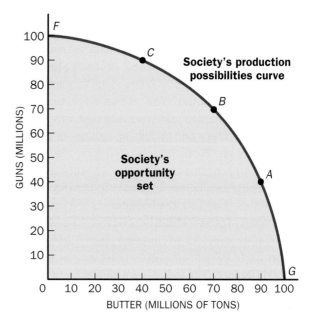

Figure 2.3

THE GUNS AND BUTTER TRADE-OFF

A production possibilities curve can show society's opportunity set. This one describes the trade-off between military spending ("guns") and civilian spending ("butter"). Points *F* and *G* show the extreme choices, where the economy produces all guns or all butter. Notice that unlike the budget and time constraint lines, the production possibilities line curves, reflecting diminishing returns.

Diminishing returns is an important concept in economics. The phenomenon occurs in many situations. You have probably discovered that you usually get more out of the first hour of studying than the tenth, and that studying a few hours may bring big payoffs when you are preparing for an exam; but if you stay up all night to cram, your concentration is likely to decrease, and you may be so tired in the morning that you actually do worse on the exam than if you had quit studying sooner. Having one of your roommates help you fix dinner cuts the preparation time; but if all your roommates try to help, they may end up just getting in each other's way. In Chapter 6, where we examine the factors that affect the costs of producing goods and services, the notion of diminishing returns will help us understand why a rise in price is necessary to induce firms to increase the amount they produce.

Table 2.3 shows the output of the corn- and wheat fields as labor is increased in each. Assume the firm has 6,000 workers to divide between wheat production and corn production. Thus, the second and fourth columns together give the firm's production possibilities, which are depicted in Figure 2.4.

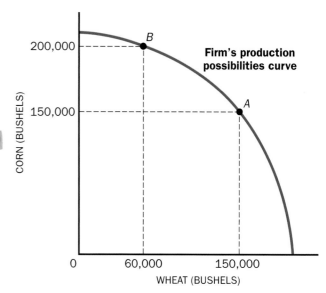

Figure 2.4

THE WHEAT AND CORN TRADE-OFF

This production possibilities curve shows that as wheat production increases, it becomes necessary to give up larger and larger amounts of corn. Or to put the same point a different way, as corn production falls, the resulting increase in wheat production gets smaller.

Costs

Making trade-offs always involves weighing costs and benefits. What you gain is the benefit; what you give up is the cost. Often, the benefits depend on an individual's personal preferences—some people would gladly skip a tennis game to go play golf, and others would just as gladly make the opposite choice. Economists generally do not try to explain why people have different preferences; instead, when it comes to understanding the choices individuals make, economists focus on costs. An opportunity set, like the budget constraint, the time constraint, or the production possibilities curve, specifies the cost of one option in terms of another. If the individual,

TABLE 2.3

DIMINISHING RETURNS

Labor in cornfield (no. of workers)	Corn output (bushels)	Labor in wheat field (no. of workers)	Wheat output (bushels)
1,000	60,000	5,000	200,000
2,000	110,000	4,000	180,000
3,000	150,000	3,000	150,000
4,000	180,000	2,000	110,000
5,000	200,000	1,000	60,000

the firm, or society is operating on the constraint or curve, then it is possible to get more of one thing only by sacrificing some of another. The "cost" of one more unit of one good is how much you have to give up of the other.

Economists think about costs in terms of trade-offs within opportunity sets. Let's go back to Michelle choosing between CDs and DVDs in Figure 2.1. The trade-off is given by the **relative price,** the ratio of the prices of CDs and DVDs. In our example, a CD costs $10, and a DVD $20. The relative price is $20/$10 = 2. For every DVD Michelle gives up, she can buy 2 CDs. Likewise, societies and firms face trade-offs along the production possibilities curve, like the one shown in Figure 2.3. There, point A is the choice where 40 million guns and 90 million tons of butter are produced. The trade-off can be calculated by comparing points A and B. Society can have 30 million more guns by giving up 20 million tons of butter.

Trade-offs are necessary because resources are scarce. If you want something, you have to pay for it—you have to give up something. If you want to go to the library tomorrow night, you have to give up going to the movies. If a sawmill wants to make more two-by-four beams from its stock of wood, it will not be able to make as many one-by-four boards.

OPPORTUNITY COSTS

If someone were to ask you right now what it costs to go to a movie, you would probably answer, "Ten dollars," or whatever you last paid for a ticket. But the concept of trade-offs suggests that a *full* answer is not that simple. To begin with, the cost is not the $10 but what that $10 could otherwise buy. Furthermore, your time is a scarce resource that must be figured into the calculation. Both the money and the time represent opportunities forgone in favor of going to the movie, or what economists refer to as the **opportunity cost** of the movie. To apply a resource to one use means that it cannot be put to any other use. Thus, we should consider the next-best, alternative use of any resource when we think about putting it to any particular use. This next-best use is the formal measurement of opportunity cost.

Some examples will help clarify the idea of opportunity cost. Consider a college student, Sarah, who works during the summer. She has a chance to go surfing in Costa Rica with friends, but to do so she has to quit her summer job two weeks early. The friends have found a cheap airfare and place to stay, and they tell Sarah the trip will cost only $1,000. To the economist, $1,000 is not the total cost of the trip for Sarah. Since she would have continued working in her summer job for an extra two weeks if she did not go to Costa Rica, the income she would have earned is part of the opportunity cost of her time. This forgone income must be added to the airfare and hotel costs in calculating the total economic cost of the surfing trip.

Now consider a business firm that has bought a building for its headquarters that is bigger than necessary. If the firm could receive $3 per month in rent for each square foot of space that is not needed, then that is the opportunity cost of leaving the space idle.

Thinking Like an Economist

TRADE-OFFS

Whenever you see an opportunity set, a budget or time constraint, or a production possibilities curve, think *trade-off*. The variables on the two axes identify the objects of the trade-offs, whether those are CDs and DVDs, guns and butter, or something else. The line or curve drawn from one axis to the other provides quantities for the trade-off. The opportunity set shows the choices that are available. The budget constraint illustrates the trade-offs that must be made because of limited money to spend, while the time constraint reflects the limited time we all have. The production possibilities curve gives the trade-offs faced in deciding what to produce when the amount of land, labor, and other inputs is limited. All three focus attention on the necessity of making trade-offs.

Many people think economists study only situations that involve money and budget constraints, but often time constraints are very important in defining trade-offs. Political elections provide a good example of the importance of time constraints. As the 2004 presidential election campaign entered its final stages, each candidate faced tough choices because of the time constraint. The election date was fixed leaving only so much time available for campaigning. Ohio was one of the critical states for both John Kerry and George W. Bush, and both candidates visited it frequently in the months leading up to the election. But time spent in Ohio was time that could not be spent in the other toss-up states. Each candidate had to decide how best to allocate the time remaining before the election.

President George W. Bush greets well-wishers.

Economists find it useful to distinguish between budget constraints and time constraints, but often we study trade-offs that involve both time *and* money. Choosing how to spend your Saturday evening usually involves both. You might decide to go to a movie that lasts for 2 hours and costs $10 or go to a concert that lasts 4 hours and costs $40. Both your budget and time constraints are important for defining your opportunity set.

The analysis can be applied to the government as well. The federal government owns a vast amount of wilderness. In deciding whether it is worthwhile to convert some of the land into a national park, the government needs to take into account the opportunity cost of the land. The land might be used for growing timber or for grazing sheep. Whatever the value of the land in its next-best use, this is the economic cost of the national park. The fact that the government does not have to buy the land does not mean that the land should be treated as a free good.

Thus, in the economist's view, when rational firms and individuals make decisions—whether to undertake one investment project rather than another, whether to buy one product rather than another—they take into account *all* of the costs (the full opportunity costs), not just the direct expenditures.

Case in Point

THE OPPORTUNITY COST OF ATTENDING COLLEGE

Opportunity cost is a key concept in economics. It is the correct measure of the cost of everything we do. As a college student, what is your opportunity cost of attending college? If you (or your parents) are asking how much your college costs, you probably think of the tuition, room and board, and books as major costs. But a consideration of the opportunity cost suggests that such a list includes both too much and too little.

Since you would need a place to live, and you would certainly need to eat, even if you were not in school, these costs do not represent part of the opportunity cost of attending college. Only if your college charges higher rent than you would otherwise pay would your dorm costs be part of your opportunity cost.

To correctly evaluate opportunity cost, you need to think about what you would be doing if you had decided not to continue in school. The economist's mind immediately turns to the job you might have had if you had not enrolled in college and the income you could have earned. That amount will vary from student to student; but in 2004, eighteen- to twenty-four-year-olds with a high school diploma who were working full-time earned just under $15,000 per year.[3] This *forgone income* must be added to the direct costs such as tuition to obtain the opportunity cost of attending school. For most students, this forgone income is a major component of the opportunity cost of college.

Test your understanding: Use the concept of opportunity cost to explain why great college basketball players often fail to complete four years of college.

Opportunity Cost and International Trade The concepts of opportunity cost and exchange play a pivotal role in helping to understand why economists argue that all countries can gain from international trade. Consider the case of two fictional countries, which we will call North and South. North is highly developed with skilled workers and modern capital equipment. South is much poorer; its workers are generally unskilled and have little capital equipment to aid them in production. For simplicity, assume further that these two countries produce only two goods,

---

[3]U.S. Census Bureau, Annual Demographic Survey, Table PINC-04, March 2004 (http://pubdb3.census.gov/macro/032004/perinc/new04_001.htm).

computers and textiles. The developed country is more productive than the less-developed country at producing both computers and textiles. Despite the fact that North can produce either good more efficiently than South can, economists argue that it will still pay for the two countries to trade, and opportunity cost provides the key to understanding why.

Let's make our example more concrete by assuming that in North, 100 hours of labor can produce either 5 computers or 100 shirts. In South, 100 hours of labor can produce only 1 computer or 50 shirts. These numbers reflect our assumption that North is more productive in producing both computers and textiles (in this case, shirts). These numbers are listed in the top half of Table 2.4. We describe this situation by saying that North has an **absolute advantage** in producing both computers and textiles. But the key insight to understanding international trade is that trade patterns are not based on absolute advantage. Instead, they are based on a comparison of the opportunity cost in each country of producing the two goods. In North, the opportunity cost of producing 100 shirts is 5 computers; shifting 100 hours of labor into textile production to produce the 100 extra shirts would reduce computer production by 5 computers. In contrast, the opportunity cost of producing 100 shirts in South is only 2 computers; shifting 200 hours of labor into textile production to produce the extra 100 shirts would reduce computer production by 2 computers. The opportunity cost of producing more shirts is lower in South than it is in North. We describe this by saying South has a **comparative advantage** in producing textiles. South is *relatively* more efficient in producing shirts than North is.

While South has a comparative advantage in producing shirts, North has a comparative advantage in producing computers; it is relatively more efficient in producing computers. To see this, consider the opportunity cost in North of producing 1 more computer. To produce an additional computer, North must shift 20 hours of labor out of textile production and into computer production, reducing shirt production by 20 shirts. The opportunity cost of the computer in North is 20 shirts. To produce an additional computer, South must shift 100 hours of labor out of textile production and into computer production, reducing shirt production by 50. The opportunity cost of a computer is higher in South (50 shirts) than it is in North (20 shirts). North has a comparative advantage in computer production.

The bottom half of Table 2.4 shows the opportunity cost of producing computers (expressed in terms of shirts) and the opportunity cost of producing shirts (expressed in terms of computers) for each country. While North has an absolute advantage in producing both goods, its comparative advantage lies in producing computers. South's comparative advantage lies in producing shirts.

Because South has a comparative advantage in shirt production and North has a comparative advantage in computer production, both countries can benefit by trading. By shifting 100 hours of labor from computer production to shirt production, South produces 1 less computer and 50 more shirts. By shifting 20 hours of labor from shirt production into computer production, North produces 1 more computer and 20 fewer shirts. By this move toward specialization in each country, total computer production has remained unchanged (1 less produced in South, 1 more produced in North), but total shirt production has risen by 30 shirts (50 more in South, 20 fewer in North). These extra shirts represent (in our example), the gains to specialization. Because the opportunity cost of a computer in North is 20 shirts,

TABLE 2.4

LABOR PRODUCTIVITY IN PRODUCING COMPUTERS AND SHIRTS

	North	South
Computers produced with 100 hours of labor	5	1
Shirts produced with 100 hours of labor	100	50

OPPORTUNITY COST OF PRODUCING COMPUTERS AND SHIRTS

	North	South
Opportunity cost of a computer (in terms of shirts)	20	50
Opportunity cost of 100 shirts (in terms of computers)	5	2

North will be willing to accept no less than 20 shirts from South in exchange for 1 computer. If South were to offer fewer than 20 shirts for a computer, North would be better off producing its own shirts. Because the opportunity cost of a computer in South is 50 shirts, South will be willing to pay no more than 50 shirts to obtain a computer from North. As long as the price for a computer lies between 20 and 50 shirts per computer, both countries can gain if North shifts labor into computer production, South shifts labor into textile production, and the two then engage in trade. For example, if the price of a computer is 30 shirts, South can buy 1 computer from North (leaving South with the same number of computers as it had previously) and it will still have 20 shirts left over to better clothe its own residents. Meanwhile, North reduced its own shirt production by 20 shirts, but was able to obtain 30 shirts in exchange for the extra computer it produced. So North is also better off. North will benefit by exporting computers to South, and South will benefit by exporting textiles to North.

By recognizing the important role of opportunity cost, we can understand why both North and South gain from specializing in production and engaging in international trade. Despite the economists' argument that free trade can benefit both countries, many people oppose moves to promote international trade. Their arguments, and the role of various government policies that affect international trade, will be the subject of Chapter 19.

SUNK COSTS

Economic cost includes costs, as we have just seen, that noneconomists often exclude, but it also ignores costs that noneconomists include. If an expenditure has already been made and cannot be recovered no matter what choice is made, a rational person would ignore it. Such expenditures are called **sunk costs.**

To understand sunk costs, let's go back to the movies, assuming now that you have spent $10 to buy a movie ticket. You were skeptical about whether the movie was worth $10. Half an hour into the movie, your worst suspicions are realized: the movie is a disaster. Should you leave the movie theater? In making that decision, the $10 should be ignored. It is a sunk cost; your money is gone whether you stay or leave. The only relevant choice now is how to spend the next 60 minutes of your time: watch a terrible movie or go do something else.

Or assume you have just purchased a fancy laptop computer for $2,000. But the next week, the manufacturer announces a new computer with twice the power for $1,000; you can trade in your old computer for the new one by paying an additional $400. You are angry. You feel you have just paid $2,000 for a computer that is now almost worthless, and you have gotten little use out of it. You decide not to buy the new computer for another year, until you have gotten at least some return for your investment. Again, an economist would say that you are not approaching the question rationally. The past decision is a sunk cost. The only question you should ask yourself is whether the extra power of the fancier computer is worth the additional $400. If it is, buy it. If not, don't.

MARGINAL COSTS

The third aspect of cost that economists emphasize is the extra costs of doing something, what they call the **marginal costs.** These are weighed against the (additional) **marginal benefits** of doing it. The most difficult decisions we make are not whether to do something or not. They are whether to do a little more or a little less of something. Few of us waste much time deciding whether or not to work. We have to work; the decision is whether to work a few more or a few less hours. A country does not consider whether or not to have an army; it decides whether to have a larger or smaller army.

Polly is considering flying to Colorado for a ski weekend. She has three days off from work. The airfare is $200, the hotel room costs $100 a night, and the ski ticket costs $35 a day. Food costs the same as at home. She is trying to decide whether to go for two or three days. The *marginal* cost of the third day is $135, the hotel cost plus the cost of the ski ticket. There are no additional transportation costs involved in staying the third day. She needs to compare the marginal cost with the additional enjoyment she will have from the third day.

Internet Connection

THE ECONOMISTS' VOICE

One way to start thinking like an economist is to read what economists have to say about current events. The Economists' Voice at www.bepress.com/ev/ provides articles about current economic issues.

People, consciously or not, think about the trade-offs at the margin in most of their decisions. Economists, however, bring them into the foreground. Like opportunity costs and sunk costs, marginal analysis is one of the critical concepts that enable economists to think systematically about the costs of alternative choices.

This kind of marginal analysis has come to play an increasingly important role in policy discussions. For instance, the key issue in various environmental regulations and safety standards is not whether there should be such regulations, but how tight they should be. Higher standards have both marginal benefits and marginal costs. From an economic standpoint, justification of higher standards hinges on whether the marginal benefits outweigh the marginal costs. Consider, for instance, auto safety. For the past three decades, the government has taken an active role in ensuring auto safety. It sets standards that all automobiles must meet. For example, an automobile must be able to withstand a side collision of a particular velocity. One of the most difficult problems the government faces is deciding what those standards should be. It recently considered tightening standards for withstanding side collisions on trucks. The government calculated that the higher standards would result on average in 79 fewer deaths per year. It calculated that meeting the higher standards would increase the cost of each vehicle by $81. (In addition, the heavier trucks would use more fuel.) In deciding whether to impose the higher standard, it used marginal analysis. It looked at the *additional* lives saved and at the *additional* costs.

BASIC STEPS OF RATIONAL CHOICE

Identify the opportunity sets.
Define the trade-offs.
Calculate the costs correctly, ignoring sunk costs, taking into account opportunity costs and marginal costs.

Review and Practice

SUMMARY

1. The basic competitive model consists of rational, self-interested individuals and profit-maximizing firms, interacting in competitive markets.
2. The profit motive and private property provide incentives for rational individuals and firms to work hard and efficiently. Ill-defined or restricted property rights can lead to inefficient behavior.
3. Society often faces choices between efficiency, which requires incentives that enable people or firms to receive different benefits depending on their performance, and equality, which entails people receiving more or less equal benefits.
4. The price system in a market economy is one way of allocating goods and services. Other methods include rationing by queue, by lottery, and by coupon.
5. An opportunity set illustrates what choices are possible. Budget constraints and time constraints define individuals' opportunity sets. Both show the trade-offs of how much of one thing a person must give up to get more of another.
6. A production possibilities curve defines a firm or society's opportunity set, representing the possible combinations of goods that the firm or society can produce. If a firm or society is producing below its production possibilities curve, it is said to be inefficient, since it could produce more of either good without producing less of the other.
7. The opportunity cost is the cost of using any resource. It is measured by looking at the next-best use to which that resource could be put.
8. A sunk cost is a past expenditure that cannot be recovered, no matter what choice is made in the present. Thus, rational decision makers ignore them.
9. Most economic decisions concentrate on choices at the margin, where the marginal (or extra) cost of a course of action is compared with its extra benefits.

KEY TERMS

competition
basic competitive model
rational choice
perfect competition
price taker
price system
private property
property rights
tragedy of the commons
rationing systems
opportunity set
budget constraints
time constraints
production possibilities
production possibilities curve
diminishing returns
relative price
opportunity cost
sunk costs
marginal costs
marginal benefits

REVIEW QUESTIONS

1. What are the essential elements of the basic competitive model?
2. Consider a lake in a state park where everyone is allowed to fish as much as they want. What outcome do you predict? Might this problem be averted if the lake were privately owned and fishing licenses were sold?
3. Why might government policy to make the distribution of income more equitable lead to less efficiency?
4. List advantages and disadvantages of rationing by queue, by lottery, and by coupon. If the government permitted a black market to develop, might some of the disadvantages of these systems be reduced?
5. What are some of the opportunity costs of going to college? What are some of the opportunity costs a state should consider when deciding whether to widen a highway?
6. Give two examples of a sunk cost, and explain why they should be irrelevant to current decisions.
7. How is marginal analysis relevant in the decision about which car to purchase? After deciding the kind of car to purchase, how is marginal analysis relevant?

PROBLEMS

1. Imagine that many businesses are located beside a river, into which they discharge industrial waste. There is a city downstream, which uses the river as a water supply and for recreation. If property rights to the river are ill-defined, what problems may occur?

2. Suppose an underground reservoir of oil may reside under properties owned by several different individuals. As each well is drilled, it reduces the amount of oil that others can take out. Compare how quickly the oil is likely to be extracted in this situation with how quickly it would be extracted if one person owned the property rights to drill for the entire pool of oil.

3. In some states, hunting licenses are allocated by lottery; if you want a license, you send in your name to enter the lottery. If the purpose of the system is to ensure that those who want to hunt the most get a chance to do so, what are the flaws of this system? How would the situation improve if people who won licenses were allowed to sell them to others?

4. Imagine that during time of war, the government imposes coupon rationing. What are the advantages of allowing people to buy and sell their coupons? What are the disadvantages?

5. Kathy, a college student, has $20 a week to spend; she spends it either on junk food at $2.50 a snack, or on gasoline at $2 per gallon. Draw Kathy's opportunity set. What is the trade-off between junk food and gasoline? Now draw each new budget constraint she would face if
   (a) a kind relative started sending her an additional $10 per week;
   (b) the price of a junk food snack fell to $2;
   (c) the price of gasoline rose to $2.50 per gallon.
   In each case, how does the trade-off between junk food and gasoline change?

6. Why is the opportunity cost of going to medical school likely to be greater than the opportunity cost of going to college? Why is the opportunity cost of a woman with a college education having a child greater than the opportunity cost of a woman with just a high school education having a child?

7. Bob likes to divide his recreational time between going to movies and listening to compact discs. He has 20 hours a week available for recreation; a movie takes two hours, and a CD takes one hour to listen to. Draw his "time-budget constraint" line. Bob also has a limited amount of income to spend on recreation. He has $60 a week to spend on recreational activities; a movie costs $10, and a CD costs $15. (He never likes to listen to the same CD twice.) Draw his budget constraint line. What is his opportunity set?

Appendix: Reading Graphs

Whether the old saying that a picture is worth a thousand words under- or overestimates the value of a picture, economists find graphs extremely useful.

For instance, look at Figure 2.5; it is a redrawn version of Figure 2.1, showing the budget constraint—the various combinations of CDs and DVDs that an individual, Michelle, can buy. More generally, a graph shows the relationship between two variables: here, the number of CDs and the number of DVDs that can be purchased. The budget constraint gives the maximum number of DVDs that she can purchase, given the number of CDs that she has bought.

In a graph, one variable (here, DVDs) is put on the horizontal axis and the other variable on the vertical axis. We read a point such as E by looking across to the vertical axis and seeing that it corresponds to 6 CDs, and by looking down to the horizontal axis and seeing that is corresponds to 3 DVDs. Similarly, we read point A by looking across to the vertical axis and seeing that it corresponds to 8 CDs, and by looking down to the horizontal axis and seeing that it corresponds to 2 DVDs.

In the figure, each of the points from the table has been plotted, and then a curve has been drawn through those points. The "curve" turns out to be a straight line in this case, but we still use the more general term. The advantage of the curve over the individual points is that with it, we can read off from the graph points on the budget constraint that are not in the table.

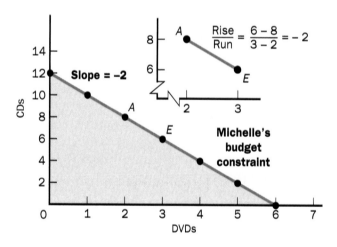

Figure 2.5

READING A GRAPH: THE BUDGET CONSTRAINT

Graphs can be used to show the relationship between two variables. This one shows the relationship between the variable on the vertical axis (the number of CDs) and the variable on the horizontal axis (the number of DVDs). The slope of the curve—here, the budget constraint—gives the change in the number of CDs Michelle can purchase if she buys another DVD. The slope of the budget constraint is negative. A small portion of the graph has been blown up to illustrate how to calculate the curve's slope. (The jagged sections of the axes near the blown-up graph's origin indicate that the distance from the origin to the first value on each axis is not drawn to scale.)

Sometimes, of course, not every point on the graph is economically meaningful. You cannot buy half a DVD or half a CD. For the most part, we ignore these considerations when drawing our graphs; we simply pretend that any point on the budget constraint is actually possible.

SLOPE

In any diagram, the amount by which the value along the vertical axis increases from a change in a unit along the horizontal axis is called the *slope*, just like the slope of a mountain. Slope is sometimes described as "rise over run," meaning that the slope of a line can be calculated by dividing the change on the vertical axis (the "rise") by the change on the horizontal axis (the "run").

Look at Figure 2.5. As we move from E to A, increasing the number of CDs by 2, the number of DVDs purchased falls from 3 to 2. For every two additional CDs bought, the feasible number of DVDs that can be purchased falls by 1. So the slope of the line is

$$\frac{\text{rise}}{\text{run}} = \frac{6-8}{3-2} = \frac{-2}{1} = -2.$$

When, as in Figure 2.5, the variable on the vertical axis falls when the variable on the horizontal axis increases, the curve, or line, is said to be *negatively sloped*. A budget constraint is always negatively sloped. But when we describe the slope of a budget constraint, we frequently omit the term "negative." We say the slope is 2, knowing that since we are describing the slope of a budget constraint, we should more formally say that the slope is negative 2. Alternatively, we sometimes say that the slope has an absolute value of 2.

Figure 2.6 shows the case of a curve that is *positively sloped*. The variable along the vertical axis, income, increases as schooling increases, giving the line its upward tilt from left to right.

In later discussions, we will encounter two special cases. A line that is very steep has a very large slope; that is, the increase in the vertical axis for every unit increase in the horizontal axis is very large. The extreme case is a perfectly vertical line, and we say then that the slope is infinite (Figure 2.7, panel A). At the other extreme is a flat, horizontal line; since there is no increase in the vertical axis no matter how large the change along the horizontal, we say that the slope of such a curve is zero (panel B).

Figures 2.5 and 2.6 both show straight lines. Everywhere along the straight line, the slope is the same. This is not true in Figure 2.8, which repeats the production possibilities curve shown originally in Figure 2.3. Panel B of the figure blows up the area around point E. From the figure, you can see that if the output of butter increases by 1 ton, the output of guns decreases by 1 million guns. Thus, the slope is

$$\frac{\text{rise}}{\text{run}} = \frac{69-70}{71-70} = -1.$$

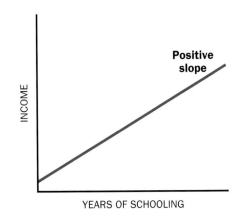

Figure 2.6

POSITIVELY SLOPED CURVE

Incomes increase with the number of years of schooling.

Now look at point *A,* where the economy is producing more butter. The area around *A* has been blown up in panel C. Here, we see that when we increase butter by 1 more unit, the reduction in guns is greater than before. The slope at *A* (again, millions of fewer guns produced per extra ton of butter) is

$$\frac{\text{rise}}{\text{run}} = \frac{38-40}{91-90} = -2.$$

With curves such as the production possibilities curve, the slope differs as we move along the curve.

INTERPRETING CURVES

Look at Figure 2.9. Which of the two curves has a steeper slope? The one on the left appears to have a slope that has a larger absolute value. But look carefully at the axes. Notice that in panel A, the vertical axis is stretched relative to panel B. The same distance that represents 20 CDs in panel B represents only 10 CDs in panel A.

Figure 2.7
LIMITING CASES

In panel A, the slope of a vertical line is infinite. In panel B, the slope of a horizontal line is zero.

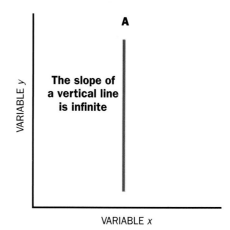

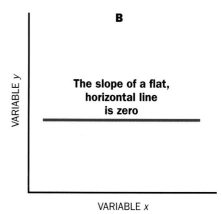

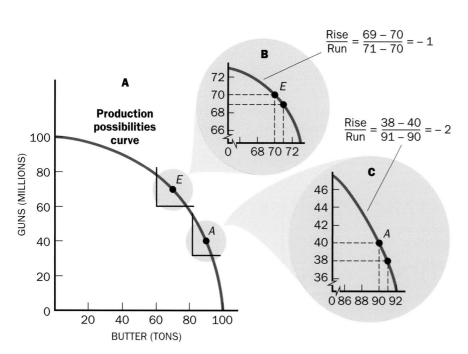

FIGURE 2.8

THE GUNS AND BUTTER TRADE-OFF

Panel A shows a trade-off between military spending ("guns") and civilian spending ("butter"), where society chooses point *E.* Panel B is an enlargement of the area around *E,* which focuses on the slope there, which also measures the marginal trade-offs society faces near that point. Similarly, panel C is an enlargement of the area around *A* and shows the marginal trade-offs society faces near that point.

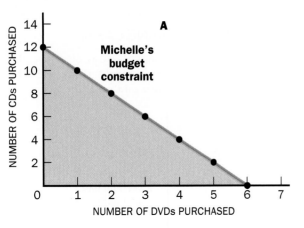

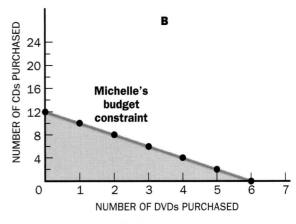

Figure 2.9
SCALING AND SLOPE

Which of these two lines has the steeper slope? The units along the vertical axis have changed. The two curves have exactly the same slope.

In fact, both panels represent the same budget constraint. They have exactly the same slope.

This kind of cautionary tale is also important in looking at graphs of data. Compare, for instance, panels A and B of Figure 2.10. Both graphs show the level of passenger car production from 1980 to 1990. Which one exhibits more variability? Which looks more stable? Panel B appears to show that car production does not change much over time. But again, a closer look reveals that the axis has been stretched in panel A. The two curves are based on exactly the same data, and there is really no difference between them.

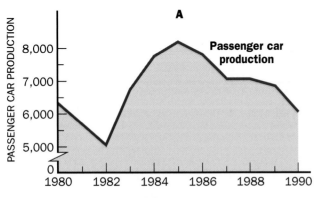

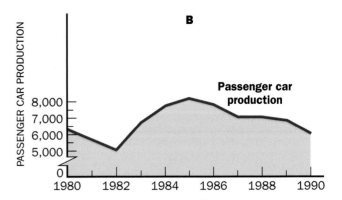

Figure 2.10
SCALING AND GRAPHS OF DATA

Which of these two curves shows greater variability in the output of cars over time? The two curves plot the same data. The vertical scale has again been changed.
SOURCE: *Ward's Automotive Reports* (1991).

Part 2

PERFECT MARKETS

Learning goals

In this chapter, you will learn

1 What a demand curve is, why demand curves normally slope downward, and what other factors, besides price, affect the quantity demanded

2 What a supply curve is, why supply curves normally slope upward, and what other factors, besides price, affect the quantity supplied

3 How the demand and supply curves can be used to determine the equilibrium price of a good

4 How shifts in the demand and supply curve affect the equilibrium price

Chapter 3

DEMAND, SUPPLY, AND PRICE

Choice in the face of scarcity is the fundamental concern of economics. But if scarcity is such a concern for economists, why is it that whenever I go to my local grocery store it has all the tomatoes I want to buy? Tomatoes might be more expensive one week and less expensive the next, but they are always available. In what sense are tomatoes scarce? The same is true for most goods most of the time; as long as I am willing to pay the market price, I can buy the good. A key economic insight is that when the forces of supply and demand operate freely, the price of a good measures its scarcity. If bad weather destroys part of the tomato crop, tomatoes *are* more scarce, and their price will rise to reflect that condition. But price does more than simply measure scarcity. Prices also convey critical economic information. When the price of a resource—such as land, labor, or capital—used by a firm is high, the company has a greater incentive to economize on its use. When the price of a good that the firm produces is high, the company has a greater incentive to produce more of that good, and its customers have an incentive to economize on its use. Thus, prices provide our economy with incentives to use scarce resources efficiently, and a major objective of economists is to understand the forces that determine prices. This chapter describes how prices are determined in competitive market economies.

The Role of Prices

The **price** of a good or service is what must be given in exchange for the good. Usually we identify the price of something with how much it costs in dollars. But price can include other factors—for example, if you have to wait to buy something, the total price includes the value of your time spent in line. For most of our discussion, however, we will keep things simple and just think of the price as the number of dollars paid to obtain a good or service.

Prices are the way participants in the economy communicate with one another. Assume a drought hits the country, drastically reducing the supply of corn. Households will need to lower their consumption of corn or there will not be enough to go around. But how will they know this? Suppose newspapers across the country ran an article informing people they would have to eat less corn because of a drought. What incentive would they have to pay attention to it? How would each family know how much it ought to reduce its consumption? Alternatively, consider the effect of an increase in the price of corn. The higher price conveys all the relevant information. It simultaneously tells families corn is scarce and provides incentives for them to consume less of it. Consumers do not need to know anything about why corn is scarce, nor do they need to be told how much to reduce their consumption of it.

Price changes and differences present interesting problems and puzzles. In the early 2000s, while the price of an average house in Los Angeles went up by 76 percent, the price of a house in Milwaukee, Wisconsin, increased by only 32 percent. Why? During the same period, the price of computers fell dramatically, while the price of bread rose, but at a much slower rate than the price of housing in Los Angeles. Why? The "price" of labor is just the wage or salary that is paid. Why does a physician earn three times as much as a college professor, though the college professor may have performed better in the college courses they took together? Why is the price of water, without which we cannot live, very low in most cases, but the price of diamonds very high? The simple answer to all these questions is that in market economies like that of the United States, price is determined by supply and demand. Changes in prices are determined by changes in supply and demand.

Understanding the causes of changes in prices and being able to predict their occurrence are not just matters of academic interest. One of the events that precipitated the French Revolution was the rise in the price of bread, for which the people blamed the government. And gas price increases were a topic of political debate in the 2004 U.S. presidential election.

Demand

Economists use the concept of **demand** to describe the quantity of a good or service that a household or firm chooses to buy at a given price. It is important to understand that economists are concerned not just with what people desire but with what they choose to buy given the spending limits imposed by their budget constraint and given the prices of various goods. In analyzing demand, the first question economists ask is how the quantity of a good purchased by an individual changes as the price changes, when everything else is kept constant.

THE INDIVIDUAL DEMAND CURVE

Think about what happens as the price of candy bars changes. At a price of $5.00, you might never buy one. At $3.00, you might buy one as a special treat. At $1.25, you might buy a few, and if the price declined to $0.50, you might buy a lot. The table in Figure 3.1 summarizes the weekly demand of one individual, Roger, for candy bars at these different prices. We can see that the lower the price, the larger the quantity demanded. We can also draw a graph that shows the quantity Roger demands at each price. The quantity demanded is measured along the horizontal axis, and the price is measured along the vertical axis. The graph in Figure 3.1 plots the points.

A smooth curve can be drawn to connect the points. This curve is called the **demand curve.** The demand curve gives the quantity demanded at each price. Thus, if we want to know how many candy bars a week Roger will demand at a price of $1.00, we simply look along the vertical axis at the price $1.00, find the corresponding point A along the demand curve, and then read down the horizontal axis. At a price of $1.00, Roger buys 6 candy bars each week. Alternatively, if we want to know at what price he will buy just 3 candy bars, we look along the horizontal axis at the quantity 3, find the corresponding point B along the demand curve, and then read across to the vertical axis. Roger will buy 3 candy bars at a price of $1.50.

As the price of candy bars increases, the quantity demanded decreases. This can be seen from the numbers in the table in Figure 3.1 and in the shape of the demand curve, which slopes downward from left to right. This relationship is typical of demand curves and makes common sense: the cheaper a good is (the lower down we look on the vertical axis), the more of it a person will buy (the farther right on the horizontal axis); the more expensive, the less a person will buy.

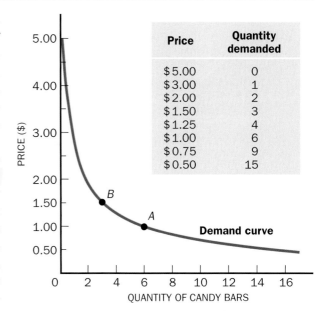

Price	Quantity demanded
$5.00	0
$3.00	1
$2.00	2
$1.50	3
$1.25	4
$1.00	6
$0.75	9
$0.50	15

Figure 3.1

AN INDIVIDUAL'S DEMAND CURVE

This demand curve shows the quantity of candy bars that Roger consumes at each price. Notice that quantity demanded increases as the price falls, and the demand curve slopes down.

Wrap-Up

DEMAND CURVE

The demand curve gives the quantity of the good demanded at each price.

THE MARKET DEMAND CURVE

Suppose there was a simple economy made up of two people, Roger and Jane. Figure 3.2 illustrates how to add up the demand curves of these two individuals to obtain a demand curve for the market as a whole. We "add" the demand curves horizontally by taking, at each price, the quantities demanded by Roger and by Jane and adding the two together. Thus, in the figure, at the price of $0.75, Roger demands 9 candy bars and Jane demands 11, so that the total market demand is 20 candy bars. The same principles apply no matter how many people there are in the economy. The **market demand curve** gives the total quantity of the good that will be demanded at each price. The table in Figure 3.3 summarizes the information for our example of candy

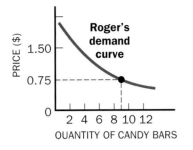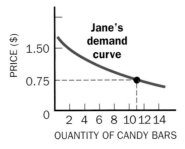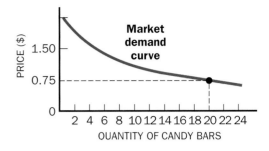

Figure 3.2

DERIVING THE MARKET DEMAND CURVE

The market demand curve is constructed by adding up, at each price, the total of the quantities consumed by each individual. The curve here shows what market demand would be if there were only two consumers. Actual market demand, as depicted in Figure 3.3, is much larger because there are many consumers.

bars; it gives the total quantity of candy bars demanded by everybody in the economy at various prices. If we had a table like the one in Figure 3.1 for each person in the economy, we would construct Figure 3.3 by adding up, at each price, the total quantity of candy bars purchased. Figure 3.3 tells us, for instance, that at a price of $3.00 per candy bar, the total market demand for candy bars is 1 million candy bars, and that lowering the price to $2.00 increases market demand to 3 million candy bars.

Figure 3.3 also depicts the same information in a graph. As in Figure 3.1, price lies along the vertical axis, but now the horizontal axis measures the quantity demanded by everyone in the economy. Joining the points in the figure together, we get the market demand curve. If we want to know what the total demand for candy bars will be when the price is $1.50 per candy bar, we look on the vertical axis at the price $1.50, find the corresponding point *A* along the demand curve, and read down to the horizontal axis; at that price, total demand is 4 million candy bars. If we want to know what the price of candy bars will be when the demand equals 20 million, we find 20 million along the horizontal axis, look up to find the corresponding point *B* along the market demand curve, and read across to the vertical axis; the price at which 20 million candy bars are demanded is $0.75.

Notice that just as when the price of candy bars increases, the individual's demand decreases, so too when the price of candy bars increases, market demand decreases. At successively higher prices, more and more individuals exit the market. Thus, the market demand curve also slopes downward from left to right. This general rule holds both because each individual's demand curve is downward sloping and because as the price is increased, some individuals will decide to stop buying altogether. In Figure 3.1, for example, Roger *exits the market*—consumes a quantity of zero—at the price of $5.00, at which his demand curve hits the vertical axis.

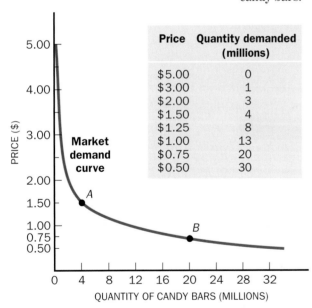

Price	Quantity demanded (millions)
$5.00	0
$3.00	1
$2.00	3
$1.50	4
$1.25	8
$1.00	13
$0.75	20
$0.50	30

Figure 3.3

THE MARKET DEMAND CURVE

The market demand curve shows the quantity of the good demanded by all consumers in the market at each price. The market demand curve is downward sloping, for two reasons: at a higher price, each consumer buys less, and at high-enough prices, some consumers decide not to buy at all—they exit the market.

SHIFTS IN DEMAND CURVES

When the price of a good increases, the demand for that good decreases—when everything else is held constant. But in the real world, everything is not held constant. Any changes other than in the price of the good in question shift the (whole) demand curve—that is, they alter the amount that will be demanded at each price. How the demand curve for candy has shifted as Americans have become more weight conscious provides a good example. Figure 3.4 shows hypothetical demand curves for candy bars in 1960 and in 2000. We can see from the figure that the demand for candy bars at a price of $0.75 has decreased from 20 million candy bars (point E_{1960}) to 10 million (point E_{2000}), as people have reduced their taste for candy.

SOURCES OF SHIFTS IN DEMAND CURVES

Two of the factors that shift the demand curve—changes in income and in the price of other goods—are specifically economic factors. As an individual's income increases, she normally purchases more of any good. Thus, rising incomes shift the demand curve to the right, as illustrated in Figure 3.5. At each price, more of the good is consumed.

Changes in the price of other goods, particularly closely related goods, will also shift the demand curve for a good. For example, when the price of margarine increases, some individuals will substitute butter. Two goods are **substitutes** if an increase in the price of one *increases* the demand for the other. Butter and margarine are thus substitutes. When people choose between butter and margarine, one important factor is the relative price, that is, the ratio of the price of butter to the price of margarine. An increase in the price of butter and a decrease in the price of margarine increase the relative price of butter. Thus, both induce individuals to substitute margarine for butter.

Candy bars and granola bars can also be considered substitutes, as the two goods satisfy a similar need. Thus, an increase in the price of granola bars makes candy bars relatively more attractive, and hence leads to a rightward shift in the demand curve for candy bars. (At each price, the demand for candy is greater.)

Sometimes, however, an increase in a price of other goods has just the opposite effect. Consider an individual who takes sugar in his coffee. In deciding on how much coffee to demand, he is concerned with the price of a cup of coffee *with* sugar. If sugar becomes more expensive, he will demand less coffee. For this person, sugar and coffee are **complements;** an increase in the price of one *decreases* the demand for the other. A price increase for sugar shifts the

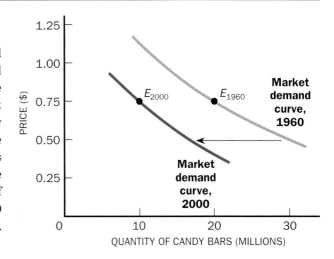

Figure 3.4

SHIFTS IN THE DEMAND CURVE

A leftward shift in the demand curve means that a lesser amount will be demanded at every given market price.

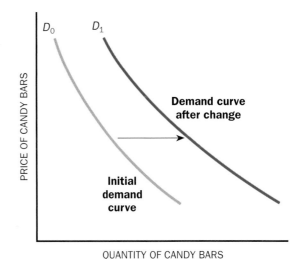

Figure 3.5

A RIGHTWARD SHIFT IN THE DEMAND CURVE

If, at each price, there is an increase in the quantity demanded, then the demand curve will shift to the right, as depicted. An increase in income, an increase in the price of a substitute, or a decrease in the price of a complement can cause a rightward shift in the demand curve.

demand curve for coffee to the left: at each price, the demand for coffee is less. Similarly a *decrease* in the price of sugar shifts the demand curve for coffee to the right.

Market demand curves can also be shifted by noneconomic factors. The major ones are changes in tastes, cultural factors, and changes in the composition of the population. The candy example discussed earlier reflected a change in tastes. Other taste changes in recent years in the United States include shifts in food choices as a result of new health information or (often short-lived) fads associated with diets. Health concerns led to a shift from high-cholesterol to low-cholesterol foods, and the Atkins diet produced a temporary shift away from high-carbohydrate foods such as bread. Cultural factors also affect demand curves. During the late twentieth century, increasing numbers of women entered the workforce as attitudes toward married middle-class women working outside the home shifted; and with this change, the demand curves for child care services shifted.

Population changes that shift demand curves are often related to age. Young families with babies purchase disposable diapers. The demand for new houses and apartments is closely related to the number of new households, which in turn depends on the number of individuals of marriageable age. The U.S. population has been growing older, on average, both because life expectancies are increasing and because birthrates fell somewhat after the baby boom that followed World War II. So there has been a shift in demand away from diapers and new houses. Economists working for particular firms and industries spend considerable energy ascertaining such **demographic effects** on the demand for the goods their firms sell.

Sometimes demand curves shift as the result of new information. The shifts in demand for alcohol and meat—and even more strongly for cigarettes—are related to improved consumer information about health risks.

Changes in the cost and available of credit can also shift demand curves—for goods such as cars and houses that people typically buy with the help of loans. When interest rates rise and borrowing money becomes more expensive, the demand curves for cars and houses shift; at each price, the quantity demanded is less.

Finally, what people expect to happen in the future can shift demand curves. If people think they may become unemployed, they will reduce their spending. In this case, economists say that their demand curves depend on expectations.

Wrap-Up

SOURCES OF SHIFTS IN MARKET DEMAND CURVES

A change in income
A change in the price of a substitute
A change in the price of a complement
A change in the composition of the population
A change in tastes or cultural attitudes
A change in information
A change in the availability of credit
A change in expectations

GASOLINE PRICES AND THE DEMAND FOR SUVS

When demand for several products is intertwined, conditions affecting the price of one will affect the demand for the other. Changes in gasoline prices in the United States, for example, have affected the types of cars Americans buy.

Gasoline prices soared twice in the 1970s, once when the Organization of Petroleum Exporting Countries (OPEC) shut off the flow of oil to the United States in 1973 and again when the overthrow of the shah of Iran in 1979 led to a disruption in oil supplies. The price of gasoline at the pump rose from $0.35 a gallon in 1971 to $1.35 a gallon by 1981 (see Figure 3.6). In response to the price increases, Americans had to cut back demand. But how could they conserve on gasoline? The distance from home to office was not going to shrink, and people had to get to their jobs. One solution was for American drivers to replace their old cars with smaller cars that offered more miles to the gallon.

Analysts classify car sales according to car size, and usually the smaller the car, the better the gas mileage. Just after the first rise in gas prices, about 2.5 million large cars, 2.8 million compacts, and 2.3 million subcompacts were bought each year. By 1985, the proportions had shifted dramatically. About 1.5 million large cars were sold that year, representing a significant decline from the mid-1970s. The number of subcompacts sold was relatively unchanged at 2.2 million, but the number of compacts sold soared to 3.7 million.

The demand curve for any good (like cars) assumes that the price of complementary goods (like gasoline) is fixed. The rise in gasoline prices caused the demand curve for small cars to shift out to the right and the demand curve for large cars to shift back to the left.

By the late 1980s, the price of gasoline had fallen significantly from its peak in 1981, but in the 1990s, gasoline prices again rose markedly. However, the prices of other goods were also rising over the thirty-five-year period shown in the figure. When

Low gas prices in 1990s and early 2000s led to higher demand for SUVs.

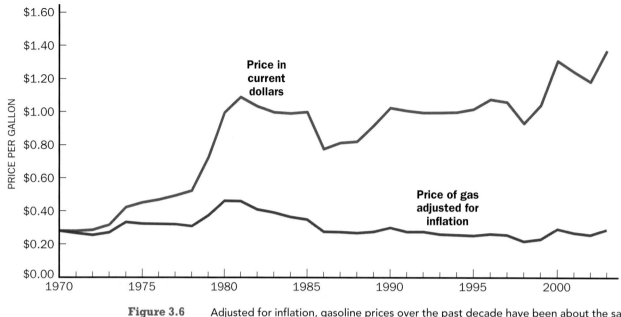

Figure 3.6

U.S. GASOLINE PRICES

Adjusted for inflation, gasoline prices over the past decade have been about the same as they were before the price increases of the 1970s.

SOURCE: Department of Energy, *Annual Energy Review 2003*, September 7, 2004 (www.eia.doe.gov/emeu/aer/petro.html).

gas prices are adjusted for inflation, the real price of gasoline—the price of gas *relative* to the prices of other goods—was lower in the 1990s than it had been *before* the big price increases of the 1970s (Figure 3.6). As a consequence, the demand curve for large cars shifted back to the right. This time, the change in demand was reflected in booming sales of sports utility vehicles, or SUVs. The registrations of light-duty trucks (which include SUVs, minivans, and pickups) jumped from less than 20 percent of all vehicles in 1980 to 46 percent in 1996.[1]

SHIFTS IN A DEMAND CURVE VERSUS MOVEMENTS ALONG A DEMAND CURVE

The distinction between changes that result from a *shift* in the demand curve and changes that result from a *movement along* the demand curve is crucial to understanding economics. A movement along a demand curve is simply the change in the quantity demanded as the price changes. Figure 3.7A illustrates a movement along the demand curve from point *A* to point *B*; *given a demand curve*, at lower prices, more is consumed. Figure 3.7B illustrates a shift in the demand curve to the right; *at a given price*, more is consumed.

---

[1] P. S. Hu, S. D. Davis, and R. L. Schmoyer, *Registrations and Vehicle Miles of Travel for Light-Duty Vehicles, 1985–1995* (publication ORNL-6936) (Oakridge, Tenn.: Center for Transportation Analysis, February 1998), p. 1.

In practice, both effects are often present. Thus, in panel C of Figure 3.7, the movement from point A to point C—where the quantity demanded has been increased from Q_0 to Q_2—consists of two parts: a change in quantity demanded resulting from a shift in the demand curve (the increase in quantity from Q_0 to Q_1), and a movement along the demand curve due to a change in the price (the increase in quantity from Q_1 to Q_2).

The distinction will be important for understanding how quantities and prices are determined once we combine our analysis of demand with an analysis of supply. For example, along a given demand curve for gasoline, a rise in the price of gasoline causes a reduction in the quantity demanded. In contrast, the introduction of a new rapid transit system in a city would shift the demand curve for gasoline to the left; in this example, at each price of gasoline, the quantity demanded would be less because alternative transportation services are available.

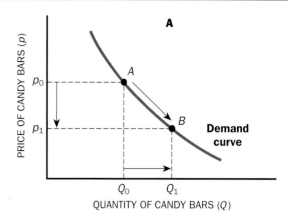

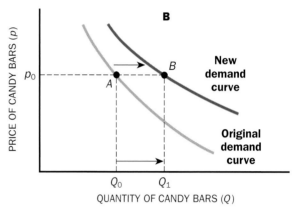

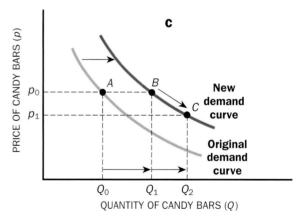

Figure 3.7

MOVEMENT ALONG THE DEMAND CURVE VERSUS SHIFT IN THE DEMAND CURVE

Panel A shows an increase in quantity demanded caused by a lower price—a movement along a given demand curve. Panel B illustrates an increase in quantity demanded caused by a shift in the entire demand curve, so that a greater quantity is demanded at every market price. Panel C shows a combination of a shift in the demand curve (the movement from point A to B) and a movement along the demand curve (the movement from B to C).

SHIFTS VERSUS MOVEMENTS ALONG DEMAND CURVES

A change in price, given a demand curve, is reflected in a movement along the given demand curve.

A shift in the demand curve causes the quantity demanded to change, at a given price.

DEMAND DECLINES AS PRICE RISES

As the price of a good increases, the quantity demanded falls. Changes in factors other than price—such as incomes, consumer tastes, or the prices of other substitutes or complements—shift the demand curve.

Supply

Economists use the concept of **supply** to describe the quantity of a good or service that a household or firm would like to sell at a particular price. Supply in economics refers to such seemingly

e-Insight

THE DEMAND FOR COMPUTERS AND INFORMATION TECHNOLOGY

The demand for computers and other information technology investments rose markedly during the 1980s and 1990s. Panel A shows an index of real investment in computers and related equipment; the index is scaled so that it equals 100 in the year 2000. Real investment has grown an aver-

age of 29 percent over the period shown (1990–2003). This growth in the demand for computers occurred for a simple reason: the effective price of computers fell enormously. Even though the average price of a personal computer remained relatively stable, today's computer delivers much

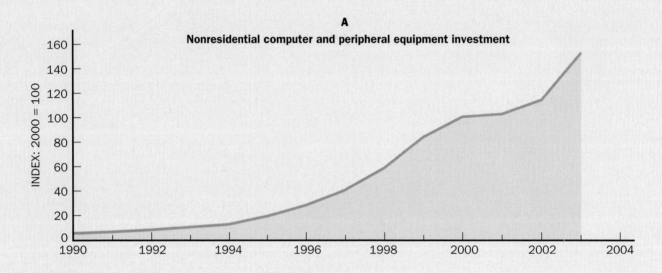

A
Nonresidential computer and peripheral equipment investment

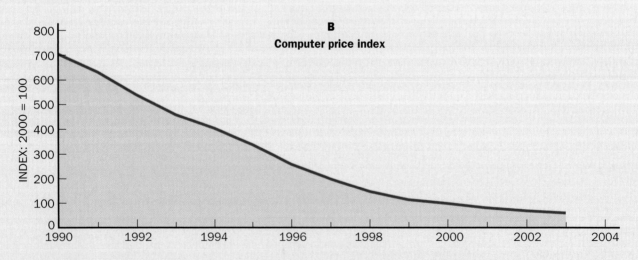

B
Computer price index

The demand for computers rose markedly during the 1980s and 1990s.

higher performance at that price. Adjusting for this change in quality, between 1990 and 2003 the price of computers is estimated to have fallen an average of 17 percent per year (see panel B). At the lower price, we see a higher quantity demanded.

A major reason for the decline in computer prices is technological innovations that have lowered the cost of producing computers. Firms able to take advantage of these technological improvements have increased their profits, as their costs have fallen faster than the prices of the computers they sell. Other firms have been less successful, and the fall in prices has forced them to leave the market.

disparate choices as the number of candy bars a firm wants to sell and the number of hours a worker is willing to work. As with demand, the first question economists ask is, How does the quantity supplied change when price changes, if everything else is kept the same?

Figure 3.8 shows the number of candy bars that a candy company would like to sell, or supply to the market, at each price. If the price of a candy bar is only 75 cents, the firm does not find it profitable to produce and sell any candy bars. At a higher price, however, the firm can make a profit. If the price is $2.00, the firm wants to sell 85,000 candy bars. At an even higher price—for example, $5.00 per candy bar—it wants to sell even more candy bars, 100,000.

Figure 3.8 also depicts these points in a graph. The curve drawn by connecting the points is called the firm's **supply curve.** It shows the quantity that the candy company will supply at each price, when all other factors are held constant. For this curve, like the demand curve, we put the price on the horizontal axis. Thus, we can read point *A* on the curve as indicating that at a price of $1.50, the firm would like to supply 70,000 candy bars.

In direct contrast to the demand curve, the typical supply curve slopes upward from left to right; at higher prices, firms will supply more. This is because higher prices yield suppliers higher profits—giving them an incentive to produce more.

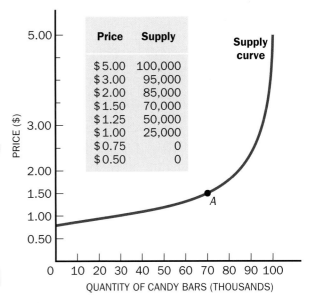

Price	Supply
$5.00	100,000
$3.00	95,000
$2.00	85,000
$1.50	70,000
$1.25	50,000
$1.00	25,000
$0.75	0
$0.50	0

Figure 3.8

ONE FIRM'S SUPPLY CURVE

The supply curve shows the quantity of a good a firm is willing to produce at each price. Normally a firm is willing to produce more as the price increases, which is why the supply curve slopes upward.

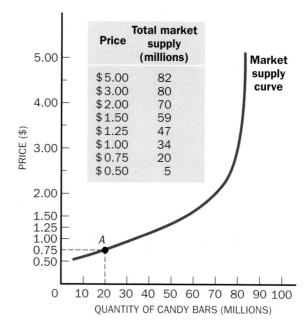

Price	Total market supply (millions)
$5.00	82
$3.00	80
$2.00	70
$1.50	59
$1.25	47
$1.00	34
$0.75	20
$0.50	5

Figure 3.9

THE MARKET SUPPLY CURVE

The market supply curve shows the quantity of a good all firms in the market are willing to supply at each price. The market supply curve is normally upward sloping, both because each firm is willing to supply more of the good at a higher price and because higher prices entice new firms to produce.

MARKET SUPPLY

The *market supply* of a good is the total quantity that all the firms in the economy are willing to supply at a given price. Similarly, the market supply of labor is the total quantity of labor that all the households in the economy are willing to supply at a given wage. Figure 3.9 tells us, for instance, that at a price of $2.00, firms will supply 70 million candy bars, while at a price of $0.50, they will supply only 5 million.

Figure 3.9 also shows the same information graphically. The curve joining the points in the figure is the **market supply curve.** The market supply curve gives the total quantity of a good that firms are willing to produce at each price. Thus, we read point *A* on the market supply curve as showing that at a price of $0.75, the firms in the economy would like to sell 20 million candy bars.

As the price of candy bars increases, the quantity supplied increases, other things being equal. The market supply curve slopes upward from left to right for two reasons: at higher prices, each firm in the market is willing to produce more; and at higher prices, more firms are willing to enter the market to produce the good.

The market supply curve is calculated from the supply curves of the different firms in the same way that the market demand curve is calculated from the demand curves of the different households: at each price, we add horizontally the quantities that each of the firms is willing to produce.

SUPPLY CURVE

The supply curve gives the quantity of the good supplied at each price.

SHIFTS IN SUPPLY CURVES

Just as demand curves can shift, supply curves too can shift, so that the quantity supplied at each price increases or decreases. Suppose a drought hits the bread-basket states of mid-America. Figure 3.10 illustrates the situation. The supply curve for wheat shifts to the left, which means that at each price of wheat, the quantity firms are willing to supply is smaller.

SOURCES OF SHIFTS IN SUPPLY CURVES

There are several sources of shifts in market supply curves, just as we saw for market demand curves. One is changing prices of the inputs used to produce a good. Figure 3.11 shows that as corn becomes less expensive, the supply curve for cornflakes shifts to the right. Producing cornflakes costs less, so at every price, firms are willing to supply

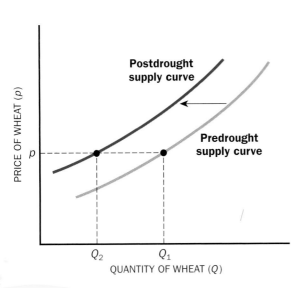

Figure 3.10

SHIFTING THE SUPPLY CURVE TO THE LEFT

A drought or other disaster (among other possible factors) will cause the supply curve to shift to the left, so that at each price, a smaller quantity is supplied.

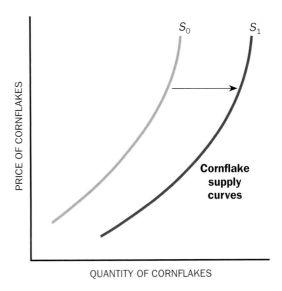

Figure 3.11

SHIFTING THE SUPPLY CURVE TO THE RIGHT

An improvement in technology or a reduction in input prices (among other possible factors) will cause the supply curve to shift to the right, so that at each price, a larger quantity is supplied.

a greater quantity. That is why the quantity supplied along the curve S_1 is greater than the quantity supplied, at the same price, along the curve S_0.

Another source of shifts is changes in technology. The technological improvements in the computer industry over the past two decades have led to a rightward shift in the market supply curve. Yet another source of shifts is nature. The supply curve for agricultural goods may shift to the right or left depending on weather conditions, insect infestations, or animal diseases.

Firms often borrow to obtain inputs needed for production, and a rise in interest rates will increase the cost of borrowing. This increase too will induce a leftward shift in the supply curve. Finally, changed expectations can also lead to a shift in the supply curve. If firms believe that a new technology for making cars will become available in two years, they will discourage investment today, leading to a temporary leftward shift in the supply curve.

Wrap-Up

SOURCES OF SHIFTS IN MARKET SUPPLY CURVES

A change in the prices of inputs
A change in technology

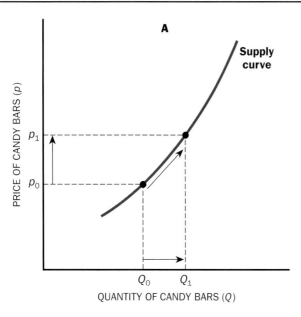
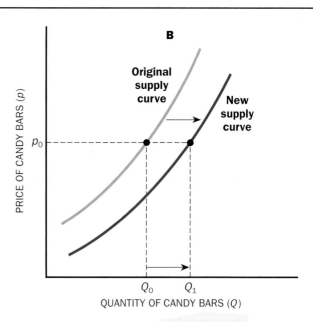

Figure 3.12

MOVEMENT ALONG THE SUPPLY CURVE VERSUS SHIFT IN THE SUPPLY CURVE

Panel A shows an increase in quantity supplied caused by a higher price—a movement along a given supply curve. Panel B illustrates an increase in quantity supplied caused by a shift in the entire supply curve, so that a greater quantity is supplied at every market price.

A change in the natural environment
A change in the availability of credit
A change in expectations

SHIFTS IN A SUPPLY CURVE VERSUS MOVEMENTS ALONG A SUPPLY CURVE

Distinguishing between a movement *along* a curve and a *shift* in the curve itself is just as important for supply curves as it is for demand curves. In Figure 3.12A, the price of candy bars has gone up, with a corresponding increase in quantity supplied. Thus, there has been a movement along the supply curve.

By contrast, in Figure 3.12B, the supply curve has shifted to the right, perhaps because a new production technique has made it cheaper to produce candy bars. Now, even though the price does not change, the quantity supplied increases. The quantity supplied in the market can increase either because the price of the good has increased, so that for a *given supply curve,* the quantity produced is higher; or because the supply curve has shifted, so that at a *given price,* the quantity supplied has increased.

FUNDAMENTALS OF DEMAND, SUPPLY, AND PRICE 2

SUPPLY INCREASES AS PRICE RISES

As the price of a good increases, the quantity firms are willing to supply rises. Changes in factors other than price—such as the costs of production or changes in technology—shift the supply curve.

Law of Supply and Demand

This chapter began with the assertion that supply and demand work together to determine the market price in competitive markets. Figure 3.13 puts a market supply curve and a market demand curve on the same graph to show how this happens. The price actually paid and received in the market will be determined by the intersection of the two curves. This point is labeled E_0, for equilibrium, and the corresponding price ($0.75) and quantity (20 million) are called, respectively, the **equilibrium price** and the **equilibrium quantity.**

Since the term **equilibrium** will recur throughout the book, it is important to understand the concept clearly. Equilibrium describes a situation where there are no forces (reasons) for change. No one has an incentive to change the result—the price or quantity consumed or produced, in the case of supply and demand.

Physicists also speak of equilibrium in describing a weight hanging from a spring. Two forces are working on the weight. Gravity is pulling it down; the spring is pulling

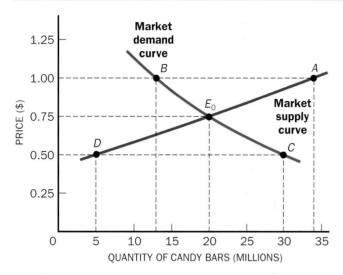

Figure 3.13

SUPPLY AND DEMAND EQUILIBRIUM

Equilibrium occurs at the intersection of the demand and supply curves, at point E_0. At any price above E_0, the quantity supplied will exceed the quantity demanded, the market will be out of equilibrium, and there will be excess supply. At any price below E_0, the quantity demanded will exceed the quantity supplied, the market will be out of equilibrium, and there will be excess demand.

it up. When the weight is at rest, it is in equilibrium, with the two forces just offsetting each other. If someone pulls the weight down a little bit, the force of the spring will be greater than the force of gravity, and the weight will spring up. In the absence of any further interventions, the weight will bob back and forth and eventually return to its equilibrium position.

An economic equilibrium is established in the same way. At the equilibrium price, consumers get precisely the quantity of the good they are willing to buy at that price, and producers sell precisely the quantity they are willing to sell at that price. The market clears. To emphasize this condition, economists sometimes refer to the equilibrium price as the **market clearing price.** In equilibrium, neither producers nor consumers have any incentive to change.

But consider the price of $1.00 in Figure 3.13. There is no equilibrium quantity here. First find $1.00 on the vertical axis. Now look across to find point A on the supply curve, and read down to the horizontal axis; point A tells you that a price of $1.00, firms want to supply 34 million candy bars. Now look at point B on the demand curve. Point B shows that at a price of $1.00 consumers want to buy only 13 million candy bars. Like the weight bobbing on a spring however, this market will work its way back to equilibrium in the following way. At a price of $1.00, there is **excess supply.** As producers discover that they cannot sell as much as they would like at this price, some of them will lower their prices slightly, hoping to take business from other producers. When one producer lowers prices, his competitors will have to respond, for fear that they will end up unable to sell their goods. As prices come down, consumers will also buy more, and so on until the market reaches the equilibrium price and quantity.

Similarly, assume that the price is lower than $0.75, say $0.50. At the lower price, there is **excess demand:** individuals want to buy 30 million candy bars (point C), while firms want to produce only 5 million (point D). Consumers unable to purchase all they want will offer to pay a bit more; other consumers, afraid of having to do without, will match these higher bids or exceed them. As prices start to increase, suppliers will also have a greater incentive to produce more. Again the market will tend toward the equilibrium point.

To repeat for emphasis: at equilibrium, no purchaser and no supplier has an incentive to change the price or quantity. In competitive market economies, actual prices tend to be the equilibrium prices at which demand equals supply. This is called the **law of supply and demand.** Note: this law does not mean that at every moment of time the price is precisely at the intersection of the demand and supply curves. Like the weight on a spring described above, the market may bounce around a little bit when it is in the process of adjusting. What the law of supply and demand does say is that when a market is out of equilibrium, there are predictable forces for change.

USING DEMAND AND SUPPLY CURVES

The concepts of demand and supply curves—and market equilibrium as the inter-section of demand and supply curves—constitute the economist's basic model of demand and supply. This model has proved to be extremely useful. It helps explain why the price of a given commodity is high, and that of some other commodity is low. It also helps *predict* the consequences of certain changes. Its predictions can then be tested against what actually happens. One of the reasons that the model is so useful is that it gives reasonably accurate predictions.

Figure 3.14 repeats the demand and supply curve for candy bars. But assume now that sugar becomes more expensive. As a result, at each price the amount of candy firms are willing to supply is reduced. The supply curve shifts to the left, as in panel A. There will be a new equilibrium, at a higher price and a lower quantity of candy consumed.

Alternatively, assume that Americans become more health conscious, and as a result, at each price fewer candy bars are consumed: the demand curve shifts to the left, as shown in panel B. Again, there will be a new equilibrium, at a lower price and a lower quantity of candy consumed.

This illustrates how changes in observed prices can be related either to shifts in the demand curve or to shifts in the supply curve. To take a different example, when the war in Kuwait interrupted the supply of oil from the Middle East in 1990, the supply curve shifted. The model predicted the result: an increase in the price of oil. This increase was the natural outcome of the law of supply and demand.

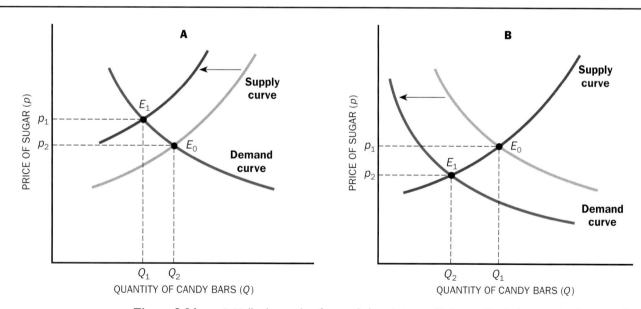

Figure 3.14

USING SUPPLY AND DEMAND CURVES TO PREDICT PRICE CHANGES

Initially the market for candy bars is in equilibrium at E_0. An increase in the cost of sugar shifts the supply curve to the left, as shown in panel A. At the new equilibrium, E_1, the price is higher and the quantity consumed is lower. A shift in taste away from candy results in a leftward shift in the demand curve as shown in panel B. At the new equilibrium, E_1, the price and the quantity consumed are lower.

CONSENSUS ON THE DETERMINATION OF PRICES

The law of supply and demand plays such a prominent role in economics that there is a joke about teaching a parrot to be an economist simply by training it to say "supply and demand." That prices are determined by the law of supply and demand is one of the most long-standing and widely accepted ideas of economists. *In competitive markets, prices are determined by the law of supply and demand. Shifts in the demand and supply curves lead to changes in the equilibrium price. Similar principles apply to the labor and capital markets. The price for labor is the wage, and the price for capital is the interest rate; thus in later chapters we can use the same principles of demand and supply developed in this chapter to study labor and capital markets.*

FUNDAMENTALS OF DEMAND, SUPPLY, AND PRICE 3

THE MARKET CLEARS AT THE EQUILIBRIUM PRICE

The price at which the quantity demanded and the quantity supplied are equal is the equilibrium price. At the equilibrium price, consumers are able to obtain the quantity they wish to purchase and firms are able to sell the quantity they wish to produce. When the market clears, there are no shortages or surpluses. The law of supply and demand allows us to predict how price and quantity will change in response to shifts in the demand and supply curves.

Price, Value, and Cost

To an economist, price is what is given in exchange for a good or service. Price, in this sense, is determined by the forces of supply and demand. Adam Smith, often thought of as the founder of modern economics, called our notion of price "value in exchange," and contrasted it to the notion of "value in use":

> The things which have the greatest value in use have frequently little or no value in exchange; and on the contrary, those which have the greatest value in exchange have frequently little or no value in use. Nothing is more useful than water: but it will purchase scarce any thing; scarce any thing can be had in exchange for it. A diamond, on the contrary, has scarce any value in use; but a very great quantity of other goods may frequently be had in exchange for it.[2]

The law of supply and demand can help to explain the diamond-water paradox and many similar examples where "value in use" is very different from "value in

---

[2]*The Wealth of Nations* (1776), Book One, Chapter IV.

THE DEMAND AND SUPPLY IN THE OIL MARKET

The U.S. Energy Information Administration (EIA) has a slide presentation at www.eia.doe.gov/emeu/25opec/anniversary.html that illustrates some of the major ways that the energy price increases during the 1970s affected the types of cars Americans bought and how they heated their homes.

---

exchange." Figure 3.15 presents a demand and a supply curve for water. Individuals are willing to pay a high price for the water they need to live, as illustrated by point *A* on the demand curve. But above some quantity, *B,* people will pay almost nothing more for additional water. In most of the inhabited parts of the world, water is readily available, so it is supplied in plentiful quantities at low prices. Thus, the supply curve of water intersects the demand curve to the right of *B,* as in the figure—hence, the low equilibrium price. (Of course, in the desert the water supply may be very limited and the price, as a result, very high.)

To an economist, the observations that the price of diamonds is high and the price of water is low are statements about supply and demand conditions. They say nothing about whether diamonds are "more important" or "better" than water. In Adam Smith's terms, they are not statements about value in use.

Price is related to the *marginal* value of an object: that is, the value of an additional unit of the object. Water has a low price not because the *total* value of water is low—it is obviously high, since we could not live without it—but because the marginal value, what we would be willing to pay to be able to drink one more glass of water a year, is low.

Just as economists take care to distinguish between the words "price" and "value," so they also distinguish the *price* of an object (what it sells for) from its *cost* (the expense of making the object). This is another crucial distinction in economics. The costs of producing a good affect the price at which firms are willing to supply that good. An increase in the costs of production will normally cause prices to rise. And in the competitive model, *in equilibrium,* the price of an object will normally equal its (marginal) cost of production (including the amount needed to pay a firm's owner to stay in business rather than seek some other form of employment). But there are important cases—as we will see in later chapters—where price does not equal cost.

As we think about the relationship of price and cost, it is interesting to consider the case of a good in fixed supply, such as land. Normally, land is something that cannot be produced, so its cost of production can be considered infinite (though sometimes land can be produced, as when Chicago filled in part of Lake Michigan to expand its lake shore). Yet there is still an equilibrium price of land—where the demand for land is equal to its (fixed) supply.

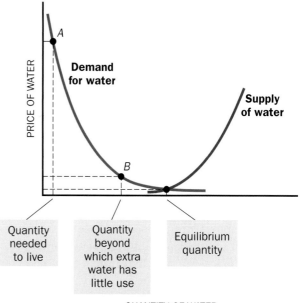

Figure 3.15

SUPPLY AND DEMAND FOR WATER

Point *A* shows that people are willing to pay a relatively high price for the first few units of water. But to the right of *B,* people have plenty of water already and are not willing to pay much for an additional amount. The price of water will be determined at the point where the supply curve crosses the demand curve. In most cases, the resulting price is extremely low.

Review and Practice

SUMMARY

1. An individual's demand curve gives the quantity demanded of a good at each possible price. It normally slopes down, which means that the person demands a greater quantity of the good at lower prices and a lesser quantity at higher prices.

2. The market demand curve gives the total quantity of a good demanded by all individuals in an economy at each price. As the price rises, demand falls, both because each person demands less of the good and because some people exit the market.

3. A firm's supply curve gives the amount of a good the firm is willing to supply at each price. It is normally upward sloping, which means that firms supply a greater quantity of the good at higher prices and a lesser quantity at lower prices.

4. The market supply curve gives the total quantity of a good that all firms in the economy are willing to produce at each price. As the price rises, supply rises, both because each firm supplies more of the good and because some additional firms enter the market.

5. The law of supply and demand says that in competitive markets, the equilibrium price is that price at which quantity demanded equals quantity supplied. It is represented on a graph by the intersection of the demand and supply curves.

6. A demand curve shows *only* the relationship between quantity demanded and price. Changes in tastes, in demographic factors, in income, in the prices of other goods, in information, in the availability of credit, or in expectations are reflected in a shift of the entire demand curve.

7. A supply curve shows *only* the relationship between quantity supplied and price. Changes in factors such as technology, the prices of inputs, the natural environment, expectations, or the availability of credit are reflected in a shift of the entire supply curve.

8. It is important to distinguish movements along a demand curve from shifts in the demand curve, and movements along a supply curve from shifts in the supply curve.

KEY TERMS

price
demand
demand curve
market demand curve
substitutes
complements
demographic effects
supply
supply curve
market supply curve
equilibrium price
equilibrium quantity
equilibrium
market clearing price
excess supply
excess demand
law of supply and demand

REVIEW QUESTIONS

1. Why does an individual's demand curve normally slope down? Why does a market demand curve normally slope down?

2. Why does a firm's supply curve normally slope up? Why does a market supply curve normally slope up?

3. What is the significance of the point where supply and demand curves intersect?

4. Explain why, if the price of a good is above the equilibrium price, the forces of supply and demand will tend to push the price toward equilibrium. Explain why, if the price of the good is below the equilibrium price, the market will tend to adjust toward equilibrium.

5. Name some factors that could shift the demand curve out to the right.

6. Name some factors that could shift the supply curve in to the left.

PROBLEMS

1. Imagine a company lunchroom that sells pizza by the slice. Using the following data, plot the points and graph

the demand and supply curves. What is the equilibrium price and quantity? Find a price at which excess demand would exist and a price at which excess supply would exist, and plot them on your diagram.

Price per slice	Demand (number of slices)	Supply (number of slices)
$1	420	0
$2	210	100
$3	140	140
$4	105	160
$5	84	170

2. Suppose a severe drought hits the sugarcane crop. Predict how this will affect the equilibrium price and quantity in the market for sugar and the market for honey. Draw supply and demand diagrams to illustrate your answers.

3. Imagine that a new invention allows each mine worker to mine twice as much coal. Predict how this will affect the equilibrium price and quantity in the market for coal and the market for heating oil. Draw supply and demand diagrams to illustrate your answers.

4. Americans' tastes have shifted away from beef and toward chicken. Predict how this change has affected the equilibrium price and quantity in the market for beef, the market for chicken, and the market for roadside hamburger stands. Draw supply and demand diagrams to illustrate your answers.

5. During the 1970s, the postwar baby boomers reached working age, and it became more acceptable for married women with children to work. Predict how this increase in the number of workers is likely to affect the equilibrium wage and quantity of employment. Draw supply and demand curves to illustrate your answers.

6. In 2001, Europeans became very concerned about what is called mad cow disease, and thus about the dangers posed by eating contaminated meat. What would this concern do to the demand curve for beef? to the demand curves for chicken and fish? to the equilibrium price of beef, chicken, and fish?

Mad cow disease is spread by feeding cows food that contains parts from infected animals. Presumably the reason why cows are fed this food is that doing so is cheaper than relying exclusively on grain. What is the

consequence for the supply curve of beef of restricting feed to grain? What are the consequences for the price of beef (a) if the new restrictions fail to restore confidence in beef and (b) if the new restrictions succeed in restoring confidence so that the demand curve returns to its original position?

At about the same time in Europe, there was an outbreak of hoof-and-mouth disease; to stop the spread of the disease, large numbers of cattle were killed. What does this do to the supply curve of beef? to the equilibrium price of beef?

7. Many advanced industrialized countries subsidize farmers. Assume that the effect of the subsidy is to shift the supply curve of agricultural products by farmers in the advanced industrialized countries to the right. Why might less-developed countries be unhappy with such policies?

8. Farm output is extremely sensitive to the weather. In 1988, the midwestern region of the United States experienced one of the worst droughts ever recorded; corn production fell by 35 percent, wheat production by more than 10 percent, and oat and barley production by more than 40 percent. What do you suppose happened to the prices of these commodities?

These grains are an input into the production of cattle. The higher cost of grain led many ranchers to slaughter their cattle earlier. What do you think happened to the price of beef in the short run? In the intermediate run?

Why did the drought in the Midwest lead to increased prices for vegetables and fruits?

9. Suppose that there are 1,000 one-bedroom apartments in a small town and that this number is fixed. The table gives the quantity demand in the market for one-bedroom apartments.

Price (Rent per month)	Demand (Apartment units)
$500	1,600
$600	1,400
$700	1,200
$800	1,000
$900	800
$1,000	600
$1,200	400

(a) What is the equilibrium rental for a one-bedroom apartment?

(b) Suppose 200 new one-bedroom apartments are constructed. What happens to the equilibrium rent?

(c) Suppose more people move into the town, increasing the demand for one-bedroom apartments by 200 units at each price. What is the new equilibrium price? (Assume the supply remains fixed at 1,200 units.)

10. Suppose a town decides to give a $100 subsidy to each renter to help with rent payments. Thus if initially the rent had been $1,000, with the $100 subsidy the out-of-pocket cost to the renter of a one-bedroom apartment is only $900. Using the data from Problem 9, answer each of the following questions.

(a) Using the data from Problem 9, draw the demand curve before the subsidy. How does this subsidy affect the demand for one-bedroom apartments? Draw the new demand curve after the subsidy is introduced.

(b) If the supply of apartments is fixed at 1,200 units, what is the equilibrium price *before* the subsidy? What is the equilibrium price *after* the subsidy?

(c) At the new equilibrium price, what is the out-of-pocket cost to a renter for a one-bedroom apartment?

(d) Have renters benefited from the town's rent subsidy? Have apartment owners (suppliers)?

Learning Goals

In this chapter, you will learn

1 What is meant by the concept of elasticity

2 How elasticity helps explain the effects on prices and quantities of shifts in demand and supply

3 How government policies such as rent control or agricultural price supports that interfere with market outcomes lead to shortages and surpluses

Chapter 4

USING DEMAND AND SUPPLY

Why are doctors, on average, paid more than lawyers? And why are lawyers paid more than schoolteachers? Why does your economics professor probably make more than your literature professor? And why has the wage gap between college graduates and those with only a high school education widened in recent years? The concepts of demand and supply developed in the previous chapter can help us answer these questions. Moreover, these concepts help us predict what will happen if the government increases the tax on cigarettes or the tax on gasoline. But economists are usually interested in more specific predictions. They want to know how much the tax on gasoline would need to be raised if the goal is to lower gasoline consumption by, say, 10 percent, or how much a frost in Florida that reduces the orange crop will increase the price of orange juice.

In this chapter, we develop some of the concepts needed to make these sorts of predictions. In addition, we examine what happens when governments intervene with the workings of competitive markets. High rents and expensive food may seem to block poor people's access to adequate housing and nutrition, farmers may feel that the prices of their crops are too low, and textile workers may object to competing with laborers producing similar goods in low-wage countries. Political pressures are constantly brought to bear on government to intervene on behalf of groups that feel disadvantaged by the workings of the market. In the second part of this chapter, we track some of the consequences of these political interventions.

The Price Elasticity of Demand

To predict the effects of a tax on gasoline on how much people drive or of a frost on the price of orange juice, we must start by asking what substitutes exist for the good in question. If the price of orange juice rises, consumers have an incentive to buy less orange juice and to buy apple juice, cranberry juice, or any one of a number of other drinks instead. If a new tax pushes up the price of gasoline, drivers likewise have an incentive to reduce their consumption of gas; but doing so may be difficult for those who have to drive to work in cars with conventional engines. Some may be able to ride the bus, but many will be hard-pressed to find an alternative means of transportation. And switching to an electric or hybrid vehicle can be costly.

As these examples illustrate, substitutes exist for almost every good or service, but substitution will be more difficult for some goods and services than for others. When substitution is difficult, an increase in the price of a good will not cause the quantity demanded to decrease by much, and a decrease in the price will not cause the quantity demanded to increase much. In terms of the demand curves we discussed in Chapter 3, the demand curve for a good with few substitutes will be relatively steep: changes in price do not cause very large changes in the quantity demanded.

When substitution is easy, as in the case of orange juice, an increase in price may lead to a large decrease in the quantity demanded. Ice cream is another example of a good with many close substitutes. A price increase for ice cream means that frozen yogurt, gelato, and similar products become relatively less expensive, and the demand for ice cream would thus significantly decrease. The demand curve for a good with many substitutes will be relatively flat: changes in price cause large changes in the quantity demanded.

For many purposes, economists need to be precise about how steep or how flat the demand curve is. They therefore use the concept of the **price elasticity of demand** (for short, the price elasticity or the elasticity of demand), which is defined as the percentage change in the quantity demanded divided by the percentage change in price. In mathematical terms,

$$\text{elasticity of demand} = \frac{\text{percentage change in quantity demanded}}{\text{percentage change in price}}.$$

If the quantity demanded changes 8 percent in response to a 2 percent change in price, then the elasticity of demand is 4.

(Price elasticities of demand are really *negative* numbers; that is, when the price increases, quantities demanded are reduced. But the convention is to simply give the elasticity's absolute value with the understanding that it is negative.)

It is easiest to calculate the elasticity of demand when there is just a 1 percent change in price. Then the elasticity of demand is just the percentage change in the quantity demanded. In the telescoped portion of Figure 4.1A, we see that increasing the price of orange juice from $2.00 a gallon to $2.02—a 1 percent increase in price—reduces the demand from 100 million gallons to 98 million, a 2 percent decline. So the price elasticity of demand for ice cream is 2.

By contrast, assume that the price of gas increases from $2.00 a gallon to $2.02 (again a 1 percent increase in price), as shown in the telescoped portion of Figure 4.1B. This reduces demand from 100 million gallons per year to 99.8 million. Demand has gone down by 0.2 percent, so the price elasticity of demand is therefore 0.2. Larger values for price elasticity indicate that demand is more sensitive to changes in price. Smaller values indicate that demand is less sensitive to price changes.

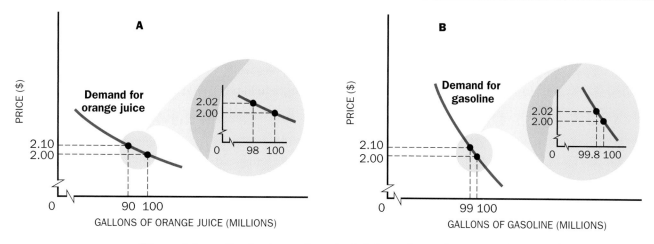

Figure 4.1

ELASTIC VERSUS INELASTIC
DEMAND CURVES

Panel A shows a hypothetical demand curve for orange juice. Note that the quantity demanded changes greatly with fairly small price changes, indicating that demand for orange juice is elastic. The telescoped portion of the demand curve shows that a 1 percent rise in price leads to a 2 percent fall in quantity demanded. Panel B shows a hypothetical demand curve for gasoline. Note that the quantity demanded changes very little, regardless of changes in price, indicating that demand for gas is inelastic. The telescoped portion of the demand curve shows that a 1 percent rise in price leads to a 0.2 percent fall in quantity demanded.

PRICE ELASTICITY AND REVENUES

The revenue received by a firm in selling a good is its price times the quantity sold. We can write this definition in a simple equation. Letting R denote revenues, p price, and Q quantity:

$$R = pQ.$$

Thus when price goes up by 1 percent, the effect on revenues depends on the magnitude of the decrease in quantity. If quantity decreases by more than 1 percent, then total revenues decrease; by less than 1 percent, they increase.

We can express this result in terms of the concept of price elasticity. When the elasticity of demand is greater than 1, the change in quantity more than offsets the change in prices; we say that the demand for that good is **relatively elastic,** or *sensitive* to price changes, and revenues decrease as price increases and increase as price decreases. For example, the demand for different brands of personal computers is judged to be relatively elastic.

In the case in which the price elasticity is 1, the decrease in the quantity demanded just offsets the increase in the price, so price increases have no effect on revenues. This is called **unitary elasticity.** Many basic food products and entertainment activities, such as going to the movies, are considered to have unitary elasticities of demand. If the price elasticity is less than 1, then a 1 percent increase in the price of a good will reduce the quantity demanded by less than 1 percent. Since demand falls little when elasticities are in this range, between 0 and 1, price increases for such goods will increase revenues. And price decreases will decrease revenues. We say the demand for these goods is **relatively inelastic,** or *insensitive* to price changes.

Business firms must pay attention to the price elasticity of demand for their products. Suppose a cement producer, the only one in town, is considering a 1 percent increase in price. The firm hires an economist to estimate the elasticity of demand so that it will know what will happen to sales after the increase. The economist tells the firm that its demand elasticity is 2. This means that if the price of cement rises by 1 percent, the quantity sold will decline by 2 percent.

The firm's executives will not be pleased by the findings. To see why, assume that initially the price of cement was $1,000 per ton, and 100,000 tons were sold. To calculate revenues, you multiply the price times the quantity sold. So initially revenues were $1,000 × 100,000 = $100 million. With a 1 percent increase, the price will be $1,010. If the elasticity of demand is 2, then a 1 percent price increase results in a 2 percent decrease in the quantity sold: sales drop to 98,000 tons. Revenues are down to $98.98 million ($1,010 × 98,000), a fall of just slightly over 1 percent. Because of the high elasticity, this cement firm's price *increase* leads to a *decrease* in revenues.

The price elasticity of demand works the same way for price decreases. Suppose the cement producer decided to lower the price of cement 1 percent, to $990. With an elasticity of demand of 2, sales would then increase 2 percent, to 102,000 tons. Thus, revenues would *increase* to $100,980,000 ($990 × 102,000)—that is, by a bit less than 1 percent.

There are two extreme cases that deserve attention. One is that of a flat demand curve, a curve that is perfectly horizontal. We say that such a demand curve is perfectly elastic, or has **infinite elasticity,** since even a slight increase in the price results in demand dropping to zero. The demand curve facing a firm that produces computer memory chips is perfectly elastic, if the manufacturer tried to charge a slightly higher price for its chips, sales would fall to zero as buyers would simply buy their memory chips elsewhere. The other extreme case is that of a demand curve that is perfectly vertical. We say that such a demand curve is perfectly inelastic, or has **zero elasticity,** since whatever the price, demand remains the same. The rabid sports fan's demand for a Super Bowl ticket may in effect be perfectly inelastic; no matter how much it costs, the fan will buy a ticket. Table 4.1 summarizes the different cases that we have discussed, together with some illustrative examples of goods with differing elasticities of demand.

The Determinants of the Elasticity of Demand

In our earlier discussion, we noted one of the important determinants of the elasticity of demand: the availability of substitutes. There are, in turn, two important determinants of the degree of substitutability: the relative price of the good consumed and the length of time it takes to make an adjustment.

When the price of a commodity is low, and its consumption is high, a variety of substitutes exist. Figure 4.2 illustrates the case for aluminum. When the price of aluminum is low, it is used as a food wrap (aluminum foil), in containers for canned

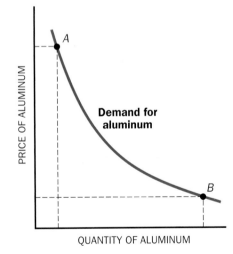

Figure 4.2

CHANGING ELASTICITY ALONG A DEMAND CURVE

Near point *A*, where the price is high, the demand curve is quite steep and inelastic. In the area of the demand curve near *B*, the demand curve is very flat and elastic.

Table 4.1

PRICE ELASTICITY OF DEMAND

Elasticity	Description	Effect on Quantity Demanded of 1% Increase in Price	Effect on Revenues of 1% Increase in Price	Examples
Zero	Perfectly inelastic (vertical demand curve)	Zero	Increased by 1%	Superbowl Tickets
Between 0 and 1	Inelastic	Reduced by less than 1%	Increased by less than 1%	gasoline
1	Unitary elasticity	Reduced by 1%	Unchanged	
Greater than 1	Elastic	Reduced by more 1%	Reduced; the greater the elasticity, the more revenue is reduced	Brands of PCs
Infinite	Perfectly elastic (horizontal demand curve)	Reduced to zero	Reduced to zero	Brands of memory chips

goods, and in airplane frames because it is lightweight. As the price increases, customers seek out substitutes. At first, substitutes are easy to find, and the demand for the product is greatly reduced. For example, plastic wrap frequently can be used instead of aluminum foil. As the price rises still further, tin replaces aluminum for cans. At very high prices, say near point *A,* aluminum is used only where its properties are essential, such as in airplane frames. At this point, it may take a *huge* price increase before some other material becomes an economical substitute.

A second important determinant of the elasticity of demand is time. Because it is always easier to find substitutes and to make other adjustments when a longer time is available to make them, the elasticity of demand is normally larger in the *long run*—in the period in which all adjustments can be made—than it is in the *short run,* when at least some adjustments cannot be made. Figure 4.3 illustrates the difference in shape between short-run and long-run demand curves for gasoline.

The sharp increase in oil prices in the 1970s beautifully exemplifies this point. The short-run price elasticity of gasoline was 0.2 (a 1 percent increase in price led to only a 0.2 percent decrease in quantity demanded), while the long-run elasticity was 0.7 or more; the short-run elasticity of fuel oil was 0.2, and the long-run elasticity was 1.2. In the short run, consumers were stuck with their old gas-guzzling cars, their drafty houses, and their old fuel-wasting habits. In the long run, however, consumers bought smaller cars, became used to houses kept at slightly lower

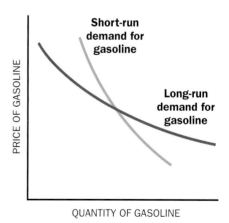

Figure 4.3

ELASTICITY OF DEMAND OVER TIME

Demand curves tend to be inelastic in the short run, when there is little time to adapt to price changes, but more elastic in the long run.

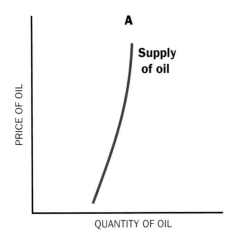

A

Supply
of oil

PRICE OF OIL

QUANTITY OF OIL

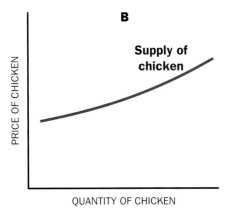

B

Supply of
chicken

PRICE OF CHICKEN

QUANTITY OF CHICKEN

Figure 4.4

DIFFERING ELASTICITIES OF
SUPPLY

Panel A shows a supply curve for oil. It is
inelastic: the quantity supplied increases
only a small amount with a rise in price.
Panel B shows a supply curve for chicken.
It is elastic: the quantity supplied increases substantially with a rise in price.

temperatures, installed better insulation in their homes, and turned to alternative energy sources. The long-run demand curve was therefore much more elastic (flat) than the short-run curve. Indeed, the long-run elasticity turned out to be much larger than anticipated.

The duration of "the long run" will vary from product to product. In some cases, adjustments can occur rapidly; in other cases, they are very gradual. As old gas-guzzlers wore out, they were replaced with fuel-efficient compact cars. As furnaces broke, they were replaced with more efficient ones. New homes are now constructed with better insulation, so that gradually, over time, the fraction of houses that are well insulated is increasing.

Some of these changes are reversible: in the 1990s, in response to low gas prices, fuel-efficient cars were replaced by gas-guzzling sport utility vehicles (SUVs). But when higher prices induce innovations—for example, manufacturers of cars discover ways of increasing mileage per gallon—then the benefits of those innovations remain even when prices subsequently fall.

The Price Elasticity of Supply

Supply curves normally slope upward. Like demand curves, they are steep in some cases and flat in others. The degree of steepness reflects sensitivity to price changes. A steep supply curve, like the one for oil in Figure 4.4A, indicates that a large change in price generates only a small change in the quantity firms want to supply. A flatter curve, like the one for chicken in Figure 4.4B, indicates that a small change in price generates a large change in supply. Economists have developed a precise way of representing the sensitivity of supply to prices in a way that parallels the one already introduced for demand. The **price elasticity of supply** is defined as the percentage change in quantity supplied divided by the percentage change in price (or the percentage change in quantity supplied corresponding to a price change of 1 percent):

$$\text{Elasticity of supply} = \frac{\text{percentage change in quantity supplied}}{\text{percentage change in price}}.$$

The elasticity of supply of oil is low—an increase in the price of oil will not have a significant effect on the total supply. The elasticity of supply of chicken is high, as President Richard Nixon found out when he imposed price controls in August 1971. When the price of chicken was forced almost 10 percent below the market equilibrium price, farmers found that producing and selling chickens at that price was simply unprofitable; there was a large decrease in the quantity supplied, and huge shortages resulted.

As is the case with demand, if a 1 percent increase in price results in more than a 1 percent increase in supply, we say the supply curve is elastic. If a 1 percent increase in price results in less than a 1 percent increase in supply, the supply curve is inelastic. In the extreme case of a vertical supply curve—where the amount supplied does not depend at all on price—the curve is said to be perfectly inelastic, or to have *zero*

International Perspective

COMPARING REACTIONS TO THE OIL PRICE SHOCK OF 2000

When gasoline prices soared in the fall of 2000, in response to the increase in oil prices, people in Great Britain and other countries in Europe took to the streets. Truckers blocked roads and entrances to refineries. There was a massive political outcry. One might have thought, given Americans' greater dependence on oil (Americans use far more gasoline per capita) and given the far smaller *percentage* increase in prices in Europe (since taxes constitute a far larger fraction of the total price), that the outcry would have been louder in the United States. But this brings home an important point: the consequences of the massive price increase depend not only on the level of consumption but also on consumers' ability to absorb the price increase. Europeans already had cut their use of oil down to low levels, because prices of gasoline were already so high. Hence, the cost to them of a further increase in price may be far greater than to individuals who can easily find ways of conserving on the use of oil.

For instance, Americans can easily conserve on gasoline by switching from high-consuming sports utility vehicles, many of which get as few as 15 miles to the gallon, to efficient diesel cars, which can get 50 miles or more to the gallon. Americans can conserve on fuel oil by keeping the temperature in their homes at 68 degrees rather than 72 degrees. But what are Europeans to do, when they already drive small, fuel-efficient cars and already keep their homes at colder temperatures?

These ideas can be related to demand curves. The elasticity of demand is the percentage reduction in the demand resulting from a 1 percent increase in the price. When the price is very low, the demand curve is very elastic; that is, the elasticity of demand is high because there are many ways of conserving on the good (here, oil). When the price is very high, the demand curve is very inelastic; that is, the elasticity of demand is very low because all of the obvious methods of conservation have already been employed.

Truckers in Newcastle, England, protested high prices for fuel in September 2000.

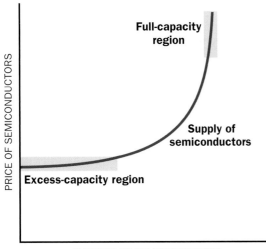

PRICE OF SEMICONDUCTORS

Full-capacity region

Supply of semiconductors

Excess-capacity region

QUANTITY OF SEMICONDUCTORS

Figure 4.5

CHANGING ELASTICITY ALONG A SUPPLY CURVE

When output is low and many machines are idle, a small change in price can lead to a large increase in quantity produced, so the supply curve is flat and elastic. When output is high and all machines are working close to their limit, it takes a very large price change to induce even a small change in output; the supply curve is steep and inelastic.

elasticity; and in the extreme case of a horizontal supply curve, the curve is said to be perfectly elastic, or to have *infinite* elasticity.

Table 4.2 summarizes the different cases for the price elasticity of supply. Paintings by Rembrandt, who died in 1669, and new songs by John Lennon, who died in 1980, have a zero elasticity of supply because no more original Rembrandts can be produced or Lennon songs written. The supply elasticity of labor is estimated to be low; a 1 percent increase in wages leads to a less than 1 percent increase in the total supply of labor. The elasticity of some agricultural crops, such as spinach, is estimated to be greater than 1 because resources (mainly land) used for growing spinach can relatively easily be switched to growing other crops if the price of spinach falls. Finally, the supply of a music CD is close to being infinitely elastic. While producing a greater number of different CDs may require that new artists be developed, new songs be written, and new recording studios be built, a CD, once recorded, can easily be copied at little additional cost.

Just as the demand elasticity varies at different points of the demand curve, so too the supply elasticity varies at different points on the supply curve. Figure 4.5 shows a typical supply curve in manufacturing—perhaps a semiconductor manufacturer. At very low prices, the semiconductor plant is just producing enough to cover its operating costs. Some plants may shut down. Under these circumstances, a small increase in the price of semiconductors elicits a large increase in supply. The supply curve is relatively flat (elastic). But eventually, the plant will reach full capacity, as the company uses three shifts of workers a day to run it around the clock. At this point, it may be very hard to increase supply further, so

Table 4.2

PRICE ELASTICITY OF SUPPLY

Elasticity	Description	Effect on Quantity Supplied of 1% Increase in Price	Examples
Zero	Perfectly inelastic (vertical supply curve)	Zero	Works by Rembrandt
Between 0 and 1	Inelastic	Increased by less than 1%	Labor
1	Unitary elasticity	Increased by 1%	
Greater than 1	Elastic	Increased by more than 1%	Spinach
Infinite	Perfectly elastic (horizontal supply curve)	Infinite increase	A CD recording

the supply curve becomes close to vertical (inelastic). That is, however much the price increases, the supply will not change very much.

Short Run Versus Long Run Economists distinguish between the responsiveness of supply to price in the short run and in the long run, just as they do with demand. Here, too, the long-run elasticity is greater than the short-run elasticity. We define the short-run supply curve as the supply response *given the current stock of machines* and *buildings.* The long-run supply curve assumes that firms can adjust the stock of machines and buildings.

Farm crops are a typical example of a good whose supply in the short run is not very sensitive to changes in price; that is, the supply curve is steep (inelastic). After farmers have done their spring planting, they are committed to a certain level of production. If the price of their crop goes up, they cannot go back and plant more. If the price falls, they are stuck with the crop they have. In this case, the supply curve is relatively close to vertical, as illustrated by the steeper curve in Figure 4.6.

The long-run supply curve for many crops, in contrast, is very flat (elastic). A relatively small change in price can lead to a large change in the quantity supplied. A small increase in the price of soybeans relative to the price of corn may induce many farmers to shift their planting from corn and other crops to soybeans, generating a large increase in the quantity of soybeans. This is illustrated in Figure 4.6 by the flatter curve.

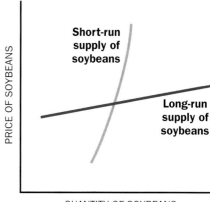

Figure 4.6

ELASTICITY OF SUPPLY OVER TIME

Supply curves may be inelastic in the short run and very elastic in the long run, as in the case of agricultural crops like soybeans.

ELASTICITY

Price elasticity of demand: the percentage change in the quantity of a good demanded as a result of a 1 percent increase (change) in the price charged. When elasticity is low, price changes have little effect on demand. When elasticity is high, price changes have a large effect on demand.

Price elasticity of supply: the percentage change in the quantity of a good supplied as a result of a 1 percent increase (change) in the price charged. When elasticity is low, price changes have little effect on supply. When elasticity is high, price changes have a large effect on supply.

Using Demand and Supply Elasticities

When the demand curve for a good such as beef shifts to the right—when, for instance, beef becomes more popular so that at each price the demand is greater—there is an increase in both the equilibrium price of beef and the quantity demanded, or consumed. Similarly, when the supply curve for a good such as corn shifts to the left—because, for instance, of a drought that hurt the year's crop so that at each price farmers supply

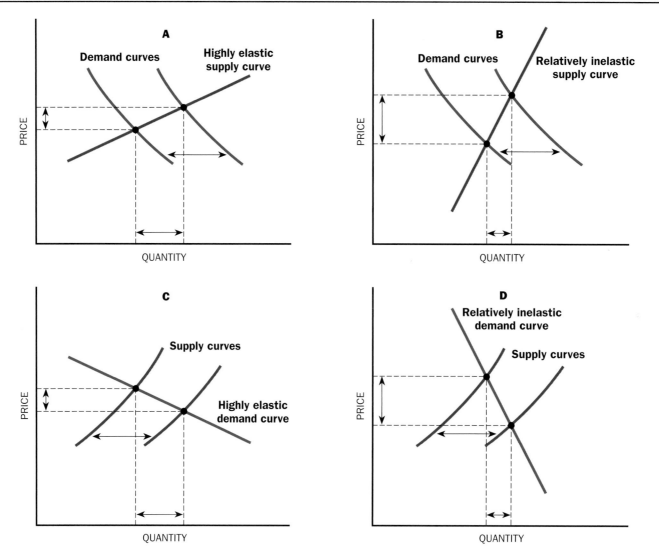

Figure 4.7

ELASTICITY OF DEMAND
AND SUPPLY CURVES:
THE NORMAL CASES

Normally, shifts in the demand curve will be reflected in changes in both price and quantity, as seen in panels A and B. When the supply curve is highly elastic, shifts in the demand curve will result mainly in changes in quantities; if it is relatively inelastic, shifts in the demand curve will result mainly in price changes. Likewise, shifts in the supply curve will be reflected in changes in both price and quantity, as seen in panels C and D. If the demand curve is highly elastic, shifts in the supply curve will result mainly in changes in quantities; if it is relatively inelastic, shifts in the supply curve will result mainly in price changes.

less—there is an increase in the equilibrium price of corn and a decrease in quantity. Knowing that the shifts in the demand or supply curve will lead to an adjustment in both price *and* quantity is helpful, but it is even more useful to know whether most of the impact of a change will be on price or on quantity. To make this determination, we have to consider the price elasticity of both the demand and supply curves.

Figure 4.7 illustrates the typical range of outcomes. If the supply curve is highly elastic (approaching the horizontal, as in panel A), shifts in the demand curve will be reflected more in changes in quantity than in price. If the supply curve is *relatively* inelastic (approaching the vertical, as in panel B), shifts in the demand curve will be reflected more in changes in price than in quantity. If the demand curve is highly elastic (approaching the horizontal, as in panel C), shifts in the supply curve will be reflected more in changes in quantity than in price. Finally, if the demand curve is *relatively* inelastic (approaching the vertical, as in panel D), shifts in the supply curve will be reflected more in changes in price than in quantity.

The extreme cases can be easily seen by extending the graphs in Figure 4.7. If one tilts the supply curve in panel A to be completely flat (perfectly elastic), a shift in the demand curve will have no effect on price. If one tilts the supply curve in panel B to be vertical (perfectly inelastic), a shift in the demand curve will have no effect on quantity.

Long-Run Versus Short-Run Adjustments Because demand and supply curves are likely to be less elastic (more vertical) in the short run than in the long run, shifts in the demand and supply curves are more likely to be reflected in price changes in the short run and in quantity changes in the long run. In fact, price increases in the short run signal firms to increase their production. Therefore, short-run price increases can be thought of as responsible for the output increases that occur in the long run.

Tax Policy and the Law of Supply and Demand For many questions of public policy, understanding the law of supply and demand is vital. One of the important ways economists use this law is in projecting the effect of taxes. Assume that the tax on a pack of cigarettes is increased by 10 cents, that the tax is imposed on cigarette manufacturers, and that all the companies try to pass on the cost increase to consumers by raising the price of a pack by 10 cents. At the higher price, fewer cigarettes will be consumed; the precise decrease depends on the price elasticity of demand. As demand falls, firms must reduce their price if demand is to equal supply; the size of the reduction depends on the price elasticity of supply. The new equilibrium is depicted in Figure 4.8A.

For firms to produce the same amount as before, they must receive 10 cents more per pack (which they pass on to the government). Thus, the supply curve is shifted up by 10 cents. Since the demand for cigarettes is relatively inelastic, this shift will result in a large increase in price and a relatively small decrease in quantity demanded.

When a tax on producers results in consumers' paying a higher price, economists say the tax is "passed on" or "shifted" to consumers. That the consumer bears the tax (even though it is collected from the producers) does not mean that the producers are "powerful" or have conspired together. It simply reflects the system of supply and demand. Note, too, that the price does not rise the full 10 cents. Producers receive slightly lower after-tax prices and therefore bear a small fraction of the tax burden.

A tax imposed on a good for which the demand is very elastic leads to a different result. Assume, for instance, that the government decides to tax cheddar cheese (but not other cheeses). Since many cheeses are similar to cheddar,

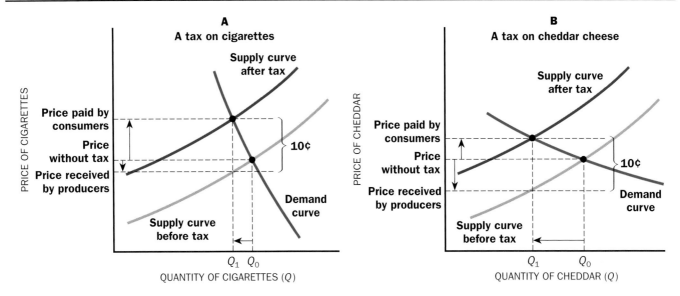

A
A tax on cigarettes

PRICE OF CIGARETTES

Supply curve
after tax

Price paid by
consumers

Price
without tax

Price received
by producers

10¢

Supply curve
before tax

Demand
curve

Q_1 Q_0

QUANTITY OF CIGARETTES (Q)

B
A tax on cheddar cheese

PRICE OF CHEDDAR

Supply curve
after tax

Price paid by
consumers

Price
without tax

Price received
by producers

10¢

Supply curve
before tax

Demand
curve

Q_1 Q_0

QUANTITY OF CHEDDAR (Q)

Figure 4.8

PASSING ALONG A TAX TO
CONSUMERS

A tax on the output of an industry shifts the supply curve up by the amount of the tax. Panel A shows that if the demand curve is relatively inelastic, as it is for cigarettes, then most of the tax will be passed on to consumers in higher prices. Panel B shows that if the demand curve is relatively elastic, as it is for cheddar cheese, then most of the tax cannot be passed along to consumers in higher prices, and must instead be absorbed by producers.

the demand curve for cheddar cheese is very elastic. In this case, as Figure 4.8B makes clear, most of the tax is absorbed by the producer, who receives (after the tax is paid) a lower price. Production of cheddar cheese is reduced drastically as a consequence.

Shortages and Surpluses

In general, the law of supply and demand works so well in a developed modern economy that everyone can take it for granted. A buyer willing to pay the "market price"— the prevailing price of the good, determined by the intersection of demand and supply—can obtain almost any good or service. Similarly, if a seller of a good or service is willing to charge no more than the market price, she can always sell what she wants to.

When the price is set so that demand equals supply—so that any individual can get as much as he wants at that price, and any supplier can sell the amount she wants at that price—economists say that the market clears. But when the market does not clear, there are shortages or surpluses. To an economist, a **shortage** means that people would like to buy something but simply cannot find it for sale at the going price. A **surplus** means that sellers would like to sell their product, but they cannot sell as much of it as they would like at the going price. These cases that seem to illustrate the market's failure to work in fact often underscore most forcefully the importance of the law of supply and demand. The problem is that the "going price" is not the market equilibrium price.

Shortages and surpluses can be seen in the standard supply and demand diagrams shown in Figure 4.9. In both panels A and B, the market equilibrium price is p^*. In panel A, the going price, p_1, is below p^*. At this price, demand exceeds supply; you can see this by reading down to the horizontal axis. Demand is Q_d; supply is Q_s. The gap between the two points is the "shortage." The shortage forces consumers to scramble to get the limited supply available at the going price.

In panel B, the going price, p_1, is above p^*. At this price, demand is less than supply. Again we denote the demand by Q_d and the supply by Q_s. There is a surplus in the market of $Q_s - Q_d$. Now sellers are scrambling to find buyers.

At various times and for various goods, markets have not cleared. There have been shortages of apartments in New York; farm surpluses have plagued both western Europe and the United States; in 1973, a shortage of gasoline led to cars waiting in long lines at U.S. gas stations. Unemployment is a type of surplus, when people who want to work find that they cannot sell their labor services at the going wage.

In some markets, like the markets for agricultural goods, the adjustment of prices to shifts in the demand and supply curves tends to be very rapid. In other cases, such as in the housing market, the adjustments tend to be sluggish. When price adjustments are sluggish, shortages or surpluses may appear as prices adjust. Houses tend not to sell quickly, for instance, during periods of decreased demand, as that lower demand translates only slowly into lower housing prices.

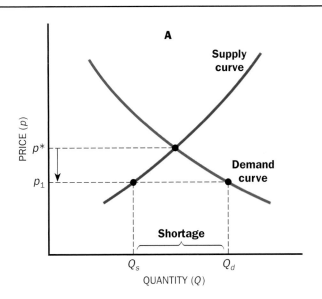

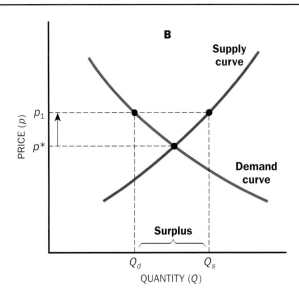

Figure 4.9

SHORTAGES AND SURPLUSES

In panel A, the actual price p_1 is below the market-clearing price p^*. At a price of p_1, quantity demanded exceeds quantity supplied, and a shortage exists. In panel B, the actual price p_1 is above the equilibrium price of p^*. In this case, quantity supplied exceeds quantity demanded, and there is a surplus, or glut, in the market.

Even when the market is not adjusting quickly toward equilibrium, the analysis of market equilibrium is useful. It indicates the direction of the changes—if the equilibrium price exceeds the current price, prices will tend to rise. Moreover, the rate at which prices fall or rise is often related to the gap, at the going price, between the quantity demanded and the quantity supplied.

Interfering with the Law of Supply and Demand

The law of supply and demand, which governs how prices are determined, can produce results that some individuals or groups do not like. For example, a reduction in supply may lead to a higher equilibrium price for oil. The higher price reflects the law of supply and demand; the price increase gives firms and consumers an incentive to reduce their consumption of products, like gasoline, that are derived from oil. That such consequences are predictable does not make them welcome. Truck drivers, many of whom own and operate their own rigs, will be forced to spend more on fuel; in the short run, their demand is likely to be very inelastic (they can't suddenly improve their mileage or shorten the distance between their destinations). Some may be forced into bankruptcy. Low demand for unskilled labor may lead to very low wages for unskilled workers. An increase in the demand for apartments in

Thinking Like an Economist

INCENTIVES AND THE WINDOW TAX

The city of Bath in England predates the Roman occupation of the British Isles. Because naturally heated springs are located at its site, the Romans built baths there. During the late eighteenth and early nineteenth centuries, the city became a popular watering hole for the well-to-do.

One of the city's striking features is the beautiful brick used to build many of the buildings. But a visitor's attention is also caught by the number of houses with windows that appear to have been bricked up. The story behind them illustrates how taxation affects incentives and people's behavior.

In the eighteenth century, Bath imposed taxes on houses, windows, and male servants—a set of taxes called the *assessed taxes*. People with more windows (and more male servants)

presumably had larger houses and were wealthier. Thus, a tax based on the number of windows was intended to force the wealthy to pay more than the poor.

The effect of the tax was to raise the cost of having a window. Anyone planning to build a new house would need to factor in that higher cost and could design their house with fewer windows. Those whose houses were already built might seem unable to avoid the tax—but individuals can be extremely inventive in finding ways to lower their consumption of goods whose price has risen. People living in houses could and did reduce their taxes by bricking up some of their windows. The reduced demand for windows caused by the tax explains the blank walls that replaced window frames in many homes in Bath.

New York City leads, in the short run (when supply is inelastic), to an increase in rents, a consequence again of the law of supply and demand—one that will please landlords and leave tenants angry.

In each of these cases, pressure from those who did not like the outcome of supply and demand has led government to act. The price of oil and natural gas was, at one time, regulated; minimum wage laws set a minimum limit on what employers can pay, even if the workers are willing to work for less; and rent control laws limit what landlords can charge. The concerns behind these interferences with the market are understandable, but the agitation for government action is based on two errors.

First, someone (or some group) was assigned responsibility for the change: the oil price rises were blamed on the oil companies, low wages on the employer, and rent increases on the landlord. As already explained, economists emphasize the role of anonymous market forces in determining these prices. After all, if landlords or oil companies are basically the same people today as they were last week, there must be some reason why they started charging different prices this week. To be sure, sometimes the price increase does result from producers' collusion. That was the case in 1973, when the oil-exporting countries got together to raise the price of oil. But far more often, the explanation lies in the market—as in 2004, when faster economic growth in the United States, Japan, and China led to an increase in the demand for oil that pushed up oil prices.

The second error is to forget that as powerful as governments may be, they can no more repeal the law of supply and demand than they can repeal the law of gravity. When they interfere with its workings, the forces of supply and demand will remain out of balance, with either excess supply or excess demand. Surpluses and shortages create problems of their own. Indeed, if shortages develop, individuals may find that instead of paying the high prices that triggered the government intervention, they cannot obtain the desired good at any price.

Two straightforward examples of government attempts to control the market are **price ceilings,** which impose a maximum price that can be charged for a product, and **price floors,** which impose a minimum price. Rent control laws are price ceilings, and minimum wage laws and agricultural price supports are price floors. A closer look at each will help highlight the perils of interfering with the law of supply and demand.

PRICE CEILINGS

Price ceilings—setting a maximum charge—are always tempting to governments because they seem an easy way to ensure that everyone will be able to afford a particular product. If the price ceiling is effective—that is, it is below the market clearing price—the result is to create shortages at the controlled price. People want to buy more of a good than producers want to sell. Those who can buy at the cheaper price benefit; producers and those unable to buy suffer.

Cities from San Francisco to New York have instituted controls on rents in the hopes of making housing more affordable. The effect of rent control laws—setting the maximum rent that a landlord can charge for a one-bedroom apartment, for example—is illustrated by Figure 4.10. In panel A, R^* is the market equilibrium rental rate, at which the demand for housing equals the supply. However, the local government is concerned that at R^*, many poor people cannot afford housing in the city; it therefore passes a law that caps rents at R_1. But at R_1, there is an excess demand for apartments. While the motives behind its action may well have been praiseworthy, the government has created an artificial scarcity.

The problems caused by rent control are likely to be worse in the long run than in the short run, because long-run supply curves are more elastic than short-run supply curves. In the short run, the quantity of apartments does not change much. But in the long run, the quantity of apartments can decline for several reasons. Apartments may be abandoned as they deteriorate; they can be converted to condominiums and sold instead of rented; and apartment owners may not wish to undertake new construction if they cannot charge enough in rent to cover their costs.

Figure 4.10B illustrates how the housing shortages under rent control will increase over time. Rent control results in all *existing* renters being better off, at least as long as the landlord stays in the business. But the quantity of available rental housing will decrease, leaving many would-be residents unable to find rental housing in the market. Since renters tend to be poorer than those who buy their homes, a shortage of rental housing will tend to hurt the poor most.

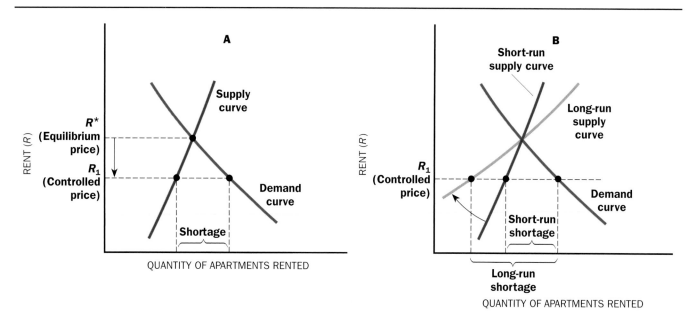

Figure 4.10

A PRICE CEILING: RENT CONTROL

Rent control laws limit the rents apartment owners may charge. If rents are held down to R_1, below the market-clearing level R^*, as in panel A, there will be excess demand for apartments. Panel B shows the long-run response. The supply of rental housing is more elastic in the long run, since landlords can refuse to build new apartment buildings or they can sell existing apartments as condominiums. The price ceiling eventually leads to the quantity supplied being even farther below the quantity demanded.

RENT CONTROL IN NEW YORK CITY

Rent control is widespread in New York City.

Rent control creates a housing shortage while, at the same time, it discourages the construction of new rental housing. In cities with rent control such as New York, vacancy rates for rental units are quite low, usually around 2 to 3 percent. In contrast, the vacancy rate normally averages around 7 percent in cities such as Chicago, San Diego, and Philadelphia that do not have rent control. With many people struggling to obtain one of the few available apartments, poor people tend to lose out. Some studies have indicated that rent control in Californian cities such as Santa Monica and Berkeley lead to increased gentrification as highly educated professionals hold on to rent-controlled apartments, forcing working-class families (and students, in the case of Berkeley) to look for housing in surrounding communities.

It is difficult for newcomers to find rental housing in New York, San Francisco, and other cities with rent control. Fewer apartments are available, and those that are tend to be very expensive. For example, a 1997 survey of rents found that the median rent for an advertised apartment in New York City was about two and a half times the median rent for all apartments in the city ($1,350) per month for advertised apartments versus $545 per month for all apartments). In contrast, in Philadelphia, a city that does not have rent control, the median rent for advertised apartments was only $2 more per month than the median for all apartments ($500 per month versus $498 per month). There were many more inexpensive and reasonably priced apartments available in Philadelphia than there were in New York City. The lack of affordable housing due to rent control forces individuals to share apartments or live farther away from where they work, thereby contributing to commuter congestion.[1]

PRICE FLOORS

Just as consumers try to get government to limit the prices they pay, so sellers would like the government to put a floor on the prices they receive: a minimum wage for workers and a minimum price on wheat and other agricultural products for farmers. Both groups appeal to fairness, arguing that the price they are receiving is inadequate to cover the effort (and other resources) they are contributing.

In many countries, farmers, because of their political influence, have succeeded in persuading government to impose a floor on the prices of numerous agricultural products—a price that is above the market equilibrium, as illustrated in

---

[1]William Tucker, "We All Pay for Others' Great Apartment Deals," *Newsday,* May 24, 1986; Tucker, "Moscow on the Hudson," *The American Spectator,* July 1986, pp. 19–21; Tucker, "How Rent Control Drives Out Affordable Housing," *Cato Policy Analysis* No. 274, May 21, 1997.

Internet Connection

FLAWED DEREGULATION

The California electricity market became a major national news story in 2001 as Californians suffered rolling blackouts, a major utility declared bankruptcy, and the state government spent as much as $70 million per day to purchase electricity. Rising demand, shrinking supply, and a price ceiling on what utilities could charge consumers produced electricity shortages. Information on the California electric industry may be found at the California Public Utilities Commission Web site: www.cpuc.ca.gov. The University of California Energy Institute provides data on daily demand and supply curves for electricity in California from 1998 to 2003 at www.ucei.berkeley.edu/ucei/datamine/datamine.htm.

Figure 4.11. The consequences should be obvious: supply exceeds demand. To sustain the price, government has had to purchase and stockpile huge amounts of agricultural goods. The cost of supporting the price at these above-market levels has been in the billions.

As government interferes with the law of supply and demand, it enters a labyrinth of problems. To reduce supplies, it has imposed production limitations. Such limitations not only are administratively cumbersome but also prevent the market from adapting quickly to changing conditions. Because quotas are based on past production, the appropriate adjustments cannot be made easily. Worse still, wheat farmers have to keep producing wheat to maintain their quota. But doing so prevents them from rotating their crops to protect the soil and the environment. To avoid the buildup of surpluses, exports are subsidized. But these subsidies have angered other countries, which view them as evidence of unfair competition. Our subsidies of wheat exports to Mexico have hurt our economic relations with Argentina. Even Mexico has viewed them with alarm, as they have interfered with Mexico's attempts to reform its agricultural sector.

ALTERNATIVE SOLUTIONS

The examples of government attempts to interfere with the workings of supply and demand yield an important cautionary moral: one ignores the workings of the law of supply and demand only at one's peril. This is not to say that the government should simply ignore the distress caused by large price and wage changes. But government must take care in addressing the problems; relying on price controls, including price ceilings and floors, is unlikely to be effective.

Later chapters will discuss ways in which the government can mitigate the sometimes painful consequences of the law of supply and demand—by making use of the power of the market rather than trying to fight against it. For example, if the government is concerned with low wages paid to unskilled workers, it can try to increase the demand for these workers. A shift to the right in the demand curve will increase their price—that is, the wages they receive. The government can either subsidize firms that hire unskilled workers or provide more training to these workers and thus increase their productivity.

If the government wants to increase the supply of housing to the poor, it can provide them with housing subsidies, which will elicit a greater supply. If the government wants drivers to conserve on the use of gasoline, it can impose a tax on gasoline. Noneconomists often object that these sorts of economic incentives have other distasteful consequences, and sometimes they do. But government policies will tend to be more effective, with fewer unfortunate side effects, when they take into account the law of supply and demand rather than ignoring its predictable economic consequences.

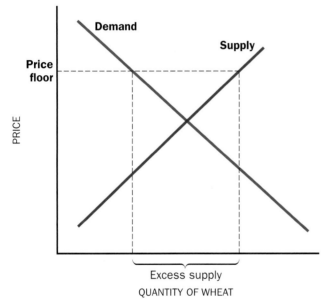

Figure 4.11

PRICE FLOORS

If the government imposes a price floor on, say, wheat—at a price in excess of the market equilibrium—there will be excess supply. Either the government will have to purchase the excess, to be stored or somehow disposed of, or it will have to limit production.

Review and Practice

SUMMARY

1. The price elasticity of demand describes how sensitive the quantity demanded of a good is to changes in the price of the good. When demand is inelastic, an increase in the price has little effect on the quantity demanded and the demand curve is steep; when demand is elastic, an increase in the price has a large effect on the quantity demanded and the curve is flat.

2. The price elasticity of supply describes how sensitive the quantity supplied of a good is to changes in the price of the good. If price changes do not induce much change in supply, the supply curve is very steep and is said to be inelastic. If the supply curve is very flat, indicating that price changes cause large changes in supply, supply is said to be elastic.

3. The extent to which a shift in the supply curve affects price or affects quantity depends on the shape of the demand curve. The more elastic the demand, the more a given shift in the supply curve will be reflected in changes in equilibrium quantities and the less it will be reflected in changes in equilibrium prices. The more inelastic the demand, the more a given shift in the supply curve will be reflected in changes in equilibrium prices and the less it will be reflected in changes in equilibrium quantities.

4. Likewise, the extent to which a shift in the demand curve affects price or affects quantity depends on the shape of the supply curve.

5. Demand and supply curves are likely to be more elastic in the long run than in the short run. Therefore a shift in the demand or supply curve is likely to have a larger price effect in the short run and a larger quantity effect in the long run.

6. Elasticities can be used to predict how much consumer prices will rise when a tax is imposed on a good. If the demand curve for a good is very inelastic, consumers in effect have to pay the tax. If the demand curve is very elastic, the quantities produced and the price received by producers are likely to decline considerably.

7. Government regulations may prevent a market from moving toward its equilibrium price, leading to shortages or surpluses. Price ceilings lead to excess demand. Price floors lead to excess supply.

KEY TERMS

price elasticity of demand
relatively elastic
unitary elasticity
relatively inelastic
infinite elasticity
zero elasticity
price elasticity of supply
shortage
surplus
price ceilings
price floors

REVIEW QUESTIONS

1. What is meant by the elasticity of demand and the elasticity of supply? Why do economists find these concepts useful?

2. Is the slope of a perfectly elastic demand or supply curve horizontal or is it vertical? Is the slope of a perfectly inelastic demand or supply curve horizontal or is it vertical? Explain.

3. If the elasticity of demand is 1, what happens to total revenue as the price increases? What if the demand for a product is very inelastic? What if it is very elastic?

4. Under what condition will a shift in the demand curve result mainly in a change in quantity? in price?

5. Under what condition will a shift in the supply curve result mainly in a change in price? in quantity?

6. Why do the elasticities of demand and supply tend to change from the short run to the long run?

7. Under what circumstances will a tax on a product be passed along to consumers?

8. Why do price ceilings tend to lead to shortages? Why do price floors tend to lead to surpluses?

PROBLEMS

1. Suppose the price elasticity of demand for gasoline is 0.2 in the short run and 0.7 in the long run. If the price of gasoline rises 28 percent, what effect on quantity demanded will this have in the short run? in the long run?

2. Imagine that the short-run price elasticity of supply for a farmer's corn is 0.3, while the long-run price elasticity is 2. If prices for corn fall 30 percent, what are the short-run and long-run changes in quantity supplied? What are the short- and long-run changes in quantity supplied if prices rise by 15 percent? What happens to the farmer's revenues in each of these situations?

3. Assume that the demand curve for hard liquor is highly inelastic and the supply curve for hard liquor is highly elastic. If the tastes of the drinking public shift away from hard liquor, will the effect be larger on price or on quantity? If the federal government decides to impose a tax on manufacturers of hard liquor, will the effect be larger on price or on quantity? What is the effect of an advertising program that succeeds in discouraging people from drinking? Draw diagrams to illustrate each of your answers.

4. Suppose a government wishes to ensure that its citizens can afford adequate housing. Consider three ways of pursuing that goal. One method is to pass a law requiring that all rents be cut by one-fourth. A second method offers a subsidy to all builders of homes. A third provides a subsidy directly to renters equal to one-fourth of the rent they pay. Predict what effect each of these proposals would have on the price and quantity of rental housing in the short run and the long run.

5. In 1990, the U.S. government imposed a 10 percent tax on certain luxuries such as pleasure boats. Sales of pleasure boats fell by nearly 90 percent in southern Florida as prospective buyers bought boats in the Bahamas to avoid paying the tax. What does this imply about the size of the elasticity of demand?

6. Assume the elasticity of demand for oil is 0.7 and the initial quantity demanded is 100 million barrels a day. What is the impact of a 10 percent increase in the price of oil on the quantity of oil demanded? What happens to total expenditures? Assume that the United States initially imports 50 million barrels a day and that production remains unchanged. What happens to the level of imports and to expenditures on imports?

   Assume that in the long run, the elasticity of demand increases to 1. How does this change your answers?

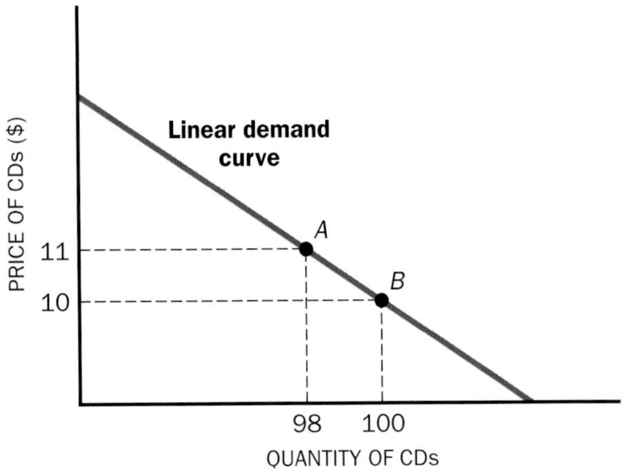

Figure 4.12

LINEAR DEMAND CURVE

The linear demand curve is a straight line; it is represented algebraically by the equation $Q = a - bp$. The slope of the demand curve is a constant. However, the elasticity varies with output. At low outputs (high prices), it is very high. At high outputs (low prices), it is very low.

Appendix: Elasticity and Slope

The elasticity of a curve is not the same as its slope. The best way to see the distinction is to look at a *linear* demand curve. A linear demand curve is a straight line, as depicted in Figure 4.12. With a linear demand curve, a $1 change in price always leads to the same change in quantity demanded, whether we start from a price of $2 or a price of $10. Table 4.3 contains information on price and quantity demanded for such a curve, and we can use this information to calculate the elasticity of demand at different prices. When the price increases from $1 to $2, a 100 percent increase, demand falls by 5 units, from 45 to 40. This represents an 11 percent fall in demand. The elasticity of demand is 11 percent divided by 100 percent, or 0.11. A $1 increase in price from $5 to $6 represents a 20 percent price increase. Because the demand curve is linear, the $1 price increase again reduces demand by 5 units, from 20 to 15 units. This is a 20 percent change in the quantity demanded. The elasticity of demand is 20 percent divided by 20 percent, or 1. As the price goes higher, a $1 change represents a smaller percentage change in the price; moreover, quantity demanded drops, so the 5-unit

Table 4.3

ELASTICITY AND A LINEAR DEMAND CURVE

Price	Quantity demanded	Change in price (%)	Change in quantity (%)	Elasticity
1	45			
		100	−11	0.11
2	40			
		50	−13	0.25
3	35			
		33	−14	0.43
4	30			
		25	−17	0.67
5	25			
		20	−20	1.00
6	20			
		17	−25	1.50
7	15			
		14	−33	2.33
8	10			
		13	−50	4.00
9	5			

fall represents a larger percentage change in demand. Thus, at higher prices, the elasticity—the percentage change in quantity divided by the percentage change in price—becomes larger.

At times, however, we can use information about the slope of the demand curve to draw a conclusion about elasticity. Figure 4.13 shows two demand curves going through the same point. Consider a 1 percentage point change in the price at the point of intersection. The quantity demanded changes more along the flatter demand curve. Because price and quantity were initially the same for the two curves, the percentage change in quantity is larger along the flatter one. We can conclude that at the point of intersection, the flatter demand curve (the one with the smaller slope) has the greater elasticity.

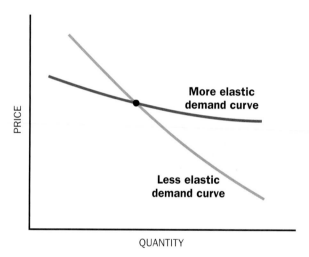

Figure 4.13

COMPARING ELASTICITIES

If two demand curves intersect, at the point of intersection the flatter demand curve has the greater price elasticity.

Learning Goals

In this chapter, you will learn

1 Where demand curves come from

2 Why demand curves are downward sloping

3 What factors cause demand curves to shift

4 What is meant by behavioral economics

Chapter 5

THE CONSUMPTION DECISION

ow many economic decisions have you made today? Did you decide to ride the bus to campus rather than drive, buy a bagel for breakfast rather than a muffin, or eat in a local café rather than at home? Perhaps you decided to look for a new job or ask for more hours at your current one. You may have decided to take out another student loan, or apply for a bank loan to buy a car. Maybe you set aside some money to finance a trip this summer. If so, you then had to decide whether to put your savings into an account at a bank or to invest in the stock market.

These decisions—about spending, about working, about saving, and about investing—represent the basic economic choices all individuals face. In this chapter, we focus on spending decisions. By studying these decisions, we will gain a better understanding of the demand curves that were introduced in Chapter 3 and used in Chapter 4. While our main focus will be on the basic model used by economists to explain how consumers make their spending decisions, we will also see that in recent years, new insights from fields such as psychology have enriched our understanding of these choices.

The Basic Problem of Consumer Choice

The basic framework for analyzing economic decision making was introduced in Chapter 2. Consumers start by defining an opportunity set: they determine what is *possible* given the constraints they face. In most cases we will discuss, what consumers can purchase is constrained by their income. And for many decisions, the time available to consumers also constrains their choices. Once the opportunity set is defined, the consumer selects the most preferred option within it. Because opportunity sets play such an important role in making decisions, this chapter begins by reviewing how they are defined. We then ask how the opportunity set changes when income and prices change, and how these changes affect the choices that consumers make.

THE BUDGET CONSTRAINT

The individual's opportunity set is defined by the budget constraint. If, after taxes, a person's weekly paycheck comes to $300 and he has no other income, that sum is his budget constraint. Total expenditures on food, clothing, rent, entertainment, travel, and all other categories cannot exceed $300 per week. (For now we ignore the possibilities that individuals may borrow money, or save money, or change their budget constraints by working longer or shorter hours.)

The line *BC* in Figure 5.1A shows a simplified individual budget constraint. A student, Fran, has a total of $300 each month to spend on "fun" items. Figure 5.1 assumes that there are two goods, candy bars and compact discs. This simplification enables us to highlight the main points of the analysis.

Let's say that a candy bar costs $1, while a compact disc costs $15. If Fran spent all her income on candy bars, she could purchase 300 candy bars (point *B* on the budget constraint). If she spent all her income on CDs, she could buy 20 CDs (point *C* on the budget constraint). Fran can also choose any of the intermediate choices on line *BC*. For example, she could buy 10 CDs (for $150) and 150 candy bars (for $150), or 15 CDs ($225) and 75 candy bars ($75). Each combination of purchases along the budget constraint totals $300.

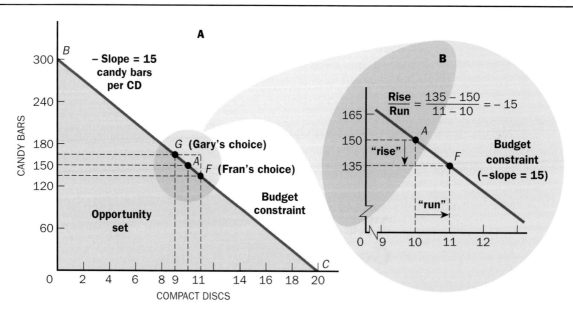

Figure 5.1

AN INDIVIDUAL'S BUDGET CONSTRAINT

Panel A is a budget constraint that shows the combinations of compact discs (at $15) and candy bars (at $1) that an individual could buy with $300. Fran chooses point *F*, with a relatively large number of CDs; Gary chooses point *G*, with a relatively large number of candy bars. Panel B shows that the trade-off of moving from 10 CDs to 11 (point *A* to *F*) is 15 candy bars.

As we learned in Chapter 2, a budget constraint diagram has two important features. First, although any point in the shaded area of Figure 5.1A is feasible, only the points on the line *BC* are really relevant, because Fran is not consuming her entire budget if she is inside her budget constraint. Second, by looking along the budget constraint, we can see her trade-offs—how many candy bars she has to give up to get 1 more CD, and vice versa. Look at points *F* and *A*, a part of the budget constraint that is blown up in panel B. At point *A*, Fran has 10 CDs; at *F*, she has 11. At *F*, she has 135 candy bars; at *A*, 150. To get 1 more CD, she has to give up 15 candy bars.

These are her trade-offs, and they are determined by the relative prices of the two goods. If one good costs twice as much as another and we went 1 more unit of the costly good, we have to give up 2 units of the cheaper good. If, as here, one good costs fifteen times as much as another, and we want 1 more unit of the costly good, we have to give up 15 units of the less costly good.

The **slope** of the budget constraint, which measures how steep it is, also tells us what the trade-off is. As we move 1 unit along the horizontal axis (from 10 to 11 CDs), the slope represents the size of the change along the vertical axis. It is the rise (the movement up or down on the vertical axis) divided by the run (the corresponding horizontal movement). The slope of this budget constraint is thus 15.[1] It tells us how much of one good, at a given price, we need to give up if we want 1 more unit of the other good: it tells us, in other words, what the trade-off is.

Note that the relative price of CDs to candy bars is 15; that is, a CD costs fifteen times as much as a candy bar. But we have just seen that the slope of the budget constraint is 15, and that the trade-off (the number of candy bars Fran has to give up to get 1 more CD) is 15. It is no accident that these three numbers—relative price, slope, and trade-off—are the same.

This two-product example was chosen because it is easy to illustrate with a graph. But the same logic applies to any number of products. Income can be spent on one item or a combination of items. The budget constraint defines what a certain amount of income can buy, a balance that depends on the prices of the items. Giving up some of one item would allow the purchase of more of another item or items.

Economists represent these choices by putting the purchases of the good to which they are paying attention, say CDs, on the horizontal axis and "all other goods" on the vertical axis. By definition, what is not spent on CDs is available to be spent on all other goods. Fran has $300 to spend altogether. A more realistic budget constraint for her is shown in Figure 5.2. The intersection of the budget constraint with the vertical axis, point *B*—where purchases of CDs are zero—is $300. If Fran spends nothing on CDs, she has $300 to spend on other goods. The budget constraint intersects the horizontal axis at 20 CDs (point *C*); if she spends all her income on CDs and CDs cost $15 each, she can buy 20. If Fran chooses a point such a *F*, she will buy 11 CDs, costing $165, and she will have $135 to spend on other goods ($300–$165). The distance 0*D* on the vertical axis measures what she spends on other goods; the distance *BD* measures what she spends on CDs.

---

[1]We ignore the negative sign. See the appendix to Chapter 2 for a more detailed explanation of the slope of a line.

CHOOSING A POINT ON THE BUDGET CONSTRAINT: INDIVIDUAL PREFERENCES

The budget constraint and a recognition of possible trade-offs are the starting points for the study of consumer behavior. The process of identifying the budget constraints and the trade-offs is the same for *any* two people. Any individual will choose *some* point along the budget constraint. But the point actually chosen depends on the individual's preferences: Fran, who likes to listen to music, might choose point *F* in Figure 5.1, while Gary, who loves candy, might choose *G*.

Few people will choose either of the extreme points on the budget constraint, *B* or *C* in Figure 5.1, where only one of the goods is consumed. The reason for this is that the more you have of a good—say, the more CDs you have relative to another good such as candy—the less valuable you will find an additional unit of that good relative to additional units of another good. At points near *C*, it seems safe to assume that to most individuals, an extra CD does not look as attractive as some candy bars. Certainly, at *B*, most people would be so full of candy bars that they would prefer an extra CD.

Where the individual's choice lies depends on how she values the two goods. Chapter 2 emphasized the idea that in making decisions, people look at the *margin:* they look at the extra costs and benefits. In this case, the choice at each point along the budget constraint is between 1 more CD and 15 more candy bars. If Gary and Fran choose different points along the budget constraint, it is because they value the marginal benefits (how much better off they feel with an *extra* CD) and the marginal costs (how much it hurts to give up 15 candy bars) differently. Gary chooses point *G* in Figure 5.1 because that is the point where, for him, the marginal benefit of an extra CD is just offset by what he has to give up to get the extra CD, which is 15 candy bars. When Fran, who loves listening to music, considers point *G*, she realizes that for her, at that point, CDs are more important and candy bars less important than they are for Gary. So she trades along the line until she feels that the marginal benefits of an extra CD and the marginal costs of 15 fewer candy bars are equal. This point, in our example, is *F*.

The same reasoning holds for a budget constraint like the one shown in Figure 5.2. Here, Gary and Fran are choosing between CDs and all other goods, measured in dollar terms. Again, the decision to buy an extra CD hinges on comparing the marginal benefit of an extra CD with the marginal cost—here, what has to be given up in other goods. With CDs priced at $15, choosing to buy a CD means giving up $15 of other goods. For Gary, the marginal benefit of an extra CD equals the cost, $15, when he has only 9 CDs and can therefore spend $165 on other goods. For Fran, who has more of a taste for CDs, the marginal benefit of an extra CD does not equal this marginal cost until she reaches 11 CDs, with $135 to spend elsewhere. Price thus serves as a quantitative measure of marginal benefit.

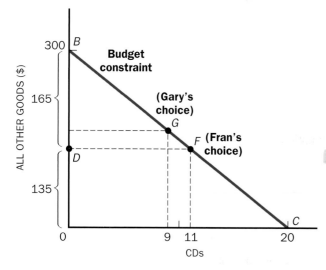

Figure 5.2

ALLOCATING A BUDGET BETWEEN A SINGLE GOOD AND ALL OTHERS

Some budget constraints show the choice between a particular good, in this case CDs, and all other goods. The other goods that might be purchased are collectively measured in money terms, as shown on the vertical axis.

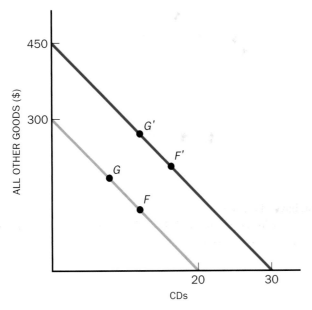

Figure 5.3

THE EFFECT ON CONSUMPTION WHEN INCOME CHANGES

If the amount Gary and Fran have to spend on CDs and other good rises from $300 to $450, the budget line shifts to the right. Because the price of CDs is still $15, the slope of the budget line does not change. The points Gary and Fran choose on the new budget line are *G'* and *F'*. With additional income, they both choose to buy more CDs *and* to spend more on other goods.

WHAT HAPPENS TO CONSUMPTION WHEN INCOME CHANGES?

When an individual's income increases, he has more to spend on consumption. Figure 5.3 shows the effect on the budget constraint of an increase in income. The original budget line is the same as that used in Figure 5.2: Gary and Fran have $300 to spend on CDs or other goods. If the total amount they have to spend increases to $450, the new budget line is farther to the right. Now, Gary and Fran could purchase 30 CDs if they spend the entire $450 on CDs, or they could spend it all on other goods. Because the price of a CD has not changed, the slope of the new budget line is the same as that of the old budget line. Changes in income shift the budget line but do not alter its slope.

The new choices of Gary and Fran are at points *G'* and *F'*. Because they have more to spend, Gary and Fran each decide to purchase more CDs *and* more of other goods. Their behavior is typical; when people's incomes increase, they will buy a little more of many goods, although the consumption of some goods will increase more than that of others, and different individuals will spend their extra income in different ways.

The **income elasticity of demand** (which parallels the price elasticity of demand presented in Chapter 4) measures how much consumption of a particular good increases with income:

$$\text{income elasticity of demand} = \frac{\text{percentage change in consumption}}{\text{percentage change in income}}.$$

The income elasticity of demand, in other words, is the percentage change in consumption that would result from a 1 percent increase in income. If the income elasticity of demand of a certain good is greater than 1, a 1 percent increase in an individual's income results in a more than 1 percent increase in expenditures on that good. That is, the amount he spends on that good increases more than proportionately with income. By definition, if the income elasticity of demand is less than 1, then a 1 percent increase in income results in a less than 1 percent increase in expenditures. Thus the share of income a consumer spends on that good decreases with a rise in income.

As people's incomes increase, the types of goods they choose to buy also change. In particular, they have more money to spend on goods other than those required just to survive. For instance, while they may spend some of the extra income to improve the quality of necessities they buy, such as food, more money goes toward movies, more expensive automobiles, vacations, and other luxuries. Accordingly, poor individuals spend a larger percentage of their income on food and housing and a smaller percentage of their income on perfume. In other words, the income elasticity of necessities is less than 1, and the income elasticity of luxuries is greater than 1.

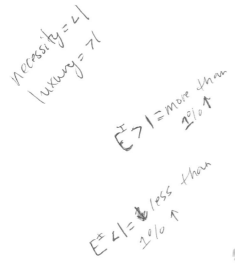

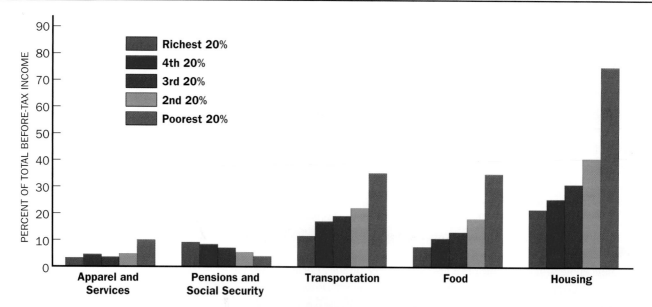

Figure 5.4

HOW HOUSEHOLDS OF DIFFERENT INCOMES SPEND THEIR MONEY

The poor spend far higher proportions of their income on basic necessities such as food and housing than do the rich.

SOURCE: U.S. Department of Labor, Bureau of Labor Statistics, *Consumer Expenditure Survey* (2002).

The consumption of some goods actually decreases as income increases and increases as income decreases; these are called **inferior goods.** In sharp contrast, the consumption of **normal goods** increases with income. In other words, goods for which the income elasticity is *negative* are, by definition, inferior, while all other goods are called normal. For instance, if Fran, who has been riding the bus to work, gets a large raise, she may find that she can afford a car. After buying the car, she will spend less on bus fare. Thus, in this particular sense, bus rides represent an inferior good.

Figure 5.4 shows how typical families at different income levels spend their income. We see that *on average,* the poorest 20 percent of the population spend almost 80 percent of their before-tax income on housing. Yet the richest 20 percent spend only a fifth of their income on housing. Similarly, the poorest 20 percent spend 38 percent of their before-tax income on food, while the richest 20 percent spend less than a tenth. The total spending of the poorest 20 percent on food and housing adds up to more than 100 percent of their income; this is possible only because of government subsidies.

Information like that contained in Figure 5.4 is of great practical importance. For example, it helps determine how a tax will affect different groups. Anybody who purchases food will be hurt by a tax on it. But if the poor spend a larger fraction of their income on food, as the figure suggests, they will bear a disproportionately large share of the tax.

INCOME ELASTICITY OF DEMAND

The *income elasticity of demand* for a good is the percentage change in consumption that would result from a 1 percent increase in income.

When income elasticity of demand is *greater than 1,* a 1 percent increase in an individual's income results in a more than 1 percent increase in expenditures on the good.

When income elasticity of demand is *less than 1,* a 1 percent increase in an individual's income results in a less than 1 percent increase in expenditures on the good.

Normal goods have a positive income elasticity of demand.

Inferior goods have a negative income elasticity of demand.

THE FATE OF THE BTU TAX

Some of the differences in choices along a budget constraint reflect nothing more than differences in tastes—Fran likes CDs more than Gary does. But some differences in choices are systematic, and many of these reflect differences in circumstances. Eleanor lives in New England and spends more on oil to heat her apartment than does Jim, who lives in Florida; Amy, who lives in Montana, 200 miles from the nearest town, buys more gas and spends more on cars than does Tom, who travels from home to work by subway in New York City.

Understanding such systematic determinants in how people spend their money helps us understand the markedly different responses in different regions of the country to government proposals to tax different goods. A case in point arose in 1993 after the Clinton administration took office with a pledge to reduce the huge federal deficit. Many policy analysts, both inside and outside government, favored a tax on energy. Most energy sources are relatively cheap in the United States compared to many other industrialized countries. Low energy prices lead Americans to consume high quantities of energy, thus increasing urban congestion, air pollution, and greenhouse gas emissions. A tax on energy would provide incentives to conserve energy—making such a tax an environmentally sound way of raising revenue.

The administration proposed a BTU tax—named after the British thermal unit, a standard measure of energy. The intent was to levy the tax on the basis of energy used, treating all energy sources alike. The tax proposal generated immediate opposition from heavy energy users. Americans living in the Northeast, who needed to heat their homes for much of the year, claimed that the tax would hit them unfairly. The aluminum industry, a heavy user of energy, strongly opposed it; so did other energy-intensive industries.

In an effort to make the tax more politically palatable—and increase its chance of passage through the Congress—policymakers whittled it down to a single-form-of-energy tax—on gasoline. The proposal turned into a 6.5 cents per gallon increase in the gasoline tax, from 14.1 cents to 20.6 cents per gallon. Americans in the West, who drive much longer distances in a typical day than people in other parts of the country, were up in arms. Politics dictated a reduction in the proposed gas tax. Congress finally passed, and the president signed, a mere 4.3 cents per gallon increase in the tax on gasoline, which raises only an added $5 billion a year in federal revenue.

Low energy prices in the United States lead Americans to consume high quantities of energy.

Internet Connection
WHAT WE CONSUME

The Bureau of Labor Statistics conducts regular surveys to discover what households spend their income on. Information from these Consumer Expenditure Surveys is available at www.bls.gov/cex/home.htm. If you follow the link to "Consumer Expenditures Annual Reports," you will discover that the average expenditure of the households surveyed in 2002 was $40,677, of which 7.6 percent was spent on food at home, 5.1 percent on food away from home, 32.7 percent on housing, and 1.0 percent on public transportation. How do your expenditures compare to those of a typical American household?

A Closer Look at the Demand Curve

In Chapter 3, we saw the principal characteristic of the demand curve: when prices rise, the quantity of a good demanded normally falls. Here, we take a closer look at why. Doing so will help us understand why some goods respond more strongly to price changes, that is, have a greater price elasticity.

Let us return to our earlier example of Fran buying CDs, shown in Figure 5.2. If the price of CDs rises from $15 to $20, Fran will face a new budget constraint. If she buys no CDs, she will still have $300 to spend on other goods; but if she decides to spend all of her income on CDs, she can buy only 15 rather than 20. Figure 5.5 shows Fran's original budget constraint in light green and her new budget constraint in dark green.

The increase in the price of CDs has one obvious and important effect: Fran cannot continue to buy the same number of CDs and the same amount of other goods as she did before. Earlier, Fran bought 11 CDs. If she again buys the same number of CDs, it will cost her $55 more, and she will have $55 less to spend on other goods. No matter what she does, Fran is worse off as a result of the price increase. It is *as if* she had less income to spend. When she has less income to spend, she reduces her expenditure on each good, including CDs. This part of the response to the higher price is called the **income effect.** An increase in income of about $55, or 18 percent ($55 out of $300), would offset the price increase.[2] Assume the income elasticity is approximately 1; that is, with income reduced by 18 percent, she would reduce purchases of CDs by 18 percent, which is about 2 CDs. This part of the reduction of the demand of CDs, from 11 to 9, is the income effect.

The magnitude of the income effect depends on two factors: how important the commodity is to the individual—that is, how large a fraction of the individual's income

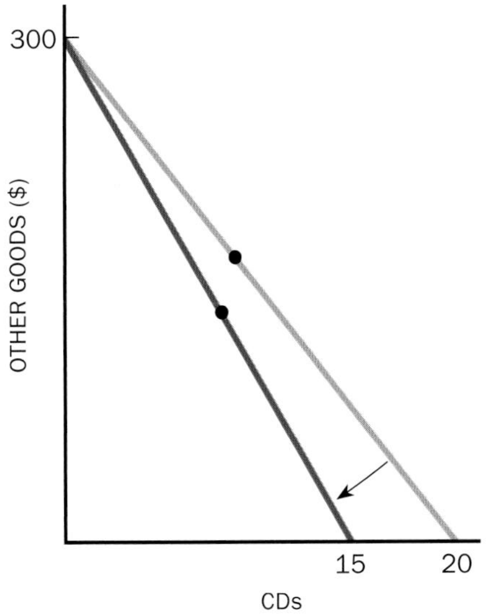

Figure 5.5
EFFECT OF PRICE INCREASE

An increase in the price of CDs moves the budget constraint down as shown. Fran must cut back on the consumption of some goods. Here, using the black dots to mark her consumption points, we show her cutting back on the consumption of both CDs and other goods.

[2]Actually, it would slightly overcompensate. With the $55 increase, Fran could buy exactly the same bundle of goods as before, but as we will soon see, she will *choose* to reallocate her spending. The reallocation will make her better off.

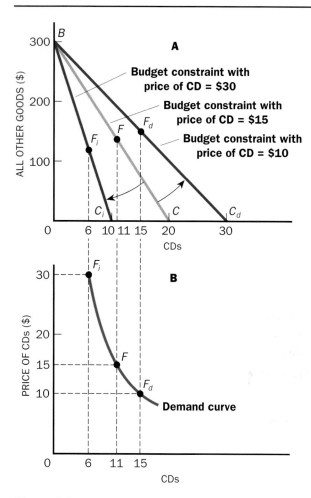

Figure 5.6

DERIVING DEMAND CURVES FROM SHIFTING BUDGET CONSTRAINTS

In panel A, the budget constraint rotates down to the left as the price of CDs increases, leading Fran to change consumption from F to F_i. The budget constraint rotates to the right when the price of CDs decreases, and Fran moves from F to F_d. Panel B shows the corresponding demand curve for CDs, illustrating how the rising prices lead to a decline in quantity consumed.

is spent on the good—and how large the income elasticity is. Since, in most cases, individuals spend a relatively small fraction of their income on any particular good, the income effect is relatively small. But sometimes the income effect of a price increase can be significant—in the case of housing, for example, a good on which most individuals spend between a fourth and a third of their income.

Let us return to Fran and the CDs. At the higher price, giving up one CD gets her more of other goods—more candy bars, more movies, more DVDs, more sweaters. The relative price of CDs, or the trade-off between CDs and other goods, has changed. At the higher price, she *substitutes* goods that are less expensive for the more expensive CDs. Not surprisingly, this effect is called the **substitution effect.** Its magnitude depends on how easily Fran can substitute other goods. If Fran can subscribe to an online music service that allows her to purchase songs and download them to her MP3 player, and the price of the subscription remains unchanged when the price of CDs rises, the substitution effect might be large. She might reduce the number of CDs she purchases to 2. But if Fran does not have an MP3 player, if her sole source of entertainment is listening to her music, and if she dislikes the music played by the local radio stations, the substitution effect may be small. Fran may cut her purchases of CDs far less sharply, only to 8.

DERIVING DEMAND CURVES

We can now see both how to derive the demand curve and why it has the shape it does. At each price, we draw the budget constraint and identify the point along the budget constraint that is chosen. In panel A of Figure 5.6, budget constraints are drawn for three different prices for CDs. If the price of a CD is $10, Fran purchases 15 CDs, indicated by point F_d. If the price rises to $15, the budget constraint shifts and Fran chooses to buy 11 CDs (point F). If the price is $30, Fran only buys 6 CDs (point F_i). As the price of CDs increases, Fran will purchase fewer CDs, as represented by points along successive budget constraints. Higher prices mean she is less well-off, and therefore she decreases her purchases of all goods, including CDs. This is the income effect. The higher price of CDs *relative to other goods* means she will substitute other goods for CDs. This is the substitution effect.

Panel B plots the number of CDs purchased at each price. This is Fran's demand curve for CDs, and it is derived directly from the information in panel A. Because Fran purchases more CDs as the price falls, the demand curve is downward sloping. The case illustrated in panel B is the normal case. As price falls, the quantity demanded increases through *both* the income effect and the substitution effect. For *inferior goods,* such as cheap cuts of meat and bus travel, the income effect goes in the opposite direction. As the price is lowered, the substitution effect leads to more consumption, but the income effect leads to less. The net effect can be either positive or negative. Generally, though, as individuals become better off, they typically reduce their consumption of these goods.

THE IMPORTANCE OF DISTINGUISHING BETWEEN INCOME AND SUBSTITUTION EFFECTS

Distinguishing between the income and substitution effects of a change in price is important for two reasons.

Understanding Responses to Price Changes First, the distinction improves our understanding of consumption responses to price changes. Thinking about the substitution effect helps us understand why some demand curves have a low price elasticity and others a high price elasticity. It also helps us understand why the price elasticity may well differ at different points along the demand curve. Recall from Chapter 4 that when an individual is consuming large amounts of one good, substitutes for it are easy to find, and a small increase in price leads to a large reduction in the quantity demanded; but as consumption falls, finding good substitutes becomes increasingly difficult.

Or consider the effect of an increase in the price of one good on the demand for *other* goods. There is always an income effect; the income effect, by itself, would lead to reduced consumption of all commodities. But the substitution effect leads to *increased* consumption of substitute commodities. Thus, an increase in the price of Coke will lead to increased demand for Pepsi at each price; the demand curve for Pepsi shifts to the right, because the substitution effect outweighs the slight income effect.

Understanding Inefficiencies Associated with Taxes A second reason to focus on income and substitution effects is to identify some of the inefficiencies associated with taxation. The purpose of a tax is to raise revenue so that the government can purchase goods; it represents a transfer of purchasing power from the household to the government. If the government is to obtain more resources, individuals have to consume less. Thus, any tax must have an income effect.

But beyond that, taxes often distort economic activity. The distortion caused by taxation is associated with the substitution effect. Take the window tax discussed in Chapter 4. Intended to raise revenue, it instead led people to cover up their windows—a major distortion of the tax. Most of the distortions associated with modern taxes are somewhat more subtle. Consider a tax on airline tickets or on telephone calls. Reducing consumption of things that are against society's interest can be a legitimate goal of taxation. But the government does not think flying or making telephone calls is a bad thing. The tax is levied simply to raise revenues. But it results in fewer air flights and telephone calls anyway—an unintentional consequence. Any tax leads to *some* reduction in consumption, through the income effect. But most taxes also change relative prices; so they have a substitution effect. It is the substitution effect that gives rise to the distortion. If the substitution effect is small, the distortion is small; if the substitution effect is large, the distortion is large.

Thinking Like an Economist

INCENTIVES, INCOME EFFECTS, AND SUBSTITUTION EFFECTS

Economists focus on incentives because they want to understand how choices are made. By using the concepts of income and substitution effects, economists are able to analyze the way that prices affect incentives, and therefore choices. The best way to understand income effects and substitution effects—and to begin thinking like an economist—is to use them, as the following example illustrates.

During the winter of 2001, the state of California was hit with an energy shortage, the result of both bad weather and market manipulation by energy traders such as Enron. Under a partial deregulation of the electrical market, the state's major electrical utilities were required to buy electricity on the open market and to sell to consumers at prices that were capped. As the cost of wholesale electricity rose sharply during 2001, the price the utilities had to pay for electricity soared above what they were allowed to charge their customers. Demand outstripped the available supply.

When demand exceeds supply, two solutions are possible—increase supply or reduce demand. In a deregulated market system, the price of electricity would have risen, and the higher prices would have provided consumers with the incentive to conserve. A higher price for electricity reduces demand through two channels. As electricity prices rise relative to the prices of other goods that households purchase, each household has an incentive to economize on electricity. This is the *substitution effect*. But there is an income effect as well. Because electricity is more expensive, the household's real income is reduced—it has to spend more to obtain the same set of consumer goods (including electricity). With a reduced real income, the household cuts back its spending on all types of goods, including electricity. This is the *income effect*.

Because higher energy costs may have a disproportionate impact on low-income families, politicians are often reluctant to let energy prices rise. The solution is not to cap prices—keeping prices low simply reduces the incentives to all households to conserve a scarce resource. Instead, suppose the added energy costs for each household average $200. The income effect can be eliminated, while still allowing the substitution effect to do its job in reducing demand, by giving each household a refund of $200. On average, households' real income no longer falls—the impact of higher electricity prices is offset by the refund of $200. But the substitution effect still operates. In spending its income, a household faces a higher relative price of electricity. It has an incentive to conserve on its use of electricity.

INCOME AND SUBSTITUTION EFFECTS AND THE SHAPE OF DEMAND CURVES

The *income effect* refers to a change in consumption arising from a change in the consumer's real income. When the price of a good you consume increases, your real income is reduced because you can no longer afford the same level of consumption. By the same logic, when the price of a good that you consume falls, your real income is increased.

The *substitution effect* refers to a change in consumption arising from a change in the relative prices of goods. When the price of a good you consume increases, that good becomes more expensive relative to other goods, inducing you to consume less of the expensive good and more of the other goods.

Normally, demand curves are downward sloping. As the price is lowered, consumers are better off and so consume more of the good (the income effect); and the lower *relative* price induces a further increase in consumption (the substitution effect).

Utility and the Description of Preferences

We have seen that people choose a point along their budget constraint by weighing the benefits of consuming more of one good against the costs—what they have to forgo of other goods. Economists refer to the benefits of consumption as the **utility** that individuals get from the combination of goods they consume. Presumably a person can tell you whether or not he prefers a certain combination of goods to another. Economists say that the preferred bundle of goods gives that individual a higher level of utility than the other bundle of goods he could have chosen. Similarly, economists say that the individual will choose the bundle of goods—within the budget constraint—that maximizes his utility.

In the nineteenth century, social scientists, including the British philosopher Jeremy Bentham, hoped that science would someday develop a machine that could actually measure utility. A scientist could simply hook up some electrodes to an individual's head and read off a unique measure of "happiness." Modern economists have several useful ways of measuring changes in how well-off a person is.

For our purposes, one simple approach will suffice: we ask how much an individual would be willing to pay to be in one situation rather than another. For example, if Joe likes chocolate ice cream more than vanilla, it stands to reason that he would be willing to pay more for a scoop of chocolate ice cream than for a scoop of vanilla. Or if Diane would rather live in California than in New Jersey, it stands to reason that she would be willing to pay more for the West Coast location.

Note that how much a person is willing to pay tells us nothing about the price actually paid. What Joe has to pay for chocolate ice cream depends on market prices; what he is willing to pay reflects his preferences. Willingness to pay is a useful measure of utility, often helpful for purposes such as thinking about how individuals allocate income along budget constraints. But the hopes of nineteenth-century economists, that we could find some way of measuring utility that would enable us to compare how much utility Fran got from a bundle of goods with how much utility Gary obtained, are now viewed as pipe dreams.

Using willingness to pay as our measure of utility, we can construct a diagram like Figure 5.7A, which shows the level of utility Mary receives from sweatshirts as the number of sweatshirts she buys increases. This information is also given in Table 5.1. Here we assume that Mary is willing to pay $400 for 5 sweatshirts, $456 for 6 sweatshirts, $508 for 7 sweatshirts, and so on.[3] Thus, 5 sweatshirts give her a

---

[3]If these dollar amounts seem high relative to typical market prices, keep in mind that they reflect Mary's willingness to pay for sweatshirts, which is our measure of the utility she derives from them. Market prices may be lower.

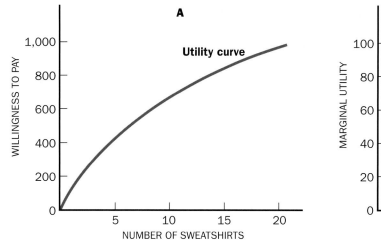

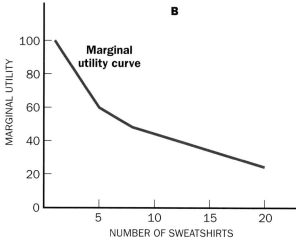

Figure 5.7

UTILITY AND MARGINAL UTILITY

Panel A shows that utility increases continually with consumption but tends to level off as consumption climbs higher. Panel B explicitly shows marginal utility; notice that it declines as consumption increases.

utility of 400, 6 a utility of 456, and 7 sweatshirts a utility of 508. Mary's willingness to pay increases with the number of sweatshirts, reflecting the fact that additional sweatshirts give her additional utility. The extra utility of an additional sweatshirt, measured here by the additional amount she is willing to pay, is the **marginal utility.** The numbers in the third column of Table 5.1 give the marginal (or extra) utility she received from her most recently purchased sweatshirt. When Mary owns 5 sweatshirts, an additional sweatshirt yields her an additional or marginal utility of 56 (456–400); when she owns 6 sweatshirts, an additional one gives her a marginal utility of only 52 (508–456). Figure 5.7B traces the marginal utilities of each of these increments.[4]

As an individual's bundle of goods includes more and more of a good, each successive increment increases her utility less. This is the law of **diminishing marginal utility.** The first sweatshirt is very desirable, and additional ones are attractive as well. But each sweatshirt does not increase utility by as much as the one before, and at some point, Mary may get almost no additional pleasure from adding to her sweatshirt wardrobe.

When Mary has a given budget and must choose between two goods that cost the same, say sweatshirts and pizza, each of which costs $15, she will make her choice so that the marginal utility of each good is the same. Table 5.1 shows Mary's willingness to pay (utility) for both sweatshirts and pizza. Suppose Mary has a $300 budget for sweatshirts and pizza. Look at what happens if she buys 20 sweatshirts with her money and no pizza. The marginal utility of the last sweatshirt is 24, and that of the first pizza is 36. If she switches $15 from sweatshirts to pizza, she loses a utility of 24 from the decreased sweatshirt, but gains 36 from her first pizza. It obviously pays for her to switch.

Now look at the situation when she has decreased her purchases of sweatshirts to 17 and increased purchases of pizza to 3. The marginal utility of the last sweatshirt

---

[4]Since marginal utility is the extra utility from an extra unit of consumption, it is measured by the slope of the utility curve in panel A.

is 30, and that of the last pizza is also 30. At this point, she will not want to switch anymore. If she buys another sweatshirt, she gains 28, but the *last* pizza, her 3rd, which she will have to give up, has a marginal utility of 30; she loses more than she gains. If she buys another pizza, she gains 28, but the last sweatshirt (her 17th) gave her a marginal utility of 30; again, she loses in net. We can thus see that with her budget, she is best off when the marginal utility of the two goods is the same.

The same general principle applies when the prices of two goods differ. Assume that a sweatshirt costs twice as much as a pizza. So long as the marginal utility of sweatshirts is more than twice that of pizzas, it still pays for Mary to switch to sweatshirts. To get one more sweatshirt, she has to give up two pizzas, and we reason, as before, that she will adjust her consumption until she gets to the point where the marginal utilities of the two goods, *per dollar spent,* are equal. This is a general rule: in choosing between two goods, consumers adjust choices to the point at which the marginal utilities are proportional to the prices. Thus, the last unit purchased of a good that costs twice as much as another must generate twice the marginal utility as the last unit purchased of the other good; the last unit purchased of a good that costs three times as much must generate three times the marginal utility as the last unit purchased of the other good; and so on.

Table 5.1

UTILITY AND MARGINAL UTILITY

Number of sweatshirts	Mary's willingness to pay (utility)	Marginal utility	Number of pizzas	Mary's willingness to pay (utility)	Marginal utility
0	0	100	0	0	36
1	100	90	1	36	32
2	190	80	2	64	30
3	270	70	3	98	28
4	340	60	4	126	26
5	400	56	5	152	24
6	456	52	6	176	22
7	508	48	7	198	20
8	556	46	8	218	18
9	602	44	9	236	16
10	646	42	10	252	14
11	688	40	11	266	12
12	728	38	12	272	10
13	766	36	13	288	8
14	802	34	14	296	
15	836	32			
16	868	30			
17	898	28			
18	926	26			
19	952	24			
20	976				

We can write this result simply as

$$\frac{MU_x}{P_x} = \frac{MU_y}{P_y},$$

where MU_x is the marginal utility of good x, MU_y is the marginal utility of good y, P_x is the price of good x, and P_y is the price of good y. The ratio of marginal utility to price should be the same for all goods. When this condition is met, Mary's consumption problem is solved—she has found the combination of the two goods that make her best off.

We have already seen that when the prices of sweatshirts and pizzas are the same, Mary is best off when she buys 17 sweatshirts and 3 pizzas. At that point, the marginal utility of the last sweatshirt purchased is the same as the marginal utility of the last pizza purchased. But let's suppose instead that a pizza costs only $7.50, while sweatshirts continue to cost $15. Using the information in Table 5.1, we can see the combination of 17 sweatshirts and 3 pizzas is no longer the best one for Mary when the prices of the two goods differ. She could give up 1 sweatshirt, which reduces her utility by 30. With the $15 she saved, she can buy 2 more pizzas, for a gain in utility of 54. On net, her utility has gone up by 24, so it pays her to give up that last sweatshirt and buy more pizzas. Does it pay to give up more sweatshirts? Yes. By giving up a second sweatshirt, she reduces her utility by 32, but she gains 46 from the 2 additional pizzas she can buy. Now look at Mary's situation if she buys 14 sweatshirts and 9 pizzas. By Mary giving up the last sweatshirt, her utility drops by 34, but by buying 2 more pizzas, going from 7 to 9, her utility gained 38. She is better off. Does it pay to reduce purchases of sweatshirts any more? No. Giving up 1 more sweatshirt leads to a loss in utility of 36 and the 2 extra pizzas only give a gain in utility of 30. She is best off with 14 sweatshirts and 9 pizzas. The marginal utility of the last sweatshirt is 36; the marginal utility of the last pizza is 18. Since sweatshirts cost twice as much as pizzas, the ratio of the marginal utility of each good to its price is the same, just as our formula said it should be.

In the example we have just analyzed, we relied on the simplifying assumption that Mary's willingness to pay for sweatshirts—her measure of utility—does not depend on how many pizzas, or other goods, she has. This is seldom the case. The utility, and hence marginal utility, of sweatshirts will depend on all her other possessions. Thus, even when the price of sweatshirts remains the same, if the price of other goods changes, she will change her consumption of those other goods *and* sweatshirts. Similarly, a change in Mary's income will affect the marginal utility of the goods she consumes.

MARGINAL UTILITY AND CONSUMER CHOICE

Consumers allocate their income among different goods so that the marginal utility associated with the last unit purchased, per dollar spent, is the same for all goods.

CONSUMER SURPLUS

In Chapter 1, we learned that one of the basic principles of economics is that people are better off as a result of voluntary trade. Now that we have developed the fundamental ideas of consumer choice, we can use the demand curve to show how we can measure some of the gains that arise from economic exchange.

Assume you go into a store to buy a can of soda. The store charges you $0.75. If you are particularly thirsty, you might be willing to pay as much as $1.25 for that can of soda. The difference between what you paid and what you would have been willing to pay is called **consumer surplus.** It provides a measure of how much you gained from the trade. In this example, you only had to pay $0.75 for something for which you would have been willing to pay $1.25; the difference, or $0.50, is your consumer surplus.

Earlier, we used the concept of marginal utility to determine Mary's choice of sweatshirts and pizzas. We can calculate from her demand curve the consumer surplus that goes to Mary when she buys pizza. Suppose a pizza costs $10 and Mary buys 13. From the information in Table 5.1, we can see that the 13th pizza gives her a marginal utility of 10 and costs $10. But the 12th pizza she purchased also only cost her $10, yet it yielded a marginal utility of 12. Mary is getting a bargain; she would have been willing to pay more for the earlier pizzas. She would have been willing to pay $12 for the 12th pizza. In fact, for her first pizza, she would have been willing to pay $36, for the second $32, and so on. She would have been willing to pay a total of $288 ($36 + $32 + $30 + $28 + $26 + $24 + $22 + $20 + $18 + $16 + $14 + $12 + $10) for the 13 pizzas. The difference between what she has to pay for 13 pizzas—$10 × 13 = $130—and what she would have been willing to pay, $288, is her consumer surplus. In this example, her surplus is $158.

Figure 5.8 shows Mary's demand curve for pizzas. If the price of pizzas is $36, she would purchase 1 pizza; if the price falls to $20, she would buy 8; and at a price of $10, she would buy 13. The total amount Mary would have been willing to pay for 13 pizzas is the total area under the demand curve between the vertical axis and 13, the combination of the blue and yellow areas. This area is the sum as detailed in the previous paragraph. The amount Mary actually has to pay is represented by the blue area—the price, $10, times the quantity, 13 pizzas. Her consumer surplus is the *difference,* the yellow area above the price line and below the demand curve, over the range of the quantity purchased.

There is always some consumer surplus so long as the consumer has to pay only a fixed price for all the items she purchases. The downward slope of demand curves means the previous units the consumer purchases are more valuable than the marginal units. She would have been willing to pay more for the earlier units than for the last unit, but she does not have to.

We can use the concept of consumer surplus to measure the effect on consumers of the type of agricultural price floor we analyzed in Chapter 4

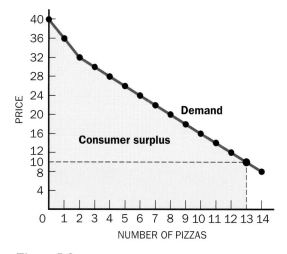

Figure 5.8

CONSUMER SURPLUS

The demand curve plots the amount Mary would be willing to pay for her 1st, 2nd, 3rd, and so on pizza. The total amount she is willing to pay for 13 pizzas is the area under the demand curve up to the 13th pizza. The amount she actually has to pay is the *blue shaded* area. The consumer surplus is the difference between the two, the *yellow shaded* area above the line and below the demand curve, over the range of the quantity purchased.

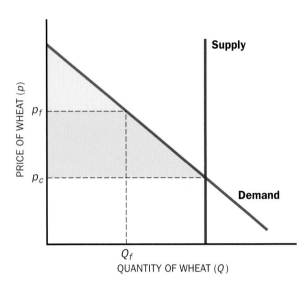

Figure 5.9

CONSUMER SURPLUS AND A PRICE FLOOR

The demand and supply of wheat are equal if the price is p_c. At this price, total consumer surplus is equal to the area between the demand curve, showing willingness to pay, and the market price, p_c. This is the sum of the yellow and orange areas. With a price floor at p_f, the quantity demanded is only Q_f. At the price p_f, consumer surplus is the yellow area. The orange area measures the fall in consumer surplus due to the price floor.

using demand and supply. Figure 5.9 shows the demand and supply curves for wheat. For the sake of simplicity, supply is drawn as a vertical line (inelastic supply). In the absence of a price floor, the equilibrium price will be p_c, and the consumer surplus is the total of the yellow and orange areas. If the government imposes a price floor, at p_f, then the quantity demanded is Q_f. Consumer surplus is equal to the yellow area, the area under the demand curve from the vertical axis to the quantity purchased. The price floor reduces consumer surplus. The orange area measures the cost to consumers of the price floor.

CONSUMER SURPLUS

Consumer surplus is the difference between what individuals would have been willing to spend to purchase a given amount of a good and what they actually had to spend. It is measured by the area under the demand curve, but above the price.

Consumer surplus provides a measure of the benefit to consumers of the market exchange for the good.

Looking Beyond the Basic Model

In the market economy, "For whom are goods produced?" has a simple answer: goods are produced for consumers. Thus to understand market economies, we must understand how consumers make choices. The model of budget constraints and individual preferences sketched in this chapter is the economist's basic approach to consumer choice, a powerful one whose insights carry well beyond this course. Still, it has been criticized, and in the past few decades, alternative models of consumer choice have been proposed. In the remainder of this chapter, we discuss four criticisms of the basic model before turning to recent work that goes under the name *behavioral economics*.

HOW WELL DO THE UNDERLYING ASSUMPTIONS MATCH REALITY?

The first criticism of the basic model of consumer choice is that it fails to reflect the actual thought processes of consumers. This line of criticism is like the claim of a pool player that the physicist's model of motion, which predicts with great precision how billiard balls will interact, is invalid because players do not work through the equations before taking a shot. The appropriate question is whether the economic model of consumer choice can be used to make accurate predictions. By and large, it can. Many businesses, for example, have found the model useful for predicting the demand for their products. And economists have used the model with remarkable success to predict consumer behavior in a variety of circumstances. Sometimes, however, it does not make reliable predictions, and we will consider some of these instances when we discuss behavioral economics.

The second criticism questions the model's assumption that individuals know what they like—that is, that they have *well-defined preferences*. Given a choice between two bundles of goods—one consisting of two T-shirts and three sweatshirts and the other containing one pair of jeans and two sweatshirts—they could tell you quickly which they preferred. Moveover, their answer would be the same tomorrow or next week. But in many cases, someone asked which of two things is preferred replies, "I don't know. Let me try them out." And what people like may change from day to day. In addition, their preferences may be affected by what others like. How else can we account for the short-lived fads so common in food and fashion as well as in other spheres?

The third criticism focuses on the model's assumption that individuals know the prices of each good in the market. In fact, people often lack this knowledge. And even when they know that bargains can be found, it is costly to search for them. While we can talk meaningfully about the price of a barrel of oil, what do we mean by the "price" of a couch, computer, or house? If we are lucky and stumble onto a good deal, we may find a leather couch for $600. If unlucky, even after looking all day, we may not find one for under $1,000. The ability to search on the Internet for prices at various stores before we go shopping has helped lower the costs of finding bargains and has made it easier for consumers to know the prices of goods.

The final criticism points out that sometimes the interactions of prices and preferences are more complicated than this chapter has depicted. In particular, people's attitudes toward a good can depend on its price. More expensive goods may be attractive simply because they have snob appeal. And when the quality of certain goods cannot easily be ascertained, people use price as their yardstick. Because, on average, better (more durable) products are more costly, a cheap item is assumed to be of poorer quality than its more expensive counterpart. In either case, demand curves will look quite different from those described in this chapter. Lowering the price for a good may actually lower its demand.

The need to extend or modify the basic economic model for some goods in some instances does not detract from its overall utility: in the vast majority of situations, it provides just the information that businesses and governments need to make important decisions. Even when it is less effective, the model provides a basic framework that enhances our understanding of the behavior of households. We will build on this framework in Part Three. And asking which of its underlying assumptions may be inappropriate whenever we apply it will help us search for a better model.

BEHAVIORAL ECONOMICS

In recent years, a growing number of economists have combined insights from psychology and economics to gain new understanding into how people make choices. Those engaged in this new field, called **behavioral economics,** reject the simple model of consumer choice that was developed in this chapter. Instead, they argue that a theory of consumer choice should be based on how people actually make decisions. Behavioral economists therefore draw on the findings of psychologists who conduct laboratory experiments to study that question. As a sign of the growing importance of this work, the 2002 Nobel Prize in Economics was shared by a psychologist, Daniel Kahneman, whose research has heavily influenced the new field.

Behavioral economics takes as its starting point a number of findings that appear to be inconsistent with the basic model of consumer choice we have developed in this chapter. A few of them, discussed below, illustrate the types of evidence on which behavioral economists focus.

Endowment Effects A large body of evidence suggests that the simple act of possessing something can alter a person's preferences. Consider the following experiment involving a group of college undergraduates, half of whom were given college coffee mugs that sold for $6.00 at the college bookstore. The students were then allowed to participate in a market in which mugs could be bought and sold. One might expect that those students with mugs who valued them least would end up selling them to those without mugs who valued them most. Since the coffee mugs had been distributed randomly, about half should trade hands. In fact, very few trades took place. The experimenters found that the median price demanded by mug sellers was $5.25, and the median amount buyers were willing to spend was around $2.25. Initially, there were no reasons to expect predictable differences in how students valued coffee mugs; but the mere fact of being given a mug seemed to make individuals value mugs more highly.

This phenomenon is called the *endowment effect*. In the standard model of consumer choice, individuals purchase those goods that they value more than the dollars they have to give up to make the purchase. But people are not expected to value more highly those items that they happen to possess. In another experiment, college students were given either a lottery ticket or $2.00. They were then allowed to exchange whichever they had received for the other; that is, a student who had been given a lottery ticket could turn it in and get $2.00, or a student who had received $2.00 could exchange it for a lottery ticket. Surprisingly, at least from the perspective of the standard model of consumer choice, very few students wanted to make the trade. Those who received lottery tickets seemed to prefer them to the cash; those who received the cash preferred it to the ticket. Since the two groups of students were otherwise similar, there was no reason to expect that those who happened to receive lottery tickets would value them more than did the students given cash.

Loss Aversion The standard model of consumer choice assumes that individuals' well-defined preferences for goods do not depend on whether they actually have those items. The endowment effect may reflect what psychologists have called *loss aversion*. Individuals seem to be particularly sensitive to losses. Once the students had mugs in their possession, they didn't want to give them up; thus they set the sale price above what they would have been willing to pay for a mug in the first place. Similarly, a person with $1,100 who then loses $100 feels worse than someone with $900 who then finds $100. Even though both ultimately have the same amount of money, their feelings about their situations are very different.

The Status Quo Bias Loss aversion and endowment effects lead to behavior that exhibits a bias in favor of the status quo. In the example just given, the status quo or reference point of the first person is the $1,100 he had, so he feels worse off when he has only $1,000. The reference level of the second person was $900, so she feels better off when she has $1,000. In the basic model of consumer choice outlined in this chapter, we assumed that individuals' utility depended on the absolute level of their consumption. If reference points are important, utility may instead depend on the difference between an individual's current consumption and a reference level of consumption. This reference level might be recent levels of consumption—a certain standard of living to which people become accustomed. Or it might be the consumption levels of an individual's peer group, an idea captured in the phrase "keeping up with the Joneses."

The tendency of individuals to accept whatever happens to be the default among a number of options illustrates the importance of the status quo. For example, many employers offer their employees the option of participating in a 401(k) savings plan, a way to set aside before-tax income for retirement. If the default is automatic participation, so that employees must actively decide to opt out of the plan, then most employees end up contributing. If the default is to not participate, requiring employees to sign up for the plan, the fraction of employees who participate is much lower. Ignoring status quo effects may undercut major public policy initiatives. In 2003, the U.S. federal government introduced a medical drug benefit as part of Medicare, the health insurance program for older Americans. To obtain discounts on prescription drugs, seniors had to sign up for a "drug discount card." The default option was to not sign up. According to a survey conducted by the Harvard School of Public Health and the Kaiser Family Foundation, only about 10 percent of eligible seniors had signed up by the middle of 2004. The status quo effect may have been one factor at work.

Implications These examples, and many others that behavioral economists have investigated, suggest the economist's simple model of choice is incomplete. But what is critical for an analysis of market economies is understanding how the behavior uncovered by psychologists and behavioral economists affects market demand curves. Do we need to change the basic ideas developed in this chapter about how consumers respond to changes in prices? Broadly speaking, the answer is clearly no. Individuals do respond to incentives—as the price of a good falls, we expect more consumers will purchase it. As price rises, less is demanded. The findings from behavioral economics do suggest, however, that preferences can depend on what individuals view as the status quo, and that consumers may display a greater reluctance to change than the basic economic model would predict. This reluctance to change, reflected in the endowment effect and the status quo effect, may reduce their sensitivity to incentives. These effects may help explain why economists often observe individuals passing up the opportunity to make exchanges that appear to be advantageous.

Behavioral economists have developed new insights into saving behavior, as well. We will consider some of them in Chapter 9, where we will discuss the factors that affect household decisions about how much to save.

Review and Practice

SUMMARY

1. The amount of one good a person must use to purchase another good is determined by the relative prices of the two goods, and is illustrated by the slope of the budget constraint.
2. As a good becomes more expensive relative to other goods, an individual will substitute other goods for the higher-priced good. This is the substitution effect.
3. As the price of a good rises, a person's buying power is reduced. The response to this lower "real" income is the income effect. Consumption of a normal good rises as incomes rises. Thus, usually, when price rises, both the substitution and income effects lead to decreased consumption of that good.
4. When substitution is easy, demand curves tend to be elastic, or flat. If substitution is difficult, demand curves tend to be inelastic, or steep.
5. Economists sometimes describe the benefits of consumption by referring to the utility that people get from a combination of goods. The extra utility of consuming one more unit of a good is referred to as the marginal utility of that good.
6. Consumers will allocate their income so that the marginal utility per dollar spent is the same for all goods.
7. Consumer surplus measures the difference between what a consumer would be willing to pay and what she has to pay (the market price).

KEY TERMS

slope
income elasticity of demand
inferior goods
normal goods
income effect
substitution effect
utility
marginal utility
diminishing marginal utility
consumer surplus
behavioral economics

REVIEW QUESTIONS

1. How is the slope of the budget constraint related to the relative prices of the goods on the horizontal and vertical axes?
2. How can the budget constraint appear the same even for individuals whose tastes and preferences differ dramatically?
3. Is the income elasticity of demand positive or negative for an inferior good?
4. If the price of a normal good increases, how will the income effect cause the quantity demanded of that good to change?
5. What is the substitution effect? Why do the substitution and income effects normally reinforce each other? Is this true for an inferior good?
6. Does a greater availability of substitutes make a demand curve more elastic or less elastic? Explain.
7. Why does marginal utility tend to diminish?
8. What is meant by consumer surplus?

PROBLEMS

1. A student has an entertainment budget of $200 per term and spends it on either concert tickets at $40 apiece or movie tickets at $10 apiece. Suppose movie tickets decrease in price, first falling to $5, then $2. Graph the three budget constraints, with movies on the horizontal axis. If the student's demand for movies, D, is represented by the function $D = 10 - 1.0p$, where p is the price, graph both the demand curve for movies and the point she will choose on the budget line corresponding to each price.
2. Choose two normal goods and draw a budget constraint illustrating the trade-off between them. Show how the budget line shifts if income increases. Arbitrarily choose a point on the first budget line as the point a particular consumer will select. Now find two points on the new budget line such that the new preferred choice of the consumer must fall between these points.
3. Compare one poor person, with an income of $10,000 per year, with a relatively wealthy person who has an income

of $60,000 per year. Imagine that the poor person drinks 15 bottles of wine per year at an average price of $10 per bottle, while the wealthy person drinks 50 bottles of wine per year at an average price of $20 per bottle. If a tax of $1 per bottle is imposed on wine, who pays more in taxes? Who pays the greater amount as a percentage of income? If a tax equal to 10 percent of the value of the wine is imposed, who pays more in taxes? Who pays the greater amount as a percentage of income?

4. The income elasticity for alcoholic beverages is 0.62. Consider two people with incomes of $20,000 and $40,000. If all alcohol is taxed at the same rate, by what percentage more will the tax paid by the $40,000 earner be greater than that paid by the $20,000 earner? Why might some people think this unfair?

5. The following table gives Sarah's willingness to pay for music CDs and movie DVDs. Calculate Sarah's marginal utility for CDs and DVDs by filling in the columns of the table labeled "marginal utility." Suppose the price of a CD is $10 and the price of a DVD is $30. How many CDs and how many DVDs should Sarah purchase if she has a fixed budget of $150 to spend on these two items? Suppose her budget for these two goods is only $80. How many CDs and how many DVDs should she purchase?

CDs	Willing-ness to pay	Marginal utility	DVDs	Willing-ness to to pay	Marginal utility
0	0		0	0	
1	24		1	42	
2	46		2	78	
3	66		3	108	
4	84		4	132	
5	100		5	150	
6	114		6	162	
7	126		7	168	
8	136		8	168	
9	144				
10	150				
11	154				
12	156				
13	156				

Appendix: Indifference Curves and the Consumption Decision[5]

This chapter explained the consumption decision in terms of the budget constraint facing the individual and the individual's choice of her most preferred point on the budget constraint. Effects of changes in prices on the quantity demanded were analyzed in terms of income and substitution effects.

To help them more rigorously analyze choices and the consequences of changes in prices, economists have developed an extremely useful tool called **indifference curves.** Indifference curves give the combinations of goods among which an individual has no preference (that is, is indifferent) or which yield the same level of utility. This appendix shows how indifference curves can be used to derive the demand curve and to separate more precisely changes in consumption into income and substitution effects.

USING INDIFFERENCE CURVES TO ILLUSTRATE CONSUMER CHOICES

In this chapter solutions to consumer choice problems were characterized as having two stages: first, identify the opportunity set, and second, find the most preferred point in the opportunity set. The budget constraint defines the opportunity set for consumers with a given income to spend on goods. Figure 5.10 repeats the budget constraint for Fran, who must divide her income between candy bars and CDs. In the chapter, we simply said that Fran would choose the most preferred point along the budget constraint. If she likes CDs a lot, she might choose point B; if she has a stronger preference for candy, she might choose point A.

The concept of the indifference curve can help us see which of these points she chooses.

The indifference curve shows the various combinations of goods that make a person equally happy. For example, in Figure 5.11, the indifference curve I_0 gives all those combinations of candy bars and compact discs that Fran finds just as attractive as 150 candy bars and 10 CDs (point A on the curve). At B, for instance, she has 12 CDs but only 130 candy bars—not so much candy, but in her mind the extra CDs make up for the loss. The fact that B and A are on the same indifference curve means that Fran is indifferent to the choice between them. That is, if you asked her whether she preferred A to B or B to A, she would answer that she couldn't care less.

Indifference curves simply reflect preferences between pairs of goods. Unlike demand curves, they have nothing to do with budget constraints or prices. The different combinations of goods along the indifference curve cost different amounts of money. The indifference curves are drawn by asking an individual which he prefers: 10 candy bars and 2 CDs or 15 candy bars and 1 CD? or 11 candy bars and 2 CDs or 15 candy bars and 1 CD? or 12 candy bars and 2 CDs or 15 candy bars and 1 CD? When he answers, "Given those options, I am indifferent," the two points that represent those choices are on the same indifference curve.

---

[5]Skipping this appendix will not affect your understanding of later chapters.

Moving along the curve in one direction, Fran is willing to accept more CDs in exchange for fewer candy bars; moving in the other direction, she is willing to accept more candy bars in exchange for fewer CDs. Any point on the same indifference curve, by definition, makes her just as happy as any other—whether it is point A or C or an extreme point like D, where she has many candy bars and very few CDs, or F, where she has relatively few candy bars but more CDs.

However, if Fran were to receive the same number of candy bars but more CDs than at A—say 150 candy bars and 15 CDs (point E)—then she would be better off, on the principle that "more is better." The new indifference curve I_1 illustrates all those combinations of candy bars and CDs that make her just as well-off as the combination of 150 candy bars and 15 CDs.

Figure 5.11 shows two indifference curves for Fran. Because more is better, Fran (or any individual) will prefer a choice on the indifference curve that is higher than another curve. On the higher indifference curve, she can have more of both items. By definition, we can draw an indifference curve for *any* point in the space of an indifference curve diagram. Also by definition, indifference curves cannot cross, as Figure 5.12 makes clear. Assume that the indifference curves I_0 and I_1 cross at point A. That would mean that Fran is indifferent to a choice between A and all points on I_0, and between A and all points on I_1. In particular, she would be indifferent when choosing between A and B, between A and C, and accordingly between B and C. But B is clearly preferred to C; therefore, indifference curves cannot cross.

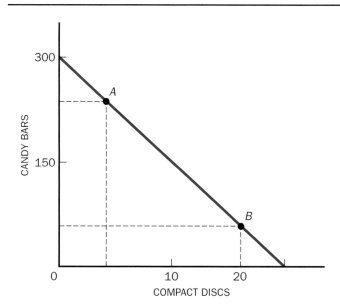

Figure 5.10

BUDGET CONSTRAINT

The budget constraint defines the opportunity set. Fran can choose any point on or below the budget constraint. If she has strong preferences for CDs, she might choose B; if she has strong preferences for candy bars, she might choose point A.

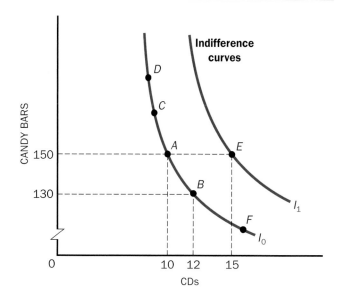

Figure 5.11

INDIFFERENCE CURVES

An indifference curve traces combinations of goods to which an individual is indifferent. Each reflects Fran's taste for CDs and for candy bars. She is just as well-off (has an identical amount of utility) at all points on the indifference curve I_0: A, B, C, D, or F.

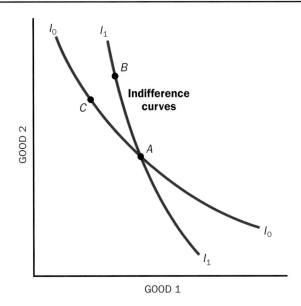

Figure 5.12

WHY INDIFFERENCE CURVES CANNOT CROSS

If two indifference curves crossed, a logical contradiction would occur. If curves crossed at point A, then Fran would be indifferent between A and B, between A and C, and therefore between B and C. But since B involves higher consumption of both goods than C, B is clearly preferred to C.

Indifference Curves and Marginal Rates of Substitution

The slope of the indifference curve measures the number of candy bars that the individual is willing to give up to get another compact disc. The technical term for the slope of an indifference curve is the **marginal rate of substitution.** The marginal rate of substitution tells us how much of one good an individual is *willing* to give up in return for one more unit of another. The concept is quite distinct from the amount a consumer *must* give up, which is determined by the budget constraint and relative prices.

If Fran's marginal rate of substitution of candy bars for CDs is 15 to 1, this means that if she is given 1 more CD, she is willing to give up 15 candy bars. If she only had to give up 12 candy bars, she would be happier. If she had to give up 20, she would say, "That's too much—having one more CD isn't worth giving up twenty candy bars." Of course, Gary could have quite different attitudes toward CDs and candy bars. His marginal rate of substitution might be 25 to 1. He would be willing to give up 25 candy bars to get 1 more CD.

The marginal rate of substitution rises and falls according to how much of an item an individual already has. For example, consider point *F* back in Figure 5.11, where Fran has many CDs and few candy bars. In this case, Fran already has bought all her favorite CDs; the marginal CD she buys now will be something she likes but not something she is wild over. In other words, because she already has a large number of CDs, having an additional one is less important. She would rather have some candy bars instead. Her marginal rate of substitution of candy bars for CDs at *F* is very low; for the sake of illustration, let's say that she would be willing to give up the marginal CD for only 10 candy bars. Her marginal rate of substitution is 10 to 1 (candy bars per CD).

The opposite holds true when Fran has lots of candy bars and few CDs. Since she is eating several candy bars almost every day, the chance to have more is not worth much to her. But since she has few CDs, she does not yet own all of her favorites. The marginal value of another candy bar is relatively low, while the marginal value of another CD is relatively high. Accordingly, in this situation, Fran might insist on getting 30 extra candy bars before she gives up 1 CD. Her marginal rate of substitution is 30 to 1 (candy bars per CD).

As we move along an indifference curve, we increase the amount of one good (like CDs) that an individual has. In Fran's case, she requires less and less of the other good (candy bars) to compensate her for each one-unit decrease in the quantity of the first good (CDs). This principle is known as the **diminishing marginal rate of substitution.** As a result of the principle of diminishing marginal rate of substitution, the slope of the indifference curve becomes flatter as we move from left to right along it.

Using Indifference Curves to Illustrate Choices

By definition, an individual does not care where he sits on any *given* indifference curve. But he would prefer to be on the highest indifference curve possible. What pins him down is his budget constraint. As Figure 5.13 illustrates, the highest indifference curve that a person can attain is the one that just touches the budget constraint—that is, the indifference curve that is *tangent* to the budget constraint. The point of tangency (labeled *E*) is the point the individual will choose. Consider any other point on the budget constraint, say *A*. The indifference curve through *A* is below the curve through *E*; the individual is better off at *E* than at *A*. But consider an indifference curve above I_0—for instance, I_1. Since every point on I_1 lies above the budget constraint, there is no point on I_1 that the individual can purchase given his income.

When a curve is tangent to a line, the curve and line have the same slope at the point of tangency. Thus, the slope of the indifference curve equals the slope of the budget constraint at the point of tangency. The slope of the indifference curve is the marginal rate of substitution; the slope of the budget constraint is the relative price. This two-dimensional diagram therefore illustrates a basic principle of consumer choice: *individuals choose the point where the marginal rate of substitution equals the relative price.*

This principle makes sense. If the relative price of CDs and candy bars is 15 (CDs cost $15 and candy bars cost $1) and Fran's marginal

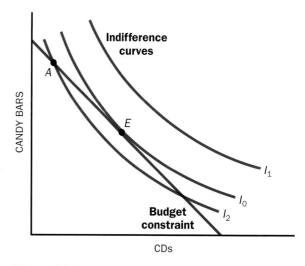

Figure 5.13

INDIFFERENCE CURVES AND THE BUDGET CONSTRAINT

The highest feasible indifference curve that can be reached is the one just tangent to the budget constraint, or indifference curve I_0 here. This individual's budget constraint does not permit her to reach I_1, nor would she want to choose point *A*, which would put her on I_2, since along I_2 she is worse off.

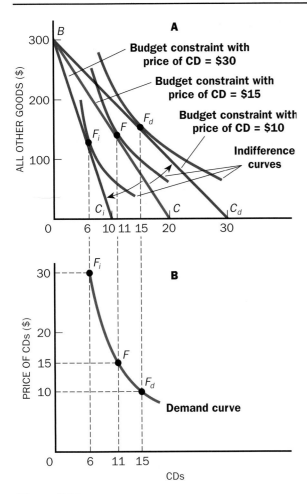

Figure 5.14

DERIVING DEMAND CURVES FROM SHIFTING BUDGET CONSTRAINTS

In panel A, the budget constraint rotates down to the left as the price of CDs increases, leading Fran to change consumption from F to F_i. The budget constraint rotates to the right when the price of CDs decreases, and Fran moves from F to F_d. Panel B shows the corresponding demand curve for CDs, illustrating how the rising prices lead to a decline in the quantity consumed.

rate of substitution is 20, Fran is willing to give up 20 candy bars to get 1 more CD, but only *has* to give up 15; it clearly pays her to buy more CDs and fewer candy bars. If her marginal rate of substitution is 10, she is willing to give up 1 CD for just 10 candy bars; but if she gives up 1 CD, she can get 15 candy bars. She will be better off buying more candy bars and fewer CDs. Thus, if the marginal rate of substitution exceeds the relative price, Fran is better off if she buys more CDs; if it is less, she is better off if she buys fewer CDs. When the marginal rate of substitution *equals* the relative price, it does not pay for her to either increase or decrease her purchases.

USING INDIFFERENCE CURVES TO DERIVE DEMAND CURVES

Indifference curves and budget constraints can be used to derive the demand curve, and thus to show what happens when prices increase. The analysis consists of two steps.

First, we identify what happens to the budget constraint as, say, the price of CDs increases. We did this earlier in Figure 5.6, but now we can add indifference curves to the analysis. In the budget constraint drawn in Figure 5.14A, we find CDs on the horizontal axis and all other goods on the vertical axis. If Fran buys no CDs, she has $300 to spend on all other goods. At a CD price of $15, she can buy up to 20 CDs, producing the budget line running from point B to C. As the price of CDs increases, the budget constraint rotates in and becomes steeper. If she buys no CDs, she still has $300 to spend on other goods. But if she buys only CDs, the number of CDs she can buy falls as their price rises. If the price of CDs falls, the budget constraint rotates out and becomes flatter.

For each budget constraint, we find the point of tangency between the indifference curve and the budget constraint, here labeled F_i, F, and F_d. This shows the point chosen along each budget constraint. Looking at the horizontal axis, we see, at each price, the quantity of CDs purchased. Panel B then plots these quantities for each price. At the price of $15, Fran chooses 11 CDs; at a price of $30, she chooses to buy only 6.

SUBSTITUTION AND INCOME EFFECTS

Indifference curves also permit a precise definition of the substitution and income effects. Figure 5.15 plots some of Jeremy's indifference curves between CDs and candy bars. Jeremy's original budget constraint is line BC and his indifference curve is I_0; the point of tangency, the point he chooses, is point E_0. Suppose the price of candy increases. Now he can buy fewer candy bars; but the number of CDs he can buy, were he to spend all of his income on CDs, is unchanged. Thus, his budget constraint becomes flatter; it is now line B_2C. While Jeremy originally chose point E_0 on the indifference curve I_0, now he chooses E_1 on the *lower* indifference curve I_1.

The price change has moved Jeremy's choice from E_0 to E_1 for two reasons: the substitution effect and the income effect. To see how this has happened, let's isolate the two effects. First, we focus on the substitution effect by asking what would happen to Jeremy's consumption if we changed relative prices but did not change how well-off he was. To keep him just as well-off as before the price change, we must keep him on the same indifference curve, I_0. Thus, the substitution effect is a movement along an indifference curve. As the price of candy rises, Jeremy, moving down the indifference curve, buys more CDs and fewer candy bars. The movement from E_0 to E_2 is the substitution effect. The budget constraint B_1C_1 represents the *new* prices, but it does not account for the income effect, by definition, since Jeremy is on the same indifference curve that he was on before.

To keep Jeremy on the same indifference curve when we increase the price of candy requires giving Jeremy more income. The line B_1C_1 is the budget constraint with the *new* prices that would leave Jeremy on the same indifference curve. Because prices are the same, the budget constraint B_1C_1 is parallel to B_2C. We now need to take away the income that left Jeremy on the same indifference curve. We keep prices the same (at the new levels), and we take away income until we arrive at the new budget constraint B_2C, and the corresponding new equilibrium E_1. The movement from E_2 to E_1 is called the income effect, since only income is changed. We have thus broken down the movement from the old equilibrium, E_0, to the new one, E_1, into the movement from E_0 to E_2, the substitution effect, and the movement from E_2 to E_1, the income effect.

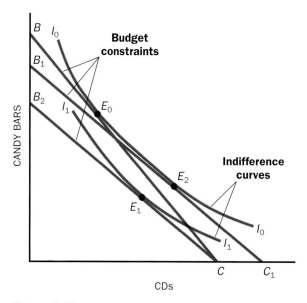

Figure 5.15

SUBSTITUTION AND INCOME EFFECTS WITH INDIFFERENCE CURVES

As the price of candy bars increases, the budget constraint rotates down. The change of Jeremy's choice from E_0 to E_1 can be broken down into an income and a substitution effect. The line B_1C_1 shows the substitution effect, the change in the budget constraint that would occur if relative prices shifted but the level of utility remained the same. (Notice that Jeremy stays on the same indifference curve in this scenario.) The substitution effect alone causes a shift from E_0 to E_2. The shift in the budget constraint from B_1C_1 to B_2C shows the income effect, the change that results from changing the amount of income but leaving relative prices unchanged. The income effect alone causes a shift from E_2 to E_1.

Learning Goals

In this chapter, you will learn

1 The different types of costs a firm faces

2 The relationship between average and marginal costs

3 How costs differ in the short run and long run

4 How firms minimize cost when they have many factors of production

Chapter 6

THE FIRM'S COSTS

Imagine the situation facing a firm in the basic competitive model. There are many other firms that make the identical product, all trying to sell what they produce to well-informed consumers who respond to any price differences. Each firm must accept the price set by the forces of supply and demand in the market as a whole. In a competitive market, a firm will lose all its customers if it charges a price even slightly above the market price. And there is no point in lowering its price, since at the market price it can already sell as much as it wants to produce. Selling at a lower price would just reduce the firm's profits.

In a competitive market, each firm is a *price taker.* No individual firm is large enough to affect the price. A firm that produces standardized memory chips or an agricultural product such as milk or almonds does not have to decide what price to set—the market sets the price; the firm decides only how much to produce.

A key factor in that decision will be the costs of producing memory chips or milk. The firm's total costs are affected by its level of production, how much labor and capital it uses in production, and the prices (wages and interest) of these inputs. Whatever output level it chooses, a firm that tries to maximize profits will seek to minimize its costs of production. This chapter focuses on how firms minimize costs and how costs are affected by the level of production. In the following chapter, we will show how a firm chooses the level of production that maximizes its profits.

Even though we talk in terms of "production" and "goods," it is important to bear in mind that only one-third of the U.S. economy consists of industries that produce goods in the conventional sense—manufacturing, mining, construction, and agriculture. The other two-thirds of the economy produces primarily services, in industries such as transportation, education, health care, wholesale and retail trade, and finance. The principles laid out here, however, apply equally to these other sectors.

Profits, Costs, and Factors of Production

A business that over time continually incurs losses will cease to exist, because it will not have enough money to pay its bills. Businesses are under constant pressure to make money. The need to make as much money as possible—maximizing profits—provides a useful starting point for discussing the behavior of firms in competitive markets.

The definition of **profits** is simple. Profits are equal to the money the business receives from selling its products—its **revenues**—minus the costs of producing those products:

$$\text{profits} = \text{revenues} - \text{costs}.$$

If a computer memory chip manufacturer sells 1 million chips at $0.20 each, its revenues would be $200,000—$0.20 times the 1 million chips sold. The revenue a business receives is just the quantity of the product it sells multiplied by the actual price the firm received for the product that it sold. A firm's *costs* are defined as the total expenses of producing the good.

What the firm uses to produce the goods are called inputs or *factors of production:* labor, materials, and capital goods. The firm's total costs are simply the sum of the costs of these inputs. Labor costs are what the company pays for the workers it hires and the managers it employs to supervise them. The costs of materials include raw materials and intermediate goods. Intermediate goods are whatever supplies the company purchases from other firms—such as seeds, fertilizer, and gasoline for a farm; or iron ore, coal, coke, limestone, and electric power for a steel company. The costs of capital goods include the cost of machinery and structures such as buildings and factories.

All firms work to keep their costs as low as possible. For given prices and levels of output, a firm maximizes its profits by finding the least costly way of producing its output. Thus, profit-maximizing firms are also cost-minimizing firms. Within limits, firms can vary the mix of labor, materials, and capital goods they use; and they will do so until they find the lowest-cost method of producing a given quality and quantity of product.

PRODUCTION WITH ONE VARIABLE INPUT

The simplest way of understanding how firms find the lowest cost point is to look at a firm with only two factors of production, one fixed (such as the amount of land a farmer has or the number of plants a manufacturer has) and one that varies with the level of production (such as the number of workers the firm hires). Not surprisingly, inputs that vary with the level of production are said to be *variable.*

A wheat farmer with a fixed amount of land who uses only labor to produce his crop is our example. The more labor he applies to the farm (his own time, plus the time of workers that he hires), the greater the output. Labor is the single variable factor (input).

The relationship between the quantity of inputs used in production and the level of output is called the **production function.** Figure 6.1 shows the farmer's production function; the data supporting the figure are set forth in Table 6.1. The increase in output corresponding to a unit increase in any factor of production, labor in this case, is the **marginal product** of that factor. For example, when the number of hours worked per year rises from 8,000 to 9,000, output increases by 10,000 bushels, from 155,000 to 165,000. The marginal product of an extra 1,000 hours of labor is thus 10,000 bushels. The marginal product is given in the last column of the table. Diagrammatically, it is given by the slope of the production function. The slope of a curve is the change along the vertical axis (the increase in output) from a unit increase along the horizontal axis (the increase in labor input).

Diminishing Returns In the case of the wheat farmer, as more labor is added to a fixed amount of land, the marginal product of labor diminishes. This is another application of the concept of *diminishing returns,* which we originally encountered in Chapter 2. In the case of a firm's production function, diminishing returns implies that each additional unit of labor generates a smaller increase in output than the last. Increasing the number of hours worked from 7,000 to 8,000 raises output by 15,000 bushels, but increasing the hours worked from 8,000 to 9,000 raises output by only 10,000 bushels. Diminishing returns sets in with a vengeance at higher levels of input; moving from 10,000 to 11,000 hours worked adds nothing. Diagrammatically, diminishing returns are represented by the slope's flattening out as the amount of labor increases. It is clear that because of diminishing returns, increases in input lead to less than proportionate increases in output; doubling the input results in output that is less than twice as large.

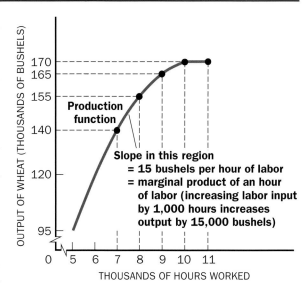

Figure 6.1

PRODUCTION FUNCTION WITH DIMINISHING RETURNS TO AN INPUT

As the amount of the input (labor) increases, so does the output (wheat). But there are diminishing returns to labor: each increase in labor results in successively smaller increases in wheat output. Since the slope of the curve is the marginal product of labor, the slope on the graph flattens out as the amount of labor increases.

Table 6.1

LEVEL OF OUTPUT WITH DIFFERENT AMOUNTS OF LABOR

Number of hours worked	Amount of wheat produced (bushels)	Marginal Product (additional bushels produced by 1,000 additional hours of labor)
5,000	95,000	
6,000	120,000	25,000
7,000	140,000	20,000
8,000	155,000	15,000
9,000	165,000	10,000
10,000	170,000	5,000
11,000	170,000	0

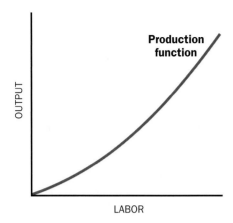

Figure 6.2

PRODUCTION FUNCTION WITH INCREASING RETURNS TO AN INPUT

As the amount of labor increases, so does output. But the returns to labor are increasing in this case; successive increases in labor result in successively larger increases in output. The slope on the graph therefore becomes steeper as the amount of labor increases.

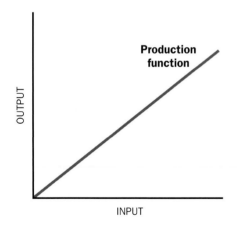

Figure 6.3

PRODUCTION FUNCTION WITH CONSTANT RETURNS TO AN INPUT

The marginal product of the input is constant, neither increasing nor diminishing as the firm expands production. The slope on the graph therefore does not change.

DIMINISHING RETURNS

As more and more of one input is added, *while other inputs remain unchanged,* the marginal product of the added input diminishes.

Increasing Returns Although a production function with diminishing returns is the most important case, other functions are possible. Figure 6.2 shows a production function where increasing an input (here, labor) raises output more than proportionately. A firm with this kind of production function has *increasing returns.* In the single-input case depicted, it is clear that the marginal product of the input increases with the amount produced; that is, adding one more worker increases output by more when the firm is producing a lot than it does when the firm is producing little.

Imagine a business that picks up garbage. If this business counts only one out of every five houses as customers, it will have a certain cost of production. But suppose the company can expand to picking up the garbage from two out of every five houses: while it will need more workers, the workers will be able to drive a shorter distance per customer and pick up more garbage faster. Thus, a doubling of output can result from a less than doubling of labor. Many examples of increasing returns, like garbage collection, involve providing service to more people in a given area. Telephone companies and electric utilities are two other familiar instances.

Constant Returns In between the cases of diminishing and increasing returns lies the case of *constant returns,* shown in Figure 6.3. Each additional unit of input increases output by the same amount, and the relationship between input and output is a straight line.

Even though we have discussed the cases of diminishing, increasing, and constant returns separately, it is important to recognize that most production functions can display all three types of returns at different levels of production. For example, at low levels of output, the addition of a unit of input may lead to a more than proportionate increase in output. As more and more of the input is added, however, diminishing returns eventually sets in. The use of fertilizer as an input into agriculture provides a good example, and one that has been well studied by agricultural economists. Imagine a large plot of land planted in corn. With the addition of only 5 pounds of nitrogen fertilizer per acre, the corn yield might be quite low, say 35 bushels per acre. Doubling the amount of fertilizer to 10 pounds per acre might more than double yields to 80 bushels per acre—an example of increasing returns. Doubling the use of fertilizer again to 20 pounds per acre increases yields to 160 bushels per acre. The impact is proportionately less than when fertilizer use was increased from 5 to 10 pounds per acre. Doubling the use of fertilizer from 10 to 20 pounds doubled the yield, a case of constant returns to scale. If the farmer again doubles the fertilizer applied, to 40 pounds per acre, yields again rise, say to 200 bushels per acre. Now yields less than double, so diminishing returns to fertilizer use have set in.

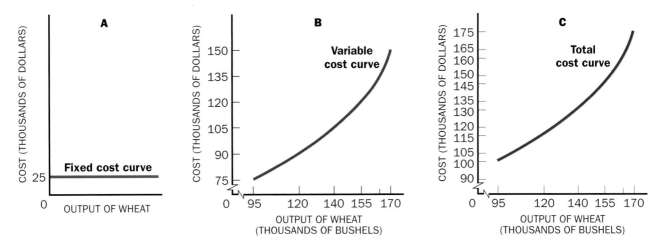

Figure 6.4

FIXED, VARIABLE, AND
TOTAL COST CURVES

Panel A shows a firm's fixed cost; by definition, fixed costs do not depend on the level of output. Panel B shows a firm's variable costs, which rise with the level of production. The increasing slope of the curve indicates that it costs more and more to produce at the margin, which is a sign of diminishing returns. Panel C shows a total cost curve. It has the same slope as the variable cost curve but is higher by the amount of the fixed costs.

TYPES OF COSTS AND COST CURVES

The production function is important to the firm because the inputs determine the cost of production. These costs are key determinants of the firm's profits and its decisions about how much to produce.

Fixed and Variable Costs Some costs associated with inputs do not vary as the firm changes the level of production. For instance, the firm may need to hire someone to run the personnel office and someone to supervise the workers, and the cost of these inputs remain constant as production varies (within limits). These costs are called **fixed costs.** Whether the firm produces nothing or produces at maximum capacity, it antes up the same fixed costs. Figure 6.4 shows how costs depend on output. Panel A depicts fixed costs as a horizontal line—by definition, they do not depend on the level of output. As an example, consider a would-be farmer who has the opportunity to buy a farm and its equipment for $25,000. Her fixed costs are $25,000.

Variable costs correspond to inputs that vary with the level of production. Any cost that the firm can change during the time period under study is a variable cost. To the extent that the costs of such items as labor and materials can go up or down as output does, these are variable costs. If our farmer has only one input to vary, labor, then her variable cost would be, say, $15 per hour for each worker. The variable costs corresponding to levels of output listed in Table 6.1 are shown in Table 6.2 and plotted in Figure 6.4B. As output increases, so do variable costs, and therefore the curve slopes upward.

Total Costs Table 6.2 also includes a column labeled "Total cost." **Total costs** are defined as the sum of fixed and variable costs, so this column is obtained by adding the farmer's fixed costs of $25,000 to the variable costs. Thus, total costs = total variable costs + fixed costs.

The total cost curve, summarizing these points, is shown in Figure 6.4C.

Marginal Cost and the Marginal Cost Curve Having come this far in studying economics, you know that rational decision making depends on evaluating trade-offs in terms of *marginal* costs and *marginal* benefits. If you have the opportunity to work more hours at your part-time job, you need to evaluate the marginal cost—the other things you could do during those extra hours you will be working (like studying economics perhaps)—against the marginal benefit, here the extra income you will earn. Firms apply this same logic in their decision making: they focus on marginal costs and benefits. Thus, one of the most important cost concepts is **marginal costs,** which are defined as the extra cost corresponding to each additional unit of production.

In the case of the wheat farmer's costs (see Table 6.2), as he increases labor input from 7,000 hours to 8,000 hours, output increases from 140,000 bushels to 155,000 bushels. Thus, the *marginal product* of the extra 1,000 hours of labor is 15,000 bushels. If the wage is $15 per hour, the cost of increasing output by 15,000 bushels is $15,000 ($15 × 1,000 extra hours). The marginal cost of the extra 15,000 bushels is $15,000. To determine the marginal cost per bushel, we divide the change in cost (C) by the change in output (Q):

$$\frac{\Delta C}{\Delta Q} = \frac{\$15,000}{15,000} = \$1 \text{ per bushel}$$

The *marginal cost curve* traces out the marginal cost for each additional unit of output. To derive the marginal cost curve using a graph, we start with the total cost curve. The marginal cost is the change in total cost (movements along the vertical axis) resulting from each unit increase in output (movements along the horizontal axis). This is shown in panel A of Figure 6.5. Panel B of Figure 6.5 shows the same relationship in a different way. The slope of the line tangent to the total cost curve at Q_1

Table 6.2

COST OF PRODUCING WHEAT

Output (bushels)	Labor required (hours)	Total variable cost (at a wage of $15 per hour)	Total cost ($)	Marginal cost ($ per bushel)	Average cost ($ per bushel)	Average variable cost ($ per bushel)
95,000	5,000	75,000	100,000	—	1.05	0.79
120,000	6,000	90,000	115,000	0.60	0.96	0.75
140,000	7,000	105,000	130,000	0.75	0.93	0.75
155,000	8,000	120,000	145,000	1.00	0.94	0.77
165,000	9,000	135,000	160,000	1.50	0.97	0.82
170,000	10,000	150,000	175,000	3.00	1.03	0.88

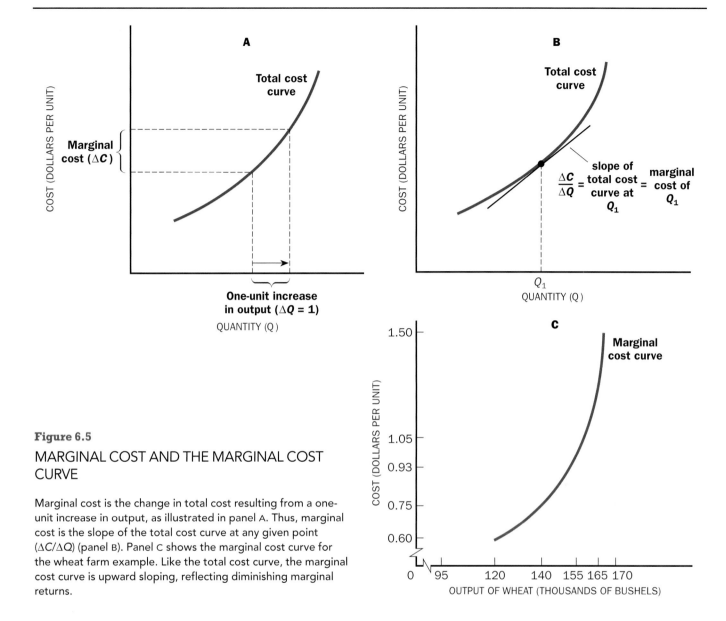

Figure 6.5

MARGINAL COST AND THE MARGINAL COST CURVE

Marginal cost is the change in total cost resulting from a one-unit increase in output, as illustrated in panel A. Thus, marginal cost is the slope of the total cost curve at any given point ($\Delta C/\Delta Q$) (panel B). Panel C shows the marginal cost curve for the wheat farm example. Like the total cost curve, the marginal cost curve is upward sloping, reflecting diminishing marginal returns.

gives the marginal cost of Q_1. Thus, the marginal cost curve represents the slope of the total cost curve at each quantity of output.

Panel C of Figure 6.5 shows the marginal cost curve for the wheat farm example. Note that the curve is upward sloping, like the total cost curve, which reflects the fact that as more is produced, it becomes harder and harder to increase output further. This is an application of the familiar principle of diminishing marginal returns. In our wheat farm example, suppose the farmer is considering increasing production by 1,000 bushels. If his current level of output is 140,000 bushels, the marginal cost of this increase will be $1,000. But if his current level of output is 155,000 bushels, increasing production by 1,000 units will entail a marginal cost of $1,500. At the higher level of output, the marginal cost is greater because of diminishing marginal returns to labor.

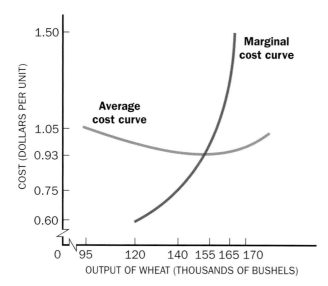

Figure 6.6

MARGINAL AND AVERAGE COST CURVES

This figure shows the marginal cost curve and average cost curve for the wheat farm example of Table 6.2. With diminishing returns to an input, marginal costs increase with the level of output, giving the marginal cost curve its typical, upward-sloping shape. Average costs initially fall with increased output, as fixed costs are spread over a larger amount of output, and then begin to rise as diminishing returns to the variable input become increasingly important. Thus, the average cost curve is typically U-shaped. With a U-shaped average cost curve, the marginal cost curve will cross the average cost curve at its minimum.

Average Cost and the Average Cost Curve A business firm also is concerned with its **average cost.** This is the total cost (*TC*) divided by output (*Q*), or

$$\text{average cost} = TC/Q.$$

The *average cost curve* gives average costs corresponding to different levels of output. Figure 6.6 shows the average cost curve for our wheat farm example (along with the marginal cost curve, for reasons indicated below). Working from the total cost curve (see Figure 6.4C and Table 6.2), we derive the average cost curve by dividing total costs (*TC*) by quantity (*Q*) at each level of output. Thus, since it takes 7,000 hours of labor to produce 140,000 bushels of wheat, and the wage is $15 per hour, the total cost is $105,000 + $25,000 (the fixed cost), for an average cost of $0.93 per bushel ($130,000/140,000 bushels). When output increases to 155,000 bushels, costs increase to $145,000, for an average cost of $0.94 per bushel.

The typical average cost curve is U-shaped, like the one in Figure 6.6. To understand why, we need to think about the two parts of total costs—fixed costs and variable costs. Just to start production usually requires a significant expense on inputs. These fixed costs do not vary with the level of output. As output increases, these costs are spread over more units of output, so the average cost of each unit of output that is due to the firm's fixed costs will fall. If these were the only costs the firm faced, average costs would decline as output increases.

Firms also face variable costs. Because of diminishing returns, beyond some level of output the firm requires more and more labor to produce each additional unit of output. Eventually, it may be almost impossible to increase output. This is why the production function in Figure 6.1 flattens out as output rises and the total cost curve in Figure 6.4C becomes steeper as output increases.

Just as we defined average costs as total costs divided by output, we define **average variable costs** as total variable costs divided by output:

$$\text{average variable costs} = \frac{\text{total variable costs}}{\text{output}}.$$

Average variable costs increase with output as the law of diminishing returns sets in strongly. The final column of Table 6.2 gives the average variable costs associated with producing wheat. At low levels of output, the falling average fixed costs dominate, and average total costs decline. But once a high-enough level of output is achieved, rising average variable costs start to dominate and average total costs increase. The result is the typical U-shape of the average cost curve, as shown in Figure 6.6.

Even if the average cost curve is U-shaped, the output at which average costs are lowest may be very great—so high that there is not enough demand to justify producing that much. As a consequence, the industry will produce at an output level below that at which average cost are lowest. When the average cost curve is U-shaped, average costs are declining at output levels that are less than the minimum average cost level of production. Thus an industry producing less than the output that results in minimum average costs will be operating in the region where average costs are declining. When economists say that an industry has declining average costs, they usually do not mean that average costs are declining at all levels of output. Instead, they typically mean that costs are declining at the output levels at which the industry is currently producing.

Relationship Between Average and Marginal Cost Curves The relationship between average costs and marginal costs is reflected in Figure 6.6. The marginal cost curve intersects the average cost curve at the bottom of the U—the *minimum* average cost. To understand why the marginal cost curve will *always* intersect the average cost curve at its lowest point, consider the relationship between average and marginal costs. As long as the marginal cost is below the average cost, producing an extra unit of output will pull down average costs. Thus, everywhere the marginal cost is below the average cost, the average cost curve is declining. If the marginal cost is above the average cost, then producing an extra unit of output will raise average costs. So everywhere that the marginal cost is above the average cost, the average cost curve must be rising.

Changing Input Prices and Cost Curves The cost curves shown thus far are based on the fixed prices of the inputs (factors) the firm uses. An increase in the price of a variable input like labor would shift the total, average, and marginal cost curves upward, as shown in Figure 6.7. An increase in fixed costs, such as an increase in the cost of the wheat farmer's land, shifts the total cost and average cost curves upward. Since fixed costs do not vary with output (by definition), a change in fixed costs does not affect the marginal cost curve.

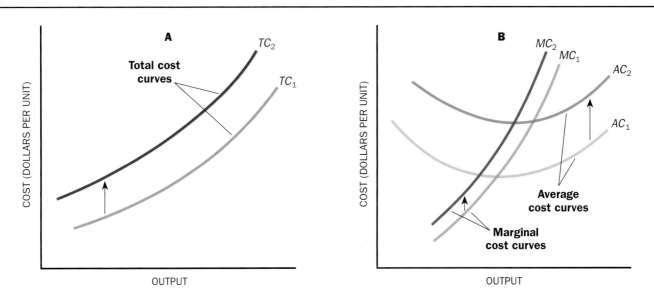

Figure 6.7

HOW CHANGING INPUT PRICES AFFECT COST CURVES

An increase in the price of a variable factor shifts the total, average, and marginal cost curves upward.

Table 6.3

DEBORAH'S COSTS IF SHE WORKS 10 HOURS DOING WEB CONSULTING

	Fixed Costs	Variable Costs	Total
Sunk costs			
Software	$125.00		$125.00
Laptop lease	$ 60.00		$ 60.00
Opportunity costs			
Forgone earnings		$50.00	$ 50.00
Total	$185.00	$50.00	$235.00
Revenue			$200.00
Profit			$ (35.00)

Example: Deborah's Web Consulting Business A simple example illustrates these various cost concepts and relates them to the notions of opportunity costs introduced in Chapter 2.

Deborah tutors for the computer science department at her college, earning $5 per hour. She works a total of 20 hours per week, which is the most she can devote to working while still maintaining good grades in her own courses. Recently, she decided to start her own business helping professors create Web pages for their classes. Deborah plans to charge $20 per hour for this service.

To get started, she had to purchase $125 worth of software, and she needed to obtain a faster laptop. A local computer store leased her the laptop she needs for $60 per month.

Tables 6.3 and 6.4 set out the costs Deborah faces in her first week of business if she works 10 hours for her new business (and continues to work 10 hours tutoring) and if she works 20 hours for her new business (and so quits tutoring completely).

Since Deborah has already purchased the software and leased the computer, these are fixed costs; they remain the same whether she decides to work 10 hours or 20 hours on her new business. These are also sunk costs; even if she decides to quit, she will be out the cost of the software and the first month's lease on the laptop.

What are her variable costs? Variable costs are costs that depend on the number of hours Deborah devotes to her Web business. For each additional hour she spends on her Web business, she works 1 hour less tutoring. The *opportunity cost* of each hour working in her new business is the $5 she could have made if she had instead spent the hour tutoring. So her variable costs consist of the $5 per hour she gives up by not tutoring.

We can now calculate Deborah's profits for the week. If she works 10 hours, her revenue is $200 (10 hours × $20 per hour). Her total costs are $125 + $60 + $50 = $235. She suffers a loss of $35. If she works 20 hours, her revenue rises to $400, while her total costs rise only to $125 + 60 + $100 = $285. She makes a profit of

Table 6.4

DEBORAH'S COSTS IF SHE WORKS 20 HOURS DOING WEB CONSULTING

	Fixed Costs	Variable Costs	Total
Sunk costs			
Software	$125.00		$125.00
Laptop lease	$ 60.00		$ 60.00
Opportunity costs			
Forgone earnings		$100.00	$100.00
Total	$185.00	$100.00	$285.00
Revenue			$400.00
Profit			$115.00

$400 − $285 = $115. So she would be better off working the entire 20 hours she has available for her new business and quitting her tutoring job completely. Note that since Deborah has $185 in sunk costs, she is better off consulting for 10 hours than closing up her business entirely. If she works 10 hours doing Web consulting, her revenues are $200, more than enough to cover her variable costs of $50.

Wrap-Up

COST CONCEPTS

Fixed costs:	Costs that do not depend on output, such as office space
Variable costs:	Costs that depend on output, such as labor costs
Total costs:	Total costs of producing output = fixed costs + variable costs
Marginal costs:	Extra cost of producing an extra unit
Average costs:	Total costs divided by output
Average variable costs:	Total variable costs divided by output

Short-Run and Long-Run Cost Curves

Up to this point, we have referred to the distinction between inputs that are fixed (their cost does not vary with quantity produced) and inputs that are variable (their cost does depend on quantity produced). We have sidestepped the fact that inputs, and costs, may be fixed for some period of time but can vary with production over a longer period. Take the inputs of labor and machines, for example. In the short run, the supply of machines may be fixed. Output is then increased only by increasing labor. In the longer run, the numbers of both machines and workers can be adjusted. The short-run cost curve, then, is the cost of production with a *given* stock of machines. The long-run cost curve is the cost of production when all factors are adjusted.[1]

SHORT-RUN COST CURVES

If we think of the number of machines as being fixed in the short run, and labor as the principal input that can be varied, our earlier analysis of production with a single variable factor provides a good description of short-run cost curves. Thus, short-run *average* cost curves are normally U-shaped.

LONG-RUN COST CURVES

Though short-run average cost curves for a given manufacturing facility are typically U-shaped, the firm's long-run average cost curve may have a quite different shape. As production grows, it will pay at some point to build a second plant, and then a third, a fourth, and so on. The curve labeled TC_1 in panel A of Figure 6.8 shows the total cost of producing different levels of output, assuming the firm has only one manufacturing plant. The panel also shows the total costs of producing different levels of output when the firm builds two plants; this cost curve is labeled TC_2. If production is very low, it is cheaper to produce using only a single plant (TC_1 is below TC_2), but as the level of production increases, it becomes more and more costly to try to handle all production in a single plant; total costs are lower if two plants are used, so TC_1 eventually rises above TC_2. The total cost curve when the firm builds three plants is shown by TC_3. How many plants should the company build? Clearly, the firm wishes to minimize the total cost of producing at any output level. If it produces less than Q_1, total costs are lowest if the firm has only one plant. Between Q_1 and Q_2, total costs are lowest if the firm has two plants. And if the firm produces more than Q_2, total costs are lowest if it uses three plants. Thus, the relevant *long-run* total cost curve when the firm is able to adjust the number of plants it has is the lower boundary of the three curves in the figure. The long-run total cost curve is the darker curve.

Panel B of Figure 6.8 shows the same result using average cost curves. If the firm minimizes the total costs of producing any particular output, it minimizes the average cost of producing that level of output. The figure shows the average cost curves corresponding to using one, two, or three plants. Once the company has

---

[1]The distinction between short-run and long-run costs corresponds to the distinction between short-run and long-run supply curves introduced in Chapter 3. Chapter 7 will make clear the relationship. It is an exaggeration to think that only capital goods are fixed in the short run while all of labor is variable. In some cases, capital goods may easily be varied; a firm can, for instance, rent cars. And in some cases, as when a company has long-term contracts with its workers, it may be very difficult to vary labor in the short run.

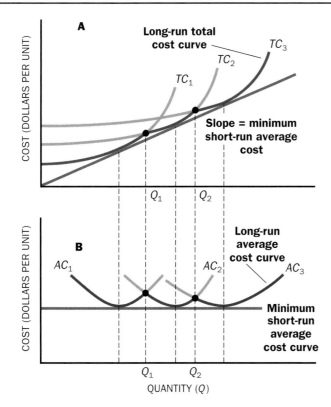

Figure 6.8

SHORT-RUN AND LONG-RUN COST CURVES

Panel A shows a series of short-run total cost curves, TC_1, TC_2, and TC_3, each representing a different level of fixed capital input. In the long run, a cost-minimizing firm can choose any of these, so the long-run total cost curve will be the lowest cost of producing any level of output, as shown by the darkened lower boundary of the curves. Panel B shows a series of short-run average cost curves, AC_1, AC_2, and AC_3, each representing a different level of fixed capital input. In the long run, a cost-minimizing firm can choose any of these, so the long-run average cost curve will be the darker lower boundary of the curves.

decided how much output it plans to produce, it will choose the number of plants that minimizes its average costs. Thus, if the firm plans to produce less than Q_1, it builds only one plant; AC_1 is less than AC_2 for all outputs less than Q_1. If the firm plans to produce between Q_1 and Q_2, it builds two plants, because in this interval, AC_2 is less than either AC_1 or AC_3. For outputs greater than Q_2, the firm builds three plants. The long-run average cost curve is the darker bumpy curve in Figure 6.8B.

The bumps in the long-run average cost curve arise because we have assumed the only alternatives in the long run that are available to the firm involve building one, two, or three plants. We have ignored the many other options a firm has. If the firm is operating one plant, it can expand by, say, adding a new assembly line rather than building a whole new plant. Or it can add new machines to its current plant. These types of adjustments would lead to a series of total cost curves between TC_1 and TC_2 in Figure 6.8A. When we take into account all the options a firm typically has to adjust its fixed costs, the bumps in the long-run average cost curve will become progressively smaller, enabling us to ignore them in most cases. Thus, when we draw a long-run average cost curve, we will typically ignore the bumps and draw a smooth curve.

But what does a smooth long-run average cost curve look like? Does it slope upward or downward? Or is it flat? A good way to answer these questions is to ask what happens to average costs if the firm doubles all its inputs. That is, it doubles the number of workers it employs and the number of plants it operates. If output also doubles when inputs are doubled, then average costs will remain unchanged. More generally, if all inputs are increased in proportion and output then increases by the same proportion, average costs will be constant. In this case, the long-run average cost curve is flat, and we say there are **constant returns to scale.** Under these conditions, changing the scale of production leaves average costs constant. Many economists argue that constant returns to scale are most prevalent in manufacturing; a firm can increase its production simply by replicating its plants. Similarly, the average cost of teaching introductory economics to 500 students is the same as it is for teaching it to 250 students. Just add another lecture hall and hire another lecturer. When long-run average cost is constant, then the marginal cost of additional output must be equal to the average cost (otherwise average costs would be changing); thus the long-run average cost curve and the long-run marginal cost curve are the same.

While constant returns to scale are common, other patterns are also possible. Suppose all inputs are increased in proportion but output increases proportionately less. For example, suppose all inputs are increased by 20 percent but output rises by only 15 percent. Costs will have risen more than output, and average costs therefore will have risen. This case is an example of **diminishing returns to scale.** If there are diminishing returns to scale, the long-run average cost curve slopes upward since long-run costs rise more than output as the firm expands production. With diminishing returns to scale, small is beautiful and big is bad. As the firm tries to grow, adding additional plants, management becomes more complex. It may have to add layer upon layer of managers, and each of these layers increases costs. When the firm is small, the owner can supervise all the workers. When the firm grows, the owner can no longer supervise everyone and will have to hire a new employee to help supervise. As the firm grows even larger, and more supervisors are hired, eventually the owner needs someone to help supervise the supervisors. Doubling the output of the firm may require not just doubling existing inputs but adding new layers of bureaucracy that can slow decision making in the firm, adding further to costs. Many small firms find they face these difficulties as they grow and that their average costs increase. Firms that attempt to grow quickly often just as quickly run into problems trying to contain costs, and many do not succeed. A recent example of a company that faltered after expanding rapidly is the Krispy Kreme Doughnut Corporation, which grew in the 1990s from a regional to a national chain. Because long-run average costs rise with output when there are diminishing returns to scale, the long-run marginal cost curve is above the long-run average cost curve.

There is one last case to consider. Suppose that increasing all inputs in proportion leads to a more than proportionate increase in output. Suppose, for example, that when all inputs are increased by 20 percent, output jumps by 25 percent. This is a case of **increasing returns to scale,** sometimes described as **economies of scale.** Big is beautiful in this case, since average costs decline as the scale of the firm is increased. Increasing returns to scale are common at low and moderate levels of production. As a company expands from one plant to ten plants, it still needs only one corporate headquarters building. Moreover, it has to pay the cost for the basic design of its plants only once. Companies with many outlets or stores, such as McDonald's or Wal-Mart, typically use a very small number of store designs, whether they are opening in Florida or Minnesota. Since these costs associated with running the firm—the overhead costs—do not increase in proportion to the increase in production, long-run average cost curves may be slightly downward sloping, as illustrated in Figure 6.9A.

For most firms, however, diminishing returns to scale eventually set in as production levels become very large. As the firm increases its size, adding additional plants, it starts to face increasing managerial problems; it may have to add layer upon layer of management, and each of these layers increases costs. Long-run average costs start to rise with output at high levels of output, as illustrated in Figure 6.9B.

Yet in some industries, increasing returns to scale are possible even for very large outputs. As the firm produces a higher output, it can take advantage of machines that are larger and more efficient than those used by smaller firms. Software companies may enjoy increasing returns to scale. Once the program code is written, the firms can expand production with very little additional costs—just the costs of blank CDs to hold the programs and the costs for distribution. At higher production levels, the initial costs of developing and writing the software are spread over a larger output, leading to declining average costs. If there are increasing returns to scale, the long-run average cost curve and the marginal cost curve will be downward sloping, as in Figure 6.9C.

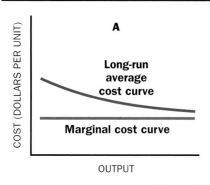
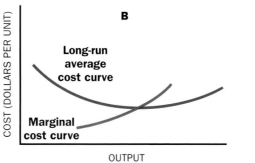
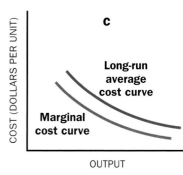

Figure 6.9

LONG-RUN AVERAGE COSTS

Panel A shows that with overhead costs, long-run average costs may be declining, but they flatten out as output increases. In panel B, with managerial costs increasing with the scale of the firm, eventually average and marginal costs may start to rise. Panel C shows that if there are increasing returns to scale, long-run costs may be continuously falling.

Wrap-Up

THE FIRM'S COSTS: KEY IDEAS

1. Profits are equal to total revenues minus total costs.
2. Marginal cost is the extra cost of producing one more unit of output. Marginal cost normally increases at higher levels of output as diminishing returns set in.
3. Average fixed costs decline as output increases, but average variable costs eventually rise. As a result, the average total cost curve is typically U-shaped.
4. The long-run average cost curve traces out the lower boundaries of the short-run average cost curve.
5. Returns to scale: There are economies of scale if doubling all inputs more than doubles output, and when there are economies of scale, the long-run average total cost curve slopes downward. There are diseconomies of scale if doubling all inputs less than doubles output, and when there are diseconomies of scale, the long-run average total cost curve slopes upward. There are constant returns to scale if doubling all inputs doubles output; in that case, the long-run average total cost curve is flat.

Relationships between the cost curves

1. The marginal cost at output level Q is the slope of the total cost curve at output level Q.
2. The average cost curve is falling when the marginal cost is less than the average cost; the average cost curve is rising when the marginal cost is greater than the average cost. Consequently, the marginal cost curve always intersects the average cost curve at the point where average costs are at their minimum.

Production with Many Factors

The basic principles of the case with only two factors—one fixed, one variable—apply also to firms producing many products with many different inputs. The only fundamental difference is that the presence of many factors makes it possible to produce the same output in several different ways. To minimize cost, firms must therefore weigh the costs of different mixes of inputs.

COST MINIMIZATION

There are usually several ways a good can be produced, using different quantities of various inputs. Table 6.5 illustrates two alternative ways of making car frames, one a highly automated process requiring little labor and the other a less-automated process that uses more assembly-line workers. The table shows the daily wage and capital costs for each process. Each method produces the same quantity of output (say, 10,000 car frames per day). In this simple example, we assume all workers are identical (of equal skill) and hence get paid the same wage, and that all machines cost the same. As we can see from the table, the less-automated process clearly costs more at the given costs of labor ($20 per worker per hour) and machines (rental costs equal $1,000 per day).

Although this table provides only two stark alternatives, it should be clear that in some cases the alternative possibilities for production will form a continuum along which the input of one increases a bit, the input of another falls a bit, and output remains the same. In other words, the firm can smoothly substitute one input for another. For instance, in producing cars, different machines vary slightly in their degree of automation. The less labor required to run a machine, the more it tends to cost. When firms make their decisions about investment, they thus have a wide range of intermediate choices between the two described in the table.

THE PRINCIPLE OF SUBSTITUTION

In the case of multiple factors of production, the principle of cost minimization has a particularly important consequence: when the price of one input (say, labor) increases relative to that of other factors of production, firms will substitute cheaper inputs for the more costly factor. This is an illustration of the general *principle of substitution* we encountered in Chapter 3.

The principle of substitution can be illustrated using the information in Table 6.5. If the wage is $20 per hour and each machine costs $1,000, output can be produced at less cost by using the more-automated process. But suppose the price of

Table 6.5

COSTS OF PRODUCTION

Inputs	More-automated process	Less-automated process
Labor	50 man-hours @ $20 = $1,000	500 man-hours @ $20 = $10,000
Machines	5 machines @ $1,000 = $5,000	2 machines @ $1,000 = $ 2,000
Total	$6,000	$12,000

machines increases to $3,500 each. Then, the more-automated process will cost $17,500, while the less-automated process will cost $17,000. Both processes rise in cost, but the less-automated process rises less. It now becomes the less costly method. As a consequence, firms will switch from the more-automated process to the less-automated process. In this way, they are able to substitute away from the factor whose price has risen (machines, in this case).

An increase in the price of any input shifts the cost function up. The amount by which the cost function shifts up depends on several factors, including how much of the input was being used in the first place and how easy it is to substitute other inputs. If the production process uses a great deal of the input, then the shift will be large. If there is a large increase in the price of an input, and the firm cannot easily substitute other inputs, then the cost curve will shift up more than it would if substitution of other inputs were easy.

In some cases, substitution is quick and easy; in other cases, it may take time and be difficult. When the price of oil increased fourfold in 1973 and doubled again in 1979, firms found many ways to economize on the use of oil. For instance, companies switched from oil to natural gas (and in the case of electric power companies, often to coal) as a source of energy. More energy-efficient cars and trucks were constructed, often using lighter materials such as aluminum and plastics. These substitutions took time, but they did eventually occur.

The principle of substitution should serve as a warning to those who think they can raise prices without bearing any consequences. For example, Argentina has almost a world monopoly on linseed oil. At one time, linseed oil was universally used for making high-quality paints. Since there was no competition, Argentina decided that it would raise the price of linseed oil, assuming everyone would have to pay it. But as the price increased, paint manufacturers learned to substitute other natural oils that could do almost as well.

Raising the price of labor (wages) provides another example. Unions in the auto and steel industries successfully demanded higher wages for their members during the boom periods of the 1960s and 1970s, and firms paid the higher wages. But at the same time, the firms redoubled their efforts to mechanize their production and to become less dependent on their labor force. Over time, these efforts were successful and led to a decline in employment in those industries.

Case in Point

THE PRINCIPLE OF SUBSTITUTION AND GLOBAL WARMING

In the two hundred years since the beginning of the industrial revolution, the amount of carbon dioxide (CO_2) in the atmosphere has increased enormously, and concentrations continue to rise. There is growing agreement among scientists that the higher concentration of CO_2 and related gases (called greenhouse gases) will lead to global warming, with potentially significant impacts on the environment. Reflecting this consensus, the countries of the world signed an agreement in Rio de Janeiro in

Hydroelectric power being generated at the Grand Coulee Dam.

1992 to work toward limiting the growth of greenhouse gases; in a subsequent meeting in 1997, in Kyoto, Japan, an effort was made to strengthen the international commitment to greenhouse gas reductions. In order for it to take effect, the Kyoto agreement had to first be ratified by countries that account for at least 55 percent of the world's greenhouse gas emissions. While President Bill Clinton supported the aims of the Kyoto agreement, he did not submit it for approval to the Senate, where it faced certain defeat; and in 2001 President George W. Bush announced that he opposed the treaty, effectively ensuring that the United States would not ratify the agreement. It eventually did take effect in early 2005 after being ratified by Russia. The agreement commits industrialized nations to make significant cuts in emissions by 2012.

From an economic perspective, the principle of substitution is at the heart of the problem of greenhouse gas reductions. Slowing down the rate of increase in greenhouse gases entails using less energy, and substituting away from sources of energy that produce large amounts of greenhouse gases, like coal, toward sources of energy that produce less, like natural gas, or even none at all, like hydroelectric power. Increasing the cost of greenhouse gas–producing energy sources by, for example, imposing a tax on fuels in proportion to how much they contribute to greenhouse gases would create an incentive for firms to substitute alternative energy sources that produce fewer greenhouse gases.

Wrap-Up

THE PRINCIPLE OF SUBSTITUTION

An increase in the price of an input will lead the firm to substitute other inputs in its place.

Economies of Scope

Most firms produce more than one good. Deciding which goods to produce and in what quantities, as well as how to produce them, are central problems facing firm managers. The problems would be fairly straightforward were it not for some important interrelations among the products. The production of one product may affect the costs of producing another.

In some cases, products are produced naturally together; we say they are **joint products.** From crude oil, a petroleum refinery can produce gasoline, lubricating oils, and diesel fuel. If more crude oil is distilled into gasoline, more lubricating oil and diesel fuel will also be produced as by-products of the process.

If it is less expensive to produce a set of goods together than separately, economists say there are **economies of scope.** The concept of economies of scope helps us understand why certain activities are often undertaken by the same firm. Your mobile phone company probably also provides text-messaging services. A company like PeopleSoft, now part of Oracle, provides software for a variety of business needs, such as human resources, finance, information technology, procurement, marketing, services, and sales. It is less expensive for one company to produce all these software services together than it would be to produce each one separately.

Review and Practice

SUMMARY

1. A firm's production function specifies the level of output resulting from any combination of inputs. The increase in output corresponding to a unit increase in any input is the marginal product of that input.
2. Short-run marginal cost curves are generally upward sloping, because diminishing returns to a factor of production imply that it will take ever-increasing amounts of the input to produce a marginal unit of output.
3. The typical short-run average cost curve is U-shaped. When an average cost curve is U-shaped, the marginal and average cost curves will intersect at the minimum point of the average cost curve.
4. Economists often distinguish between short-run and long-run cost curves. In the short run, a firm is generally assumed not to be able to change its capital stock. In the long run, it can. Even if short-run average cost curves are U-shaped, long-run average cost curves can take on a variety of shapes, including flat and continuously declining as well as declining and then increasing.
5. When a number of different inputs can be varied, and the price of one input increases, the change in relative prices of inputs will encourage a firm to substitute relatively less expensive inputs; this is an application of the principle of substitution.
6. Economies of scope exist when it is less expensive to produce two products together than it would be to produce each one separately.

KEY TERMS

profits
revenues
production function
marginal product
fixed costs
variable costs
total costs
marginal costs
average costs
average variable costs
constant, diminishing, **or** increasing returns to scale (economies of scale)
joint products
economies of scope

REVIEW QUESTIONS

1. What is a production function? When there is a single (variable) input, why does output normally increase less than in proportion to input? What are the alternative shapes that the relationship between input and output takes? What is the relationship between these shapes and the shape of the cost function?
2. What is meant by these various concepts of cost: total, average, average variable, marginal, and fixed? What are the relationships between these costs? What are short-run and long-run costs? What is the relationship between them?
3. Why are short-run average cost curves frequently U-shaped? Assume that the average cost curve is U-shaped: What is the relationship between the average and marginal costs? What does the total cost curve look like?
4. What happens to average, marginal, and total costs when the price of an input rises?
5. If a firm has a number of variable inputs and the price of one of them rises, will the firm use more or will it use less of this input? Why?
6. What are diminishing, constant, and increasing returns to scale? When might you expect each to occur? What is the relationship between these properties of the production function and the shape of the long-run average and total cost curves?
7. What are economies of scope, and how do they affect what a firm chooses to produce?

PROBLEMS

1. Tom and Dick, who own the Tom, Dick, and Hairy Barbershop, need to decide how many barbers to hire.

The production function for their barbershop looks like this:

Number of barbers	Haircuts provided per day	Marginal product
0	0	
1	12	
2	36	
3	60	
4	72	
5	80	
6	84	

Calculate the marginal product of hiring additional barbers, and fill in the last column of the table. Over what range is the marginal product of labor increasing? constant? diminishing? Graph the production function. By looking at the graph, you should be able to tell at what point the average productivity of labor is highest. Calculate average productivity at each point to illustrate your answer.

2. The overhead costs of the Tom, Dick, and Hairy Barbershop are $160 per day, and the cost of paying a barber for a day is $80. With this information, and the information in Problem 1, make up a table with column headings in this order: Output, Labor required, Total variable cost, Total cost, Marginal cost, Average variable cost, and Average cost. If the price of a haircut is $10 and the shop sells 80 per day, what is its daily profit?

3. Using the information in Problems 1 and 2, draw the total cost curve for the Tom, Dick, and Hairy Barbershop on one graph. On a second graph, draw the marginal cost curve, the average cost curve, and the average variable cost curve. Do these curves have the shape you would expect? Do the minimum and average cost curves intersect at the point you expect?

4. Suppose a firm has the choice of two methods of producing: one method entails a fixed cost of $10 and a marginal cost of $2; the other entails a fixed cost of $20 and a marginal cost of $1. Draw the total and average cost curves for both methods. At what levels of output will the firm use the low-fixed-cost technology? At what levels of output will it use the high-fixed-cost technology?

5. The cost data below are from the Acme Pizza Company. Fill in the information on the firm's total costs, marginal costs, average total costs, and average variable costs. Draw the total cost curve on one graph. On another graph, draw the marginal cost, average cost, and average variable cost curves. Are there output levels that exhibit increasing returns to scale? Are there output levels that display decreasing returns to scale?

Pizzas	Fixed costs	Variable costs	Total costs	Marginal costs	Average total costs	Average variable costs
0	$1,000	$–				
200	$1,000	$360				
400	$1,000	$840				
600	$1,000	$1,440				
800	$1,000	$2,160				
1,000	$1,000	$3,000				
1,200	$1,000	$3,960				
1,400	$1,000	$5,040				
1,600	$1,000	$6,240				
1,800	$1,000	$7,560				
2,000	$1,000	$9,000				

Learning Goals

In this chapter, you will learn

1 What determines the level of output a firm will supply at any given price

2 What determines whether a firm enters or exits a market

3 How the market supply curve is derived and why it is upward sloping

4 How competition drives economic profits to zero, and how economic profits and accounting profits differ

Chapter 7

THE COMPETITIVE FIRM

Whether it is a flower seller at a local farmer's market, a memory chip manufacturer in China, or a huge corporation such as Microsoft, Citibank, or Intel, every firm is in business to make profits. In competitive markets, firms are price takers—they are too small to affect the market price of the goods they produce. They also take as given the prices they have to pay for the inputs they purchase. The chief decision such a firm needs to make is how much to produce. In this chapter, we develop the principles that govern this decision, which will be guided by the aim of maximizing the firm's profits. Chapter 6 looked at the cost curves of the firm. Because profits are the difference between the firm's revenues and its costs, we focus here on the firm's revenues. By comparing revenues and costs, we will be able to determine the level of output the firm will supply at any given price.

This chapter examines firms in highly competitive markets. Accordingly, economists sometimes refer to the principles developed here as the *theory of the competitive firm*.

Revenue

Consider the hypothetical example of the High Strung Violin Company, manufacturers of world-class violins. The company hires labor; it buys wood, utilities, and other materials; and it rents a building and machines. Its violins sell for $40,000 each. Last year the company sold 7 of them, for a gross revenue of $280,000. Table 7.1 gives a snapshot of the firm's financial health, its profit-and-loss statement for last year.

We see that High Strung's revenues were $280,000, and its costs were $175,000, so its profits were $105,000. If its costs had been $400,000 instead of $175,000, its profits would have been –$120,000. The firm would have made a negative profit—in other words, a loss.

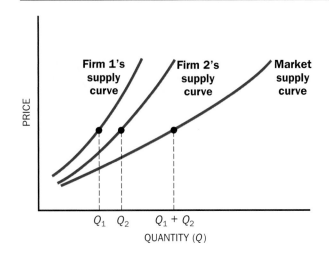

PRICE

Firm 1's supply curve

Firm 2's supply curve

Market supply curve

Q_1 Q_2 $Q_1 + Q_2$

QUANTITY (Q)

FIGURE 7.1

THE REVENUE CURVE

The revenue curve shows a firm's revenues at each level of output. For the firm in a competitive industry, price does not change as more is produced, so the revenue curve is a straight line with a constant slope. In this example, the revenue yielded by each additional violin is always $40,000.

The relationship between revenue and output is shown by the **revenue curve** in Figure 7.1. The horizontal axis measures the firm's output, while the vertical axis measures the revenues. When the price of a violin is $40,000 and the firm sells 9 violins, its revenue is $360,000; when it sells 10, revenue rises to $400,000.

The extra revenue that a firm receives from selling an extra unit is called its **marginal revenue.** Thus, $40,000 is the extra (or marginal) revenue from selling the tenth violin. It is no accident that the marginal revenue equals the price of the violin. A fundamental feature of competitive markets is that firms receive the same market price for each unit they sell, regardless of the number of units they sell. Thus, the extra revenue that firms in competitive markets receive from selling one more unit—the marginal revenue—is the same as the market price of the unit.

Costs

High Strung's costs increase as it expands its level of output. Total costs are given in column 1 of Table 7.2 and depicted diagrammatically in Figure 7.2A. Panel B shows the corresponding average and marginal costs. High Strung's average cost curve exhibits the typical U-shape that we associate with manufacturing firms.

Even before it builds its first violin, the company must spend $90,000. Space must be rented. Some employees will have to be hired. Equipment must be purchased. No matter how many or how few violins High Strung produces, its fixed costs will remain $90,000.

TABLE 7.1

PROFIT-AND-LOSS STATEMENT FOR THE HIGH STRUNG VIOLIN COMPANY

Gross revenue		$280,000
Costs		$175,000
Wages (including fringe benefits)	$150,000	
Purchases of wood and other materials	$ 15,000	
Utilities	$ 1,000	
Rent of building	$ 5,000	
Rent of machinery	$ 2,000	
Miscellaneous expenses	$ 2,000	
Profits		$105,000

The *extra* cost of producing an additional violin, the marginal cost, is shown in column 3. Marginal cost is always associated with the extra cost of producing a *particular* unit of output. The marginal cost of increasing production from 1 to 2 violins, for example, is $10,000. Each additional violin costs $10,000 more to produce until production reaches 6 violins. The extra (marginal) cost producing the seventh violin is $25,000 (perhaps another violin maker needs to be hired; or perhaps only limited quantities of the special wood the company uses in its violins are available, and finding enough of the wood for more than 6 violins is difficult and expensive). The marginal cost of producing the eighth violin is $40,000.

The High Strung Violin Company's average costs initially decline as its production increases, since the fixed costs can be divided among more units of production.

Table 7.2

HIGH STRUNG VIOLIN COMPANY'S COSTS OF PRODUCTION (THOUSANDS OF DOLLARS)

Output	(1) Total cost	(2) Average cost	(3) Marginal cost	(4) Total variable cost	(5) Average variable cost
0	90				
1	100	100.0	10	10	10.0
2	110	55.0	10	20	10.0
3	120	40.0	10	30	10.0
4	130	32.5	10	40	10.0
5	140	28.0	10	50	10.0
6	150	25.0	10	60	10.0
7	175	25.0	25	85	12.1
8	215	26.9	40	125	15.6
9	270	30.0	55	180	20.0
10	400	40.0	130	310	31.0

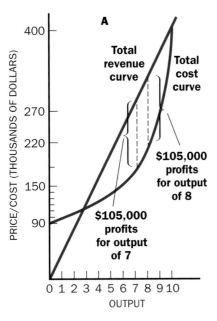

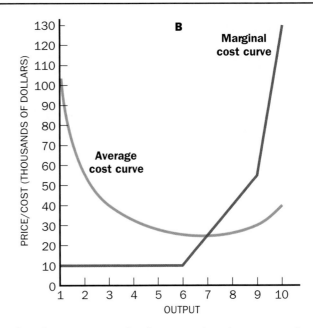

Figure 7.2

RELATING REVENUES
AND COSTS

The firm's revenue and total cost curves can be diagrammed on the same graph, as in panel A. When total revenue exceeds total costs, the firm is making profits at that level of output. Profits, the difference between revenues and costs, are measured by the distance between the two curves; in this case, the highest level of profit is being made at a production level of 7 or 8. When total costs exceed total revenue, the firm is making losses at that level of output. When the two lines cross, the firm is making zero profits. The marginal and average cost curves for this company have their expected shape in panel B. Marginal costs are constant until a production level of 6, and then they begin to increase. The average cost curve is U-shaped.

But after 7 violins, average costs begin to increase, as the effect of the increasing average variable costs dominates the effect of the fixed costs.

Basic Conditions of Competitive Supply

In choosing how much to produce, a profit-maximizing firm will focus its decision at the margin. Because it has already incurred the fixed cost of getting into this market, its decision is generally not the stark one of whether or not to produce, but whether to produce one more unit of a good or one less. For a firm in a competitive market, making this choice is relatively easy: the company simply compares the marginal revenue it will receive by producing an extra unit—which is just the price of the good—with the extra cost of producing that unit, the marginal cost. As long as the marginal revenue exceeds the marginal cost, the firm will make additional profit by producing more. If marginal revenue is less than marginal cost, then producing an extra unit will cut profits, and the firm will reduce production. In short, the firm will produce to the point where the marginal cost equals marginal revenue, which in a competitive market is equal to price.

Figure 7.3 develops the graphical analysis underlying this principle. Panel A shows the firm's marginal cost curve. If the price of the good in a competitive market is p_1, the profit-maximizing output level will be Q_1. This is the level of output at which price and marginal cost are equal. An upward-sloping marginal cost curve clearly leads the firm to produce more as price increases.

The marginal cost curve is upward sloping, just as the supply curves in Chapter 3 were upward sloping. This too is no accident: a firm's marginal cost curve is actually the same as its supply curve. The marginal cost curve shows the additional cost of producing one more unit at different levels of output. A competitive firm chooses to produce at the level of output where the cost of producing an additional unit (that is, the marginal cost) is equal to the market price. We can thus read from the marginal cost curve what the firm's supply will be at any price: it will be the quantity of output at which marginal cost equals that price.

Before we turn to Figure 7.3B, look once more at Figure 7.2A, which shows total revenues as well as total costs of the High Strung Violin Company. We can see that profits—the gap between revenues and costs—are maximized at an output of either 7 or 8. If the price were just slightly lower than $40,000, profits would be maximized at 7, and if the price were just slightly higher than $40,000, profits would be maximized at 8.

The profit-maximizing level of output can also be seen in panel B of Figure 7.3, which shows the total revenue and total cost curves. Profits are the difference between revenues and costs. In panel B, profits are the distance between the total revenue curve and the total cost curve. The profit-maximizing firm will choose the

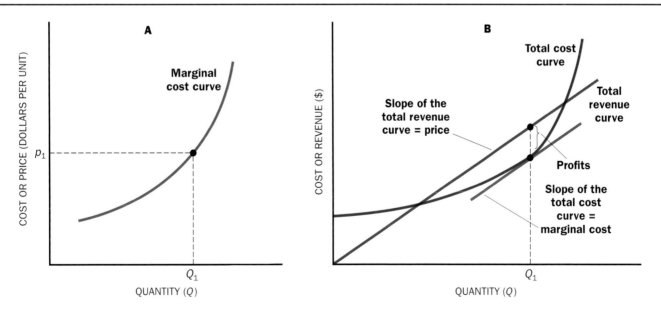

Figure 7.3

THE PROFIT-MAXIMIZING LEVEL OF OUTPUT

A competitive firm maximizes profits by setting output at the point where price equals marginal cost. In panel A, at the price of p_1, this quantity is Q_1. Panel B shows total revenue and total costs. Profits are maximized when the distance between the two curves is maximized, which is the point where the two lines are parallel (and thus have the same slope).

output where that distance is greatest. This occurs at Q_1. Below Q_1, price (the slope of the revenue curve), exceeds marginal costs (the slope of the total cost curve), so profits increase as output increases; above Q_1, price is less than marginal cost, so profits decrease as output increases.

Entry, Exit, and Market Supply

We are now in a position to tackle the market supply curve. To do so, we need to know a little more about each firm's decision to produce. First, let's consider a firm that is currently not producing. Under what circumstances should it incur the fixed costs of entering the industry? This is a relatively easy problem: the company simply looks at the average cost curve and the price. *If price exceeds minimum average costs, it pays for the firm to enter.* A company that enters the industry can sell the goods for more than the cost of producing them, thus making a profit.

Book publishing and the restaurant business are two industries that are easy to enter. If book prices are above minimum average costs, new publishers will enter the market, as it is relatively easy to produce a book. Similarly, if prices of restaurant meals in an area exceed minimum average cost, new restaurants will open up or restaurant chains will expand with branches in new locations.

Figure 7.4A shows the U-shaped average cost curve. Minimum average cost is c_{min}. If the price is less than c_{min}, then there is no level of output at which the firm could produce and make a profit. If the price is above c_{min}, then the firm will produce at Q^*, the level of output at which price (p) equals marginal cost. At Q^*, marginal costs exceeds average costs. (This is always true at output levels greater than that at which average costs are minimal.) Profit per unit is the difference between price and average costs. Total profits are the product of profit per unit and the level of output (the shaded area in the figure).

Different companies may have different average cost curves. Some will have better management. Some will have a better location. Accordingly, firms will differ in their minimum average cost. As prices rise, additional firms will find it attractive to enter the market. Figure 7.4B shows the U-shaped average cost curves for three different firms. Firm 1's minimum average cost is AC_1, firm 2's minimum average cost is AC_2, and firm 3's minimum average cost is AC_3. Thus, firm 1 enters at the price p_1, firm 2 at the price p_2, and firm 3 at the price p_3.

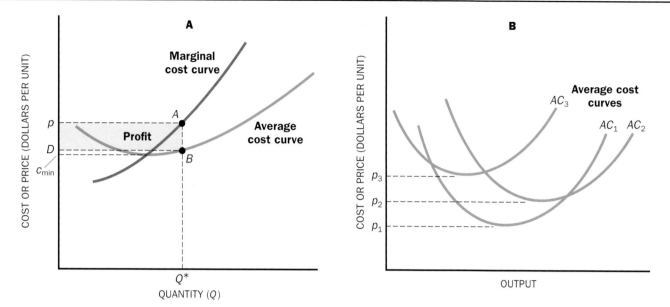

Figure 7.4

COST CURVES, PROFITS, AND ENTRY

Panel A shows that if price is above the minimum of the average cost curve, profits will exist. Profits are measured by the area formed by the shaded rectangle, the profit per unit (price minus average cost, corresponding to the distance AB) times the output, Q^*. Thus, profits are the shaded rectangle, $ABDp$. Panel B shows average cost curves for three different firms. At price p_1, only one firm will enter the market. As price rises to p_2 and then to p_3, first the firm whose cost curve is AC_2 and then the firm whose cost curve is AC_3 will enter the market.

SUNK COSTS AND EXIT

The converse of the decision of a firm to enter the market is the decision of a firm already producing to exit the market. *Sunk costs* are costs that are not recoverable, even if a firm goes out of business. The High Strung Violin Company, for example, may have had an extensive television advertising campaign. The cost of this campaign is a sunk cost. There is no way this expenditure can be recouped even if production ceases. If there were no sunk costs, the decision to enter and the decision to exit would be mirror images of each other. Firms would exit the market when their average costs rose above the good's price. But if some costs remain even after a firm exits the market, the question facing that firm is whether it is better off continuing to produce or exiting.

Let us assume for the sake of simplicity that all fixed costs are sunk costs. A firm with no fixed costs has an average cost curve that is the same as its average variable cost curve. It will shut down as soon as the price falls below minimum average costs—the cost at the bottom of its U-shaped variable cost curve. But a firm *with* fixed costs has a different decision to make. Figure 7.5A depicts both the average variable cost curve and the average cost curve for such a case. As in the case with no sunk costs, the firm shuts down when price is below minimum average *variable* costs (costs that vary with the level of output), p_1. But if the price is

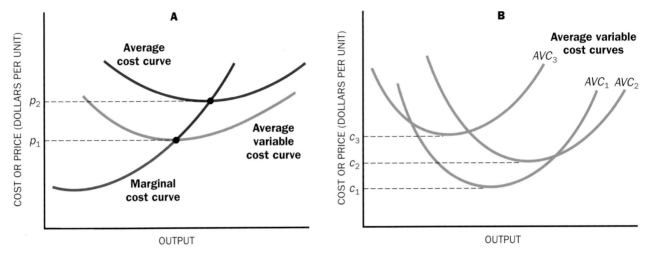

Figure 7.5

AVERAGE VARIABLE COSTS
AND THE DECISION
TO PRODUCE

Panel A shows a firm's average variable cost curves. In the short run, firms will produce as long as price exceeds average variable costs. Thus, for prices between p_1 and p_2, the firm will continue to produce, even though it is recording a loss (price is less than average cost). Panel B shows that firms with different average variable cost curves will decide to shut down at different price levels. As price falls below c_3, the minimum average variable cost for firm 3, firm 3 shuts down; as price falls still lower, below c_2, firm 2 shuts down. Finally, when price falls below c_1, firm 1 shuts down.

between average variable costs and average costs, the firm will continue to produce, even though it will show a loss. It continues to produce because it would show an even bigger loss if it ceased operating. Since price exceeds average variable costs, the revenues it obtains exceed the additional costs it incurs from producing.

Different firms in an industry will have different average variable costs, and so will find it desirable to exit the market at different prices. Figure 7.5B shows the average variable cost curves for three different firms. Their cost curves differ; some may, for instance, have newer equipment than others. As the price falls, the firm with the highest minimum average variable costs finds it is no longer able to make money at the going price, and decides not to operate. Thus, firm 3 (represented by the curve AVC_3) shuts down as soon as the price falls below c_3, firm 2 shuts down as soon as the price falls below c_2, and firm 1 shuts down as soon as the price falls below c_1.

THE FIRM'S SUPPLY CURVE

We can now draw the firm's supply curve. As Figure 7.6A shows, for a firm contemplating entry into the market, supply is zero up to a critical price, equal to the minimum average cost. Thus, for prices below $c_{\min} = p$, the firm produces zero output. For prices greater than $c_{\min} = p$, the firm produces up to the point where price equals

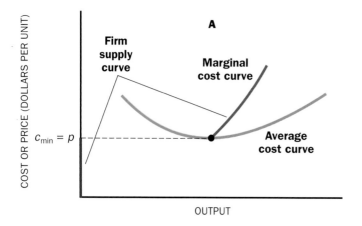

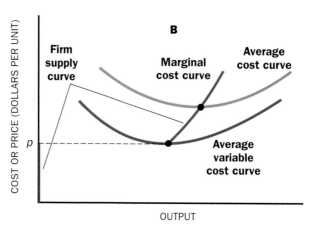

FIGURE 7.6

THE SUPPLY CURVE FOR A FIRM

Panel A shows that for a firm contemplating entry into the market, supply is zero up to a critical price, equal to the firm's minimum average cost, after which the firm's supply curve coincides with the marginal cost curve. Panel B shows a firm that has already entered the market, incurring positive sunk costs; this firm will produce as long as price exceeds the minimum of the average variable cost curve.

marginal cost, so the firm's supply curve coincides with the marginal cost curve. For a firm that has incurred sunk costs in entering the market (panel B), the supply curve coincides with the marginal cost curve so long as price exceeds the minimum value of average *variable* costs; when price is below the minimum value of average variable costs, the firm exits, so supply is again zero.

THE MARKET SUPPLY CURVE

With this information about the cost curves of individual firms, we can derive the overall market supply curve. Back in Chapter 3, the market supply curve was defined as the sum of the amounts that each firm was willing to supply at any given price. Figure 7.7 provides a graphical description of the supply curve for a market with two firms. More generally, if the price rises, the firms already in the market (firms 1 and 2) will find it profitable to increase their output, and new firms (with higher average variable cost curves) will find it profitable to enter the market. Because higher prices induce more firms to enter a competitive market, the market supply response to an increase in price is greater than if the number of firms were fixed. In the same way, as price falls, there are two market responses. The firms that still find it profitable to produce at the lower price will produce less, and the higher-cost firms will exit the market. In this way, the competitive market ensures that whatever the product, it is produced at the lowest possible price by the most efficient firms.

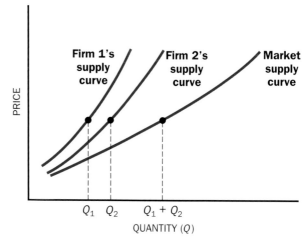

FIGURE 7.7

THE MARKET SUPPLY CURVE

The market supply curve is derived by horizontally adding up the supply curves for each of the firms. More generally, as price rises, each firm produces more and new firms enter the market.

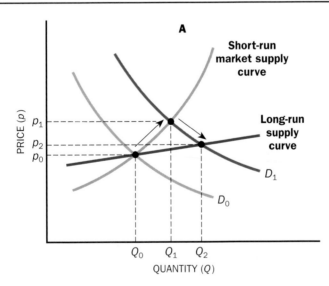

Long-Run Versus Short-Run Supply

As we saw in Chapter 6, in the short run the typical firm will have a U-shaped average cost curve, and a rising marginal cost curve at output levels above the lowest point of the U. But its long-run marginal cost curve is flatter because adjustments to changes in market conditions take time, and some adjustments take longer than others. In the short run, a firm can add workers, work more shifts, and run the machines harder (or reduce the rate at which these things are done), but it is probably stuck with its existing plant and equipment. In the long run, it can acquire more buildings and more machines (or sell them). Thus, the long-run supply curve for a firm is more elastic (flatter) than the short-run supply curve, as shown in Figure 7.8.

The same difference, only more marked, is seen for the industry—again because the number of firms is not fixed. Even if each firm can operate only one plant, the industry's output can be increased by 5 percent by increasing the number of firms by 5 percent. The extra costs of increasing output by 5 percent are approximately the same as the average costs. Accordingly, the long-run market supply curve is roughly horizontal. Under these conditions, even if the demand curve for the product shifts drastically, the market will supply much more of the

FIGURE 7.8

ELASTICITY OF SHORT-RUN AND LONG-RUN SUPPLY CURVES FOR A FIRM

Because there is a greater chance for a firm to adjust to changes in price in the long run, the price elasticity of the supply curve is greater in the long run than in the short run.

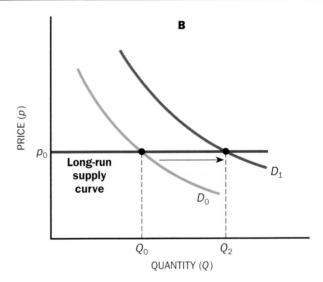

Figure 7.9

MARKET EQUILIBRIUM IN THE SHORT RUN AND LONG RUN

In panel A, the market equilibrium is originally at a price p_0 and an output Q_0. In the short run, a shift in the demand curve from D_0 to D_1 raises the price to p_1 and quantity to Q_1. In the long run, the supply elasticity is greater, so the increase in price is smaller—price is only p_2—and quantity is greater, Q_2. If supply is perfectly elastic in the long run, as shown in panel B, shifts in demand will change only the quantity produced in the long run, not the market price.

THE 2001 RECESSION: CUTBACKS VERSUS SHUTDOWNS

In late 2000, the economy seemed to slow down, and by early 2001 some parts of the economy were actually contracting. Many dot-com firms that had opened in the late 1990s found themselves struggling. Some businesses shut down, while others cut back. How do we explain the difference?

Hit particularly badly were publishers of magazines, which depend heavily on advertisements for revenues. Ad revenues for one magazine that focused on the new economy, *The Industry Standard,* fell by more than 60 percent. Publishing firms cut back on employment, but even the most adversely affected in this sector did not shut down. Why? The reason was simple: though they were showing losses, their revenues exceeded their variable costs. Much of their costs were sunk costs that would not be recovered if they closed. It paid them to continue publishing, even if on a smaller scale.

On the other hand, many Internet companies (dot-coms) did shut down. Some that had depended on advertising revenue closed because although their variable costs were low, their revenues were even lower. They could not cover their variable costs.

The online grocery service Webvan closed its doors for good during the economic slowdown of 2001.

product at close to the same price, as additional plants are constructed and additional firms enter the market.

Thus, the market supply curve is much more elastic in the long run than in the short run. Indeed, in the *very* short run, a firm may find it impossible to hire more skilled labor or to increase its capacity. Its supply curve, and the market supply curve, would be nearly vertical. In the short run, machines and the number of firms are fixed, but labor and other inputs can be varied. Figure 7.9A shows the short-run supply curve. Contrast the short-run market supply curve with the long-run market supply curve: the short-run curve slopes up much more sharply. A shift in the demand curve has a larger effect on price and a smaller effect on quantity than it does in the long run. In the long run, the market supply curve may be horizontal. In that case, shifts in the demand curve have an effect *only* on quantity, as in panel B. Price remains at the level of minimum average costs; *competition leads to entry up to the point where there are zero profits.*

Again, it is worth asking, "How long is the long run?" The answer depends on the industry. It takes an electric power company years to change its capacity. For most other firms, buildings and equipment can be added if not within months, then certainly within a year or two. Recent improvements in technology, such as computer-aided design and manufacturing, have made it possible for many companies to change what they are producing more rapidly, and thus have reduced the length of the long run and made supply curves more elastic than they had been in the past.

ADJUSTMENTS IN THE SHORT RUN AND THE LONG RUN

In the very short run, firms may be unable to adjust production at all; only the price changes.

In the short run, firms may be able to hire more labor and adjust other variable inputs.

In the long run, firms may be able to buy more machines, and firms may decide to enter or to exit.

The times required for these adjustments may vary from industry to industry.

Accounting Profits and Economic Profits

This chapter has shown how firms enter and exit markets in pursuit of profits. The result of this process is that competition among firms drives profits to zero—in an apparent contradiction of the basic competitive model. If firms are profit maximizers, as we learned in Chapter 6, why would they ever choose to produce when there are no profits to be made? Moreover, how can it be true that profits are zero when firms in the real world routinely report making profits?

The answer to these questions is that accountants and economists think about profits differently in two important respects. The first is that economists take opportunity costs into account. The second has to do with the economic concept of rent. Both deserve a closer look.

OPPORTUNITY COSTS

To begin to see how opportunity costs affect the economist's view of profits, consider a small firm in which the owner has invested $100,000. Assume the owner receives a small salary and devotes sixty hours a week to running the enterprise. An economist would argue that the owner ought to calculate his opportunity costs related to his investment of time and money into the business. The opportunity cost of his time is the best wage available to him if he worked sixty hours a week at an alternate job. The opportunity cost of his capital is the return that the $100,000 invested in this enterprise would produce in another investment. These are the true costs of the owner's time and capital investment. To calculate the firm's profits as the economist sees them, these opportunity costs have to be subtracted out.

One can easily imagine a business whose accountant reports a profit equal to 3 percent of the capital investment. An economist would note that if the investment capital had been put in a bank account, it would have earned at least 5 percent. Thus, the economist would say the business is operating at a loss. Because they generally fail to take into account opportunity costs, reported profits often are frequently higher than true economic profits.

Taking opportunity costs into account is often not a simple matter; it is not always easy to determine the alternative uses of a firm's resources. Managerial time spent in expanding the firm in one direction, for example, might have been spent in controlling costs or expanding the firm in another direction. Land that is used for a golf course for the firm's employees might have been used for some other purpose, and the money saved could have more than covered golf club memberships for all employees who want them. In making decisions about resources like these, firms must constantly ask what price the resources might fetch in other uses.

Sometimes market data can provide appropriate prices for calculating opportunity costs. For example, the opportunity cost of giving huge offices to top executives can be gauged by the money those offices would bring if they were rented to some other company. But often the calculation involves imponderables, such as the opportunity cost of the vice president who cannot be fired and will not retire for five years.

What about the costs associated with an expenditure already made, say on a building that is no longer really needed by the firm? The relevant opportunity cost of this building is not the original purchase or lease price, but instead the value of the building in alternate uses, such as the rent that could be earned if the building were leased to other firms.

The fundamental point is that past expenditures cannot be used to calculate opportunity costs. Consider a computer manufacturer that has purchased a parcel of land for $1 million an acre. It turns out, however, that the company made a mistake: the land is worth only $100,000 an acre. The firm now must choose between two different plants for producing new computers, one of which uses much more of the land than the other. In figuring opportunity costs, should the property be valued at the purchase price of $1 million an acre, or at what it could be sold for—$100,000 an acre? The answer can help determine whether the firm chooses to conserve on land. From an economics viewpoint, the answer to this valuation problem should be obvious: the firm should evaluate costs according to its *current* opportunity costs. The fact that the company made a mistake in purchasing the land is irrelevant.

Yet individuals and firms frequently do compound their economic errors by continuing to focus on past expenditures. Business executives who were originally responsible for making a bad decision may be particularly reluctant to let bygones be bygones. Publicly declaring that the correct market price of land is $100,000 an acre, for example, would be tantamount to announcing that a major mistake had been made. Acknowledging such a mistake could jeopardize a business executive's future with the firm.

ECONOMIC RENT

A second difference between an economist's and an accountant's definition of profit concerns **economic rent.** Economic rent is the difference between the price that is actually paid and the price that would have to be paid in order for the good or service to be produced.

Economic rent has far broader applications than its historic use to refer to payments made by farmers to their landlords for the use of their land, but the example of rent for land use is still instructive. The critical characteristic of land in this context is that its supply is inelastic. Higher payments for land (higher rents) will not elicit a greater supply. Even if landlords received virtually nothing for their land, the same land would be available. Many other factors of production have the same inelastic character. Even at double the salary, Shaquille O'Neal would not "produce" more baskets for the Miami Heat. The extra payments for this kind of rare talent fall into the economist's definition of rent.

While the supersalaries of movie stars and professional athletes consist largely of economic rent, many workers with more mundane salaries also receive it. For example, suppose Jim has just finished his degree in education and has offers to teach high school from two school districts in California, one in Santa Cruz on the Pacific Ocean and one in San Jose, a forty-minute drive from the beach. Both districts offer Jim the same starting salary. If Jim loves to surf, he will take the job in Santa Cruz, where he can surf before and after work. In fact, he would have taken the job in Santa Cruz even at a slightly lower salary than was offered by the school in San Jose. The difference between what he actually is paid and his opportunity cost—the value of his next best-alternative—is economic rent.

The concept of opportunity cost explains our claim that the salaries of movie stars and top professional athletes are mainly economic rent. Before Brad Pitt became a famous and highly paid actor, he supported himself as a limo driver and by dressing as a giant chicken for an L.A. restaurant chain. He studied journalism in college but left before graduating. None of these occupations would have paid anything near what he earns as an actor. The value of his next-best opportunity is low, making almost all his income economic rent. The same is true of people like Kobe Bryant; his income in his next-best alternative to basketball is probably trivial compared to what he is paid by the Lakers. Anyone who is in a position to receive economic rents is fortunate indeed, because these "rents" are unrelated to effort. They are payments determined entirely by demand.

Firms earn economic rent to the extent that they are more efficient than other firms. We saw earlier that a firm is willing to produce at a price equal to its minimum average cost. Some firms might be more efficient than others, so their average cost curves are lower. Consider a market in which all firms except one have the same average cost curve, and the market price corresponds to the minimum average cost of these firms. The remaining firm is super-efficient, pushing its average costs far below those of the other firms. The company would have been willing to produce at a lower price, at its minimum average cost. What it receives in excess of what is required to induce it to enter the market are rents—returns on the firm's superior capabilities.

In some cases, supplies of inputs are inelastic in the short run but elastic in the long run. An example is payment for the use of a building. In the short run, the supply of buildings does not depend on the return, and hence payments for the use of the building are rents, in the economist's sense. But in the long run, the supply of buildings does depend on the return—investors will not construct new buildings unless they receive a return equal to what they could obtain elsewhere. So the "rent" received by the building's owner is not really a rent, in the sense in which economists use the term.

Thus, when economists say that competition drives profits to zero, they are focusing on the fact that in competitive equilibrium, price equals marginal cost for every firm producing. A company will not increase profits by expanding production, and firms outside the industry will not gain by entering it. We say that competition drives profits to zero at the margin.

Case in Point

ENTERING THE PAINTING BUSINESS AND OPPORTUNITY COSTS

Individuals often forget to include opportunity costs when they are making important decisions, as the following story illustrates.

House painting is a summer business, for days that are hot and long, using available low-skilled labor on vacation from high school and college. As a way of picking up some cash, Michael decided to start Presto Painters during the summer, after taking introductory economics.

Just getting started involved some substantial fixed costs. Michael ran the business out of his parents' home so he had no costs for office space. His fixed costs ended up looking like this:

Fixed costs	
Used van	$5,000
Paint and supplies	$2,000
Flyers and signs	$1,200
Business cards and estimate sheets	$ 500
Phone line and answering machine	$ 300
Total	$9,000

Michael went to work drumming up business. He took calls from potential customers and knocked on doors, made estimates of what he thought it would cost to paint someone's home, and then offered them a price. Of course, he was in direct competition with many other painters and had to meet the competition's price to get a job.

Michael found that the going rate for labor was $10 per hour. In the real world, labor is not the only variable input required for house painting—there are also the costs of buying additional paint and brushes—but for the sake of simplicity, let's assume that he started off the summer with all the paint he needed. Thus, his variable costs were related to the labor he needed to hire.

Variable costs are also related to the amount of time it takes to paint a house, which depends in part on the quality of the labor available. The variable costs for Presto Painters were as follows:

Houses painted	Hours of labor hired	Payroll cost
5	100	$ 1,000
10	300	$ 3,000
15	600	$ 6,000
20	1,000	$10,000
25	1,500	$15,000
30	2,100	$21,000

Number of homes	Total cost	Average cost	Marginal cost (per house)
0	$ 9,000		
5	$10,000	$2,000	$ 200
10	$12,000	$1,200	$ 400
15	$15,000	$1,000	$ 600
20	$19,000	$ 950	$ 800
25	$24,000	$ 960	$1,000
30	$30,000	$1,000	$1,200

Given this information, Michael could calculate cost curves for Presto Painters (see above).

Based on his marginal and average cost curves, Michael figured that if market conditions allowed him to charge $1,000 or more for a typical house, then he could make a profit by painting at least 25 houses. Roughly speaking, that is how his summer worked out; painting 25 houses for $1,000 apiece. Thus, he earned $1,000 in profits.

Or so he thought. Nowhere on this list of costs did Michael consider the opportunity cost of his time. He was not getting paid $10 an hour for painting houses; he was out there stirring up business, hiring and organizing workers, taking calls from customers, dealing with complaints.

Imagine that Michael had an alternate job possibility: waiting on tables. He could earn $6 per hour (including tips) and work 40-hour weeks during a 12-week summer vacation. Thus, he could have earned $2,880 during the summer with little stress or risk. If this opportunity cost is added to the fixed costs of running the business, then his apparent profit turns into a loss. Since Presto Painters did not cover Michael's opportunity cost *and* compensate him for the risk and aggravation of running his own business, he would have been financially better off sticking to the business of filling people's stomachs rather than painting their houses.

ACCOUNTANTS' VERSUS ECONOMISTS' PROFITS

Accounting profits: revenues minus expenditures

Economic profits: revenues minus rents minus economic costs (including opportunity costs of labor and capital)

The Theory of the Competitive Firm

We now have completed half of our description of the theory of the competitive firm. The firm takes as given the prices it pays for the inputs it uses, including the wages it pays workers and the costs of capital goods. From these figures, it can calculate the costs of producing different levels of output. Taking the prices it receives for the goods it sells as given, the firm chooses the level of output to maximize its profits—that is, it sets price equal to marginal cost. From this information, we can derive the supply curves that were used in Chapters 3 and 4. As prices increase, output increases; firms produce more, and more firms produce. Thus, supply curves are upward sloping.

But as the firm produces more, it will also demand more labor and more capital. Deriving firms' demand curves for labor and capital is our next task, which we take up in the following chapters.

Review and Practice

SUMMARY

1. A revenue curve shows the relationship between a firm's total output and its revenue. For a competitive firm, the marginal revenue it receives from selling an additional unit of output is the price of that unit.
2. A firm in a competitive market will choose the level of output at which the market price—the marginal revenue it receives from producing an extra unit—equals the marginal cost.
3. A firm will enter a market if the market price for a good exceeds its minimum average costs, since it can make a profit by selling the good for more than it costs to produce the good.
4. If the market price is below minimum average costs and a firm has no sunk costs, the firm will exit the market immediately. If the market price is below minimum average costs and a firm has sunk costs, it will continue to produce in the short run as long as the market price exceeds its minimum average variable costs.
5. For a firm contemplating entering a market, its supply is zero up to the point at which price equals minimum average costs. Above that price, the supply curve is the same as the marginal cost curve.
6. The market supply curve is constructed by adding up the supply curves of all firms in an industry. As prices rise, more firms are willing to produce, and each firm is willing to produce more, so that the market supply curve is normally upward sloping.
7. The economist's and the accountant's concepts of profits differ in how they treat opportunity costs and economic rents.

KEY TERMS

revenue curve
marginal revenue
economic rent

REVIEW QUESTIONS

1. In a competitive market, what rule determines the profit-maximizing level of output? What is the relationship between a firm's supply curve and its marginal cost curve?
2. What determines firms' decisions to enter a market? to exit a market? Explain the role of the average variable cost curve in determining whether firms will exit the market.
3. Why is the long-run supply curve more elastic than the short-run supply curve?
4. What is the relationship between the way accountants use the concept of profits and the way economists use that term?

PROBLEMS

1. The market price for painting a house in Centerville is $10,000. The Total Cover-up House-Painting Company has fixed costs of $4,000 for ladders, brushes, and so on, and the company's variable costs for house painting follow this pattern:

Output (houses painted)	2	3	4	5	6	7	8	9	10
Variable cost (in thousands of dollars)	26	32	36	42	50	60	72	86	102

Calculate the company's total costs, and graph the revenue curve and the total cost curve. Do the curves have the shape you expect? Over what range of production is the company making profits?

2. Calculate and graph the marginal cost, the average costs, and the average variable costs for the Total Cover-up House-Painting Company. Given the market price, at what level of output will this firm maximize profits? What profit (or loss) is it making at that level? At what price will the firm no longer make a profit? Assume its fixed costs are sunk; there is no market for used ladders, brushes, etc. At what price will the company shut down?

3. Draw a U-shaped average cost curve. On your diagram, designate at what price levels you would expect entry and at what price levels you would expect exit if all the fixed costs are sunk. What if only half the fixed costs are sunk? Explain your reasoning.

4. José is a skilled electrician at a local company, a job that pays $50,000 per year, but he is considering quitting to start his own business. He talks it over with an account-

ant, who helps him to draw up the following chart with their best predictions about costs and revenues.

Predicted annual costs		Predicted annual revenues
Basic wage	$20,000	$75,000
Rent of space	$12,000	
Rent of equipment	$18,000	
Utilities	$ 2,000	
Miscellaneous	$ 5,000	

The basic wage does seem a bit low, the accountant admits, but she tells José to remember that as owner of the business, José will get to keep any profits as well. From an economist's point of view, is the accountant's list of costs complete? From an economist's point of view, what are José's expected profits?

Learning Goals

In this chapter, you will learn

1 What determines the number of hours an individual works

2 How income and substitution affect labor supply decisions in opposing ways

3 What determines a firm's demand for labor

4 How wages ensure that demand and supply balance in the labor market

CHAPTER 8

LABOR MARKETS

The previous three chapters examined demand and supply in the markets for goods and services. Choosing what goods to purchase and how much of them are among the most basic decisions of households. The amount of money available to spend depends on two other basic decisions: how much to work (and earn) and how much to save (or spend from savings). The decisions that people make about work determine the economy's supply of labor. Their decisions about saving determine the economy's supply of funds in the capital market. Understanding the factors that influence these decisions will give us insight into the supply side of the economy's labor and capital markets.

In this chapter, we focus on the labor market and the decisions that determine both the demand for labor and the supply of labor. We will find that the approach developed in Chapter 5 to understand how households decide about consuming can also offer insights into how they decide how much to work. We will also look into the factors that determine the firm's demand for labor. By bringing together the demand and supply sides of the labor market, we will see how wages are determined in a competitive market economy. Chapter 9 will then examine saving decisions and the capital market.

The Labor Supply Decision

At one time, going to college was a full-time job. Students were supported by their families or by scholarships and loans, with few students holding down jobs. Today, most college students work to help pay their tuition and living expenses. In addition to deciding which classes to take, students have to decide whether to work; and if they decide to work, they need to decide how many hours to work each week. Working more helps pay the bills, but it also takes time away from studies, perhaps even delaying graduation. Understanding the forces that affect decisions about how much to work—how much labor to supply to the market—is central to understanding how labor markets function.

The increase in student employment is just one of many changes in the pattern of labor supply that have taken place over the past half century. The average workweek has declined from 39 hours in 1959 to just under 34 hours in 2004. At the same time, the fraction of women in the labor force has increased enormously. In 1950, just 34 percent of women over the age of sixteen were in the labor force. Today, that figure is close to 60 percent. Many of the changes in American society in recent decades are reflections of the decisions individuals make about how much labor to supply.

THE CHOICE BETWEEN LEISURE AND CONSUMPTION

Economists use the basic model of choice to help understand these patterns of labor supply. This is the model we used in Chapter 5 to examine the consumption decision. The decision about how much labor to supply is a choice between consumption (or income) and leisure. (*Leisure* to an economist means all the time an individual could potentially work for pay that is not actually spent working.) By giving up leisure, a person receives additional income, and this enables her to increase consumption. By working less and giving up some consumption, a person obtains more leisure. Her increase in income does not necessarily translate *immediately* into consumption; she has to decide whether to spend the extra income now or in the future. We will tackle that choice in Chapter 9. Here, we assume the person spends all her income.

Even though the typical job seems to entail set hours of work, people have many ways to influence how much labor they will supply. Many workers may not have discretion as to whether they will work full-time, but they have some choice in whether they will work overtime. In addition, many individuals moonlight, taking second jobs that provide them with additional income. Most of these jobs—for example, driving a taxi—provide considerable discretion in the number of hours worked. Hence, people still have choices even when they lack control of their work hours at their primary job. And because jobs differ in their normal workweek, a worker has some flexibility in choosing a job that allows her to work the number of hours she wishes. Finally, economists believe that social conventions concerning the "standard" workweek—the 40-hour week that has become the 35-hour week—respond over time to the attitudes (preferences) of workers.

We now apply the analysis of Chapter 5 to an individual's choice between work and leisure. Figure 8.1 shows the budget constraint of Steve, who earns an hourly wage of $7. Accordingly, for each hour less of leisure Steve enjoys—for each extra hour he works—he earns $7 more. That is, his consumption increases by $7. Underlying this budget constraint is his time constraint. He has only so many hours a day, say 16, to spend either working or at leisure. For each extra hour he works, he has 1 less hour of leisure. If he works 1 hour, his income is $7; if he works 2 hours, his income is $14; and so forth. If he works 16 hours—he has no leisure—his income is $7 × 16 = $112. The trade-off between income and leisure given by his budget constraint is $7 per hour.

Steve will choose a point on the budget constraint according to his own preferences, just as a consumer chooses between two goods (see Chapter 5). Let's suppose that he chooses point E_0. At E_0 he has 10 hours of leisure, which means that he works 6 hours out of the total available time of 16 hours. His income is $42 per day.

In deciding which of the points along the budget constraint to choose, Steve balances the marginal benefits of what he can buy with an additional hour's wage against the marginal costs—the value of the hour's worth of leisure that he will have to forgo. Steve and his brother, Jim, assess the marginal benefits and marginal costs differently. Steve chooses point E_0, while his brother chooses point E_1. Jim values the material things in life more and leisure less.

For Steve, at E_0, the marginal benefit of the extra concert tickets or other goods he can buy with the money he earns from working an extra hour just offsets the marginal costs of that hour—the extra leisure he has to give up. At points to the left of E_0, Steve has less leisure (so the marginal value of leisure is greater) and he has more goods (so the marginal value of the extra goods he can get is lower). The marginal benefit of working less exceeds the marginal costs, and so he works less—he moves toward point E_0. The converse arguments apply to Steve's thinking about points to the right of E_0.

We can apply the same kind of reasoning to see why the workaholic Jim chooses a point to the left of E_0. At E_0, Jim values goods more and leisure less. The marginal benefit of working more exceeds the marginal costs. At E_1, the marginal benefit of working an extra hour (the extra consumption) just offsets the marginal costs.

We can use this framework to derive a *labor supply curve* that shows the quantity of labor supplied at different wages. Changes in wages have both an income effect and a substitution effect. An increase in wages makes individuals better off. When individuals are better off, they purchase more of all goods. One of the "goods" they will want more of is leisure, so they work less. This is the income effect. But an increase in wages also changes the trade-offs. By giving up one more hour of leisure, the individual can get more goods. Because of this, individuals are willing to work more. This is the substitution effect.

When we looked at the case of a typical good in Chapter 5, we saw that the income and substitution effects reinforce each other. A higher price

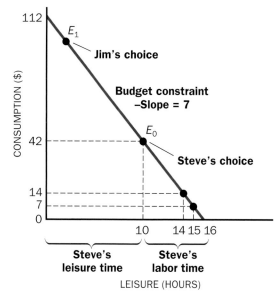

FIGURE 8.1

A BUDGET CONSTRAINT BETWEEN LEISURE AND INCOME

Individuals are willing to trade leisure for an increase in income, and thus in consumption. The budget constraint shows Steve choosing E_0, with 10 hours of daily leisure, 6 hours of work, and $42 in daily wages.

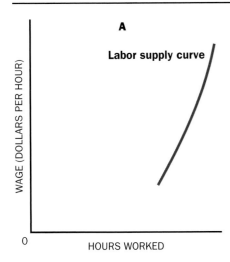

A

Labor supply curve

WAGE (DOLLARS PER HOUR)

0   HOURS WORKED

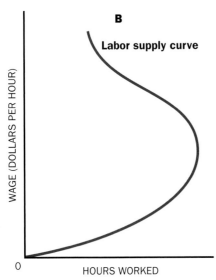

B

Labor supply curve

WAGE (DOLLARS PER HOUR)

0   HOURS WORKED

Figure 8.2

THE LABOR SUPPLY CURVE

Panel A shows the case where the substitution effect exceeds the income effect by just a bit, so increases in wages lead to only a small change in labor supply, and the labor supply curve is very steep. In panel B, the substitution effect dominates the income effect at low wages, so that the labor supply curve is upward sloping; and the income effect dominates the substitution effect at high wages, so that the labor supply is downward sloping over that range. Thus, the labor supply curve bends backward.

means that individuals are worse off—this income effect leads to reduced consumption of the good; and individuals substitute away from the good whose price has increased—the substitution effect also leads to reduced consumption of the good. *With labor supply, income and substitution effects work in opposite directions, so the net effect of an increase in wages is ambiguous.*

If your wage goes up by 5 percent and you cut back on your hours of work by 5 percent, your total wage income (the hourly wage multiplied by the number of hours you work) will be unchanged: you would have the same income while gaining some extra leisure time. Alternatively, you could work the same number of hours as before and enjoy a higher income. Here, the income effect acts to reduce labor supply. But the opportunity cost of leisure also rises when the wage increases, for the cost of enjoying an extra hour of leisure is the wage income you are giving up. At lower income levels, people generally prefer not to cut back their hours of work when their wage rises; instead, they increase their hours to take advantage of the opportunity to earn the higher wage (the substitution effect of the higher hourly wage dominates the income effect). Labor supply increases as the wage increases. This normal case of an upward-sloping labor supply curve is shown in Figure 8.2A. People choose to work more as their wage rises, trading off leisure for more income.

If income is already very high, however, people often prefer to work less and enjoy more leisure when their wage increases (the income effect dominates the substitution effect). For examples of individuals whose labor supply curve is backward-bending at high wage levels, think of those doctors, dentists, and other high-income professionals who work only a four-day week. This case is illustrated in Figure 8.2B.

If income and substitution effects just balance each other, then labor supply will be relatively unaffected by wage changes. The evidence is that at least for men, the labor supply curve elasticity—the percentage increase in hours worked as a result of a 1 percent increase in wages—is positive but small. For this reason, the average hours that men work has changed little over the past fifty years despite the huge increase in their wages. For women, the evidence suggests that a rise in wages increases labor supply.

So far, we have discussed the impact of a change in wages on labor supply while implicitly assuming that the prices of consumer goods remain unchanged. But in assessing the trade-off between leisure and consumption, an individual is concerned with the actual goods and services that can be purchased, not simply the number of dollars available to spend on consumption. If wages and the prices of all consumer goods double at the same time, then the trade-off between leisure and consumption has not changed. If Jim's wage rises from $7 per hour to $14 per hour, but the price of a compact disc goes up from $10.50 to $21.00, Jim must still give up an hour and a half of leisure to obtain one CD. What is important for labor supply decisions is the average dollar wage, called the **nominal wage,** corrected for changes in the prices of consumer goods. This corrected wage is called the **real wage.** Since 1980, the average nominal wage has risen by more than 100 percent, from $6.84 to $15.38 per hour. Yet the prices of the things we buy have also risen; in fact, the average real wage has remained constant over the past twenty years.

WAGE CHANGES AND LABOR SUPPLY

Labor supply decisions depend on the real wage—the nominal wage corrected for the price of consumer goods.

As real wages rise, individuals become better off. This income effect induces them to work less. Offsetting it is the substitution effect—the higher return to working provides an incentive to work longer hours. Either effect may dominate. Thus, the quantity of labor supplied may increase or decrease with wage increases.

LABOR FORCE PARTICIPATION

The decision about how much labor to supply can be divided into two parts: whether to work and, if so, how much to work. For men, the first question traditionally has had an obvious answer. Unless they were very wealthy, they had to work to support themselves (and their families). Accordingly, the wage at which they decided to work rather than not to work was very low. A change in wage still does not affect the decision of most men about whether to work. It influences only their decision about how many hours to work, and even that effect is small.

Thinking Like an Economist

TRADE-OFFS

The relevant trade-off for deciding how much labor to supply is that between consumption and leisure, as delineated in the budget constraint in Figure 8.1. To gain more consumption, you have to work more, and as a result you have to give up leisure. To gain more leisure time, you have to give up consumption as you work fewer hours and earn less money.

Like all trade-offs, this one reflects an opportunity cost, a concept we introduced in Chapter 2. In the present case, the opportunity cost of an extra hour of leisure is the consumption you have to give up by working one hour less. Similarly, the opportunity cost of an extra $25 of consumption is the leisure time you have to give up to earn the extra $25.

Because the opportunity cost of leisure is the forgone consumption, this opportunity cost depends on the wage you can earn. If your wage is $7 per hour, the opportunity cost of an hour of leisure is $7. If your wage is $25 per hour, the opportunity cost of an hour of leisure is $25. So the opportunity cost of leisure is greater for someone who earns a high wage than it is for someone who earns a lower wage.

Another key idea to remember is that economic decisions are determined by marginal trade-offs (see Chapter 2). If you want to consume more, the benefit of the *extra* consumption must be weighed against the (opportunity) cost of the *diminished* leisure. On the basis of individual preferences for consumption and leisure, the worker chooses the point on the budget constraint where the marginal benefits and costs are equal.

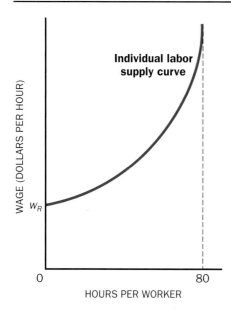

Figure 8.3

THE LABOR PARTICIPATION DECISION

The reservation wage W_R is the minimum wage at which an individual supplies labor.

The decision about *whether* to work is called the **labor force participation decision.** Figure 8.3 shows the labor supply curve for an individual—it shows how many hours that person is willing to supply at each real wage. The minimum wage at which the individual is willing to work, W_R, is called the **reservation wage.** Below the reservation wage, the individual does not participate in the labor force. For men, the reservation wage traditionally has been very low.

Today, most women also work for pay, but for them, unlike men, such employment is not traditional. Only a few decades ago, the social presumption was that middle-class women, if they worked at all, would drop out of the labor market after they began to bear children. And many mothers did not reenter the market even after their children were grown.

The increased quantity of labor supplied by women over the past fifty years can be viewed partly as a *movement* along the labor supply curve and partly as a *shift* in the curve. Job opportunities for women have burgeoned over the past thirty years, and relative wages have risen. Thus, the remuneration from working has increased, raising by the same amount the *opportunity cost* of being out of the labor force. For women already in the labor force, these wage increases have opposing income and substitution effects, just as they do for men. But for women who were not previously part of the labor force, only the substitution effect operates: if a woman was working zero hours, an increase in wages does not raise her income—there is no income effect. Therefore, the substitution effect acts to draw more women into the labor force.[1] The aggregate effect of increased wages on the quantity of labor supplied by women represents a movement along the labor supply curve.

There has been a large increase in labor force participation by women over the past thirty years.

---

[1]It is important to note here that the labor force, as economists define it, includes not only those who have jobs but also those who are looking for jobs. It is also important to note that when we refer to "labor supply," we refer to "market" labor supply—that is, work for pay. Many people perform tasks at home that are comparable to those they perform at work; nonetheless, these are not included in the analysis of labor supply.

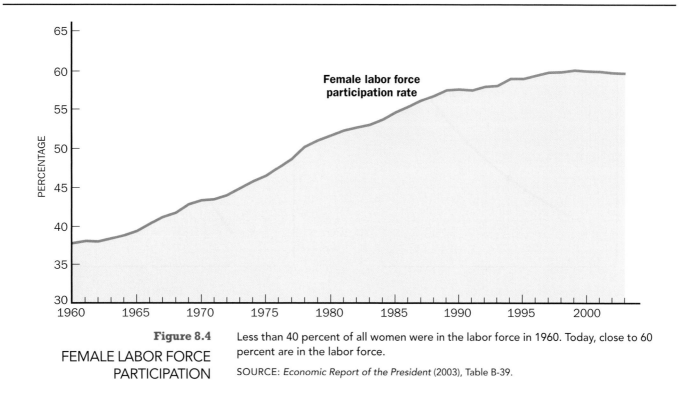

Figure 8.4

FEMALE LABOR FORCE
PARTICIPATION

Less than 40 percent of all women were in the labor force in 1960. Today, close to 60 percent are in the labor force.

SOURCE: *Economic Report of the President* (2003), Table B-39.

The labor supply curve for women also has shifted, increasing the labor supply at each value of the wage. Two changes have shifted the labor supply curve to the right and contributed to the dramatic increase in labor force participation of women that is shown in Figure 8.4. Beginning around 1973, (real) wages stopped growing at the rate they had been increasing during the period following World War II. Individuals and families had come to expect regular increases in their material standards of living. When these increases stopped, they felt the loss. This development encouraged married women to take part-time or full-time jobs as a way of keeping the family income increasing or, in many cases, to prevent it from falling.

Attitudes about the role of women, both among women themselves and among employers, have changed significantly. Outright discrimination against women was barred by federal law in 1964; as more careers were open to them, entering the labor force became more attractive. Changed attitudes are also reflected in the dramatic increase in the enrollment of women in professional schools. Most women without small children participate in the labor market, and many with children leave the labor force only for relatively short periods of time. These changes contributed to the shift in the labor supply curve for women and, along with the effects of higher wages, led to the large increases in labor supply by women over the past thirty years.

Firms and the Demand for Labor

Having explored the supply side of the labor market, we now turn to the demand side. What factors influence firms' decisions about how much labor to hire? Once

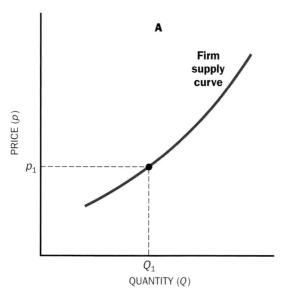

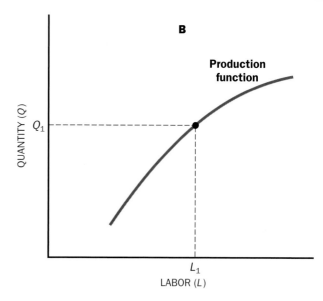

FIGURE 8.5

THE DEMAND FOR LABOR

The demand for labor can be calculated from the firm's supply curve and its production function. Panel A shows how the firm, given a market price p_1, chooses a level of output Q_1 from its supply curve. Panel B shows that to produce the output Q_1 requires L_1 units of labor. L_1 is the demand for labor.

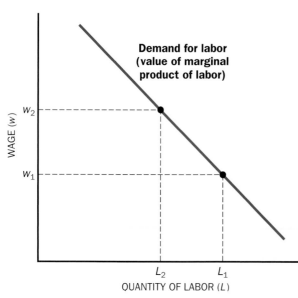

FIGURE 8.6

THE DEMAND CURVE FOR LABOR

The value of the marginal product of labor declines with the level of employment. Since labor is hired up to the point at which the wage equals the value of the marginal product, at wage w_1, employment is L_1, and at wage w_2, employment is L_2, The demand curve for labor thus traces out the values of the marginal product of labor at different levels of employment.

we have examined these decisions, the basic law of supply and demand can be used to show how the wage is determined in the labor market. Labor is one of the primary inputs that firms use in producing output. So our discussion begins by considering what determines a firm's demand for inputs.

FACTOR DEMAND

In the process of deciding how much of each good to supply and determining the lowest-cost method of producing those goods, firms also decide how much of various inputs they will use. This is called **factor demand.** In Chapter 6, the analysis of costs was broken up into two cases, one in which there was a single variable input, or factor of production, and one in which there were several factors. We proceed along similar lines here. Labor is used as our main example of an input, but the same principles apply to any factor of production.

When there is only a single factor of production—here labor—then the decision about how much to produce is the same as the decision about how much labor to hire. As soon as we know the price of the good, we can calculate the supply (output) from the marginal cost curve. As soon as we know the output the firm plans to produce, we know the labor required simply by looking at the production function, which gives the labor input required to produce any level of output.

Thus, in Figure 8.5, at the price p_1, the output is Q_1 (panel A), and the labor required to produce that output (factor demand) is L_1 (panel B).

There is another way to derive the demand for a factor. If the firm hires one more worker, for example, the extra (or marginal) cost to the firm is her wage. The extra benefit of the worker is the additional revenue that the firm receives from selling the output she produces. This is equal to the price at which the good sells multiplied by the amount of extra output she produces. The extra output produced by the worker is the marginal product of labor—the amount of output produced by the last worker added by the firm. Thus the marginal benefit to the firm of adding an extra worker is the price of the firm's good multiplied by the marginal product of labor. If adding an extra employee at the local Jiffy Lube enables the owner to handle an extra 50 oil changes a month, and the price of each oil change is $25, then the marginal benefit to the owner of adding the worker is $40 times 50, or $1,250 per month. This dollar amount is called the **value of the marginal product of labor.** While the marginal product of labor is measured in units of output (e.g., 50 oil changes per month), the value of the marginal product is measured in dollars.

As long as the value of the marginal product of labor is greater than the marginal cost of hiring the extra worker, the firm can increase its profits by hiring an extra worker. In the Jiffy Lube example, as long as the added wage is less than $1,250 per month, it pays the owner to hire another worker. The firm hires labor up to the point at which the value of the marginal product (the marginal benefit to the firm) is equal to the price of labor, the wage (the marginal cost to the firm).

Using p for the price of the good, MPL for the marginal product of labor, and w for the wage of the worker, we can write this equilibrium condition as

$$\text{value of marginal product} = p \times MPL = w = \text{wage}.$$

From this equilibrium condition, we can derive the demand curve for labor. Figure 8.6 plots the value of the marginal product of labor for each level of labor. Since the marginal product of labor decreases as labor increases, the value of the marginal product also decreases. When the wage is w_1, the value of the marginal product of labor equals the wage with a level of labor at L_1. This is the firm's demand for labor at a wage w_1. Thus, the curve giving the value of the marginal product of labor at each level of employment *is* the demand curve for labor.

It is easy to use this diagram to see the effect of an increase in the price of the good the firm produces. In Figure 8.7, the higher price increases the value of the marginal product of labor at each level of employment, and it immediately follows that at each wage, the demand for labor increases. The demand curve for labor shifts to the right.

Thus, the demand for labor depends on both the wage and the price the firm receives for the goods it sells. In fact, the demand for labor depends only on the ratio of the two, as we will now see.

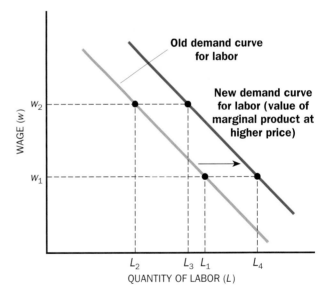

FIGURE 8.7

EFFECT OF PRICE CHANGE ON THE DEMAND CURVE FOR LABOR

An increase in the price received by a firm shifts the value of the marginal product of labor curve up, so that at each wage, the demand for labor is increased. At wage w_1, employment rises from L_1 to L_4; at wage w_2, employment rises from L_2 to L_3.

FIGURE 8.8

THE FIRM'S DEMAND CURVE FOR LABOR AND THE REAL PRODUCT WAGE

Firms hire labor up to the point at which the real product wage equals the marginal product of labor. As the real product wage increases, the demand for labor decreases.

If we divide both sides of the previous equation giving the equilibrium condition by the price, we obtain the condition

$$MPL = w/p.$$

The wage divided by the price of the good being produced is defined as the **real product wage.** It measures what firms pay workers in terms of the goods the worker produces rather than in dollar terms. Thus, the firm hires workers up to the point at which the real product wage equals the marginal product of labor.

This principle is illustrated in Figure 8.8, which shows the marginal product of labor. Because of diminishing returns, the marginal product diminishes as labor (and output) increases. As the real product wage increases, the demand for labor decreases.

FACTOR DEMAND

A factor of production will be demanded up to the point at which the value of the marginal product of that factor equals its price. In the case of labor, this is the same as saying that the marginal product of labor equals the real product wage.

FROM THE FIRM'S FACTOR DEMAND TO THE MARKET'S FACTOR DEMAND

Once we have derived the firm's demand curve for labor, we can derive the total market demand for labor. At a given set of prices, we simply add up the demand for labor by each firm at any particular wage rate. The total is the market demand at that wage. Since each firm reduces the amount of labor that it demands as the wage increases, the market demand curve is downward sloping.

Labor Supply, Demand, and the Equilibrium Wage

We have now discussed the factors that determine labor supply decisions and those that determine the demand for labor by firms. Households decide how much labor to supply to the marketplace, at each value of the wage. If the substitution effect dominates, higher real wages increase the quantity of labor supplied. Firms decide how much labor to demand at each value of the wage. At higher real wages, the quantity of labor that firms demand is lower. The labor market is in equilibrium when the wage has adjusted to balance labor supply and labor demand. When the labor market is in equilibrium, the demand for labor equals the supply of labor. No worker who wishes to get a job (for which he is qualified) at the going market wage will fail to get one. No firm that wants to hire a worker at the going wage will fail to find a qualified employee.

If demand and supply are not equal at the going market wage, the wage will adjust. If, at the going wage, the number of hours of labor that households wish to supply is greater than the number of hours of labor that firms wish to employ, those in the labor force without jobs will offer to work for less than the going wage. The process of competition will lead to lower wages, until eventually demand again equals supply. Likewise, if firms in the economy demand more labor at the going wage than is supplied, competition by firms to hire scarce labor services will bid the wage up until demand and supply are equal.

This basic model of the labor market makes clear predictions for the consequences of shifts in the demand and supply of labor. Consider first shifts in the supply curve of labor. Such shifts can occur because the total labor force grows, as the number of young people reaching working age exceeds the numbers of workers retiring, because of new immigrants, or because of social changes such as the entry of more women into the labor force. The U.S. labor force expanded rapidly in the 1970s, for example, as the baby boomers entered the labor force and more and more women worked outside the home. An increase in the labor force shifts the supply curve of labor to the right; at each real wage, the total number of labor hours that individuals wish to supply is greater. The equilibrium real wage falls. This fall in the price of labor indicates to firms that labor is less scarce than it was before, and firms should therefore economize less in the use of labor. Firms respond to the lower real wage by creating more jobs. Employment rises to absorb the increase in labor supply.

Consider now the effects of a shift in the demand curve for labor. Suppose technological progress makes workers more productive, raising the marginal product of labor. At each wage, firms now wish to hire more labor, and the labor demand curve shifts to the right. Real wages rise to restore equilibrium in the labor market.

Over the past quarter century, increases in the American labor force have shifted the labor supply curve to the right. At the same time, increases in worker productivity have shifted the labor demand curve to the right as well. The basic model predicts that the total quantity of labor employed will rise, but real wages may either fall (if supply shifts more than demand) or rise (if demand shifts more than supply). Average real wages in the United States in fact have fallen slightly over this period.

Review and Practice

SUMMARY

1. The decision about how to allocate time between work and leisure can be analyzed using the basic ideas of budget constraints and preferences. Individuals face a trade-off along a budget constraint between leisure and income. The amount of income a person can obtain by giving up leisure is determined by the wage rate.

2. In labor markets, the substitution and income effects of a change in wages work in opposite directions. An increase in wages makes people better-off, and they wish to enjoy more leisure as well as more consumption; this is the income effect. But an increase in wages raises the opportunity cost of leisure and encourages more work; this is the substitution effect. The overall effect of a rise in wages will depend on whether the substitution or income effect is actually larger.

3. An upward-sloping labor supply curve represents a case in which the substitution effect of higher wages outweighs the income effect. A relatively vertical labor supply curve represents a case in which the substitution and income effects of higher wages are nearly equal. A backward-bending labor supply curve represents a case in which the substitution effect dominates at low wages (labor supply increases as the wage increases), but the income effect dominates at high wages (labor supply decreases as the wage increases).

4. The basic model of choice between leisure and income also can be used to analyze decisions concerning labor force participation, including when to enter the labor force and when to retire.

5. The demand for labor arises from the firm's demand for the factors of production. To maximize profits, the firm will use labor up to the point at which the value of the marginal product of labor equals the wage. This means the marginal product will equal the *real* wage.

6. In this basic competitive model, the real wage adjusts in labor markets to balance supply and demand.

KEY TERMS

nominal wage
real wage
labor force participation decision
reservation wage
factor demand
value of the marginal product of labor
real product wage

REVIEW QUESTIONS

1. How do people make choices about the amount of time to work, given their personal tastes and real wages in the market?

2. How will the income effect of a fall in wages affect hours worked? How will the substitution effect of a fall in wages affect hours worked?

3. What does the labor supply curve look like if the income effect dominates the substitution effect? What will it look like if the substitution effect dominates the income effect?

4. How does a technological change that makes workers more productive affect the demand for labor at a given wage and price?

5. How does an increase in the price of a firm's output affect the firm's demand for labor at a given wage?

6. Why is the labor demand curve downward sloping?

PROBLEMS

1. Imagine that a wealthy relative dies and leaves you an inheritance in a trust fund that will provide you with $20,000 per year for the rest of your life. Draw a diagram to illustrate this shift in your budget constraint between leisure and consumption. After considering the ideas of income and substitution effects, decide whether this inheritance will cause you to work more or less.

2. Most individuals do not take a second job (moonlight), even if they can get one—say, as a taxi driver—even though their "basic job" may require them to work only 37 hours a week. Most moonlighting jobs pay less per hour than the worker's basic job. Draw a typical worker's budget constraint. Explain why the budget

constraint has a kink at 37 hours of work. Discuss the consequences of the kink in the budget constraint.

3. Under current economic conditions, let's say that an unskilled worker will be able to get a job at a wage of $6 per hour. Now assume the government decides that all people with a weekly income of less than $180 will be given a check from the government to bring them up to the $180 level. Draw one such worker's original budget constraint and the constraint with the welfare program. Will this welfare program be likely to cause a recipient who originally worked 30 hours to work less? How about a recipient who worked less than 30 hours? more than 30 hours? Explain how the government might reduce these negative effects by offering a wage subsidy that would increase the hourly wage to $7 per hour for each of the first 20 hours worked, and draw a revised budget constraint to illustrate.

4. There is a negative relationship between a woman's real wage and her family size. Two possible explanations have been put forth. One is that women with higher real wages *choose* to have smaller families. Explain why this might be so. The second explanation is that larger family sizes might cause women to receive lower wages, perhaps because they can accept only jobs that allow them the flexibility to stay home when their children are sick.

What evidence might help you choose between these two explanations?

5. John is a college student who has decided that at current wage levels, it is not worthwhile getting a part-time job. Now suppose the wage increases. Explain how the substitution effect of the wage increase affects John's decision. Is there an income effect on John of the wage increase?

6. Over the past twenty years, the income gap between workers with college degrees and those without a college education has grown. Draw two supply and demand diagrams, one for workers with college degrees and one for workers without degrees. Now suppose new information technologies raise the marginal product of highly educated workers but do not affect the marginal product of less-educated workers. Use your supply and demand diagrams to illustrate what happens to the wage gap between the two types of workers.

7. Suppose an increase in educational opportunities increases the supply of college-educated workers and reduces the supply of workers without college educations. Using supply and demand diagrams, illustrate how this change would affect the gap between the wages of workers with and those without college educations.

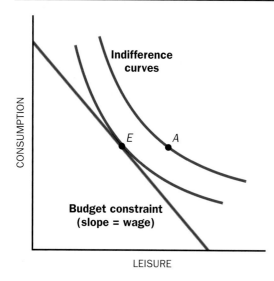

Figure 8.9

INDIFFERENCE CURVES AND LEISURE-INCOME CHOICES

An individual will choose the combination of leisure and income at E. Point A would be more desirable, but it is not feasible. Other points on the budget line or inside it are feasible, but they lie on lower indifference curves and are therefore not as desirable.

Appendix: Indifference Curves and the Labor Supply Decision[2]

This appendix investigates the labor supply decision using the indifference curve approach applied in the appendix to Chapter 5 to the consumption decision.

Figure 8.9 shows Tom's budget constraint between leisure and consumption. The slope of the budget constraint is the wage. The figure also shows two indifference curves; each gives the combination of leisure and consumption choices toward which Tom is indifferent. As usual, since people prefer more of both consumption and leisure if that is possible, Tom will move to the highest indifference curve he can attain—the one that is just tangent to his budget constraint.

The slope of the indifference curve is the marginal rate of substitution between leisure and consumption. It measures the amount of extra consumption Tom requires to compensate him for forgoing one additional hour of leisure. At the point of tangency between the indifference curve and the budget constraint, point E, both have the same slope. That is, the marginal rate of substitution equals the wage at this point.

As in the appendix in Chapter 5, we can easily see why Tom chooses this point. Assume his marginal rate of substitution is $15 (dollars per hour), while his wage is $20 (dollars per hour). If he works an hour more—gives up an hour's worth of leisure—his consumption goes up by $20. But to compensate him for the forgone leisure, he requires only $15. Since he gets more than he requires by working, he clearly prefers to work more.

DECIDING WHETHER TO WORK

Figure 8.10 shows how to use indifference curves to analyze how people decide whether or not to work. Consider a low-wage individual facing a welfare system that provides a fixed level of benefits to those whose income is below a threshold. Benefits are cut off once income exceeds a certain level. The indifference curve I_0 is tangent to the budget constraint without welfare, and the point of tangency is E_0. The curve I_1 is the highest indifference curve consistent with the person receiving welfare.

The three possible cases are illustrated in panels A, B, and C. In panel A, the indifference curve through point E_0, I_0, is higher than the curve I_1. The individual chooses to work at E_0 and is unaffected by the welfare program. In panels B and C, the person works sufficiently little to be eligible for welfare; that is, I_1 is higher than I_0, and so he chooses point E_1. In panel B, the individual realizes that if he works more, he will lose his welfare benefits. He earns just (little) enough to be eligible for welfare. In panel C, the welfare system has only an income effect. If the welfare benefits are large enough, the individual may choose not to work at all.

---

[2]You will need to have read the appendix to Chapter 5 in order to follow this appendix.

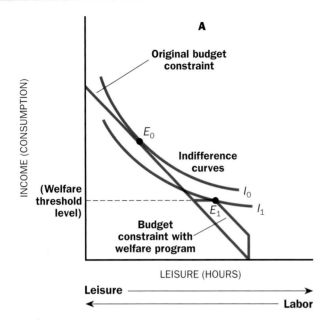

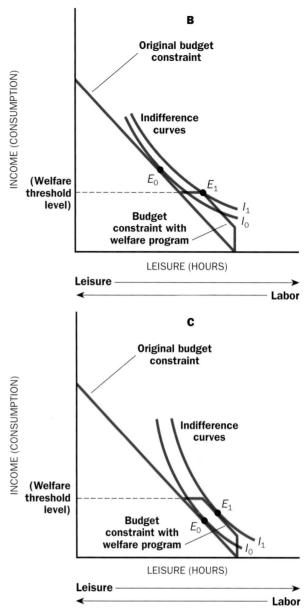

Figure 8.10

INDIFFERENCE CURVES AND WELFARE PROGRAMS

Panel A shows the case of an individual who chooses to work whether or not the welfare program exists. In panel B, before a welfare program is introduced, the individual is earning more than the welfare threshold. With the availability of welfare, this individual relies on welfare benefits to work less and move to a higher indifference curve. Panel C shows the case of someone who is earning less than the welfare threshold but would choose to work still less if the welfare program existed.

Learning Goals

In this chapter, you will learn

1 How the basic tools introduced in Chapter 5 can be used to analyze decisions about saving and education

2 What economists mean by the time value of money

3 How income and substitution affect saving decisions in opposing ways

4 What determines the firm's demand for capital

5 How interest rates ensure that demand and supply balance in capital markets

6 Why education is an investment that leads to what economists call human capital

Chapter 9

CAPITAL MARKETS

At any given time, there are some people and companies who would like to borrow to enable them to spend more than their current income. John has his first job and knows he needs a car for transportation; Jill is borrowing money to buy a new home; Chad needs to purchase kitchen equipment, tables, and chairs to open his new restaurant; Intel needs to build a new chip-assembly plant. Others would like to save, spending less than their current income. Julie is putting money aside for her children's college education and for her retirement; Bill is putting aside money to make a down payment on a house.

The basic tools we have developed in previous chapters to explain how households and firms make decisions about which goods to buy, which to produce, how much to work, and how many workers to hire can also be used to explain saving and borrowing decisions. When households save, spending less than they earn in income, they provide funds for those who want to spend more than their income. When an individual household puts its savings in a bank or into the stock market, it might not think of itself as lending money, but that is exactly what it is doing. Firms that wish to buy new machines or build new factories or office buildings borrow the savings of the household sector. The **capital market**—or, as it is also called, the **loanable funds market**—is the market in which the funds made available when households save are directed to those who wish to borrow, whether to build a new home, to buy a new car, to build a new factory, or to install new machinery.

Supply in the Capital Market

To understand the supply of saving to the loanable funds market, we will focus on households; even though many individual households borrow, households as a group

191

typically save. This is not always the case, though: in 1999 U.S. households actually dissaved, spending more than they earned in income. We will focus on firms as the major borrowers in the economy.

THE HOUSEHOLD DECISION TO SAVE

The assumption that individuals spend their money in a rational manner, thinking through the alternatives clearly, holds for decisions about saving as well as about spending and working. In making their saving decisions, individuals are making a choice about *when* to spend or consume. If they consume less today—that is, if they save more today—they can consume more tomorrow.

We use the budget constraint to analyze this decision. Instead of showing a choice between goods, the budget constraint now shows, as in Figure 9.1, a choice between spending in two time periods: here, "working years" and "retirement years." Consider the case of Joan. She faces the lifetime budget constraint depicted in the figure. The first period is represented on the horizontal axis, the second on the vertical axis. Her wages during her working life (the first period) are w. Thus, at one extreme, she could consume all of w in the first period (point C) and have nothing for her retirement. At the other extreme, she could consume nothing in the first period, save all of her income, and consume her savings, together with any accumulated interest she has earned on her savings, in the second period (point B). If we use r to denote the rate of interest, her consumption in the second period at point B is $w(1+r)$. In between these extremes lies a straight line that defines the rest of her choices. She can choose any combination of first- and second-period consumption on this line. This is Joan's two-period budget constraint.

By postponing consumption—that is, by saving—Joan can increase the total amount of goods that she can obtain, because she is paid interest on her savings. The cost, however, is that she must wait to enjoy the goods. But what is the relative price, the trade-off between future and current consumption? To put it another way, how much extra future consumption can she get if she gives up one unit of current consumption?

If Joan decides not to consume one more dollar today, she can take that dollar, put it in the bank, and get back at the end of the year that dollar plus interest. If the interest rate is 5 percent, then for every dollar of consumption that Joan gives up today, she can get $1.05 of consumption next year. The relative price (of consumption today relative to consumption tomorrow) is thus 1 plus the interest rate. Because Joan must give up more than $1.00 of consumption in the second period to get an additional $1.00 worth of consumption today, current consumption is more expensive than future consumption. The opportunity cost of current consumption is the future consumption that is forgone, and this cost depends on the rate of interest.

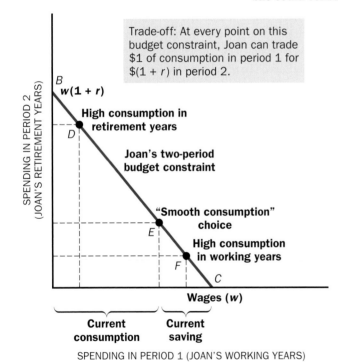

Trade-off: At every point on this budget constraint, Joan can trade $1 of consumption in period 1 for $(1 + r)$ in period 2.

Figure 9.1

THE TWO-PERIOD BUDGET CONSTRAINT

The two-period budget constraint *BC* describes the possible combinations of current and future consumption available. Wages not spent in period 1 become savings, which earn interest. As a result, forgoing a dollar of consumption today increases future consumption by more than a dollar.

Joan chooses among the points on this budget constraint according to her personal preferences. Consider, for example, point D, where Joan is consuming very little during her working life. Since she is spending very little in the present, any additional consumption now will have a high marginal value. She will be relatively eager to substitute present consumption for future consumption. At the other extreme, if she is consuming a great deal in the present, say at point F, additional consumption today will have a relatively low marginal value, while future consumption will have a high marginal value. Hence, she will be relatively eager to save more for the future. She chooses a point in between, E, where consumption in the two periods is not too different. She has *smoothed* her consumption. That is, consumption in each of the two different periods is about the same. This kind of saving, intended to smooth consumption over a worker's lifetime and to provide for retirement, is called **life-cycle saving.** In Figure 9.1, the difference between the first-period income, w, and what she consumes in the first period is her saving.

The Time Value of Money   Because you can earn interest on your savings, the cost of a dollar of current consumption is more than simply $1.00 of future consumption. As we learned in Chapter 2, calculating costs correctly is one of the basic steps in making rational decisions. But what if we are comparing costs that occur at different times, such as the cost of current versus future consumption? Or to take a more specific example, suppose one store advertises a car stereo system for $400 and another advertises it for $425 with no payment for a full year. How can we compare these two? If you have the $400 to spend today, is it cheaper to pay $400 right now for the stereo or to pay $425 in one year?

To think about this comparison, consider what you could do with your $400 if you opted to buy from the store that lets you delay your payment. You might put the money in a bank. When you deposit money in a bank, you have lent it your money. In return, the bank pays you **interest.** If the interest rate is 5 percent per year, you will receive $420 in a year—the $20 is the interest payment, while the $400 is the repayment of the **principal,** the original amount you lent to the bank.

The interest rate is a price, and like other prices, it describes a trade-off. If the interest rate is 5 percent, by giving up $1.00 worth of consumption today, a saver can have $1.05 worth of consumption next year. Thus, the rate of interest tells us how much future consumption we can get by giving up $1.00 worth of current consumption. It tells us the relative price of purchases in the present and in the future.

Because interest rates are normally positive, $1.00 today becomes more than a dollar in the future. Thus a dollar today is worth more than a dollar in the future. Economists call this phenomenon the **time value of money.** The concept of **present discounted value** tells us precisely how to measure the time value of money. The present discounted value of $100 a year from now is what you would pay today for $100 in a year. Suppose the interest rate is 5 percent. If you put $95.24 in the bank today, then at the end of a year you will receive $4.76 in interest, which together with the original principal will total $100. Thus, $95.24 is the present discounted value of $100 one year from now, if the interest rate is 5 percent.

There is a simple formula for calculating the present discounted value of any amount to be received a year from now: just divide the amount by 1 plus the annual rate of interest (often denoted by r).

To check this formula, consider the present discounted value of $100. According to the formula, it is $100/(1 + r)$. In other words, take the present discounted value, $100/(1 + r)$, and put it in a bank. At the end of the year you will have

$$\frac{\$100}{1+r} \times (1 + r) = \$100,$$

confirming our conclusion that $100/(1 + r)$ today is worth the same as $100 one year from now.

We can now evaluate the two options for purchasing the stereo. To compare $400 today with $425 in one year, we need to calculate the present discounted value of $425. If the interest rate is 5 percent, the present discount value of $425 is $404.76. Since this is greater than $400, you are better off paying for the stereo today.

Present discounted values depend on the rate of interest. If the interest rate increases, the present discounted value of future amounts will decrease. If the interest rate rises to 10 percent, the present discounted value of $425 falls to $386.96. Now it is cheaper to postpone payment for the stereo. You can take your $400, put it in the bank, and earn 10 percent interest. In one year, you will have $440. After paying $425 for the stereo, you are left with $15 more than if you had paid for it immediately.

The concept of present discounted value is important because so many decisions in economics are oriented to the future. Whether a person is buying a car or a house or saving for retirement, or a company is building a factory or making an investment, the decision maker must be able to value money that will be received one, two, five, or ten years in the future.

Wrap-Up

PRESENT DISCOUNTED VALUE

Present discounted value of $1.00 next year = $1.00/(1 + interest rate).

Inflation and the Real Rate of Interest The interest rate, we have seen, is a price. It tells us how many dollars we can get in the next period if we give up one dollar today. But dollars are of value only because of the goods that can be bought with them. If prices rise, then a dollar will buy less. Suppose a couple has been saving so that in a year they will have $40,000, which they plan to use to buy a BMW. If prices double between now and next year, their $40,000 will get them only a Honda Civic. Thus, to know how much we can actually purchase in the future if we save today, we need to take into account more than just the interest rate: we also need to consider how the general level of prices will change. The rate at which the general level of prices increases each year is the *rate of inflation*. If the inflation rate is 5 percent, then prices on average will be 5 percent higher in one year; if inflation is 10 percent, prices will go up 10 percent. Some prices will rise faster than the overall inflation rate; others will rise more slowly or even decline. For example, over the past twenty years computer prices have fallen while housing prices in many parts of the country have risen very rapidly. The inflation rate measures what is happening on average to prices in the economy.

Individuals want to know how much *consumption* they get tomorrow if they give up a dollar's worth of consumption today. The answer is given by the **real rate of interest.** This is distinguished from the **nominal rate of interest,** the rate posted at banks and printed in newspapers, which simply describes the number of dollars received next year in exchange for a dollar today. There is a simple relationship between the real interest rate and the nominal interest rate: the real interest rate equals the nominal interest rate minus the rate of inflation. If the nominal interest rate is 10 percent and the rate of inflation is 6 percent, then the real interest rate is 4 percent. By saving a dollar today, you can increase the amount of goods that you get in one year's time by 4 percent.

Consider an individual who decides to deposit $1,000 in a savings account. At the end of the year, at a 10 percent interest rate, she will have $1,100. But prices meanwhile have risen by 6 percent. A good that cost $1,000 in the beginning of the year now costs $1,060. In terms of "purchasing power," she has only $40 extra to spend ($1,100 – $1,060)—4 percent more than she had at the beginning of the year.

REAL INTEREST RATE

Real interest rate = nominal interest rate – rate of inflation.

Using the Model: Saving and the Interest Rate We can use the budget constraint to understand how Joan's saving decision will be affected if the interest rate changes. Keep in mind two points as we apply this model, however. First, just as we saw earlier that the relevant wage for labor supply decisions is the real wage, so the relevant interest rate for saving decisions is the real interest rate—that is, the interest rate adjusted for inflation. Also keep in mind that we have simplified the saving decision with our two-period model (current consumption on the one hand, future consumption on the other). In the real world, individuals usually earn interest on their savings year after year as they save for retirement. If you begin saving at the age of twenty-five, you might earn interest for forty years before retiring. Typically, the interest is compounded annually (or monthly), which means that each year you earn interest on the interest paid in previous years. Compounding makes a huge difference over long periods of time. If you set aside $100 at 5 percent interest for forty years, you might think that each year you would earn $5 in interest (5 percent of $100) and that at the end of the forty years you would have your $100 plus $200 in interest (40 × $5), or $300 in total. In fact, because you earn interest for thirty-nine years on the $5 of interest earned in year one, plus interest for thirty-eight years on the interest earned in year two, and so on, after forty years you end up with not $300 but $704!

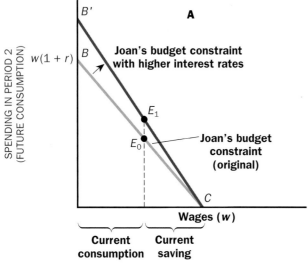

FIGURE 9.2

SAVING AND THE INTEREST RATE

An increase in interest rates rotates the budget constraint out from BC to $B'C$. Because the individual is better off, there is an income effect, leading to greater consumption in the present (and in the future). However, the higher interest rate makes future consumption cheaper; the substitution effect associated with the change in the slope of the budget constraint leads to greater current saving. In the typical case, the substitution effect is larger than the income effect; Joan's new choice will be on the new budget constraint to the left of E_1 and her saving increases. The saving function in panel B gives the level of saving at each real interest rate. The saving function in panel B illustrates this case, in which the saving function has a positive slope.

To focus on the key factors important for understanding saving decisions, we will continue to distinguish current from future consumption and apply interest only once. This simplification captures the essential characteristic of the saving decision, the choice between consumption now and in the future.

When the interest rate increases, Joan's budget constraint changes. Her new budget constraint is shown in Figure 9.2A as line $B'C$. If she does not save, the interest rate has no effect on her consumption. She simply consumes her income during her working years, with nothing left over for retirement. But for all other choices, the higher interest rate enables her to consume more during her retirement years.

The increased interest rate has both an income effect and a substitution effect. Because Joan is a saver, higher interest rates make her better off. Because she is better off, she consumes more today; that is, she reduces her saving. This is the income effect. But her return to savings—to postponing consumption—is increased. For each dollar of consumption she postpones, she gets more consumption when she retires. The opportunity cost of current consumption is now higher. This increase induces her to consume less—to save more. This is the substitution effect. Thus, the substitution and income effects work in opposite directions, and the *net* effect is ambiguous. Either may dominate. A higher interest rate may lead to more or to less saving.

What happens on *average* is a difficult empirical question. Most estimates indicate that the substitution effect outweighs the income effect, and thus an increase in real interest rates has a slightly positive effect on the rate of savings.

Panel B of Figure 9.2 shows the saving function, which gives the level of saving for each level of the real interest rate. It is derived by finding the choices between consumption today and in the future for different real interest rates, represented by rotating the budget constraint. The curve depicted has the typical shape. Increases in the real interest rate lead to slight increases in saving; the substitution effect slightly outweighs the income effect. But the saving curve could be vertical; the income effect and the substitution effect balance. Or it can even be backward bending; the income effect slightly outweighs the substitution effect.

THE SAVING DECISION

The saving decision is a decision of *when* to consume: today or tomorrow.

The slope of the budget constraint between consumption today and consumption tomorrow is determined by the real rate of interest.

A principal motive of saving is to smooth consumption to ensure that one's consumption while working and during retirement is about the same.

Other Factors Affecting Saving We have now seen how the techniques of consumer choice analysis presented in Chapter 5 can be applied to individuals' decisions about saving. The two basic determinants are income and interest rates. As incomes rise, individuals want to consume more in their retirement, and hence must save more. As interest rates change, the income and substitution effects work in different directions, so the net effect is ambiguous.

The saving decision in the United States also involves an even more important determinant: Social Security. How much individuals need to save for their retirement depends in part on how large a check they will get from the Social Security Administration when they stop working. A generous government system reduces the individual need to save for retirement, so one effect of Social Security is to reduce the overall level of saving in the United States. The Social Security checks mailed out each month to retired workers are paid for by taxes on individuals who currently work. As the members of the large baby boom generation born after World War II

Thinking Like an Economist

WEALTH DISTRIBUTION AND INTEREST RATES

Government policies aimed at increasing the interest rate individuals receive, such as exempting certain forms of savings from taxation, are based on the belief that an increase in the interest rate on savings will significantly increase total (aggregate) saving in the economy. Though the impact of these provisions on the aggregate saving rate is debatable, the distributional impact is not. Since wealthy people save more, a reduction in taxes on interest—which increases the effective interest rate the saver receives—obviously benefits them more and increases the degree of income inequality. According to the Survey of Consumer Finances (2001), almost 80 percent of households in the top 20 percent of the income distribution saved. These families had an average income in 2001 of just over $200,000 and an average net worth of $2 million. In contrast, only 30 percent of households in the bottom 20 percent of the income distribution saved. These families had an average income of $10,000 and an average net worth of just $52,000.

Low-income households save little and therefore enjoy little direct benefit from policies designed to increase the returns on saving.

HOUSEHOLD SAVING

The Federal Reserve Board conducts a survey of households every three years, called the Survey of Consumer Finances. Each one provides a wealth of information on household saving.

The most recently available survey was conducted in 2001, and you can find it and information about it at www.federalreserve.gov/pubs/oss/oss2/2001/scf2001home.html.

begin to retire, many are raising concerns about the future financial health of the entire system. The problems with the Social Security program and the reforms proposed by President George W. Bush and others are discussed in Chapter 17.

Even as Social Security payments have become more generous, private saving schemes have grown over the last fifty years. Three explanations are commonly put forward for this development. First, as individuals' life spans have increased well beyond normal retirement age, the need for more income late in life has increased faster than the generosity of Social Security. In fact, to reduce the financial burden on the system, the age at which a worker qualifies to receive Social Security benefits has gradually been increased. Individuals born in 1937, for example, could receive full benefits at age 65; those born in 1967 must wait until they are 67. Second, as we saw in Chapter 8, individuals who earn higher incomes may decide to enjoy more leisure, one form of which is earlier retirement—a choice that increases their need for retirement income. Finally, surveys indicate that many younger workers are concerned that the Social Security benefits received by their parents and grandparents will not be available to them. If the huge cost of the program forces cuts in the benefits of future retirees, younger workers will have to rely more on their own savings rather than on Social Security in their retirement.

Case in Point

WHY IS THE U.S. SAVING RATE SO LOW?

Between 1959 and 1992, the personal saving rate for U.S. households averaged 7.4 percent of disposable income (income after taxes). Since 1993, the saving rate has averaged only 3.6 percent (Figure 9.3). Why?

Economists have given several reasons for the low and falling saving rate among U.S. households. First, Social Security benefits are relatively generous, reducing the need for individuals to save for their retirement, and that generosity grew markedly in the 1970s. Second, it has become much easier to borrow for all kinds of purchases. In other words, the capital market in this country has improved its capacity to serve individual borrowers. Third, Americans prefer to consume now rather than later. Fourth, the value of household wealth from investments in housing and corporate stocks in the United States rose dramatically through the 1980s and 1990s. As people saw their wealth rise, they spent more and saved less. The figure suggests that the personal saving rate rose after the stock market crashed in 2001. Finally, there is the effect of the new economy. Many who observed increases in productivity as a result of new technologies concluded that the economy would grow faster, leading to higher incomes in the future. The income effect of higher expected future income works to increase current consumption, reducing saving today.

Aggregate Saving The sum of the saving of all individuals in society is **aggregate saving.** At any time, some individuals are saving and others are spending their savings (or, as economists say, *dissaving*). Aggregate saving is the two activities taken together. The *aggregate saving rate* is aggregate saving divided by aggregate income. *Demographic* factors—that is, factors relating to population—in particular the rate of growth of the population, are important determinants of the aggregate saving rate. Retirees typically dissave. That is, they withdraw money from savings accounts and cash in stocks and bonds if they have any (to supplement their main income sources, Social Security and interest on investments). There is considerable concern about the low aggregate saving rate in the United States (discussed further below), which is explained in part by our aging population. A slowly growing population, like that of the United States, has a larger proportion of elderly and, on that account, a lower aggregate saving rate than faster-growing populations with higher birthrates.

Forms of Savings To simplify our discussion, we have assumed that savings earns a single rate of interest, r. In fact, there are many different ways in which individuals can save, and these may offer different interest rates. For example, if you

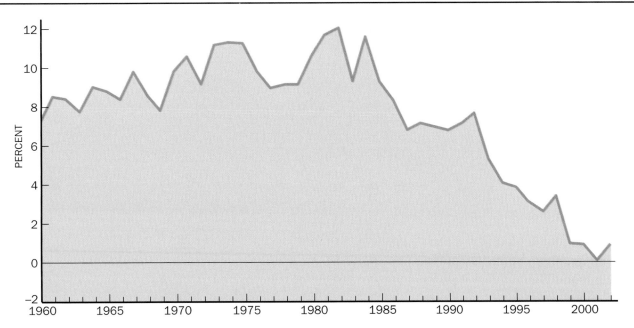

FIGURE 9.3

U.S. PERSONAL SAVING RATE, 1980–2002

U.S. households saved far less of their disposable income throughout the 1990s and into the first years of the twenty-first century than they had done in earlier decades.

SOURCE: *Economic Report of the President* (2005).

want to save, you can put money into a savings account at a bank. This earns interest and is very safe, because the federal government insures savings accounts with balances up to $100,000. The tremendous boom in the stock market in the 1990s encouraged many people to put some of their savings into stocks. Stocks earn a higher return on average than savings accounts, but they are much riskier. The stock market can go down as well as up. Real estate has also been an attractive place to put savings, but it too is risky. Rather than discussing the various savings options that are available to households, our focus in this chapter is on the broad outlines of the capital market and the role played by the interest rate in affecting saving decisions.

Demand in the Capital Market

Our goal here is to understand how the supply of savings by households and the demand for savings by firms result in a market equilibrium. In the preceding sections we worked through the supply side of the market. Now we turn to demand. The demand side of the capital market is driven by firms that borrow the savings of households to fund their purchases of **capital goods**—the machines, tools, buildings, and other equipment used in the production process. We therefore begin our analysis with firms' demand for capital goods.

Applying the same principle we used earlier to derive the demand for labor, we know that firms will demand capital (capital goods) up to the point at which the value of the marginal product of capital is equal to the price. The marginal product of capital is just the additional output obtained if one more unit is employed. It is the extra output obtained by adding another machine. But what is the price of capital?

A quick answer is that the price of a piece of equipment is simply what it costs to buy it. If a new computer server to handle Internet orders costs the firm $20,000, isn't that the price of this particular piece of capital? The answer is no—and to see why more is involved, let's think about the decision of a new start-up company as it evaluates whether to buy this computer. To keep things simple, suppose Andrea and Bryan, the company founders, plan to sell the server after one year for $12,000. They can borrow the $20,000 to buy the server from their bank, and the bank charges them interest on this loan. Let's suppose for our example that the interest rate the bank charges is 5 percent. What has it cost them to use the equipment?

Andrea and Bryan pay $20,000 for the server. At the end of the year, they sell the server for $12,000, but they also have to repay the bank. Since the bank charged them 5 percent interest, at the end of the year they owe the bank $21,000 (the $20,000 they borrowed plus $1,000 in interest). So the net cost of using the server is $21,000 − $12,000 = $9,000. A critical part of this cost is the interest Andrea and Bryan had to pay the bank. If the interest rate had been 10 percent, the cost of the computer would have been $10,000 ($20,000 + $2,000 − $12,000, since interest now totals $2,000). *The user cost of capital increases when the interest rate rises.*

The interest rate would have played exactly the same role if Andrea and Bryan had not needed to borrow from the bank. Suppose they had savings of their own that they could use to purchase the computer. When they use their own savings to buy the computer, there is an opportunity cost associated with the purchase. Andrea and Bryan could have left their $20,000 in the bank. If the interest rate is 5 percent, they would have earned $1,000 in interest over the year. This opportunity cost must be included in calculating the cost of capital. So when the interest rate is 5 percent, the total cost of the server is $9,000, regardless of whether they borrow from the bank or use their own funds. An increase in the interest rate raises the cost (including opportunity costs) of using the server.

This simple example illustrates an important point—the user cost of capital will increase with the interest rate. At a higher interest rate, firms will demand less capital and will need to borrow less. At lower interest rates, firms will demand more capital and need to borrow more.

Figure 9.4 shows the demand for loanable funds in the capital market as a downward-sloping relationship between the interest rate and the quantity of funds firms borrow. The figure also shows the supply of loanable funds as an upward-sloping line; it is shown as a steep line because the income and substitution effects of a change in the interest rate have opposing effects on saving. The net effect, though, is some increase in saving as the interest rate increases. In the loanable funds or capital market, the "price" is the interest rate, and the interest rate will adjust to bring supply and demand into balance. In the figure, the equilibrium interest rate is r^*.

We can now explain why the equilibrium interest rate is positive. If it were zero or negative, prospective borrowers would demand more funds than prospective savers would be willing to supply. Indeed, negative interest rates would enable borrowers to consume today and pay back less in the future, and force savers to receive less in the future than the amount they saved. Only at a positive interest rate can the demand for loans be made equal to the supply.

In our economy, borrowers and savers do not usually meet face-to-face. Instead, banks and other financial institutions serve as intermediaries, collecting savings from those who want to save and disbursing money to those who want to borrow. These intermediaries help make the market for loans work smoothly. For their services, the intermediaries charge fees, which can be measured as the difference between the interest rate they pay savers and the interest rate they charge borrowers.

New Technologies and the Demand for Capital Modern economies have undergone tremendous changes as new computer and information technologies have transformed the ways goods are produced and sold. The development of new technologies has led firms to undertake investments in new equipment. To analyze the impact this change might have on the interest rate, we can use our model of the loanable funds market.

Figure 9.5 shows demand and supply as a function of the rate of interest. The new technology increases the marginal product of capital and increases firms' demand for capital at each rate of interest. To purchase this additional capital, firms borrow more. At each rate of interest, the demand for funds shifts to the right. The equilibrium rate of interest rises.

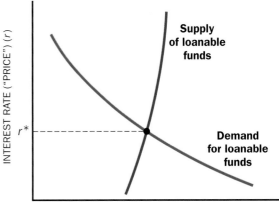

Figure 9.4

SUPPLY AND DEMAND FOR LOANABLE FUNDS

The amount of money loaned (or borrowed, from the other perspective) is the quantity, and the interest rate is the price. At the equilibrium interest rate r^*, the supply of loanable funds equals the demand.

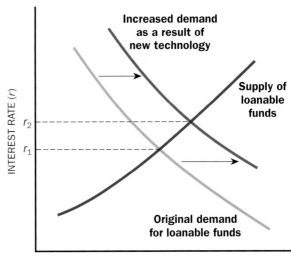

FIGURE 9.5

THE EFFECTS OF NEW TECHNOLOGIES THAT INCREASE THE DEMAND FOR CAPITAL

If new technologies increase the demand for capital by firms, the demand for funds will shift to the right as firms attempt to borrow more to purchase new equipment. If the supply of funds from saving does not shift, the equilibrium interest rate rises from r_1 to r_2.

A Behavioral Perspective on Saving

In Chapter 5, we introduced some of the new insights on how people behave that have come from research in psychology and behavioral economics. Many of these insights have proven particularly useful in understanding household saving decisions.

Earlier we discussed the importance of the desire to smooth consumption over a person's lifetime in influencing saving. A basic implication of the economist's standard model of saving is that people should save during their peak earning years so that when they retire, and their income drops, they will have accumulated enough to ensure that their consumption does not fall. Yet there is a great deal of evidence that when people retire, their income *and* their consumption drops. They have not saved enough for their retirement and so are forced to scale back the amount they consume. Behavioral economics offers some interesting perspectives that help explain why individuals undersave.

One reason may be that people simply lack the self-control necessary to postpone consumption. The standard model of choice that economists employ assumes people can rationally balance the benefits of consuming today versus the advantages of saving so that more consumption can be enjoyed in the future. But people often find it very difficult to make sacrifices in the present, even if they recognize the benefits to be gained in the future. Smoking provides a good example. There is a saying that the best time to quit smoking is tomorrow—the smoker is always tempted to have that cigarette today and promise (himself) that tomorrow will be different and he will quit. Of course, when tomorrow comes around, he falls into the same pattern. The result is that many people never are able to quit smoking. The self-control assumed by the standard model of rational choice appears to be in short supply.

Lack of self-control would make reducing current consumption quite difficult, for the benefits of such self-denial may not be seen for ten or twenty years. It may also explain why most saving done by American households takes the form of *forced savings,* occurring automatically without the need for an explicit decision every month. There are three common forms of forced saving. First, many workers participate in pension plans through their place of employment. Each month, the employer sets aside funds for the worker's pension, to which a certain amount deducted from the worker's paycheck may also be added. This is a form of saving for the worker. Second, Americans who own their own homes typically buy those homes by borrowing ("taking out a mortgage"), and they make a mortgage payment each month. Part of this payment represents the interest on the amount that was borrowed; the rest goes toward repaying the principal. This repayment builds the family's equity in their home, another common form of saving. A final example of forced saving is provided by the automatic withholding of income tax from paychecks for salaried jobs. Many people have too much withheld each pay period so that when they file their tax return in April of each year, they are owed a refund from the government. These refunds are often used to purchase a big-ticket item that the taxpayer might otherwise not have had the willpower to save up for.

Despite offering important insights into how people actually make choices, behavioral economics in some ways may explain too much. Lack of self-control makes intuitive sense as an explanation for low savings, but how do we then account for the many countries with high rates of saving? Many Asian countries, for example, have saving rates that average 30 to 40 percent of income. A traditional economic approach would focus on differences in the returns to saving (perhaps due to differences in the way taxes are structured in different countries), average family size, or the age distribution of the population to explain why saving rates differ so markedly across countries. A behavioral perspective suggests that cultural factors might also be important.

One area in which the insights of behavioral economics may be very useful is in designing public policies to increase the level of saving. For example, behavioral economists have identified the importance of the status quo effect (see Chapter 5), which predicts that people resist changes to their current circumstances. In particular they resist making choices that actively require a decision to be made. As a consequence, when presented with a number of options, many people will simply pick whatever option is the default—the one that is chosen automatically without further action on their part. The status quo effect can help explain why many people do not take advantage of some of the best ways to save for retirement, such as participating in what is called a 401(k) plan. In 1978, section 401(k) of the U.S. Internal Revenue Code created a new saving account that allowed workers to put aside some of their income for retirement. Its big advantage is tax deferral: the worker pays taxes not on the income put into the 401(k) or on any interest earned on the account but on the money when it is taken out of the account—after the worker is retired, when she usually has a lower tax rate. Many employers will match workers' contributions to 401(k) accounts, making them even more valuable. When workers are offered the option to participate in a 401(k) plan via an automatic paycheck deduction, the number that do so can depend on what the default option happens to be. If workers must explicitly choose to sign up for the account, fewer end up participating than when enrollment in the plan is automatic and deliberate action must be taken to opt out. This is an example of the status quo effect at work—peoples' choices are shaped not just by their rational evaluation of the pros and cons of different options but also by their reluctance to make changes. Policies designed to encourage saving need to increase the incentives to save, as suggested by the economist's basic model of consumer choice; but to be fully effective, they also must take into account the status quo effect.

Education and Human Capital

Why go to college? Many answers spring to mind, but to tackle this question from an economic perspective, and to understand why educational choices are similar to saving decisions, we will focus on the costs and benefits of education.

Education is one of the most important determinants of workers' productivity. Staying in school longer, which usually means delaying entry into the labor force, increases expected annual income. On average, high school graduates earn more than those without high school degrees; those with some college earn more than

This dental student improves his human capital by acquiring valuable skills and knowledge.

those who only have a high school degree; those with a college degree earn more than those who started college but never finished. A student has lower income while in school but can expect to earn high incomes in the future. In addition, working *harder* in school, and giving up leisure, may result in better grades and skills, which in turn will result in higher wages in the future. Thus, students face a trade-off between leisure and income today and income and consumption in the future.

Spending a year in college has its obvious costs—tuition, room, and board. But there are also opportunity costs, in particular the income that would have been received from a job. These are just as much part of the cost of going to school as any direct tuition payments. Economists say that the investment in education produces **human capital,** making an analogy to the *physical capital* investments that businesses make in plant and equipment. Human capital is developed by formal schooling, on-the-job training, and many other investments of time and money that parents make in their children, individuals make in themselves, and employers make in their employees.

The United States invests an enormous amount in human capital. In fact, the cumulative value of human capital is greater than that of physical capital. As much as two-thirds to three-fourths of all capital is human capital. This investment is financed both publicly and privately. Local, state, and federal governments spend about one-quarter of a trillion dollars a year on education. Government spending on primary and secondary education is the largest category of expenditure at the local and state levels, accounting for more than 20 percent of the total.

The enormous increase in education in the past fifty years is illustrated in Table 9.1. Among those 65 and older, more than 30 percent do not have a high school degree; of those 25 to 44, only one in eight has not received a high school degree. Similarly, the percentage with at least a bachelor's degree is more than one and a half times as high for those 25 to 44 as for those 65 and older.

e-Insight

FINANCING THE NEW ECONOMY

We have seen how the capital market links households who save with firms that invest, so that saving equals investment at the equilibrium interest rate. But how do firms actually get their hands on household saving? The answer is that financial intermediaries such as banks and investment companies perform the function of transferring funds between households and firms. Their job is to make sure that the households' money is well invested, so that the households can get it back with a return.

Banks are perhaps the most important financial intermediary. In the nineteenth century, banks mainly lent money to firms to help finance their inventories. The inventories were held as collateral—that is, if the borrower defaulted on the loan, the lender could seize the inventories. Gradually, banks expanded their lending activities—for instance, to finance houses and commercial real estate, in such cases holding the buildings as collateral. The past decade's revolution in information technology has presented special problems to these traditional forms of finance. Today firms invest heavily in software and new ideas. If the idea does not pan out, the firm may go bankrupt, but there is no collateral: there is little of value that the creditor can seize.

In the United States, financial markets have adapted, and there now is a new form of financial institution—venture capital firms. Typically, the funds are provided by either wealthy private investors or institutions, such as universities, seeking high returns. The venture capital firms have developed expertise in assessing new ideas in the new economy—the most successful of the venture capital firms have an impressive record of picking winners. But they offer more than capital; they typically also give managerial assistance and take an active role in oversight. After providing the initial capital that enables a firm to get established, the firm supported by the venture capital firms typically "goes public"—that is, it sells at least some of its shares on the market. It is at this point that venture capitalists reap their gains.

While the first venture capital firms concentrated on Silicon Valley (the area surrounding Stanford University where much of the early development of computers occurred), more recently they have expanded their focus to other areas of the country and other sectors.

Table 9.1

YEARS OF SCHOOLING BY AGE

Age group (in 2003)	% with less than a high school degree	% with a high school degree but no bachelor's degree	% with at least a bachelor's degree
25–34	13	57	30
35–44	12	59	29
45–54	11	59	30
55–64	15	58	27
65–74	25	56	19
75 and older	33	52	15

SOURCE: *Statistical Abstract of the United States, 2004*

(www.census.gov/prod/2004pubs/04statab/educ.pdf).

EDUCATION AND ECONOMIC TRADE-OFFS

The production possibilities curve introduced in Chapter 2 can illustrate how decisions concerning investments in human capital are made. To accomplish this, we divide an individual's life into two periods: "youth" and "later working years." Figure 9.6 depicts the relationship between consumption in youth and in later life. As the individual gives up consumption in his youth, staying in school longer increases his expected future consumption because he can expect his income to go up. The curve has been drawn with a rounded shape. It shows diminishing returns: spending more on education today (reducing consumption) raises future income, but each additional investment in education provides a smaller and smaller return.

Point *A* represents the case in which Everett is a full-time student through four years of college, with little income until graduation (his youth) but with a high income in later life. Point *B* represents the consequences of dropping out of school after high school. When he does this, Everett has a higher income in his youth but a lower income in later life. Other possible points between *A* and *B* represent cases where Everett drops out of college after one or two years.

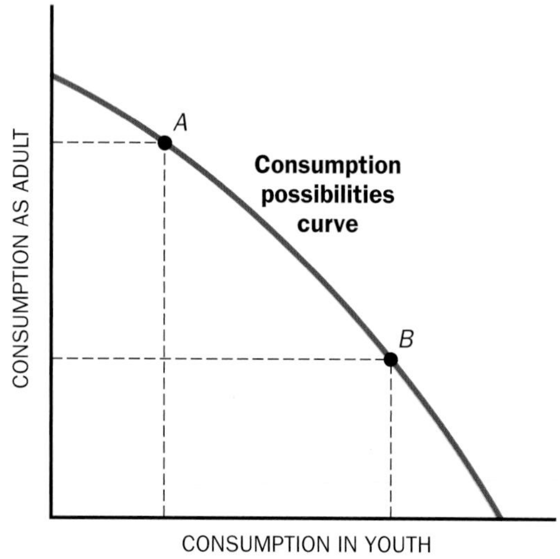

Figure 9.6

EDUCATION AND THE TRADE-OFF BETWEEN CURRENT AND FUTURE CONSUMPTION

Point A represents a choice of a reduced consumption and better education in the present, with a higher consumption in the future. Point B represents the choice of higher consumption and less education now, with a lower level of consumption in the future.

The Basic Competitive Model

We now have completed our description of the basic competitive model. Households make decisions about how much to consume and what goods to purchase. They decide how much labor to supply and how much to save. The firm in the competitive model takes the price it receives for the goods it sells as given. The firm also takes the prices of the inputs it uses, including the wages it pays workers and the cost of capital goods, as given. At these prices, the firm chooses its outputs and inputs to maximize profits. Prices adjust to ensure that demand and supply are equal. In the labor market, wages bring demand and supply into balance; in the capital market, the interest rate is the "price" that adjusts to balance supply and demand.

We have now seen where the supply and demand curves that were introduced in Chapters 3 and 4 come from, and why they have the shapes they do. Whether we examine the household's demand for goods, its supply of labor, or its savings decision, the effects of price changes on the household's choices can be analyzed in terms of income and substitution effects. We also demonstrated that firms balance marginal cost and price in deciding on production levels, and they set the value of the marginal product equal to the price of an input in deciding on their demand for factors of production such as labor and capital. An increase in the real wage reduces the firm's demand for labor. An increase in the interest rate reduces the demand for capital. In the next chapter, we will put all these results together to sketch a model of the complete economy.

Review and Practice

SUMMARY

1. The interest rate is determined in the capital market—also called the loanable funds market. The supply of loanable funds comes from savings, as some households and firms spend less than their income. The demand arises from those households and firms that spend more than their income.

2. In making a decision to save, people face a trade-off between current and future consumption. The amount of extra consumption an individual can obtain in the future by reducing present consumption is determined by the real rate of interest.

3. A dollar received in the future is worth less than a dollar received today. The present discounted value tells us how much a future dollar amount is worth today. The present discounted value of a future amount falls when the rate of interest rises.

4. The real interest rate adjusts to balance supply and demand in the capital market.

5. The interest rate is an important part of the cost of using capital. If the interest rate increases, the cost of using capital increases. Firms' demands for funds for investment decrease as they cut back on their purchases of capital goods.

6. Human capital adds to economic productivity just as physical capital does. It is developed by education, on-the-job training, and investments of time and money that parents make in their children.

KEY TERMS

capital market
loanable funds market
life-cycle saving
interest
principal
time value of money
present discounted value
real rate of interest
nominal rate of interest
aggregate saving
capital goods
human capital

REVIEW QUESTIONS

1. How does a choice to consume in the present determine the amount of consumption in the future?
2. What is the price of future consumption in terms of present consumption?
3. For savers, how will the income effect of a higher interest rate affect current saving? How will the substitution effect of a higher interest rate affect current savings?
4. What are some of the factors, besides incomes and interest rates, that affect saving?
5. Describe how students invest time and money to acquire human capital.

PROBLEMS

1. This chapter focused on how interest rates affect savers. If an individual is a net debtor (that is, she owes money), what is the income effect of an increase in interest rates? Will an increase in the interest rates that she has to pay induce her to borrow more or borrow less?
2. In the context of the life-cycle model of saving, explain whether you would expect each of the following situations to increase or decrease household saving.
   (a) More people retire before age 65.
   (b) There is an increase in life expectancy.
   (c) The government passes a law requiring private businesses to provide more lucrative pensions.
3. Explain how each of the following changes might affect people's saving.
   (a) Inheritance taxes are increased.
   (b) A government program allows college students to obtain student loans more easily.
   (c) The government promises to assist anyone injured by natural disasters such as hurricanes, tornadoes, and earthquakes.
   (d) More couples decide against having children.
   (e) The economy does far worse than anyone was expecting in a given year.
4. Economists are fairly certain that a rise in the price of most goods will cause people to consume less of those goods, but they are not sure whether a rise in interest rates will cause people to save more. Use the ideas of substitution and income effects to explain why economists are confident of the conclusion in the first case but not in the second.

5. Suppose a new technology makes capital more productive, leading firms to want to borrow more at each rate of interest in order to purchase more capital. Using supply and demand diagrams of the loanable funds market, show what the likely effect on the equilibrium rate of interest would be.

6. Suppose younger households decide that they cannot rely on Social Security and must save more on their own for their retirement years. What is the likely effect on the equilibrium rate of interest? Will the equilibrium amount of borrowing rise or will it fall?

7. We have all heard about winners of $10 million jackpot lotteries. The winner, however, does not get $10 million in cash on the spot, but rather typically gets a measly $500,000 for twenty years. Why is the present discounted value of the prize much less than $10 million? Calculate the present discounted value if $r = 5$ percent.

8. Consider an individual who is borrowing. Assume the nominal interest rate remains the same but the rate of inflation increases. What happens to the real interest rate? Why do you expect the individual to borrow more?

Appendix A: Indifference Curves and the Saving Decision[1]

This appendix investigates the saving decision using the indifference curve approach applied in the appendix to Chapter 5 to the consumption decision and in Chapter 8 to the labor supply discussion. Let's first look at the choice between leisure and consumption.

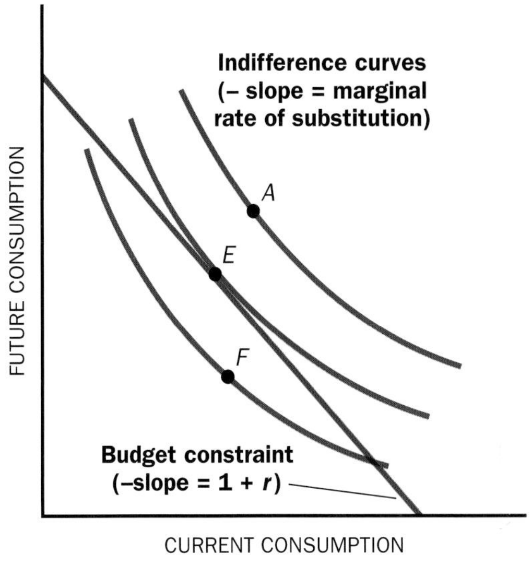

DECIDING HOW MUCH TO SAVE

Choosing how much to save is a decision about how much of lifetime income to consume now and how much to consume in the future. This trade-off is summarized in the two-period budget constraint introduced in the chapter, with present consumption measured along the horizontal axis and future consumption along the vertical axis. The slope of the budget constraint is $1 + r$, where r is the rate of interest, the extra consumption we get in the future from forgoing a unit of consumption today.

Figure 9.7 shows three indifference curves. The indifference curve through point A gives all the combinations of consumption today and consumption in the future about whose choice the individual is indifferent (she would be just as well off, no better and no worse, at any point along the curve as at A). Since people generally prefer more to less consumption, they would rather be on a higher than a lower indifference curve. The highest indifference curve a person can attain is one that is tangent to the budget constraint. The point of tangency we denote by E. The individual would clearly prefer the indifference curve through A, but no point on that curve is attainable because the whole indifference curve is above the budget constraint. She could consume at F, but the indifference curve through F lies below that through E.

As we learned in the appendix to Chapter 5, the slope of the indifference curve at a certain point is the marginal rate of substitution at that point. In this case, it tells us how much future consumption a person requires to leave him just as well off after his current consumption decreases by 1 unit. At the point of tangency, the slope of the indifference curve is equal to the slope of the budget constraint. The marginal rate of substitution at that point, E, equals $1 + r$. If the individual forgoes a unit of consumption, he gets $1 + r$ more units of consumption in the future, and this is exactly the amount he requires to compensate him for giving up current consumption. On the other hand, if the marginal rate of substitution is less than $1 + r$, it pays the individual to save more. To see why, assume $1 + r = 1.5$, while the person's marginal rate of substitution is 1.2. By reducing his consumption by a unit, he gets 1.5 more units in the future, but he would have been content getting only 1.2 units. He is better off saving more.

Figure 9.7

INDIFFERENCE CURVES AND SAVING BEHAVIOR

An individual will choose the combination of present and future consumption at E. Point A would be more desirable, but it is not feasible. Point F is feasible, but it lies on a lower indifference curve and is therefore less desirable.

---

[1]You will need to have read the appendix to Chapter 5 in order to follow this appendix.

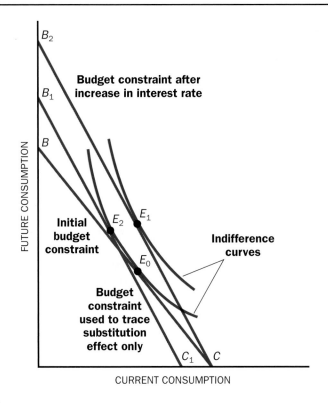

Figure 9.8

INCOME AND SUBSTITUTION EFFECTS OF A HIGHER INTEREST RATE

An increase in the interest rate rotates the budget constraint, moving it from BC to B_2C. The substitution effect describes what happens when relative prices are changed but Maggie remains on the same indifference curve; there is a shift in the budget line from BC to B_1C_1, and an increase in saving from E_0 to E_2. The income effect is the result of an outward shift of the budget line, keeping relative prices the same; the income effect is described by the shift from B_1C_1 to B_2C, and the increase in present consumption from E_2 to E_1.

CHANGING THE INTEREST RATE

Indifference curves and budget constraints enable us to see the effect of an increase in the interest rate. Figure 9.8 shows the case of an individual, Maggie, who works while she is young and saves for her retirement. The vertical axis gives consumption during retirement years, the horizontal axis consumption during working years. An increase in the rate of interest rotates the budget constraint, moving it from BC to B_2C. It is useful to break the change down into two steps. In the first, we ask what would have happened if the interest rate had changed but Maggie remained on the same indifference curve. This is represented by the movement of the budget constraint from BC to B_1C_1. As a result of the increased interest rate, Maggie consumes less today—she saves more. This is the substitution effect, and it is seen in the movement from E_0 to E_2 in the figure.

In the second step we note that since Maggie is a saver, the increased interest rate makes her better off. To leave Maggie on the same indifference curve after the increase in the interest rate, we needed to reduce her income. Her true budget constraint, after the interest rate increase, is B_2C, parallel to B_1C_1. The two budget constraints have the same slope because the after-tax interest rates are the same. The movement from B_1C_1 to B_2C is the second step. It induces Maggie to increase her consumption from E_2 to E_1. At higher incomes and the same relative prices (interest rates), people consume more every period, which implies that they save less. The movement from E_2 to E_1 is the income effect.

Thus, the substitution effect leads her to save more, the income effect to save less, and the net effect is ambiguous. In this case, there is no change in saving.

Appendix B: Calculating Present Discounted Value

In the text, we described how to calculate the present discounted value (PDV) of a dollar received a year from now. The present discounted value of a dollar received two years from now can be calculated similarly. But how much *today* is equivalent to, say, $100 two years from now? If I were given $PDV today and I put it in the bank, at the end of the year I would have PDV(1 + r)$. If I left it in the bank for another year, in the second year I would earn interest on the total amount in the bank at the end of the first year, $r \times PDV(1 + r)$. Therefore, at the end of the two-year period I would have:

$$PDV(1 + r) + [r \times PDV(1 + r)]$$
$$= PDV(1 + r)(1 + r)$$
$$= PDV(1 + r)^2.$$

Thus, the $PDV of $100 in two years is $100/(1 + r)^2$. If I put $100/(1 + r)^2$ in the bank today, I would have $100/(1 + r)^2 \times (1 + r)^2 = \$100$ in two years. In performing these calculations, we have taken account of the interest on the interest. This is called **compound interest.** (By contrast, **simple interest** does not take into account the interest earned on interest that has been previously earned.)

TABLE 9.2

PRESENT DISCOUNTED VALUE OF $100

Year received	Present discounted value
Next year	$\dfrac{1}{1 + r} \times 100 = \dfrac{100}{1 + r}$
Two years from now	$\dfrac{1}{1 + r} \times \dfrac{100}{1 + r} = \dfrac{100}{(1 + r)^2}$
Three years from now	$\dfrac{1}{1 + r} \times \dfrac{100}{(1 + r)^2} = \dfrac{100}{(1 + r)^3}$

Table 9.3

CALCULATING PRESENT DISCOUNTED VALUE OF A THREE-YEAR PROJECT

Year	Return	Discount factor $(r = 0.10)$	Present discounted value $(r = 0.10)$
1	$10,000	$\dfrac{1}{1.10}$	$ 9,091
2	$15,000	$\dfrac{1}{(1.10)^2} = \dfrac{1}{1.21}$	$12,397
3	$50,000	$\dfrac{1}{(1.10)^3} = \dfrac{1}{1.331}$	$37,566
Total	$75,000	—	$59,054

If the rate of interest is 10 percent and is compounded annually, $100 today is worth $110 a year from now and $121 (*not* $120) in two years' time. Thus, the present discounted value today of $121 two years from now is $100. Table 9.2 shows how to calculate the present discounted value of $100 received next year, two years from now, and three years from now.

We can now see how to calculate the value of an investment project that will yield a return over several years. We look at what the returns will be each year, adjust them to their present discounted values, and then add these values up. Table 9.3 shows how this is done for a project that yields $10,000 next year and $15,000 the year after, and that will be sold in the third year for $50,000. The second column of the table shows the return in each year. The third column shows the discount factor—what we multiply the return by to obtain the present discounted value of that year's return. The calculations assume an interest rate of 10 percent. The fourth column multiplies the return by the discount factor to obtain the present discounted value of that year's return. In the bottom row of the table, the present discounted values of each year's return have been added up to obtain the total present discounted value of the project. Notice that it is much smaller than the number we obtain simply by adding up the returns, which is the "undiscounted" yield of the project.

Learning Goals

In this chapter, you will learn

1 How competitive markets maximize consumer and produce surplus

2 How competitive markets result in economic efficiency

3 How taxes create deadweight losses that reduce efficiency

4 How governments may intervene in markets to combine efficiency with acceptable distribution of wealth and income

5 How markets are interrelated, and how changes in one market will affect other markets in the economy

Chapter 10

THE EFFICIENCY OF COMPETITIVE MARKETS

In earlier chapters, we focused on the product market and saw that supply and demand come into balance at an equilibrium price and quantity. In equilibrium, the quantity of goods demanded by consumers equals the quantity supplied by firms. We have also seen that labor and capital markets achieve equilibrium similarly. In the labor market, labor supply and demand come into balance at an equilibrium wage; in equilibrium, the supply of labor by households equals the demand for labor by firms. In the capital market, equilibrium is achieved through adjustment in the interest rate; in equilibrium, the amount of savings supplied by households equals the amount of borrowing by firms. When all three markets are in equilibrium, the basic economic questions—What gets produced? By whom? How? For whom?—are resolved through the interactions of households and firms in the marketplace. When all of the economy's central markets have achieved equilibrium in this way, economists say that the economy is in **general equilibrium.**

Understanding how markets provide answers to these basic economic questions is important. But we also are interested in evaluating whether markets do a good job. When the assumptions of the basic competitive model hold, will the economy produce the right amounts of all the thousands and thousands of different goods and services? Will society's scarce resources be used *efficiently?* Once we evaluate how markets in our basic competitive model operate, we will be ready to extend the model in Part Three to deal with situations in which markets do not work perfectly (because competition is not perfect, for instance).

Competitive Markets and Economic Efficiency

The forces of demand and supply determine what is produced, how it is produced, and who receives the goods that are produced. To many people, relying on competitive markets seems like an undesirable way of addressing the fundamental economic questions. Such critics often complain that markets result in too much of some goods being produced, or too few of others; that allowing markets free rein leads to inequalities in income and wealth; or that society's scarce resources could be used more efficiently if only the government would do something.

Economists have long been concerned with these issues. Are there circumstances in which markets do a good job in allocating society's scarce resources? Are there circumstances in which they don't? By and large, economists have concluded that *competitive* markets, the markets in our basic competitive model, make efficient use of society's scarce resources. This faith in markets can be traced back to Adam Smith's 1776 masterpiece, *The Wealth of Nations*. Smith argued that workers and producers, interested only in helping themselves and their families, were the basis of the success of the economy. As Smith put it,

> Man has almost constant occasion for the help of his brethren, and it is in vain for him to expect it from their benevolence only. He will be more likely to prevail if he can interest their self-love in his favour, and shew them that it is for their own advantage to do for him what he requires of them. . . . It is not from the benevolence of the butcher, the brewer, or the baker, that we expect our dinner, but from their regard to their own interest. We . . . never talk to them of our own necessities but of their advantages.[1]

In short, Smith argued that individuals pursuing their own self-interest would best promote the public interest. His insight was that individuals work hardest—and best—to help the overall economic production of the society when their efforts help themselves. Smith used the metaphor of the "invisible hand" to describe how self-interest leads to social good: "He intends only his own gain, and he is in this, as in many other cases, led by an invisible hand to promote an end which was no part of his intention. . . . By pursuing his own interest he frequently promotes that of the society more effectually than when he really intends to promote it."[2]

This insight is one of the most fundamental in social science, and one that is not at all obvious. There is more to running an economy efficiently than individuals simply working hard. How do they know what to produce? How is it that the *uncoordinated* pursuit of self-interest then leads to efficiency? One of the most important achievements of modern economic theory has been to establish in what sense and under what conditions the market is efficient.

---

[1]*The Wealth of Nations* (1776), Book One, Chapter II.

[2]Ibid., Book Four, Chapter II.

CONSUMER AND PRODUCER SURPLUS

To understand why competitive markets are efficient, we need to measure the benefit that consumers gain from buying goods in such a market, as well as measure the benefits that firms gain from selling in it. We will then show that equilibrium in the competitive market leads to the greatest possible total gain for consumers and firms.

To evaluate the outcome in a competitive market, we can make use of Figure 10.1, which shows the market demand and supply curves for a market in equilibrium at a quantity Q_c and a price p_c. Can we measure the benefits that accrue to consumers and firms from participating in this market? From Chapter 5, we know that the gain to consumers is measured by consumer surplus. The consumers who purchase the good will do so only if their willingness to pay is greater than the market price. The magnitude of the *net* benefit that they receive from, say, the nth unit of the good they purchase is the difference between what they have to pay for that good—the market price—and what they were willing to pay for that good, as reflected in the demand curve. Accordingly, the area shaded in blue measures the total consumer surplus.

Firms also gain from participating in the market. As we learned in Chapter 7, the market supply curve reflects the marginal costs of producing the good. At the equilibrium quantity, Q_c, the marginal cost of producing the last unit of output is p_c, the equilibrium price. Just as the demand curve shows consumers' willingness to pay, so the supply curve shows firms' willingness to produce; if the market price were p_1, firms would be willing to produce only the quantity Q_1. The supply curve has a positive slope, reflecting the fact that marginal cost rises as output increases. At an output of Q_1, the marginal cost of production is equal to p_1, so the marginal cost of producing Q_1 is less than the competitive equilibrium price p_c. Since the firm is able to sell all it produces at the competitive market price p_c, it sells all but the last (marginal) unit for more than its marginal cost production. The magnitude of the profit, the net benefit, that firms receive from selling, say, the nth unit of the good is the difference between what they receive, the market price, and the price at which they would have been willing to produce the good, the marginal cost. The total gain to firms, called **producer surplus,** is the difference between the supply curve and the market price. The producer surplus is the green area in the figure.

We measure the total gain to both consumers and producers by adding together consumer surplus and producer surplus. We can now state an important result: *The equilibrium price and quantity in a competitive market lead to the highest possible level of total surplus.* At quantities such as Q_1, which are below the market equilibrium quantity Q_c, consumers are willing to pay p_2 while firms are willing to sell at p_1. The value to consumers exceeds the cost to firms of producing an extra unit. Total surplus could be increased if the quantity were increased. At output levels greater

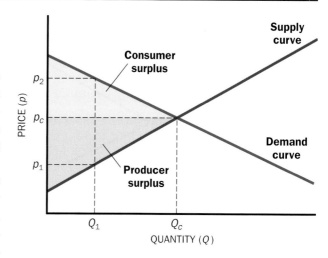

Figure 10.1

THE COMPETITIVE MARKET EQUILIBRIUM MAXIMIZES CONSUMER AND PRODUCER SURPLUS

When a competitive market is in equilibrium at the price p_c and quantity Q_c, at which demand and supply are equal, the sum of consumer surplus and producer surplus reaches its highest possible value. Consumer surplus is the blue area between the demand curve, showing willingness to pay, and the market price. Producer surplus is the green area between the supply curve (showing marginal cost) and the market price. If quantity is Q_1, firms are willing to supply an additional unit at a price p_1, while consumers are willing to pay p_2. The value to consumers exceeds the cost to producers, and total surplus can be increased if production expands. At quantities above Q_c, surplus can be increased by reducing output. At the market equilibrium, p_c and Q_c, the sum of consumer and producer surplus is maximized.

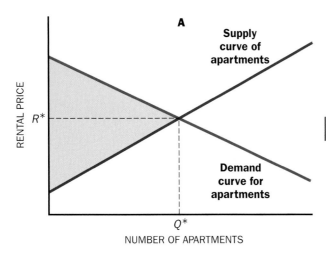

A

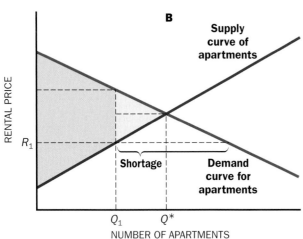

B

Figure 10.2

THE EFFECTS OF RENT CONTROL

Panel A of Figure 10.2 shows the supply and demand curves for rental apartments. The equilibrium rent at which supply equals demand is R^*. At this rent, the total surplus to renters and landlords is maximized. In panel A, the blue area is the consumer surplus—the value of apartments to renters in excess of the actual rent, R^*, they have to pay. The green area is the surplus that goes to landlords.

than Q_c, the marginal cost exceeds what consumers are willing to pay for the last unit, and so total surplus would be increased by reducing output. At Q_c and p_c, the sum of consumer and producer surplus reaches its highest level.

HOUSEHOLDS AND FIRMS ARE PRICE TAKERS

In competitive markets, there are many firms and many consumers. Because each consumer and each firm is small relative to the size of the market, each takes prices as given. Firms, maximizing profits, produce at the level where price equals marginal cost. Households, making rational choices, purchase up to the point where the marginal willingness to pay equals the market price.

Example: Efficiency Losses from Rent Control In Chapter 4, we used the basics of supply and demand to illustrate why rent control interferes with the workings of a competitive market. We showed how rent control could create an artificial scarcity of housing, reducing the supply of low- and moderately priced apartments and making it more difficult for newcomers to find a place to live at a reasonable price. Now we can use the concepts of consumer and producer surplus to see how rent control reduces economic efficiency.

Panel A of Figure 10.2 shows the supply and demand curves for rental apartments. The equilibrium rent at which supply equals demand is R^*. At this rent, the total surplus to renters and landlords is maximized. In panel A, the blue area is the consumer surplus—the value of apartments to renters in excess of the actual rent, R^*, they have to pay. The green area is the surplus that goes to landlords.

Panel B illustrates what happens when the local government imposes a law that prevents rents from rising above R_1. A rental shortage results, as there will be an excess of demand over supply at R_1. We can use this simple supply and demand model of the market for apartments to see what happens to consumer surplus and producer surplus. The blue area of panel B equals consumer surplus at the rent R_1. The green area is the landlords' surplus. Comparing panels A and B, we can see that *total surplus is smaller as a result of rent control.* Total surplus has fallen by the area shown in yellow. The reduction in total surplus measures the inefficiency resulting from rent control.

Our analysis also highlights the distributional impact of policies such as rent control. Look again at panel B. Total surplus falls when the rent ceiling is R_1, and the available supply of apartments also falls, from Q^* to Q_1. Some consumers may be unable to find an apartment when rent control is imposed. Few apartments are available at or below the median rental in cities with rent control; in cities without rent control, it is much easier to find an apartment that is reasonably priced. Those consumers who do happen to get a rent-controlled apartment benefit from the policy. They would have been willing to pay more to get an apartment, but they only have to pay R_1. Renters who are fortunate enough to find a rent-controlled apartment gain, while landlords and those who cannot find housing lose.

In the long run, the supply of apartments is more elastic. Low rents discourage the construction of new apartments and cause some landlords to remove units from the rental market (converting them to condominiums and selling them, for example). Consumer surplus falls as rent control leads to a decline in the quantity of apartments available for rent. Thus, the cost of rent control in terms of the inefficient allocation of resources and its distributional impact can change in the long run. In general, the distributional impact is smaller in the long run, while the efficiency cost is greater. In the long run, landlords will put their money elsewhere—where they will get a normal return on their capital. The benefits to rent control will diminish, as the decreasing supply of rental apartments will result in more and more of those who would like to get rent-controlled apartments simply finding that none are available.

Fundamentals of Competitive Markets 2

THE EQUILIBRIUM PRICE MAXIMIZES CONSUMER PLUS PRODUCER SURPLUS

When the market clears, firms are able to sell the quantity that maximizes their profits at the market price, and households are able to purchase the quantity that maximizes their utility at the market price. At the equilibrium price, marginal cost equals consumers' willingness to pay. At a price above the equilibrium price, the marginal cost of producing one more unit is less than consumers' marginal willingness to pay. At a price below the equilibrium price, the marginal cost of producing one more unit is greater than consumers' marginal willingness to pay. At the equilibrium price in a competitive market, consumer plus producer surplus is maximized.

Internet Connection

DIGITAL ECONOMIST

The Digital Economist provides an online graphic demonstration of consumer surplus. You can test your understanding of how consumer surplus is calculated at www.digital economist.com/cs_4010.html.

TAXES AND EFFICIENCY

Economists use the law of demand and supply to study the impact of taxes on consumers and producers. In Chapter 4 we learned that taxes imposed on producers can be passed on, or shifted, to consumers in the form of higher prices. There, two examples were contrasted. In the first, the law of supply and demand was used to study the impact of a tax on cigarette producers. When the demand for the taxed good is very inelastic, as is true of cigarettes, most of the burden of the tax is shifted to consumers. The second example involved a tax on one particular type of cheese, cheddar. In this case, the demand for the taxed good is very elastic, since close substitutes for cheddar cheese are available. When demand is elastic, most of the tax is borne by producers. Using the concepts of consumer surplus, producer surplus, and efficiency, we can gain additional insights into the effects of a tax.

Figure 10.3 shows the markets for cigarettes in panel A and the market for cheddar cheese in panel B. In each case, the equilibrium quantity without a tax is denoted by Q_0. The tax on the output of an industry paid by firms can be thought of as increasing the costs of production. This increase in cost shifts the supply curve up by the amount of the tax. Because the demand curve for cigarettes is relatively inelastic, the main impact of the tax is to raise the price to consumers. The price received by producers falls slightly, as does the quantity produced in the new equilibrium. In contrast, when the demand curve is relatively elastic, as shown in panel B for cheddar cheese, the effect is to cause a larger fall in the price producers receive and a smaller rise in the price paid by consumers.

The figure also shows what happens to consumer surplus when a good is taxed. In panel A, the entire blue area is equal to consumer surplus without the tax. After the tax, consumer surplus is equal only to the blue hatched area. Producer surplus is also reduced. It is equal to the entire orange region without the tax and the orange hatched area with the tax. Because the demand curve for cigarettes is inelastic, the reduction in consumer surplus is greater than the reduction in producer surplus, reflecting the fact that here the burden of the tax is shifted mainly to consumers.

While both consumer surplus and producer surplus fall, not all of this is lost to society—after all, the government collects revenue from the tax on cigarettes, and this revenue is then available to spend on government services. The tax revenue that is collected equals the tax per unit of output times the quantity of output produced. The difference between the price consumers pay and the price received by producers is equal to the tax on each unit of output. So the tax revenues collected will equal the area outlined in green. When we add up consumer surplus, producer surplus, and the revenue collected by the government, we can see that this total is less than the total surplus without the tax—the efficiency cost of the tax is measured by the area outlined in orange. This is called the **deadweight loss** caused by a tax. A tax thus has a cost beyond the revenue actually collected by the government.

Panel B illustrates the situation for a market in which the demand curve is relatively elastic. Here, the deadweight loss of the tax (the area outlined in orange) is larger. Because consumers are more sensitive to price when the demand curve is elastic, the tax causes them to substitute away from the taxed good. The tax "distorts" consumers' choices more in this case, and the resulting efficiency loss is larger.

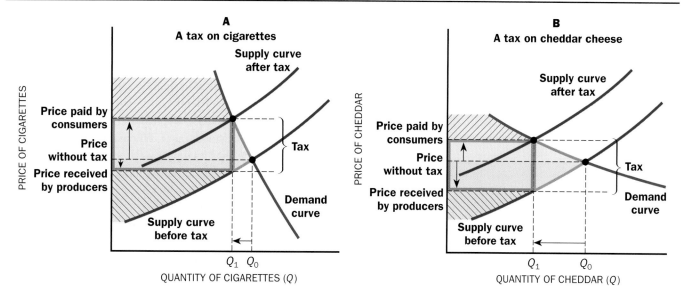

Figure 10.3

TAXES AND EFFICIENCY

A tax on the output of an industry shifts the supply curve up by the amount of the tax. Panel A shows that if the demand curve is relatively inelastic, as is the case with cigarettes, most of the tax is passed on to consumers. Both consumer surplus and producer surplus fall, but most of the tax burden falls on consumers. The area outlined in green is equal to the revenue the government collects from the tax. Consumer and producer surplus fall by more than the revenue collected by the government. The deadweight loss due to the tax is shown as the area outlined in red. Panel B repeats the analysis for a good whose demand curve is relatively elastic. More of the burden of the tax falls on producers, and the deadweight loss is larger.

Efficiency

In the basic competitive model, with each consumer and each firm taking the market price as given, the equilibrium between demand and supply ensures the largest possible joint gain to consumers and firms. This is why most economists believe that the basic competitive model provides an important benchmark for evaluating how well resources are allocated. Taxes on specific goods create efficiency losses, as does interfering with the law of supply and demand through policies such as rent control. These policies may have desirable effects (a tax on cigarettes helps to reduce smoking, for instance), but those effects must be balanced against the inefficiencies they create. As we have seen before, trade-offs must be made.

If the conditions of the basic competitive model are satisfied, markets do a good job of allocating society's resources efficiently. But the benchmark provided by the basic competitive model is also useful because it helps us understand how markets can fail when the basic assumptions of the model do not hold. In Part Three, we consider a number of factors that cause markets to be inefficient. But first, we need to examine more closely what economists mean when they talk about the efficiency of markets.

PARETO EFFICIENCY

In everyday usage, we say something is efficient if it involves little waste. Economists relate the concept of efficiency to concern with the well-being of those in the economy. When no one can be made better off without making someone else worse off, the allocation of resources is called **Pareto efficient,** after the great Italian economist and sociologist Vilfredo Pareto (1848–1923). Typically, economists' use of the term refers to Pareto efficiency. Saying that a market is efficient is a compliment. In the same way that an efficient machine uses its inputs as productively as possible, an efficient market leaves no way of increasing output with the same level of inputs. The only way one person can be made better off is by taking resources away from another, thereby making the second person worse off.

It is easy to see how an allocation of resources might not be Pareto efficient. Assume that the government is given the job of distributing chocolate and vanilla ice cream and pays no attention to people's preferences. Assume, moreover, that some individuals love chocolate and hate vanilla, while others love vanilla and hate chocolate. Some chocolate lovers will get vanilla ice cream, and some vanilla lovers will get chocolate ice cream. Clearly, this arrangement is Pareto inefficient. Allowing people to trade resources—in this case, ice cream—makes both groups better off.

There is a popular and misguided view that *all* economic changes represent nothing more than redistributions. Gains to one only subtract from another. Rent control is one example. In this view, the only effect of rent control is redistribution—landlords receive less and are worse off by the same amount that their tenants' rents are reduced (and the tenants are better off). In some countries, unions have expressed similar views and see wage increases as having no further consequences than redistributing income to workers from those who own or who manage firms. This view is mistaken because it ignores consequences beyond the redistribution in each of these instances. Rent control that keeps rents below the level that clears the rental housing market does more than just take money out of the pocket of landlords and put it into the pocket of poor renters. It affects the amount of housing that landlords are willing to supply. It results in inefficiencies. For those concerned about renters who cannot afford the going rate, there are better approaches, such as vouchers to help those with low incomes pay for rent, that make the renters as well as the landlords better off than under rent control. Thus, with rent control, the economy is not Pareto efficient.

CONDITIONS FOR THE PARETO EFFICIENCY OF THE MARKET ECONOMY

For the economy to be Pareto efficient, it must meet the conditions of exchange efficiency, production efficiency, and product-mix efficiency. Considering each of these conditions separately shows us why the basic competitive model attains Pareto efficiency. (Recall the basic ingredients of that model: rational, perfectly informed households interacting with rational, profit-maximizing firms in competitive markets.)

Exchange Efficiency **Exchange efficiency** requires that whatever the economy produces must be distributed among individuals in an efficient way. If I like chocolate ice cream and you like vanilla ice cream, exchange efficiency requires that I get the chocolate and you get the vanilla. When there is exchange efficiency, there is no scope for further trade among individuals.

The price system ensures that exchange efficiency is attained. In deciding how much of a good to buy, people balance the marginal benefit they receive by buying an extra unit with the cost of that extra unit, its price. Hence, price can be thought of as a rough measure of the *marginal* benefit an individual receives from a good—that is, the benefit she receives from one more unit of the good. For those who like chocolate ice cream a great deal and vanilla ice cream very little, this will entail consuming many more chocolate ice cream cones than vanilla ones. And conversely for the vanilla lover. Notice that no single individual or agency needs to know who is a chocolate lover and who is a vanilla lover for the goods to get to the right person. Not even the ice cream stores have to know individual preferences. Each consumer, by his own action, ensures that exchange efficiency is attained.

Production Efficiency For an economy to be Pareto efficient, it must also be **production efficient.** That is, it must not be possible to produce more of some goods without producing less of other goods. In other words, Pareto efficiency requires that the economy operate along the production possibilities curve first introduced in Chapter 2.

Figure 10.4 shows the production possibilities curve for a simple economy that produces only two goods, SUVs and sedans. If the economy is at point *I,* inside the production possibilities curve, it cannot be Pareto efficient. At *I* society could produce more of both SUVs and sedans; and by distributing them to different individuals, it could make people better off. Prices signal to firms the scarcity of each of the inputs they use. When all firms face the same prices of labor, capital goods, and other inputs, they will take the appropriate actions to economize on each of these inputs, ensuring that the economy operates along its production possibilities curve.

Product-Mix Efficiency The third condition for Pareto efficiency is **product-mix efficiency.** That is, the mix of goods produced by the economy must reflect the preferences of those in the economy. The economy must produce along the production possibilities curve at a point that reflects what consumers want. The price system again ensures that this condition will be satisfied. Both firms and households look at the trade-offs. Firms look at how many extra sedans they can produce if they reduce their production of SUVs. The result is given by the slope of the production possibilities curve, and is called the **marginal rate of transformation.** Firms compare this trade-off with the relative benefits of producing the two goods—given by the relative prices. Similarly, households look at the relative costs of SUVs and sedans—again given by the relative prices—and ask, given those trade-offs, whether they would like to consume more SUVs and fewer sedans or vice versa.

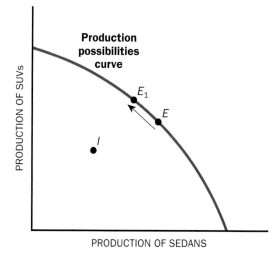

Figure 10.4

THE PRODUCTION POSSIBILITIES CURVE

The production possibilities curve shows the maximum level of output of one good given the level of output of other goods. Production efficiency requires that the economy be on its production possibilities curve. Along the curve, the only way to increase production of one good (here, SUVs) is to decrease the production of other goods (sedans).

Thinking Like an Economist

EXCHANGE AND DISTRIBUTION

The concepts of consumer surplus and producer surplus remind us that *exchange* in competitive markets can benefit both buyers and sellers. The demand curve for a good shows the total willingness to pay for each unit of the good. Though consumers are willing to pay more for the marginal unit at lower quantities, all units are purchased at the market price, which reflects the value of the last unit purchased. Thus, the total utility of the units purchased by consumers is greater than the total cost to consumers. Similarly, the supply curve reflects the marginal cost of producing each unit of a good. The market equilibrium price will equal the marginal cost of the last unit produced. Because marginal cost increases as the firm produces more, the price the firm receives is greater than the marginal cost of producing every unit except the last.

Consumer surplus and producer surplus also remind us that exchange has *distributional effects*. The gains from exchange need not be evenly distributed. If demand is relatively elastic while supply is inelastic, consumer surplus is small while producer surplus is large. If demand is relatively inelastic while supply is very elastic, consumer surplus is large while producer surplus is small.

Changes in preferences are reflected quickly—through the operation of demand and supply curves—in changes in prices. These changes are then translated by firms into changes in production. Assume that the economy is initially producing at point E along the production possibilities curve in Figure 10.4. Consumers decide that they like SUVs more and sedans less. The increased demand for SUVs will result in the price of SUVs increasing, and this price rise will lead to an increased output of SUVs; at the same time, the decrease in demand for sedans will result in the price of sedans falling, and this change in turn will lead to a decreased output of sedans. The economy will move from E to a point such as E_1, where there are more SUVs and fewer sedans produced; the mix of goods produced in the economy will have changed to reflect the changed preferences of consumers.

Wrap-Up

THREE CONDITIONS FOR PARETO EFFICIENCY

1. Exchange efficiency: Goods must be distributed among individuals in a way that leaves no scope for gains from further trade.
2. Production efficiency: The economy must be on its production possibilities curve.
3. Product-mix efficiency: The economy must produce a mix of goods reflecting the preferences of consumers.

COMPETITIVE MARKETS AND PARETO EFFICIENCY

We now know that when economists say that market economies are efficient, or that the price system results in economic efficiency, they mean that the economy is Pareto efficient: no one can be made better off without making someone else worse off. We have also shown why competitive markets ensure that all three of the basic conditions for Pareto efficiency—exchange efficiency, production efficiency, and product-mix efficiency—are attained.

The argument that competitive markets ensure Pareto efficiency can be put somewhat loosely in another way: a rearrangement of resources can benefit only people who voluntarily agree to it. But in competitive equilibrium, people have already agreed to all the exchanges they are willing to make; no one wishes to produce more or less or to demand more or less, at the prices given.

Pareto efficiency does *not* say that there are no ways to make one or many individuals better off. Obviously, resources could be taken from some and given to others, and the recipients would be better off. We have seen how, for instance, government interventions in the market, such as rent control, do benefit some individuals—those who are lucky enough to get the rent-controlled apartments. But in the process, others are made worse off.

Fundamentals of Competitive Markets 3

THE COMPETITIVE MARKET ECONOMY IS PARETO EFFICIENT

The equilibrium in the competitive market economy is Pareto efficient—no one can be made better off without making someone else worse off. In the competitive economy, the conditions for exchange efficiency, production efficiency, and product-mix efficiency are all satisfied.

COMPETITIVE MARKETS AND INCOME DISTRIBUTION

Efficiency is better than inefficiency, but it is not everything. In the competitive equilibrium, some individuals might be very rich, while others live in dire poverty. One person might have skills that are highly valued, while another does not. Competition may result in an efficient economy with a very unequal distribution of resources.

The law of supply and demand in a competitive economy determines how the available income will be divided up. It determines how much workers are paid for their labor and the return to owners of capital on their investments. By determining wages and the return to capital, the market thus determines the distribution of income.

Knowing how the distribution of income is determined is important, because it tells us how the nation's economic pie is divided: it provides the answer to the question "For whom are goods produced?" While competitive markets produce economic *efficiency*—no one can be made better off without making someone else worse off—competitive markets may also produce distributions of income that seem, at least to some, morally repugnant. An economy in which some individuals live in mansions while others barely eke out a living may be efficient, but that hardly makes the situation desirable. Left to themselves, competitive markets may provide an answer to the question "For whom are goods produced?" that seems unacceptable.

This unacceptable response does not mean that the mechanism should be abandoned, at least not under the conditions assumed in our basic model—perfectly informed, rational consumers and firms interacting in competitive markets. Even if society as a whole wishes to redistribute income, it should not dispense with competitive markets. Instead, *all* that is needed is to redistribute in any way desired the wealth that people possess, and then leave the rest to the workings of a competitive market.

Of course, redistributing wealth is easier said than done; and as a practical matter, virtually all of the ways that the government engages in redistribution affect the workings of the market economy. Taxes on wages affect the labor market; taxes on capital, the capital market; taxes on luxuries, markets for specific goods.

Perhaps the most important impact of government on the distribution of "wealth" is in the sphere of education—in ensuring that everyone has a certain amount of human capital. By providing all individuals, regardless of the wealth of their parents, with a free basic education, government reduces the degree of inequality that otherwise would exist. Still, as we will see in Chapter 17, the magnitude of inequality in the United States remains high—larger than in most other developed countries.

Frequently government interferences with the market are justified on the grounds that they increase equality. These government policies are often based on the widely held but mistaken (as we have already seen) view that all redistributions are just that—some individuals get more and others get less with no further repercussions. We now know that changing relative prices to achieve redistribution—say, by imposing rent control—will have other effects as well. Such changes interfere with the economy's efficiency. One consequence of lower rents for apartments, for example, is that the return on capital invested in rental housing will fall. As a result, the economy will invest too little in rental housing and therefore too few apartments will be made available. Because of this underinvestment, the economy is not efficient.

Thus, interventions in the economy justified on the grounds that they increase equality need to be treated with caution. To attain an efficient allocation of resources with the desired distribution of income, *if* the assumptions of the competitive model are satisfied by the economy, the *sole* role of the government is to alter the initial distribution of wealth. Not only can it rely on the market mechanism thereafter, but its interference with the market may actually result in the economy not being Pareto efficient.

Both of the results just presented—that competitive markets are Pareto efficient and that every Pareto-efficient allocation, regardless of the desired distribution of income, can be obtained through the market mechanism—are *theorems*. That is, they are logical propositions that follow from basic definitions and assumptions, such as what is meant by a competitive economy and what is meant by Pareto efficiency. When these assumptions are not satisfied, market economies may not be Pareto efficient, and more extensive government interventions may be required to obtain Pareto-efficient allocations. Later chapters will explore these circumstance in greater detail.

Still, two important lessons that emerge are worth noting here: there are costs associated with redistributions that entail interventions in market mechanisms, and those costs have to be weighed against the benefits; and redistributions can make use of the price mechanism, rather than trying to override it. One cannot repeal the laws of supply and demand. Interventions like rent control can impose large costs. Some alternative forms of interventions, such as housing subsidies, may achieve comparable distributional objectives at less cost. If government cannot *costlessly* redistribute, it should look for efficient ways of redistributing—that is, ways that reduce the costs as much as possible. This is one of the main concerns of the branch of economics called the *economics of the public sector.*

General Equilibrium Analysis

When we applied the idea of market equilibrium in earlier chapters, we focused on one market at a time. The price of a good is determined when the demand for that good equals its supply. The wage rate is determined when the demand for labor equals its supply. The interest rate is determined when the demand for savings equals its supply. This kind of analysis is called **partial equilibrium analysis.** In studying what is going on in one market, we ignore what is going on in other markets—as we did earlier in this chapter when we analyzed the efficiency cost of rent control and the impact of a tax on cigarettes. In each case, we focused just on the demand and supply in the market for apartments and the market for cigarettes.

Interdependencies in the economy make partial equilibrium analysis overly simple, because demand and supply in one market depend on prices determined in other markets. For instance, the demand for skis depends on the price of ski tickets, ski boots, and possibly even airline tickets. Thus, the equilibrium price of skis will depend on the price of ski tickets, ski boots, and airline tickets. By the same token, the demand for ski tickets and ski boots will depend on the price of skis. **General equilibrium analysis** broadens our perspective, taking into account the interactions and interdependencies throughout the various parts of the economy.

THE BASIC COMPETITIVE EQUILIBRIUM MODEL

Economists view the entire economy as made up of numerous different markets, all interrelated. Individuals and firms interact in these different markets. In the labor market, for example, the supply of labor reflects the outcome of decisions by households as they determine the amount of labor they wish to supply. Households supply labor because they want to buy goods. Hence, their labor supply depends on both wages and *prices.* It also depends on other sources of income. If we assume, for the sake of simplicity, that households also have savings that yield a return, then we can see that the labor supply is connected to the product market and the capital market.

Equilibrium in the labor market requires that the demand for labor equal the supply. Normally, when we draw the demand curve for labor, we simply assume that *p*, the price of the good(s) being produced, and the interest rate (here, *r*) are kept fixed. We focus our attention solely on the wage rate, the price of labor. Given *p* and *r*, we look for the wage at which the demand and supply for labor are equal. This is a *partial equilibrium analysis* of the labor market. But in fact all markets are interrelated; the demand for labor depends on the wage, on the interest rate, and on the price at which the firm sells its output.

The labor market is only one of the three markets, even in our highly simplified economy. There is also the market for capital to consider. In Chapter 9, we saw how

Thinking Like an Economist

INDIRECT TRADE-OFFS AND AIR SAFETY FOR CHILDREN

General equilibrium analysis calls attention to the fact that trade-offs often exist across markets. The benefits of an action taken in one market may be offset by related costs that arise in another market. This same reasoning applies to government policies, as policymakers work to balance the costs and benefits of expenditure programs and regulations. Sometimes the costs of a policy arise through its indirect repercussions. Such indirect trade-offs helped determine regulations related to air safety for children.

States require small children in cars to ride in specially designed safety seats. So why shouldn't small children traveling by plane be required to ride in safety seats as well? It seems clear that in at least a few cases, such seats would save a child's life in an airplane crash. Nevertheless, after considering the full potential consequences of requiring child safety seats in planes, the Federal Aviation Administration (FAA) argued against it.

On the benefit side, the FAA estimated that mandatory safety seats would save the life of one child in one airline crash every ten years. But parents would have to pay as much as $185 to buy the safety seats themselves, in addition to paying for a regular airplane seat for the child. Under current regulations, children under two years old are allowed to sit in their parents' laps, avoiding the expense of an airline ticket. With those extra costs, the FAA estimated that 20 percent of the families who now fly with small children would either stay home or drive. The additional driving would lead to 9 additional highway deaths, 59 serious injuries, and 2,300 minor injuries over the same ten-year period, according to FAA estimates.

Even those who feel that saving an additional child's life has a value that cannot be reduced to a price tag, however

high, must look beyond the market being regulated. Looking beyond airlines makes it clear that reducing airline deaths by requiring child safety seats for infants and toddlers is almost certain to cause even greater total loss of life.

households determine their saving, which in turn determines the available supply of capital. The supply of capital is affected, in general, by the return it yields (the interest rate r) plus the income individuals have from other sources, in particular from wages. Since the amount individuals are willing to save may depend on how well-off they feel, and how well-off they feel depends on the wage rate relative to prices, we can think of the supply of capital, too, as depending on wages, interest rates, and prices. In Chapter 9 we learned how to derive firms' demand for capital. This depends not just on the interest they must pay but also on the price at which goods can be sold, and on the cost of other inputs such as labor.

Equilibrium in the capital market occurs at the point at which the demand and supply for capital are equal. Again, partial equilibrium analysis of the capital market focuses on the return to capital, r, at which the demand and supply of capital are equal, but both the demand and supply depend on the wage rate and the price of goods as well.

Finally, there is the market for goods. Chapter 5 showed how to derive households' demand for goods. We can think of the household at first deciding on how much to spend and then deciding how to allocate what it spends over different goods. Of course, with a single consumption good, the second choice does not exist. In our simplified model, then, we can think of the demand for goods at any price as being determined by household income, which in turn depends on the wage and the interest rate.

Similarly, in Chapter 7, we analyzed how firms determine how much to produce. They set price equal to marginal cost, where marginal cost depends on wages and the interest rate. Equilibrium in the goods market requires that the demand for goods equal the supply of goods. Again, while in the simple partial equilibrium analysis we focus on how the demand and supply of goods depend on price, p, we know that the demand and supply of goods also depend on both the wage rate and the return to capital.

The labor market is said to be in equilibrium when the demand for labor equals the supply. The product market is in equilibrium when the demand for goods equals the supply. The capital market is in equilibrium when the demand for capital equals the supply. The economy as a whole is in equilibrium only when all markets clear simultaneously (demand equals supply in all markets). The general equilibrium for our simple economy occurs at a wage rate, w; price, p; and interest rate, r, at which all three markets are in equilibrium.

In the basic equilibrium model, there is only a single good, but it is easy to extend the analysis to the more realistic case where there are many goods. The same web of interconnections exists between different goods and between different goods and different inputs. Recall from Chapter 3 that the demand curve depicts the quantity of a good—for instance, soda—demanded at each price; the supply curve shows the quantity of a good that firms supply at each price. But the demand curve for soda depends on the prices of other goods and the income levels of different consumers; similarly, the supply curve for soda depends on the prices of inputs, including the wage rate, the interest rate, and the price of sugar and other ingredients. Those prices, in turn, depend on supply and demand in their respective markets. The general equilibrium of the economy requires finding the prices for each good and for each input such that the demand for each good equals the supply, and the demand for each input equals the supply. *General equilibrium entails prices, wages, and returns to capital that ensure all markets for goods, labor, and capital (and other factors of production) clear.*

EQUILIBRIUM IN THE BASIC COMPETITIVE MODEL

The labor market clearing condition: The demand for labor must equal the supply.
The capital market clearing condition: The demand for capital must equal the supply.
The goods market clearing condition: The demand for goods must equal the supply.

THE LABOR MARKET AND THE WIDENING WAGE GAP

A general equilibrium perspective can help us understand how changes in one market affect other markets. Often those repercussions on other markets feed back to cause further changes in the market originally affected. As a case in point, a general equilibrium analysis is needed to analyze how wages for skilled and unskilled workers are affected by changes in technology.

Those who have a college education are paid more on average than those who fail to complete high school. The average wage of workers with at least four years of college is two-thirds higher than that of workers whose education ended with a high school diploma. Because unskilled workers generally cannot perform the same jobs as skilled workers, it is useful to think about the wages of these two groups as determined in separate labor markets, as illustrated in Figure 10.5. Panel A shows the demand and supply curves of unskilled workers, and panel B those for skilled workers. The equilibrium wage for skilled workers is higher than that for unskilled workers.

What happens if a change in technology shifts the demand curve for skilled labor to the right, to DS_1, and the demand curve for unskilled labor to the left, to DU_1? The wages of unskilled workers will decrease from wu_0 to wu_1, and those of skilled workers will increase from ws_0 to ws_1. In the long run, this increased wage gap induces more people to acquire skills, so the supply of unskilled workers shifts to the left, and that of skilled workers shifts to the right. As a result, the wage of unskilled workers rises from wu_1 to wu_2, and that of skilled workers falls from ws_1 to ws_2. These long-run supply responses thus dampen the short-run movements in wages.

Over the past two decades, the ratio of wages of college graduates to high school graduates, as well as the ratio of wages of high school graduates to nongraduates, has increased enormously. Indeed, the real wages (that is, wages adjusted for changes in the cost of living) of unskilled workers have fallen dramatically (by as much as 30 percent). Though there have been shifts in both demand and supply curves, the primary explanation of these shifts is a change in the relative demand for skilled labor, probably attributable largely to changes in technology.

While we can be fairly confident of the predicted shifts in long-run labor supply, how fast they will occur is less clear. At the same time that these supply shifts occur,

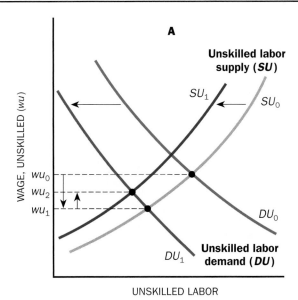

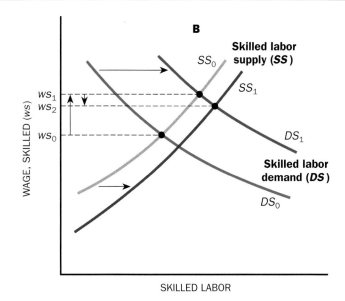

Figure 10.5

THE MARKET FOR SKILLED AND UNSKILLED LABOR

In panel A, new advanced technology shifts the demand curve for unskilled labor to the left, and reduces wages from wu_0 to wu_1. In panel B, the new technology shifts the demand curve for skilled labor out to the right, and thus raises wages from ws_0 to ws_1. Over time, this increased difference in wages may lead more individuals to obtain skills, shifting the supply curve for unskilled labor back to the left, raising wages for unskilled labor somewhat from wu_1 to wu_2, and shifting the supply curve for skilled labor to the right, reducing wages for skilled labor from ws_1 to ws_2.

there may be further shifts in the demand curves, exacerbating wage differences. The question is, How long will it take for the wage gap to be reduced to the levels that prevailed in the 1960s? In the meantime, many worry about the social consequences of steadily increasing wage (and income) inequality.

THE MINIMUM WAGE AND GENERAL EQUILIBRIUM

When the first minimum wage law was adopted by passage of the Fair Labor Standards Act of 1938, it had general equilibrium effects that altered the character of the country.

Initially the minimum wage law required that wages be no lower than 32.5 cents per hour. Because wages were much lower in the South than in the North, many more workers were affected there. For example, 44 percent of southern textile workers were paid below the minimum wage, but only 6 percent of northern textile workers were. The law had a particularly strong impact on African Americans in the South. Many lost their jobs and migrated North. The way to boost employment in

The effects of the first minimum wage were far reaching, and included the migration of many African Americans to the North.

the South was to raise the productivity of the workforce, so southern states were eager to attract new capital investment that would increase labor productivity and restore employment.

Gavin Wright, a professor of economics at Stanford University, described the situation this way: "The overall effect of this history on black Americans is complex, mixed, and ironic. Displacement and suffering were severe. Yet in abolishing the low-wage South, the federal government also destroyed the nation's most powerful bastion of racism and white supremacy. The civil rights movement of the 1960s was able to use the South's hunger for capital inflows as an effective weapon in forcing desegregation. Similarly, migration to the North allowed dramatic increases in incomes and educational opportunities for many blacks; yet the same migration channeled other blacks into the high-unemployment ghettos which if anything have worsened with the passage of time."[3]

A partial equilibrium analysis of the effects of enacting a minimum wage would look only at how the law affected labor markets. But for society as a whole, the effects of enacting such a law were far more momentous, touching on issues such as racial desegregation and the growth of urban ghettos.

GENERAL EQUILIBRIUM OVER TIME

A general equilibrium perspective focuses on the interrelationships among markets, including markets at different points in time. For example, the supply (and demand) for exhaustible natural resources like oil will depend on the price of oil

[3]Gavin Wright, "The Economic Revolution in the American South," *Journal of Economic Perspectives 1* (Summer 1987): 161–78.

today, but it will also depend on prices expected in the future. The role played by prices expected in the future is important for understanding how quickly the limited supply of a natural resource will be used.

Just as we did in Chapter 9 when we discussed household saving, we will simplify by considering only two periods, today and the future. Let's also assume that known reserves of oil are one billion barrels. The oil can be sold now or left in the ground and sold in the future. Oil producers will want to sell the oil today if they think prices in the future will be lower, and they will want to leave it in the ground today and sell it in the future if they expect prices then will be higher. Of course, we learned in Chapter 9 that we cannot compare prices today and in the future directly—a dollar in the future is not worth as much as a dollar today because today's dollar could always be invested, earning interest and thus yielding more than a dollar in the future. To compare prices in the future with prices today we need to look at the *present discounted value* of the future price (Chapter 9 explained how to calculate this figure). If the expected price of oil in one year is $55 per barrel and the interest rate is 10 percent, then the present discounted value of that $55 is $55/1.1 = $50.

We can now restate the comparison that oil producers will make. Oil producers will compare the current price with the present discounted value of the future price of oil. If the current price is above the present discounted value of the future price, they have an incentive to sell all one billion barrels today. But an attempt to sell all the oil reserves today will depress the current price of oil, pushing it down toward the present discounted value of the future price. In the opposite case, when the current price is less than the present discounted value of the future price, oil producers have an incentive to save the oil and sell it in the future. But because the oil is withheld from the market today, the current price will rise, until it equals the presented discounted value of the future price. Thus, market forces will tend to make the current price and the present discounted future price equal. By definition, in equilibrium an oil producer must be indifferent between the choices of selling an extra barrel today and saving it to sell in the future. This tells us that the current price and the presented discounted future price will be equal in equilibrium.

If the current price and the present discounted future price are equal, oil producers have no preference as to when they sell the oil. What then determines how much oil will actually be sold today? To answer this question we need to know something about the demand for oil, both today and in the future. In equilibrium, the quantity demanded today and in the future, when the current and present discounted future prices are equal, must add up to the total amount of oil—in our example, one billion barrels.

We can now understand how the price of oil is affected by such factors as the development of new technologies or more fuel-efficient cars. Suppose these developments lower the demand for oil in the future. The demand curve for oil in the future then shifts to the left, lowering the future price of oil. Whenever the present discounted future price of oil falls, oil producers will want to sell more of their oil today. As we have seen, an increase in the supply of oil today causes the current price of oil to fall. The current price must adjust until it again equals the present discounted future price, and total demand today and in the future equals one billion barrels. Because reduced demand in the future lowers the current price of oil, it leads to higher current consumption of oil and an increase in the quantity of oil produced today.

WHEN PARTIAL EQUILIBRIUM ANALYSIS WILL DO

In the examples of the widening wage gap and the price of oil, general equilibrium analysis is clearly important. But can we ever focus on what goes on in a single market, without worrying about the reverberations in the rest of the economy? Are there circumstances in which partial equilibrium analysis will provide a fairly accurate answer to the effect of, say, a change in a tax? When will the sort of analysis we used earlier in this chapter to analyze the impact of a tax on cigarettes and cheddar cheese be sufficiently accurate?

Partial equilibrium analysis is adequate, for example, when the reverberations from the initial imposition of a tax are so dispersed that they can be ignored without distorting the analysis. Such is the case when individuals shift their demand away from the taxed good toward many, many other goods. Each of the prices of those goods changes only a very little. And the total demand for the factors of production (such as capital and labor) changes only negligibly, so that the second-round changes in the prices of different goods and inputs have a very slight effect on the demand and supply curve of the industry analyzed. In these circumstances, partial equilibrium analysis will provide a good approximation of what will actually happen.

Our earlier analysis of a tax on cigarettes is an example of partial equilibrium analysis providing a good approximation. Since expenditures on cigarettes are a small proportion of anyone's income, an increase in their price will have a small effect on overall consumption patterns. While the reduced quantity demanded of cigarettes (and the indirect changed demand for other goods) will slightly change the total demand for labor, this effect is so small that it will have no noticeable impact on the wage rate. Similarly, the tax will have virtually no effect on the return to capital.

Under these circumstances, when more distant general equilibrium effects are likely to be so faint as to be indiscernible, a partial equilibrium analysis of a tax on cigarettes is appropriate.

Looking Beyond the Basic Model

This chapter has brought together the pieces of the basic competitive model. It has shown how the competitive equilibrium in an ideal economy is achieved. To the extent that conditions in the real world match the assumptions of the basic competitive model, there will be economic efficiency. Governments will have little role in the economy beyond establishing a legal framework within which to enforce market transactions.

What are the consequences when the underlying assumptions are not valid? Which of the assumptions are most suspect? What evidence do we have to assess either the validity of the model's underlying assumptions or its implications? The next part of this book is devoted to these questions, and to the role of government that emerges from the answers.

Review and Practice

SUMMARY

1. General equilibrium in the basic competitive model occurs when wages, interest rates, and prices are such that demand is equal to supply in all labor, capital, and product markets. All markets clear.
2. The competitive equilibrium maximizes the sum of consumer and producer surplus.
3. Under the conditions of the basic competitive model, the economy's resource allocation is Pareto efficient: that is, no one can be made better off without making someone worse off.
4. The distribution of income that emerges from competitive markets may be very unequal. However, under the conditions of the basic competitive model, a redistribution of wealth can move the economy to a more equal allocation that is also Pareto efficient.
5. Changes in one market will have effects on other markets. To analyze the effects of a tax, for example, general equilibrium analysis takes into account the effects in all markets. But when the secondary repercussions of a change are small, partial equilibrium analysis, focusing on only one or a few markets, is sufficient.

KEY TERMS

general equilibrium
producer surplus
deadweight loss
Pareto efficient
exchange efficiency
production efficiency
product-mix efficiency
marginal rate of transformation
partial equilibrium analysis
general equilibrium analysis

REVIEW QUESTIONS

1. How does the economy in general equilibrium answer the four basic economic questions: What is produced, and in what quantities? How are these goods produced?

For whom are they produced? Who makes the economic decisions?
2. What is meant by Pareto efficiency? What is required for the economy to be Pareto efficient? If the conditions of the basic competitive model are satisfied, is the economy Pareto efficient?
3. What is the difference between partial and general equilibrium analysis? When is each one especially appropriate?
4. If the distribution of income in the economy is quite unequal, is it necessary to impose price controls or otherwise change prices in the competitive marketplace to make it more equal?

PROBLEMS

1. Decide whether partial equilibrium analysis would suffice in each of these cases, or whether it would be wise to undertake a general equilibrium analysis.
   (a) A tax on alcohol
   (b) An increase in the Social Security tax
   (c) A drought that affects farm production in the midwestern states
   (d) A rise in the price of crude oil
   (e) A major airline going out of business
   Explain your answers.
2. Explain how each of the following might interfere with exchange efficiency.
   (a) Airlines that limit the number of seats they sell at a discount price
   (b) Doctors who charge poor patients less than rich patients
   (c) Firms that give volume discounts
   In each case, what additional trades might be possible?
3. Assume that in the steel industry, given current production levels and technology, 1 machine costing $10,000 can replace 1 worker. Given current production levels and technology in the automobile industry, 1 machine costing $10,000 can replace 2 workers. Is this economy Pareto efficient; that is, is it on its production possibilities curve? If not, explain how total output of both

goods can be increased by shifting machines and labor between industries.

4. Consider three ways of helping poor people to buy food, clothing, and shelter. The first way is to pass laws setting price ceilings to keep these basic goods affordable. The second is to have the government distribute coupons that give poor people a discount when they buy these necessities. The third is for the government to distribute income to poor people. Which program is more likely to have a Pareto-efficient outcome? Describe why the other programs are not likely to be Pareto efficient.

5. Suppose the supply of rental apartments is completely inelastic in the short run. Show that imposing a ceiling on rents that is below the equilibrium rent does not cause any inefficiency by demonstrating that total consumer and producer surplus is not reduced by the rent ceiling. If the supply of rental apartments is more elastic in the long run, explain why a ceiling on rents would reduce the total surplus.

6. If you do not know whether you would be able to get a rent-controlled apartment, under what circumstances might you nonetheless vote for rent control? Why would your enthusiasm for rent control wane over time?

Part 3

IMPERFECT MARKETS

Learning Goals

In this chapter, you will learn

1 The key ways many markets fall short of the perfect competition envisioned in the basic competitive model

2 The different forms of imperfect competition and their consequences

3 How imperfect information can affect markets

4 What economists mean by externalities, and how they affect markets

5 What a public good is, and why markets undersupply public goods.

Chapter 11

INTRODUCTION TO IMPERFECT MARKETS

In the two centuries since Adam Smith enunciated the view that markets ensure economic efficiency, economists have investigated the basic competitive model with great care. Nothing they have discovered has shaken their belief that markets are, by and large, the most efficient way to coordinate an economy. However, economists have also found significant ways in which modern economies do not fit the basic competitive model. These differences can cause markets to operate inefficiently, and they may provide a rationale for government involvement in the economy.

Before we can understand the role of government in the economy, we need to understand how the differences between modern economies and the world envisioned in our basic competitive model affect the ways markets work. If competition is less than perfect, do markets still produce efficient outcomes? If they do not produce efficient outcomes, is too much produced or is too little produced? If people do not have enough information about, say, the quality of goods, will markets be efficient? And if the outcomes when information is imperfect are not efficient, what can government do about it? What sorts of policies will improve the situation?

In this part of the book, we address these questions. We begin by outlining four important ways in which some markets may differ from the basic competitive model. These differences can help account for the important role that government plays in our economy. We examine how these differences affect the ability of private markets to efficiently use society's scarce resources. Subsequent chapters explore each of these differences in greater depth. By considering when markets fail to produce efficient outcomes and why, we can greatly extend the range of insights that economics has to offer and better understand some of the dissatisfactions with markets and some of the roles of public policy. And going beyond the competitive model will help us make sense of many of the economic changes associated with new technologies and the information revolution.

As we explore the economics of imperfect markets, the five key concepts introduced in Chapter 1—trade-offs, incentives, exchange, information, and distribution—continue to serve as guides to thinking like an economist. Individuals, firms, and government still face trade-offs when markets are imperfect, though perhaps different ones from those in the world of the basic competitive model, and they must be weighed in any economic analysis. Trade-offs necessitate choices, which we can understand if we focus on incentives. Gaining an understanding of how market imperfections affect the outcome of market exchange will be especially critical. Throughout, we will highlight the effects of market imperfections on not only the level but also the distribution of economic welfare. The basic concepts of economics apply beyond the basic competitive model in which competition is perfect and everyone has all the information they need. In exploring the role of imperfect competition and imperfect information in market economies, economists have continued to find that these foundational concepts are crucial.

Extending the Basic Competitive Model

In Part Two, we made several simplifying assumptions to enable us to focus on key factors that explain how markets work. So that we could better understand how prices and quantities are determined and evaluate the nature of market outcomes, we concentrated on the essence of the market rather than on detailed descriptions of actual markets. In any field, theorizing often ordinarily takes place on a high level of generality.

The main assumptions in the basic competitive model include the following:

1. Firms and individuals take market prices as given—because each is small relative to the market because their decisions do not affect the market price.
2. Individuals and firms have perfect information about the quality and availability of goods, and about the prices of all goods.
3. Actions by an individual or firm do not directly affect other individuals or firms except through prices.
4. Goods can be enjoyed only by the buyer—if I buy and eat a slice of pizza, it is no longer available for you to eat; if you buy a bike, we cannot both use it at the same time.

Frequently, however, we would like to analyze what happens if a firm has the power to set prices, or consumers are uninformed about the quality of different goods, or actions by one individual directly affect others (a cigarette smoker creating secondhand smoke, for example), or there are goods we can all consume simultaneously (like national defense). We can extend our basic competitive model to deal with these cases, and we begin by considering each of our main assumptions in turn.

First, most markets are not as competitive as those envisioned by the basic model. In Part Two, we assumed markets have so many buyers and sellers that no individual household or firm believes its actions will affect the market equilibrium price. The basic competitive model focuses on products such as wheat or pig iron, which may be produced by different firms but are essentially identical and are perfect substitutes for one another. If a firm raises its price slightly above that of other firms, it loses all its customers. In that model, there is no room for brand loyalty, yet it is hard to think of a consumer product without attaching a brand name to it. If BMW raises the price of its cars, it may lose some customers to other makes, but it won't lose them all. A BMW enthusiast would probably pay more for a BMW than for an Audi. Likewise, if Nike charges slightly more than Adidas for running shoes, it will not lose every customer. Because it takes the market price as given, a firm in the competitive model does not need to consider how other firms will react when it considers changing the quantity it produces. However, when BMW and Nike make production and pricing decisions, they must worry about how their rivals will react. In the real world, many firms devote enormous resources to efforts designed to anticipate others' actions and reactions.

Second, buyers and sellers seldom have all the information that the basic competitive model assumes. In the basic competitive model, buyers know everything about what they are buying, whether it is stocks or bonds, a house, a used car, or a refrigerator. Firms know the productivity of each worker they hire; and when workers take employment at a firm, they know exactly what is expected of them in return for the promised pay. Yet in most markets, participants do not have complete information. A buyer of a used car may not know the true condition of the car, a high school student choosing among colleges doesn't have complete information about the quality of the teachers or the availability of courses she desires, and a firm hiring a new worker doesn't know precisely how productive he will be.

Third, firms and consumers bear all the consequences of their actions in the basic competitive model—but not in reality. Whenever an individual or firm can take an action that directly affects others but for which it neither pays nor is paid compensation, economists say that an **externality** is present. (The effect of the action is "external" to the individual or firm.) Externalities are pervasive. A hiker who litters, a driver whose car emits pollution, a child whose play leaves a mess behind, a person who smokes a cigarette in a crowded room, a student who talks during a lecture—each creates externalities. In each case, others—not just the agent—suffer the consequences of the action. Externalities can be thought of as instances when the price system works imperfectly. The hiker is not "charged" for the litter she creates. The car owner does not pay for the pollution his car makes.

While these examples are of negative externalities, externalities also can be positive. A homeowner tending a well-kept garden that provides a benefit to the neighbors creates a positive externality; so does a hiker who picks up litter along a trail.

Fourth, in the basic competitive model, when one person consumes a good, it is not available for others to consume. If John buys a gallon of gas for his car, Sarah cannot also use that gallon of gas. But some goods, called **public goods,** do remain available for others to consume. They represent extreme cases of externalities. (Normally, we think of these as positive externalities—for example, all *benefit* from the provision of national defense. However, some individuals—equally affected— may dislike the public good; for them, it acts like a negative externality.) The consumption (or enjoyment) of a public good by one individual does not subtract from that of other individuals (in this case, consumption is said to be *nonrivalrous*). Public goods also have the property of *nonexcludability*—that is, it costs a great deal to exclude any individual from enjoying the benefits of a public good. The standard example of a public good is national defense. Once the United States is protected from attack, it costs nothing extra to protect each new baby from foreign invasion. Furthermore, it would be virtually impossible to exclude a newborn from the benefits of this protection.

Imperfect competition, imperfect information, externalities, and public goods all represent cases in which the market does not produce economic efficiency. Economists refer to these problems as **market failures** and have studied them closely. The market "fails" not by ceasing to exist but by failing to produce efficient outcomes. Government *may* be able to correct such a market failure and improve economic efficiency. But before considering government policies to correct these failures, we first need to understand clearly how it is that market outcomes may be inefficient.

Though it describes an oversimplified world, the basic competitive model continues to provide important and powerful insights. For that reason, most economists use it as the starting point for building a richer, more complete model of the modern economy. This richer model is the focus of Part Three. In the next several chapters, we will examine how adding the complications of imperfect competition, imperfect information, externalities, and public goods to the basic model increases the ability of economics to explain our economy.

IMPERFECT MARKETS LEAD TO MARKET FAILURES

When the market is perfectly competitive, consumers and firms have perfect information, and there are no externalities (positive or negative) and no public goods, market outcomes will be efficient. When these conditions do not hold, markets are inefficient and there can be a role for government policies that lead to more efficient outcomes.

Imperfect Competition and Market Structure

When economists look at markets, they look first at the **market structure**—that is, how the market is organized. The market structure that formed the basis of the competitive model of Part Two is called **perfect competition.** For example, there are so many wheat farmers (producers) that no individual farmer can realistically hope to move the price of wheat from that produced by the law of supply and demand.

Frequently, however, competition is not "perfect" but limited. Economists group markets in which competition is limited into three broad categories. In the most extreme case, there is no competition: a single firm supplies the entire market. This is called **monopoly.** Your local electrical company may have a monopoly in supplying electricity in your area. In a court case in 1999, Microsoft was found to have a near monopoly in the market for personal computer operating systems. Because the profits of a monopolist would normally attract other businesses into the market, the firm must take advantage of some barrier to entry to maintain its monopoly position. In Chapter 12, we will discuss some of those barriers.

In the second structure, several firms supply the market, so there is *some* competition. This is called **oligopoly.** The automobile industry is an example, with a relatively small number of global producers. The defining characteristic of oligopoly is that the small number of firms forces each to be concerned with how its rivals will react to any action it takes. If General Motors offers low-interest-rate financing, for instance, other companies may feel compelled to match the offer, a predictable response that General Motors will have to take into account before acting. By contrast, a monopolist has no rivals and considers only whether special offers help or hurt itself. And a firm facing perfect competition never needs to resort to any special offer—it can always sell as much as it wants at the market price.

The third market structure contains more firms than an oligopoly but not enough for perfect competition. This is called **monopolistic competition.** An example is the market for laptop computers. IBM, HP, Toshiba, Sony, Gateway, Dell, and others produce their own brand of laptops. Each is slightly different from the others, similar enough that there is considerable competition—so much that profits may be driven down to zero—but different enough to make competition limited and prevent the companies from being price takers. The degree of competition under monopolistic competition is greater than that in oligopoly, because monopolistic competition involves a sufficiently large number of firms that each firm can ignore the reactions of any rival. If one company lowers its price, it may gain a large number of customers. But the number of customers it takes away from any single rival is so small that none of the rivals is motivated to retaliate.

Both oligopolies and monopolistic competition are in-between market structures, allowing some but not perfect competition. They thus are referred to as **imperfect competition.**

Wrap-Up

ALTERNATIVE MARKET STRUCTURES

Perfect competition: Many, many firms, each believing that nothing it does will have any effect on the market price.

Monopoly: One firm.

Imperfect competition: Several firms, each aware that its sales depend on the price it charges and possibly other actions it takes, such as advertising. There are two special cases:

Oligopoly: Sufficiently few firms that each must be concerned with how its rivals will respond to any action it undertakes.

PRICE AND QUANTITY WITH IMPERFECT COMPETITION

In the basic model of perfect competition, each firm takes the market price as given. If one firm tries to raise its price, even slightly, it will lose all of its customers. When competition is imperfect, a firm will lose some but not all of its customers if it charges a slightly higher price. In conditions of imperfect competition, firms do not simply "take" the price as dictated to them by the market. They "make" the price. They are the *price makers.*

Whether a firm is a price taker or a price maker, it tries to maximize profits. In determining output, the firm will compare the extra or **marginal revenue** that it will receive from an extra unit of output with the extra or marginal cost of producing that extra unit. If marginal revenue exceeds marginal cost, it pays to expand output. Conversely, if marginal revenue is less than marginal cost, it pays to reduce output. Whether the firm operates in a market characterized by perfect or imperfect competition, it will produce at the output level at which marginal revenue equals marginal costs.

The essential difference between a firm facing perfect competition and one facing imperfect competition lies in the relationship between marginal revenue and price. For a competitive firm, marginal revenue equals the price. For instance, the marginal revenue received by a wheat farmer for one more bushel of wheat is just the price of a bushel of wheat. But under imperfect competition, a firm knows it cannot simply sell as much as it would like at the current price. The firm recognizes that its demand curve is downward sloping; if it wants to sell more, it has to be more proactive—for example, by lowering its price. Or it might try to shift its demand curve to the right by spending more on advertising. For the sake of simplicity, in this chapter and the next two we will focus on the case in which the firm lowers its price if it wants to increase sales. (Chapter 15 will investigate the role of advertising.) By changing its price, the firm will influence its sales. What needs to be emphasized here is that the firm cannot sell an extra unit of output at the present market price. Thus marginal revenue is not equal to the present market price when competition is imperfect.

In the case of a monopoly, for example, the firm controls the entire market; a doubling of its output therefore doubles industry output, which will have a significant effect on price. If Alcoa, in the days when it had a monopoly on aluminum, had increased its production by 1 percent, the total market supply of aluminum would have increased by 1 percent. If Alcoa leaves its price unchanged, that extra aluminum will not be sold; buyers were already purchasing the quantity they demanded. An increase in market supply will cause the equilibrium price to fall. Market price will continue to fall until the quantity demanded has increased by 1 percent.

How much the price must change as sales change will depend on whether the firm is a monopolist, a monopolistic competitive firm, or an oligopolist. If the firm is a monopolist, it controls the entire market, by definition, so the demand curve it faces is the market demand curve. By contrast, a firm such as PepsiCo will need to know how rivals like Coca-Cola will respond before it can determine how its sales will be affected if it changes its price. In either case, *marginal revenue will be less than price*. To sell more, the firm must lower its price, reducing the revenue it receives on all units that it produces.

To maximize profits, firms will set marginal cost equal to marginal revenue. When competition is imperfect, however, marginal revenue is less than price. Consequently, at the output level that maximizes profit, marginal cost is also less than price. In other words, the market price will be too high—it exceeds the cost of producing the last unit sold. Under conditions of perfect competition, producers would have an incentive to increase production when price exceeds marginal cost: an efficient outcome. Imperfect competition, in contrast, results in too little being produced at too high a price.

GOVERNMENT POLICIES

Because imperfect competition leads to an inefficient outcome, with too little produced at too high a price, government has taken an active role in promoting competition and in limiting the abuses of market power.

Antitrust laws are designed to break up monopolies, to prevent monopolies from forming, and to restrain firms from engaging in practices that restrict competition. For instance, before two large firms in an industry can merge, or before one can acquire another, they must seek government approval. The government will seek to determine whether the merger of the two firms will *significantly* reduce competition. The most recent highly publicized antitrust case involved the U.S. government and Microsoft, with the government arguing that Microsoft had a near monopoly in the market for operating systems and that it had abused that market power—not only setting prices above the competitive levels but also using its market power to deter and destroy rivals.

Internet Connection

THE FEDERAL TRADE COMMISSION

The Federal Trade Commission (FTC) enforces consumer protection and antitrust laws and plays an important role in eliminating unfair or deceptive practices while ensuring that American markets function competitively. The FTC provides articles at www.ftc.gov/bcp/menu-internet.htm on what to watch out for in e-commerce and when making purchases or seeking information over the Internet.

TRADE AND COMPETITION

As a result of the increasing globalization of the world economy, firms must compete with both foreign and domestic rivals. Even a firm that is the sole domestic producer of a product may be unable to take advantage of its monopoly position because of competition from foreign producers. Government actions to open a country to trade can therefore help promote competition. New Zealand provides a case in point.

New Zealand had a long history of restricting imports to protect domestic firms. Since the New Zealand economy was small, many industries had very few firms—sometimes only one. Besides the typical problems that accompany monopolies (too little produced at a price that is too high), domestic firms frequently offered only a narrow range of products. For example, suppose you wanted to buy some auto paint to touch up a scratch on your car. Because New Zealand had a domestic paint producer, imports of paint were restricted. But the small size of the New Zealand market limited the demand for any given type of paint. Consequently, the New Zealand paint industry offered few colors. If your car was an unusual hue, you were out of luck.

In 1984, a new Labour government was elected in New Zealand that implemented a new strategy to improve competition. The government realized that the regulatory structure that had developed to address the inefficiencies of monopoly could be eliminated; competition could be increased simply by removing the country's many trade barriers. There is no need to worry if only a single paint firm is located in New Zealand—that firm's market power will be limited if it must compete with foreign paint producers. Today, consumers can choose from a wide variety of products, and the prices of domestic firms are kept down by competition from foreign firms that can now sell their goods in New Zealand.

In some cases, the government may decide not to break up a firm even if it is a monopoly. It may believe, for instance, that it is more efficient for a single firm to provide the service. In this case, the firm is called a **natural monopoly.** Typically the government establishes a regulatory body to oversee such a monopoly. Industries that have been characterized in the past as *regulated monopolies* include local cable TV, electrical utility, and telephone. Firms in these industries normally must obtain the approval of the regulatory agency before they can raise the price they charge.

In Chapters 12 and 13 we will discuss some of the ways government attempts to limit the power of monopolies and promote competition. The policies that government uses depend on the source of imperfect competition and on the structure of the market.

Fundamentals of Imperfect Markets 2

IMPERFECT COMPETITION

Imperfectly competitive markets are characterized according to their market structure as monopolies, oligopolies, or monopolistic competition. In all cases, firms maximize profits by setting marginal cost equal to marginal revenue. Because marginal revenue is less than the market price, too little is produced at too high a price.

Imperfect Information

The model of perfect competition that was developed in Part Two assumed that market participants, whether consumers, firms, or the government, had *perfect information*. They had full information about the goods being bought and sold. Seldom do we actually approach this standard, and economists have gained new insights into how markets function by incorporating **imperfect information** into their models. Interestingly, economists' understanding of the importance of imperfect information deepened at almost the same time that new technologies improved the ability of firms and households to gather, process, and transmit information.

THE INFORMATION PROBLEM

The basic competitive model assumes that households and firms are well informed: they know their opportunity set, or what is available and at what price. More strikingly, they know every characteristic of every good, including how long it will last. For some purchases, we do have very good information, so the assumption of the basic model is a reasonable one. When I buy my favorite breakfast cereal at the grocery store, I know all I need to know.[1] Typically, though, we must make decisions about what to buy with much less than perfect information.

The model also assumes that consumers know their preferences; that is, they know what they like. They know not only how many oranges they can trade for an apple but also how many oranges they want to trade. In the case of apples and oranges, this assumption may make sense. But how do students know how much they are going to enjoy, or even benefit from, a college education? How does an individual know whether she would like to be a doctor, a lawyer, or a writer? She gets some idea about the different professions by observing those who practice them, but her information is at best incomplete.

According to the basic model, firms too are perfectly well informed. They know the best available technology. They know the productivity of each applicant for a job. They know precisely how hard every worker is working and how good a job each is doing. They know the prices at which inputs can be purchased from every possible supplier (and all the input's characteristics). And they know the prices at which they can sell the goods, not only today but in every possible circumstance in the future.

HOW BIG A PROBLEM?

That individuals and firms are not perfectly well informed is, by itself, not necessarily a telling criticism of the competitive model, just as the observation that markets are not perfectly competitive does not cause us to discard the model. The relevant issues are as follows: Can the competitive model mislead us in these situations? Are there important economic phenomena that can be explained only by taking into account

---

[1]Of course, to gain information about the cereal, I had to try it initially. So even in this example, the information was not automatically available. Often, gaining information about a good requires actually using it.

One benefit of this degree is that it conveys information about its recipient.

imperfect information? Are there important predictions of the model that are incorrect as a result of the assumption that consumers and firms are well informed?

Increasingly, over the past two decades, economists have come to believe that the answer to these questions is yes. For example, college graduates receive a higher income on average than high school graduates, perhaps not only because they have learned things in college that make them more productive but also because their college degree conveys valuable information to employers. Employers cannot easily learn in an interview which applicants for a job will be productive workers. They therefore use a college degree as a criterion to judge applicants. College graduates *are,* on average, more productive workers. But it is wrong to conclude from this that college has necessarily *increased* students' productivity. It may simply have aided firms in sorting those students who are more productive from the less productive.

HOW PRICES CONVEY INFORMATION

The price system provides brilliant solutions for some information problems. We have seen how prices play an important role in coordinating production and communicating information about economic scarcity. Firms do not have to know what John or Julia likes, or what their trade-offs are. The price tells the producer the marginal benefit of producing an extra unit of the good, and that is all the firm needs to know. Similarly, a firm does not need to know how much iron ore is left in Minnesota, the cost of refining iron ore, or a thousand other details. All it needs to know is the price of iron ore. This tells the company how scarce the resource is, and how much effort it should expend in conserving it. Prices and markets provide the basis of the economy's incentive system. But there are some information problems that markets do not handle, or do not handle well. And imperfect information sometimes inhibits the ability of markets to perform the tasks that they carry out so well when information is complete.

MARKETS FOR INFORMATION

Information has value; people are willing to pay for it. In this sense, we can consider information to be a good like any other. There is a market for information, at a price—just as there is a market for labor and a market for capital. Indeed, our economy is sometimes referred to as an *information economy*. And every year, investors spend millions of dollars on newsletters that give them information about stocks, bonds, and other investment opportunities. Magazines sell specialized information about hundreds of goods. One of the major impacts of the growth of the Internet has been to reduce the cost of all types of information.

Yet even with all the new information technologies, the markets for information are far from perfect, and for good reasons. Most obviously information is *not* just like any other good. When you buy a chair, the furniture dealer is happy to let you look at it, sit on it, and decide whether you like it. When you buy information, you cannot do the same. The seller can either say, "Trust me. I'll tell you what you need to know," or show you the information and say, "Here's what I know. If this is what you wanted to know, please pay me." You would rightfully be skeptical in the first scenario and might be unwilling to pay in the second. After you were given the information, what incentive would you have to pay?

e-Insight

INFORMATION, COMPETITION, AND THE INTERNET

The Internet is having a profound effect on consumer choices and on the nature of competition. One way it has done so is by providing consumers with easily accessible information at a low cost. For example, rather than pay a series of time-consuming visits to various car dealers when you want to shop for a car, you can now do your shopping from home over the Internet. Consumers can comparison shop using Web sites that provide car reviews and pricing information. They can even buy a car online and have it delivered to their doorstep. Many economists argue that by increasing the information consumers have, the new information technologies will enable actual markets to more closely approximate the basic competitive model, with its assumption that consumers are fully informed.

The Internet also increases competition. Local retail (bricks-and-mortar) stores must now compete against online sellers. Consumers can easily check prices at various online sellers, and there are even digital agents called "bots" that search Internet sites for the best available deals. Because consumers can comparison shop on the Web with little effort, Internet sellers are forced to offer low prices.

In business-to-business (B2B) commerce, the sheer number of firms linked through the Internet enables larger pools of buyers and sellers to be brought together, creating new marketplaces and lower costs for many businesses. For instance, the major U.S. auto manufacturers are moving their purchasing operations online, forming a marketplace for parts and other items that is estimated to handle almost $250 billion of purchases each year. As competition among parts suppliers increases, the auto manufacturers expect to gain significant cost savings. But some antitrust experts worry that to the extent that the U.S. auto manufacturers *cooperate* in purchasing, they may actually reduce competition among the buyers. Single buyers (called *monopsonists*) or limited competition among buyers is just as bad for economic efficiency as monopoly sellers or limited competition among sellers.

Some cases present a basic problem of credibility. You might think, If a stock tipster *really* knows that a stock's price is going to go up, why should he tell me, even if I pay him for the information? Why doesn't he go out and make his fortune with the information? Or is it that he really is not sure, and would just as soon have me risk my money rather than risk his?

Most important, even after the firm or consumer buys all the information thought to be worth paying for, the information is still far from perfect. Some information is simply too costly to obtain relative to the benefit of having it. So imperfect information is a fact of life, and in Chapter 15 we will examine the ways it can affect economic behavior and the structure of markets.

GOVERNMENT POLICIES

The market inefficiencies resulting from imperfect information can take a number of forms. Government concern about the pitfalls for ill-informed consumers has motivated a number of pieces of **consumer protection legislation.** For example, the Wheeler-Lea Act of 1938 made "deceptive" trade practices illegal and gave the Federal Trade Commission power to stop false and deceptive advertising. Truth-in-lending legislation requires lenders to disclose the true interest rate being charged. Truth-in-packaging legislation makes it less likely that consumers will be misled by what is printed on an item's package.

The Securities and Exchange Commission, which regulates the sale of stocks and bonds, requires the firms selling these securities to disclose a considerable amount of information. Of course, simply publishing the information is not enough—the public must be confident of its accuracy. For that reason, companies must hire accounting firms to audit their financial statements. Not surprisingly, many of the largest busi-

The Enron scandal shocked the American public.

ness scandals in recent years have involved misleading accounting practices. The best-known case is that of the energy-trading firm Enron. Between 1996 and 1999, Enron used accounting tricks to report profits of $2.3 billion to potential investors, while reporting to the U.S. tax authorities that it had lost $3 billion. In one of the many legal cases that resulted from Enron's collapse, the accounting firm Arthur Andersen, once one of the world's five largest, was found guilty of obstructing justice by destroying documents related to its role in auditing and approving Enron's financial statements (the Supreme Court later overturned the conviction on the grounds that the judge's instructions to the jury were too broad). And the Enron case is not unique. In January 2005, McKesson Corporation, the largest drug distributor in the United States, agreed to pay almost $1 billion to former investors who, in a single day in 1999, lost $8.6 billion—the value of McKesson stock had collapsed after it became known that the company had misreported its revenues.

Often, legislation mandating that more information be supplied is of only limited effectiveness. One problem occurs when consumers try to take in and process the information. A cereal manufacturer may disclose not only what is required but also vast amounts of other information, which may or may not be important. How are consumers to know what to pay attention to? They cannot absorb everything. Occasionally, as in the case of warnings about the dangers of smoking, government regulators for this reason have required the disclosures to be of a specific form and lettering size to make them stand out. But making this kind of intervention universal would be, at the very least, extremely costly.

Another problem with outlawing deceptive advertising is the difficulty of drawing a clear line between persuasion and deception. Advertisers are good at walking along the edge of any line—a suggestive hint may be legal but an explicit claim might be called deceptive. Congress or the courts cannot be expected to draw a line between informative and noninformative advertising for every product in the economy.

Most of the problems arising from imperfect information are not easily remedied. For example, firms will have imperfect information concerning potential employees, no matter what the government does. However, the government often must deal with the consequences. Imperfect information can lead to imperfect competition. In some markets, such as the health insurance market, the consequences are severe, and there has been considerable dissatisfaction with the way these markets work. Government has intervened in a variety of ways, but these efforts clearly have not remedied the problems—and some observers question whether they have even improved matters.

Fundamentals of Imperfect Markets 3

IMPERFECT INFORMATION

Consumers and firms must constantly make decisions based on less-than-perfect information. Markets for information exist, but information is not like normal goods—you cannot usually "try before you buy." Many government policies are designed to help improve the information on which consumers and investors base their decisions.

Externalities

Even when there is perfect competition and information, the market may supply too much of some goods and too little of others. One of the reasons for this is externalities. Externalities arise whenever an individual or firm can take an action that directly affects others without paying for a harmful outcome or being paid for a beneficial one. When externalities are present, firms and individuals do not bear all the consequences of their action.

A common example of a negative externality is the air pollution emitted by a factory. The factory benefits from not installing pollution-control devices, which would raise the cost of its product. When firms do not have to pay for the pollution they emit, society as a whole bears the negative consequences. If firms had to pay for their pollution, they would find ways to produce less of it—by adopting cleaner technologies, for instance. Government environmental regulations, which we will discuss in Chapter 18, are usually designed to ensure that firms bear the costs of the pollution they create.

When there are externalities, the market's allocation of goods will be inefficient, because the producer fails to take into account "social costs" in deciding how much to produce. To put it another way, the price of a good such as steel, determined in competitive markets by the law of supply and demand, reflects only *private costs,* the out-of-pocket costs to the firms. If firms do not have to pay *all* the costs (including the costs of pollution), equilibrium prices will be lower and output higher than they would be if firms took social costs into account. When the production of a good like steel entails a negative externality—such as smoke and its effects on the air—the market level of production is too high.

The inefficiency of market outcomes in the presence of externalities can be understood by considering an important characteristic of market outputs in the basic competitive model. There, the market price is equal both to the value consumers place on the last unit of output and to the cost to firms of producing that last unit. Thus, at the margin, the value of the last good produced is just sufficient to cover the costs of producing it. When an externality is present, this balance no longer holds. If the price consumers pay does not fully reflect the costs of producing the good (a negative externality), consumers will demand too much of the good and too much will be produced. If there are social benefits in addition to the private benefits to consumers (a positive externality), too little will be produced.

GOVERNMENT POLICIES TOWARD EXTERNALITIES

Because externalities lead to market inefficiencies, they can justify the government's intervention in markets. The government can prevent the overproduction of goods that accompanies negative externalities either by establishing regulations (for instance, environmental regulations that restrict the levels of pollution) or by providing incentives (for instance, imposing fees or fines on polluters).

practical matter, this can be done only on toll roads, and ironically, the tollbooths often contribute to the congestion.[2]

Many of the goods that are publicly provided, such as education and health services, have high costs associated with providing the service to additional individuals. For most of these goods, exclusion is also relatively easy. In fact, many of these goods and services are provided privately in some countries, or provided both publicly and privately. Though they are provided publicly in this country, they are not *pure* public goods, in the term's technical sense.

Private markets undersupply public goods. If a shipowner uses a port near which a lighthouse should be located, he could weigh the costs and benefits of constructing the lighthouse. But if there were one large shipowner and many smaller owners, it would not pay any one of the small owners to build the lighthouse; and the large shipowner, in deciding whether to construct the lighthouse, would take into account only the benefits she would receive, not the benefits to the small shipowners. If the costs of construction exceeded the benefits she alone would receive, she would not build the lighthouse. But if the benefits accruing to *all* the shipowners, large and small, were taken into account, those benefits might exceed the costs. It would then be desirable to build the lighthouse.

One can imagine a voluntary association of shipowners getting together to construct a lighthouse in these circumstances. But what happens if some small shipowner refuses to contribute, thinking that even if he does not contribute, the lighthouse will still be built anyway? This is the **free-rider problem** that accompanies public goods; because it is difficult to preclude anyone from using them, those who benefit from the goods have an incentive to avoid paying for them. Every shipowner has an incentive to free ride on the efforts of others. When too many decide to do this, the lighthouse will not be built.

Governments bring an important advantage to bear on the problem of public goods. They have the power to coerce citizens to pay for them. There might be *some* level of purchase of public goods—lighthouses, highways, parks, even police or fire services—in the absence of government intervention. But such societies would be better off if the level of production were increased, and if citizens were forced to pay for that increased level of public services through taxes.

Fundamentals of Imperfect Markets 5

PUBLIC GOODS

A pure public good can be provided to an additional person at a zero marginal cost and it is impossible to exclude people from receiving the good. Private markets undersupply public goods because of the free-rider problem.

---

[2]New technologies enable drivers to be charged for tolls without stopping at tollbooths. Scanners identify cars equipped with special tags as they pass, automatically billing the driver. Thus, new technologies can convert what was a public good into a private good.

Looking Ahead

We have now examined four situations in which markets may fail to develop an efficient allocation of society's scarce resources. In each of these cases—imperfect competition, imperfect information, externalities, and public goods—a role for government exists. Government can employ a variety of policies to promote competition, address the problems created by externalities and imperfect information, and supply public goods.

In the next several chapters, we will study market failures in more detail, beginning, in Chapter 12, with the analysis of imperfect competition—including the extreme case, that of a monopoly. Chapter 13 shows how public policy mitigates the results of imperfections of competition. Subsequent chapters will deal with strategic behavior when competition is imperfect (Chapter 14), with imperfect information in the product market (Chapter 15), and with the effects of imperfect competition and imperfect information on labor markets (Chapter 16).

Review and Practice

SUMMARY

1. By and large, private markets allocate resources efficiently. However, in a number of areas they do not, as in the cases of imperfect competition, imperfect information, externalities, and public goods.
2. Economists identify four broad categories of market structure: perfect competition, monopoly, oligopoly, and monopolistic competition.
3. When competition is imperfect, the market will produce too little of a good and the market price will be too high.
4. The basic competitive model assumes that participants in the market have perfect information about the goods being bought and sold and their prices. However, information is often imperfect.
5. Individuals and firms produce too much of a good with a negative externality, such as air or water pollution, since they do not bear all the costs. They produce too little of a good with positive externalities since they cannot receive all the benefits.
6. Public goods are goods that cost little or nothing for an additional individual to enjoy, but that cost a great deal to exclude an individual from enjoying them. National defense and lighthouses are two examples. Free markets underproduce public goods.

KEY TERMS

externality
public goods
market failures
market structure
perfect competition
monopoly
oligopoly
monopolistic competition
imperfect competition
marginal revenue
antitrust laws
natural monopoly
imperfect information
consumer protection legislation
free-rider problem

REVIEW QUESTIONS

1. What is the difference between perfect competition and imperfect competition?
2. What does it mean when an economist says that monopoly output is "too little" or a monopoly price is "too high"? By what standard? Compared with what?
3. What role does information play in the basic competitive model? How does the market for information differ from the market for a good such as wheat?
4. What is an example of a positive externality? of a negative externality? Why are goods with negative externalities often overproduced? Why are goods with positive externalities often underproduced? Give an example for each.
5. What sorts of policies can government use to address the problem of externalities?
6. What two characteristics define a public good? Give an example. Why will private markets not supply the efficient level of public goods?

PROBLEMS

1. Which do you think best describes each of the following markets—perfect competition, monopoly, oligopoly, or monopolistic competition?
   (a) The market for automobiles
   (b) The market for soy beans
   (c) The market for portable music players
   (d) The market for dining out in a large city
2. Briefly explain why marginal revenue is equal to the market price for a firm in a perfectly competitive market but is less than the current market price for a firm in an imperfectly competitive market.
3. Colleges and universities compete for students, and students shop for colleges. Is the market for college placements characterized by perfect competition? Does Harvard face a horizontal demand curve or a downward-sloping demand curve? Is the market for college placements characterized by perfect information? Describe how students' information about colleges might be imperfect. Describe how colleges' information about prospective students might be imperfect.

4. Each of the situations below involves an externality. Tell whether it is a positive or a negative externality, or both, and explain why a free market will overproduce or underproduce the good in question.
   (a) A business undertaking research and development projects
   (b) A business that discharges waste into a nearby river
   (c) A concert given in the middle of a large city park
   (d) An individual who smokes cigarettes in a meeting
5. When some activity causes a negative externality like pollution, would it be a good idea to ban the activity altogether? Why or why not? (Hint: Consider marginal costs and benefits.)
6. Do highways provide an example of a public good? Can you describe a situation in which the marginal costs of an additional driver on the highway might be high? How might society deal with this problem?
7. Many highways have designated car pool or high-occupancy lanes. Generally, only cars containing at least two people can use these lanes. Single drivers are fined heavily if they are caught using these lanes. With new technologies, it is possible to charge drivers using car pool lanes by recording identifying markings on the car and billing the owners. Would allowing single drivers to pay to use car pool lanes increase economic efficiency? Explain.
8. Group projects are often assigned in classes, with everyone in the group receiving the same grade for the project. Explain why a free-rider problem might arise in this situation.

Learning Goals

In this chapter, you will learn

Chapter 12

MONOPOLY, MONOPOLISTIC COMPETITION, AND OLIGOPOLY

As we discussed in Chapter 11, many markets in our economy are not well described by the perfectly competitive model. For years, AT&T was the only long-distance telephone carrier. Kodak controlled the market for film, and Alcoa the market for aluminum. Some firms so dominated a product that their brand name became synonymous with the product—for example, Kleenex, or Jell-O. These firms did not simply take the market price as given: they recognized that their actions could affect the market price. And the power to affect prices will influence a firm's decision about how much to produce.

In some industries, a handful of firms dominate the market, producing similar but not identical products: think of soft drinks (Coca-Cola, Pepsi, Canada Dry) or running shoes (Nike, Adidas, Reebok). Other industries may include a large number of firms, each producing a similar but slightly different product. When one firm raises its price a little—say, by 2 or 3 percent—it loses some customers, but it does not lose all customers, as would happen under perfect competition. If such a firm lowers its price by 2 or 3 percent, it gains additional customers but not the entire market.

Picking up where the discussion in Chapter 11 left off, this chapter explores markets in which there is either limited competition or no competition at all. It explains why output in these markets is typically lower than it would be under more competitive conditions, and it identifies the various factors that limit competition.

Monopoly Output

Economists' concerns about monopolies and other forms of restricted competition stem mainly from their observation that the output, or supply, of firms within these market structures is less than that of firms that face perfect competition, and prices

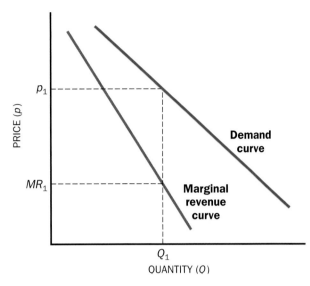

Figure 12.1

DEMAND CURVE AND MARGINAL REVENUE CURVE FOR A MONOPOLIST

Because the monopolist faces a downward-sloping demand curve, marginal revenue is less than price. To sell an extra unit of output, the monopolist must accept a lower price on every unit sold. At the quantity Q_1, the market price is p_1 and the marginal revenue is MR_1.

are higher as well. To understand these concerns, we consider a monopolist that charges the same price to all its customers, and show how it decides on its level of output.

A monopolist, just like a competitive firm, will try to maximize profits. Both compare the marginal revenue and the marginal cost of producing more. For both, the basic principle for determining output is the same. Each produces at the output level at which marginal revenue equals marginal cost. The key difference lies in their marginal revenue. When a competitive firm decides on its output level, it takes the market price as given. Such a firm faces a horizontal demand curve—it can sell as much as it wants at the market price. In contrast, the monopolist is the sole supplier to the market, so its demand is the *market demand curve*. As we have already seen, market demand curves are downward sloping. The monopolist can increase its sales only by lowering its price.

Because the monopolist faces a downward-sloping demand curve, its marginal revenue is not equal to the market price. To understand why, we can break the marginal revenue a monopolist receives from producing one more unit into two separate components. First, the firm receives revenue from selling the additional output. This additional revenue is just the market price. But to sell more, the monopolist must reduce its price. Unless it does so, it cannot sell the extra output. Marginal revenue is the price it receives from the sale of the one additional unit *minus* the loss in revenue from the price reduction on all other units. Thus, for a monopolist, the marginal revenue for producing one extra unit is always less than that unit's price.

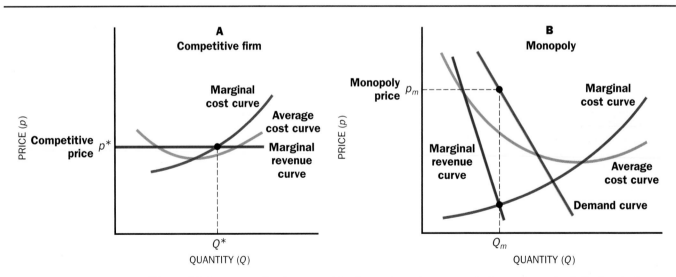

Figure 12.2

MARGINAL REVENUE EQUALS MARGINAL COST

A perfectly competitive firm gains or loses exactly the market price (p^*) when it changes the quantity produced by one unit. To maximize profits, the firm produces the quantity where marginal cost equals marginal revenue, which in the competitive case also equals price. Panel B shows the downward-sloping marginal revenue curve for a monopolist. A monopolist also chooses the level of quantity where marginal cost equals marginal revenue. For a monopolist, however, marginal revenue is lower than price.

In Chapter 7, we used a graph that showed the firm's marginal cost together with the market price to determine how much output the firm should produce to maximize profits (see Figure 7.3). We can use a similar graph to illustrate how much a monopoly will produce, once we recognize that for a monopolist, marginal revenue will be less than the market price.

Figure 12.1 shows the relationship between the demand curve and the marginal revenue of the monopolist. If the monopolist wants to sell the quantity Q_1, the market price must be p_1. Marginal revenue is less than price, so the marginal revenue curve lies below the demand curve. At the quantity Q_1, marginal revenue is MR_1, less than the price p_1.

Figure 12.2A shows the output decision of a competitive firm. Marginal revenue is just equal to the market price, p^*. The competitive firm produces at Q^*, where marginal cost is equal to the market price. Panel B shows the output decision of a monopolist. Marginal revenue is always less than price. The monopolist produces an output of Q_m, since at that output level, marginal cost is equal to marginal revenue. Both the monopolist and the competitive firm maximize profits by producing where marginal cost equals marginal revenue. The difference is that for the monopolist, marginal revenue is less than price.

Note that in the case of a monopolist, since marginal revenue is less than price and marginal revenue is equal to marginal cost, marginal cost is less than price. The price is what individuals are willing to pay for an extra unit of the product; it measures the marginal benefit to the consumer of an extra unit. Thus, the marginal benefit of an extra unit exceeds the marginal cost of producing that extra unit. This is the fundamental reason why monopolies reduce economic efficiency.

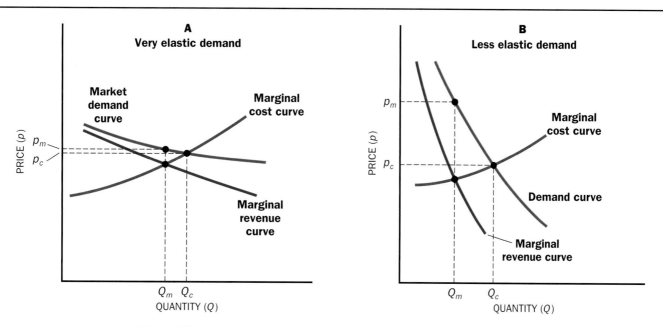

Figure 12.3

MONOPOLY AND THE ELASTICITY OF DEMAND

In panel A, a monopoly faces a very elastic market demand; prices therefore do not fall much as output increases, and monopoly price is not much more than the competitive price. In panel B, showing a monopoly that faces a less elastic market demand, price falls quite a lot as output increases, and the monopolist maximizes profit at a price substantially above the competitive price.

The extent to which output is curtailed depends on the magnitude of the difference between marginal revenue and price. This in turn depends on the shape of the demand curve. When demand curves are very elastic (relatively flat), prices do not fall much when output increases. As shown in Figure 12.3A, marginal revenue is not much less than price. The firm produces at Q_m, where marginal revenue equals marginal cost. Q_m is slightly less than the competitive output, Q_c, where price equals marginal cost. When demand curves are less elastic, as in panel B, prices may fall a considerable amount when output increases, and then the extra revenue the firm receives from producing an extra unit of output will be much less than the price received from selling that unit.

The larger the elasticity of demand, the smaller the discrepancy between marginal revenue and price.

THE FIRM'S SUPPLY DECISION

All firms maximize profits at the point where marginal revenue (the revenue from selling an extra unit of the product) equals marginal cost. For a competitive firm, marginal revenue equals price. For a monopoly, marginal revenue is less than price.

AN EXAMPLE: THE ABC-MENT COMPANY

Table 12.1 gives the demand curve facing the ABC-ment Company, which has a monopoly on the production of cement in its area. There is a particular price at which it can sell each level of output. As it lowers its price, it can sell more cement. Local builders will, for instance, use more cement and less wood and other materials in constructing a house.

For the sake of simplicity, we assume cement is sold in units of 1,000 cubic yards. At a price of $10,000 per unit (of 1,000 cubic yards), the firm sells 1 unit; at a price

TABLE 12.1

DEMAND CURVE FACING THE ABC-MENT COMPANY

Cubic yards (thousands)	Price	Total revenues	Marginal revenues	Total costs	Marginal costs
1	$10,000	$10,000	$8,000	$15,000	$2,000
2	$ 9,000	$18,000	$6,000	$17,000	$3,000
3	$ 8,000	$24,000	$4,000	$20,000	$4,000
4	$ 7,000	$28,000	$2,000	$24,000	$5,000
5	$ 6,000	$30,000	0	$29,000	$6,000
6	$ 5,000	$30,000		$35,000	

of $9,000, it sells 2 units; and at a price of $8,000, 3 units. The third column of the table shows the total revenues at each of these levels of production. The total revenues are just price multiplied by quantity. The marginal revenue from producing an extra unit (of 1,000 cubic yards) is just the difference between, say, the revenues received at 3 units and 2 units or 2 units and 1 unit. Note that in each case, the marginal revenue is less than the price.

Figure 12.4 shows the firm's demand and marginal revenue curves, using data from Table 12.1. At each level of output, the marginal revenue curve lies below the demand curve. As can be seen from the table, not only does price decrease as output increases, but so does marginal revenue.

The output at which marginal revenue equals marginal cost—the output chosen by the profit-maximizing monopolist—is denoted by Q_m. In our example, $Q_m = 4,000$ cubic yards. When the number of cubic yards increases from 3,000 to 4,000, the marginal revenue is $4,000, and so is the marginal cost. At this level of output, the price, p_m, is $7,000 (per 1,000 cubic yards), which is considerably in excess of marginal costs, $4,000. Total revenues, $28,000, are also in excess of total costs, $24,000.[1]

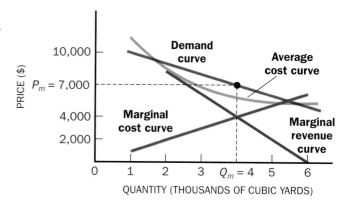

Figure 12.4

DEMAND AND MARGINAL REVENUE

At each level of output, the marginal revenue curve lies below the demand curve.

MONOPOLY PROFITS

Monopolists maximize their profits by setting marginal revenue equal to marginal cost. The total level of monopoly profits can be seen in two ways, as shown in Figure 12.5. Panel A shows total revenues and total costs (from Table 12.1) for each level of output of the ABC-ment Company. The difference between revenues and costs is profits—the distance between the two curves. This distance is maximized at the output $Q_m = 4,000$ cubic yards. We can see that at this level of output, profits are $4,000 ($28,000 − $24,000). Panel B calculates profits using the average cost diagram. Total profits are equal to the profit per unit multiplied by the number of units produced. The profit per unit is the difference between the unit price and the average cost, and total monopoly profits is the shaded area *ABCD*. Again, the sum is $4,000: ($7,000 − $6,000) × 4.

A monopolist enjoys an extra return because it has been able to reduce its output and increase its price from the level that would have prevailed under competition. This return is called a **pure profit.** Because these payments do not elicit greater effort or production on the part of the monopolist (in fact, they derive from the monopolist's *reducing* the output from what it would be under competition), they are also called **monopoly rents.**

---

[1] In this example, the firm is indifferent to the choice between producing 3,000 or 4,000 cubic yards. If the marginal cost of producing the extra output exceeds $4,000 by a little, then it will produce 3,000 cubic yards; if the marginal cost is a little less than $4,000, then it will produce 4,000 cubic yards.

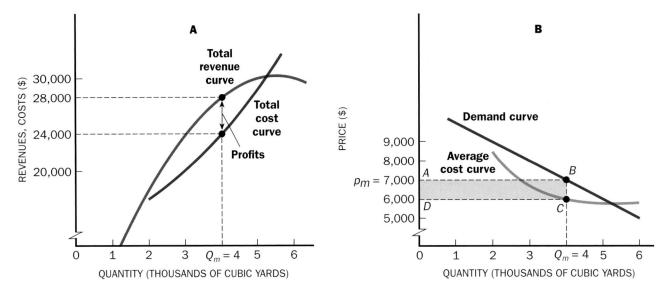

Figure 12.5

PRICE EXCEEDING AVERAGE
COST LEADS TO PROFIT

Panel A shows profits to be the distance between the total revenue and total cost curves, maximized at the output $Q_m = 4{,}000$ cubic yards. Profits occur when the market price is above average cost, as in panel B, so that the company is (on average) making a profit on each unit it sells. Monopoly profits are the area *ABCD*, which is average profit per unit times the number of units sold.

PRICE DISCRIMINATION

The basic objective of monopolists is to maximize profits, and they accomplish this by setting marginal revenue equal to marginal cost, so price exceeds marginal cost. Monopolists can also engage in a variety of other practices to increase their profits. Among the most important is **price discrimination:** that is, charging different prices to different customers or in different markets.

Figure 12.6 shows a monopolist setting marginal revenue equal to marginal cost in the United States and in Japan. The demand curves in the two countries are different. Therefore, though marginal costs are the same, the firm will charge different prices for the same good in the two countries. (By contrast, in competitive markets, price equals marginal cost, so that regardless of the shape of the demand curve, price remains the same except for the different costs of delivering the good to each market.) Because prices in the two countries differ, middleman firms will enter the market, buying the product in the country with the low price and selling it in the other country. A company may attempt to thwart the middlemen—as many Japanese companies do—by, for instance, having distinct labels on the two products and refusing to provide service or honor any guarantees outside the country in which the good is originally delivered.

Within a country, a monopolist can also practice price discrimination *if* resale is difficult and *if* it can distinguish between buyers with high and low elasticities of demand. Because the retransmission of electricity is restricted, an electricity company can make its charge for each kilowatt hour depend on how much electricity the

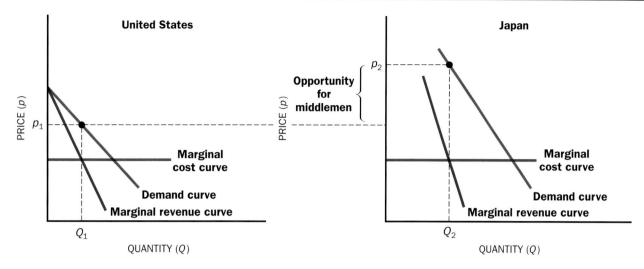

Figure 12.6

PRICE DISCRIMINATION

A monopolist that sells products in two different countries may find itself facing different demand curves. Though it sets marginal revenue equal to the same marginal cost in both countries, it will charge different prices.

customer uses. If the company worries that large customers charged the same high prices as its small customers might install their own electric generators, or switch to some other energy source, it may lower the price to them. An airline with a monopoly on a particular route may not know whether a customer is buying a ticket for business purposes or for a holiday trip, but by charging more for refundable tickets or tickets purchased at the last minute, it can effectively discriminate between business travelers and vacationers. Business customers are more likely to need the flexibility of a refundable ticket or to make their travel plans at the last minute, while vacationers have many alternatives. They can travel elsewhere, on another day, or by car or train. Such business practices enable the monopolist to enjoy greater profits than it could if it charged a single price in the market. Firms facing imperfect competition also engage in these practices, as we will see. Airlines again provide a telling example. Though the Robinson-Patman Act, which Congress passed in 1936, was designed to restrict price discrimination, it is only partially successful.

Economies of Scale and Natural Monopolies

The technology needed to produce a good can sometimes result in a market with only one or very few firms. For example, it would be inefficient to have two firms construct power lines on each street in a city, with one company delivering electricity to one house and another company to the house next door. Likewise, in most locales, there is only one gravel pit or concrete plant. These situations are called **natural monopolies.**

SOUTH AFRICA, AIDS, AND PRICE DISCRIMINATION

In perfectly competitive and well-functioning markets, goods cannot be sold at two different prices. Those who purchased the good at the low price could resell the good in the high-price market, making a pure profit. But in some markets, reselling the good is difficult; in others, governments prohibit or limit resale.

Research and testing account for the major cost of producing drugs. These are fixed costs that the drug manufacturers recoup by charging prices that are considerably in excess of the manufacturing costs. If they can practice price discrimination, the price they charge in each market will depend on the price elasticity *in that market*. But if they worry about resale, they may charge the same price in all markets.

Drug companies have developed some effective remedies against AIDS—not cures but treatments that can substantially prolong life. They charge $10,000 and more a year for treatment, a cost few in the developing countries can afford. The actual cost of manufacturing the drugs is much, much less. But the drug companies have been reluctant to sell the drugs at lower prices in these countries for two reasons. They worried that it would lower profits *in those countries;* and, probably more importantly, they worried about resale, which would lower profits in their own home markets (the United States, Europe). But charging high prices in, say, South Africa, the country with one of the highest incidence of HIV infection in the world, in effect condemned millions in that country to a premature death. Naturally, South Africa balked. It passed a law allowing the importation of drugs at lower prices, drugs possibly made by manufacturers that had ignored standard patent protections. The drug companies sued on the grounds that the law violated their basic economic rights. But protesters around the world argued that intellectual property rights must be designed to balance the rights of potential users and the rights of producers, that the benefits to the poor in Africa far outweighed the loss in profits. In April 2001 they successfully pressured the drug companies to drop their suit against South Africa.

Protesters in South Africa objected to the high price of AIDS drugs.

A natural monopoly occurs whenever the average costs of production for a single firm decline as output increases up to levels beyond those likely to emerge in the market. When the average costs of production fall as the scale of production increases, we say there are economies of scale, a concept first introduced in Chapter 6. In Figure 12.7, the demand curve facing a monopoly intersects the average cost curve at an output level at which average costs are still declining. At large enough outputs, average costs might start to increase; but that level of output is irrelevant to the actual market equilibrium. For instance, firms in the cement industry have U-shaped average cost curves, and the level of output at which costs are minimized is quite high. Accordingly, in smaller, isolated communities, there is a natural monopoly in cement.

A natural monopolist is protected by the knowledge that it can undercut its potential rivals. Since entrants typically are smaller and average costs decline with size, the average costs of new firms are higher. Therefore, the monopolist feels relatively immune from the threat of entry. So long as it does not have that worry, it acts like any other monopolist, setting marginal revenue equal to marginal cost.

In some cases, even when a market is occupied by a natural monopolist, competition can still exist *for the market*. Competition to be that single supplier is so keen that price is bid down to average cost, at p_r. If the firm were to charge a slightly higher price, another firm would enter the market, steal the entire market with its lower price, and still make a profit. Markets for which there is such fierce competition are said to be *contestable*. Contestability requires that sunk costs be low or zero. If they are significant, a firm that entered the market could be undercut by the incumbent firm, which might lower price to its marginal cost (since so long as price exceeds marginal cost, it makes a profit on the last unit sold). The lower prices that result are sometimes referred to as a *price war,* and the result of a price war is that the entrant encounters a loss—when set equal to marginal cost, price is substantially below average cost. The entrant knows that even if it leaves at this juncture, it loses its sunk costs, which are, by definition, the expenditures that are not recovered when the firm shuts down. But anticipating this outcome, the potential rival does not enter the market. Thus, despite sustained current profits, other firms may choose not to enter the market. In fact, sunk costs appear to be sufficiently important that few markets are close to perfectly contestable. Even in the airline industry, where sunk costs are relatively low—airlines can fly new planes into markets that seem profitable or out of markets that seem unprofitable—they act as a sufficiently large barrier to entry that there are sustained profits in certain routes, especially those out of airline hubs (like American Airlines' hub in Dallas–Fort Worth). Just as most markets are not perfectly competitive, so most natural monopolies are not perfectly contestable, though the threat of competition (or potential competition) may limit the extent to which an incumbent monopolist exercises its monopoly power.

Whether a particular industry is a natural monopoly depends on the size of the output at which average costs are minimized relative to the size of the market.

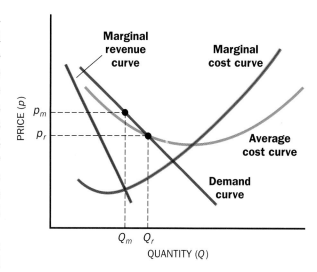

Figure 12.7

NATURAL MONOPOLY

In a natural monopoly, average cost curves are downward sloping in the relevant range of output. A firm can charge the monopoly price p_m. If the market is *contestable,* potential competition prevents the firm from charging a price higher than average costs. The equilibrium price is p_r.

The size of the market depends largely on transportation costs. If, somehow, the cost of transporting cement were lowered to close to zero, then there would be a national cement market. Many firms then would be competing against each other—the size of the national market is far larger than the output at which average costs are minimized.

The size of output at which costs are minimized depends in part on the magnitude of fixed costs. Since research is a fixed cost, its growing importance in many industries has increased the size of output at which average costs are minimized. At the same time, new technologies and business arrangements are enabling many firms to reduce their fixed costs. Today, firms need not have a personnel department for routine matters like paying checks; they can contract for such services as needed.

Because both technology and transportation costs can change over time, the status of an industry as a natural monopoly also can change. Telephone service used to be a natural monopoly. Telephone messages were transmitted over wires, and installing and using duplicate lines would have been inefficient. As the demand for telephone services increased, and as alternative technologies such as satellites and cell phones developed, telephone services ceased to be a natural monopoly. Today, consumers in most communities can choose from among several firms that provide telephone service.

Assessing the Degree of Competition

In the real world, few industries match the extreme cases of monopoly and perfect competition. Usually industries have some degree of competition. How then should that degree of competition in an industry be assessed?

One way to do this is to ask, What will happen if a firm in that industry raises its price? How much will sales of its product fall? In other words, what is the elasticity of demand for the firm's output? The lower the elasticity of demand—the less the quantity demanded falls when price is increased—the greater the firm's market power.

Two factors affect the elasticity of the firm's demand curve and, therefore, its market power. The first is the number of firms in the industry—more generally, how concentrated production is within a few firms. The second is how different the goods produced by the various firms in the industry are.

NUMBER OF FIRMS IN THE INDUSTRY

Competition is likely to be greater when there are many firms in an industry (textiles, shoes) than when a few companies dominate (home refrigerators and freezers, greeting cards, soft drinks). Table 12.2 gives the percentage of output that is

Table 12.2

DEGREE OF COMPETITION IN VARIOUS INDUSTRIES

	Market share of top 4 firms (percent)
Motor vehicle manufacturers	
Book publishers	41.8
Grocery stores	30.9
Electronic shopping and mail-order houses	19.0
Air transportaation	18.7
Furniture stores	8.1
Truck transportation	7.6
Florists	1.7
SOURCE: 2002 Economic Census (www.census.gov/epcd/www/concentration.html).	

produced by the top four firms in a variety of industries ranging from books to furniture. This fraction is called the **four-firm concentration ratio,** one of several measures used to study industry concentration. When the four-firm percentage is high, as in the automobile or book publishing industry, companies have considerable market power. When it is low, as in the case of furniture or florists, market power is low; each firm faces a practically horizontal demand curve.[2]

PRODUCT DIFFERENTIATION

The amount of competition also depends on the extent of differences between the products of an industry. In some industries, the goods produced are essentially identical, as in the case of agricultural goods such as wheat and corn. More typically, the firms in an industry with imperfect competition produce goods that are **imperfect substitutes**—goods sufficiently similar that they can be used for many of the same purposes, but different in ways that reflect consumer preferences. Kellogg's Corn Flakes and the store brand may look alike, but more people purchase the Kellogg's version, even though it is more expensive. Many of the goods people buy belong to clusters of imperfect substitutes: beverages (Coke, Pepsi, and store-brand colas), cars (Toyota Camry, Honda Accord, Ford Taurus, and other four-door sedans), clothing (Land's End, L.L. Bean, and Eddie Bauer), computers, cameras, telephone service, building materials, and many more. Economists refer to this phenomenon as **product differentiation.**

Because product differentiation is a source of market power, firms devote considerable effort to producing goods that are slightly different from those of their

---

[2]In both theory and practice, a critical issue in evaluating the extent of competition is defining the relevant market.

e-Insight

NETWORK EXTERNALITIES, THE NEW ECONOMY, AND MONOPOLY POWER

Network externalities arise whenever an individual benefits from an increase in the number of individuals that are part of the network. A telephone is not much use if there is no one at the other end of the line. The value of a telephone is increased as more people have telephones.

Assume there are two different telephone systems that do not interconnect. A new subscriber having to decide between them is likely to sign up with the one with the larger number of subscribers. Thus, a firm that is initially in the lead will, over time, increase its dominance; an entrant will find it difficult to make headway. And this in turn will enable the dominant company to exercise monopoly power. It can charge a price considerably in excess of its costs of production without worrying about a new entrant coming in and stealing its customers.

Government can limit the ability of this firm to abuse its monopoly power by imposing restrictions—for example, by insisting that the dominant telephone network allow an entrant to interconnect, so that the subscribers in the new network can talk to the subscribers of the dominant network. Effective enforcement of these restrictions may be difficult, however; for example, the dominant firm might provide low-quality interconnectivity but blame the problems on the entrant.

The problem of network externalities is common in the new economy. If more people use the Windows operating system, then independent software developers will write more applications that work with Windows. If relatively few people use Apple's operating system (or Unix), then developers have little incentive to write software that works on that operating system. But if there are many applications that work on Windows, and few that work on Apple, customers will be induced to employ Windows. In fact, Windows has become the dominant operating system: more than 90 percent of all personal computers use it.

But such market dominance almost invites abuse, and Microsoft evidently found the invitation difficult to resist. Such abuse can take a number of forms. Many in the software industry realized that Microsoft's market power would be reduced if they could create a computer language that would enable programs to work on many alternative operating systems with equal, or almost equal, effectiveness. Sun Microsystems developed Java to do just that. Had this effort been successful, it would have broken the network externality. Microsoft sought to frustrate these efforts by developing a version of Java that was specifically adapted to Windows.

Another innovation that might have served as a platform for other applications and been applicable across operating systems was Netscape, an early entrant into Internet browsers. Microsoft sought to quash Netscape, not only by developing its own competing browser but also by delivering its browser free and insisting that computer manufacturers who purchased its operating system (to be installed on the computers they sell) *not* install Netscape as well. (This stipulation is called an *exclusionary practice.*) Microsoft's behavior led to legal suits being filed against it by the U.S. Justice Department, as well as by several individual states. As a result of these challenges, Microsoft agreed to stop some of its abusive practices; however, the company has faced additional legal problems in Europe, where the European Union Commission has found the company guilty of exploiting its monopoly power in the market for media players. Microsoft must now offer a version of its Windows XP operating system in Europe that does not include its media player software.

competitors. When goods are perfect substitutes, individuals will choose whichever is cheapest. In an imaginary world where all brands of cornflakes really are perfect substitutes for all consumers, they would all sell at the same price. By contrast, if most consumers view the different brands as imperfect substitutes, the demand curve facing each firm will be downward sloping, which means that each firm has some degree of market power.

Equilibrium with Monopolistic Competition

In most industries there is some but limited competition. The number of firms in the industry is perhaps the most important determinant of the nature of competition. If the fixed costs are large—not so large as to result in a single firm but sufficiently large that there are only two, three, or four firms—then the outcome is a natural oligopoly. We discuss oligopolies in the next section; we here consider the case in which fixed costs are relatively small—sufficiently small that the numerous firms drive profits to zero, but sufficiently large that only a single firm produces any single product. However, because these products are *close* but not perfect substitutes, each firm faces a downward-sloping demand curve. This is the case of monopolistic competition, first analyzed by Edward Chamberlin of Harvard University in 1933.

The market for women's dress shoes is one such industry. The producers include Steve Madden, Bass, Diverse, Naturalizer, Bruno Magli, Nine West, and many more. No two firms produce exactly the same shoes, but the shoes made by the different companies are close substitutes. Each producer faces a downward-sloping demand curve, but each firm has a small portion of the overall market. The market for fine pens provides another example. There are many manufacturers (Montblanc, Parker, Cross, Aurora, Pelikan, etc.). Each produces pens that differ from the pens of the others, each has a downward-sloping demand curve, and each is small relative to the total market for fine writing instruments.

Figure 12.8 illustrates a market in which there is monopolistic competition. Assume initially that all firms are charging the same price, say p_1. If one firm were to charge a slightly lower price, it would steal some customers away from other businesses. And if it should raise its price above that of its rivals, it would lose customers to them. Each firm assumes that the prices charged by other firms will remain unchanged as it changes its price or the quantity it produces. The demand curve facing each firm is thus the one shown in the figure.

In deciding how much to produce, the firm sets marginal revenue equal to marginal cost. The market equilibrium is (p_1, Q_1), with marginal revenue equaling marginal cost. In the equilibrium depicted in the figure, price exceeds average costs. One can think of this situation as a sort of minimonopoly, where each firm has a monopoly on its own brand name or its own store location.

But if existing firms are earning monopoly profits, there is an incentive for new competitors to enter the market until profits are driven to zero, as in the perfectly competitive model. *This is the vital distinction between monopolies and firms in monopolistic competition.* In both cases, firms face downward-sloping demand curves. In both cases, they set marginal revenue equal to marginal cost. But monopolistic competition raises no barriers to entry, which continues so long as profits are positive. As firms enter, each firm's share of the industry demand is reduced. The demand curve of each firm thus shifts to the left, as depicted in panel B. This process continues until the demand curve just touches the average cost curve, at point (p_e, Q_e), where profits are zero.

The figure also shows the firm's marginal revenue and marginal cost curves. As we have said, the firm sets its marginal revenue equal to its marginal cost. This equality

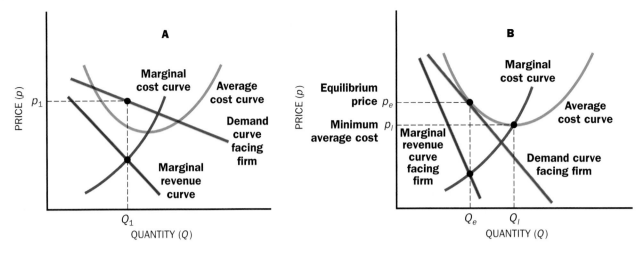

Figure 12.8

PROFIT MAXIMIZING FOR A MONOPOLISTIC COMPETITOR

A monopolistic competitor chooses the quantity it will produce by setting marginal revenue equal to marginal cost (Q_1), and then selling that quantity for the price given on its demand curve (p_1). In panel A, the price charged is above average cost, and the monopolistic competitor is making a profit, enticing other firms to enter the market. As firms enter, the share of the market demand of each firm is reduced, and the demand curve facing each firm shifts to the left. Entry continues until the demand curve just touches the average cost curve (panel B). When the firm produces the quantity Q_e, it just breaks even; there is no incentive for either entry or exit.

occurs at exactly the level of output at which the demand curve is tangent to the average cost curve. At any other point, average costs exceed price, so profits are negative. Only at this point are profits zero. Accordingly, this is the profit-maximizing output.

The monopolistic competition equilibrium has some interesting characteristics. Note that in equilibrium, price and average costs exceed the minimum average costs at which the goods could be produced. *Less is produced at a higher price.* But there is a trade-off here. Whereas in the perfectly competitive market every product was a perfect substitute for every other one, the world of monopolistic competition offers variety in the products available. People value variety and are willing to pay a higher price to obtain it. Thus, that goods are sold at a price above the minimum average cost does not necessarily indicate that the economy is inefficient.

Oligopolies

In oligopolies there are just a few firms, so each worries about how its rivals will react to anything it does. This is true of the airline, cigarette, aluminum, and automobile industries, as well as a host of others.

If an oligopolist lowers its price, it takes the chance that rivals will do the same and deprive it of any competitive advantage. Worse still, a competitor may react to a price cut by engaging in a price war and cutting the price still further. Different oligopolies behave quite differently. The oligopolist is always torn between its desire to outwit competitors and the knowledge that by cooperating with other oligopolists to reduce output, it will earn a portion of the higher industry profits.

A firm that is part of an oligopolistic market must think *strategically*. In deciding what to do, it faces four key questions: (1) Should it cooperate with other firms or compete? When firms cooperate rather than compete, economists say the firms are *colluding*. (2) If it cannot collude explicitly (because there are laws barring such behavior), how can it reduce the effectiveness of competition through *restrictive practices* or other means? (3) How can it deter entry? Like a monopolist, it knows that the entry of other firms will erode profits. (4) How will rivals react to whatever it does? Will they, for instance, match price decreases? In the next four subsections, we take up each of these questions in turn.

Note the contrast between both competitive and monopolistic competitive models on the one hand and pure monopoly on the other. In the latter, there is no competition, hence no need to take actions to restrict competition; in the former, by assumption, there are so many competing firms that attempts to restrict competition are fruitless.

COLLUSION

In some cases, oligopolists enter into **collusion** to maximize their profits. In effect, they act jointly as if they were a single monopoly, and split up the resulting profits. The prevalence of collusion was long ago noted by Adam Smith, the founder of modern economics: "People of the same trade seldom meet together, even for merriment and diversion, but the conversation ends in a conspiracy against the public, or in some contrivance to raise prices."[3] A group of companies that formally operate in collusion is called a **cartel.** The Organization of Petroleum Exporting Countries (OPEC), for instance, acts collusively to restrict the output of oil, thereby raising oil prices and hence the profits of member countries.

In the late nineteenth century, two or more railroads ran between many major cities. When they competed vigorously, profits were low. So it did not take them long to discover that if they acted collusively, they could raise profits by raising prices.

In the steel industry at the turn of the century, Judge Elbert H. Gary, who headed the U.S. Steel Company, the largest of the firms, regularly presided over Sunday dinners for prominent members of his industry at which steel prices were set. In the 1950s, a cartel that included General Electric and Westinghouse colluded in setting the prices of electrical generators. And in the 1990s, the government uncovered price-fixing by Archer Daniel Midland (ADM).

But the mere fact that collusion is illegal inhibits it. Because the members of the cartel cannot get together to discuss price-fixing or restricting output, they typically must rely on *tacit collusion*—each restricting output with an understanding that the others will too. They cannot sign a contract that can be enforced in a court of law, simply because collusion to fix prices is illegal; hence they must rely on self-enforcement, which can be difficult and costly. Moreover, their artificially high prices—well in excess of the marginal cost of production—tempt each firm to cheat, to expand production. The members of the cartel may try to discipline those that cheat. They may even incur losses in the short run to punish the cheater, in the belief

---

[3]*Wealth of Nations* (1776), Book One, Chapter X, Part II.

OPEC leaders met in Caracas, Venezuela, in September 2000.

that the long-run gains from "cooperation" (that is, collusion) are worth the temporary sacrifice. For instance, if a firm cuts its price or expands its output *and the cheating is detected,* the other firms in the cartel may match, or even more than match, the price cuts or capacity expansions. The cheater ends up not only with lower profits than anticipated but also with lower profits than it would have obtained had it cooperated.

A variety of *facilitating practices* can make collusion easier by making punishment for cheating easier. Some industries maintain cooperative arrangements—one firm, for instance, may draw on the inventories of another, in the case of an unanticipated shortfall—from which cheaters are excluded.

Sometimes, policies that *seem* to be highly competitive actually have exactly the opposite effect. Consider the "meeting-the-competition clauses" by which some members of the oligopoly commit themselves to charging no more than any competitor. This sounds highly competitive. But think about it from the perspective of rival firms. Assume one firm is selling for $100 an item that costs only $90 to produce, so it is making a $10 profit. Consider another firm that would like to steal some customers away. It would be willing to sell the item for $95, undercutting its rival. But then it reasons that if it cuts its price, it will not gain any customers, since its rival has already guaranteed to match the lower price. Further, the second firm knows that it will make less money on each sale to its current customers. Price-cutting simply does not pay. Thus, a practice that appears highly competitive in fact facilitates collusion.

Circumstances are always changing, necessitating adjustments in outputs and prices. The cartel must coordinate these changes. The illegality of collusion makes this coordination particularly difficult, all the more so since the interests of the members of the cartel may not coincide—some may find their costs lowered more than others and therefore seek a greater expansion of output than others. Were there to be perfect collusion, in which industry profits were maximized, some might have to contract production and others expand it, with profits of some firms actually decreasing and others increasing. The gainers could, in principle, make payoffs to the losers and still be better off. However, these side payments are also illegal, and thus must be subtle and hard to detect if they occur at all. While perfect coordination is seldom possible, some industries have found a partial solution by allowing one firm to play the role of the *price leader*. In the airline industry, American Airlines for a long time acted as a price leader. As it increased or decreased prices, others followed suit.

Using Game Theory to Model Collusion Economists apply a branch of mathematics called **game theory** to study collusion among oligopolists. Its basic aim is to shed light on strategic choices—that is, on how people or organizations behave when they expect their actions to influence the behavior of others. For instance, when executives at a major airline decide to change fares for flights on a certain route, they have to consider how their competitors might respond to the price change. And the competitors, when deciding how to respond, have to consider how the first airline might answer in turn. These are strategic decisions, just like those typical of players in various sorts of games, such as chess, football, or poker.

Using game theory, the economist views the participants in a given situation as players in a game, whose rules define certain moves. The outcomes of the game—what each participant receives—are referred to as its payoffs, and they depend on what each player does. Each participant in the game chooses a strategy; he decides what moves to make. In games in which each player has the chance to make more than one move (there is more than one round, or period), moves can depend on what has happened in previous periods. Game theory begins with the assumption that each player in the game is rational and knows that her rival is rational. Each is trying to maximize his own payoff. The theory then tries to predict what each player will do. The actions depend on the rules of the game and the payoffs.

One example of such a game is called the **prisoner's dilemma.** Two prisoners, A and B, alleged to be conspirators in a crime, are put into separate rooms. A police officer goes into each room and makes a little speech: "Now here's the situation. If your partner confesses and you remain silent, you'll get five years in prison. But if your partner confesses and you confess also, you'll only get three years. On the other hand, perhaps your partner remains silent. If you're quiet also, we can send you to prison for only one year. But if your partner remains silent and you confess, we'll let you out in three months. So if your partner confesses, you are better off confessing, and if your partner doesn't confess, you are better off confessing. Why not confess?" This deal is offered to both prisoners.

Figure 12.9 shows the results of this deal. The upper left box, for example, shows the result if both A and B confess. The upper right box shows the result if prisoner A confesses but prisoner B remains silent. And so on.

From the combined standpoint of the two prisoners, the best option is clearly that they both remain silent and each serves one year. But the self-interest of each individual prisoner says that confession is best, whether his partner confesses or not. However, if they both follow their self-interest and confess, they both end up

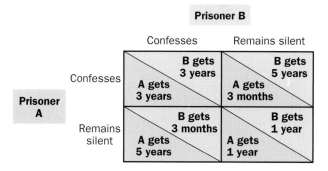

Figure 12.9

THE PRISONER'S DILEMMA

Both prisoners would be better off if both remained silent, but their individual incentives lead each one to confess. From the standpoint of prisoner A, confessing is the better strategy if prisoner B confesses, and confessing is the better strategy if prisoner B remains silent. The same holds for prisoner B.

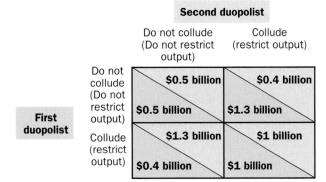

Second duopolist

	Do not collude (Do not restrict output)	Collude (restrict output)
First duopolist Do not collude (Do not restrict output)	$0.5 billion / $0.5 billion	$0.4 billion / $1.3 billion
Collude (restrict output)	$1.3 billion / $0.4 billion	$1 billion / $1 billion

Figure 12.10

THE PROBLEM OF COLLUSION AS A PRISONER'S DILEMMA

The payoffs for the duopolists delineate a prisoner's dilemma. Both firms would be better off if both colluded (restricted output), but their individual incentives lead each to not collude (not restrict output).

worse off, each serving three years. The prisoner's dilemma is a simple game in which both parties are made worse off by independently following their own self-interest. Both would be better off if they could get together to agree on a story, and to threaten the other if he deviated from the story.

The prisoner's dilemma game can be used to illustrate the problem of collusion among oligopolists. Let us work with the example of a *duopoly*, which is a market with two firms. Figure 12.10 shows the level of profits of each if both collude and restrict output (both get $1 billion), if neither restricts output (both get $0.5 billion), or if one restricts output and the other does not (the one that does not gets $1.3 billion, the one that does gets $0.4 billion). As each firm thinks through the consequences of restricting output, it will quickly realize that if the other firm restricts output, its best strategy is to expand output; and if the other firm fails to restrict output, its best strategy is also to expand output. Thus the firm finds that regardless of what the other does, it pays to expand output rather than to restrict it. Since the other firm will reach the same conclusion, both will conclude that it does not pay to restrict output. Hence, both will expand output; they do not collude to restrict output.

The central point is that even though the firms see that they could both be better off colluding, the individual incentive to cheat dictates the strategy that each follows.

So far we have considered the prisoner's dilemma when each player makes only a single move to complete the game. But if firms interact over time, then they have additional ways to try to enforce their agreement. For example, suppose each oligopolist announces that it will refrain from cutting prices as long as its rival does. But if the rival cheats on the collusive agreement, then the first oligopolist will respond by increasing production and lowering prices. This strategy is called *tit for tat*. If this threat is credible—as it may well be, especially after it has been carried out a few times—the rival may decide that it is more profitable to cooperate and keep production low than to cheat. In the real world, such simple strategies may play an important role in ensuring that firms do not compete too vigorously in markets that have only three or four dominant firms.

The commonness and success of such strategies have puzzled economists. The logic of game theory suggests that these approaches would not be effective. Consider what happens if the two firms expect to compete in the same market over the next ten years, after which time a new product is expected to come along and shift the entire configuration of the industry. It will pay each firm to cheat in the tenth year, when there is no possibility of retaliation, because the industry will be completely altered in the next year. Now consider what happens in the ninth year. Both firms can figure out that it will not pay either one of them to cooperate in the tenth year. But if they are not going to cooperate in the tenth year anyway, then the *threat* of not cooperating in the future is completely ineffective. Hence in the ninth year, each firm will reason that it pays to cheat on the collusive agreement by producing more than the agreed-on amount. Collusion breaks down in the ninth year. As they reason backward through time, this logic will lead collusion to break down almost immediately. However, if there is no certain date at which the collusion will end, it is possible for collusion to carry on indefinitely. Whenever the firms contemplate cheating, on any agreement to collude, each will compare the initial increase in profits from cheating with the future reduction in profits when the other firm retaliates. The firms therefore may decide to continue colluding.

It is not just among traditional business firms that collusion occurs. A few years ago, the U.S. Justice Department investigated collusion by a group of colleges and universities, including several Ivy League schools. The claim was that these schools colluded to set financial aid awards. The schools had agreed to all offer the same scholarship package to students who had been accepted by more than one of the schools. Thus, the colleges were agreeing not to use larger financial awards to compete for these students. Their collusion helped the schools hold down their costs. In 1991, the eight Ivy League universities signed an agreement with the Justice Department in which they agreed to no longer cooperate in setting their financial aid offers.

RESTRICTIVE PRACTICES

If members of an oligopoly could easily get together and collude, they would. Their joint profits would increase. We have seen, however, that there are significant impediments to collusion. As a result, oligopolists typically resort to other ways of increasing profits. One approach is to restrict competition.

Firms engage in a number of **restrictive practices** to limit competition. Some were made illegal by the Federal Trade Commission Act of 1914. While these practices may not increase profits for the firms quite as successfully as the collusive arrangements discussed above, they do raise prices. In some cases, consumers may be even worse off than under outright collusion. Many restrictive practices are aimed at the wholesalers and retailers who sell a producer's goods. When one firm buys or sells the products of another, the two companies are said to have a "vertical" relationship. Such restrictive practices are called *vertical restrictions,* in distinction to the price-fixing arrangements among producers or among wholesalers selling in the same market, which are referred to as *horizontal restrictions.*

One example of a vertical restriction is the use of *exclusive territories:* a producer gives a wholesaler or retailer the exclusive right to sell a good within a certain region. Beer and soft drink producers, for instance, typically give their distributors exclusive territories. Coca-Cola manufactures its own syrup, which it then sells to bottlers who add the soda water. Coca-Cola gives these bottlers exclusive territories, so the supermarkets in a particular area can buy Coke from only one place. A store in Michigan cannot buy the soft drink from Coca-Cola bottlers in New Jersey, even if the price in New Jersey is lower. In 1979, Indiana passed a law prohibiting exclusive territories for beer within the state. As a result, beer prices there are substantially lower (adjusting for other differences) than in other states.

Another restrictive practice is *exclusive dealing:* a producer insists that any firm selling its products not sell those of its rivals. When you go into an Exxon gas station, for instance, you can be sure you are buying gas refined by the Exxon Corporation, not Texaco or Sunoco. Like most refiners, Exxon requires stations that want to sell Exxon to sell only its brand of gasoline.

A third example of a restrictive practice is *tie-ins,* which force a customer who buys one product to buy another. Mortgage companies, for example, used to insist that those who obtained mortgages from them purchase fire insurance as well. Nintendo designs its console so that it can be used with only Nintendo games. In effect, it forces a tie-in sale between the console and the software. In the early days of computers, IBM designed its computers so that they could be used only with IBM "peripherals," such as printers.

A final example is *resale price maintenance.* Under this restrictive practice, a producer insists that any retailer selling his product must sell it at the "list" price. Like exclusive territories, it is designed to reduce competitive pressures at the retail level.

Consequences of Restrictive Practices Firms engaging in restrictive practices *claim* they are doing so not because they wish to restrict competition but because they want to enhance economic efficiency. Exclusive territories, they argue, provide companies with a better incentive to "cultivate" their territory. Exclusive dealing contracts, they say, provide incentives for firms to focus their attention on one producer's goods.

Despite these claims, restrictive practices often reduce economic efficiency. Exclusive territories for beer, for example, have limited the ability of very large firms, with stores in many different territories, to set up a central warehouse and distribute beer to their stores more efficiently. And regardless of whether they enhance or hurt efficiency, restrictive practices may lead to higher prices by limiting competitive pressures.

Some restrictive practices work by increasing the costs of, or otherwise impeding, one's rivals. In the 1980s, several major airlines developed computer reservation systems that they sold at very attractive prices to travel agents. If the primary goal of these systems had been to serve consumers, they would have been designed to display all the departures near the time the passenger desired. Instead, each airline's system provided a quick display for only its own flights—United's, for instance, focused on United flights—although with additional work, the travel agent could find out the flights of other airlines. Airlines benefited from these computer systems not because they best met the needs of the consumer, but because they put competitors at a disadvantage and thereby reduced the effectiveness of competition.

An exclusive dealing contract between a producer and a distributor also exemplifies how one firm may benefit from hurting its rivals. The contract might force a rival producer to set up its own distribution system, at great cost, when the already-existing distributor might have been able to undertake the distribution of the second product at relatively low incremental cost. The exclusive dealing contract increases total resources spent on distribution.

Courts have responded inconsistently to these and similar practices—in some circumstances ruling that they are illegal because they reduce competition, while in others allowing them, having been persuaded that they represent reasonable business practices.

FORMS OF RESTRICTIVE PRACTICES

Exclusive territories
Exclusive dealing
Tie-ins
Resale price maintenance

ENTRY DETERRENCE

Oligopolists use restrictive practices to reduce competition and thereby increase profits. Another way to reduce competition is to prevent other firms from entering the market. This is called **entry deterrence.**

Entry deterrence is intended to limit the number of firms—the fewer the firms, presumably the weaker the competitive pressure. Natural barriers to entry, such as the large fixed costs discussed earlier in the chapter, put some limits on competition, but they are not so impermeable as to block it entirely. Businesses already in the market often try to supplement the natural barriers by *strategic barriers*—that is, acting in ways that make the market unattractive for new firms.

The issue of entry barriers is at the center of the theory of monopoly and oligopoly, which must explain why new firms don't enter the market despite the pull of profits. What are the barriers to their entry? Thus, our discussion of entry deterrence applies to both monopolies and oligopolies.

Government Policies as Barriers to Entry Many early monopolies were established by governments. For example, in the seventeenth century, the British

---

Internet Connection

KEEPING TRACK OF OLIGOPOLIES

The Web site www.oligopolywatch.com provides numerous articles and news stories about oligopolies. Many of the stories report on the latest mergers and acquisitions by large corporations, describing how these often serve to reduce the number of sellers in a market to just a few different producers. For example, more than 80 percent of all the music titles produced in the United States are controlled by just five major record label conglomerates: Time Warner, EMI Group, Universal Music Group (UMG), Bertelsmann Music Group (BMG), and Sony. In 2000, Time Warner and EMI announced plans to merge, further consolidating the industry, but opposition from European Union regulators led the two companies to eventually call off the proposed merger.

These same corporations also own distribution companies that control more than 80 percent of the wholesale market.

government gave the East India Company a monopoly on trade with India. More recently, governments have often granted monopolies to providers of such services as electricity, telephones, and cable television. Today, however, the most important monopolies granted by governments are patents. A patent gives inventors the exclusive right to produce or license others to produce their discoveries for a limited period of time (generally twenty years). The argument for patents is that without property rights in their discoveries, inventors would have no economic incentive to innovate. The framers of the U.S. Constitution thought promoting "the Progress of Science and useful Arts" to be so important that they included the granting of patents among the powers of the newly created Congress.

Single Ownership of an Essential Input Another barrier to entry is a firm's exclusive ownership of some raw material. For example, an aluminum company might attempt to become a monopolist by buying all the sources of bauxite, the main ore of aluminum. A single South African company, De Beers, has come close to monopolizing the world's supply of diamonds.

Information as a Barrier to Entry Information can act as a barrier to entry when consumers do not know and cannot easily assess the quality of a new product. In the computer printer market, for example, firms such as HP, Epson, and Canon dominate; because these firms have already established reputations for producing high-quality printers, a new entrant unknown to consumers would need to sell at a price significantly below those of the other firms. Imperfect information about the production costs and responses of incumbent firms too can act as a barrier to entry. Potential entrants may know that they can undercut the incumbent firm's current price, but they do not know how much the incumbent will (or can afford to) lower its prices.

Market Strategies for Entry Deterrence Established firms often pursue strategies to convince potential entrants that even though they are currently making high levels of profits, these profits will disappear if the new firm enters the market. Two major forms of such **entry-deterring practices** are *predatory pricing* and *excess capacity*.

In predatory pricing, an incumbent firm deliberately lowers its price below the new entrant's cost of production in order to drive the new arrival out and discourage future entry. The incumbent may lose money in the process, but it hopes to recoup its losses when the entrant leaves and it is free to raise prices back to the monopoly level. Predatory pricing is an illegal trade practice, but changing technologies and shifting demand often make it difficult to ascertain whether a firm has actually engaged in predatory pricing or has simply lowered its price to meet the competition (see the following Thinking Like an Economist box).

Firms can also build more production facilities than are currently needed. By readying extra plants and equipment—excess capacity—even if they are rarely used, the incumbent sends a signal to potential entrants that it is willing and able to engage in fierce price competition.

These strategies are most likely to be effective if there are some sunk costs. Assume the incumbent firm has constant marginal costs and can respond to the entry of another firm by lowering its unit price to marginal cost. A potential entrant,

Thinking Like an Economist

TRADE-OFFS, AMERICAN AIRLINES, AND PREDATION

Firms with market power like to keep it that way, as they can earn high profits by being the only, or the dominant, firm in a market. One of the ways in which they do this is to be a *predator*. Like a predatory animal that eats up rivals, predatory firms lower their prices in an attempt to drive out competitors. A firm may find it can earn higher profits overall if it sacrifices some profit in the short run by cutting its prices to keep rivals out of its market.

This behavior is illegal. For instance, in 1999 the U.S. Justice Department accused American Airlines of predation. The Justice Department alleged that repeatedly, when a new, low-cost carrier entered a market, American Airlines would slash its prices and increase the number of its flights, in an attempt to drive the entrant out of the market. As soon as it was successful, it would cut back on its flights and raise prices. While consumers benefited in the short run from the price war, in the long run they suffered from higher prices caused by lack of competition. Courts have the difficult task of trying to determine whether the lowering of prices is just a normal response to competition, or a predatory action intended to kill a firm entering the market.

One part of the test that is commonly employed asks, Did the predatory firm give up profits today in anticipation of earning them back later from its monopoly position? One way of answering is to compare price and average variable cost. If price is below average variable cost, clearly the firm could not be maximizing its profits, because it would have been better off simply shutting down.

A more refined approach looks at price in comparison with marginal cost. If price is less than marginal cost, a firm should reduce production. Marginal cost is often hard to observe, however, and courts have had to rely on proxies. If the firm is operating at or near an efficient level of production, so that average total costs are minimized, then marginal cost equals average total costs (recall Figure 6.6).

The American Airlines case involved an expansion of output. In competitive markets, so long as the marginal cost curve is upward sloping, a lower price will be associated with lower output, since price must equal marginal cost. But predation occurs in markets that are not competitive. Still, it seemed peculiar that as a new entrant stole some of the demand facing American Airlines, it reacted by increasing supply. The Justice Department alleged that a closer look at American Airlines's behavior showed that it had given up profitable opportunities in order to drive out its rival. The additional revenue that it received from expanding its output was lower than the costs it incurred (including the opportunity cost associated with the profits the planes would have earned on alternative routes).

Predation cases present courts with difficult trade-offs because they assess the risk of finding an innocent party guilty versus that of finding a guilty party innocent. Consumers benefit from the lower prices in the first phase of predation. Courts worry that if firms that really were not engaged in predation are found guilty, competition will be stifled. But if predation really is occurring, then competition in the long run will be suppressed, and consumers will face higher prices and worse service. In most of the airline routes where the Justice Department alleged predation, after the entrant left, prices returned to high levels and service was cut back.

The courts ultimately ruled in favor of American Airlines and dismissed the suit brought by the Justice Department. The ruling was upheld on appeal on the grounds that the airlines did not set fares below average variable cost. Thus, the Justice Department failed to establish that American was pricing below an appropriate measure of cost.

American Airlines planes at Miami International Airport

with marginal costs equal to those of the incumbent, will realize that once it enters, it too must set price equal to marginal cost and therefore will be unable to recover even a small sunk cost. Hence, it chooses not to enter. And the incumbent firm, aware of this calculation, can charge a monopoly price unchallenged.

ENTRY DETERRENCE

Government policies: These include grants of monopoly (patents) and restrictions on entry (licensing).

Single ownership of an essential input: When a single firm owns the entire supply of a raw material, entry is by definition precluded.

Information: Lack of technical information by potential competitors inhibits their entry; lack of information by consumers concerning the quality of a new entrant's product discourages consumers from switching to the new product, and thus inhibits entry.

Market strategies: These include actions such as predatory pricing and excess capacity aimed at convincing potential entrants that entry would be met with resistance, and thus would be unprofitable.

The Importance of Imperfections in Competition

Many of the features of the modern economy—from frequent-flier mileage awards to offers to match prices of competitors, from brand names to the billions spent every year on advertising—not only cannot be explained by the basic competitive model but also are inconsistent with it. They reflect the imperfections of competition that affect so many parts of the economy. Most economists agree that the extreme cases of monopoly (no competition) and perfect competition (where each firm has *no* effect on the market prices) are rare, and that most markets are characterized by some, but imperfect, competition.

Review and Practice

SUMMARY

1. Both monopolists and firms in conditions of perfect competition maximize their profits by producing at the quantity at which marginal revenue is equal to marginal cost. However, marginal revenue for a perfect competitor is the same as the market price of an extra unit, while marginal revenue for a monopolist is less than the market price.

2. Since in a monopoly price exceeds marginal revenue, buyers pay more for the product than the marginal cost to produce it; there is less production in a monopoly than there would be if price were set equal to marginal cost.

3. Imperfect competition occurs when a relatively small number of firms dominate the market or when firms produce goods that are differentiated in ways that reflect consumer preferences.

4. An industry in which fixed costs are so large that only one firm can operate efficiently is called a natural monopoly. Even when there is only one firm (or a few firms), the threat of potential competition may be sufficiently strong that price is driven down to average costs; there are no monopoly profits. Such markets are said to be contestable. If, however, there are sunk costs or other barriers to entry, markets will not be contestable, and monopoly profits can persist.

5. With monopolistic competition, barriers to entry are sufficiently weak that entry occurs until profits are driven to zero; there are few enough firms that each faces a downward-sloping demand curve, but a sufficiently large number of firms that each ignores rivals' reaction to what it does.

6. Oligopolists must choose whether to seek higher profits by colluding with rival firms or by competing. They must decide what their rivals will do in response to any action they take.

7. A group of firms that have an explicit and open agreement to collude is known as a cartel. While the gains from collusion can be significant, important limits are posed by the incentives to cheat and the need to rely on self-enforcement, and by the difficulty of coordinating the responses necessitated by changing economic circumstances. Although cartels are illegal under U.S. law, firms have tried to find tacit ways of facilitating collusion—for example, by relying on price leaders and "meeting-the-competition" pricing policies.

8. Even when they do not collude, firms attempt to restrict competition with practices such as exclusive territories, exclusive dealing, tie-ins, and resale price maintenance. In some cases, a firm's profits may be increased by raising its rival's costs and making the rival a less effective competitor.

KEY TERMS

pure profit *or* monopoly rents
price discrimination
natural monopoly
four-firm concentration ratio
imperfect substitutes
product differentiation
collusion
cartel
game theory
prisoner's dilemma
restrictive practices
entry deterrence
entry-deterring practices

REVIEW QUESTIONS

1. Why is price equal to marginal revenue for a perfectly competitive firm but not for a monopolist?

2. How should a monopoly choose its quantity of production to maximize profits? Explain why producing either less or more than the level of output at which marginal revenue equals marginal cost will reduce profits. Since a monopolist need not fear competition, what prevents it from raising its price as high as it wishes to make higher profits?

3. What are the primary sources of product differentiation?

4. Under what circumstances will price be equal to average costs, so that even though there is a single firm in the market, it earns no monopoly rents?

5. What is a natural monopoly?

6. Describe market equilibrium under monopolistic competition. Why does the price charged by the typical firm exceed the minimum average cost, even though other firms may enter the market?

7. What are the gains from collusion? Why is there an incentive for each member of a cartel to cheat by producing more than the agreed-on amount? What is the "prisoner's dilemma" and how is it related to the problem of cheating? What are the other problems facing cartels?

8. Name some ways that firms might facilitate collusion, if explicit collusion is ruled out by law.

9. What are barriers to entry? How can firms try to deter entry?

10. Name and define three restrictive practices.

PROBLEMS

1. Explain how it is possible that at a high enough level of output, if a monopoly produced and sold more, its revenue would actually decline.

2. Assume there is a single firm producing cigarettes, and the marginal cost of producing cigarettes is a constant. Suppose the government imposes a 10-cent tax on each pack of cigarettes. If the demand curve for cigarettes is linear (that is, $Q = a - bp$, where Q = output, p = price, and a and b are constants), will the price rise by more or by less than the tax?

3. With what strategies might a furniture firm differentiate its products?

4. Suppose a gas station at a busy intersection is surrounded by many competitors, all of which sell identical gas. Draw the demand curve the gas station faces, and draw its marginal and average cost curves. Explain the rule for maximizing profit in this situation. Now imagine that the gas station offers a new gasoline additive called zoomine, and begins an advertising campaign that says: "Get zoomine in your gasoline." No other station offers zoomine. Draw the station's demand curve after this advertising campaign. Explain the rule for maximizing profit in this situation, and illustrate it with an appropriate diagram.

5. Explain how consumers may benefit from predatory pricing in the short run, but not in the long run.

6. Assume the demand curve faced by a monopolist is given by the following table:

Price	Demand	Total revenue	Marginal revenue
55	45		
60	40		
65	35		
70	30		
75	25		
80	20		
85	15		
90	10		
95	5		
100	0		

(a) Fill in the columns of the table for total revenue and marginal revenue.

(b) Draw the demand curve and the marginal revenue curve.

(c) If the firm's marginal cost is $75, what is the equilibrium monopoly price? How much does a monopolist produce?

(d) What would be the price and quantity produced if this were a competitive market (assume marginal costs to be $75)?

7. How might cooperative agreements between firms—to share research information, share the costs of cleaning up pollution, or address shortfalls of supplies—end up helping firms to collude in reducing quantity and raising price?

8. Explain why each of the following might serve to deter entry of a competitor.

(a) Maintaining excess production capacity

(b) Promising customers that you will undercut any rival

(c) Selling your output at a price below that at which marginal revenue equals marginal cost (Hint: Assume entrants are unsure about what your marginal costs are. Why would they be deterred from entering if they believed you have low marginal costs? Why might a lower price lead them to think that you had low marginal costs?)

(d) Offering a discount to customers who sign up for long-term contracts

9. Explain why frequent-flier programs (in which airlines give credits, convertible into travel awards for each mile traveled) might reduce competition among airlines. Put yourself in the role of consultant to one of the airlines in the days before any airline had such programs. Would you have recommended that the airline adopt the program? What would you have *assumed* about the responses of other airlines? Would this have been important to your assessment?

10. At various times, Nintendo has been accused of trying to stifle its competitors. Among the alleged practices have been (a) not allowing those who produce games for Nintendo to produce games for others; and (b) discouraging stores that sell Nintendo from selling competing games—for instance, by not fulfilling their orders as quickly, especially in periods of shortages. Explain why these practices might increase Nintendo's profits.

11. Consider two oligopolists, with each choosing between a "high" and a "low" level of production. Given their choices of how much to produce, their profits will be:

Firm A

	High production	Low production
High production	A gets $2 million profit B gets $2 million profit	A gets $1 million profit B gets $5 million profit

Firm B

	High production	Low production
Low production	A gets $5 million profit B gets $1 million profit	A gets $4 million profit B gets $4 million profit

Explain how firm B will reason that it makes sense to produce the high amount, regardless of what firm A chooses. Then explain how firm A will reason that it makes sense to produce the high amount, regardless of what firm B chooses. How might collusion assist the two firms in this case?

Learning Goals

In this chapter, you will learn

1 The sources of economic inefficiency that result from imperfect competition

2 The different policies that governments have adopted to deal with imperfect competition

3 The role of antitrust policies in limiting market domination and curbing practices that restrict competition

Chapter 13

GOVERNMENT POLICIES TOWARD COMPETITION

Motivated by both political and economic concerns, governments have taken an active role in promoting competition and in limiting the abuses of market power. In this chapter, we review the economic effects of limited competition and look at government policies to reduce its negative effects.

The Drawbacks of Monopolies and Limited Competition

Four major sources of economic inefficiency result from monopolies and other imperfectly competitive industries: restricted output, managerial slack, insufficient attention to research and development, and rent-seeking behavior. The problems stand out most plainly in the context of monopolies (the focus here), but they also arise in imperfectly competitive markets.

RESTRICTED OUTPUT

Monopolists, like competitive firms, are in business to make profits by producing the kinds of goods and services that customers want. But monopolists can make profits in ways not available to competitive firms. One way is to drive up the price of a good by restricting output, as discussed in Chapters 11 and 12. They can, to use the popular term, gouge their customers. Consumers, by *choosing* to buy the monopolist's good, are revealing that they are better off than they would be without the product. But they are paying more than they would if the industry were competitive.

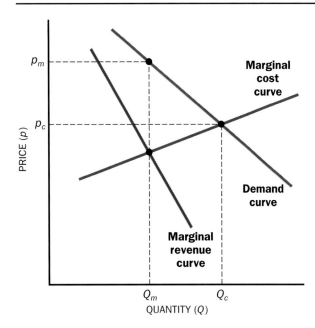

FIGURE 13.1

WHY MONOPOLY OUTPUT IS INEFFICIENT

With perfect competition, price is set equal to marginal cost: output is at quantity Q_c, and price at p_c. A monopolist will set marginal revenue equal to marginal cost, and will produce at quantity Q_m and price p_m, where the market price exceeds marginal cost.

A monopolist who sets marginal revenue equal to marginal cost produces at a lower level of output than a corresponding competitive industry—an industry with the same demand curve and costs but in which there are many producers rather than one—where price equals marginal cost. Figure 13.1 shows that the monopoly output, Q_m, is smaller than the competitive output, Q_c, where the price under competition, p_c, equals marginal cost. The price under monopoly, p_m, is higher than p_c.

The price of a good, by definition, measures how much an individual is willing to pay for an extra unit of it. It measures, in other words, the marginal benefit of the good to the purchaser. With perfect competition, price equals marginal cost, so that in equilibrium the marginal benefit of an extra unit of a good to the individual (the price) is just equal to the marginal cost to the firm of producing it. At the monopolist's lower level of output, the marginal benefit of producing an extra unit—the price individuals are willing to pay for an extra unit—exceeds marginal cost.

By comparing the monopolist's production decision with the collective decisions regarding output made by firms in a competitive market, we can estimate the value of the loss to society incurred by a monopoly. To simplify the analysis, in Figure 13.2 marginal cost is assumed to be constant, the horizontal line at the competitive price p_c. The monopolist produces an output of Q_m, at the point where marginal revenue equals marginal cost, and finds that it can charge p_m, the price on the demand curve corresponding to the output Q_m.

Two kinds of loss result, both related to the concept of consumer surplus introduced in Chapter 5. There we saw that the downward-sloping demand curve implies a bounty to most consumers. At points to the left of the intersection of the price line and demand curve, people are willing to pay more for the good than they have to. With competition, the consumer surplus in Figure 13.2 is the entire shaded area between the demand curve and the line at p_c.

The monopolist cuts into this surplus. First, it charges a higher price, p_m, than would be obtained in the competitive situation. This loss is measured by the rectangle *ABCD*, the extra price multiplied by the quantity actually produced and consumed. It is not a loss to society as a whole but a transfer of income, as the higher price winds up as revenues for the monopoly. But the monopolist also reduces the quantity produced. While production in a competitive market would be Q_c, a monopoly produces the lower amount, Q_m. This second kind of loss is a complete loss to society, and is called the *deadweight loss* of a monopoly. Consumers lose the surplus to the right of Q_m, denoted by triangle *ABG*, with no resulting gain to the monopolist.

Some economists, such as Arnold Harberger of UCLA, have argued that these costs of monopoly are relatively small, amounting to perhaps 3 percent of the monopolist's output value. Others believe the losses from restricting output are higher. Whichever argument is right, output restriction is only one source of the inefficiencies monopolies introduce into the economy.

MANAGERIAL SLACK

Chapter 6 argued that any company wants to minimize the cost of producing whatever level of output it chooses to produce. But in practice, companies already earning a great deal of money without much competition often lack the incentive to hold costs as low as possible. The lack of efficiency when firms are insulated from the pressures of competition is referred to as **managerial slack.**

In the absence of competition, it can be difficult to tell whether managers are being efficient. How much, for instance, should it cost for AT&T to put a call through from New York to Chicago? In the days when AT&T had a monopoly on long-distance telephone service, it might have claimed that its costs were as low as possible. However, not even trained engineers could really tell whether this was true. When competition developed for intercity telephone calls, shareholders in AT&T could compare its costs with those of Sprint, MCI, and other competitors; competition therefore provided each company with an incentive to be as efficient as possible.

REDUCED RESEARCH AND DEVELOPMENT

Competition motivates firms to develop new products and less expensive ways of producing goods. A monopoly, by contrast, may be willing to let the profits roll in, without aggressively encouraging technological progress.

Not all monopolists stand pat, of course. Bell Laboratories, the research division of AT&T, was a fountain of important innovations throughout the period during which AT&T was a virtual monopolist in telephone service. The laser and the transistor are but two of its innovations. But AT&T was also in a unique position. The prices it charged were determined by government regulators, and those prices were set to encourage the expenditure of money on research. From this perspective, AT&T's research contribution was largely a consequence of government regulatory policy.

In contrast to Bell Labs, the American automobile and steel industries are often blamed for falling behind foreign competition because of their technological complacence. By the end of World War II, these industries had attained a dominant position in the world. After enjoying high profits for many years, they lost a significant share of the market to foreign firms in the 1970s and 1980s. Foreign automobile and steel firms, for example, were able to undersell their U.S. counterparts during the 1980s, not only because they paid lower wages but also because their technological advances had made production processes more efficient.

More recently, analysts have expressed concern that firms with monopoly power not only engage in less innovation than they would under competition but also seek actively to quash innovations by rivals that could reduce their market power. And even if they do not

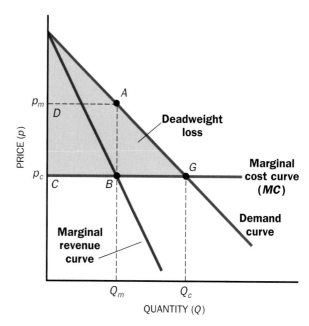

FIGURE 13.2

MEASURING THE SOCIAL COST OF MONOPOLY

The higher, monopoly price removes some of the consumer surplus. Part of this loss (the rectangle *ABCD*) is simply a transfer of income from consumers to the monopolist; the remainder (the triangle *ABG*) is known as the deadweight loss of monopoly.

deliberately try to inhibit innovative activities of potential rivals, they may stifle progress indirectly. Some of the most important inputs into the innovation process are prior innovations themselves, and by raising the "price" associated with these earlier discoveries (through their market power), monopolists reduce the incentives for follow-up inventions.

RENT SEEKING

The final source of economic inefficiency under monopoly is the temptation for monopolists to expend resources in economically unproductive ways. In particular, they may seek to deter the entry of other firms into their market. Because the profits a monopolist receives are called *monopoly rents,* the attempt to acquire or maintain already-existing rents by acquiring or maintaining a monopoly position in some industry is referred to as **rent seeking.**

Sometimes a firm's monopoly position is at least partly the result of government protection. Many less-developed countries grant a company within their country a monopoly to produce a good, and they bar imports of that good from abroad. In these circumstances, firms will give money to lobbyists and politicians to maintain regulations that restrict competition so that they can keep their profits high. Such activities are socially wasteful. Real resources (including labor time) are used to win favorable rules, not to produce goods and services. There is thus legitimate concern that the willingness of governments to restrict competition will encourage firms to spend money on rent-seeking activities rather than on making a better product.

To gain and hold a monopoly position, the firm would be willing to spend up to the amount it would receive as monopoly profits. The waste from this rent-seeking activity can be much larger than the loss from reduced output.

FURTHER DRAWBACKS OF LIMITED COMPETITION

We saw in Chapter 12 that markets in which a few firms dominated were more common than monopolies, and some of the inefficiencies discussed above are smaller under limited competition. Output is lower than under perfect competition but higher than under monopoly, for example. And competition to produce new products (research and development) is often intense, as we will see in Chapter 20. But other inefficiencies are worse in markets with limited competition than in monopoly markets. Firms under imperfect competition, for example, devote much attention to practices designed to deter entry, to reduce the force of competition, and to raise prices. Their expenditures may increase profits but they waste resources and make consumers worse off. Under imperfect competition firms may, for instance, maintain excess capacity to deter entry. A firm may gain a competitive advantage over its rival not by lowering its own costs but by raising the rival's—for instance, by denying it the use of existing distribution facilities. A firm may also spend money on uninformative (but persuasive) advertising.

e-Insight

USING THE INTERNET TO ENHANCE PRICE DISCRIMINATION

In 2000, the online retailer Amazon.com conducted a marketing test that generated an immediate outcry of foul play from consumer advocates. Amazon.com had offered different customers different prices on DVDs; and when the pricing strategy became public, it claimed that the prices were set randomly in an attempt to determine how consumers would respond to different prices. Analysts were skeptical, fearing that Amazon.com was using information collected from the previous purchases of individual consumers to fine-tune its prices. Customers from wealthier neighborhoods with a record of buying more expensive items might be receiving higher price quotes. Newspaper commentators accused Amazon.com of "unfair" pricing, and the marketing test was suspended.

Consumers have long accepted that airlines will offer different fares to travelers on the same flight, according to when tickets were purchased. Travelers who can plan in advance receive discount fares, while business travelers who need to get to a newly scheduled meeting pay much more. Because the business traveler's demand is highly inelastic, airlines can charge her a higher price. People who can plan ahead and easily adjust travel dates and times will be more price sensitive—their demand curve is more elastic. By offering only price-sensitive customers lower fares, airlines can sell more seats without having to offer the same low price to everyone.

In imperfectly competitive markets, as we saw in Chapter 12, firms can try to boost profits through price discrimination—charging different prices to different consumers. The Internet is opening up new opportunities for this sales strategy. Here's an example of how it might work. Knowing that a blizzard is predicted for the weekend, early in the week you log onto a hardware site to order extra lanterns, batteries, and candles. The Web site is programmed to check orders of emergency supplies from your zip code against a national weather database. Knowing that you are facing a blizzard, the hardware online retailer decides that your demand is inelastic, and raises the prices for the purchase and delivery of the items you need.

By providing firms with more detailed information about their customers, the Internet may open new possibilities for firms in imperfectly competitive markets to engage in price discrimination.

Policies Toward Natural Monopolies

If imperfect competition is as disadvantageous as the previous analysis has suggested, why not simply require that competition be perfect? To answer this question, we need to recall the reasons, discussed in Chapter 11, why competition is imperfect.

One reason is that the cost of production may be lower if there is a single firm in the industry, leading to a natural monopoly. In the case depicted in Figure 13.3, average costs are declining throughout the relevant levels of output, though marginal costs are constant; there are very large fixed costs. Natural monopolies present a difficult policy problem. Like any other firm, a natural monopolist will produce at the level where marginal revenue equals marginal cost—at Q_m, in Figure 13.3. At this level, it will charge a price of p_m, which is higher than the marginal cost at that point. Thus, it will produce less and charge more than it would if price were equal to

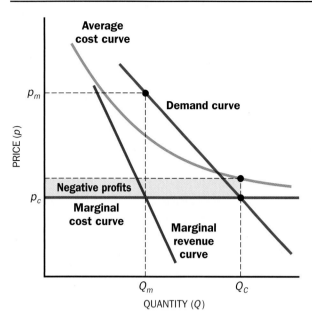

FIGURE 13.3

A PROBLEM WITH REGULATING A NATURAL MONOPOLY

A natural monopoly will set marginal revenue equal to marginal cost, and produce at quantity Q_m and price p_m. In perfect competition, price would be equal to marginal cost, at Q_c and p_c. However, the perfectly competitive outcome is not possible in this case, since it would force the natural monopoly to produce at below its average cost, and thus to be making losses.

marginal cost, as would be true under perfect competition (the output level Q_c and the price p_c in the figure).

However, a decreasing average cost curve necessarily precludes perfect competition. To understand why, recall that under perfect competition, price equals marginal cost. Now look again at Figure 13.3 and consider what would happen if price were driven down to marginal cost. In the figure, marginal cost is equal to p_c. At a price equal to p_c, the quantity demanded is equal to Q_c. But at that quantity, the firm's average costs are greater than p_c. When average costs are declining, marginal costs are less than average costs. Hence, a price equal to marginal cost would be less than average costs. But if the firm sells its output at a price that fails to cover its average costs, it will lose money. So when average costs are declining, profits will be negative when price equals marginal cost, as shown by the shaded area in the figure. No firm will be able to stay in business if it always loses money.

There is old joke about a firm that loses money on every sale but makes it up in volume. Of course, selling more when there is a loss on each sale just makes the firm even worse off. And that would be exactly the condition of a firm with declining average costs that set price equal to marginal cost.

If the government wanted a natural monopoly to produce at the point where marginal cost equaled price, it would have to subsidize the firm to offset its losses. But the taxes that would have to be raised to provide the subsidy impose other economic costs; thus the severity of the two distortions—caused either by a firm charging a price above marginal cost or by the taxes required to fund the subsidy to eliminate the first distortion—would have to be compared. Moreover, the government would likely have a difficult time ascertaining the magnitude of the subsidy needed. Managers and workers in the firm would have an incentive to exaggerate the wage and other costs necessary to produce the required output, because exaggeration would win them a bigger subsidy from the government.

Governments have found three different solutions to the problem of natural monopolies.

PUBLIC OWNERSHIP

In some countries, government simply owns natural monopolies, such as electric power, gas, and water. There are problems with public ownership, however. Governments often are not particularly efficient as producers.

Managers of such monopolies commonly lack adequate incentives to cut costs and modernize vigorously, particularly since government is frequently willing to subsidize the industry when it loses money. In addition, public ownership tends to politicize business decisions. Political influence may affect where public utilities, for example, locate their plants—politicians like to see jobs created in their home districts—and whether they prune their labor force to increase efficiency. Publicly run firms may also be under pressure to provide some services at prices below marginal cost and to make up the deficit with revenues from other services, a practice referred to as **cross subsidization.** Thus, business customers of utilities are sometimes charged more, relative to the actual costs of serving them, than are households. This practice in effect involves a hidden tax and a hidden subsidy; businesses are taxed to subsidize households. The same phenomenon can be seen in our most important public monopoly, the U.S. Postal Service. It charges the same price for delivering mail to small rural communities as it does to major cities, in spite of the large differences in costs. Small communities have their mail services subsidized by larger ones.

How much less efficient the government is as a producer than the private sector is difficult to determine. Efficiency comparisons between government-run telephone companies in Europe and America's private firms provided much of the motivation for the late-twentieth-century **privatization** movement—the movement to convert government enterprises into private firms. Britain sold its telephone services and some other utilities, Japan its telephones and railroads, France its banks and many other enterprises. Not all publicly run enterprises are less productive than their private counterparts, however. For example, Canada has two major rail lines, one operated by the government and one private, which differ little in the efficiency with which they are run—perhaps because of competition between the two. Many of the publicly owned enterprises in France seem to run as efficiently as private firms, perhaps because the high prestige afforded to those who work in the French civil service enables it to recruit from among the most talented people in the country. There may also be less difference between government enterprises and large corporations—particularly when both are subjected to some market pressure and competition—than popular conceptions of governmental waste would suggest.

REGULATION

Some countries leave the natural monopolies in the private sector but regulate them. This is generally the U.S. practice. Local utilities, for instance, remain private, but their rates are regulated by the states. Federal agencies regulate interstate telephone services and the prices that can be charged for interstate transport of natural gas.

The aim of regulation is to keep the price as low as possible, commensurate with the monopolist's need to obtain an adequate return on its investment. In other words, regulators try to keep price equal to average costs—where average costs include a "normal return" on what the firm's owners have invested in the firm. If they are successful, the natural monopoly will earn no monopoly profits. Such a regulated output and price are shown in Figure 13.4 as Q_r and p_r.

Two criticisms have been leveled against regulation as a solution to the natural monopoly problem. The first is that regulations often introduce inefficiencies in several ways. The intent is to set prices so that firms obtain a "fair" return on their capital. But to make the highest level of profit, firms respond by investing as much capital as

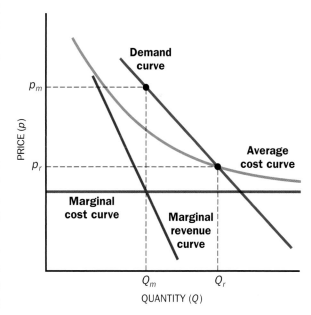

FIGURE 13.4

REGULATING A NATURAL MONOPOLY

Government regulators will often seek to choose the point on the market demand curve where the firm provides the greatest quantity at the lowest price consistent with the firm covering its costs. The point is the quantity Q_r and price p_r, where the demand curve intersects the average cost curve.

possible—sometimes too much. In addition, some groups, often businesses, may be required to pay extra-high prices so that other groups can be subsidized. Cross subsidies are no less a problem for natural monopolies if they are privately owned and regulated than if they are owned and operated by the government. Furthermore, companies have little incentive to innovate if their success in lowering costs is always followed by lower regulated prices rather than by higher profits. U.S. regulators have recognized that unless they reward innovation, it will not happen. They have agreed to allow the utilities to retain much of the increased profits they obtain from improved efficiency, at least for a few years.

The second criticism is that the regulators lose their focus on the public interest. The theory of **regulatory capture** argues that regulators are frequently pulled into the camps of those they regulate. Sometimes bribery and corruption are to blame, but far more common is that over time, employees of a regulated industry develop personal friendships with the regulators, who in turn come to rely on their expertise and judgment. Worse, regulatory agencies (of necessity) tend to hire from among those in the regulated industry. By the same token, regulators who demonstrate an "understanding" of the industry may be rewarded with good jobs in that industry after they leave government service.

ENCOURAGING COMPETITION

The final way government deals with the hard choices posed by natural monopolies is to encourage competition, even if it is imperfect. To understand this strategy,

International Perspective

THE DARKER SIDE OF PRIVATIZATION

In many countries around the world, where government used to own a large share of industry, privatization has had a marked impact on the economic landscape. Those favoring privatization argued that it would not only improve efficiency but also reduce corruption, by eliminating government enterprises as a source of income and patronage.

But privatization itself has turned out to be a major source of corruption; indeed, in many parts of the world it has come to be called *briberization*. When state assets are sold at below market prices, those who are lucky enough to get control of them win a huge bonanza. (In Russia, instant billionaires were created.) And to be sure, those who control the privatization process get ample kickbacks.

The problem is that the sale of a large corporation involves a host of technical details. To begin with, potential buyers have to be certified—will they really come up with the cash they promise? The rules for conducting the sales have routinely been written and implemented in ways that serve the interests of some at the expense of others. As a result, rather than being those most capable of managing the corporation, the winners are the most politically connected or are willing to bribe the most. This in turn has meant that the promised benefits of privatization—increased efficiency—often have not been realized. In many countries in the former Soviet Union and Eastern Europe, privatization has led more often to the stripping away of assets than to the creation of more efficient firms.

let us first review why competition may not be viable when average costs are declining over the relevant range of output.

If two firms divide the market between them, each faces higher average costs than if either one controlled the whole market. By undercutting its rival, a firm would be able to capture the entire market *and* reduce its average costs. By the same token, a natural monopolist knows that it can charge a price above its average cost without worrying about entry. Rivals that might enter the market, trying to capture some of the profits, know that the natural monopolist has lower costs because of its larger scale of production, and so can always undercut them.

Even under these conditions, some economists have argued that a monopolist would not in fact charge higher than average costs, because a rival could enter any time and grab the whole market. Analysts have argued that in the software industry, such a worry leads Microsoft to lower its prices. By keeping its prices lower than it would if no potential rival could enter the market, Microsoft promotes the wider use of its software. As people use programs such as Microsoft's Word and Excel, they become familiar with them and more reluctant to switch to something new, thereby creating a greater obstacle for a new entrant to overcome. Similarly, in small countries such as New Zealand, the threat that a large foreign firm could enter the market and take it over if the local monopoly charged above average costs restrains the monopoly's ability to raise its prices. On this argument, all that is required to keep prices low is potential competition.

Most economists are not so optimistic about the effectiveness of potential, as opposed to actual, competition. They note that potential competition has not been able to keep airline prices down in those markets in which actual competition is limited to one or two carriers.

In the late 1970s and 1980s, many governments became convinced that competition, however imperfect, might be better than regulation, and they began a process of deregulation. Deregulation focused on industries such as airlines, railroads, and trucking in which increasing returns to scale are limited. Recall that it is increasing returns to scale that lead to declining average costs. Thus, reformers believed that competition had a chance of succeeding in these industries. Government also sought to distinguish parts of an industry where competition might work from parts where competition was unlikely to be effective. In the telephone industry, for example, competition among several carriers was strong for long-distance telephone service, and there were few economies of scale in the production of telephone equipment. Accordingly, regulation in these areas was reduced or eliminated.

The virtues of competition have been realized, for the most part. Trucking—where the arguments for government regulation seemed most suspect—was perhaps the most unambiguous success story, as prices have fallen significantly. Railroads appear more financially sound than they did under regulation. But coal producers, who rely on railroads to ship their coal, complain that railroads have used their monopoly power to charge them much higher tariffs.

Airline deregulation has become more controversial. After its initial success—marked by new firms, lower fares, and more extensive routings—a rash of bankruptcies has reduced the number of airlines. Many airports, including those at St. Louis, Atlanta, and Denver, are dominated by one or two carriers, and travelers from these communities often must pay extremely high fares. A pattern of discriminatory pricing has developed, and businesspeople who cannot make reservations weeks in advance are charged four or more times the fare of a vacationer for the same seat.

Deregulation has not yet extended to natural monopolies like water. But the deregulation of electricity is well under way, implemented in more than half the U.S. states.

Case in Point

CALIFORNIA ELECTRICITY DEREGULATION

California was among the states in the forefront of electricity deregulation. Economists recognized that there were many potential suppliers of generating capacity and many potential retailers of electricity services. The only natural monopoly was in the transmission between the generators of electricity and the retailers. Breaking up the old electricity companies, which integrated all these functions, could lead to competition in all areas except transmission. Increased competition in the parts of the system where it was possible would lead to greater efficiency, and ultimately to lower prices and better service—or so it was hoped.

In 2000, deregulation appeared to be a disaster: electricity prices soared, shortages of generating capacity led to brownouts and interrupted service, electricity companies went bankrupt, and a massive government bailout was needed. Clearly, things had not gone as planned. Not surprisingly, there was plenty of finger-pointing. Critics blamed deregulation. Proponents said that even with

Shasta Dam is a hydroelectric facility in California.

deregulation, government had retained too large a role—it had put ceilings on the prices companies could charge consumers and prevented the use of long-term contracts. Well-intentioned or not, these restrictions exposed electricity companies like Pacific Gas and Electric to an impossible squeeze: high gas prices led to high wholesale prices for electricity that were greater than the controlled retail prices. And the way deregulation was done allowed energy traders like Enron to manipulate the market. Enron was doing more than just gouging California—it was also engaging in a variety of allegedly fraudulent accounting practices that were designed to boost its stock price. Eventually, the company collapsed, and the schemes that enabled Enron to create profits by exploiting the partially deregulated California energy market were revealed during the court cases that attended its bankruptcy.

Wrap-Up

APPROACHES TO THE PROBLEM OF NATURAL MONOPOLY

Public ownership
Regulation
Encouraging competition

Antitrust Policies

Only some of the failures of competition arise from natural monopolies. Other imperfections, as we have seen, are the result of sharp business practices intended to develop market power by deterring entry or promoting collusion. When encouraging competition does not work, government sometimes resorts to enforcing competition through *antitrust law,* the body of law designed to restrict anticompetitive practices.

As we will see, these policies have often been controversial. Consumer groups and injured businesses tend to support them, arguing that without them, firms would focus more on competition-reducing strategies than on efficiently producing products that customers like. But many businesses claim that such policies interfere with economic efficiency. For instance, even if the most efficient way to distribute its products is through exclusive territories for distributors, the firm might worry that such a contract might be ruled illegal.

Table 13.1 lists the major landmarks of U.S. antitrust policy. These take the form of legislation and relevant judicial decisions. They fall into two categories: (1) limiting market domination and (2) curbing restrictive practices.

Table 13.1

MAJOR ANTITRUST LEGISLATION AND LANDMARK CASES

Sherman Antitrust Act, 1890	Made acts in restraint of trade illegal.
Standard Oil and American Tobacco cases, 1911	Broke up both firms (each of which accounted for more than 90% of its industry) into smaller companies.
Clayton Act, 1914	Outlawed unfair trade practices. Restricted mergers that would substantially reduce competition.
Establishment of the Federal Trade Commission, 1914	Established to investigate unfair practices and issue orders to "cease and desist."
Robinson-Patman Act, 1936	Strengthened provisions of the Clayton Act, outlawing price discrimination.
Alcoa case, 1945	Alcoa, controlling 90% of the aluminum market, was found to be in violation of the Sherman Act.
Tobacco case, 1946	The tobacco industry, a concentrated oligopoly, was found guilty of violation of the Sherman Act on the basis of tacit collusion.
Celler-Kefauver Antimerger Act, 1950	Placed further restrictions on mergers that would reduce competition.
Du Pont Cellophane case, 1956	Broadened the definition of market. Ruled that a 20% market share was insufficient to establish market power.

LIMITING MARKET DOMINATION

In this section, we look at how government tries to limit economic power. In the decades following the Civil War, entrepreneurs in several industries attempted to form **trusts.** These were organizations that controlled a market. One individual had a controlling interest in a firm, which in turn had a controlling interest in all the other firms in the industry. Through the addition of more layers—firms that controlled firms that controlled firms, and so on—a relatively small ownership stake could be leveraged into enormous economic power.

Among the most famous of the nineteenth-century trusts was the oil industry trust; John D. Rockefeller and his partners eventually controlled 90 percent of all oil sold in America between 1870 and 1899. In the early 1900s, Andrew Carnegie and J. P. Morgan merged many smaller steel companies to form U.S. Steel, which in its heyday sold 65 percent of all American steel.

Concern about these so-called robber barons led to passage of the Sherman Antitrust Act of 1890, which outlaws "every contract, combination in the form of a trust or otherwise, or conspiracy in restraint of trade or commerce." Further, "every person who shall monopolize, or attempt to monopolize, or combine or conspire with any other person or persons, to monopolize any part of the trade or commerce among the several States, or with foreign nations, shall be deemed guilty of a misdemeanor." (A 1974 amendment made violations felonies.) Two important decisions based on the Sherman Act led to the breakups of Standard Oil and American Tobacco in 1911, each of which had dominated its respective industry.

The Sherman Act was supplemented by the Clayton Act in 1914, which forbade any firm to acquire shares of a competing firm when that purchase would substantially reduce competition. The act also outlawed interlocking directorates (in which the same individuals serve as directors of several firms) among firms that were supposedly in competition. These antimerger provisions were further strengthened in 1950 by the Celler-Kefauver Antimerger Act.

The government does not care about absolute size itself. In the 1960s, huge firms called *conglomerates* were formed that brought together such disparate enterprises as a steel company, an oil company, and a company making films. For example, United Airlines for a few years owned Hertz rental cars and Westin Hotels (both sold in the late 1980s). But while large, these conglomerates generally did not have a dominant position in any one market, and thus the antitrust laws were not concerned with them. The early antitrust laws were particularly concerned with **horizontal mergers,** and thus with competition within a market. These are distinguished from **vertical mergers,** in which a firm buys a supplier or a distributor, thereby amalgamating the various stages in the production process within a firm. Thus, Ford made its own steel, and General Motors bought out Fisher Body (the maker of GM's car bodies), as well as many of the specialized firms that produced batteries, spark plugs, and other components.

Under current court interpretations, market power per se is also not a primary concern. To be convicted of an antitrust violation, the firm must be shown to have acquired its market position by anticompetitive practices or to have used its market power to engage in anticompetitive practices.

DEFINING MARKETS

We have seen that the extent to which a firm's demand curve is downward sloping, enabling it to raise its price without losing all its customers—its market power—is related to the number of firms in the industry and the extent of product differentiation. Both factors are important for purposes of antitrust enforcement, since the government must first define "the market" before it can determine whether a firm dominates its market.

Thinking Like an Economist

INCENTIVES AND THE REMEDY TO THE MICROSOFT MONOPOLY PROBLEM

In 1999, Judge Thomas Penfield Jackson found Microsoft guilty of violating U.S. antitrust laws. He then was faced with a difficult problem: what remedy to impose. Jackson was keenly aware of the *incentives* that Microsoft faced; its profitability depended on its ability to preserve its market power, and it therefore had strong incentives to stifle innovations that might reduce that market power. For instance, Sun Microsystems had developed a language, Java, that would enable programmers to develop applications to run not just on Microsoft's Windows operating system but on other operating systems as well. One of the reasons why Microsoft's operating system was so dominant was that rivals started with a marked disadvantage—a lack of applications to run on their operating systems. By changing all of that, Java would result in real competition in the market for operating systems. Microsoft similarly worried that Netscape might serve as a platform through which competition in the operating system might be enhanced, and it sought to quash this threat by bundling its own browser,

Internet Explorer, free with the Windows operating system. Microsoft had done what comes naturally to monopolists—it simply sought to maximize its long-run profits by reducing the threat of competition. The judge worried that no matter how he scolded Microsoft, or what fines he imposed, Microsoft had every incentive to continue these anticompetitive practices. Moreover, he was aware of how difficult detecting and proving anticompetitive behavior can be, and Microsoft had already demonstrated its willingness to face risks of antitrust prosecution. Hence, the only way to alter behavior was to alter incentives, and doing so entailed changing the structure of the enterprise. The Department of Justice proposed splitting Microsoft into two, with one company focusing on applications and the other focusing on the operating system. The application company would have every incentive to ensure that its applications could be used on as many operating systems as possible. The hope was that Microsoft Word might then be written to work on more operating systems, like Linux, so that

Market Bounds and Globalization Over the past two hundred years, the geographical scope of markets has grown enormously. Technological improvements in transportation, from steam-powered ships to railroads to airplanes, have lowered the cost of transportation and expanded the boundaries of markets. As a market expands, it may become more competitive—as happened in the U.S. auto industry during the 1980s and 1990s, when the big three domestic firms (Ford, General Motors, and Chrysler) faced increasing competition from Japanese, European, and Korean manufacturers. Today, the degree of competition in a market must be judged by a global assessment rather than by a simple examination of how many firms produce a good in the United States. Because of the Internet, many markets have enlarged even more. Twenty years ago, a local bookstore might have been the only bookseller in a town; now that same business must face competition from online vendors such as Amazon.com and Borders.com.

Product Differentiation All firms that produce the same good and sell in the same location are clearly in the same market, but definitions become more ambigu-

demand for them would increase. And restraining the operating system company from writing applications would at least prevent a repeat of what had happened with Netscape and the browser market.

Some critics thought the judge, in approving the Justice Department's recommendations in 2000, went too far; others thought he did not go far enough. Those in the former camp worried that he overlooked important economies of scope—efficiencies that arose from the close interaction between those writing the operating system and those developing applications. These advantages, they contended, more than offset the disadvantages from the loss in competition. Moreover, they believed that Microsoft's monopoly power was temporary; within a few years, surely competition would erode its dominant position. Already, Linux was rapidly growing as an alternative operating system. They argued that Microsoft had achieved its dominant position by strong innovation, and it was wrong to punish this success now by breaking the company up.

But critics on the other side said that at least a significant part of Microsoft's success was due to its ruthless business practices, and such behavior should not go unpunished. And more was at stake: Microsoft represented a threat to innovation. Few would invest in innovation if they believed that any innovation threatening Microsoft's competitive position would be suppressed by Microsoft. Many Silicon Valley firms shared this fear.

These critics worried that the Microsoft application company still might not write programs for other operating systems, that there might be sweetheart deals between the two companies; they argued for other approaches to changes Microsoft's incentives. For instance, some suggested limiting intellectual property protection—and requiring the disclosure of the code—for operating systems of a firm with a dominant position (like Microsoft) to, say, three to five years. Doing so would automatically create a competitor to, say, Windows XP—the freely available Windows 2000. Only if Windows XP were markedly better than Windows 2000 would people pay anything for it. This approach would enhance Microsoft's incentives to innovate. Meanwhile, application programmers would have an incentive to write programs that worked better and better with the freely available 2000 operating system. The hope was that out of this competition, consumers would benefit not only from lower prices but also from innovations, possibly leading to programs that crash less often and are tailored better to the needs of particular groups of users, that run faster, and that perform new tasks.

ous when goods produced by different firms are imperfect substitutes. What, for example, is the market for beer? Those in the industry might claim that premium beers and discount beers really constitute two different markets, as relatively few customers cross over from one to the other. In the 1950s, DuPont had a virtual monopoly on the market for clear wrapping paper, but it fought off charges of monopoly by arguing that its product was one among several "wrapping materials." It claimed that brown paper was a good, though not perfect, substitute for clear wrapping paper, and that DuPont did not have a particularly large share of this larger market.

Legal Criteria Today, the courts look at two criteria in defining a market and market power. First, they consider the extent to which a change in price for one product affects the demand for another. If an increase in the price of aluminum has a large positive effect on the demand for steel, then steel and aluminum may be considered to be in the same market—the market for metals. Second, if a firm can raise its price, say by 5 percent, and lose only a relatively small fraction of its sales, then it is "large"—that is, it has market power.

Before one large company can acquire or merge with a competitor, it must convince the government that the acquisition would not seriously interfere with the overall competitiveness of the market.

CURBING RESTRICTIVE PRACTICES

In addition to promoting competition by limiting the degree of concentration within an industry, the government works to limit restrictive practices. The history here begins with the 1914 Federal Trade Commission Act. The first ten words of the act read: "Unfair methods of competition in commerce are hereby declared unlawful." President Woodrow Wilson defined the purpose of the new commission as being to "plead the voiceless consumer's case." Since then, a number of laws have been passed by Congress to specify what is "unfair."

Many of the restrictive practices targeted by the government involve the relations between a firm and its distributors and suppliers. Such practices include tie-ins, exclusive dealing, and price discrimination. We have already encountered all three in Chapter 12. Tie-ins require a consumer to purchase additional items when she buys a product. In exclusive dealing, a producer says to a firm that wants to sell its product, "If you sell my product, you cannot sell that of my rival." Price discrimination entails charging different customers different prices on grounds unrelated to the costs of serving those customers. The Robinson-Patman Act of 1936 strengthened the provisions outlawing price discrimination, making it easier to convict firms engaged in the practice. Other practices discussed in Chapter 12 designed to deter entry or promote collusion are illegal as well.

The precise definition of an illegal restrictive practice has changed over time with varying court interpretations of the antitrust laws. Some practices are illegal per se—firms conspiring to fix prices, for example. In 1961, General Electric, Westinghouse, and other producers of electrical equipment were found guilty of such conspiracy. More recently, several huge price-fixing cases were prosecuted successfully, most notably one against ADM (Archer Daniel Midland) involving lysine, citric acid, and high-fructose corn syrup. The corporations paid more than $100 million in fines, and some of their officials went to prison. Most practices, however, are not so clear-cut, and today a "rule of reason" prevails: they are acceptable if they can be shown to be reasonable business procedures, designed to promote economic efficiency. The efficiency gains are balanced against the higher prices resulting from the reduced competition.

Consider the example of Budweiser beer, which delivers its product through distributors. In any area, there is only one distributor, and the distributors are not allowed to compete against one another. The New York attorney general has argued that this system, by restricting competition, raises prices. Anheuser-Busch has replied that the system of exclusive territories enhances the efficiency with which beer is delivered and is necessary to ensure that customers receive fresh beer. They have maintained that their distribution system satisfies the rule of reason, and thus far their view has prevailed in the courts.

States have also been accused of adopting laws that restrict competition in ways designed to favor in-state firms. In December 2004, the U.S. Supreme Court heard arguments brought by a small Virginia winery against New York's laws restricting direct sales by out-of-state wineries to residents of New York. A challenge to a similar law in Michigan was also heard by the courts. The states argued that they were given regulatory power over the sale of alcoholic beverages by the Twenty-first Amendment to the Constitution, adopted to repeal Prohibition in 1933. However, because the New York and Michigan restrictions apply only to out-of-state producers while allowing in-state producers to ship directly to consumers, the laws have the effect of limiting competition. In May 2005, the Supreme Court ruled in favor of the Virginia winery and struck down the New York and Michigan laws that had restricted sales by out-of-state wineries.

ENFORCING THE ANTITRUST LAWS

Today antitrust laws are on the books at both state and federal levels, and they are enforced by both criminal and civil courts. The government takes action not only to break up existing monopolies but also to prevent firms from obtaining excessive market power.

The Federal Trade Commission (FTC) and the Antitrust Division of the Department of Justice are at the center of the government's efforts to promote competition. The FTC works like a law enforcement agency, investigating complaints it receives. It can provide advisory opinions on how an individual business should interpret the law, provide guidelines for entire industries, and even issue specific rules and regulations that businesses must follow. When necessary, the FTC enforces these decisions in court.

One interesting and controversial aspect of the antitrust laws is the use they make of *private* law enforcement. Any firm that believes it has been injured by the anticompetitive practices of another firm can sue; if successful, it can receive three times the dollar value of the damages and attorney fees incurred. The treble damages provision helps encourage private firms to call violations to the attention of the government. For example, in 1974 MCI sued AT&T, claiming that the latter had used unfair trade practices to hurt MCI in its attempt to enter the long-distance telephone business. In 1982, the jury estimated that MCI had, as a result of AT&T's activities, lost $600 million in profits, and ordered AT&T to pay triple that amount—$1.8 billion—in damages to MCI. The award was subsequently reduced on appeal to higher courts.

Two arguments favor private enforcement of antitrust laws. First, those who are injured by anticompetitive practices are in the best position to detect a violation of the law. Second, government may be lax in the enforcement of these laws because cartels and dominant firms may wield a great deal of political influence.

On the other side of the argument are concerns about the rising costs of antitrust litigation—the number of private suits doubled between the 1960s and the 1970s. And many worry that businesses use the threat of an antitrust suit as a way of raising a rival's costs. Thus, Chrysler charged General Motors with an antitrust violation when GM proposed a joint venture with a Japanese firm, only to drop the action when it found a Japanese partner for its own joint venture.

ANTITRUST POLICIES

Antitrust policies are designed to ensure competition in the marketplace by
    Limiting market dominance
    Curbing restrictive trade practices

The problems faced in designing and enforcing antitrust policies include
    The problem of defining the market
    Determining how to deal with firm practices that may *both* reduce competition *and* enhance efficiency

Enforcement of antitrust regulations can involve criminal or civil penalties.

Case in Point

COKE AND PEPSI PLAY MERGER

The Coca-Cola Company and PepsiCo, Inc., dominate the market for carbonated soft drinks. Early in 1986, each proposed to grow larger through acquisition. In January, PepsiCo proposed buying 7-Up, the fourth-largest soft drink manufacturer, for $380 million. In February, Coca-Cola proposed buying Dr. Pepper, the third-largest, for $470 million.

The mergers would have made the big even bigger. Coca-Cola and PepsiCo already held 39 percent and 28 percent of the market, respectively, while Dr. Pepper had 7 percent and 7-Up had 6 percent. The next largest firm in the market after 7-Up was R. J. Reynolds (known for Canada Dry and Sunkist), which held 5 percent of the soft drink market.

The Federal Trade Commission announced that it would oppose the mergers. To assess the impact on competition in such cases, the government often uses what is called the Herfindahl-Hirschman index (HHI). The HHI is calculated by summing the squares of the market shares. If the industry consists of a single firm, then the HHI is $(100)^2 = 10,000$. If the industry consists of 1,000 firms, each with 0.1 percent of the market, then the HHI is $(0.1)^2 \times 1,000 = 10$. Thus, higher values of the HHI indicate less competitive industries.

Merger guidelines used by the federal government divide markets into three categories, with different policy recommendations. The divisions and policy recommendations are given in Table 13.2.

Before the mergers, assuming that the 15 percent of the market not accounted for by the big five was divided equally among fifteen small producers, a somewhat simplified HHI for the soft drink industry was

$$HHI = 39^2 + 28^2 + 7^2 + 6^2 + 5^2 + 15 \, (1)^2 = 2,430.$$

If we plug in the 34 percent share that PepsiCo would have after acquiring 7-Up, the PepsiCo–7-Up merger would raise the HHI to 2,766. The two proposed mergers together would raise the HHI to 3,312.

After the FTC announced its opposition, PepsiCo immediately gave up on purchasing 7-Up. Coca-Cola pushed ahead with its plan to buy Dr. Pepper until a federal judge ruled that it was a "stark, unvarnished" attempt to eliminate competition that "totally [lacked] any apparent redeeming feature."

The court case did bring a secret to the surface, however. The trial disclosed certain Coca-Cola company memos written after PepsiCo's offer for 7-Up had been made. In the memos, Coca-Cola executives expressed fear that the FTC might allow the PepsiCo merger, despite the agency's guidelines. By announcing plans to buy Dr. Pepper, Coca-Cola hoped that the FTC would step in and block *both* mergers, as it did, thereby preventing PepsiCo from using a merger to catch up in size to Coca-Cola.[1]

Table 13.2

HERFINDAHL-HIRSCHMAN INDEX

Level of HHI	Policy recommendation
Less than 1,000, unconcentrated	Mergers allowed without government challenge
Between 1,000 and 1,800, moderately concentrated	Mergers challenged if they raise the industry HHI by more than 100 points
Above 1,800, concentrated	Mergers challenged if they raise the industry HHI by more than 50 points

---

[1]See the following *Wall Street Journal* articles: Timothy K. Smith and Scott Kilman, "Coke to Acquire Dr. Pepper Co. for $470 Million," February 21, 1986, p. 2; Andy Pasztor and Timothy K. Smith, "FTC Opposes Purchase Plans by Coke, Pepsi," June 23, 1986, p. 2; Pasztor and Smith, "Coke Launched Dr. Pepper Bid to Scuttle Plans by PepsiCo, Documents Indicate," July 29, 1986, p. 3; Pasztor and Smith, "Coke's Plan to Buy Dr. Pepper Is Blocked by U.S. Judge, Pending Decision by FTC," August 1, 1986, p. 3.

Review and Practice

SUMMARY

1. Economists have identified four major problems resulting from monopolies and imperfect competition: restricted output, managerial slack, lack of incentives to make technological progress, and wasteful rent-seeking expenditures.

2. Since for a natural monopoly average costs are declining over the range of market demand, a large firm can undercut its rivals. And since marginal cost for a natural monopoly lies below average cost, an attempt by regulators to require it to set price equal to marginal cost (as in the case of perfect competition) will force the firm to make losses.

3. Taking ownership of a natural monopoly enables the government to set price and quantity directly. But it also subjects an industry to political pressures and the potential inefficiencies of government operation.

4. In the United States, natural monopolies are regulated. Government regulators seek to keep prices as low and quantity as high as is consistent with the natural monopolist being able to cover its costs. However, regulators are under political pressure to provide cross subsidies and are prone to being "captured" by the industry they are regulating.

5. In some cases, potential competition may be as effective as public ownership or government regulation at keeping prices low.

6. Antitrust policy is concerned with promoting competition, both by making it more difficult for any firm to dominate a market and by restricting practices that interfere with competition.

7. Under the "rule of reason," companies may seek to defend themselves from accusations of anticompetitive behavior by claiming that the practice in question also leads to greater efficiency. In such cases, courts must often decide whether the potential efficiency benefits of restrictive practices outweigh their potential anticompetitive effects.

KEY TERMS

managerial slack
rent seeking
cross subsidization
privatization
regulatory capture
trusts
horizontal mergers
vertical mergers

REVIEW QUESTIONS

1. What does it mean when an economist says that monopoly output is "too little" or a monopoly price is "too high"? By what standard? Compared with what?

2. Why might a monopoly lack incentives to hold costs as low as possible?

3. Why might a monopoly lack incentives to pursue research and development opportunities aggressively?

4. What might an economist regard as a socially wasteful way of spending monopoly profits?

5. Explain why the marginal cost curve of a natural monopoly lies below its average cost curve. What are the consequences of this?

6. If government regulators of a natural monopoly set price equal to marginal cost, what problem will inevitably arise? How might government ownership or regulation address this problem? What are the problems of each?

7. What is the regulatory capture hypothesis?

8. Explain the difference between a horizontal and a vertical merger.

9. Explain how the government uses antitrust policies to encourage competition, by making it more difficult for a firm to dominate a market and by curbing restrictive practices. What are some of the problems in implementing antitrust policy and some of the current controversies surrounding it?

PROBLEMS

1. Before deregulation of the telephone industry in 1984, AT&T provided both local and long-distance telephone service. A number of firms argued that they could provide

long-distance service between major cities more cheaply than AT&T, but AT&T argued against allowing firms to enter only the long-distance market. If those other firms (which had no technological advantage) could actually have offered long-distance service more cheaply, what does that imply about cross subsidies in AT&T's pricing of local and long-distance service? What would have happened if AT&T had been required to continue offering local service at the same price, but competition had been allowed in the long-distance market?

2. Explain the incentive problem involved if regulators ensure that a natural monopoly will be able to cover its average costs.

3. Explain how some competition, even if not perfect, may be an improvement for consumers over an unregulated natural monopoly. Explain why such competition will not be as good for consumers as an extremely sophisticated regulator, and why it may be better than many real-world regulators.

4. Smalltown, USA, has one bookstore, one newspaper, one movie theater, one nightclub, one grocery store, one hair salon, one college, and one department store. Does it follow that each of these is a monopolist? In each case, explain what sources of competition the firm might face that would limit its market power.

5. For each pair, explain whether you think they are part of the same or separate markets.
   (a) Ice cream manufacturers and frozen yogurt manufacturers
   (b) Doctors and dentists
   (c) Doctors and chiropractors
   (d) Public universities and private universities
   (e) Trade schools and universities

6. Before the 1980s, many industries in New Zealand were dominated by a single firm. To limit the social cost of monopoly, these firms were heavily regulated by the government. After winning election in the 1980s, New Zealand's Labour Party shifted the government's focus from regulating domestic firms to eliminating restrictions on imports. Explain why reducing the barriers that had prevented New Zealanders from buying imported goods could reduce the market power of the domestic firm, even if there continues to be only one domestic firm in the industry.

Learning Goals

In this chapter, you will learn

1 How game theory can help us understand strategic behavior

2 What the Nash equilibrium is in the prisoner's dilemma game

3 Why backward induction is critical for thinking strategically

4 How reputation can play a role in repeated games

5 How game theory can help us understand why threats and promises may not always be credible

Chapter 14

STRATEGIC BEHAVIOR

During the 2000 television season, viewers were enthralled by the first season of the show *Survivor*. Sixteen contestants were marooned on Pulau Tiga, an uninhabited island off the coast of Borneo, and at the end of each episode, the survivors voted to kick out one of their members. The last surviving contestant collected $1 million. By episode 13, the original group had been reduced to just three final contestants: Kelly, Rudy, and Rich. In the course of a trial that involved answering questions about the thirteen previously evicted castaways, Kelly won immunity in the first round of voting that would reduce the group to the final pair. She still had to decide, though, how to cast her own vote. If, as seemed certain, Rudy votes against Rich and Rich votes against Rudy, Kelly's vote would decide who stays and who leaves. How should Kelly vote?

To know whom she should vote out in the first round, Kelly must think about how she was likely to fare in the final round. Kelly must think backward from the end of the contest. Rudy seemed popular with the audience and with the other thirteen contestants who would get to vote for the final winner. So Kelly would reason that if the final contest came down to her and Rudy, Rudy would probably win. On the other hand, Rich seemed to be very unpopular. So Kelly would reason that if it came down to a choice between her and Rich, she would probably win. Her best chance would be to face off against Rich, not Rudy, in the final voting. Even if Kelly really dislikes Rich, her best strategy is to oust Rudy. As it turned out, that is exactly what happened. Rich and Kelly voted against Rudy. Unfortunately for Kelly, the voters ended up picking Rich over her, but her strategy was still the right one.

The participants in *Survivor* had to think strategically. They needed to anticipate how their rivals would respond to the decisions they themselves made. They had to consider how their own position would depend on who else survived and who didn't, and they had to use that information in deciding how to vote.

Thinking strategically doesn't help just in a made-up environment such as a television show. We all face situations that call for strategic thinking. Economists try to understand the choices individuals and firms make, and researchers studying strategic behavior have extended the reach of economics into many new areas.

Economists examine the choices made by rational individuals and profit-maximizing firms. In the basic competitive model presented in the first two parts of this book, individuals and firms do not need to behave strategically. Consumers and firms can buy or sell as much as they want at the market price. A firm does not need to worry about how its rivals will react if it decides to produce more. Nor does a monopoly, but for a different reason: a monopoly has no rivals. In the basic competitive model and in a monopoly model, **strategic behavior**—decisions that take into account the possible reactions of others—plays no role.

Things were different in Chapter 12 when we studied oligopolies. With only a few firms in the industry, each firm needs to be concerned about how its rivals might react whenever it contemplates expanding production or cutting its price. Strategic behavior becomes important. When AMD considers cutting the prices of its various computer processor chips, it must try to assess how Intel will respond. If Intel reacts by also cutting prices, then AMD may not gain much market share and its revenues will decline as a result of the lower prices. But if Intel keeps its prices unchanged, AMD may gain market share and its revenues might rise as it sells more chips.

Because oligopolies engage in strategic behavior, Chapter 12 used game theory—and the simple prisoner's dilemma game—to demonstrate why it may be difficult for firms to collude. In this chapter, we return to the prisoner's dilemma and see how its basic insights can be applied to other areas of economics. The usefulness of game theory goes well beyond this simple model, however, for decisions and choices often must incorporate the potential reactions of others. You will learn more about game theory and how it helps us understand the choices made by individuals, firms, unions, and governments. Game theory provides a framework for studying strategic behavior. Using this framework, economists have found that many instances of strategic behavior can be understood by relying on the core concepts of incentives and information.[1]

Review of the Prisoner's Dilemma

Let's very briefly recall the prisoner's dilemma game introduced in Chapter 12. Two prisoners, A and B, are alleged by the police to be conspirators in a crime. After being taken into custody, the two are separated. A police officer tells each, "Now here's the situation. If your partner confesses and you remain silent, you'll get five years in prison. But if your partner confesses and you confess also, you'll both get three years. On the other hand, if both you and your partner remain silent, we'll be able to convict you only of a lesser charge and you'll get one year in prison. But if your partner remains silent and you confess, we'll let you out in three months." The same deal is offered to both prisoners.

---

[1]If you would like to learn even more about game theory, an accessible textbook is available: Avinash Dixit and Susan Skeath, *Games of Strategy*, Second Edition (New York: W. W. Norton, 2004).

Figure 14.1, which reproduces a diagram from Chapter 12, shows the results of the deal the police have offered the prisoners. This type of grid, showing the payoffs to each player, is called a **game table.** In Chapter 12, we saw that based on self-interest, each individual prisoner believes that confession is best, whether his partner confesses or not. But by following self-interest and confessing, each ends up worse off than if neither had confessed. The prisoner's dilemma is a simple game in which both parties suffer because they independently act in self-interest. Both would be better off if they could get together to agree on a story and if each could threaten to punish the other if he deviates from the story.

This simple game has been widely applied in economics and in other fields such as international relations and political science. In Chapter 12, we used it to explain why two oligopolists would find it difficult to sustain an agreement to collude. We will discuss some further examples of the prisoner's dilemma and then consider other types of game situations. First, though, we will need to clarify our method of analyzing strategic situations to make predictions about how individuals and firms will behave.

		Prisoner B: Confesses	Prisoner B: Remains silent
Prisoner A	Confesses	B gets 3 years / A gets 3 years	B gets 5 years / A gets 3 months
	Remains silent	B gets 3 months / A gets 5 years	B gets 1 year / A gets 1 year

FIGURE 14.1
PRISONER'S DILEMMA GAME
Each prisoner's dominant strategy is to confess.

DOMINANT STRATEGIES

Behaving strategically means that each player must try to determine what the other player is likely to do. Will your accomplice confess or keep quiet? Will your rival match price reductions if you cut your prices? The decision of one player depends on how she thinks the other player will respond.

In the basic prisoner's dilemma game, we assume that players reason along the following lines: "For each choice that I might make, what is the best choice for the other player to make?" In analyzing the prisoner's dilemma, we ask, "If prisoner A doesn't confess, what is the best strategy for prisoner B? If prisoner A confesses, what is the best strategy for prisoner B?" In both cases, we conclude that confessing is prisoner B's *best response.* If B's best response is to confess, no matter what prisoner A does, then A will conclude that B will confess, so A needs to decide what his best response is to prisoner B confessing. As we saw, prisoner A's best option is also to confess.

Such a strategy—one that works best no matter what the other player does—is called a **dominant strategy.** Recall that an objective of game theory is to predict what strategy each player will choose. When a player has a dominant strategy, that is the strategy we should predict a rational decision maker will choose.

NASH EQUILIBRIUM

It is easy to predict the outcome of a game—its equilibrium—if each player has a dominant strategy. Each will play his dominant strategy. Thus, in the prisoner's dilemma, the equilibrium is both players confessing. The situation is not quite so simple when only one player has a dominant strategy, or when neither player has one; we will learn about such games later. To predict the equilibrium outcomes in these more complex games, we need to look more closely at why confessing is the equilibrium in the prisoner's dilemma.

In the prisoner's dilemma, each prisoner confesses because doing so leads to the best, or *optimal* payoff—the least amount of time in prison—given what the other prisoner can be expected to do. The outcome is an equilibrium in the sense that neither prisoner would change her chosen strategy if offered the chance to do so at the end of the game. By confessing, both have played their best response. Such an equilibrium is called a **Nash equilibrium,** and it is the most fundamental idea for predicting the actions of players in a strategic game.

John Nash developed the notion that bears his name when he was just twenty-one years old and a graduate student in mathematics at Princeton University. Economists have found the concept of Nash equilibrium extremely useful for predicting the outcomes of games and understanding economic problems. In recognition of its importance, John Nash shared the 1994 Nobel Prize in Economics. Nash is not an economist; he is a mathematician and the only winner of the Nobel Prize in Economics whose life has been the subject of a best-selling biography and a popular movie. Published in 1998, *A Beautiful Mind* by Sylvia Nasar chronicles Nash's early mathematical brilliance, his struggle with mental illness, and his eventual recovery. On being informed he had won the Nobel Prize, Nash commented that he hoped it would improve his credit rating.

The prisoner's dilemma arises in many contexts, both in economics and in other social sciences. The following examples, briefly sketched, provide some illustrations.[2]

Example: Collusion In Chapter 12, we studied an application of the prisoner's dilemma to the problem faced by two rivals who can benefit by colluding to restrict output. Colluding results in a higher price and therefore greater profits for each. The higher price can be maintained only if both firms continue to restrict output. But at the higher price, each firm perceives that it would be even better off if it could expand its output a little and sell more at the high price. Of course, this means that each firm has an incentive to cheat on their agreement to restrict output, just as each prisoner had an incentive to confess. And if both firms fail to stick to their bargain, their expansion causes the price, and their profits, to fall, thereby making each worst off than if they had continued to collude. In this game, each firm has a dominant strategy—cheat on the agreement by expanding output. Here, the outcome in which each firm expands is the Nash equilibrium; each firm is choosing its best response, given the actions of its rival. When both players have a dominant strategy, as in the prisoner's dilemma, both will choose to play it; no other outcome would satisfy the definition of a Nash equilibrium. In this case, there is only one Nash equilibrium, a situation economists describe by saying there is a *unique Nash equilibrium.*

Example: Politicians and Negative Ads Why do politicians engage in negative advertising even though they all promise not to?

---

[2]You should test your understanding of each example by filling out a game table, identifying the dominant strategy for each player, and finding the Nash equilibrium.

Consider the case of politicians A and B. If neither runs a negative campaign, the public thinks highly of both of them, but neither gains any advantage over the other. If both run negative campaign ads, the public thinks poorly of both, but again neither gains an advantage. Each is tarred by the other's ads. If politician A runs a clean campaign, politician B can gain an advantage by running a negative ad that tarnishes A's reputation. Conversely, A gains by running a negative ad if politician B runs a clean campaign.

Each politician will reason as follows: "If my opponent runs a negative ad, I'm better off if I also run negative ads. And if my opponent doesn't run a negative ad, then I can gain an advantage if I run negative ads. Either way, I'm better off if I run negative ads." Each politician has a dominant strategy, and in this unique Nash equilibrium both run negative campaign ads, despite their promises not to.

Example: Military Spending Two countries, A and B, are locked in a military balance. Each must decide whether to build a new generation of missiles. If neither builds the missile system, the military balance is preserved and each country will remain secure. If one builds the system while the other does not, one will gain a military advantage. If they both build the system, they each spend billions of dollars, but neither gains an advantage: each country now has the new missile system, preserving the military balance.

Each country reasons that if the other country fails to build the system, it can gain an advantage by going ahead and building the system. Both also know that if one country builds the new missiles, the other will be worse off if it fails to build the missile system as well. Each country has a dominant strategy—build the missile system. Both countries spend billions, only to find themselves left in the same military balance as before.

Example: Sports Owners and Player Salaries Sports teams compete to hire the best players. Suppose there are just two teams, the Yankees and the Athletics. If both teams collude and keep salaries low, the owners' profits go up. If the Yankees' owner instead offers high salaries while the Athletics owner does not, the Yankees will attract all the good players and will generate higher profits for the owner. Meanwhile, the Athletics end up with weaker players and have a poor season. Low attendance causes the owner to lose money. Conversely, if the Athletics offer high salaries and the Yankees do not, the Athletics get all the good players and earn the higher profits, while the Yankees lose money. If both offer high salaries, neither team gets all the good players, but increased salary costs cut into the owners' profits.

In a Nash equilibrium, both team owners offer players high salaries, and the owners are worse off than if they been able to collude to keep salaries down. Of course, our simple example ignores all the other factors—TV revenues, cable deals, sales of team paraphernalia, and so on—that support total payrolls and thus affect salaries and profits. But the example does suggest one of the factors behind the desire of owners in most professional sports to institute caps on player salaries. Without such caps, each owner has an incentive to try to outbid the others for the best players. A salary cap enables the owners to collude more effectively.

THE PRISONER'S DILEMMA

In the prisoner's dilemma, each player has a dominant strategy. In a unique Nash equilibrium, the players choose their dominant strategy. Yet the players are worse off in this Nash equilibrium than if they had chosen their alternative strategy. Applications of the prisoner's dilemma arise in many branches of economics, as well as in other social sciences and in everyday life.

Strategic Behavior in More General Games

In the prisoner's dilemma, both players have a dominant strategy. In most games, however, this is not the case. What each player finds it best to do depends on what the other player does, and determining the outcome of a game is therefore harder. But we can often make an accurate prediction by thinking through the consequences from each player's perspective, just as we did in the prisoner's dilemma.

GAMES WITH ONLY ONE DOMINANT STRATEGY

Consider the positions of two firms deciding on whether to cut prices. Discounters Delux and Quality Brands compete with each other. Discounters Delux promises its customers the lowest prices; it would suffer a large loss of customers if it failed to deliver on that promise. Quality Prices has higher costs; perhaps it provides better health care benefits to its workers or spends more on the displays in its stores. Because of these higher costs, it would prefer not to cut prices. However, it risks losing some of its business if it does not match Discounters Delux's price reductions. The profits each expects to earn are shown in Figure 14.2. The payoffs to Discounters Delux are below the diagonal lines, while those of Quality Brands are above the diagonals.

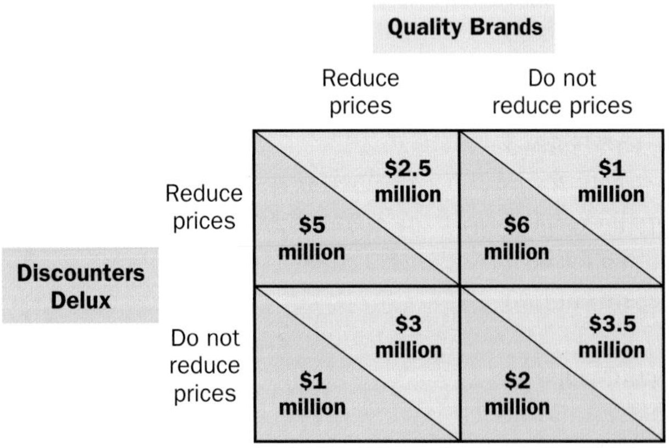

Discounters Delux has a dominant strategy—reduce prices. It makes more in profits under this strategy, regardless of what Quality Brands does. Quality Brands, in contrast, does not have a dominant strategy. If Discounters Delux reduces prices, Quality Brand's best response is to cut prices as well, since otherwise it would lose too many sales. However, if Discounters Delux does not reduce prices, then Quality Brands is better off not reducing its prices.

Even though Quality Brands does not have a dominant strategy, we can predict its move if we reason as follows. Quality Brands

FIGURE 14.2

PRICE-CUTTING GAME

Discounters Delux has a dominant strategy, which is to reduce prices. Thus, the best response for Quality Brands is also to cut prices.

International Perspective
BEGGAR-THY-NEIGHBOR TARIFF POLICIES

During the international depression of the 1930s, many countries debated whether to impose restrictions on international trade. Some argued that restricting imports from other countries would boost the demand for goods produced domestically. Increased demand, in turn, would enable domestic firms to expand employment and production. By reducing the demand for goods produced in other countries, such policies would lead to fewer sales by foreign firms, who would then have to cut production and employment. The gains at home would come at the expense of foreign producers and workers, so these were often called "beggar-thy-neighbor" policies. The trade wars of the 1930s can be understood as another example of the prisoner's dilemma.

In 1930, the United States passed the Smoot-Hawley Tariff Act. This act raised tariffs on imported goods, making them more expensive for American consumers and thereby providing an incentive for Americans to shift their demand to domestically produced goods. Other countries did not stand by idly while American tariffs reduced their market in the United States. They retaliated by raising their tariffs on goods produced in the United States. The result was that all countries suffered from the decline in world trade. By imposing tariffs that reduced trade, all countries lost the benefits of trade.

The outcome in the sort of trade war set off by the Smoot-Hawley Act can be illustrated in terms of a simple game. The diagram shows the payoffs to each of two countries that are deciding whether to impose trade restrictions. Payoffs to country A are shown below the diagonal line in each box; payoffs to country B, above the diagonal. The payoffs are defined as the gains (or losses) to a country's income relative to what that income would be if neither imposed trade restrictions. The numbers are hypothetical and can be thought of as, say, tens of billions of dollars. Each country gains the most if it is the only one to impose restrictions. Both are worse off if both impose restrictions and better off if neither imposes them.

Each country has a dominant strategy—impose trade sanctions. Country A, for example, would reason as follows: "If country B imposes trade restrictions, our country will be better off if we also impose restrictions. If country B does not impose restrictions, we are also better off if we impose restrictions. Therefore, we should impose trade restrictions regardless of what country B does." Country B would reason in exactly the same manner. Unfortunately, when they both impose restrictions, both are left worse off than if no restrictions had been imposed.

Another way to look at this situation is to recognize that both countries would be better off if they could cooperate and mutually agree not to impose trade restrictions. The problem is, our simple example provides no mechanism to ensure that they cooperate. Just as in the collusion example discussed in Chapter 12, each player has an incentive to violate any voluntary agreement not to impose trade restrictions. One of the roles of international organizations such as the World Trade Organization (WTO) is to lay down rules designed to promote international trade and cooperation, enabling nations to make credible commitments not to raise tariffs or other barriers to trade. The WTO can impose sanctions on the countries that violate these rules.

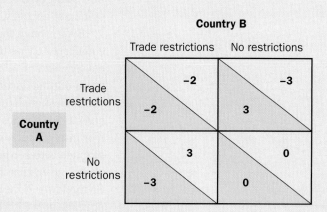

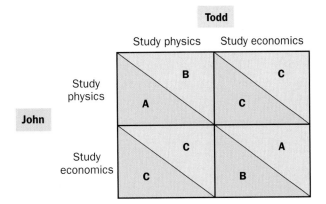

FIGURE 14.3

THE STUDY GAME

Neither player has a dominant strategy, but there are two Nash equilibria: both study physics or both study economics.

knows that Discounters Delux will reduce prices, since that is Discounters Delux's dominant strategy. So the fact that Quality Brands would find it best to keep prices high if Discounters Delux keeps its prices high is irrelevant. Quality Brands knows that Discounters Delux will cut prices, and therefore its best strategy is also to cut prices. The outcome, or equilibrium, in this game will have both firms reducing their prices.

GAMES WITHOUT DOMINANT STRATEGIES

Both the prisoner's dilemma game and the price-cutting game have unique Nash equilibria. Often, however, a game will have more than one Nash equilibrium, as the following example illustrates.

Two friends are enrolled in the same physics and economics classes. They both know that studying together is much more efficient than studying alone. By working through problems together, each will greatly improve his performance on upcoming tests in the two classes. However, John is really worried about his physics grade and would prefer that he and Todd focus on physics. Conversely, Todd is most worried about economics and would rather devote their study time to it. The game table for their circumstances is shown in Figure 14.3, with the payoffs expressed in the average grade for the two courses (the letter below the diagonal line in each box is the payoff to John).

Does either John or Todd have a dominant strategy? No. If John insists on studying physics, Todd is better off joining John in hitting the physics books than in going it alone and studying economics. On the other hand, if John is willing to study economics, then Todd's best response is obviously to study economics too. Similarly, John's best strategy is to study physics if that is what Todd also does, while John's best strategy is to study economics if Todd does that instead. Neither player has a dominant strategy, one that is best regardless of what the other does.

Even though there are no dominant strategies in this game, there are two Nash equilibria—either both friends study physics or both study economics. If Todd pulls out Stiglitz and Walsh's economics textbook and starts reviewing the material on trade-offs and incentives, John's best strategy is to join him. Studying economics is John's best choice, given that Todd is studying economics. After all, if he goes off and studies physics by himself, his average grade in the two classes will be a C; while if he instead studies economics with Todd, he will do worse in physics, but he will do so much better in economics that his average grade will be a B. The same is true for Todd—given that John is studying economics, Todd's best strategy is to join him. So the lower right box in the diagram is a Nash equilibrium. But it is not the only one. The upper left box, where both end up studying physics together, is also a Nash equilibrium. While it may not enable us to predict a *unique* equilibrium in a game, the concept of a Nash equilibrium can help eliminate some outcomes. Neither the upper right nor the lower left box in the diagram is a Nash equilibrium. If Todd studies physics, then studying economics alone is not John's best response.

THE ZERO-SUM GAME SOLVER

Some games have a fixed total payoff: in *Survivor,* the winner receives $1 million and the next few survivors receive smaller amounts. Nothing the contestants do can affect the total prize money available. If one contestant receives more, another receives less. Games like this are called *zero-sum games.* When we think of games, we usually think of sports or chess, or perhaps gambling—all zero-sum games. In sports, one team wins and the other loses. In gambling, every dollar you win is someone else's loss. While many people think that economic exchange is a zero-sum game, you should understand by now that it is not—exchange can leave *both* parties better off. On the Web site of Professor David Levine at UCLA, you can find a program that will find the solution to any two-person zero-sum game. Invent a game yourself and find its solution at http://levine. sscnet.ucla.edu/Games/zerosum.htm.

Wrap-Up

THE BASIC TYPES OF GAMES

1. The prisoner's dilemma—both players have dominant strategies and the game has one Nash equilibrium. Application: understanding why collusion is difficult.
2. The price-cutting game—only one player has a dominant strategy and the game has one Nash equilibrium. Application: understanding competition between duopolists.
3. The study game—neither player has a dominant strategy and there are two Nash equilibria. Application: understanding banking panics (see p. 322).

Repeated Games

In the basic prisoner's dilemma game, each party makes only one decision. The game is played just a single time. The two players could do better if they could somehow cooperate and agree not to pick the dominant strategy. But when the game is actually played, each has an incentive to break any prior agreement and do what is in his own best interest. If the players or parties interact many times, then the strategies for each can become more complicated. There may be additional ways to try to enforce cooperation that would benefit both parties. Games that are played many times over by the same players are called **repeated games.**

To see how the nature of the game is changed when it is repeated, let us consider the actions of two politicians running for the Senate. At the start of an election campaign, suppose each candidate announces that she will refrain from running negative ads as long as her rival does. But if the rival cheats on this agreement and runs a negative ad, the other candidate responds by running her own negative attack ads. Can this threat of retaliation ensure that the two candidates run clean campaigns?

Imagine that there are several weeks remaining until the date of the election. Each candidate will figure that she should run negative ads in the last week of the campaign: this is her best strategy, because the threat of retaliation carries no force after the election. There is no longer any payoff in continuing to cooperate, since the campaign (and the game) ends on election day. The agreement breaks down the week before the election.

Now consider what happens two weeks before the election. Both candidates know that the other will start running negative ads the following week. But if they are not going to honor their agreement during the last week of the campaign anyway, then the threat of future retaliatory attacks is completely meaningless. Hence, each candidate will reason that it pays to cheat on the agreement by running a negative ad. The agreement breaks down two weeks before the election. Reasoning backward through time, we see that the agreement not to run negative ads will break down almost immediately, no matter when the election is held.

This example illustrates an important principle of strategic thinking: think first about the end of the game and work backward from there to identify the best current choice. Making decisions in this way is called **backward induction.** For each decision a player can make, she needs to work out her opponent's optimal response and what her own payoff will be. Then, in the first stage of the game, she can adopt the strategy that gives her the highest payoff.

Backward induction also applies in the various games considered earlier, from Kelly making her decision in *Survivor* to the players in a prisoner's dilemma game. For example, prisoner A reasoned, "Suppose my partner confesses; what is my best strategy? And if my partner does not confess, then what is my best strategy?" Each thought about the consequences of his opponent's choices and worked backward to determine what he should do.

Our analysis of collusion in a repeated game setting may seem too pessimistic about the ability of firms or individuals to cooperate. Certainly we see that individuals often do find ways to cooperate, trading a short-term gain to establish longer-term relationships that yield higher benefits. And firms behave similarly, offering services or providing higher-quality products that lower their immediate profits but contribute to higher profits in the future. In strategic games that do not have a finite end—that always offer the possibility of another round—a variety of strategies may enable players to cooperate to achieve better outcomes.

Wrap-Up

BACKWARD INDUCTION

When strategic interactions occur for a repeated but fixed number of times, the best approach is to start from the end of the game and work backward to determine the optimal strategy. Backward induction helps the player focus on the future consequences of his current decision.

REPUTATIONS

Developing good reputations can be useful when players are engaged in repeated interactions. A firm that relies on local customers for repeat business has more of an incentive to develop a reputation for good service than does one with little repeat business. A car mechanic might have an incentive to pad the bill or otherwise cheat a customer if he never expects to service that particular car again, but in the long run he might profit more by gaining a reputation for good service and relying on repeat business from his customers.

Gaining a reputation is costly in the short run—initially the car mechanic will be unable to charge any more than do garages unconcerned about their reputations. His lower profits in the short run are like an investment: they will pay off in the future when the reputation he has developed enables him to charge more than most mechanics.

TIT FOR TAT

Economists have set up laboratory experiments, much like those used in other sciences, to test how individuals actually behave in these different games. The advantage of this sort of **experimental economics** is that the researcher seeking the crucial determinants of behavior can change one aspect of the experiment at a time. One set of experiments has explored how individuals cooperate in situations like the prisoner's dilemma. These experiments tend to show that participants often evolve simple strategies that, although sometimes apparently irrational in the short run, can be effective in inducing cooperation (collusion) as the game is repeated a number of times. One common strategy is tit for tat. In the case of two oligopolists, one might threaten to increase output if the other does, even if doing so does not maximize its short-term profits. If the rival finds this threat credible—as it may well be, especially after it has been carried out a few times—the firm may decide that it is more profitable to cooperate and keep production low than to cheat. In the real world, such simple strategies may play an important role in ensuring that firms do not compete too vigorously in markets in which there are only three or four dominant firms.

Internet Connection

THE PRISONER'S DILEMMA

You can play a repeated game version of the prisoner's dilemma against a computer at www. princeton.edu/-mdaniels/PD/PD.html.

Try a tit-for-tat strategy and see how the computer responds.

INSTITUTIONS

In many situations, institutions ensure that a cooperative outcome is reached. International organizations such as the World Trade Organization (WTO) serve to enforce agreements that promote international trade. Member countries agree to abide by certain rules that forbid the type of trade restrictions and beggar-thy-neighbor policies that proved so disastrous during the 1930s. Professional sports leagues impose salary caps, which limit the ability of teams to boost salaries. Deposit insurance eliminates the incentive for depositors to withdraw funds when there are rumors of financial trouble at their bank, because they know their money is protected even if their bank fails.

Case in Point

BANKING PANICS

Between 1930 and 1933, the United States suffered a massive financial panic that forced about nine thousand banks to fail. This disruption of the financial system contributed to the severity of the Great Depression, when unemployment reached levels as high as 25 percent of the labor force. As banks closed their doors, businesses that relied on bank credit to finance their inventories and investments were forced to cut back production and lay off workers. How can game theory help us understand why so many banks failed?

During the banking panics of the early 1930s, depositors rushed to withdraw their savings, leading to many bank failures.

If you have a deposit in a commercial bank today, the federal government insures it (up to $100,000): if your bank makes bad investments and goes bankrupt, the federal government will make sure that you receive all your money back. Before 1933, however, bank deposits were not insured. If your bank went bankrupt, you could lose everything—that is, unless you acted at the first hint of trouble and withdrew your deposits before the bank ran out of cash. Banks lend out most of the money they receive as deposits, holding only a small fraction as cash to meet daily unpredictable fluctuations in deposits and withdrawals. If all depositors were to suddenly demand their money back, a bank would quickly run out of cash and be forced to close. That's what almost happened to George Bailey's bank in the movie *It's a Wonderful Life,* and it is exactly what happened in real life in the 1930s as depositors raced to be the first to withdraw their deposits. When they all tried to withdraw their deposits at the same time, there simply was not enough money on hand to pay everyone. Thousands of banks had to shut their doors. Everyone would have been better off leaving their deposits alone, since in that case the banks could have remained open.

The concept of Nash equilibrium can help us understand bank runs and financial panics. Consider a simple example of a bank with just two depositors—call them A and B. Each depositor must decide whether to try to withdraw her deposits from the bank or to leave them there. Assume each has deposited $1,000 at the bank. The bank has used these funds to make loans and investments but keeps $200 on hand in its vault. If the bank's loans are repaid, the bank can pay an interest rate of 5 percent to its depositors.

If neither depositor tries to withdraw funds from the bank, let us assume they both will eventually receive the full value of their deposits plus the 5 percent interest (for a total of $1,050). If depositor A withdraws while depositor B does not, A can take out $200, all the cash the bank has on hand. The bank then must shut its doors, and depositor B receives nothing. The reverse happens if depositor B tries to withdraw its funds while A does not. If both try to withdraw their money, the most each can get is $100. The payoffs are shown in Figure 14.4.

Clearly both depositors are better off if neither attempts a withdrawal. In that case, they both would eventually receive $1,050. This is also a Nash equilibrium. If depositor A leaves her money in the bank, depositor B's best strategy is to do the same. Conversely, if depositor B leaves her money in the bank, depositor A's best strategy is to do the same. Each reasons as follows: "If the other leaves her deposits in the bank, my best strategy is also to leave my deposits in the bank." So there is an equilibrium in which neither depositor trys to withdraw funds, and the bank stays open.

Just as in the earlier example of the two friends deciding what to study, there are two Nash equilibria to the deposit withdrawal game. The second Nash equilibrium occurs when both depositors try to withdraw their money and the bank fails. In this case, each reasons as follows: "If the other depositor tries to withdraw, I'm better off if I also try to withdraw. That way, at least I get $100,

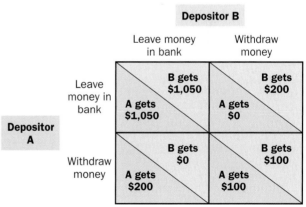

FIGURE 14.4

A BANK PANIC AS A STRATEGIC GAME

Like the study game, this game has two Nash equilibria: both withdraw money or both leave money in the bank. The equilibrium in which both leave their money in the bank leaves both better off than if they both withdraw their money.

which is better than nothing." So there is an equilibrium in which each rushes to the bank, and the bank is unable to fully meet its obligations to the two depositors. The bank fails.

In this example, there is a good equilibrium—the one in which the bank remains open and the depositors eventually receive all their money plus interest—and a bad equilibrium, when the bank is forced to close. In the prisoner's dilemma, in contrast, the only equilibrium was inferior to an alternative set of strategies (neither prisoner confesses). The example of John and Todd illustrated another possible outcome: one of the two equilibria was preferred by Todd and the other by John.

Financial panics can be thought of as shifts from the good to the bad equilibrium. Such a shift can occur if depositors start to worry about the financial soundness of the banking sector, even if such fears are unfounded. The simple argument illustrated by this game provides part of the rationale behind federal deposit insurance. Deposit insurance gives each depositor confidence that her money is safe, regardless of what other depositors do. No depositor has an incentive to try to outmaneuver others by getting her money out first.

Sequential Moves

In the prisoner's dilemma, each player must make a choice without knowing what the other has done. The players move simultaneously. In many situations, however, one player must move first, and the second player then responds directly to what the first has done. This is called a **sequential game,** since players take turns and each can observe what choices were made in earlier moves. In such a game, the player who moves first must consider how the second player will respond to each possible move he can make.

Sports offer many instances of strategic behavior. The baseball manager deciding whether to bring in a relief pitcher is a prime example of someone playing a sequential game. Conventional wisdom in baseball says that a left-handed batter has more success against a right-handed pitcher, and a right-handed batter does better against a left-handed pitcher. Does that mean that if a right-handed player is coming to bat, the manager should bring in a right-handed pitcher? Not necessarily. Once a right-handed pitcher is brought in, the manager of the other team can send a left-handed pinch hitter to the plate. So a manager considering a change of pitchers needs to think about how his counterpart will respond to each of the possible pitching choices he can make.

This example illustrates an important aspect of a sequential game. The player who moves first must anticipate how the second player will respond. Take the case of a firm facing the potential entry of a new rival into its market. Suppose a software firm, call it Redhat, is considering the launch of a new operating system that will compete with Microsoft Windows. Redhat must decide whether to enter the business or stay out. If it enters, Microsoft must decide whether to peacefully compete or to wage a price war. Suppose that Redhat enters and Microsoft competes peacefully. Assume Microsoft will earn profits of $50 billion and Redhat $10 billion on its operating system. If instead Microsoft engages in a price war, assume both firms will lose money, with Microsoft losing $1 billion and Redhat losing $500 million. If Redhat decides not to enter, it earns $0, while Microsoft earns profits of $80 billion. Will Redhat enter? And will Microsoft engage in a price war?

To simplify this complex scenario we can use a **game tree** diagram, which is the standard way to represent a sequential game. Different branches on a game tree indicate the various outcomes that could occur, given all the possible strategies the players could follow. For example, the entry game involving Microsoft and Redhat is represented by the game tree of Figure 14.5. At the end of each branch, the payoffs to Redhat and Microsoft are shown. The first number is Redhat's payoff; the second is Microsoft's.

Each node—the points at which new branches split—represents a decision point for one of the players. In this game, Redhat moves first (node 1). Microsoft moves second, after it has learned whether Redhat has entered or not. If Redhat decides to enter, we move along the upper branch of the game tree from node 1 to node 2. Microsoft must then choose whether to compete peacefully or wage a price war. From node 2, we move along the upper branch if Microsoft competes peacefully, and the payoffs are $10 billion to Redhat and $50 billion to Microsoft; or we move along the lower branch if Microsoft wages a price war, in which case the payoffs are −$500 million and −$1 billion, respectively. If Redhat decides not to enter, we move along the lower branch from node 1. Here, there is nothing further Microsoft must decide, so the game ends and the players receive the payoffs shown ($0 for Redhat and $80 billion for Microsoft).

In deciding whether to enter, Redhat's managers will reason as follows: "If we enter, Microsoft can either wage a price war or compete peacefully. In the former case, it loses $1 billion, and in the latter case it makes $50 billion. Clearly, once we enter, it will be in Microsoft's best interest to compete peacefully, so we should enter."

This example again illustrates backward induction. "Thinking strategically" requires that one think first about the end of the game, and work backward from there to determine the best current choice. Redhat asks itself what Microsoft will do if Redhat has entered. It works backward from there to determine if it should enter.

Using backward induction is easy when a game tree is employed . At each node that leads to an end to the game, determine the best strategy of the player who makes a decision at that node. Then work backward. At node 2, Microsoft's best strategy is to compete peacefully. It gets $50 billion that way, while it would lose $1 billion in a price war. Now work back to the previous node—node 1, where Redhat makes its decision. From its analysis of Microsoft's options at node 2, Redhat knows that if it enters the market, Microsoft will compete peacefully, leaving Redhat with a $10 billion profit. Redhat's other option at node 1 is not to enter, which would leave it with profits of $0. Clearly, Redhat's best strategy is to enter.

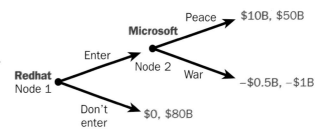

FIGURE 14.5

GAME TREE FOR A SEQUENTIAL GAME

Redhat makes the first move. If Redhat decides to enter the market, Microsoft may then choose between peaceful coexistence or a price war. By reasoning backward from these options, we can see that Redhat will enter the market and Microsoft will choose to compete peacefully.

Thinking Like an Economist

INFORMATION AND THINKING STRATEGICALLY

Information plays a critical role in strategic behavior, but sometimes in surprising ways. Take the prisoner's dilemma, for example. Each prisoner must make a decision about whether to confess without knowing what the other prisoner has done. It might seem that the outcome would change if one prisoner could know the other's choice in advance, but it turns out that providing this extra information makes no difference. It is still best to confess, because confessing is a dominant strategy: it is the best strategy for each prisoner, regardless of what the other did.

In the absence of a dominant strategy, changing the information that the player has *is* likely to alter the player's best strategy. Consider the case of an insurance company that offers health insurance. Suppose the insurance company can obtain information such as whether an individual smokes. Since smoking is associated with many health problems, the insurance company will offer different policies to smokers and nonsmokers; smokers will pay higher insurance premiums to reflect the likelihood they will incur higher medical bills. Now suppose a law is passed that forbids the insurance company from collecting such information. Governments frequently pass such laws on the grounds that collecting certain types of information is an invasion of privacy. If the company offers just a single policy to everyone, it faces an adverse selection problem of the type we will consider in Chapter 15—those with the poorest health are the ones most likely to buy the insurance. But if the firm thinks strategically, it might reason along the following lines: "If we offer only one type of policy, we run the risk that only those with health problems will buy it and we will lose money. Instead, let's offer two different policies. One will have a high deductible, so that patients themselves have to pay a large amount for doctor visits and other services before insurance kicks in. The other policy will have a low deductible, with insurance paying for most medical services. We will charge more for the policy with the low deductible. The low-deductible policy will be more attractive to individuals who think they will need lots of medical services. It will be attractive to smokers. The policy with the high deductible will be more attractive to individuals who think they are less likely to need lots of medical care. It will be attractive to nonsmokers. By offering these separate policies, we can get individuals to reveal information about their health risks."

By thinking strategically, the insurance company is able to overcome some of the information problems it faces. By offering different policies, it is able to separate individuals into high- and low-risk groups.

Time Inconsistency

Threats and promises are common components of strategic behavior. We have already discussed the case of a monopolist who threatens to wage a price war if another firm enters its market (our Redhat and Microsoft example). In that case, the firm that is considering entering the market understands that once it enters, the existing firm's best strategy is to compete peacefully. Because the potential entrant can use backward induction to make this determination, the initial threat is ineffective in deterring entry—it is not credible.

Now instead of looking at this problem from the perspective of the firm contemplating entrance, consider the situation of the monopolist trying to protect its market. It makes sense for the monopolist to try to scare off potential rivals by threatening a price war if any business attempts to enter the industry. But are these threats *time consistent;* that is, will it be in the monopolist's best interest to act in a manner consistent with its statements by actually carrying out the threat? The answer is no; as we have seen, the monopolist's best strategy if a rival enters the market is simply to compete peaceably. We can describe the threat as *time inconsistent;* it will not make sense to actually carry out the threat when it comes time to do so. The rival, knowing that the monopolist will not do as it threatened, knows that the threats can be ignored.

Time inconsistency arises in many contexts, usually in situations in which one player's promise or threat is designed to influence the other player's actions. Consider the case of Sarah, who has just graduated from high school. Her parents believe that holding down a summer job will help Sarah learn responsibility, so they offer to help pay her college tuition in the fall if she works during the summer. The implicit threat is that they will not help with her tuition if Sarah loafs around over the summer and does not work.[3] But Sarah can see that such a threat is time inconsistent. If she hangs out at the beach with her friends all summer, the only choice her parents face in the fall is whether to help her pay for college. Because Sarah knows her parents want her to receive a college education, regardless of how lazy she is, she knows they will help pay for college whatever she does. Since she would rather loaf than work, she does not get a job. Her parents' threat, designed to force her to find a job, was ineffective because it was time inconsistent. Sarah knew they would never actually carry out the threat, because it would not be their best strategy come the fall.

COMMITMENT

Consider again the situation faced by Sarah's parents at the end of the summer. At that point, it was too late to affect Sarah's summer activities, so the threat to not fund her college is no longer worth carrying out. Things would have been different if her parents could have somehow tied their hands in a way that would have prevented them from paying for Sarah's tuition unless she had actually worked during the summer. A demonstrated commitment to undertake a future action may be necessary for threats or promises to be credible.

Military strategists commonly face the problem of making threats credible. During the cold war, the United States stated that it would not rule out being the first to use nuclear weapons. This policy raised the possibility that if the Soviet Union invaded Western Europe, the United States would retaliate against the Soviet Union with nuclear weapons if necessary. Such retaliation would then lead the Soviet Union to launch a nuclear strike against the United States. A Soviet military planner using backward induction might reason that if the Soviet Union invaded Europe, the U.S. government would be faced with the choice of either launching a nuclear attack on the Soviet Union, and having millions of Americans killed in the ensuing nuclear war, or accepting a Soviet victory in Europe. Faced with that choice, the United States might decide to accept a Soviet victory. The U.S. threat to retaliate would not be credible. One argument for maintaining thousands of U.S. troops in Europe was that their loss in a Soviet invasion would force the U.S. military to launch a strike against the Soviet Union. By committing troops to Europe, the Americans made their threat more credible.

Imperfectly competitive markets provide a firm many opportunities to take concrete actions that deter rivals when threats alone would not be credible. A variant of the earlier example of Microsoft and Redhat can illustrate this point. Consider a coffee company, which we'll call Northwest Coffee, that opens a coffee store on every

---

[3]This example is from Herb Taylor, "Time Inconsistency: A Potential Problem for Policymakers," *Economic Review* (Federal Reserve Bank of Philadelphia), March/April 1985, pp. 3–12.

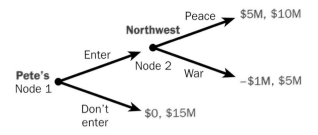

FIGURE 14.6

MARKET ENTRY GAME WITHOUT COMMITMENT

Northwest may threaten to wage a price war if Pete's Coffee enters the market, but such a threat lacks credibility.

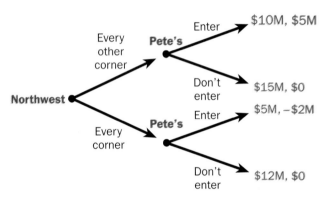

FIGURE 14.7

MARKET ENTRY GAME WITH COMMITMENT

Even though it costs more to operate stores on every street corner, Northwest will do so in order to prevent Pete's Coffee from entering the market. Opening stores on every street corner serves as a commitment mechanism.

other corner of a city's downtown. To deter a potential rival, Pete's Coffee, from opening stores on the empty corners, Northwest Coffee might threaten a price war if a rival opens up competing stores. The game tree and payoffs are shown in Figure 14.6.

Just as in our earlier example, Pete's Coffee can use backward induction to determine that if it enters, Northwest will find it more profitable to compete peacefully. Any threat by Northwest Coffee would not be credible.

Now let's change the game so that Northwest first decides whether to open on every *other* corner, or on *every* corner. The order of play now starts with Northwest's choice about how many stores to open. In the second stage of the game, Pete's Coffee must decide if it will enter. When it makes that decision, it knows whether Northwest has opened on every corner or only on every other corner. The new game tree appears in Figure 14.7.

First, note that if Northwest opens on every other corner and Pete's Coffee enters, the payoffs—$10 million for Northwest Coffee and $5 million for Pete's Coffee— reflect the previous finding that Northwest will not wage a price war. Second, the new branches of the tree show the possible outcomes if Northwest opens on every corner. Because of its added costs, Northwest's profit is smaller when it opens the additional stores and Pete's Coffee stays out of the market ($12 million) than if it opens only on every other corner and Pete's stays out ($15 million). If Northwest has a store on every corner and Pete's Coffee decides to enter the market, Northwest's profits fall to $5 million, while Pete's Coffee ends up losing $2 million.

We again use backward induction to determine the Nash equilibrium. Start from the Pete's Coffee decision node along the top branch (the branch followed if Northwest opens on every other corner). If it finds itself at this node, the best strategy is for Pete's Coffee to enter the market, earning $5 million. Now look at the Pete's Coffee decision node along the bottom branch (the branch followed if Northwest opens on every corner). Here, the best strategy is to not enter. That way, at least, it does not lose any money.

By applying backward induction, we can now analyze Northwest Coffee's decision at the start of the game. Northwest knows that if it puts a store on every other corner, Pete's will enter and Northwest will earn $10 million. If it opens on every corner, Pete's will not enter, and Northwest will earn $12 million. Northwest's best strategy therefore is to open a store on every corner. Even though the decision may appear to be counterintuitive, lowering Northwest's profits from $15 million to $12 million, the extra stores are worth opening because they deter a potential rival. Northwest's extra stores are a more credible threat to a potential rival than is a promise to engage in a price war. Stores that are open and in place serve as a commitment mechanism that deters potential rivals from entering. Northwest is worse off than if it opened fewer stores and Pete's stayed out of the market, but it is better off than if Pete's had entered.

Review and Practice

SUMMARY

1. In perfectly competitive markets, firms and consumers can decide how much to produce and how much to consume without taking into account how others might react. In imperfectly competitive markets, firms must take into account how their rivals will respond to the firms' production or pricing decisions. Firms must behave strategically in such situations. Individuals also face many situations in which they must behave strategically. Economists use game theory to predict how individuals and firms will behave.

2. In a Nash equilibrium, each player in a game is following a strategy that is best, given the strategies followed by the other players. A game may have a unique Nash equilibrium, or it may have several equilibria.

3. A dominant strategy is one that is best regardless of what the other player chooses to do. Looking for dominant strategies can help analysts predict behavior.

4. Backward induction is crucial for strategic behavior. Thinking strategically means looking into the future to predict how others will behave, and then using that information to make decisions.

5. Strategic choices are often designed to influence the choice of others. Once others have made their choices, however, carrying out the initial strategy may no longer be best. When this is the case, the original strategy was time inconsistent.

KEY TERMS

strategic behavior
game table
dominant strategy
Nash equilibrium
repeated game
backward induction
experimental economics
sequential game
game tree
time inconsistency

REVIEW QUESTIONS

1. Firms in perfectly competitive markets do not need to behave strategically. Why not? Why do oligopolists need to behave strategically? Does a monopolist need to behave strategically?

2. Professional sports leagues often have salary caps that limit the amount individual teams can pay players. Using the prisoner's dilemma game, explain why such a restriction might make the team owners better off.

3. What is a dominant strategy? Explain why each player in the prisoner's dilemma has a dominant strategy.

4. What is a Nash equilibrium? What is the unique Nash equilibrium in the prisoner's dilemma game? Can a game have more than one Nash equilibrium? Give an example to illustrate your answer.

5. In the prisoner's dilemma, each player has a dominant strategy and there is a unique Nash equilibrium in which the players choose their dominant strategy. Give an example of a game in which only one player has a dominant strategy. What is the Nash equilibrium?

6. This chapter opened with a discussion of the television show *Survivor*. What principle of strategic behavior did Kelly need to use?

7. What is a sequential game? Why does the player who moves first need to use backward induction?

8. An old saying, when a parent punishes a child, is "This hurts me more than it hurts you." Drawing on the idea of a repeated game, explain why a parent might still punish the child even if doing so really did hurt her more than the child.

9. Why might threats and promises not be credible?

PROBLEMS

1. Consider two oligopolists, each choosing between a "high" and a "low" level of production. Given their

choices of how much to produce, their profits will be as follows:

Firm B

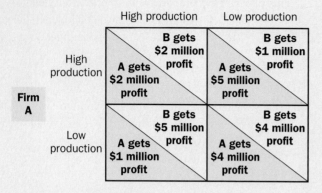

Explain how firm B will reason that it makes sense to produce the high amount, regardless of what firm A chooses. Then explain how firm A will reason that it makes sense to produce the high amount, regardless of what firm B chooses. How might collusion assist the two firms in this case?

2. Use the prisoner's dilemma analysis to describe what happens in the following two situations:

(a) Consider two rivals—say, producers of cigarettes. If Benson and Hedges alone advertises, it diverts customers from Marlboro. If Marlboro alone advertises, it diverts customers from Benson and Hedges. If they both advertise, each retains its customer base.

Are they genuinely unhappy with government regulations prohibiting advertising? In practice, cigarette firms have complained quite bitterly about such government restrictions, including those aimed at children. Why?

(b) Consider two rivals—say, producers of camera film, Fuji and Kodak. Consumers want a film that accurately reproduces colors and is not grainy. Assume that initially, the two firms had products that were comparable in quality. If one does research and improves its product, it will steal customers from its rivals. If they both do research and develop comparable products, then they will continue to share the market as before. Thus, the hypothetical payoff matrix (in millions of dollars) appears below (the profits in the case of research take into account the expenditures on research):

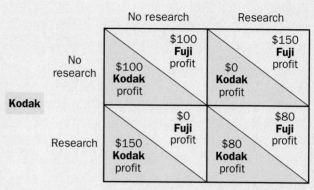

Explain why both will engage in research, even though doing so reduces their profits. Could this choice make society better off, even though their profits are lower?

3. Draw the game tree for the game discussed on pages 324–325 in which Microsoft moves first and decides whether to threaten a price war; Redhat then decides whether to enter; and finally, Microsoft decides whether to compete peacefully or wage the price war. Verify that Microsoft's decision at the first stage of the game has no effect on Redhat's strategy.

4. Suppose firm A is a monopolist. Firm A threatens a price war if any potential rival enters its market. Suppose firm B is contemplating such a move. The game tree is as follows (firm B's payoffs are shown first; firm A's are shown second):

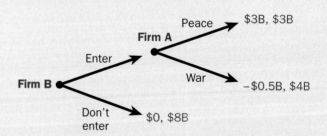

Should firm B enter? Is firm A's threat credible? Why? What makes this example different from the outcome in the Redhat-Microsoft example given in the text?

5. Draw the game tree for the sequential game between Sarah and her parents that was described on page 327. The first move is Sarah's; she decides whether to work during the summer or not work. At the end of the

summer her parents decide whether or not to pay for Sarah's tuition. Using backward induction, what is the equilibrium for this game? Now add a new first stage in which Sarah's parents announce that they will only pay for the tuition if Sarah works. Is this announcement credible? Use this example to explain what is meant by time inconsistency.

6. "Tying one's hands" can be a way to commit credibly to a certain course of action. In the 1960s film *Dr. Strangelove,* the Soviet Union deployed a dooms-day device that could destroy the world and would be automatically triggered if the United States attacked. Explain how such a device could serve as a credible threat to deter a U.S. attack. In the movie, the Soviet Union did not inform the United States that the device had been deployed. Why was this a really bad strategy?

7. Suppose Quality Brands and Discounters Delux are involved in a repeated price-cutting game. Explain what a tit-for-tat strategy would be. Is a promise to "match any available price" a way for one firm to signal that it is playing tit for tat? Explain.

8. Restaurants often locate along major highways. Since most customers at such restaurants will not return, does the restaurant have an incentive to develop a reputation for good food? If reputations are important, which restaurant will have a greater incentive to offer good service—one that is part of a national chain (such as McDonald's or Burger King) or one that is locally owned?

9. How might a cultural or group norm or expectations about "correct" behavior, such as that summarized in the old saying "honor among thieves," help enforce cooperation in the prisoner's dilemma?

Learning Goals

In this chapter, you will learn

1 About the critical ways information affects markets

2 What the adverse selection problem is, and how it affects markets

3 What the incentive problem is, and how it affects markets

4 How search and advertising are explained by imperfect information

Chapter 15

IMPERFECT INFORMATION IN THE PRODUCT MARKET

I t was never any secret to economists that the real world did not match the model of perfect competition. Theories of imperfect competition and monopoly such as those covered in Chapters 11 and 12 have been put forth from Adam Smith's time to the present.

Another limitation of the model of perfect competition has recently attracted attention: its assumption of perfect information—that market participants are fully informed about the goods being bought and sold. By incorporating *imperfect information* into their models, economists have come a long way in closing the gap between the real world and the world depicted in the perfect competition, perfect information model of Part Two.

This chapter provides an overview of the major information problems of the product market, the ways in which market economies deal with them, and how the basic model of Part Two has to be modified as a result. In Chapter 16, we will see how information problems affect labor markets. We start our analysis of information problems by examining a market you may be familiar with—the used-car market.

The Market for Lemons and Adverse Selection

Have you ever wondered why a three-month-old used car sells for so much less—often 20 percent less—than a new car? Surely cars do not deteriorate that fast. The pleasure of owning a new car may be worth something, but in three months, even the car you buy new will be "used." Several thousand dollars is a steep price to pay for this short-lived pleasure.

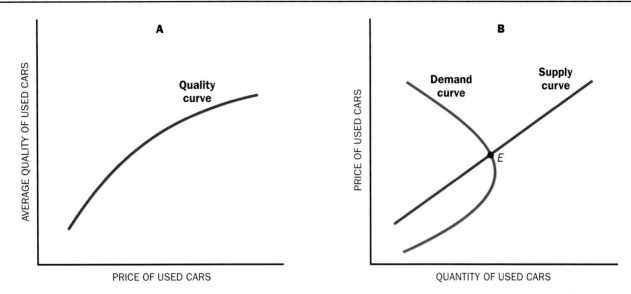

Figure 15.1

A MARKET WITH LEMONS

Panel A shows the average quality of a used car increasing as the price increases. Panel B shows a typical upward-sloping supply curve, but a backward-bending demand curve. Demand bends back because buyers know that quality is lower at lower prices, and they thus choose to buy less as the price falls. Panel B shows the market equilibrium is at point *E*.

George Akerlof of the University of California at Berkeley has provided a simple explanation, based on imperfect information. Some cars are worse than others. They have hidden defects that become apparent to the owners only after they have driven the cars for a while. Such defective cars are called *lemons*. One thing after another goes wrong with them. While warranties may reduce the financial cost of having a lemon, they do not eliminate the bother—the time it takes to bring the car into the shop, the anxiety of knowing there is a good chance of a breakdown. The owners, of course, know they have a lemon and would like to pass it along to someone else. Those with the worst lemons are going to be the most willing to sell their car. At a high used-car price, they will be joined by owners of better-quality cars, who perhaps just want to replace their cars with the latest model. As the price drops, more of the good used cars will be withdrawn from the market as the owners decide to keep them. And the average quality of the used cars for sale will *drop*. We say there is an **adverse selection** effect. The mix of those who elect to sell changes adversely as price falls.

Figure 15.1 shows the consequences of imperfect information for market equilibrium in the used-car market. Panel A depicts, for each price (measured along the horizontal axis), the average quality of used cars being sold in the market. As price increases, average quality increases. Panel B shows the supply curve of used cars. As price increases, the number of cars being sold in the market increases, for all the usual reasons. The demand curve is also shown. This curve has a peculiar shape—upward as well as downward sloping—because as price decreases, the average quality decreases. But demand depends not just on price but on quality—on the "value" being offered on the market. If, as price falls, quality deteriorates rapidly, then the quantity demanded will actually *fall* as price falls—consumers are getting less for their dollars. The equilibrium is depicted in panel B.

The situation just described is characterized by **asymmetric information** between sellers and buyers. That is, the seller of the used car has more information about the product than does the buyer. Many markets, and not just the market for used cars, are characterized by asymmetric information. The founders of a new high-tech start-up company may know more about the potential value of the company's stock than a typical investor does; an individual buying car insurance knows more about her driving abilities than the car insurance company does; the manufacturer of a kitchen refrigerator knows more about how reliable the product is than the customer who is contemplating its purchase does. One of the consequences of asymmetric information is that there may be relatively few buyers and sellers, far fewer than there would be with perfect information. Economists use the term **thin** to describe markets in which there are relatively few buyers and sellers. Sometimes particular markets may be so thin as to be essentially nonexistent. When there are important markets missing from an economy, it is said to have an **incomplete** set of markets. The used-car market, for example, is a thin one. Buyers may know that there are some legitimate sellers, people who for one reason or another prefer to always drive a new car. But mixed in with these are people who are trying to dump their lemons. The buyers cannot tell the lemons apart from the good cars. Rather than risk it, they may simply decide not to buy. (Of course, the low demand drives down the price, increasing the proportion of lemons. It is a vicious cycle.) The problems that arise when markets are thin and distorted by adverse selection, as used-car markets are, help explain why the price of a relatively new used car can be so much lower than the price of a brand-new vehicle.

SIGNALING

If you have a good car and you want to sell it, you would like to persuade potential buyers that it is good. You could tell them that it is not a lemon, but why should they believe you? There is a simple principle: *actions speak louder than words*. What actions can you take that will convince buyers of the quality of your car?

That Kia is willing to provide a ten-year, 100,000-mile warranty on its cars says something about the confidence Kia has in its product. The warranty is valuable to the buyer, not only because it reduces his risk of having to spend a mint to repair the car but also because he believes that Kia would not have provided the warranty unless the chances of defects were low. Actions such as this are said to **signal** higher quality. A signal is effective if it differentiates goods—here between high-quality cars and low-quality cars. The cost to the producer of a ten-year guarantee is much higher for a car that is likely to fall apart within ten years than for a car that is unlikely to break down. Customers know this, and thus can infer that a firm willing to provide this warranty is selling high-quality cars.

When you go to a car dealer, you want to know that it will still be around if you have trouble. Some firms signal that they are not fly-by-nights by spending a great deal of money on their showroom. Expensive furnishings lead visitors to infer that they would find it too costly to just pack up and leave.

Actions such as providing a better guarantee or a larger showroom are taken not just for the direct benefit that the consumer receives from them, but because they persuade consumers that the product is a better product or the firm is a better business to deal with. In a sense, the desire to convey information "distorts" decisions, insofar as they no longer conform to what they would have been in a world of perfect information. For example, if customers receive no direct benefit from a luxurious showroom, the cost of building and maintaining it is a waste of resources.

JUDGING QUALITY BY PRICE

There is still another clue that buyers use to judge the quality of what they are about to purchase: price. Consumers base inferences about the quality of goods on the price charged. For example, they know that on average, if the price of a used car is low, their chance of getting a lemon is higher. Many if not most sellers know that buyers know this.

In markets with imperfect information, firms *set* their prices. And in setting their prices, they take into account what customers will think about the quality of the good being sold. Concerns about the (correct or incorrect) inferences that consumers may make about quality impede the effectiveness of price competition. In the used-car example, we saw that as price rose, the average quality of cars on the market increased. But if firms think customers believe that cars being sold at a lower price are lower quality, then they will not lower the price—to do so would scare away customers who perceive that such "bargains" must be lemons. Under such circumstances, even if firms cannot sell all they would like at the going price, they still will not cut prices.

Information problems fascinate economists because they turn the basic competitive model upside down. Economists have long recognized that prices convey critical information about scarcity in a market economy. But only recently have the other informational roles of prices—and their consequences—become clear. When they can, sellers will manipulate prices to control the information conveyed. Buyers, for their part, usually see through these manipulations. And their suspicion that the seller is trying to pass off a lemon discourages trade. When these sorts of information problems are severe, markets are thin or even nonexistent. Moreover, price competition may be limited. Even when there is an excess supply of goods, firms may not cut their prices and the market may not clear.

Wrap-Up

SOLUTIONS TO ADVERSE SELECTION PROBLEMS IN MARKET ECONOMIES

Signaling
Judging quality by price

The Incentive Problem

Providing incentives that motivate individuals to make the best choices is one of the central economic problems. The central problem of incentives, in turn, is that individuals do not bear the full consequences of their actions. The multibillion-dollar collapse of many savings and loan associations in the 1980s—though fraud may have played a part—is attributable largely to incorrect incentives. Because S & L deposits were guaranteed by the government, depositors had no incentives to check on what the S & Ls were doing. For the same reason, the owners of many S & Ls had an incentive to take high risks. If they were successful, they kept the gains. If they failed, the government picked up the loss.

When there is a misalignment of incentives such as occurred in the S & Ls, we say there is a problem of **moral hazard.** The term originated in the insurance industry. Individuals who purchased insurance had an inadequate incentive to avoid the insured-against event—indeed, if they were insured for more than 100 percent of the loss, they would have an incentive to bring it about. Though the term was originally associated with insurance fraud, its use by economists today has no ethical overtones. For example, an individual who has fire insurance has less of an incentive to avoid a fire. The benefit to her, for instance, of putting in a sprinkler system may not be worth the cost—because she need not take into account the expected cost to the fire insurance company. Thus the fire insurance company is likely to require a sprinkler system; or it may change her calculations by offering a discount on the premiums of individuals with such systems, so that it would pay for her to have a sprinkler installed.

In the basic competitive model of Part Two, private property and prices provide incentives. Individuals are rewarded for performing particular tasks. Incentive problems arise when individuals are not rewarded for what they do, or when they do not have to pay the full costs for what they do. In our economy, such problems are pervasive.

In product markets, firms must be given the incentive to produce quality products, and here, too, information is an important part of the picture. If customers could always tell the quality of the product they were getting, firms that produced higher-quality products would always be able to charge a higher price, and no company could get away with producing shoddy goods.

MARKET SOLUTIONS

In simple transactions, incentive problems can be solved by stipulating penalties and rewards. For example, many companies need to have goods delivered. They contract with trucking firms, promising to pay a certain amount if the goods are delivered safely and on time to their destination. The contract might stipulate how much will be deducted from the total payment for each day the goods are late or for any damage that occurs while they are in the truck. The agreement thus has built-in incentives for the trucking firm to perform adequately.

But most transactions, even relatively simple ones, are more complex than this one. The more complicated the transaction, the more difficult it is to solve the incentive problem. Say you want your grass mowed, and your neighbor's twelve-year-old son wants to mow it. You want him to take good care of your power mower. When he sees a rock in the mower's path, he should pick it up. But what incentive does he have to take care of the mower? If you plan to charge him for repairs if the mower does hit a rock, how can you tell whether the rock was hidden by the grass? If he owned his own mower, he would have the appropriate incentives—an illustration of why private property combined with the price system provides such an effective solution to the incentive problem. But your neighbor's son probably does not have the money to buy his own power mower. Under these conditions, an incentive problem is inevitable. Either you let him use your lawn mower and bear the risk of his mistreating it. Or you lend him money to buy his own, in which case you bear the risk of his not paying you back.

Many private companies must hire people to run machinery worth hundreds or thousands of times more than a lawn mower. Every company would like its workers to exert effort and care, to communicate clearly with one another and take responsibility for their actions. Beyond a reliance on private property and prices, the market economy has other partial solutions to these incentive problems, loosely categorized as contract solutions and reputation solutions.

CONTRACT SOLUTIONS

When one party (firm) agrees to do something for another, it typically signs a contract, which specifies the conditions of the transaction. For example, a firm will agree to deliver a product of a particular quality at a certain time and place. There will normally be "escape" clauses. If there is a strike, if the weather is bad, and so on, the delivery may be postponed without penalty. These *contingency clauses* may also make the payment depend on the circumstances and manner in which the service is performed.

Contracts attempt to deal with incentive problems by specifying what each of the parties is to do in each situation. But no one can think of every contingency. And even if such foresight was possible, writing down all the possibilities would be prohibitively time-consuming.

There are times when complying with all the terms of the contract would be extremely expensive for the supplier. He could make the promised delivery on time, but only at a very great cost; a delay of just one day would save him a great deal. To provide suppliers with the incentive to violate the terms only when doing so is really economically worthwhile, most contracts allow delivery delays, but with a penalty. The penalty gives the supplier the incentive to provide timely, but not overly costly, deliveries.

Sometimes the supplier may think it simply is not worth complying with the contract. If she violates the agreement, she is said to be in *breach* of the contract. When a contract has been breached, the parties usually wind up in court, and the legal system stipulates what damages the party breaking the contract must pay to the other side. Contracts, by specifying what parties are supposed to do in a variety of circumstances, help resolve incentive problems. But no matter how complicated the contract, ambiguities and disputes will always remain. Contracts are incomplete and enforcement is costly, and thus they provide only a partial resolution of the incentive problem.

REPUTATION SOLUTIONS

Reputation plays an extremely important role in providing incentives in market economies. A reputation is a form of guarantee. Even though no particular individual or firm can collect anything from this guarantee—it is not a "money-back" guarantee—all know that the reputation of the person or company will suffer if it does not perform well. The desire to maintain a good reputation is what provides firms with an incentive to produce high-quality goods. It provides contractors with an incentive to complete a house on or near the promised date.

For reputation to be an effective incentive mechanism, firms must lose something if their reputation suffers. The "something" is, of course, profits. For reputations to provide incentives, there must be profits to lose.

Thus, we see another way in which markets with imperfect information differ from markets with perfect information. In competitive markets with perfect information, competition drives price down to marginal cost. In markets, competitive or not, in which quality is maintained as the result of a reputation mechanism, price must remain above marginal cost.

In markets where reputation is important, competition fails to lead to price-cutting, because prices that are "too low" give firms no incentive to maintain their reputation. Consumers, aware of this dynamic, come to expect low-quality goods. Here again, we see why cutting prices will not necessarily bring firms more customers. Even companies with (initially) good reputations are unlikely to find price-cutting a successful long-term strategy.

Reputation as a Barrier to Entry Competition is frequently very imperfect in markets where reputation is important. The necessity of establishing a reputation acts as an important barrier to entry and limits the degree of competition in these industries. Given a choice between purchasing the product of an established firm with a good reputation and the product of a newcomer with no reputation at the same price, consumers will normally choose the established firm's good. In selecting a new TV, at a given price you will probably choose a Sony over a new brand with no track record for quality and reliability. To win customers, the newcomer must offer a sufficiently low price, often accompanied with strong guarantees. Entering a market thus becomes extremely expensive.

Wrap-Up

SOLUTIONS TO INCENTIVE PROBLEMS IN MARKET ECONOMIES

Private property and prices
Contracts
Reputations

THE MARKET FOR HEALTH INSURANCE

The market for health insurance provides an illustration of the impact imperfect information can have. It is estimated that about 45 million Americans are without health insurance, and even those with insurance often feel dissatisfied with their coverage. Understanding the problems with health care and the policy debates that these problems have generated requires an understanding of the market for health insurance, a market in which information, or rather the lack of information, plays a major role.

The United States spends a larger fraction of its national income on health care than most other developed countries, but its figures for life expectancy are lower and for infant mortality are higher. Information problems and associated market failures are a large part of the reason. Moral hazard—the reduced incentive to economize on health care expenditures when a large fraction of the tab is picked up by insurance firms—is one source of market failure. Adverse selection—the attempt of each insurance firm to take the lowest-risk applicants, leaving those with high medical costs to others—is another. In some countries, the first of these problems is addressed by rationing the availability of health care and the second is overcome by having a universal health care system that covers everyone, not just those at low risk.

In the standard model, consumers are assumed to be well-informed. But consumers go to the doctor for information, to find out what is wrong with them. Moreover, they typically must rely on the doctor's advice. Economists worry that under a fee-for-service system, in which doctors are paid for each of the services they perform, there is an incentive to provide excessive care. *Excessive* here means the marginal cost exceeds the marginal benefit to the patient. Making sure that health care dollars are used efficiently requires that the marginal benefits of a particular treatment, prescription, or procedure are balanced against the marginal costs. Consumers can be expected to balance marginal benefits and costs when they purchase most goods, but health care differs because consumers may lack the information needed to assess the potential benefits of care and because those with insurance typically bear only a small fraction of the marginal costs.

Today, more and more doctors work in "managed care" organizations, or HMOs, where they are paid a flat fee up front. They then provide whatever care is needed and receive no extra income from doing extra procedures. On average, doctors working in managed care charge less and perform fewer surgeries, with no noticeable effect on patient health. Critics worry that under managed care, doctors have an incentive to underprovide services, since they receive no compensation at all for providing care at the margin. Newspaper accounts of managed care programs denying patients treatment have galvanized legislators to enact a patients' bill of rights. But while admitting that there may be occasional abuses, advocates argue that any managed care organization guilty of repeated abuses would lose its patients. Reputations can provide effective discipline. When employers provide a level playing field between fee-for-service and managed care plans—contributing an equal amount for each and making employees pay for the extra costs if they choose the more expensive fee-for-service plans—more than half their employees, on average, choose the managed care plan. Evidently, the employees do not feel that the benefits of the extra services provided under fee-for-service are worth the extra cost.

BUYING HEALTH INSURANCE

Have you ever seen an advertisement for health insurance which stresses that no physical exam is required? What can economics, and the notion of adverse selection, tell us about who is likely to buy such insurance and whether it is a "good" deal?

Health insurance is designed to let individuals share the risks that are associated with health needs. To see how such insurance might work, let's suppose there is a medical condition that affects 1 person in 100. This condition can be treated through surgery, but the cost of the surgery is $50,000. Let's assume that the chances of needing the surgery are the same for everyone. Without insurance, 99 of the 100 will not have to pay anything, but one unlucky person will have to pay $50,000. Under an insurance plan, 100 people could each contribute $500. Whoever ends up needing the operation has its cost paid by the insurance. The other 99 are "out" $500, but they have been insured against the much larger cost they would have had to pay had they required the surgery. If all 100 were equally likely to need the operation, and the cost of the surgery is $50,000, then charging everyone $500 is the fair price

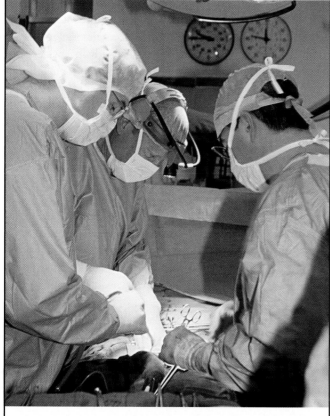

Health insurance is designed to let individuals share the risk of needing expensive health care, such as surgery.

for the insurance. A private company could offer this insurance since it will collect enough from selling the insurance to cover the amount it expects to have pay out.[1] Most people would probably find the option of paying $500 to avoid the much larger cost of the operation a good deal.

But suppose some people know that they are more likely than others to need the operation. Perhaps, like heart disease, the likelihood of needing surgery is higher if there is a family history of the disease. Suppose other individuals know they are extremely unlikely to develop the condition. Now, if an insurance company offers insurance for $500, all the individuals at high risk will see this as a good deal—they will purchase the insurance. But the individuals at low risk will not; for them, it is not worth $500. So the insurance company finds that only the bad risks buy the insurance—an example of adverse selection.

To continue our example, suppose 50 of our 100 individuals are in the high-risk group and buy the insurance. The insurance company collects $500 from each, for a total of $25,000: only half of what is needed to pay for an operation. The insurance company therefore has to charge $1,000 in order to break even. Given the overall likelihood of someone in the general population needing the operation (1 in 100), the insurance company appears to be overcharging; the ratio suggests that $500 is the fair price. And at the premium of $1,000, the low-risk people find the insurance even less attractive. They see themselves as providing a large subsidy to the high-risk individuals. But if the insurance company cannot distinguish between high-risk and low-risk individuals, the adverse selection effect will force it to charge more. So if you think you are at low risk for health problems, an insurance plan that does not require a medical exam is likely to be a bad deal. The adverse selection problem also explains why health and life insurance companies typically require medical exams—their incentive is to insure only healthy individuals, or at least to make certain that the premiums charged reflect the risks.

The Search Problem

A basic information problem is that consumers must find out what goods are available on the market, at what price, and where. Households must learn about job opportunities as well as opportunities for investing their savings. Firms, by the same token, have to figure out the demand curve they face, and where and at what price they can obtain inputs. Both sides of the market need, in other words, to find out about their opportunity sets.

In the basic competitive model of Part Two, a particular good sells for the same price everywhere. If we see what look like identical shoes selling for two different prices at two neighboring stores—$25 at one and $35 at the other—it must mean (in that model) that the stores are really selling different products. If the shoes are in fact identical, then what the customer must be getting is a combination package:

---

[1]For the sake of simplicity, this ignores any administrative cost the firm would have to include in the price charged to those who buy its insurance.

Thinking Like an Economist

INCENTIVE AND INFORMATION PROBLEMS IN THE HOUSING MARKET

For most Americans, buying or selling a house is likely to be the largest financial transaction they ever engage in. For people selling houses, setting the right price is critical. Set the price too high, and the house may remain unsold for months; set it too low, and the house sells quickly but the seller ends up with less money. Most people rely on a real estate agent to help them sell their homes, and the agent's job is to recommend a price at which to list the home, advertise it to attract potential buyers, and help the owner negotiate a final sale.

Because real estate agents know more about the local housing market than the typical client does, they can use their informational advantage to help sell the home. In their book *Freakonomics,* the University of Chicago economist Steven Levitt and his co-author Stephen Dubner highlight some of the ways real estate agents signal information about a house to other agents and to potential buyers. Words in ads such as "fantastic," "spacious," "charming," or "great neighborhood" actually are associated with lower sales prices, while "granite," "state-of-the-art," "Corian," "maple," and "gourmet" are associated with higher sales prices. Levitt and Dubner argue that the second set of descriptive terms tell potential buyers about particular attributes of the house. If all you can say about a house is that it is "spacious," potential buyers may take that as a signal that the place isn't all that great—otherwise, the ad would list its specific attractive features.

Interestingly, when real estate agents sell their *own* homes, they are much more likely to employ specific terms like "granite" or "maple," knowing that doing so is likely to yield a higher sales price.

Why then would they use adjectives like "fantastic" when they are hired to sell the homes of others? The answer lies in the incentives agents face. Suppose an agent lists her own home for $400,000. If she receives an offer of $380,000, she may decide to reject it and wait longer for the higher asking price. After all, she gives up $20,000 if she accepts the offer. But when it is *your* home she is selling, the situation is quite different. The agent typically receives a commission that is equal to a percentage of the sales price. After the costs of advertising and the share that goes to the agent's company are subtracted, only 1.5 percent of the sales price ends up in the agent's pocket. So if you reject the $380,000 offer in hopes of getting an offer of $400,000, the agent stands to gain only about an extra $300 (1.5 percent of $20,000), a far cry from the $20,000 she would gain if it were her home. In selling her own home, the agent has a big incentive to reject the lower offer; but when it comes to your home, the agent's incentive is to encourage you to accept. Giving up the chance of an extra $300 is too small a gain to make the agent want to pass up a sale that guarantees her a commission of $5,750 (1.5 percent of $380,000).

SOURCE: Steven D. Levitt and Stephen J. Dubner, *Freakonomics* (New York: William Morrow, 2005).

the shoes plus the service of having the shoes fitted. And the more expensive store is providing a higher-quality service.

Yet as we know from experience, essentially the same good may be sold at different stores for different prices, and it is not always possible to account for the observed differences in prices by differences in other attributes, such as the location of the store or the quality of the service provided. In these cases, we say there is **price dispersion.** If the act of finding out all prices were itself costless (or information were perfect, as in the standard competitive model), consumers would search until they found the cheapest price. And no store charging more than the lowest price on the market would ever have any customers. But in a world of costly information, a high-price store may still be able to keep some customers—and its higher profit per sale offsets its lower level of sales. Thus, price dispersion can persist.

Given price dispersion, combined with variations in quality, households and firms must spend considerable energy searching. Workers search for a good job. Firms look for good workers. Consumers search for the lowest prices and best values. The process by which this kind of information is gathered is called **search.**

Search is an important, and costly, economic activity. Because it is costly, a search stops before you have *all* the relevant information. A Google search may turn up thousands of references, but you are unlikely to scroll through more than the first few pages of the results. Because links that appear near the top of the list are more likely to be clicked on, the order of search results is extremely important. A site on the second or third page might be an even better source for the information you are seeking, but navigating through all the links until the perfect one is located is just too time-consuming. Similarly, after buying a new shirt for a special occasion, you may worry that you might have found an even better one if only you had visited one more store. But in truth, there should be no regrets. Going to more stores is costly in terms of your time, and there is always a chance you would not have found anything better. There is even a chance that by the time you returned to buy the shirt you had originally thought acceptable, it would have been sold to someone else. Continuing a search has benefits, but there are also costs. When deciding whether to search further, you need to compare the marginal benefits to the marginal costs.

The expected marginal benefit of searching declines with the amount of search. In general, people search the best prospects first. As they search more and more, they look at less and less likely prospects. On the other hand, the marginal cost of additional search rises with increased search. The more time people spend in search, the less time they have to do other things; thus the opportunity cost of spending an extra hour searching increases. The amount of search chosen will be at the point where the expected marginal benefit just equals the marginal cost.

An increase in price (or quality) dispersion will normally increase the marginal benefit of searching—there is a chance of picking up a really good bargain, and the difference between a good buy and a bad buy is larger. Thus, the amount of search will increase.

SEARCH AND IMPERFECT COMPETITION

Firms know and take advantage of the costliness of search. They know they will not lose all their customers if they raise their prices. And if a store lowers its price slightly, it will not immediately attract *all* the customers from the other stores. Customers have to learn about the competitive price advantage, a process that takes time. Moreover, even when people do hear of the lower price, they may worry about the quality of the goods being sold, the nature of the service, whether the goods will be in stock, and so on.

The fact that search is costly means that the demand curve facing a firm will be downward sloping. Competition is necessarily imperfect.

Consider, for instance, the demand for a portable MP3 player. When you walk into a store, you have some idea what it should sell for. The store asks $195 for it. You may know that somewhere you might be able to purchase it for $5 less. But is it worth the additional time, trouble, and gasoline to drive to the other stores that might have it, looking for a bargain? Some individuals are willing to pay the extra

$5 simply to stop having to search. As the store raises its price to, say, $200, $205, or $210, some people who would have bought the MP3 player at $195 decide that it is worth it to continue shopping around. The store, as it raises its price, loses some but not all of its customers. Thus, it faces a downward-sloping demand curve. If search were costless, everyone would go to the store selling the MP3 player at the lowest price, and any store charging more than that would have no sales. Markets in which search is costly are, accordingly, better described by the models of imperfect competition introduced in Chapters 11 and 12.

Costly search is also responsible for some of the strategic behavior by firms that was studied in Chapter 14. For example, some stores, in order not to lose customers, guarantee to match the lowest price available, if the customer can prove that another store has a better price. This common sales tactic ensures that the customer benefits from searching for a lower price; at the same time the firm, by matching the price, ensures that it does not lose a customer. In fact, while an offer to match any price sounds like a good offer, most economists believe it is simply a way for firms to keep prices high by letting any competitors know that they will not gain many sales by cutting prices.

SEARCH AND THE LABOR MARKET

The economics of search—a comparison of the costs and benefits of search—has important applications in the labor market. While older workers typically stay with an employer for years, younger workers often leave after a period of a few weeks or months. How can we explain these differences?

To begin, consider the positions of a sixty-year-old and a thirty-year-old contemplating a job search. Even should the sixty-year-old find a better job, he is likely to enjoy the job for at most a few years. For the thirty-year-old, the marginal benefit of additional search is much greater: there is at least the *possibility* that she will stay with the new employer for two decades or more. Each worker evaluates the marginal benefit and the marginal cost of additional search, but their evaluations yield different answers.

Two other factors reinforce these outcomes. First, the younger worker is likely to be less informed about her own preferences (what she likes and does not like) and about the job market. Moving from job to job provides additional information about both. Second, employers recognize such a learning process as normal, so there is little stigma associated with a younger worker moving about. By contrast, employers worry that an older worker who is looking for a new job may know that he is about to be dismissed or demoted because of inadequate job performance. Excessive job mobility for an older worker is often interpreted as a "bad" sign.

SEARCH AND INFORMATION INTERMEDIARIES

Some firms play an important role by gathering information and serving as intermediaries between producers and customers. One of the functions of stores such as Wal-Mart and Macy's, for example, is to economize on customers' search costs. The stores' buyers seek out literally hundreds of producers, looking for the best buys and the kinds of goods that their customers will like. Stores can earn a reputation for the quality of the selection they offer their buyers. Customers still have a search problem—they may have to visit several stores—but doing so is far less costly than if they had to search directly among producers. In addition, magazines like *Consumer Reports* provide readers with detailed information on product quality and price, saving consumers considerable search cost. Today, numerous Internet sites enable consumers to compare prices offered by different online sellers, again helping to reduce search costs.

Advertising

Customers have an incentive to find out where the best buys are. Firms have a corresponding incentive to tell customers about the great deals they are providing. Companies may spend large sums to bring information about their products, prices, and locations to potential customers. In the United States, many firms spend 2 percent, 3 percent, or more of their total revenue on advertising. This figure varies greatly across industries, however. Motion picture producers spend more than 12 percent of their sales revenue on advertising, but motion picture theaters spend only about 1 percent. Department stores spend more than 3 percent, while drug stores spend less than 1 percent.

Advertising can serve the important economic function of providing information about what choices are available. When a new airline enters a market, it must announce its presence to potential customers. When a new product is developed, that fact has to be publicized. When a business is having a sale, it must let people know. A firm that wants to be successful cannot just lower its prices and wait for customers. Companies need to actively recruit new customers and convey information. Thus, advertising plays an important role in improving the efficiency of markets when information is imperfect. It also supports the entire network television industry—rather than paying a direct price to watch network programs, as cable subscribers do, we pay an indirect price: we sit through the commercials that are scattered through our favorite shows, and the networks receive revenue by selling time to firms who wish to advertise.

But not all advertising is designed to convey factual information about product prices or characteristics. Take the typical beer or car advertisement. It provides almost no information about the product; instead, it seeks to create an image, one with which potential buyers will identify. That these advertisements succeed in persuading individuals either to try a product or to stick with that product rather than trying another is a reminder that consumer behavior is much more complicated than the simple theories of competitive markets suggest. Few people decide to go out and buy a car or new shoes solely because they saw a TV ad. But decisions about what kinds of clothes to wear, what beer to drink, and what car to drive are affected by a variety of considerations, including how peers view the consumers or how they see themselves. These views, in turn, can be affected by advertising.

To emphasize the different roles played by advertising, economists distinguish between *informative advertising* and *persuasive advertising*. The intent of the former is to provide consumers with information about the price of a good, where it may be acquired, or what its characteristics are. The intent of persuasive advertising is to make consumers feel good about the product. To that end, advertisers may even provide "disinformation," seeking to confuse consumers into perceiving differences among goods that are essentially the same.

ADVERTISING AND COMPETITION

Advertising is both a cause and a consequence of imperfect competition. In a perfectly competitive industry, in which many producers make identical goods, it would not pay any single producer to advertise the merits of its product. We do not see advertisements for wheat or corn. If such advertising were successful, it would simply shift the demand curve for the product out. This increase in the total demand for wheat would have a negligible effect on the wheat grower who paid for the advertisement. The industry as a whole might benefit, however, if all the wheat farmers could get together and advertise as a group. In recent years, associations representing producers of milk, oranges, almonds, raisins, and beef have done just that.

But if advertising can create in consumers' minds the perception that products are different, then firms will face downward-sloping demand curves. There will be imperfect competition. And once imperfect competition exists, advertising can be used to increase the demand for a firm's products.

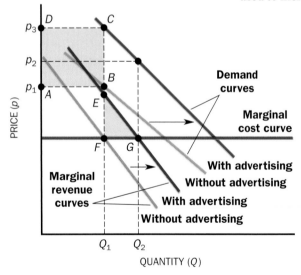

Figure 15.2

HOW ADVERTISING CAN SHIFT THE DEMAND CURVE

Successful advertising shifts the demand curve facing a firm. When the imperfect competitor equates its new marginal revenue with its old marginal cost, it will be able to raise both its price and its output.

ADVERTISING AND PROFITS

The objective of advertising is not only to change the slope of the demand curve—by creating the perception of product differentiation—but also to shift the demand curve out, as in Figure 15.2. The increase in advertising by one firm may divert customers away from rivals, or it may divert customers away from other products. Advertising a particular brand of cigarettes may succeed in inducing some smokers to switch brands and inducing some nonsmokers to smoke.

The increase in profits from shifting the demand curve consists of two parts. First, the firm can sell the same quantity it sold before but at a higher price—p_3, rather than p_1. Profits then increase by the original quantity (Q_1) times the change in price ($p_3 - p_1$), the rectangle $ABCD$ in the figure. Second, because the advertising has shifted the firm's marginal revenue curve up, it can adjust the quantity it sells. As usual, the imperfectly competitive firm sets marginal revenue equal to marginal cost, so it increases output from Q_1 to Q_2. The additional profits thus generated are measured by the area between the marginal revenue and marginal cost curves between Q_1 and Q_2. Marginal cost remains the same, so the second source of extra profits is the shaded area *EFG*. The net increase in profits is the area *ABCD* plus the area *EFG* minus the cost of advertising.

So far, in studying the effect of an increase in advertising on one firm's profits, we have assumed that other firms keep their level of advertising constant. Determining the effect of advertising on both industry and firm profits is more problematic once the reactions of other firms in the industry are taken into account. To the extent that advertising diverts sales from one firm in an industry to another, it may, in equilibrium, have little effect on demand. For example, assume that Nike shoe ads divert customers from Reebok to Nike and vice versa for Reebok ads. Figure 15.3 shows the demand curve facing Reebok (1) before advertising, (2) when only Reebok advertises, and (3) when both companies advertise. The third demand curve is the same as the first. Price and output are the same; profits are lower by the amount spent on advertising. We have here another example of a prisoner's dilemma. If the firms could cooperate and agree not to advertise, they would both be better off. But without such cooperation, it pays each to advertise, regardless of what the rival does. The government-mandated ban on cigarette advertising on radio and TV may have partially solved this prisoner's dilemma for the tobacco industry—in the name of health policy.

In practice, when all cigarette firms advertise, the ads do more than just cancel each other out. Some people who might not otherwise have smoked are persuaded to do so, and some smokers are persuaded to smoke more than they otherwise would have. But the shift in a particular firm's demand curve when all companies advertise is still much smaller than it is when only that firm advertises.

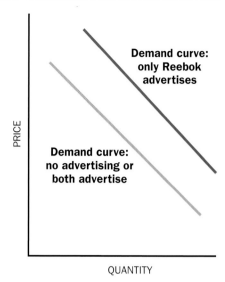

Figure 15.3

HOW ADVERTISING CAN CANCEL OUT OTHER ADVERTISING

If only one company advertises, the demand curve for its product may shift out. But if both companies advertise, the resulting demand curve may be the same as it would be if neither advertised.

Wrap-Up

CONSEQUENCES OF IMPERFECT INFORMATION

In the presence of adverse selection problems, quality may be affected by price.
  Adverse selection can lead to thin markets or the failure of markets to even exist.
  Signaling plays an important role in adverse selection problems.
In the presence of weak or misdirected incentives, moral hazard problems arise.
  Contingent contracts and reputation are important solutions for incentive problems.
In the presence of price dispersion, consumers must engage in search.
  Because searching is costly, firms face downward-sloping demand curves and competition is imperfect.
In the presence of imperfect information, firms engage in advertising.
  Advertising can be used to change perceptions of product differences, altering the slope of the demand curve.
  Advertising can be used to shift the demand curve.

The Importance of Imperfect Information

The modern economy has sometimes been called "the information economy." The name is justified in part because the major advances in computer technology have greatly enhanced the capacity to process information, and in part because such a large fraction of total economic activity now revolves around collecting, processing, and disseminating information. Personnel officers focus on finding out about potential employees; lending officers attempt to assess the likelihood that potential borrowers will default; market researchers try to determine the potential market for some new product; large retailers send buyers out to scour the world for new suppliers of the clothes they sell. But no matter how much information we have, we seldom have as much as we would like.

Not only is information imperfect, but different people have different information. Information is asymmetric. The seller of a car knows more about her car's problems than the buyer. The worker may know more about his strengths and weaknesses than does the firm where he is interviewing for a job. The borrower may know more about some of the contingencies that may affect his ability to repay the loan than the lender. Because the parties to a transaction do not always have an incentive to be perfectly truthful, it may be difficult for the more informed party to convey convincingly what she knows to others.

That individuals and firms typically make decisions based on imperfect information fundamentally affects the behavior of markets in various ways. For their part, firms and individuals attempt to compensate for the scarcity of information. In many markets in which problems of adverse selection and moral hazard arise, firms adjust prices to convey information about quality. Moreover, individuals and firms may attempt to signal information about their characteristics and work to establish a reputation.

Review and Practice

SUMMARY

1. The basic competitive model assumes that participants in the market have perfect information about the goods being bought and sold and their prices. In the real world, information is often imperfect. Economists have modified the basic model so that it includes a number of limitations on information.

2. A problem of adverse selection may arise when consumers cannot judge the true quality of a product. As the price of the good falls, the quality mix changes adversely, and the quantity demanded at a lower price may actually be lower than at a higher price.

3. Producers of high-quality products may attempt to signal that their product is better than those of competitors; for instance, they may provide better warranties.

4. When consumers judge quality by price, they may agree on some price that offers the best value. Firms will have no incentive to cut prices below this "best value" price, even when, at this price, the amount they would be willing to supply exceeds demand. As a result, the market can settle on an equilibrium with an excess supply of goods.

5. When there is perfect information, private property and prices supply the correct incentives to all market participants. When information is imperfect and incentives are not correct, two methods of adjusting them are to employ contracts with contingency clauses and to rely on reputation. For firms to have an incentive to maintain a good reputation, they must earn profits by doing so. Thus equilibrium price exceeds marginal cost. (Reputation may also serve as a barrier to entry.)

6. Costly search may lead to price dispersion and imperfections of competition as each firm faces a downward-sloping demand curve.

7. Advertising attempts to change consumers' buying behavior, either by providing relevant information about prices or characteristics, by using persuasion, or both.

KEY TERMS

adverse selection
asymmetric information
thin or incomplete markets
signal
moral hazard
reputation
price dispersion
search

REVIEW QUESTIONS

1. Why would "lemons" not be a problem for consumers in a world of perfect information? Why do they lead to a backward-bending demand curve in a world of imperfect information?

2. Why is signaling unnecessary in a world of perfect information? What does it accomplish in a world of imperfect information?

3. Explain why, if consumers think that quality increases with price, there will be cases in which firms will have no incentive to cut prices in an attempt to attract more business.

4. How do contingency clauses in contracts help provide appropriate incentives? What are some of the problems in writing contracts that provide for all the relevant contingencies?

5. What role does reputation have in maintaining incentives? What is required if firms are to have an incentive to maintain their reputations? How might the good reputation of existing firms serve as a barrier to the entry of new firms?

6. What are the benefits of searching for market information? What are the costs? How does the existence of price dispersion affect the benefits? Could price dispersion exist in a world of perfect information? How do the costs of search affect the nature of competition in a market?

7. Describe how advertising might affect the demand curve facing a firm. How do these changes affect prices? profits?

8. What is moral hazard? What is adverse selection? Give an example of each.

PROBLEMS

1. How does imperfect information help explain why used cars cost more when sold by car dealers than by private individuals?

2. For each situation, state whether it reflects a problem of adverse selection or of moral hazard.
   (a) A person drives faster because his new car has air bags.
   (b) A high school football team visits an "all you can eat" restaurant.
   (c) A real estate agent who advertises that she will buy your house from you if she fails to sell it in six weeks sets a low selling price for your house.
   (d) An insurance company that offers health insurance without requiring a medical exam finds that only people with health problems buy its insurance.

3. Explain how the incentives of someone to look after a car she is renting may not suit the company that is renting the car. How might a contingent contract help solve this problem? Is it likely to solve the problem completely?

4. L. L. Bean, a mail-order company, has a long-standing policy that it will take back anything it has sold, at any time, for any reason. Why might it be worthwhile for a profit-maximizing firm to enact such a policy?

5. Would you expect to see greater price dispersion within a metropolitan area, or between several small towns that are fifty miles apart? Why?

6. How do costs of search help explain the success of department stores?

7. Suppose a professor assigns a group project to a class. Each student in a group will receive the same grade, based on the project submitted by the group. Will this lead to a moral hazard problem? Explain.

Learning Goals

In this chapter, you will learn

1 About the economic effects of labor unions on wages and employment

2 About the factors that limit union power

3 About the factors that explain wage differentials

4 About the incentive problems that face firms seeking to motivate workers

Chapter 16

IMPERFECTIONS IN THE LABOR MARKET

Part Two emphasized the similarity between the labor market and markets for goods. Households demand goods and firms supply them, with the price system as intermediary. Likewise, firms demand labor and workers supply it, with the wage as intermediary. Firms hire labor up to the point at which the value of the marginal product of labor is equal to the wage, just as they would buy coal up to the point at which the value of the marginal product of coal is equal to the price of coal.

This chapter takes another look at the labor market. Just as we saw in the preceding five chapters some of the ways in which product markets differ from their depiction in the basic competitive model, here we will see important ways in which labor markets differ from their depiction in the basic competitive model. We will find that labor markets, like product markets, are characterized by imperfect competition. Unions are the most obvious manifestation, and we will take a look at their history as well as their impact on wages and employment—the prices and quantities of the labor market.

Information problems affect the labor market even more significantly than product markets, in part because workers are not like computer chips. They have to be motivated to work hard, and they are concerned with working conditions and how their current pay compares with that offered by other firms. Firms are aware of the importance of these considerations in attracting and keeping employees, and they design employment and compensation policies accordingly.

Labor Unions

Labor unions are organizations of workers, formed to obtain better working conditions and higher wages for their members. The main weapon they have is the threat of a collective withdrawal of labor, known as a *strike*.

A BRIEF HISTORY

Labor unions are less important institutions in our economy than they used to be, and they have always played a smaller role in the United States than in many European countries. Unionization in the United States began in the late nineteenth and early twentieth centuries. A variety of craft unions were established, consisting of skilled workers such as carpenters, plumbers, and printers. In 1886, the American Federation of Labor (AFL) was formed. Led by Samuel Gompers, the AFL gathered together a number of these craft unions to enhance their bargaining power.

The Rise of Unions In the 1930s, two events strengthened union power: the confederation of major industrial unions into the Congress of Industrial Organizations (CIO) and the passage of the Wagner Act, which provided legal status to unions. The CIO represented a major change in two respects. First, it embraced all workers, unskilled as well as skilled; and second, it represented all the workers in a company. These industrial unions, by uniting all workers across job categories, enhanced workers' bargaining strength. Their leaders, such as Walter Reuther of the United Automobile Workers (UAW), attained national prominence, and the unions were able to obtain for their workers substantial wage increases and improvements in working conditions. The 1935 Wagner Act set up the National Labor Relations Board, which established procedures for certifying labor unions and preventing certain practices on the part of firms trying to block workers from unionizing.

The Decline of Unions Prompted by concerns that the balance had swung too far in favor of unions, Congress in 1947 passed the Labor-Management Relations Act, better known as the Taft-Hartley Act. This law addressed two issues. First,

The United Auto Workers currently has 710,000 active union members.

unions had claimed that when they negotiated a better contract or better working conditions, they were providing benefits to all workers at an establishment. Thus, they demanded that all laborers at unionized companies join the union, a requirement that established **union shops.** Critics of union shops thought that the right to work should not be limited to members of unions. The Taft-Hartley Act left it to the individual states to decide whether to outlaw union shops, and many states subsequently passed **right-to-work laws.** These laws gave workers the right to hold a job without belonging to a union—or, to put it the way unions do, the right to receive union pay without paying union dues.

The second concern addressed by the Taft-Hartley Act was the devastating effect on the country of strikes by national unions. A shutdown of the railroads or the steel or coal industry could have ramifications far beyond the firms directly involved. The new law gave the president the power to declare, when national welfare was at stake, an eighty-day cooling-off period, during which workers had to return to work.

Since the mid-1950s, union power has declined steadily in the United States. Figure 16.1 traces the sharp increases of union membership in the 1930s, and again during World War II, when the government encouraged unionization in all military plants. But since then, unions have had only limited success in recruiting new members, and the union share of nonagricultural employment has thus been falling. It fell below 20 percent in 1984, where it remains today. In fact, not only the union share but also the actual number of unionized workers has been declining. Today there are about 16 million union members, 2 million fewer than there were in 1960.

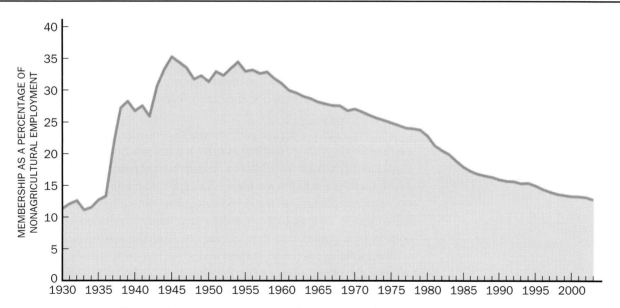

Figure 16.1

UNIONIZATION OF THE U.S. LABOR FORCE

The percentage of the U.S. labor force belonging to unions increased sharply in the 1930s and early 1940s but has been largely declining since 1950.

SOURCE: U.S. Census Bureau, *Historical Statistics of the United States, Colonial Times to 1970, Employment and Earnings* (various issues).

UNIONS ON THE INTERNET

The American Federation of Labor–Congress of Industrial Organization (AFL-CIO) is the largest union organization in the United States. Its home page is at www.aflcio.org. Traditional unions such as the United Automobile Workers (UAW) (www.uaw.org) organize workers in manufacturing industries. Today, many workers are employed in public-sector jobs, and AFSCME, the American Federation of State, County and Municipal Employees, is a major organizer of public-sector and health industry workers (www.afscme.org).

Though total union membership has fallen, today's union member is much more likely to work in the public sector than was true in the past. In 1960, the percentage of union members working in the public sector was only 6 percent. Today it is closer to 40 percent, while only about one in ten nongovernmental workers belongs to a union. Why the recent and continuing decline in union membership among workers in the private sector?

One explanation is that working conditions for workers—whether as a result of union pressure or technological progress—have improved enormously. Workers therefore see less need for unions.

A second reason is related to the changing nature of the American economy. Unions have declined as the traditionally unionized sectors (such as automobiles and steel) have weakened, and the service sector, in which unions have been and continue to be weak, has grown.

Third, unions may be less effective in competitive markets. When competition is limited, there are monopoly (or imperfect competition) profits or rents. Unions may be successful in winning a share in those rents for their workers. But when markets are competitive, firms cannot charge more than the market price for their goods; and if they are to survive, they simply cannot pay their workers more than the competitive wage.

In the late nineteenth and early twentieth centuries, for example, high wages in shoe and textile mills in New England drove plants to the nonunionized South. High wages also drive American firms to manufacture abroad. Unless unions manage to ensure that their workers are more productive than average, it is only when these sources of competition are restricted that unions can succeed in keeping their wages above average for long. In this view, the increased competition to which American industry is subjected, both from abroad and from the deregulation of trucking, oil, airlines, banking, telephone service, and so on, has led to a decline in the ability of unions in the private sector to garner higher wages for their workers.

A final explanation of the growth and decline of unions is the changing legal atmosphere. When laws support or encourage unions, unions prosper. When they do not, unions wither. Thus, the Wagner Act set the stage for the growth of unions in the 1930s. The Taft-Hartley Act paved the way for their decline in the post–World War II era.

ECONOMIC EFFECTS

The source of union power is collective action. When workers join together in a union, they no longer negotiate as isolated individuals. The threat of a strike (or a work slowdown) poses many more difficulties for an employer than does the threat of any single employee quitting.

In the perfectly competitive model of labor markets, workers are price takers; the market wage is given. But when there is a downward-sloping demand curve for labor, as in Figure 16.2,[1] unions have some power to be price setters. As a result of this power, a worker at a particular level of skill who works in a unionized establishment will be paid more than a comparable worker in a competitive industry. The firm would like to hire that lower-priced, nonunion worker, and the nonunionized worker could easily be induced to move, but the firm has a union contract that prevents it from hiring anyone at a lower wage. But as the union raises the price of labor (the wage), firms will employ fewer workers. Higher wages are obtained at the expense of lower levels of employment. In the figure, when wages rise from the competitive level w_c to w_m, employment is reduced from L_c to L_m.

Short-Run Gains at the Expense of Long-Run Losses

Sometimes unions can increase both employment and wages, at least for a time. They present the employer with, in effect, two alternatives: either pay a high wage *and* maintain an employment level above the labor demand curve for that wage, or go out of business. If the employer already has sunk costs in machines and buildings, he may accede to the union demands. In effect, the union takes away some of the employer's monopoly profits or return to capital. In competitive markets, where there are no monopoly profits, the higher wages can only come out of employers' return to capital. But these employers will lose interest in investing in more capital. As capital wears out, an employer has less and less to lose from the union threat. As she refuses to invest more, jobs decrease. Even if the union makes short-run gains, they come at the expense of a long-run loss in jobs.

Effects on Nonunion Workers
The gains of today's union members not only may cost future jobs but also may come at the expense of those in other sectors of the economy, for two reasons. First, the higher wages may well be passed on to consumers in the form of higher prices, particularly if product markets are not perfectly competitive. Second, the increased wages (and reduced employment) in the union sector drive down wages in the nonunionized sector, as the supply of nonunion labor increases. Some argue the opposite—that high union wages "pull up" wages in

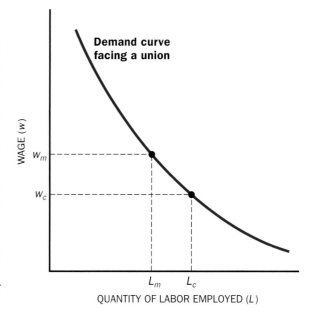

Figure 16.2

THE UNION AS A MONOPOLY SELLER OF LABOR

Unions can be viewed as sellers of labor, with market power. When they increase their wage demands, they reduce the demand for their members' labor services.

---

[1]Chapter 8 showed how the demand curve for labor is derived in competitive markets. Firms hire labor up to the point at which the wage equals the value of the marginal product of labor. The derivation of the demand curve for labor in monopolies and imperfectly competitive markets follows along similar lines. Firms hire labor up to the point at which the marginal revenue—that is, the extra revenue they obtain from selling the extra output they produce from hiring an extra unit of labor—is equal to the wage.

nonunion firms. The nonunion firms may, for instance, pay higher wages to reduce the likelihood of unionization. In particular sectors this effect is important, but most economists believe that the overall impact of union gains on nonunion workers is negative.

Job Security and Innovation The economy as a whole benefits from innovation, but particular groups within it are likely to suffer. In an innovative economy, those workers who are dislocated by new inventions are expected to learn new skills and seek out new jobs. Without the shifts of labor in response to changes in demand (resulting from either new technologies or changes in tastes), the economy will be inefficient.

Technological changes may threaten the job security that unions seek for their members. As a result, unions have attempted to retard innovations that might decrease the demand for their members' services. An efficient economy requires job transitions, but they are costly and the costs are borne largely by the workers. Before the advent of unions and laws providing unemployment compensation, the human toll was considerable. Individuals could not buy insurance against these employment risks, but they could form unions—and union attempts to enhance job security were a response to this important problem. Today many countries are looking for ways of insulating workers against the risks of job transition without impeding the labor mobility that is so important for economic efficiency.

Unions and Politics We have seen that the fortunes of unions depend, to a large extent, on the legal environment in which they operate. Unions have also learned that what they cannot get at the bargaining table they may be able to obtain through the political process. For example, they have actively campaigned for higher minimum wages.

At the same time, unions have shown in their political stances that they recognize the economic forces that determine both the strength of their bargaining positions and, more generally, the level of wages. Thus, they have been active supporters of policies of high employment. They have sought to restrict imports from abroad (believing that such restrictions will increase the demand for American products and therefore the demand for labor). And historically they have been proponents of limits on immigration (recognizing that increases in the supply of labor lead to reductions in wages).

Finally, unions have been strong advocates, through the political process, of safer working conditions. Today, the Occupational Safety and Health Administration (OSHA) attempts to ensure that workers are not exposed to unnecessary hazards. OSHA seeks to make much less likely the kinds of episodes that occurred in the asbestos industry, which knowingly exposed workers to life-threatening risks.

LIMITS ON UNION POWER

In the United States, no union has a monopoly on *all* workers. At most, a union has a monopoly on the workers currently working for a particular firm. Thus, the power of unions is partly attributable to the firm's inability to easily replace its employees.

When a union goes on strike, the firm may be able to hire some workers, but it is costly to bring in and train a whole new labor force. Indeed, most of the knowledge needed to train the new laborers is in the hands of the union members. While one bushel of wheat may be very much like another, one worker is not very much like another. Workers outside the firm are not perfect substitutes for other workers, particularly skilled ones, inside.

The Threat of Replacement   In industries in which skills are easily transferable across firms or in which a union has not succeeded in enlisting the support of most of the skilled workers, a firm can replace striking workers, and union power will be limited. Caterpillar, a manufacturer of tractors and road-making equipment, weathered a seventeen-month strike by the UAW that began in 1993. Eventually, management announced that if workers did not return to their jobs, they would be replaced. The union caved in shortly after the firm made good its threat.

In today's global economy, the threat to move jobs overseas provides another limit to union power. Even if the union has a monopoly on all workers in an industry, its reach does not extend to foreign workers. The ability of firms to relocate to other countries reduces a union's ability to gain higher wages.

In many cases, however, workers' skills are specific to the firm. Just as, from the employer's perspective, workers outside the firm are not perfect substitutes for workers within the firm, so from the workers' perspective one job is not a perfect substitute for another. Thus, there is often value to both workers and to firms in preserving ongoing employment relationships.

The Threat of Unemployment   Unions understand that in the long run, higher wages—other things being equal—mean lower levels of employment. When job opportunities in general are weak, concern about the effects of union contracts on employment increases. Maintaining jobs rather than raising wages may become the union's chief priority if the industry is shrinking, perhaps owing to increased competition from imports or owing to technological changes that have increased the industry's competition from new products. A rise in overall unemployment in the economy is also likely to limit a union's ability to seek wage hikes.

Wrap-Up

UNIONS AND IMPERFECT COMPETITION IN THE LABOR MARKET

Economic effects of unions:

    Higher wages for union members, with fewer union jobs and lower wages for nonunion members

    Improved job security, sometimes at the expense of innovation and economic efficiency

    Minimum wages, restrictions on imports, improved working conditions, and other gains achieved through the political process

Determinants of union power:
  Political and legal environment
  Economic environment: salience of the threat of replacement and unemployment

Wage Differentials

The basic competitive model suggests that if the goods being sold are the same, prices will also be the same. Wages are the price in the labor market; but even in the absence of unions, similar types of workers performing similar types of jobs are sometimes paid quite different wages. For example, some secretaries are paid twice as much as others. How can economists explain differences like these?

An understanding of wage differentials begins with the observation that although different jobs may have the same title, they can be quite different. Some are less pleasant, require more overtime, and are in a less convenient location. These are **nonpecuniary attributes** of a job. Other nonpecuniary attributes include the degree of autonomy provided the worker (that is, the closeness with which her actions are supervised) and the risk she must bear, whether from physical hazard or from variability in income. Economists expect wages to adjust to reflect the attractiveness or unattractiveness of these nonpecuniary characteristics. **Compensating wage differentials** arise because firms have to compensate their workers for the negative aspects of a job.

Other differences are accounted for by differences in the productivity of workers. These are *productivity wage differentials.* Some workers are much more productive than others, even those with the same experience and education.

Compensating and productivity wage differentials fall within the realm of the basic competitive model analysis. But other wage differentials are due to imperfect information. It takes time to search out different job opportunities. Just as one store may sell the same object for a higher price than another store, one firm may hire labor for a lower wage than another firm. The worker who accepts a lower-paying job simply because he did not know about the higher-paying one down the street illustrates an *information-based differential.*

Limited information has important implications for firms. First, in the standard competitive model, firms face a horizontal supply curve for labor. If they raise wages slightly above the "market" wage, they can obtain as much labor as they want. In practice, mobility is more limited. Even if workers at other firms knew about the higher wage offer, they might be reluctant to switch. They may worry that they are not well matched for the job, or that the employer is offering high wages because the work is unattractive.

Second, firms worry about the quality of their workforce. If an employer offers a higher wage to someone working for another firm and the worker accepts, the employer might worry about the signal the acceptance sends about the worker's quality. Did his current employer—who presumably knows a lot about the worker's productivity—fail to match the job offer because his productivity does not warrant the higher wage? Does the worker's willingness to leave demonstrate a "lack of loyalty," or an "unsettled nature"—in which case, he may not stick with the new firm long enough to make his training worthwhile? These concerns again impede labor mobility, leading employers to prefer to keep their existing labor force even when there are lower-paid workers with similar credentials whom they might recruit at a lower wage.

Different groups of individuals may differ in their mobility. For instance, older workers may be much more reluctant to move than younger workers. Sometimes, firms take advantage of these differences to cut their own costs. Knowing that older workers will not leave even if their wages fail to keep pace with inflation, employers may hold back raises from them. Their lack of mobility provides a rationale for employers to engage in age discrimination.

DISCRIMINATION

Discrimination is said to occur if two workers of seemingly similar *work-related* characteristics are treated differently. Paying higher wages to better-educated workers is not discrimination, as long as the higher level of education is related to higher productivity. If older workers are less productive, then paying them lower wages is not discrimination. But if they are just as productive as younger workers, then taking advantage of their lower mobility to pay them less *is* discrimination.

Forty years ago, there was open and outright discrimination in the labor market. Some employers simply refused to hire African Americans. Today much of the discrimination that occurs is more subtle. Firms seek to hire the best workers they can for each job at the lowest cost possible, operating with imperfect information. In making predictions about future performance, employers use whatever information they have available. Employers may have found that those receiving a degree from a well-established school are more productive, on average, than those receiving a degree from a less-established college. Of the African Americans and Hispanics who are college graduates, more may have gone to less-prestigious schools. Screening the applicant pool to pick those with degrees from well-established colleges effectively excludes many African Americans and Hispanics. This more subtle form of discrimination is called **statistical discrimination.**

Some discrimination reflects neither old-fashioned prejudice nor statistics. Employers may just feel more comfortable dealing with people with whom they have dealt in the past. Highly uncertain about who is a good worker, and knowing that a bad worker can do enormous damage, top management may rely on certain trusted employees for recommendations. And such judgments are inevitably affected by friendships and other ties. Many claim that if discrimination is to be eliminated, this associative form, based on "old boy networks," has to be broken.

When firms pay lower wages to, say, women or minorities, they are practicing **wage discrimination.** Today, wage discrimination is perhaps less common than **job discrimination,** the denial to disadvantaged groups of equal access to better-paying jobs. Women are often said to face a "glass ceiling": they can climb up to middle management jobs but can't get beyond that level to reach top management.

Some market forces tend to limit the extent of discrimination. If a woman earns less than a man of comparable productivity, it pays a firm to hire her. Not to do so costs the firm profits. To put it another way, the firm pays a price for discriminating.

If there are enough firms that put profits above prejudice, then the wages of women will be bid up toward the level of men of comparable productivity.

Beginning in the 1960s, the government has taken an active stance in combating discrimination. In 1964, Congress passed the Civil Rights Act, which banned employment discrimination and set up the Equal Employment Opportunity Commission to prosecute cases of discrimination. The reach of these laws was extended in 1975 when the government prohibited age discrimination; in 1990, job discrimination against qualified individuals with disabilities was barred.

Beyond this, the federal government has required its contractors to undertake **affirmative action.** They must actively seek out minorities and women for jobs, and actively seek to promote them to better-paying positions. Affirmative action has occasionally taken the form of quotas that specify that a certain number or fraction of positions be reserved for minorities or women. Critics claim that quotas are discriminatory—they imply that a minority individual would be chosen over a more qualified white male. One of the objectives of antidiscrimination laws was to discourage thinking in racial or gender terms. Courts have reaffirmed this aim, allowing quotas only in special circumstances such as redressing the effects of specific instances of past discrimination.

Wrap-Up

EXPLANATIONS OF WAGE DIFFERENTIALS

Unions: Unions may succeed in obtaining higher wages for their workers.

Compensating differentials: Wage differences may correspond to differences in the nature of the job.

Productivity differentials: Wage differences may correspond to differences in the productivity between workers.

Information-based differentials: Wage differences may be a reflection of workers' not having perfect information about the opportunities available in the market, and employers' not viewing all workers as perfect substitutes for one another.

Imperfect labor mobility: Differentials are preserved because of the reluctance of individuals to move between jobs.

Discrimination: Wage differentials and hiring and promotion decisions can sometimes be traced to nothing more than differences of race or sex.

Motivating Workers

The discussion to this point has treated workers as if they were machines. Workers have a price—the wage—analogous to the price of machines. But even to the most profit-hungry and coldhearted employer, people are different from machines. They bring adaptability and a multitude of skills and experiences to a job. Most machines can do only one task, and even robots can only follow their programs. However, machines have one advantage over humans: except when they break down, they do what they are told. Workers, in contrast, have to be motivated if they are to work hard and to exercise good judgment.

This requirement can be viewed as an information problem. In the basic competitive model of Part Two, workers were paid to perform particular tasks. The employer knew perfectly whether the worker performed the agreed-on task in the agreed-on manner. If the worker failed to do so, he did not get paid. The pay was the only form of motivation required. But in reality, workers frequently have considerable discretion. And because employers have limited information about what a worker is doing at each moment, they have to motivate members of their workforce to exercise their abilities to the fullest.

To motivate workers, employers use both the carrot and the stick. They may reward workers for performing well by making pay and promotion depend on performance, and they may punish workers for shirking by firing them. Sometimes a worker is given substantial autonomy; sometimes she is monitored closely. The mix of carrots and sticks, autonomy and direct supervision, varies from job to job and industry to industry. Among other factors, it depends on how easy it is to supervise workers directly and how easy it is to compensate workers on the basis of performance.

PIECE RATES AND INCENTIVES

When the pay of workers increases for higher productivity and falls for lower productivity, they will have appropriate incentives to work hard. The system of payment in which a worker is paid for each item produced or each task performed is called a **piece-rate system.** But relatively few Americans are paid largely, let alone exclusively, in this way. Typically, even workers within a piece-rate system get a base pay *plus* additional pay, which goes up as they produce more.

Why don't more employers enact a piece-rate system, if it would improve incentives? One major reason is that piece rates leave workers bearing considerable risk. A worker may have a bad week because of bad luck. For example, salespeople, who are often paid commissions on the basis of sales—a form of piece rate—may simply find little demand for their products, no matter how hard they have worked.

A firm, by providing a certain amount of guaranteed pay, gives the worker a steady income and reduces the risk she must bear. But compensation that is less dependent on a piece rate gives the worker less incentive to work hard. There is thus a trade-off between risk and incentives. Compensation schemes must find some balance between offering security and offering incentives linked to worker performance. In many jobs, employers or managers achieve this balance by providing both a guaranteed minimum compensation (including fringe benefits) and bonuses that depend on performance.

A second reason that more employers do not use piece-rate systems is their concern for quality, which can be difficult to measure even when the quantity—say, the output of workers on an assembly line—is obvious. If pay depends just on the number of items produced, the worker has an incentive to emphasize quantity over quality. The result may be less profitable for the firm than a lower level of higher-quality output.

In any case, most workers are engaged in a variety of tasks, only some of which can easily be defined and rewarded by means of a piece-rate system. For example, although employers would like experienced workers to train new workers, employees who are paid on a piece-rate system have little incentive to do this, or to help their co-workers in other ways. Similarly, when salespeople are paid on the basis of commissions, they have little incentive to provide information and service to any potential customers except those perceived as likely to buy immediately. Even if providing information enhances the likelihood that a customer will return to the store to purchase the good, there is a fair chance that someone else will get the commission. To observe this effect at work, visit a car dealer's showroom, make it clear that you are not going to buy a car that day, and see what service you get.

EFFICIENCY WAGES

When output is easily measured, then the carrot—basing pay at least partially on performance—makes sense. And when effort is easily monitored, then the stick—firing workers for not exerting adequate effort—makes sense. But monitoring effort continuously is often expensive. An alternative is to monitor less frequently, and impose a big penalty if the worker is caught shirking. One way of imposing such a penalty is to pay above-market wages and benefits. Then, if a worker is fired, he suffers a large income loss. The higher the wage, the greater the penalty from being fired. Similarly, rewarding workers with higher pay who are observed to be working hard whenever they are monitored provides incentives for workers to continue to apply themselves.

In these cases, higher wages help motivate workers and lead to increased productivity. Additional factors may persuade a firm to pay wages higher than are absolutely necessary to recruit the desired number of workers. High wages reduce labor turnover, lead to more loyalty and higher-quality work by employees, and enable the firm to attract more productive workers. The theory that higher wages increase workers' net productivity, for any or all of these reasons, is called the **efficiency wage theory.** While conventional theory emphasizes that increased productivity leads to higher wages, efficiency wage theory emphasizes that higher wages lead to increased productivity.

UPS exemplifies a firm that has adopted a conscious strategy of developing a reputation as an excellent employer. It treats its employees well, offering good benefits and salaries. It also encourages workers to gain promotions. The availability of these benefits and opportunities makes the loss of a job especially costly for UPS workers. But because employees feel they are well treated by UPS, they are likely to show more loyalty to the firm, working harder and ensuring a high level of labor productivity. In the long run, UPS benefits from this approach, even though in the short run it might be able to raise its profits by scaling back employee benefits or promotion opportunities.

Efficiency wage theory provides an explanation for some wage differentials. In jobs in which the costs of monitoring workers on a day-to-day basis are very high or the damage a worker can do is very great (for instance, by punching one wrong button the worker can destroy a machine), employers are more likely to rely on high wages to ensure that workers perform well.

These "wages of trust" may explain why pay in more capital-intensive industries (which require massive investments) is higher for workers with otherwise comparable skills than it is in industries using less capital. They may also explain why workers entrusted with the care of much cash (that they could steal) earn higher wages than other workers of comparable skills. It is not so much that they are paid more because they are trustworthy, but that they become more trustworthy because they are paid more—and the threat of losing those high wages encourages honest behavior.

MINIMUM WAGES

Legislating a minimum wage below which it is illegal to hire workers has been sharply criticized by economists as hurting exactly the people it is designed to help—those at the bottom of the wage scale.

Critics base their reasoning on the traditional demand and supply model of Part Two. There, an increase in wages above the market equilibrium results in lower employment. Those who manage to get jobs are better off; those who are forced into unemployment are worse off. If the objective is to reduce poverty, the minimum wage, from this perspective, seems counterproductive.

But as this chapter has pointed out, markets for labor are different from markets for many other commodities. Workers have to be motivated to work hard. High wages lead to increased productivity, less absenteeism, and lower labor turnover. Presumably, rational firms would take these consequences into account in setting wages. Even so, if the government forces firms to pay higher wages through minimum wage legislation, the increased productivity may largely offset the increased wages, making the employment effect very small.

In labor markets in which there is imperfect competition, minimum wages could actually lead to increased employment. Because of imperfect mobility, firms face an upward-sloping supply curve. Since all workers in a similar job have to be treated the same, the cost of hiring an additional worker may be much higher than the new

Does minimum wage legislation help or hurt low-income workers?

employee's salary. Not only must the firm raise the wage offered to the *new* worker, it must also raise the wage paid to all existing workers. This cost discourages the firm from hiring additional employees. The imposition of a minimum wage limits the expense of hiring an additional worker to just that employee's wage. And because their marginal cost of adding to their workforce is lower, firms that are required to pay a minimum wage in fact will hire more workers.

These perspectives are consistent with several recent empirical studies that have shown there to be negligible, or even positive, employment effects from a minimum wage.

Some economists have also pointed to broader positive consequences of minimum wages: they induce firms to invest more in their workers in order to increase their workers' productivity. Gavin Wright, a distinguished economic historian at Stanford University, has argued that minimum wages played a vital role in the transformation of the South. It was a region that had been vastly poorer than the North from the end of the Civil War to the Great Depression, and its economy had been largely based on very low wages. The minimum wage catalyzed dramatic changes, shifting the South away from low-wage industries to dynamic industries paying higher wages.

A further alleged advantage of raising the minimum wage is that it increases the incentive to work by increasing the income gap between someone on welfare and someone with a job.

OTHER INCENTIVES

Other important incentives to increase job performance are enhanced possibilities of promotion, and thus higher salaries, for those who perform well. But, as already noted, assessing achievement is often difficult. One way to figure out who is performing well is to set up a contest among workers and promise the winner some valuable prize, like a cash bonus. Consider a firm trying to figure out how much to pay its sales force when it is promoting a new product. If a salesperson is successful, does that success demonstrate good salesmanship, or is the new product able to "sell itself"? All sales representatives are in roughly the same position. The representative who sells the most gets a bonus—and wins the contest.

At the upper end of the corporate hierarchy, the top executives of America's largest firms are paid much more, on average, than their counterparts in many other industrial economies; their salaries often run into the millions of dollars. Economists continue to debate why this is. Some interpret these salaries as the payoffs of contests, others as reflecting the large contributions of these managers or as wages of trust. But some suspect that top managers have enough control over the firm to divert a considerable amount (though still a small fraction) of its resources to their own betterment in the form of higher compensation.

COMPENSATING WORKERS

We saw earlier that the wage a firm has to pay adjusts to take into account non-pecuniary attributes. Some of these nonpecuniary attributes reflect decisions made by the firm: the company can try to make the workplace more attractive; it can try to make it safer; it can even try to lower the stress level of its employees. Such changes may affect the workers' level of performance. In choosing how to organize the workplace, firms consider the impact of their decisions both on productivity and on how much they will have to pay to recruit workers.

Today, much of the compensation a worker receives takes the form not of direct cash but of **fringe benefits;** these include health insurance, retirement pay, and life insurance. In recent years, fringe benefits have constituted an increasing share of total compensation.

Employers' reliance on fringe benefits rather than simply paying a straight salary to workers is largely explained by the tax code. If employees are paid income and then purchase health insurance on their own, they must pay income tax on the money. But if the company buys the insurance for them, the fringe benefit is not counted as income. From the firm's perspective, it costs less to provide workers with health insurance than to raise their wages enough to enable employees to buy the insurance themselves. In addition, many employers use fringe benefits as an incentive for employees to stay with the company. For example, firms often require that the employee remain with the company for a period of several years before becoming eligible for the company pension plan. Such benefits show that employers are not eager to lose their long-term employees, and would rather offer some added benefits than go through the cost and trouble of hiring and training new workers. But why—other than for tax reasons—they should rely so heavily on rewarding their workers through better fringe benefits rather than through cash bonuses remains unclear.

e-Insight

LABOR MARKETS AND THE INTERNET

One of the main *imperfections* in the labor market is that searching for a new job is costly. Information is imperfect and is expensive to acquire. Help-wanted ads play an important role in making the labor market work, but individuals in one city often cannot easily obtain current newspapers from other cities that might have job opportunities.

Employment agencies and government employment services have helped make the labor market work better. But the Internet promises a revolution in labor markets—or at least a vast improvement. Almost without cost, individuals can see the help-wanted ads in newspapers in other cities. Employers can post free help-wanted ads and can provide far more complete descriptions both of the job and of the characteristics of the employees that they seek. Eighty percent of the world's largest 500 firms use Web sites for job recruitment, as do more than 90 percent of American firms. Existing employment agencies (including government-provided services) have used the Internet to extend their scope, and new firms have been created. Much of the information relevant both to the employer and to the employee will still be obtained by face-to-face contact, during an interview, and this process will remain costly. Still, by lowering search costs, the Internet holds out the promise of enormously increasing the efficiency of labor markets.

WAYS OF MOTIVATING WORKERS

Piece rates, or pay based on measured output.

Threats: firing workers whose efforts or performance are deemed inadequate.

Efficiency wages: introducing an extra cost to those dismissed for unsatisfactory performance.

Relative performance: promotions, contests.

Fringe benefits, such as health insurance and retirement pay.

Review and Practice

SUMMARY

1. The proportion of U.S. workers in unions has declined since the 1950s. Possible reasons include laws that have improved working conditions in general; the decline of manufacturing industries, where unions have traditionally been stronger than in service industries; increased competition in the product market, providing firms with less latitude to pay more than market wages; and a legal atmosphere that has shifted away from encouraging unions.

2. Union gains in wages are typically made at the cost of lower employment, at least in the long run, and lower wages in the nonunion sector. Unions also have played an important role in enhancing job security, though sometimes at the expense of innovation. They have accomplished some of their gains for workers through the political process; for instance, unions have pushed legislation promoting occupational safety and health as well as the minimum wage.

3. Union power is limited by the ability of companies to bring in new, nonunion workers and to threaten union workers with unemployment.

4. Explanations of why two workers doing the same job may receive different wages include compensating differentials (differences in the nature of jobs), productivity differentials (differences in productivity between workers), imperfect information (workers do not know all the job opportunities that are available), and discrimination.

5. Employers try to motivate workers and induce high levels of effort through a combination of direct supervision, incentives for doing well, and penalties for doing badly. They pay wages higher than workers could get elsewhere (efficiency wages), give promotions and bonuses, and base pay on relative performance (contests).

KEY TERMS

union shops
right-to-work laws
nonpecuniary attributes
compensating wage differentials
statistical discrimination
wage discrimination
job discrimination
affirmative action
piece-rate system
efficiency wage theory
fringe benefits

REVIEW QUESTIONS

1. Has the power of unions in the U.S. economy been shrinking or growing in the last few decades? Why? In what sector has union growth been largest? Why might this be so?

2. What effect will successful unions have on the level of wages paid by unionized companies? on the capital investment for those companies? What effect will they have on wages paid by nonunionized companies?

3. How might greater job security for union workers possibly lead them to become less efficient?

4. Does it make sense for a union to resist the introduction of an innovation in the short run? in the long run?

5. What are alternative explanations for wage differentials?

6. How do piece rates provide incentives to work hard? Why is there not a greater reliance on piece-rate systems?

7. What is efficiency wage theory?

PROBLEMS

1. In what ways are labor markets similar to product markets? In what ways are they different?

2. Explain how both these points can be true simultaneously:
   (a) Unions manage to raise the wage paid to their members.
   (b) Unions do not affect the average level of wages paid in the economy.

3. How might each of the following factors affect the power of unions?
   (a) A state passes a right-to-work law.
   (b) Foreign imports increase.
   (c) The national unemployment rate falls.
   (d) Corporate profits increase.
4. Suppose a worker holding a job that pays $15 per hour applies for a job with another company that pays $18 per hour. Why might the second company be suspicious about whether the worker is really worth $18 per hour? How might the worker attempt to overcome those fears?
5. Imagine that a company knows that if it cuts wages 10 percent, then 10 percent of its employees will leave. How might adverse selection cause the amount of work done by the company to fall by more than 10 percent?
6. Advances in computer technology have enabled some firms to monitor their typists by a system that counts the number of keystrokes they make in a given workday. Telephone operators are sometimes monitored according to how many calls they take, and how long they spend on an average call. Would you expect such information to increase productivity? Why or why not?
7. When someone is promoted from middle-management to top executive, her salary often doubles or more. Why does this seem puzzling, from the perspective of the theory of competitive markets? Why might a profit-maximizing firm offer such a large raise?

Part 4

ISSUES IN PUBLIC POLICY

Learning Goals

In this chapter, you will learn

1 The three basic reasons why governments intervene in the economy

2 The characteristics of a good tax system and how the U.S. system measures up

3 About the major transfer programs of the government

4 About current controversies in the economics of the public sector

Chapter 17

THE PUBLIC SECTOR

Throughout American history, the issue of the role of government in the economy has been at the center of political discussions. Today's debates focus on the sizable imbalance between the federal government's spending and its tax revenues and on the future financial health of government programs that provide retirement income (Social Security) and health insurance (Medicare) to the elderly.

The impact of the government on the economy is huge, much larger than raw statistics on the size of the government might suggest (e.g., federal tax receipts and expenditures have averaged around 20 percent of GDP over the past fifty years, while state and local government taxes and expenditures now total around 14 percent of GDP). The government influences the economy not only through taxes and expenditures but also through myriad regulations that affect every aspect of economic life. This chapter describes what the government does, why it does what it does, the trade-offs it faces in choosing what to do, and how those choices are made.

The United States has a federal structure in which responsibilities are divided between the federal government and state and local governments. Federal expenditures represent about two-thirds of total government spending. State and local governments are responsible for education (their single largest category of expenditures), local roads, law enforcement, and fire protection.

One way of understanding what the federal government does is to look at what it spends its money on. Figure 17.1 shows how its spending has changed over the past half century. In the 1950s, defense expenditures represented more than half of all expenditures; by 2000 defense had fallen to just 16 percent of the total. Though this figure has risen to close to 20 percent as a result of the wars in Afghanistan and Iraq, it is still a significantly smaller share of government expenditures than in earlier years. A half century ago, Social Security and welfare expenditures were about an eighth of the total; today they are three-eights. In recent years the federal

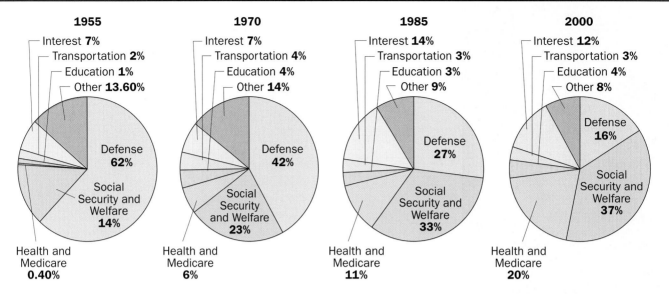

Figure 17.1

THE CHANGING PATTERN OF FEDERAL EXPENDITURES

Since 1955 there has been a steady increase in the share of federal funds allocated to Social Security, welfare, health, and Medicare. During the same period, the share allocated to defense has dropped dramatically.

SOURCE: U.S. Census Bureau, *Statistical Abstract of the United States* (1997), Table 518, and (2000), Table 533.

government has become more involved in school reform, but most spending on education in the United States is undertaken by state and local governments; it accounts for about 4 percent of federal spending.

But as already noted, the impact of the federal government cannot be gauged just by taxes and expenditures. First, it provides the legal system that enables the private sector to function. For example, the government creates and enforces contract laws, which structure agreements between two parties. The government also makes and enforces bankruptcy laws, which determine whose bills must be paid when an individual or corporation cannot meet debt obligations and files for bankruptcy.

Second, the government is responsible for maintaining the macroeconomic stability of the economy—preventing or at least minimizing recessions and depressions on the one hand, and runaway inflation on the other. Third, the government creates and enforces regulations designed to promote competition, preserve the environment, and protect consumers and workers. While there is considerable debate about the costs of these regulations, and about whether the benefits exceed those costs, few doubt that the regulations have succeeded in creating cleaner air, less-polluted waterways, and even safer cars and workplaces.

Although everyone values these benefits of government, many have worried that the taxes levied to finance government activities are a drag on the economy and interfere with its efficiency.

Why Does the Government Intervene in the Economy?

There are three basic reasons why the government intervenes in the economy: (1) to improve economic efficiency by correcting market failures; (2) to pursue social values of fairness, or equity, by altering market outcomes; and (3) to pursue other social values by mandating the consumption of some goods, called merit goods, and prohibiting the consumption of other goods, called merit bads. The next three sections address each of these reasons for government participation in the economy.

International Perspective

THE SIZE OF GOVERNMENT IN DIFFERENT COUNTRIES

The increase in central (federal) government expenditures during the twentieth century was dramatic, but expenditures in the United States are still among the smallest of any of the major industrialized economies in proportion to the size of the economy. In Denmark, Sweden, and the United Kingdom, government expenditures are more than one-third of GDP; in the United States, they are less than one-fifth. Of the major industrialized countries, only Japan and Australia spend less than one-third of GDP on the public sector. As a significant portion of U.S. federal expenditures goes to defense (about 3 percent of GDP), the relative size of its nondefense expenditures is particularly low viewed from this international perspective.

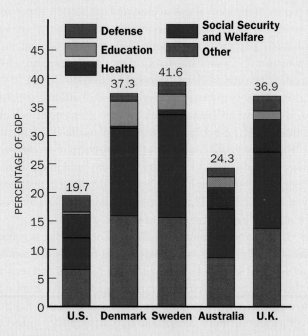

SOURCE: *Government Finance Statistics Yearbook* (2000) and *Economic Report of the President* (2001).

In the United States, federal spending on nondefense public-sector programs amounts to about 17 percent of GDP. In Sweden and the United Kingdom, this figure is 39 and 34 percent, respectively. The key difference lies in social insurance and welfare programs, which are proportionally much larger in those countries than in the United States.

These foreign comparisons prove different things to different people. Advocates of more government spending argue that the United States is out of step with global norms. Opponents of more government spending argue that other industrialized nations would do better to reduce public expenditures.

One factor to keep in mind is the smaller role played by local governments in those countries. In the United States, state and local government spending is about 14 percent of GDP, bringing total government expenditures close to 31 percent—a figure more in line with other countries.

Correcting Market Failures Chapter 11 described four sources of market failure in the economy: imperfect competition, imperfect information, externalities, and public goods. Government programs are aimed at redressing market failures in each of these major categories. For instance, under imperfect competition, firms use their market power to raise prices and reduce output. Antitrust policies set by government attempt to maintain a competitive marketplace and restrain firms from abusing their market power. Imperfect information may impede the efficient functioning of product and labor markets. Governments establish regulations to require firms to produce information on their products and on their financial condition. Moreover, governments often play a large role in providing *social insurance* that helps protect against the risks of unemployment or illness, in part to provide relief for problems caused by imperfect information. In the presence of externalities, firms produce too little of goods (like research) accompanied by positive externalities and too much of goods (such as those that generate pollution) accompanied by negative externalities. Governments subsidize the former and tax or otherwise regulate the latter.

Equity and the Redistribution of Income But even if markets were efficient, they would result in some individuals receiving too low of an income to survive at a standard of living that is viewed as socially acceptable. In the market, individuals' incomes are related to their ownership of assets and their productivity. Those with little education receive low wages. And even in the United States, most individuals have few assets: the bottom 75 percent of households by wealth own less than 15 percent of total wealth, and the average wealth of the bottom 25 percent of all households was less than $1,100 in 2001. Income in the United States is highly unequal: the top 10 percent of households receive 30 percent of the income, and the bottom 20 percent receive just 2 percent of total income. Wealth is even more concentrated, as the top 10 percent of households have 70 percent of the wealth; the bottom 50 percent, only 3 percent. Some countries have even greater inequality of income and wealth, while others, such as many European countries, have somewhat less.

Inequality raises concerns for several reasons. High levels are often associated with a variety of social and political problems, which in turn often result in a climate that does not favor investment. East Asia and Latin America illustrate the two extremes. Over the past thirty years, the countries of East Asia have grown very rapidly—at more than twice the rate of those in Latin America—and many economists believe that the greater degree of equality in East Asia provides at least part of the explanation. Many of the countries of Latin America, characterized by great inequality, are plagued by urban violence and political unrest.

In most societies, there is a concern about *social justice* or *fairness*. It seems morally wrong for so many of society's goods to go to so few. But fairness, like beauty, is often in the eye of the beholder. Many of those with high incomes and wealth believe that they *deserve* their fortunes. Attitudes toward inequality differ markedly across countries and have changed over time. In the United States, inequalities explained by individual effort are far more acceptable than inequalities linked to inheritance. Wealth that results from a brilliant innovation is more acceptable than wealth gained by the exercise of monopoly power or political influence (as wielded by the nineteenth-century "robber barons").

The lifetime prospects for children born into poor families are much bleaker than those of children born into rich families.

Concern is particularly acute about two groups—the very poor and children. The public finds it especially disturbing that even in the United States, supposedly the land of opportunity, the lifetime prospects of a child born into a poor family and a child born into a rich family are markedly different—and much bleaker for the poor child. This troubling disparity helps explain the widespread support for high-quality public education; for Pell Grants, which help make a college education affordable to students with low family incomes; and for Project Head Start, which provides preschool education for poor children.

The government provides a variety of programs aimed at the very poor. These programs attempt to provide a basic *safety net,* to ensure that all have a minimal level of income (through welfare programs), housing, food (through food stamps), and health (through Medicaid). Programs that take income from some people and *redistribute* it to others are called **transfer programs.** Many government programs, including education, have a redistributive component, which is especially important in social insurance programs. Low-wage individuals, for instance, get back more than they contribute to Social Security.

Merit Goods and Bads Some government activities, however, neither correct market failures nor redistribute income. Rather, they attempt to impose social values on individuals, to force or encourage them to do more of some things and less of others. Governments try to discourage drug taking and encourage education. These are called **merit goods.** Such merit goods (and bads) need to be distinguished from externalities: no one else may be harmed by someone smoking marijuana, yet many governments make it illegal. Moderate drinking or cigarette smoking may have an adverse effect only on the drinker or smoker, yet government still tries to discourage the consumption of alcohol and tobacco through high taxes. In these instances, the government interferes with the general principle of **consumer sovereignty,** which holds that individuals are the best judges of what is in their own interests and promote their own well-being. The government acts *paternalistically.* Many economists believe that government should limit such behavior to its oversight of minors—few object to compulsory education requirements for children but many question whether government should dictate what adults should or should not do, so long as their actions do not cause harm to others.

WRAP-UP

REASONS FOR GOVERNMENT INTERVENTION IN THE ECONOMY

To correct market failures: Market failures such as externalities provide a rationale for government intervention, which aims at improving economic efficiency.

To pursue equity: Market outcomes, even when they are efficient, might fail to satisfy social standards of equity. Government may intervene to redistribute income.

To promote and discourage merit goods and bads: Sometimes government imposes social values, by mandating the consumption of merit goods (education) and prohibiting the consumption of merit bads (illicit drugs).

EQUITY-EFFICIENCY TRADE-OFFS

We have seen that government programs have multiple objectives. If the only task of the government were to address market failures, it would face difficult technical issues—for instance, how best to reduce pollution. But the hardest problems are those that involve *trade-offs,* especially between improving the efficiency of the market and promoting equity. Equity—a sense of fairness—might suggest that the rich and wealthy should contribute not only more to support the government but proportionately more (i.e., a larger fraction of their income). The United States has a **progressive** income tax system that is designed to do exactly that; tax rates for higher-income individuals are set above those for lower-income individuals. (Conversely, tax systems in which the poor pay a higher proportion of their income to the government are **regressive.**) The inefficiencies associated with such taxation arise from the **marginal tax rate,** the extra tax that an individual pays on the last dollar earned. If the marginal tax rate is high, incentives to work harder are

e-Insight

THE NEW ECONOMY AND INEQUALITY

Income inequality in the United States has increased significantly over the past twenty years. One reason for this change has been the increasing premium earned by skilled workers. In 1980, college graduates received a wage 43 percent higher, on average, than that received by those with only a high school education; by 1990, that premium had increased to just over 70 percent. Over the 1990s, it continued to increase, rising to 75 percent by the end of the decade.

The job skills demanded by the new, information-based economy are often cited as a major cause of the growth in the wage premium for skilled workers. In fact, two opposing forces have been at play. On the supply side, there has been a marked increase in the skills of the U.S. labor force. In 1980, only 20 percent of the workforce had a college degree; by 2000, this fraction had risen to almost 30 percent. But at the same time that the supply of college-educated workers was increasing, the new economy was generating an increasing demand for skilled labor. The rise in the college wage premium since 1980 suggests that increases in demand have outpaced increases in supply (at any given wage).

Economists debate how much of the premium's rise has been caused by the introduction of new computer-related technologies. According to a survey of human resource managers, new information technologies have led many organizations to decentralize decision making, a shift that has increased the demand for highly educated workers able to use computers. Some economists believe that the wage premium associated with computer skills will erode over time as these skills become widely disseminated.

reduced. Thus, if high-income individuals have a high income because their wages are high, and their wages are high because they are more productive, then the effect of a progressive income tax on those who are the most productive is to discourage them from working.

Though governments often must make hard trade-offs, sometimes equity and efficiency go together. Providing educational opportunities for the poor may be equitable and efficient, as encouraging the use of these human resources may also improve the efficiency of the economy. And in many poor countries, large numbers of landless peasants work under sharecropping contracts in which the landlord gets one out of two dollars they earn. It is as if the sharecroppers face a 50 percent tax rate. Redistributing land to the poor may increase both efficiency and equity.

The U.S. Tax System in Practice

One out of every three dollars of the U.S. economy's total output goes to the government. Not surprisingly, the question of how the government raises its revenue attracts a great deal of attention. Nobody likes taxes, but they are necessary if the government is to provide public goods and services and if it is to reduce income inequality by redistribution.

CHARACTERISTICS OF A GOOD TAX SYSTEM

While the design of the tax system is a perennial subject of controversy—views of how to balance the equity-efficiency trade-off differ markedly, as is wholly predictable—there is broad consensus on five *principles* of a good tax system.

Fairness The first criterion is fairness. But fairness is not always easy to define. Economists focus on two points: **horizontal equity,** the notion that individuals who are in identical or similar situations should pay identical or similar taxes, and **vertical equity,** the notion that people who are better off should pay more taxes.

Efficiency The second criterion for a good tax system is efficiency. The tax system should interfere as little as possible with the economy's allocation of resources, and it should raise revenue with the least cost to taxpayers. Very high taxes may discourage work and saving, and thereby interfere with the efficiency of the economy. Taxes that narrowly target particular goods—such as excise taxes on perfume, boats, and airline tickets—discourage individuals from purchasing those goods, and thereby also interfere with efficiency.

Sometimes, taxes can be used to improve economic efficiency or to advance broader social purposes: taxes on pollution can improve the environment; taxes on cigarettes discourage smoking, leading to improvements in public health. Such taxes are said to yield a "double dividend," increasing overall efficiency or promoting social purposes at the same time that they generate revenue.

Administrative Simplicity The third criterion is administrative simplicity. Taxation is an expensive process, both to those who must pay taxes and to the government that must collect them. In addition to the costs of running the IRS, billions of hours are spent each year in filling out tax forms, hours that might be spent producing goods and services or enjoyed as additional leisure time. Billions of dollars are spent by taxpayers and by the IRS on tax software, accountants and lawyers in the annual ritual of preparing and processing tax forms. Finally, having a simple tax system reduces the likelihood that a would-be tax evader will succeed.

Flexibility The fourth criterion is flexibility. As economic circumstances change, it may be desirable to change tax rates. A good tax system should permit such adjustments with relative ease.

Transparency The fifth criterion is transparency. A good tax system is one in which it can be ascertained what each person is paying in taxes. The principle of transparency is analogous to the principle of "truth in advertising." Taxpayers are consumers of public services. They should know what they (and others) are paying for the services they are getting.

CRITERIA FOR EVALUATING A TAX SYSTEM

Fairness
Efficiency
Administrative simplicity
Flexibility
Transparency

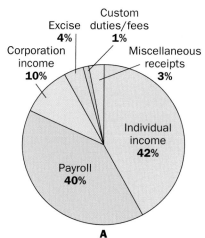

A
Sources of Federal Tax Revenues 2003

THE SCOPE OF THE U.S. TAX SYSTEM

The U.S. government raises tax revenues from a variety of sources. The earnings of individuals and corporations yield **individual income taxes** and **corporation income taxes.** Real estate—buildings and land—is subject to taxation by most states; these payments are known as **property taxes.** Large bequests and gifts are taxed, through **gift** and **estate taxes.** Special provisions apply to the taxation of capital gains (the increase in value of an asset between the time an individual purchases it and the time she sells it). Furthermore, wage income is subject not only to the income tax but also to the **payroll tax** (the tax levied on a company's payroll, half of which is deducted from employees' paychecks). Revenues from the payroll tax finance two programs: Social Security (retirement and disability income) and Medicare (medical care for the aged).

There are also taxes on the purchase of specific goods and services, known as **excise taxes.** The two heaviest excise taxes are on alcohol and tobacco, also known as **sin taxes.** The excise taxes on air travel and gasoline are sometimes called **benefit taxes** because the proceeds are spent on benefits (e.g., airports and roads) for those who purchase the good. Excise taxes on perfume, large cars, yachts, and expensive fur coats, aimed at the rich, are referred to as **luxury taxes.** Other excise taxes, such as the one on telephone services, have no particular justification other than to raise revenue. Most states impose a general tax on purchases of goods and services, known as a **sales tax,** though often some items (such as food) are exempted.

As this list indicates, few transactions in our economy escape taxation. Figure 17.2 shows the relative importance of various taxes at the federal and at the state and local levels. At the federal level (panel A), the single most important source of revenue is the tax on individuals' income (contributing almost half of total revenue), followed by the payroll tax. At the state and local levels (panel B), the sales tax is the most important revenue source.

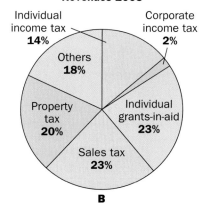

B
Sources of State and Local Tax Revenues 2003

Figure 17.2

THE IMPORTANCE OF VARIOUS TAXES

At the federal level, the largest share of taxes comes from the individual income tax, followed by the payroll tax and the corporate income tax, as shown in panel A. Sources of revenue at the state and local level are more fragmented, as seen in panel B; they include sales and property taxes, as well as revenue received from other levels of government.

SOURCE: Bureau of Economic Analysis, *National Income and Product Accounts* (2004), Tables 3.2 and 3.3 (www.doc.gov)

GRADING THE U.S. TAX SYSTEM

How well does the U.S. tax system measure up against the five principles of a good tax system? Equally important, have the major changes in the tax laws over the past decade resulted in improvements? During the past quarter century, the U.S. income tax system has undergone five major reforms, in 1981, 1986, 1993, 1997, and 2001. The announced intent of each was to make the system more efficient, more fair, and administratively more simple. But trade-offs always had to be made, and the reforms approached them differently; indeed, each tended to undo what was widely viewed as the excesses of its predecessor. Meanwhile, worries about soaring government expenditures limited the extent to which various social goals could be pursued through new programs. Hence, government instead used tax expenditures—such as tuition tax credits and deductions—to pursue these objectives in the tax bills of 1993, 1997, and 2001, inevitably complicating the tax system greatly.

Fairness As noted, the U.S. federal income tax system is, overall, progressive. Low-income individuals are exempt from paying any income tax whatsoever. Beyond a certain level of income (depending on family size—for a family of four, the critical level in 2004 was $22,100), the tax rate is then 10 percent. Thus, for each $100 an individual earns, he must pay an extra $10 of taxes; this is his *marginal tax rate.* At higher levels of income, the marginal tax rate increases further, eventually reaching 39.1 percent on incomes above $315,900 (for a family of four).

The **average tax rate** gives the ratio of taxes to taxable income. While the marginal tax rate shows big jumps, the average tax rate increases smoothly. Figure 17.3 shows the 2000 marginal and average income tax rates for a typical family of four that did not itemize its deductions.

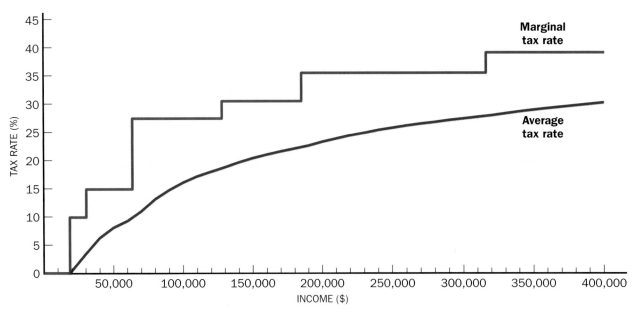

Figure 17.3

MARGINAL AND AVERAGE
FEDERAL INCOME TAX RATE

Marginal tax rates change by jumps, as shown in the table, but average tax rates increase gradually.

SOURCE: Tax Relief Act of 2001.

The income tax is only one of several income-related taxes that U.S. citizens pay. The payroll (Social Security) tax is another that increases with income up to a fixed level. An **earned-income tax credit** is designed to supplement the income of low-income workers with families; as a person's income increases beyond a given level, the payments she *receives* under this program decrease.

To assess the overall progressivity of the U.S. tax system, we have to look not only at federal taxes but at all taxes—including the corporate income tax and state and local taxes.

Many state and local taxes are regressive, because lower- and middle-income individuals spend a larger fraction of their income on items that are subject to state sales taxes than do the rich. Our current *total* tax system—combining the slightly progressive federal tax system with the slightly regressive state and local tax system—is, in the judgment of most economists, only modestly progressive.

Tax changes in recent years have alternately decreased and increased the degree of progressivity. In 1981 and 1986, marginal tax rates on upper-income individuals, for instance, were brought down markedly; in 1993, they were increased again, though to levels that were still lower than they had been in 1981. The tax cut passed by Congress in 2001 phases in lower marginal tax rates over a number of years. Prior to 1986, capital gains—the increases in the value of assets over time—were taxed at lower rates (varying from 40 to 50 percent of the "normal" rate) than were other forms of income. Reform abolished this special treatment, but in 1997 it was restored. Earlier, we noted that wealth is heavily concentrated; not surprisingly, the rich benefited enormously from this provision. At the same time, other changes in the tax law helped those with lower incomes, especially those with children, and the 2001 tax changes reduced the marginal tax rate from 15 percent to 10 percent on the first $6,000 of taxable income ($12,000 for married couples).

Efficiency The U.S. tax system today, while considerably more efficient than it was fifteen years ago, still has much room for improvement. Its inefficiencies are related to two factors: the progressivity of the tax system and the extent to which different kinds of income and different expenditures are treated differently. The *marginal* tax rates distort labor supply, for instance, and the variations in marginal tax rates discussed earlier affect this distortion.

Similarly, the distortions associated with differential taxation have increased, decreased, and again increased over time. As we noted, the 1981 tax law encouraged certain kinds of investment, while the 1986 law created a more level playing field than had existed for decades. Changes in the tax law since then have introduced new distortions—some, such as provisions favoring the oil and gas industries, largely reflect the influence of special interests while others, such as those promoting education, demonstrate the use of the tax system to pursue social objectives.

The U.S. income tax system has many provisions intended to encourage some types of economic activity and discourage others. For instance, the U.S. income tax allows certain child care payments to be taken as a credit against tax payments owed. The government thus subsidizes child care. Similarly, when firms spend money on R & D, their expenditures may reduce the amount they have to pay in taxes. Such arrangements are called **tax subsidies.** These subsidies cost the government money, just as if the government paid directly for child care or research. Accordingly, the revenue lost from a tax subsidy is called a **tax expenditure.**

Administrative Simplicity Americans live in a complex society, and their tax laws reflect and contribute to this complexity. As legislators have sought to ensure that the tax laws are fair and apply uniformly to all people in similar situations, the laws have become increasingly complex. High tax rates make it worthwhile for individuals and businesses to think hard about legal means of minimizing taxes. It may pay a businessperson to devote almost as much energy to tax avoidance as to designing and producing a better product. The tax law has evolved out of this constant battle between the government and taxpayers; as each new way of reducing tax payments is discovered, the law is modified to close the loophole. Inevitably another hole is discovered, and another repair job is attempted. Today the federal tax law fills tens of thousands of pages.

The objective of administrative simplicity seems to remain elusive. Many economists are convinced that the United States could have a tax system that is truly simple to administer, but only if other objectives are given up. Some of its complexity derives from the effort to have a progressive income tax and to tax the income from capital.

Flexibility One of the weakest aspects of the U.S. tax system is its lack of flexibility. Any time a tax change is proposed, all of the issues discussed here are raised. Its effects on different groups and on efficiency are debated. Basic issues of values—how progressive should the tax system be?—are aired once again, while special-interest groups try to take advantage of the chance to have favorable treatment written into the code. Changing the tax law is thus extremely difficult—and very time-consuming.

Transparency Though the merits of transparency are widely preached, governments often prefer citizens to be ignorant of their total tax bill. The worry is that knowledge might lead to "sticker shock" and that opposition to taxes might grow. The overall impact of some taxes is more obvious than others. For instance, individuals pay sales taxes in dribs and drabs; they never get a clear view of their total payments. That may be one reason why politicians seem to love the sales tax so much. Of all the parts of the tax system, the ultimate burden imposed by corporate income tax is perhaps the least transparent. Although corporations write the check to the IRS, most economists agree that much of the onus of paying taxes is shifted to individuals and households, through reduced wages, higher product prices, or both.

Transfers

Earlier we noted the role of government in redistributing income: very poor individuals receive more from the government than they contribute in taxes. There are five major public benefit programs for low-income Americans: welfare, Medicaid, food stamps, supplemental security income (SSI), and housing assistance. Until

1997, the program commonly known as "welfare" was AFDC (Aid to Families with Dependent Children), which provided cash assistance to poor families, mostly households with only one parent present. It was replaced by a new program called TANF (Temporary Assistance to Needy Families). Medicaid provides health care to the poor. The food stamp program offers vouchers for the purchase of food. SSI provides cash assistance to the low-income elderly and disabled, to supplement their Social Security benefits. Housing assistance programs include public housing and rental vouchers. In addition, states and localities provide different amounts of general assistance to those who fall between the cracks. Food stamps and SSI are federal programs (states can supplement SSI benefits). The other programs vary from state to state, with the federal government typically providing only broad program guidelines but footing much of the bill.

Our discussion here focuses on the most controversial program areas: welfare, housing, and social insurance.

WELFARE

From 1935 until 1997, AFDC was the primary cash program in the U.S. welfare system. The states not only administered AFDC but also set benefit levels and had some discretion over rules. The federal government provided a fraction of the funds, which varied from approximately one-half to three-fourths, depending on the state's per capita income. Programs in which federal outlays depend on state expenditures are called **matching programs.** The federal matching subsidy presumably resulted in raising the benefit levels above what they would have been if the states had been required to pay the full (marginal) costs themselves. States were given considerable discretion in determining the level of expenditures. Not surprisingly, there were considerable discrepancies in the level of benefits provided by the states; the highest benefits, in Alaska, were more than seven times the lowest benefits, in Mississippi.

Starting in 1997, TANF replaced AFDC. TANF represented a marked departure from the earlier system in two ways. First, it replaced the old system of matching grants with **block grants,** a fixed amount of money, with states given great flexibility in spending that money (including discretion in determining the eligibility of needy families and the benefits and services those families receive). Second, TANF focused on moving individuals from welfare to work. The states were given broad leeway in the design and operation of their welfare-to-work programs, but the use of TANF funds had to be consistent with the federal priorities: strong work requirements, time limits to receiving assistance, a reduction in welfare dependency, and the encouragement of two-parent families.

Under TANF, most recipients of aid must find work or participate in "work activities" such as job-training programs to keep their benefits. Among those exempt from this requirement are single parents with a child under six; they cannot be penalized for not working if they are unable to find adequate child care. In a major break with past welfare programs, TANF puts explicit time limits on participation. A family with an adult who has received federally funded assistance for a total of five years is not eligible for cash aid under the TANF program. After the introduction of TANF, employment among low-income single mothers with children under six rose significantly. The incidence of poverty among children, which had already been falling, continued to decline, although it rose slightly during the economic recession in 2001.

When the original TANF legislation was passed by Congress in 1996, the program was designed to expire in 2002. However, on nine occasions since 2002, Congress has temporarily extended it. The most recent extension, passed in March 2005, reauthorized TANF until September 30, 2005.

HOUSING

Public housing projects have been described, with some justification, as warehouses of the poor. By failing to integrate the poor thoroughly into the communities in which they live, public housing projects can help perpetuate the cycle of poverty. Moreover, many housing programs are inequitable. They provide generous benefits to those lucky enough to receive them, but many with the same income and family size get nothing. Worse still, providing a subsidy that is tied to a particular dwelling impedes labor mobility. Finally, though the costs of public housing are high, its quality is often much lower than housing of similar cost in the private sector.

All these drawbacks have led the government to reduce its role in directly supplying low-income housing and to turn increasingly to more market-based solutions. The most common is to subsidize the cost of housing for the poor by supplying rental vouchers. As recipients use the vouchers, thereby increasing demand for low-income housing, more builders are induced to provide housing for them. Vouchers have several other advantages. They allow individuals to shop for their housing over broader areas, not just in the designated projects, and they can be made "portable," so that individuals can relocate to pursue job opportunities without losing their housing subsidy. Unfortunately, vouchers are no panacea. Long waiting lists, time limits on using the voucher once it is received, and the disinclination of builders and landlords to provide low-income housing when the demand for housing generally is so strong limit their effectiveness.

Wrap-Up

GOVERNMENT TRANSFER PROGRAMS IN THE UNITED STATES

Welfare: TANF (Temporary Assistance for Needy Families)

Medicaid: health care for the poor

Food stamps: vouchers for the purchase of food

Supplemental security income: cash assistance to the low-income elderly and disabled

Housing assistance: public housing and rental vouchers

SOCIAL INSURANCE

The United States has a variety of what are referred to as middle-class **entitlement programs,** so named because individuals do not have to demonstrate poverty to receive benefits. The most important of these are the social insurance programs. Social insurance programs are like private insurance, in that people nominally pay for their own protection through a tax on wage income, the payroll tax. But in other important ways, they are *not* like private insurance, as we will see in the paragraphs that follow.

The Burden of Social Insurance Programs Social Security is supported by a tax on wages, 50 percent paid by the employer and 50 percent by the employee. This division of the tax is entirely superficial; the consequences of the tax are essentially the same as they would be if the worker paid the entire amount.

Figure 17.4 uses demand and supply curves for labor to demonstrate this point. Consider a payroll tax imposed on the employer based on what she pays her workers. The vertical axis measures the wage *received* by the employee. Since the cost of a worker is the wage received by the employee *plus* the tax, the tax shifts the demand curve down. In the new equilibrium, workers' wages have fallen. The wage received by a worker is precisely the same as it would have been had the same tax been imposed on the worker directly. While normally the wage falls by less than the amount of the tax, the extent to which it falls depends on the elasticity of the demand and supply curves. The figure shows the "normal" case where the supply of labor is relatively inelastic, in which case wages fall by almost the full amount of the tax. According to another view, Social Security has relatively little impact on labor supply, by and large, because benefits increase with contributions (though the increase in benefits may not be *fully* commensurate with the increase in contributions); the program is largely a forced savings program. Indeed, most individuals are not forced to save more, or at least much more, than they otherwise would. As we note in the next paragraph, the program has a redistributive aspect. Some individuals therefore receive back less than they contribute, and for them there is a disincentive effect not unlike the disincentive effects that would arise if a similar amount of redistribution occurred through the income tax system.

How Social Insurance Is More Than an Insurance Program In any insurance program, some individuals receive back more than they contribute, others receive less. That is, in a sense, the whole purpose of insurance. David may pay for fire insurance year after year, but if his home never burns down, he doesn't receive anything back from the insurance company. Clara may have the misfortunate to have her house burn down, and may receive back from the insurance company a payment that greatly exceeds what she had paid in. Those lucky enough not to have their houses go up in flames in effect help pay for those who do suffer a loss. Similarly,

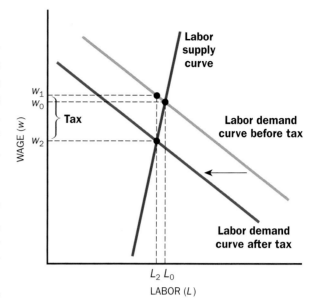

Figure 17.4

THE INCIDENCE OF PAYROLL TAXES

The payroll tax introduces a wedge between the cost to an employer of an individual working an hour more (wage plus tax) and what the worker receives. The magnitude of the wedge does not depend on whether the tax is levied on the employer or employee. The tax leads to fewer workers being hired at the equilibrium wage, reduced from w_0 to w_2.

no one knows whether the upcoming year will bring serious illness. So people buy health insurance that covers hospitalization. Those who remain healthy essentially pay for the hospitalization of those who need it. But the premiums of an individual's private insurance policy will, on average, cover the costs of what the policyholder can expect to receive (plus the costs of administration, which are often substantial). Social insurance programs, in contrast, often lack a close connection between the amount contributed and the amount contributors expect to receive. In the case of Social Security, for example, the retirement payments of single high-wage earners are less per dollar contributed than those of low-wage families with a single earner. Thus, the Social Security program performs a redistributive as well as an insurance function.

In the United States, Social Security faces a serious financial shortfall over the next several decades as the large post–World War II generation of baby boomers retires; social insurance programs in many other countries anticipate similar difficulties. Many argue that these financing problems could be solved by undertaking modest reforms, such as increasing the minimum age at which retirees can start collecting benefits. More radical proposals call for establishing individual retirement accounts for younger workers. These accounts would tie the benefits an individual receives more closely to the taxes the individual has paid, thereby diminishing the redistributive role of social insurance.

Designing Government Programs

Even when there is agreement about *what* the government should do, analysts often disagree on *how* it should do it. Take, for instance, the problem of pollution. The government can tax those who pollute, it can regulate pollution, or it can subsidize actions that abate pollution. Or consider education. At the elementary and secondary level, the government provides free public education to all; it is a *producer*. But at the university level, education is not free to all. Instead, state governments subsidize those who choose to go to state universities or colleges, and the federal government gives grants to low-income individuals to use for any university or college, public or private. A variety of considerations go into making these choices. When the government is an inefficient producer, as often happens, it makes more sense for it to provide the money to individuals, who can make purchases from the more efficient private producers. In the case of higher education, the U.S. government improves the access of those from poor or disadvantaged backgrounds by offering educational *grants* to individuals rather than by providing the education itself. Such grants to individual students are more controversial when it comes to elementary or secondary education. In school *voucher* programs, grants go directly to the parents of school-age children, to be spent at either public or private elementary and secondary schools. Many critics of school vouchers, while supporting the same basic concept in higher education, believe that such programs would weaken public schools by draining away their pupils and funds. Supporters of vouchers argue that giving parents a choice in where to send their children would force public schools to improve.

Government Failures

Decisions about whether the government should intervene and *how* it should intervene thus depend on one's views of the efficiency and efficacy of government. One of the main rationales for government action that we noted above is to correct market failures. But proponents of a limited role for government argue that government often not only fails to correct the problems of the market but makes matters even worse. Noting that many of the difficulties facing the private sector—such as imperfect information—also plague the public sector, they then point to several more that are especially acute in the public sector, such as problems relating to incentives and commitments and to budgetary constraints and processes.

In fact, the evidence on government inefficiency is mixed. Government has long played an important role in the economy, and the list of its commonly accepted successes is correspondingly long. The amazing increase in agricultural productivity over the past seventy-five years is generally attributed to the government's support of research and its outreach to train farmers in the new technologies. Key advances in computer technology and jet engines were the result of government support. The development of the vital telecommunications sector has relied on government support—from Samuel Morse's first telegraph line between Baltimore and Washington in 1842 to the birth and growth of the Internet in the 1970s and 1980s. Today we can more safely breathe the air in our cities and drink and swim in the water from our lakes and rivers, largely because of actions undertaken by government.

Critics of government draw on a number of widely cited studies comparing the efficiency of the government and the private sector in similar activities—such as collecting garbage—to suggest that the public sector is systematically less efficient. But two important caveats must be added. First, much of the government activity is in areas where output is hard to measure or the quality of an individual's contribution is hard to assess, and accordingly where the private sector too has a hard time designing effective incentive systems. Second, public enterprises are every bit as efficient as private enterprises. For instance, in the United States, the administrative and transaction costs are a much smaller percentage of contributions for Social Security than they are for privately provided annuities (insurance policies that pay a fixed amount every year of an individual's retirement). The government-run Canadian National Railroad appears to be as efficient as the privately run Canadian Pacific Railroad. And even the much-maligned U.S. Postal Service has managed to score productivity improvements in the past fifteen years that exceed the average for the U.S. economy. One reason cited for these successes is competition: the post office has to compete with private-sector competitors such as FedEx and UPS, and Canadian National Railroad had to compete with Canadian Pacific.

Still, failures of government are well-recognized, from public housing projects that rival the worst provided by any slumlord to cost overruns on defense projects. And some of the government successes have had questionable side effects: for example, the interstate highway system, while greatly reducing transportation time, contributed to the urban sprawl that blights many of our cities. Given the frequency with which government failures occur, it is natural to ask if there are *systemic* reasons for them? Four major factors underlie systemic government failure: incentive problems, budgeting problems, information problems, and the nature of political decision making. While the first three can afflict any large organization, including private-sector businesses, they often have particularly severe effects in government programs.

INCENTIVES AND CONSTRAINTS

Unlike private organizations, government has the power of coercion. It can force people to pay taxes, it can prohibit firms from paying less than the minimum wage if they engage in interstate commerce, and so on. But since this power carries with it enormous potential for abuse, certain procedures have been developed to protect the public against arbitrary use of government power. These procedures are collectively called *due process*.

Such procedures have the potential to create incentive problems, as can be seen from the set of rules governing civil service employment. These rules are designed to ensure that there is no discrimination against or other arbitrary treatment of government workers. But the rules are often inflexible and make it difficult to pay comparable salaries to public officials who do their jobs as well as similarly qualified and dedicated persons in the private sector—or to offer them the same opportunities for rapid promotion. It is even more difficult for government to demote or fire incompetent and lazy workers. Thus, the public sector's ability to recruit and manage staff with maximum efficiency typically is limited.

In addition to the constraints of due process, the government has trouble making long-term commitments that are perceived to be binding. Any Congress can reverse decisions made by previous Congresses, though it may try to design both legislation and legislative rules in ways that discourage later about-faces. Such limitations on the government's ability to make binding commitments can have major economic consequences. Take, for example, a government promise that it will pursue a policy of maintaining low inflation. The current government may convince investors of its commitment to keeping inflation low. But it has no control at all over what happens after the next election—as investors know. They therefore make their own assessments of inflation risk, which may interfere with the effectiveness of what the government is trying to do today. The current government can make it more costly for future governments to increase the rate of inflation; for instance, it can issue short-term bonds, so that the interest cost to the government would rise quickly if inflation started to pick up.

Also undermining government efficiency, and sometimes leading to perverse decisions against the broad interests of society, are the political pressures inherent in the democratic process. A prime example here is legislators' concerns about the next election. These can lead to so-called pork barrel projects that create jobs in a pivotal legislator's home district but make no economic sense from a national perspective. Moreover, the enormous cost of running for office provides incentives for elected officials to pay particular attention to the views and needs of those who contribute to their campaign funds. Thus lobbyists, among others, can wield influence far out of proportion to the importance of the interests they represent.

BUDGETING AND SPENDING PROCEDURES

The budgeting and spending constraints on government decision makers differ from those of the private sector in three major ways. The first is in their severity. Unlike a private firm, which faces the prospect of bankruptcy if enough of its ventures yield losses, a public enterprise can more easily turn to the government for budgetary help. This is the problem of *soft budget constraints*. Amtrak, for example, continues to lose money in its overall railroad operations, in spite of government promises that it will turn a profit. A major reason for the continuing loss is a set of labor rules *imposed by the government* requiring that workers be compensated if they are laid off or forced to relocate even a short distance. Soft budget constraints such as these weaken the incentives for public management to be efficient. There is nothing quite like the threat of bankruptcy to focus managerial attention.

The second budgetary difference between the private and public sectors—a factor that works in the opposite way from the soft budget constraints—is the annual appropriations process. This can force short-term spending constraints on the public sector that are not cost-effective in the long run. Limited investment flexibility is a particularly unfortunate consequence of the annual appropriations system.

The third budgetary constraint on government is the anti-efficiency effects of some of the procedures implemented to ensure strict cost control. Government has instituted detailed accounting, competitive bidding, and other procurement procedures to avoid waste and corruption. Yet these procedures can cost more than they save—and not just because of the extra bureaucracy involved. When purchasing T-shirts, for example, the government in its efforts to ensure that the specifications were accurate and precise—so that bidders were competing to supply *exactly* the same product—created thirty pages of documentation in small print that prospective bidders had to follow carefully. These forms of bureaucratic red tape reduce the supply of bidders willing to sell to the government and increase the cost to the government of goods and services.

IMPERFECTIONS OF INFORMATION

Information problems plague government just as they plague the private sector. As a result, there are often adverse *unintended* (and often unforeseen) *consequences* of even well-intentioned programs. We already noted one example: the expansion of the superhighway system in the 1950s may have led to urban sprawl, weakened the inner cities, and increased air pollution (from increased driving); none of these effects was even widely discussed, let alone anticipated. Urban renewal programs, designed to increase the quality of housing, often resulted in a decreased supply of affordable housing for the poor, thus aggravating the housing problems they faced and even contributing to homelessness.

Table 17.1

VOTING PREFERENCES

	Jessica's preferences	Ralph's preferences	Brutus's preferences
First choice:	Young and Romantic	Third and Goal to Go	Automatic Avengers
Second choice:	Third and Goal to Go	Automatic Avengers	Young and Romantic
Third choice:	Automatic Avengers	Young and Romantic	Third and Goal to Go

COLLECTIVE DECISION MAKING

A fourth important reason for public failures relates to how government decisions get made. Governments are not always consistent in their actions. This inconsistency may not be surprising, given that government choices do not reflect the preferences of a single individual. More fundamentally, majority voting may not yield a determinate outcome even when only three people choose among only three alternatives, as was noted more than two hundred years ago by the Frenchman Marquis de Condorcet—a phenomenon referred to as the **voting paradox.** Consider the simple example of three people who want to go to a movie together. They have narrowed their choices down to three possibilities, which they rank as shown in Table 17.1.

When they compare each of the films, they find that *Young and Romantic* is preferred over *Third and Goal to Go* by a two-to-one margin and *Third and Goal to Go* is preferred to *Automatic Avengers,* also by a two-to-one margin. Taking this information alone, they might reason that—since *Young and Romantic* is preferred over *Third and Goal to Go* and *Third and Goal to Go* is preferred over *Automatic Avengers*—*Young and Romantic* is also preferred to *Automatic Avengers*. But when they put it to a vote, they find that *Automatic Avengers* is preferred to *Young and Romantic* by a two-to-one margin. There is no majority winner. Majority voting can compare any two of these choices but is incapable of ranking all three of them.

The Nobel laureate Kenneth Arrow proved an even more remarkable result. All voting systems (two-thirds majority, weighted majority, or any other), under some circumstances, yield the same kind of indecision. Inconsistencies are simply inherent in the decision-making process of any democratic government. The only way around this problem is to entrust a single individual with all decisions. Such a system yields consistent choices but is hardly democratic!

Economists have looked carefully at how political processes are affected by *incentives*—for example, the incentives of politicians, of political parties, of government bureaucrats, and of special interests to curry favor with these political actors to influence legislation. *Public choice* theory is a branch of economics that analyzes the outcomes of political processes, assuming that each of the participants acts rationally. James Buchanan of George Mason University received a Nobel Prize for his contributions in developing public choice theory. As an understanding of how campaign contributions affect the behavior of politicians, and thus the outcomes of political processes, has become widespread, growing numbers of legislators and activists have argued for the need to reform campaign contribution laws.

SOURCES OF PUBLIC FAILURES

Incentives and constraints
  Due process
  Constrained ability to make long-term commitments
  Political pressures
  Pork barrel projects
  Power of lobbyists who make campaign contributions
Budgeting and spending constraints
  Soft budget constraints
  Annual appropriations process
  Rigid procurement rules
Imperfect information
  Unforeseen changes in behavior resulting from government action
Problems in collective decision making

Current and Recent Controversies in the Economics of the Public Sector

A good number of the controversies in public policy revolve around the role of the government in the economy. In the following paragraphs, we describe three of the *major* issues.

DEALING WITH THE DEFICIT

The past twenty-five years have seen large swings in the federal government's budget balance. In 1981, President Ronald Reagan engineered a large tax cut. As a result, the U.S. government's expenditures outpaced its revenues and the government ran huge deficits that continued throughout the 1980s. At its worst, the deficit reached almost $300 billion in the early 1990s. When the government runs a deficit, spending more than it collects in taxes, it must borrow to make up the difference. The federal debt is the total amount that the government owes as a result of this borrowing, and it rose from $3,500 for every man, woman, and child in the United States in 1981 to just over $14,000 in 1996.

When President Bill Clinton took office in 1993, he managed to slow the growth of expenditures, mainly by cutting defense spending (a task made far easier by the end of the cold war), and to increase taxes, mainly on individuals in the upper 2 percent of the income distribution. At the same time, the rate of growth of the U.S. economy picked up, increasing the growth in tax revenues.

By 1998, the budget situation had improved so much that the government actually ran a surplus, its first since 1969. Because the government was collecting more revenue than it was spending, it could use the excess (the surplus) to repay some of its debt. There was even talk that the government would eventually be able to repay all of its base borrowing and reduce the debt to zero. The debate over how to cut the deficit was apparently over; now the political issue was how to spend the surplus. Three views dominated the discussions. Some wanted to continue to use the surplus to reduce the debt; others wanted large tax cuts; still others wanted to use the funds to increase spending on a variety of social programs—from financing Social Security and health care for the elderly to improving education for the poor.

Tax cuts won out in the first months of President George W. Bush's presidency. In June 2001, President Bush signed into law a new tax reform that provided extensive tax cuts over a ten-year period. At the same time, the economy was entering a slowdown that caused tax revenues to decline; and the September 11, 2001, terrorist attack on the United States and the wars in Afghanistan and Iraq led to large hikes in defense spending. Rather than enjoying the expected surpluses, the U.S. government was confronted with massive deficits. By 2004, the deficit reached an all-time high of more than $400 billion, nearly $17,000 for every person in the country.

Dealing with the deficit is complicated by the other two major areas of controversy: Social Security and health care.

SOCIAL SECURITY

As President Bush began his second term in January 2005, the future of Social Security was being actively debated. The main component of Social Security, and the focus of our discussion, is the provision of retirement income to the elderly; it also supports survivors and those with disabilities. Currently, Social Security is a **pay-as-you-go program:** the taxes paid by today's workers go to pay the benefits of today's retirees. The tax rate now is 12.4 percent on all income up to $90,000 (half the tax is taken out of the worker's paychecks, and the other half is paid directly by the employer). Under a pay-as-you-go program, each generation of workers contributes to the retirement payments for previous generations. Under a **fully funded program,** in contrast, each worker has an individual account. Contributions are invested until the worker retires, when the proceeds finance that worker's retirement.

The Social Security program has been running a surplus since 1984. This will end as members of the large baby boom generation, born between the late 1940s and early 1960s, begin to retire and the program's balance between its expenditures and taxes collected starts to shift. By 2018, the program will begin paying out more in benefits than the smaller number still working are paying in; the difference will be covered from the surplus, which will be exhausted around 2040. At that point, additional sources of revenue will be needed if the current law's promises of benefits are to be honored.

While all agree that some changes to Social Security will be needed, what form those changes should take and how large they have to be are intensely debated. Calling the situation a crisis, President Bush has sought major changes to the very nature of the program. He has proposed that younger workers be allowed to divert some of the Social Security taxes they pay into individual retirement accounts, which then could be invested as each individual chooses. At retirement, benefits would be paid both from the traditional Social Security program and from the balance in the individual account. Proponents of retirement accounts argue that they will enable individuals to earn, on average, higher rates of return on their contributions than they do under the current Social Security program.

Opponents of retirement accounts make three points. First, they argue that the advocates have made unrealistic assumptions about the average returns on worker's contributions. Second, they stress that a system of individual accounts involves more risk for each individual; for example, the stock market might decline significantly just as a worker was about to retire, wiping out a large part of her account if it were invested heavily in stocks. Third, opponents point out that if younger workers divert some of their Social Security taxes into separate accounts, the funds available to provide benefits to the current retirees will go down. To come up with the money to keep paying for these promised benefits, therefore, the government will need to do one of three things: raise other taxes; borrow more now, thereby worsening the already huge budget deficit; or cut back on other government programs.

Most critics of the president's proposals recognize that if nothing is done, Social Security in time will face financial problems. However, they argue that these can be fixed with relatively minor adjustments in the program. One suggestion is to index the level of a retiree's initial benefit payment to the level of prices rather than to the general level of wages (as is currently done). Since wages on average rise faster than prices, tying payments to the latter would reduce the growth in future payments. At the same time, the indexing would ensure that the purchasing power of the benefits did not decline.

President Bush has been urging Americans to consider a major reform of the Social Security system.

A second adjustment often mentioned is to raise the age at which one can start collecting retirement benefits. Currently, that age is being gradually increased. For example, anyone born before 1937 could start receiving full benefits at age sixty-five. Someone born in 1947, however, has to wait until she is sixty-six years old, an individual born in 1957 must wait until they are sixty-six and a half, and anyone born in 1967 must be sixty-seven. The argument in favor of increasing the retirement age is that because people live much longer now than they did when the Social Security program was first established, they might reasonably expect to retire somewhat later.

A third proposal is to raise Social Security taxes, in one (or both) of two ways. First, the basic tax rate, currently 12.4 percent, could go up. It is estimated that an increase of 1 to 2 percent would cover the projected shortfall. There seems to be little political support for this approach, but somewhat less hostility toward the second: raising the income cap. Now the tax is paid only on the first $90,000 of income; taxing incomes instead up to $125,000 or $150,000 would bring in more revenue.

A fourth possibility is to accept a reduction in the level of benefits that future retirees will receive. Analysts estimate that if no adjustments are made, the system will be able to pay about 70 percent of what is now promised. This option, like an increase in the basic tax rate, lacks political support.

The Social Security program is often called the "third rail" of American politics, threatening a fatal shock to any politician who dares to propose any changes. Until some reforms are made, however, its fiscal stability will remain in doubt.

HEALTH CARE

There has long been dissatisfaction with certain aspects of the U.S. health care system, and yet it has proven hard to reform. The United States spends a larger fraction of its GDP on medical care than any country in the world, but its health indicators (such as child mortality and life span) are lower than those in many other countries of comparable income. (This outcome is explained in part by the relatively high level of inequality in the United States. Poverty and poor health are closely associated, as low income leads to poor health and poor health leads to low income. Most other countries also do a better job than the United States in making sure that all citizens have access to health care.) Health care costs have been rising faster than the cost of living in general. The federal government has two major programs: Medicaid, which provides health care for the poor, and Medicare, which provides health care for the aged. Both have become increasingly expensive.

Not only do Americans spend more, with seemingly poorer results, than do residents of other countries, but they also have a greater sense of *insecurity*. In most advanced industrialized countries, everyone is guaranteed the right to a reasonably high level of health care; that is, there is effectively some form of comprehensive insurance. While most Americans receive health care coverage from their employers, many lack any insurance. For them a major illness can be a financial disaster. Most Americans do manage to receive health care in one way or another, but it is a major source of anxiety, especially for middle-income Americans who are too well-off to receive Medicaid.

Health care is different from most other commodities in several respects. Most health care is paid for by the government or insurance companies, not by individuals. Hence, individuals do not have an incentive to economize on these expenditures. Individuals also are often not in a position to judge well the necessity or quality of the services being provided. They must rely on the judgment of a physician. But under the standard fee-for-service system, the physician has an incentive to provide services, some of which may be of marginal value. To make matters worse, since individuals do not bear much of the cost, they have little incentive to monitor value; so long as the expected benefits exceed the costs they bear, they will wish the services to be performed. Moreover, doctors fear that a medical malpractice suit may be brought if they fail to provide a service that may be of benefit. Thus for many, "defensive medicine" has become a way of life.

Early attempts to correct these problems relied on a massive increase in the use of an alternative system called the health maintenance organization (HMO), or managed care. After paying a fixed annual amount, individuals are charged nominal fees for each doctor's visit. To gain access to a specialist, a patient must sometimes be referred by a primary care physician. But while the fee-for-service system may have an incentive for excessive provision of services, HMOs have an incentive, equally worrisome, not to supply services that are needed. In principle, an HMO that is excessively restrictive would lose customers to its competitors, but in practice, competition is limited. Thus, in the early 1990s, HMOs were widely lauded as the solution to the country's soaring health care costs; but by the late 1990s, HMOs were viewed as part of the problem. They were criticized, for instance, for "drive-by deliveries"—requirements that new mothers could stay in the hospital for only a day or two after a normal birth.

Today, the high cost of pharmaceuticals is causing much concern. Drug companies are constantly introducing new prescription medications, and more and more Americans are taking them. For the elderly—up to a third of whom are thought to lack insurance that covers their drugs—the financial burden of paying for them can be crushing. The growing awareness that the identical drugs cost less in other countries has led many to argue for new laws that would allow Americans to legally purchase drugs from pharmacies outside the United States, particularly in Canada. Drug manufacturers and the Bush administration have argued that the importation of drugs from other countries poses too great a safety risk.

In 2003, Congress added a major drug benefit to the Medicare program; it comes into effect fully only in 2006. Almost immediately after the bill's passage, concerns were raised about the new benefit's long-term cost, estimated to exceed $700 billion over the next decade. As the prices of prescription drugs have soared, many have called for the government to be given the power to negotiate discounts from the drug companies, something that the 2003 legislation specifically prohibits. They also have demanded more loudly that Americans be allowed to import drugs from Canada, where the federal government imposes price ceilings on drugs under patent and where health insurers negotiate with drug companies to obtain lower prices for the specific drugs that they cover. States such as Minnesota have saved money by purchasing drugs from Canada. However, the Canadian market is smaller than that in the United States, and if more Americans purchase drugs from Canadian sources, shortages in Canada are likely to occur. Such shortages are particularly likely if U.S. manufacturers carry out their threat to stop shipping to Canadian pharmacies that sell to the United States.

Reformers cite four major tasks that remain on the health care agenda:

1. Reducing the number of uninsured Americans, particularly through programs targeted at the unemployed and at children.
2. Containing the soaring costs of health care in ways that are socially acceptable. In many countries, health care benefits are rationed to contain costs; that is, government programs provide assistance only to *some* of those who need it. For example, those over eight-five years old may not be eligible for a hip replacement or must wait until all those who are younger and need the surgery get it.
3. Developing programs for nursing home care; today, many of the elderly must rely on Medicaid, the government program for low-income elderly, for long-term care.
4. Promoting healthy habits (e.g., better diet and more exercise), while discouraging activities such as smoking that are known to cause disease. Medical care is only one factor affecting health, and perhaps not the most important. Expenditures in broader areas of living and the environment may more effectively improve health status in general than increased spending targeted at medical care.

Review and Practice

SUMMARY

1. Government plays a pervasive role in the economy, influencing the economy through taxes, expenditures, and myriad regulations that affect every aspect of economic life.

2. In the United States, federal government spending over the past fifty years has shifted away from defense and toward Social Security, health care, and welfare. These areas accounted for 57 percent of expenditures in 2000.

3. There are three basic reasons why the government intervenes in the economy: (1) to improve economic efficiency by correcting market failures, (2) to pursue social values of fairness by altering market outcomes, and (3) to pursue other social values by mandating the consumption of merit goods (such as education) and outlawing the consumption of merit bads (such as illicit drugs).

4. Sometimes government faces a trade-off between improving the efficiency of the economy and promoting equity. The U.S. income tax illustrates this trade-off. In the interest of equity, the system requires the wealthy to pay a greater share of the tax than the poor. On the other hand, the progressive income tax discourages from work those who are the most productive.

5. A tax system can be judged by five criteria: fairness, efficiency, administrative simplicity, flexibility, and transparency.

6. Government transfer programs alter the income distribution by transferring resources from those who are relatively wealthy to those who are relatively poor. In the United States, there are five major transfer programs: welfare, Medicaid, food stamps, supplemental security income, and housing assistance.

7. Just as markets may fail, attempts by the government to intervene in the economy may also fail. Four major factors underlie systematic government failure: incentive problems, budgeting problems, information problems, and the nature of political decision making.

8. Some of the most important areas of public policy debate regarding the economic role of government relate to the federal budget deficit, reform of the Social Security system, and reform of the U.S. health care system.

KEY TERMS

transfer programs
merit goods
consumer sovereignty
progressive tax system
regressive tax system
marginal tax rate
horizontal equity
vertical equity
individual income taxes
corporation income taxes
property taxes
gift and estate taxes
payroll tax
excise taxes
sin taxes
benefit taxes
luxury taxes
sales tax
average tax rate
earned-income tax credit
tax subsidies
tax expenditure
matching programs
block grants
entitlement programs
voting paradox
pay-as-you-go program
fully funded program

REVIEW QUESTIONS

1. Name some of the ways that government touches the lives of all citizens, both in and out of the economic sphere.

2. Explain the rationale for government intervention in the economy in connection with economic efficiency, equity, and the role of merit goods.

3. What are the five characteristics of a good tax system? How well does the U.S. tax system fare in terms of these criteria? What is the difference between horizontal equity and vertical equity? What is the difference between a progressive and a regressive tax?

4. How do tax and redistribution programs affect incentives? How do social insurance programs affect incentives? Describe some of the trade-offs involved.

5. How can redistribution take place through an entitlement program like Social Security, to which all workers contribute and from which all retirees receive benefits?

6. What are some of the major controversies in the realm of policy and public-sector economics?

PROBLEMS

1. In each of the following areas, specify how the government is involved, either as a direct producer, a regulator, a purchaser of final goods and services distributed directly to individuals or used within government, or in some other role.
   (a) Education
   (b) Mail delivery
   (c) Housing
   (d) Air travel
   (e) National defense
   In each of these cases, think of ways that part of the public role could be provided by the private sector.

2. Assume that a country has a simple tax structure, in which all income over $10,000 is taxed at 20 percent. Evaluate a proposal to increase the progressivity of the tax structure by requiring all those with incomes over $100,000 to pay a tax of 80 percent on income in excess of $100,000. Draw a high-wage earner's budget constraint. How does the surtax affect her budget constraint? What happens to her incentives to work? Is it possible that imposing the tax actually will reduce the tax revenues the government receives from the rich?

3. Imagine that Congress decided to fund an increase in Social Security benefits by increasing the payroll tax on employers. Would this prevent employees from being affected by the higher tax? Draw a diagram to illustrate your answer.

4. Consider an individual contemplating whether to quit her job and go on welfare. How might the fact that welfare is time limited affect her decision? Is it possible that time-limited welfare may not only lead people to leave welfare but also reduce the number who go on welfare?

5. The president is trying to decide which of three goals he should put at the top of his agenda—Social Security reform (s), a middle-class tax cut (m), and preserving the safety net for the poor (p). He puts the matter before his advisers in three separate meetings. Assume he has three advisers, and he takes a vote in each meeting. His political adviser's ranking is {m-s-p}, his economic adviser's ranking is {s-p-m}, and his health care adviser's ranking is {p-m-s}. What is the outcome?

6. What is the difference between a pay-as-you-go retirement system and a fully funded system? Explain why the former may run into problems if a large generation is followed by a generation with many fewer members.

7. Assume that initially prescription drug prices are lower in Canada than in the United States, and suppose all barriers to drug trade between the two countries are removed. In the absence of any price controls, what would you predict will happen to drug prices in the United States? in Canada? How does the difference in the size of the two countries' populations affect your answer? If Canada has a system of price controls on prescription drugs, what would you predict will happen in the Canadian drug market if barriers to trade are eliminated?

Learning Goals

In this chapter, you will learn

1. Why many environmental problems are the result of externalities that cause market failures

2. The four types of policy responses to environmental problems and their implications for economic efficiency

3. Whether natural resources are depleted too rapidly in a market economy

Chapter 18

ENVIRONMENTAL ECONOMICS

Among the most contentious issues today is the impact of the economy on the environment. Usually, the discussion portrays economic activity and environmental concerns as diametrically opposed. Producing more goods and services generates more pollution, uses up more and more land, and contributes to global warming. It may seem that the fundamental perspective of economics—that of scarcity—hardly applies to things like pollution. After all, most people think we have too much pollution, not a scarcity of it. Yet the tools of economics can provide critical insights into the causes of environmental pollution, and these insights help shape the ways that government has tried to design policies to protect the environment.

The basic competitive model yielded the conclusion that markets would produce efficient outcomes. But we have seen, in Chapter 11 and again in Chapter 17, that in some situations, markets fail to produce efficient outcomes. In those circumstances, government may have an economic role to play. This justification for government involvement in the market is known as the *market failure approach* to the role of government.

Many environmental problems are the result of a market failure that arises because of the presence of externalities—costs and benefits of a transaction that are not fully reflected in the market price. In this chapter, we focus on negative externalities and the issues of environmental protection.

Negative Externalities and Oversupply

The basic competitive model assumes that the costs of producing a good and the benefits of selling it all accrue to the seller, and that the benefits of receiving the good and the costs of buying it all accrue to the buyer. This is often not the case. As was explained in Chapter 11, the extra costs and benefits not captured by the market transaction are called *externalities*.

Externalities can be either positive or negative, depending on whether individuals enjoy extra benefits they did not pay for or suffer extra costs they did not incur themselves. Goods for which there are positive externalities—such as research and development—will be undersupplied in the market (see Chapter 20). In deciding how much of the good to purchase, each individual or firm thinks only about the benefits it receives, not the benefits conferred on others. By the same token, goods for which there are negative externalities, such as air and water pollution, will be over-supplied in the market. The inability of the market to fully capture the costs and benefits of a trade provides a classic example of a market failure and a possible role for the public sector.

Figure 18.1A shows the demand and supply curves for a good—say, steel. Market equilibrium is the intersection of the curves, the point labeled E, with output Q_p and price p_p. Chapter 10 explained why, in the absence of externalities, the equilibrium E is efficient. The price reflects the marginal benefit that individuals receive from an extra unit of steel (it measures their marginal willingness to pay for an extra unit). The price also reflects the marginal cost to the firm of producing an extra unit. At E, marginal benefits equal marginal costs.

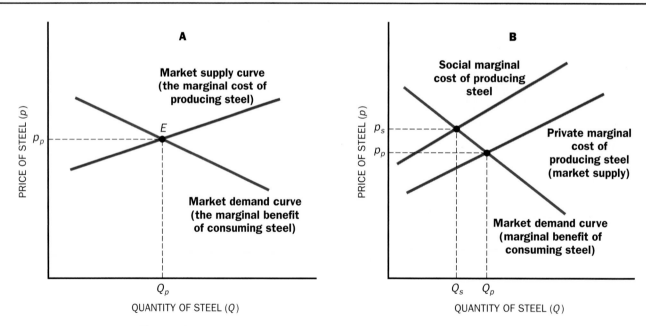

Figure 18.1

HOW NEGATIVE EXTERNALITIES CAUSE OVERSUPPLY

In a perfectly competitive market, the market supply curve is the (horizontal) sum of the marginal cost curves of all firms, while market demand reflects how much the marginal unit is worth to any consumer. In panel A, the equilibrium, at quantity Q_p and price p_p, will be where private marginal cost is equal to the marginal benefit.

If society as a whole faces broader costs, like pollution, then the social marginal costs will exceed the private costs. If the supplier is not required to take these additional costs into account (as in panel B), production will be at Q_p, and the quantity produced will exceed the amount Q_s where marginal cost is equal to marginal benefit for society as a whole.

Consider what happens if, in the production of steel, there is an externality—producers are polluting the air and water without penalty. The **social marginal cost**—the marginal cost borne by all individuals in the economy—will now exceed the **private marginal cost**—the marginal cost borne by the producer alone. Note that in a competitive industry, the supply curve corresponds to the horizontal sum of all producers' *private* marginal cost curves. Panel B contrasts the two situations. It shows the social marginal cost curve for producing steel lying above the private marginal cost curve. Thus, with social marginal costs equated to social marginal benefits, the economically efficient level of production of steel will be lower, at Q_s, than it would be, at Q_p, if private costs were the only ones.

The level of production of steel, which generates negative externalities, will therefore be too high in a free market. We can also ask, What about the level of expenditure on pollution abatement? Such expenditures confer a positive externality—the benefits of the equipment, the cleaner air, accrue mainly to others. Figure 18.2 shows a firm's demand curve for pollution-abatement equipment in the absence of government regulation. It is quite low, reflecting the fact that the firm itself derives little benefit. That is, the firm's marginal private benefit from expenditures on pollution-abatement equipment is small. The firm sets its marginal private benefit equal to the marginal cost of pollution abatement, which results in a level of expenditure on pollution abatement at E. The figure also depicts the marginal social benefit of pollution abatement, which is far greater than the marginal private benefit. Efficiency requires that the marginal social benefit equal the marginal cost, point E'. Thus, economic efficiency requires greater expenditures on pollution abatement than there would be in the free market.

One of government's major economic roles is to correct the inefficiencies resulting from externalities. Among the many types of negative externalities, perhaps the most conspicuous are those that harm the environment.

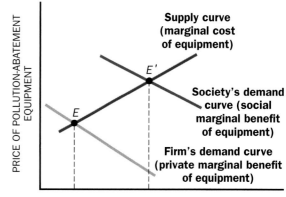

Figure 18.2

HOW POSITIVE EXTERNALITIES CAUSE UNDERSUPPLY

The private marginal benefit includes just the benefits received by the firm; but since pollution-abatement equipment provides a positive externality, it will have a social marginal benefit that is higher. If the firm takes only its private benefit into account, it will operate at point *E*, using less equipment than at the point where marginal benefits are equal to marginal costs for society as a whole (*E'*).

Policy Responses to Problems in the Environment

As the negative externalities associated with pollution and other environmental issues are increasingly recognized, the various approaches of governments seeking to curtail their bad effects have received considerable attention from economists and others. This section evaluates several of the major options.

PROPERTY RIGHTS RESPONSES

Large-scale environmental degradation is a conspicuous form of negative externalities. Having identified these market failures, what can the government do to improve

International Perspective

GLOBAL WARMING

Many environmental problems are local in nature. The pollution of a stream or a toxic waste site mainly affects people in the neighborhood. But some environmental hazards have an impact on the entire planet and therefore require international cooperation. For instance, the Montreal Convention signed in 1990 limited the emissions of chemicals that had led to the depletion of ozone in the atmosphere. Ozone depletion was linked to a higher incidence of certain types of cancer caused by radiation normally blocked by the ozone layer. The agreement was remarkably successful: with little cost to the economy, the use of these chemicals was phased out, even ahead of schedule.

Today, the most serious global environmental problem is probably global warming, the increased temperature of the earth caused by the buildup of the so-called greenhouse gases, such as carbon dioxide, that trap the sun's energy just as a greenhouse does. The evidence of the buildup of these gases is strong, and there is mounting data about the consequences. A series of international panels of experts have concluded that the impacts are likely to be large: they include the melting of the polar ice cap and a rise in the sea level, resulting in the inundation of low-lying regions of the world. In 1992 at Rio de Janeiro, an international convention was signed committing the world's governments to controlling the emission of greenhouse gases. In 1997, a further agreement, making the reductions binding, was signed in Kyoto. However, then-president Bill Clinton never submitted the Kyoto Protocol on global climate change to the Senate for ratification because opposition to it was very strong. In 2001, President George W. Bush announced formally that the United States would not ratify the treaty. The outrage from the rest of the world at this declaration was particularly strong because the United States is the largest producer of greenhouse gases, emitting 36 percent of the world's total. Opponents of the Kyoto Protocol argue that it does not do enough to limit emissions

from rapidly developing economies such as China's: while mandatory limits are set for developed economies, developing countries are subject only to voluntary limits. In 1997, the U.S. Senate had voted 95–0 to oppose any agreement that did not incorporate mandatory limits on developing countries as well. In addition, many argue that the economic costs of limiting emissions are too great.

Supporters of the treaty note that on a per capita basis, emissions from the developing economies are much lower than they are from the United States. Further, it seems unfair to ask countries struggling to boost economic growth and reduce poverty to bear the costs of limiting greenhouse gas emissions, when it is the past pollution of the rich, developed countries that has created the problem. Drawing on arguments of equity, the developing economies such as China and India called for mandatory limits on the rich countries first, combined with initially voluntary targets for the developing countries.

To come into effect, the Kyoto Protocol needed to be ratified by a set of countries that accounted for 55 percent of total greenhouse gas emissions in 1990. By 2004, industrialized countries accounting for 44 percent of 1990 emissions had ratified the treaty. It was finally pushed over the 55 percent hurdle in late 2004, when President Vladimir Putin announced that Russia, which accounted for 17 percent of 1990 emissions, would ratify the treaty. Russia had a large economic incentive to vote for the Kyoto Protocol, since it allows countries that reduce their emissions below the level of their quota to sell the unused portion to countries that fail to meet their target. Because of its economic contraction following the collapse of the former Soviet Union, Russia's emissions are 25 percent lower than the 1990 level, while the treaty required of the nation only a 5 percent reduction. Thus, Russia can potentially earn billions by selling its unused quotas.

matters? Some economists, led by the Nobel laureate Ronald Coase of the University of Chicago Law School, argue that government should simply rearrange property rights. **Coase's theorem** says that with appropriately designed property rights, markets could take care of externalities without direct government intervention. Consider, for example, the case of a small lake in which anyone can fish without charge. Each fisherman ignores the fact that the more fish he takes out of the lake, the fewer there are for others to take out. No fisherman has an incentive to worry about whether there will be fish in the lake in the future, either. Why should he? After all, if he leaves fish in the lake today, someone else might take them out tomorrow. If all fishermen think this way, the lake will quickly be overfished, likely to the point of wiping out the fish stock. If the government were to rearrange property rights and grant the right to fish to a single individual, then she would have every incentive to fish efficiently. There would no longer be any externality. She would have an incentive to take into account both the long-term and the short-term effects of her decisions. She would realize that if she fished too much today, the lake would contain fewer fish tomorrow. If it were a large lake, she might let others do the fishing and charge them for each fish caught or regulate the amount of fish they could catch. But the prices she charged and the regulations she imposed would be designed to ensure that the lake was not overfished.

The point of this example is that the problem of overfishing is solved with only limited government intervention. All the government has to do is assign the property rights correctly.

Coase envisioned that once property rights were assigned, market solutions or bargaining among potential users would ensure efficient outcomes. Consider the conflict between smokers and nonsmokers over whether to allow smoking in a room. Smokers confer a negative externality on nonsmokers. Coase suggests a simple solution. Give the rights to the air to one individual, say, a smoker. He has the right to decide whether to allow smoking or not. For the sake of simplicity, assume that there are only two individuals in the room, one a smoker and the other a nonsmoker. If the value of fresh air to the nonsmoker exceeds the value of smoking to the smoker, the nonsmoker would offer the smoker enough money to compensate him not to smoke. Conversely, if the property rights were given to the nonsmoker, and if the value of smoking to the smoker exceeded the value of fresh air to the nonsmoker, then the smoker could compensate the nonsmoker.

Coase argued not only that assigning property rights ensures an efficient outcome but also that how the property rights are assigned affects only the distribution of income, not economic efficiency. Whether smoking would be allowed would depend merely on whether the value of smoking to smokers exceeded or was less than the value of fresh air to nonsmokers.

The appeal of Coase's theorem is that it assigns a minimal role to government. Government simply makes the property rights clear, and leaves the efficient outcome to private markets. Opportunities to apply the theorem are limited, however, because the costs of reaching an agreement may be high, particularly when large numbers of individuals are involved. Imagine the difficulties of assigning property rights to the atmosphere, and arranging that all the individuals adversely affected by air pollution negotiate with all those contributing to it!

Thinking Like an Economist

ENVIRONMENTAL AND ECONOMIC TRADE-OFFS

In economics, what matters are *incentives,* not *intentions*—and well-intentioned acts often have unintended consequences. In 1973, Congress passed an important piece of legislation, the Endangered Species Act, intended to protect species that are threatened with extinction. If, for instance, a rare species, like the spotted owl, was discovered to be nesting in a tree on your property, you would not be allowed to cut down the tree. The act brought to the fore the point that we often think of private property too simplistically: If I own something, I should be able to do with it what I like, *so long as I don't harm anyone else.* But there's the rub. What you do with your property does affect others. If you build a tall building on your property, blocking out the light that your neighbors receive, you are affecting them. If you build a dirty, noisy factory in a quiet residential neighborhood, you are affecting your neighbors. Such inter-

dependence explains why most cities have *zoning laws* restricting the use of land; there are residential zones and business zones and manufacturing zones. But society as a whole benefits from the preservation of endangered species; in that sense, destroying the habitat of an endangered species has repercussions that touch others beyond the owners of the land.

In 1993, a heated dispute arose over the spotted owl in the Pacific Northwest. Environmentalists, concerned about the destruction of the spotted owl's habitat, had acted on a provision of the Endangered Species Act to halt logging, thereby threatening the livelihood of hundreds of people in the area. In the region as a whole, there were new bases for economic growth—for instance, software and other high-tech industries were moving in, attracted in part by the natural beauty of the environment. But the loggers lacked the requisite skills to join

Today there is general agreement that while assigning property rights clearly may take care of some problems, most externalities, particularly those concerning the environment, require more active government intervention.

REGULATION

Government's first response to the need for intervention to address environmental externalities was to regulate. Electric utilities that burned high-sulfur coal would not be allowed to emit sulfur dioxide into the atmosphere. They would be required to install scrubbers, devices that removed the sulfur from the fumes. And cars would be required to have catalytic converters. This approach is sometimes called the **command and control approach.**

It quickly ran into problems. The same environmental benefits often could be achieved at much lower costs in ways that were not allowed by the regulations. This weakness arose in part because the regulations did not (and could not) allow for the myriad variations in the circumstances of different firms, and in part because the regulatory process is always slow (at best) in incorporating newly developing technologies. Worse still, the command and control approach failed to provide incentives for the development of new technologies to reduce environmental

in such developments. The end of logging would have presented them with bleak prospects. There seemed to be a clear *trade-off*: which was more important, the livelihood of the loggers or the survival of the spotted owl? There was one way out of this box: if the value of preserving the spotted owl exceeded the economic damage to the loggers, those benefiting from preservation could pay off the loggers. Alternatively, the federal government might have used general tax revenues to compensate the loggers. But at the time, the government's budget was severely constrained. A compromise was sought, whereby enough area was kept closed to protect the spotted owl's habitat while enough was kept open for logging to protect many of the jobs.

Critics of the Endangered Species Act pointed out the perverse incentives created by the law. For example, if you had a tree of the type that a spotted owl might nest in, you would have an incentive to cut it down before the owl nested in it. That way, your later desire to develop your land would not be encumbered by a court injunction issued because the land contained a habitat for an endangered species. Some worried that these *unintended consequences* were so large that they reversed the act's intended effects.

Which is more important, the livelihood of loggers or the survival of the spotted owl?

damage, since it often would not allow those technologies to be used, even if they did a better job.[1]

Moreover, politics inevitably intrudes into the setting of regulations, resulting in higher than necessary costs. High-sulfur coal producers worried that the cost of scrubbers would put them at a competitive disadvantage relative to low-sulfur coal producers. (This is the correct market outcome from the viewpoint of economic efficiency, because the social cost of high-sulfur coal—including its negative environmental impacts—was greater than that of the low-sulfur coal.) So they succeeded in getting Congress to mandate that users of low-sulfur coal also had to have scrubbers, though for them such devices were unnecessary. In another example, ethanol producers (dominated by a single firm, Archer Daniels Midland) persuaded regulators to require a corn-based gasoline additive to reduce pollution rather than an oil-based one—even though the latter is cheaper and may be better environmentally.

Another reason economists are wary of regulations is that the costs they impose are often hidden. As the costs of environmental regulation rise, it becomes clear that better analysis when designing regulations is needed. Such analysis should look

---

[1]On the other side, advocates argue that in some cases the tight regulations have "forced" the development of new technologies to meet environmental standards that could not be met with existing technologies.

at cost and benefit, encouraging government to undertake regulations only when benefits exceed costs, and to focus on those areas where environmental risks are greatest. These principles, supported by most economists, would seem to be unexceptionable, and are in fact reflected in presidential Executive Orders issued to guide the implementation of regulations. But some environmentalists take a "purist" stand. They argue that a child's health should not be submitted to the cold calculus of costs and benefits. And they worry about "paralysis by analysis"—that the process of doing the cost-benefit analyses will effectively bring environmental regulation to a halt.

TAXES AND SUBSIDIES

Most economists believe that taxes and subsidies provide a better way than regulation to encourage the behavior desired by society. Taxes are the stick, while subsidies are the carrot. Both share the aim of adjusting private costs to account for social costs.

Panel A of Figure 18.3 shows the supply and demand curves for steel. If the production of steel generates a negative externality in the form of pollution, then the social marginal cost of producing steel is higher than the private marginal cost. The market equilibrium leads to a production level of Q_p, which exceeds the socially optimal quantity Q_s. Panel B illustrates how a tax on the production of steel can lead to

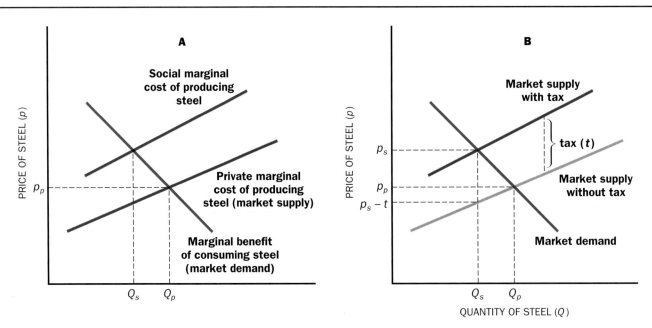

Figure 18.3

USING A TAX IN THE PRESENCE OF A NEGATIVE EXTERNALITY

When production leads to a negative externality, such as pollution in the case of steel production, the firm's costs do not reflect the total social cost of production. The market equilibrium, before a tax is imposed, is at a price p_p and quantity Q_p (see panel A). The efficient level is at quantity Q_s. Panel B depicts the effects of imposing a tax on steel producers. The tax increases their costs, and the market supply curve shifts up. The new equilibrium price is p_s and the equilibrium quantity is Q_s.

the socially optimal level of production. The tax, t, increases the firm's costs of producing steel, shifting up the market supply curve. The new market equilibrium is now at the socially optimal quantity Q_s. The equilibrium price is p_s; purchasers of steel pay a price that correctly reflects the social cost of producing steel. Doing so ensures that the marginal benefits are set equal to the marginal costs. Steel-producing firms receive the market price less the tax, $p_s - t$, an amount that equals their private marginal cost of producing steel.

Taxes on pollution are similar to fines for violating regulations in one respect—both increase the cost of and thereby discourage pollution. But taxes differ from regulation in a fundamental way. Regulations are a clumsy tool. They penalize firms for polluting over a specific level, but polluters who stay just below that level get off scot-free. Pollution taxes can be set so that they reduce aggregate pollution by the same amount as a regulator would under a command and control system. But the economic effects are very different. Taxes add the cost of pollution to the costs that a company has to cover to remain in business. As a result, companies have an incentive to reduce their pollution as far as possible and to find new, low-cost ways of reducing pollution or to devise new production methods that are less polluting, rather than keeping pollution just below the legal standard. This is "efficient pollution abatement," as the producers who pollute less gain their reward in lower costs.

Subsidies such as tax credits for pollution-abatement devices are an alternative way of providing incentives to reduce pollution. Subsidies are economically inefficient. Take the case of steel firms. When they receive subsidies, firms are not paying the full costs. Part of the costs are being picked up by the government. Producers therefore can sell (and users can buy) steel for less than its full cost of production, and steel and pollution production thus remain above the socially efficient level. Clearly, firms prefer subsidies to taxes.

THE MARKETABLE PERMIT RESPONSE

Still another approach to curbing pollution is **marketable permits.** Companies purchase (or are granted) a permit from the government that allows them to emit a certain amount of pollution. Again, the government can set the amount so that the company produces the same level of pollution as it would under the command and control approach. However, companies are allowed to sell their permits. Thus, if a company cuts its pollution in half, it can sell some of its allowance to another company that wants to expand production (and hence its emission of pollutants).

The incentive effects of marketable permits are very much like those of taxes. A market for pollution permits encourages development of the best possible anti-pollution devices, rather than keeping the pollution just under some government-set limit. If the government wishes to reduce pollution over time, the permits can be designed to reduce the amount of pollution they allow by a prescribed amount each year. In the United States, this sort of shrinking marketable permit was used to reduce the amount of lead in gasoline during the early 1980s. Variants of this idea have recently been adopted to help control other forms of air pollution, such as sulfur dioxide.

The effects of acid rain are easy to see in forests throughout the northeastern United States and Canada.

REDUCING ACID RAIN

Forests throughout the northeastern United States and Canada have been damaged by acid rain—that is, rain polluted by sulfuric and nitric acids. These acids result from the reaction of sulfur dioxide (SO_2) and nitrogen oxides in the atmosphere. In the United States, coal-fired power plants in the Northeast and Midwest are the primary sources of the SO_2 that contributes to acid rain. The Clean Air Act Amendments of 1990 established programs to reduce the emissions of SO_2.

As part of this program, owners of pollution-producing plants are given permits, called *allowances,* that give them rights to emit a certain amount of SO_2. The critical aspect of the program is that these permits are tradable. A plant that has a larger allowance than it needs can sell the unused portion to another plant that wishes to emit more than its allotted amount. A plant that finds the marginal cost of reducing SO_2 emissions to be greater than the price of a permit will choose to purchase a permit; a firm that finds the marginal cost of reducing emissions to be less than the price of a permit will want to sell a permit. As a consequence, the market price for permits will measure the marginal cost of reducing emissions.

A simple example illustrates how a system of tradable permits can reduce the total cost of lowering emissions. Consider the case of two plants with different marginal costs of cutting back on their emissions of SO_2. For the sake of illustration, suppose the relevant cost data are those given below:

Reduction in Emissions	Plant A		Plant B	
	Total Cost	Marginal Cost	Total Cost	Marginal Cost
0	$0	$0	$0	$0
1	$1	$1	$0.5	$0.5
2	$3	$2	$1.5	$1
3	$6	$3	$3	$1.5
4	$10	$4	$5	$2
5	$15	$5	$7.5	$2.5
6	$21	$6	$10.5	$3

In this example, plant B is able to reduce emissions at a lower cost than plant A.

Now suppose the goal is to reduce emissions by 6 units. One approach might be to require each plant to cut emissions by 3 units. In this case, the cost of reducing emissions would be $6 at plant A and $3 at plant B for a total cost of $9. However, the marginal cost of achieving the last reduction in emissions at plant A was $3, while plant B would be able to gain a further reduction (to 4) in its emissions at a marginal cost of only $2.

Instead of requiring each plant to reduce its emissions by the same amount, suppose the same overall reduction of 6 units is achieved by having plant A cut emissions by 2 units and plant B by 4 units. The total cost is now only $3 + $5 or $8. We have achieved the same overall reduction in pollution more efficiently by having the plant that can cut emissions at a lower marginal cost (plant B) cut back the most.

If the two plants can participate in a market for permits, plant A would find it advantageous to purchase a permit from plant B. By cutting back by only 2 units instead of 3, plant A can reduce its costs by $3. Plant B, having sold a permit to plant A, must cut its emissions back further, from a reduction of 3 to a reduction of 4. This raises its costs by $2. As long as the price of a permit is between $2 and $3, both firms gain. Society gains by achieving the desired reduction in emissions at the least cost.

While the SO_2 tradable permit system has been in place only since the mid-1990s, the evidence indicates that it has achieved emission goals in a cost-effective manner.[2]

WEIGHING THE ALTERNATIVE APPROACHES

Incentive programs, such as taxes or marketable permits, have an important advantage over direct controls, like regulations. The issue of pollution is not whether it should be allowed—after all, it is virtually impossible to eliminate all pollution in an industrial economy. Nor would such elimination be efficient; its costs would far exceed its benefits. The real issue is how sharply pollution should be limited. The *marginal* benefits have to be weighed against the marginal costs. This calculation is not performed under regulation. If instead government ascertains the marginal social cost of pollution and sets charges or marketable permits accordingly, private firms will engage in pollution control up to the point at which the marginal cost of pollution control equals the marginal social return of pollution abatement (which is just the marginal cost of pollution). Each firm will have the correct marginal incentives.

Governments often prefer direct regulations because they believe that they can control the outcomes better. But such control can be illusory. If an unreachable standard is set, it is likely to be repealed. For example, as automobile companies have found the costs of various regulations to be prohibitive, they have repeatedly appealed for a delay in the enforcement of those regulations, often with considerable success.

It must also be kept in mind that choosing the socially efficient method of pollution abatement is the easy part of the policy problem. Figuring out the "right" level of pollution to aim for is much harder. Uncertainty about the consequences of pollution abounds, and how to value certain options is hotly debated. To what extent can environmental degradation be reversed? How much value should be placed on the extinction of a species like the spotted owl, or the preservation of the Arctic wilderness? No matter what approach is chosen to externalities and the environment, such questions will remain controversial.

---

[2]See Richard Schmalensee et al., "An Interim Evaluation of Sulfur Dioxide Emissions," and Robert N. Stavins, "What Can We Learn from the Grand Policy Experiment? Lessons from SO_2 Allowance Trading," in *Journal of Economic Perspectives* 12, no. 3 (Summer 1998): 53–68, 69–88.

SOLVING THE PROBLEM OF EXTERNALITIES

Externalities, which occur when the extra costs and benefits of a transaction are not fully reflected in the market price, give rise to market failure. Four main solutions have been proposed and used:

1. The reassignment of property rights
2. Regulations that outlaw the negative externality
3. Tax and subsidy measures to encourage the behavior society wants
4. Marketable permits

Natural Resources

A recurrent theme among environmentalists is that our society is squandering its natural resources. We are using up oil and energy resources at an alarming rate, hardwood timber forests that took hundreds of years to grow are being cut down, and supplies of vital resources like phosphorus are dwindling. There are repeated calls for government intervention to enhance the conservation of our scarce natural resources. Those who believe in the infallibility of markets reply, Nonsense! Prices give the same guidance to the use of natural resources that they give to any other resource. Prices measure scarcity, and send consumers and firms the right signals about how much effort to expend to conserve resources, so long as consumers and firms are well informed, and so long as there is not some other source of market failure.

There is, in fact, some truth in both positions. Prices, in general, do provide signals concerning the scarcity of resources; and *in the absence of market failures,* those signals lead to economic efficiency. We have seen some cases in which a private market economy without government intervention will not be efficient—when there are negative externalities (pollution) or when a resource (like fish in the ocean) is not priced.

But what about a privately owned resource, such as bauxite (from which aluminum is made) or copper? The owner of a bauxite mine has a clearly defined property right. Let's assume that he pays a tax appropriate to any pollution his mining operation causes. Thus, the price he charges will reflect both social and private costs. The question of resource depletion now boils down to the question of whether his bauxite is worth more to him in the market today or left in the ground for future extraction. The answer depends on how much the owner of the bauxite thinks it will be worth in the future, say thirty years from now. If the owner expects it to be sufficiently more valuable thirty years from now to compensate him both for waiting and for all the uncertainties associated with trying to predict what the bauxite will be worth that far in the future, he will keep the bauxite in the ground.

In Chapter 9, we learned how to calculate the future value of something in terms of its present discounted value. For example, if the price of the bauxite next year is expected to be $25 per ton and the interest rate is 10 percent, the present discounted value of that $25 is found by dividing $25 by 1 plus the interest rate, or 1.1. At an interest rate of 10 percent, next year's expected price of bauxite is equivalent to a price today of $25/1.1 = $22.73. If the interest rate is 10 percent, then a dollar a year from now is worth 10 percent less than a dollar today (a dollar today could be invested and would yield $1.10 in one year). If the current price of bauxite is above $22.73, it will pay to mine the bauxite today and sell it. If the current price is less than $22.75, the owner of the bauxite mine will find it more profitable to leave the bauxite in the ground and mine it next year.

Now looking ahead to what the bauxite might be worth thirty years from now. Suppose the owner's best guess is that in thirty years bauxite will be selling for $75 per ton and that the interest rate will remain 10 percent for the next thirty years; then the present discounted value of bauxite today will be $75/(1.1)^{30} = $4.30. If the current price is greater than $4.30, it will pay to mine the bauxite now—the price expected in the future is not high enough to compensate the owner for waiting. If the interest rate falls to 5 percent, however, the present discounted value rises to $75/1.05^{30} = $17.35. Now, if the current price is less than $17.35, it will pay to leave the bauxite in the ground. At a lower interest rate, the owner of the bauxite has a greater incentive to leave the bauxite in the ground until some future time. Higher interest rates increase the incentive for firms to extract the bauxite earlier.

If this miner and all other bauxite producers choose to bring the bauxite to market today, depleting the world's supply of bauxite, there are two possible reasons for their decision. Perhaps this is the socially efficient outcome—society values bauxite more highly today than it will tomorrow. Or perhaps the miners have miscalculated the value of bauxite thirty years from now and underestimated future prices, though they have every incentive to forecast as accurately as they can. If they have indeed miscalculated, we might view the result as a market failure; but there would be no reason to expect a government bureaucracy to do any better than the firms at guessing future prices.

However, there are two plausible reasons why private owners may habitually tend to undervalue future benefits of a natural resource. First, in countries where property rights are not secure, owners of a resource may feel that if they do not sell it soon, there is a reasonable chance that it will be taken away from them. There may be a revolution, for example, in which the government will take over the resource with no or only partial compensation to the owners. Even in countries like the United States, where owners are not worried about government confiscating their property, they might fear that more stringent regulations will make it more expensive to extract the resource in the future, or that higher taxes will make it less attractive to sell the resource in the

INFORMATION AND THE ENVIRONMENT

In addition to employing regulation and taxation, some governments have sought to control pollution by requiring firms to disclose the type and level of toxic substances they are emitting into the air or water. Such information disclosure has proved to be extremely effective. Pressure brought by local communities, and worries on the part of firms about acquiring a bad reputation, have induced polluting firms to reduce their levels of emissions. In this effort, the Internet has proved to be an important tool. For instance, Environmental Defense, a not-for-profit environmental advocacy group, maintains an Internet site called Scorecard (www.scorecard.org) that provides a wide range of information on pollutants.

future. Second, individuals and firms often face limited borrowing opportunities and very high interest rates. In these circumstances, capital markets discount future returns at a high rate, far higher than society or the government would discount them.

Sometimes government has aggravated the waste of natural resources. For example, much of the timber in the United States lies on government lands. The government, in making the land available, has paid less attention to concerns about economic efficiency than it has to the pleading of timber interest groups. Government policies aimed at restricting the import of foreign oil have also encouraged the use of domestic resources, a seemingly perverse policy of "drain America first." Government policies intended to keep the price of water low for farmers has led to many negative outcomes: excessive use of water has drained water from underground basins filled over centuries, lowered the water table, and in some cases leached out the soil. In each of these instances, private property rights and market outcomes would have supplied solutions that almost everyone in society would regard as better than what happened.

Merit Goods and the Environment

In this chapter, we have explained how externalities provide a rationale for government intervention in the economy. To some people, how we treat the environment and the earth's natural resources is not just a matter of economic efficiency: it is a moral issue. They argue that the question of, say, allowing whaling should not be approached narrowly from the perspective of economic costs and benefits. This view reflects the principle of merit goods discussed in Chapter 17. The government sometimes becomes involved not just because markets have failed to produce efficient outcomes but out of a belief that there are values that supersede those reflected in individual preferences, and government has the right and duty to impose those values on its citizens. Such a view rejects the basic premise of *consumer sovereignty,* which holds that individuals are the best judges of their own welfare, and argues that in certain selected areas, there is a role for *paternalism*—government can make better choices in some matters than individuals.

Review and Practice

SUMMARY

1. Government may have a role in the economy when markets fail to produce an efficient outcome. When positive or negative externalities exist, markets will not provide an efficient outcome.
2. One way to deal with externalities is to assign clear-cut property rights.
3. Governments may deal with environmental externalities by imposing regulatory measures (the command and control approach), levying taxes and granting subsidies, or issuing marketable permits.
4. In a perfect market, natural resources are used up at an efficient rate. However, privately owned resources may be sold too soon, for two reasons. First, owners may fear that if they do not sell the resources soon, new government rules may prevent them from selling at all or, in any case, may lower the return from selling in the future. Second, interest rates facing owners may be high, so they may value future income less than society does in general. High interest rates lead to a faster exploitation of natural resources.

KEY TERMS

social marginal cost
private marginal cost
Coase's theorem
command and control approach
marketable permits

REVIEW QUESTIONS

1. Name several market failures. Why do economists see the existence of these market failures as a justification for government action?
2. Why will a free market produce too much of goods that have negative externalities, like pollution? Why will a free market produce too little of goods that have positive externalities, like pollution controls?
3. What are the advantages and limitations of dealing with externalities by assigning property rights?
4. What are the advantages of marketable permits over command and control regulation? What are the advantages of using taxes on polluting rather than subsidies for pollution-abatement equipment?
5. How do markets work to allocate natural resources efficiently? In what cases will markets fail to give the correct signals for how quickly a resource like oil should be depleted?

PROBLEMS

1. Marple and Wolfe are two neighboring dormitories. Wolfe is considering giving a party with a very loud band, which will have a negative externality in the form of a sort of sound pollution for Marple. Imagine that the school administration decides that any dormitory has the right to prevent another dorm from hiring a band. If the band creates a negative externality, how might the residents of Wolfe apply the lessons of Coase's theorem to hire the band they want?

   Now imagine that the school administration decides that no dormitory can prevent another dorm from hiring a band, no matter how loud. If the band provides a negative externality, how might the residents of Marple apply the lessons of Coase's theorem to reduce the amount of time they have to listen to the band? How would your answer change if the band provided a positive externality?

2. The manufacture of trucks produces pollution of various kinds; for the purposes of this example, let's call it all "glop." Producing a truck creates one unit of glop, and glop has a cost to society of $3,000. Imagine that the supply of trucks is competitive, and market supply and demand are given by the following data:

Price (thousand $)	19	20	21	22	23	24	25
Quantity supplied	480	540	600	660	720	780	840
Quantity demanded	660	630	600	570	540	510	480

   Graph the supply curve for the industry and the demand curve. What are equilibrium price and output? Now graph the social marginal cost curve. If the social cost of glop were taken into account, what would be the new equilibrium price and output?

   If the government is concerned about the pollution emitted by truck plants, explain how it might deal with the externality through fines or taxes and through subsidies. Illustrate the effects of taxes and subsidies by drawing the appropriate supply and demand graphs. (Don't bother worrying about the exact units.) Why are economists likely to prefer fines to subsidies?

3. Consider a small lake with a certain number of fish. The more fish that one fisherman takes out, the fewer fish are available for others to take out. Use graphs depicting private and social costs and benefits to fishing to describe the equilibrium and the socially efficient level of fishing. Explain how a tax on fishing could achieve the efficient outcome. Explain how giving a single individual the property right to the fish in the lake might also be used to obtain an efficient outcome.

   The more fish taken out this year, the fewer fish will be available next year. Explain why if there is a single owner for the lake, the fish will be efficiently extracted from it. Assume that anyone who wants to fish can do so. Would you expect that too many fish would be taken out this year?

4. Consider a crowded room with an equal number of smokers and nonsmokers. Each smoker would be willing to pay $1.00 to have the right to smoke. Each nonsmoker would be willing to pay $0.50 to have the room free from smoke. Assume there is a rule that says no smoking is allowed. Could everyone be made better off if smoking is allowed? How? If property rights to clean air are assigned to the nonsmokers, how might the efficient outcome be obtained? What difference does it make to the outcome whether there is initially a rule that smoking is allowed or that smoking is not allowed? What problems

might you envision occurring if no smoking is allowed unless all the nonsmokers agree to allow it?

5. The following table gives the demand for water for two households, the Joneses and the Lopezes. Suppose these two households are the only ones in the market. Draw the individual demand curves for each household and the market demand curve. If the total quantity of water available is 80 units, what price would equate demand and supply?

   Assume the local water authority has set the price at 3. Now suppose there is a water shortage, and the total quantity of water available falls to 60 units. Suppose the local water authority keeps the price unchanged and rations the available water supply, with each household receiving 30 units. What is the marginal benefit of an extra unit of water to the Joneses? to the Lopezes? Is the allocation of water between the two households efficient? Suppose the water authority let the price of water rise until market demand equated supply (60 units). How much would the Joneses consume? How much would the Lopezes consume? Is the allocation efficient?

Price	Demand by the Jones family	Demand by the Lopez family
2	50	40
3	45	35
4	40	30
5	35	25
6	30	20
7	25	15
8	20	10

Learning Goals

In this chapter, you will learn

1 How international trade can benefit all countries

2 The role comparative advantage plays in determining what countries produce and trade

3 Why countries erect barriers to trade and who the winners and losers are when international trade is restricted

4 Why international trade agreements are often controversial

Chapter 19

INTERNATIONAL TRADE AND TRADE POLICY

Exchange was one of the core concepts in economics discussed in Chapter 1. Economists often use the words *trade* and *exchange* interchangeably. When Chip goes to work, he exchanges, or trades, his labor services for income. When Juanita purchases a new cell phone, she exchanges, or trades, income for the product she chooses. The subject of international trade—the exchange of goods and services across national borders—is an extension of the basic principle of exchange. Individuals in our economy are involved in countless voluntary trades. They "trade" their labor services (time and skills) to their employer for dollars. They then trade dollars with a multitude of merchants for goods (such as gasoline and groceries) and services (such as plumbing and hairstyling). A firm trades the goods it produces for dollars, and then trades those dollars for labor services.

Why is it that people engage in all these complex sets of economic exchanges with one another? The answer is that people are better off as a result of trading. Just as individuals *within* a country find it advantageous to trade with one another, so too do countries find trade advantageous. And just as it is impossible for any individual to be self-sufficient, it is impossible for a country to be self-reliant without sacrificing its standard of living.

Trade Between Countries

The United States has long been part of an international economic community. Its participation has grown in recent decades—a process often referred to as *globalization*—increasing the interdependence among the United States and its trading partners. How has this development affected the three major markets in the U.S. economy?

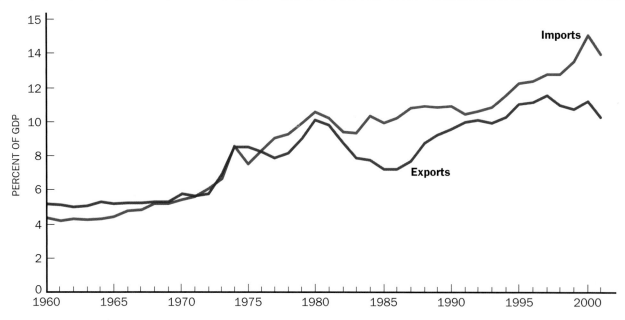

Figure 19.1
INTERNATIONAL TRADE

Here, U.S. imports and exports are expressed as a fraction of GDP. Note that trade has increased over time, and that imports have exceeded exports since the mid-1970s.

SOURCE: *Economic Report of the President* (2004).

INTERDEPENDENCE IN THE PRODUCT MARKET

Foreign-produced goods are commonplace in U.S. markets. In the 1990s, for instance, more than one-fourth of the cars sold in the United States were imported (**imports** are goods produced abroad but bought domestically), along with a third of apparel items, a third of the oil, and virtually all the diamonds. Many of the materials essential for the U.S. economy must also be imported from abroad. At the same time, American farmers export almost two-fifths of the agricultural goods they produce (**exports** are goods produced domestically but sold abroad), including almost three-fourths of the wheat and one-third of the cotton.

Imports have grown in recent decades, not only in dollar terms but also as a percentage of overall production. Exports have grown almost as much. Figure 19.1 shows how exports and imports have increased relative to the nation's total output. As a percentage of GDP, both have more than doubled over the past twenty-five years. Countries with smaller economies are even more dependent on international trade than the United States is. Britain and Canada import one-fourth of their goods, France one-fifth.

INTERDEPENDENCE IN THE LABOR MARKET

International interdependence extends beyond simply the shipping of goods between countries. More than 99 percent of U.S. citizens either came here from another country or are descended from people who did. Though the flow of immigrants, relative to the size of the population, has slowed since its peak a century ago, millions still arrive each year.

The nations of Europe have increasingly recognized the benefits that result from this international movement of workers. One of the most important provisions of the treaty establishing the European Union, an agreement initially among most of the countries in western Europe but now extended to include many in eastern Europe, allows for the free flow of workers within the member countries.

INTERDEPENDENCE IN THE CAPITAL MARKET

The United States has become a major borrower from abroad, but the country also invests heavily overseas. In 2002, for example, U.S. private investors owned approximately $180 billion worth of assets (factories, businesses, buildings, loans, etc.) in foreign countries, while foreign investors owned $707 billion worth of assets in the United States. American companies have sought out profitable opportunities abroad, where they can use their special skills and knowledge to earn high returns. They have established branches and built factories in Europe, Japan, Latin America, and elsewhere in the world. Foreign companies have likewise invested in the United States. Major automobile producers such as Toyota and BMW have built factories in the United States to manufacture cars.

MULTILATERAL TRADE

Often, we think of trade as a two-way exchange—the United States sells airplanes to Japan and buys Japanese-produced consumer electronics. Such transactions between two individuals or countries are called **bilateral trade.** But exchange between two parties is often less advantageous than that among several parties, called **multilateral trade.** Such trades are often observed among sports teams. One highly publicized trade in 2004 involved the Boston Red Sox, the Chicago Cubs, the Montreal Expos, and the Minnesota Twins. At its heart were three shortstops—Nomar Garciaparra, a five-time all-star, who went from the Red Sox to the Cubs; Alex Gonzalez, who went from the Cubs to Montreal; and Orlando Cabrera, who went from Montreal to Boston—but other players and a fourth team (the Twins) were also involved. No two of the teams were willing to make a bilateral trade, but all thought they could benefit from the multilateral deal.

Countries function similarly. China imports oil from the Arabian countries. The Arabian countries want wheat and food for their oil, not just the textiles that China can provide. So the Arabian countries use revenue obtained by selling oil to China to buy wheat and food from the United States, and the United States buys textiles from China. This three-way trade, shown in Figure 19.2, offers gains that two-way trade cannot. The scores of nations that are active in the world economy create patterns far more complex than these simple examples.

When trade is multilateral, the trade between any two countries may not balance. In Figure 19.2, the Arab nations send oil to China but get no goods (only yuan) in return. No one would fault this trade policy. Yet some members of Congress,

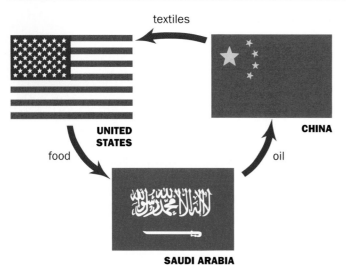

Figure 19.2

MULTILATERAL EXCHANGE

The figure illustrates exchange in international trade. Note that no two of the countries have the ingredients for a mutually beneficial exchange.

newspaper columnists, union leaders, and business executives complain that because the United States imports more from a particular country (often China or Japan) than it exports to that country, the trade balance is "unfair." According to a misguided popular cliché, "Trade is a two-way street." But trade in the world market is a complex network involving hundreds of possible streets. While the overall U.S. trade deficit raises legitimate concerns, there is no reason why U.S. exports and imports with any particular country should be balanced.

Comparative Advantage

We have so far focused on exchanges of existing goods. But clearly, most of what is exchanged must first be produced. Trade enables individuals and countries to concentrate on what they produce best.

Some countries—because they have more highly educated workers, more capital (plant and equipment), or more abundant natural resources—may be more efficient at producing almost all the different goods that their citizens wish to consume. The possession of superior production skills is called having an **absolute advantage.** Why would a country with an absolute advantage wish to trade with countries that are less efficient? And how can such disadvantaged countries successfully engage in trade? The answer to these questions lies in the principle of **comparative advantage,** which states that individuals and countries specialize in those goods in whose production they are *relatively,* not absolutely, most efficient.

To see what comparative advantage means, let's say that both the United States and Japan produce two goods, computers and wheat. The amount of labor needed to produce these goods is shown in Table 19.1. (These numbers are all hypothetical.) The United States is more efficient (spends fewer worker hours) at making both products. America can rightfully claim to have the most efficient computer industry in the world, and yet it imports computers from Japan. Why? The *relative* cost of making a computer (in terms of labor used) in Japan, relative to the cost of producing a ton of wheat, is low, compared with that in the United States. That is, in

Table 19.1

LABOR COST OF PRODUCING COMPUTERS AND WHEAT (WORKER HOURS)

	United States	Japan
Labor required to make a computer	100	120
Labor required to make a ton of wheat	5	8

DAVID RICARDO

The economist David Ricardo developed the theory of comparative advantage. Born in 1772, Ricardo was the third of seventeen children. He was a successful stockbroker before retiring at age forty-two to write about economics. The Library in the Virtual Economy at Biz/ed—a Web site devoted to business and economics education—provides a brief biography of this famous economist and discusses his contributions to the theory of comparative advantage at www.bized.ac.uk/virtual/economy/library/economists/ricardo.htm.

Japan, it takes 15 times as many hours (120/8) to produce a computer as a ton of wheat; in the United States, it takes 20 times as many hours (100/5) to produce a computer as a ton of wheat. While Japan has an absolute *dis*advantage in producing computers, it has a *comparative* advantage.

The principle of comparative advantage applies to individuals as well as countries. The president of a company might type faster than her secretary, but it still pays to have the secretary type her letters, because the president may have a comparative advantage at bringing in new clients, while the secretary has a comparative (though not absolute) advantage at typing.

PRODUCTION POSSIBILITIES CURVES AND COMPARATIVE ADVANTAGE

The easiest way to understand the comparative advantage of different countries is to use the production possibilities curve first introduced in Chapter 2. Figure 19.3 depicts parts of hypothetical production possibilities curves for two countries, China and the United States, producing two commodities, textiles (garments) and airplanes. In both, point *E* represents the current level of production. Let us look at what happens if each country changes its production by 100 airplanes.

China has a comparative advantage in producing textiles. If it reduces its airplane production by 100, its textile production can be increased by 10,000 garments. This trade-off between airplanes and garments is called the *marginal rate of transformation*. By contrast, if the United States reduces its airplane production by 100 airplanes, its textile production can be increased by only 1,000 garments. Conversely, if it increases its airplane production by 100, it will have to reduce its garment production by only 1,000 garments. We can now see why the world is better off if each country exploits its comparative advantage. If China moves from *E* to *E'* (decreasing airplane production by 100),

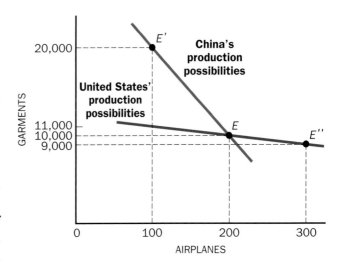

Figure 19.3

EXPLOITING COMPARATIVE ADVANTAGE

The production possibilities schedules for China and the United States, each manufacturing two commodities, textiles and airplanes, illustrate the trade-offs at different levels of production. Point *E* shows the current level of production for each country; *E'* and *E''* illustrate production decisions that better exploit each country's comparative advantage.

10,000 more garments can be produced. If the United States at the same time increases its airplane production by 100 from E to E'', it will produce only 1,000 fewer garments. In the new situation, the world production of airplanes is unchanged ($100 + 300 = 200 + 200$), but world production of garments has increased by 9,000 (the difference between $20,000 + 9,000$ and $10,000 + 10,000$). So long as the production trade-offs differ—that is, so long as the marginal rates of transformation differ—it pays for China to specialize increasingly in textiles, and the United States to specialize increasingly in airplanes. Notice that the analysis depends on knowledge only about the production trade-offs. We do not need to know how much labor or capital is required in either country to produce either airplanes or garments.

Though it pays countries to increase the production and export of goods in which they have a comparative advantage and to import goods in which they have a comparative disadvantage, doing so may not lead to complete specialization. Thus the United States continues to be a major producer of textiles, in spite of heavy imports from the Far East. Its engagement in this industry does not violate the principle of comparative advantage: not all textiles require the same skill and expertise in manufacturing. While China may have a comparative advantage in inexpensive textiles, the United States may have a comparative advantage in higher-quality textiles. At the same time, the comparative advantage of other countries is so extreme in producing some goods—TVs and VCRs, for example—that it does not pay for the United States to produce them at all.

COMPARATIVE ADVANTAGE AND SPECIALIZATION

To see the benefits of specialization, consider the pencil. A tree of the right kind of wood must be felled; it must be transported to a sawmill, and there cut into pieces that can be further processed into pencil casings. Then the graphite that runs through the pencil's center, the eraser at its tip, and the metal that holds the two together must each be produced by specially trained people. The pencil is a simple tool. But to produce it by oneself would cost a fortune.

Why Specialization Increases Productivity Specialization increases productivity, thereby enhancing the benefits of trade, for three reasons. First, specializing eliminates the time it takes a worker to switch from one production task to another. Second, by repeating the same task, the worker becomes more skilled at it. And third, specialization creates a fertile environment for invention.

Dividing jobs so that each worker can practice and perfect a particular skill (called the *division of labor*) may increase productivity hundreds or thousands of times. Almost anyone who practices activities—cooking, writing, adding a column of numbers, and so on—will be quite a lot better at them than someone who has not practiced. Similarly, a country that specializes in producing sports cars may develop a comparative advantage in their manufacture. With its relatively large scale of production, it can divide tasks into separate assignments for different people; as each becomes better at his own tasks, productivity is increased.

THE UNITED STATES' COMPARATIVE ADVANTAGE IN THE INTERNET AGE

The United States holds a comparative advantage in information technology and Internet-based commerce. Large U.S. firms such as Microsoft, Intel, and Sun Microsystems have led the surge in information technology over the past two decades, and Internet-based businesses such as Amazon, Google, and eBay have come to define the so-called new economy. How has the United States established itself as a leader in this field? Let's consider this question from the standpoint of the sources of comparative advantage described in this chapter.

The key to the United States' success in the information revolution has been its ability to innovate. U.S. firms have developed new types of computers and software, as well as new applications of these resources across various industries. This prowess in innovation derives from acquired endowments, superior knowledge, and specialization.

The human skills needed for innovation represent acquired endowments that have led to superior knowledge, some of which was gained as a by-product of America's massive expenditures on defense-related research. Another aspect of acquired endowments that has played a major role is the distinctive set of *institutions* in the United States that are particularly well suited for promoting research. These institutions include a special set of financial institutions (venture capital firms) that are better able to supply capital to new and small enterprises, which have played a pivotal role in the new economy, and strong research universities, which often have close ties to firms that can translate basic research into market applications. More broadly, both American labor and capital seem more able and willing to bear the high risks associated with new innovative enterprises, many of which may fold after a relatively brief existence. Americans' willingness to bear these risks may be

connected to the generally high levels of employment that have characterized the U.S. economy for the past two decades.

Partly as a result of these acquired advantages and of superior knowledge, the United States has developed a relative specialization in high-tech industries; it has become, to a large extent, the world's research center.

Intel's strength in computer chip production exemplifies the U.S. comparative advantage in information technology.

At the same time, the division of labor often leads to invention. As someone learns a particular job extremely well, she might figure out ways of doing it better—including devising a machine to do it. Specialization and invention reinforce each other. A slight initial advantage in the production of some good leads to greater production of that good, thence to more invention, and thence to even greater production and further specialization.

Limits of Specialization The extent of the division of labor, or specialization, is limited by the size of the market. Specialization has greater scope in mass-produced manufactured goods like picture frames than in custom-made items like the artwork that gets framed. That is one reason why the costs of production of mass-produced goods have declined so much. Similarly, there is greater scope for specialization in a big city than a small town. That is why small stores specializing in a particular food or type of clothing thrive in cities but are rare in smaller towns.

The very nature of specialization limits its benefits. Repetitive jobs can lead to bored and unproductive workers. And single-track specialization inhibits the new insights and ideas that engagement in a variety of work activities can spark.

WHAT DETERMINES COMPARATIVE ADVANTAGE?

Earlier we learned that comparative advantage determines the pattern of trade. But what determines comparative advantage? In the modern world, this turns out to be a complex matter.

Natural Endowments In first laying down the principle of comparative advantage in the early 1800s, the great British economist David Ricardo used the example of Portugal's trade with Britain. In Ricardo's example, Portugal had an absolute advantage in producing both wool and wine. But it had a comparative advantage in producing wine, and Britain had a comparative advantage in producing wool. In this and other early examples, economists tended to assume that a nation's comparative advantage was determined largely by its *natural endowments*. Countries with soil and climate that are *relatively* better for grapes than for pasture will produce wine; countries with soil and climate that are relatively better for pasture than for grapes will produce sheep (and hence wool).

In the modern economy, natural endowments still count: countries such as China that have an abundance of low-skilled labor relative to other resources have a comparative advantage in producing goods like textiles, which require a lot of handwork. But in today's technological age nations can also act to *acquire* a comparative advantage.

Acquired Endowments Japan has little in the way of natural resources, yet it is a major player in international trade, in part because it has *acquired endowments*. Japan's case underscores the principle that by saving and accumulating capital and building large factories, a nation can acquire a comparative advantage in goods like steel that need large amounts of capital for their production. And by devoting resources to education, a nation can develop a comparative advantage in those goods that require a skilled labor force. Thus, the resources—human and physical—that a country has managed to acquire for itself can also give rise to comparative advantage.

Superior Knowledge In the modern economy, comparative advantage may come simply from expertise in using resources productively. Switzerland has a comparative advantage in watches because, over the years, the people of the country have accumulated superior knowledge and expertise in watchmaking. Belgium has a comparative advantage in fine lace; its workers have developed the requisite skills. A quirk of fate might have led Belgium to acquire a comparative advantage in watches and Switzerland in lace.

Specialization Earlier we saw how comparative advantage leads to specialization. Specialization may also lead to comparative advantage. The Swiss make fine watches, and have a comparative advantage in that market because of years of unique experience. Such superior knowledge, however, does not explain why Britain, Germany, and the United States, which are at roughly the same level of technological expertise in building cars, all trade cars with one another. How can each country have a comparative advantage in making cars? The answer lies in specialization.

Both Britain and Germany may be better off if Britain specializes in producing sports cars and Germany in producing luxury cars, or the converse, because specialization increases productivity. Countries enhance, or simply develop, a comparative advantage by specializing just as individuals do. As a result, similar countries enjoy the advantages of specialization even when they specialize in different variations of products that are fundamentally similar.

Interactions The different sources of comparative advantage can serve to reinforce each other. Pittsburgh provides a good example of some of these interactions. Its rivers and deposits of bituminous coal (natural endowments) gave it an early comparative advantage as a location for industries such as steel production. George Westinghouse, founder of the corporation that bears his name, came to Pittsburgh because he needed steel for a tool he had designed to get derailed train cars back onto their tracks, and he could take advantage of Pittsburgh's established steel industry. Carnegie Technical Schools, the ancestor of today's Carnegie Mellon University, was created to help supply the area's industries with the engineers they needed. The availability of engineers (acquired endowments) made Pittsburgh an attractive place for other industries to locate.

Wrap-Up

THE FIVE BASES OF COMPARATIVE ADVANTAGE

Natural endowments, which consist of geographical determinants such as land, natural resources, and climate

Acquired endowments, which are the physical capital and human skills a nation has developed

Superior knowledge, including technological advantages, which may be acquired either as an accident of history or through deliberate policies

Specialization, which may create comparative advantages between countries that are similar in all other respects

Interactions, which reinforce the other sources of comparative advantage

The Perceived Costs of International Interdependence

If the argument that voluntary trade must be mutually beneficial is so compelling, why has there been, from time to time, such strong antitrade sentiment in the United States and many other countries? This antitrade feeling is often labeled **protectionism,** because it calls for "protecting" the economy from the effects of trade. Those who favor protectionism raise a number of concerns. Some of the objections to international trade parallel the objections to trade among individuals noted earlier. Was the trade a fair deal? Was the seller in a stronger bargaining position? Such concerns, for individuals and countries, revolve around how the *surplus* associated with the gains from trade is divided. Weak countries may feel that they are being taken advantage of by stronger countries. Their weaker bargaining position may lead to the stronger countries getting *more* of the gains from trade. But this outcome does not contradict the basic premise: both parties gain from voluntary exchange. All countries—weak as well as strong—are better off as a result of voluntary exchange.

Thinking Like an Economist

EXCHANGE AND THE GLOBALIZATION CONTROVERSY

In recent decades, transportation and communication costs have come down markedly. So too have artificial barriers to the movements of goods and services—trade barriers such as tariffs and quotas. The result is that the economies of the world are now more closely integrated than ever before.

From an economic perspective, this trend toward globalization would seem to offer a great benefit to the world. As we know, one of the core ideas of economics is that *voluntary exchange* is mutually beneficial to the parties involved. Yet globalization has been a subject of great controversy. For instance, some critics see globalization as a one-sided process mainly benefiting rich countries and large multinational firms. Others on the opposite side of the debate see it as the best opportunity to increase the standards of living in poor countries. How do we make sense of this controversy from an economic perspective? A close look at the globalization controversy shows that some of the criticisms are misplaced, while others have merit.

Globalization no doubt has made us more aware of the huge inequalities around the world. Some workers in China, Africa, and India, for instance, earn less than a dollar a day working under conditions that appear inhumane by American standards. But, for the most part, globalization has not caused their misery; it has only brought their plight to global attention. Many of these workers have moved to jobs in seemingly awful factories—some run by multinational firms, others selling their goods to multinational firms—because their previous jobs were even worse or because they had no previous jobs. It may seem cruel for corporations to exploit these workers, especially when working conditions could be improved at moderate expense. But even so, in many cases the workers have benefited from globalization.

Another economic aspect of globalization is that the *distribution* of its benefits may be highly uneven. For example, the owners of factories that make goods for multinational firms typically benefit more than the workers they employ. As a result, even if everyone is better off, inequality increases. Critics attacking the issue from a normative stance—emphasizing social values about fairness—may see increased inequality as the primary concern. In their view, the poor, who in some cases may benefit the least from globalization, are the very people who deserve to benefit more. But even if we agree with this con-

But trade among individuals and trade among countries differ in one important way. Some individuals within a country benefit from trade and some lose. Since the trade as a whole is beneficial to the country, the gains to the winners exceed the losses to the losers. Thus, in principle, those who benefit within the country could more than compensate those who don't. In practice, however, those who lose remain losers and obviously oppose trade, arguing that it results in lost jobs and reduced wages. Such worries have become particularly acute as unskilled workers face competition with low-wage unskilled workers in Asia and Latin America: how can they compete without lowering their income?

These concerns figured prominently in the debate in 1993 over ratification of the North American Free Trade Agreement (NAFTA), which allows Mexican goods into the United States with no duties at all. Advocates of NAFTA pointed out that (1) more jobs would be created by the new export opportunities than would be lost through competition from Mexican firms and (2) the jobs that were created paid higher wages, reflecting the benefits from specialization in areas where the United States had a comparative advantage.

tention, we have to recognize that it does not refute the basic economic principle about the benefits of voluntary exchange.

A further criticism of globalization maintains that some individuals are actually made worse off. Can this be? The answer is yes, and an example helps illustrate the point. The theory of comparative advantage says that countries should produce the goods that they are relatively good at producing. But when they are protected from foreign competition, firms may produce goods that are not part of the country's comparative advantage. The United States may produce cheap clothes, simply because of the limits put on importing inexpensive foreign-made clothes. Removing the protection may make the production of the inexpensive clothes unprofitable. The factory may have to shut down, and workers will be left unemployed. But in theory, these conditions should not last for long. If markets work well, some new enterprises will be created to take advantage of the country's comparative advantage. Resources are redeployed from where they are less productive to where they are more productive, a shift that increases the country's income. But this process does not happen automatically, or always quickly; in the meanwhile, those who are pushed into unemployment often object to the removal of the protection.

Such problems are especially severe in developing countries, where there is a shortage both of entrepreneurs and of capital to start new enterprises. Workers who lose their jobs can be at particular risk, since they have no unemployment insurance or welfare system to fall back on. In many cases it may be true that the gains of those who benefit from freer trade more than offset the losses of those who suffer. Therefore, in principle, the gainers could compensate the losers so that everyone could be made better off. But in practice, the compensation is seldom paid. Thus, although a country may benefit from globalization, some of its citizens may suffer until the process of redeployment works itself out.

Are the jobs of these Chinese workers a cost or a benefit of globalization?

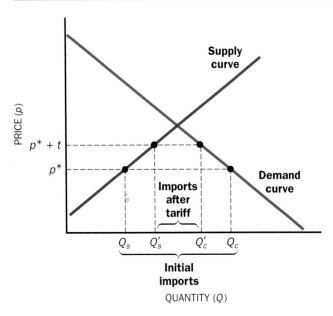

Figure 19.4

EFFECT OF TARIFFS

A small country faces a horizontal supply curve for a good at the international price, p^*. In the absence of tariffs, the price in the country will be p^*. The country will produce Q_s (the quantity along the supply curve corresponding to p^*), consume Q_c (the quantity along the demand curve corresponding to p^*), and import $Q_c - Q_s$. A tariff at the rate t increases the price in the country to $p^* + t$, lowers aggregate consumption to Q'_c (the quantity along the demand curve corresponding to $p^* + t$), and increases domestic production to Q'_s (the quantity along the supply curve corresponding to $p^* + t$). Domestic producers are better off, but consumers are worse off.

Opponents of free trade are not swayed by these arguments, but instead stress the costs to workers and communities as particular industries shrink in response to foreign imports. The textile worker in North Carolina who loses his job as a result of imports of inexpensive clothing from China cannot instantly convert himself into a computer programmer in California or an aircraft engineer working for Boeing. But the fact is that jobs are being destroyed and created all the time, irrespective of trade. Over the long run, the increased demand for computer programmers and aircraft engineers leads to higher salaries for those workers, thereby strengthening the incentives for young workers to gain the skills needed for these jobs and for others to relocate to areas where new jobs are being created. The declining demand for textile workers lowers salaries for textile workers, reducing the incentives for workers to remain in that industry. The United States is characterized by a high degree of labor mobility, and as jobs are created in one part of the country and disappear in other parts, individuals and families often move to seek new employment opportunities.

On balance, the country benefits from these changes, but the benefits are not distributed evenly. The unemployed textile worker sees only the economic hardship she faces and the cost of free trade. For this reason, many economists argue that policies must be implemented to help retrain and relocate workers displaced by trade so that they too can share in the benefits that accrue from international interdependence. To the extent that such assistance increases the number of winners, it should reduce opposition to trade.

While the perceived costs of economic interdependence cannot be ignored—especially when they become the subject of heated political debate—the consensus among the vast majority of economists is that the country as a whole benefits from freer trade. We can summarize this central tenet as follows: *There are gains from voluntary exchanges. Whether it occurs between individuals or across national borders, voluntary exchange can benefit all. Trade enables parties to specialize in activities in which they have a comparative advantage.*

Trade Policies

In spite of the gains from trade, countries have imposed a variety of barriers to it. In the remainder of this chapter, we explore some of the common trade barriers and the major initiatives to remove them.

COMMERCIAL POLICY

Countries that have *no* barriers to trade are said to practice **free trade,** but most countries engage in some form of protectionism—that is, in one way or another they restrict the importation of goods. Policies directed at affecting either imports or exports are referred to as **commercial policies.** This and the next section examine the forms that trade barriers take, their economic costs, and their economic and political rationale. The final section explores international attempts to reduce them.

There are five major categories of trade barriers—tariffs, quotas, voluntary export restraints, other *nontariff barriers,* and a set of so-called fair trade laws that, by and large, actually serve to impede trade.

TARIFFS

Tariffs are simply a tax on imports. Since a tariff is a tax that is imposed only on foreign goods, it puts the foreign goods at a disadvantage and discourages imports.

Figure 19.4 shows the effect of a tariff: a downward-sloping demand curve for the product, and an upward-sloping domestic supply curve. For the sake of simplicity, we consider the case of a country sufficiently small that the price it pays for a good on the international market does not depend on the quality purchased. In the absence of a tariff, the domestic price is equal to this international price, p^*. The country produces Q_s, consumes Q_c, and imports the difference, $Q_c - Q_s$. When a tariff is imposed, the price that consumers have to pay is increased from p^* to $p^* + t$, where t is the tariff. Domestic production is increased (to Q'_s)—producers are better off as a result. But consumers are worse off, as the price they pay is increased. Their consumption is reduced to Q'_c. Since production is increased and consumption reduced, imports are reduced; the domestic industry has been protected against foreign imports.

Quantifying the Losses to Society from Tariffs We can quantify the net loss to society caused by tariffs. The difference between the amount consumers are willing to pay and what they have to pay is called *consumer surplus.* For the last unit consumed, the marginal benefit exactly equals the price paid, and so there is no consumer surplus. But for the first units consumed, individuals typically would be willing to pay far more—reflected in the fact that the demand curve is downward sloping in Figure 19.5. Initially, the consumer surplus is given by triangle *ABC,* the area between the demand curve and the price line, p^*. After the price increase, it is given by the triangle *ADE.* The net loss is the trapezoid *BCED.*

But of this loss, the rectangle *BDHF* represents increased payments to producers (the increased price, *BD,* times the quantity that they produce), and *HFGE* is the tariff revenue of the government (imports, *HE,* times the tariff). A portion of the increased payments to domestic producers covers the cost of expanding production. The rest represents a difference between price and the marginal cost of production—increased profits. This is the area *BIHD.* Thus, the societal loss is represented by two triangles, *EGC* and *HFI.* The triangle *EGC* is similar to the loss to consumers arising from a monopolist's raising his price. The triangle *HFI* is a waste

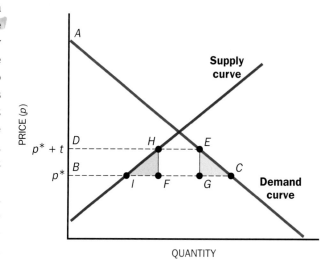

Figure 19.5

QUANTIFYING THE NET LOSS TO SOCIETY FROM IMPOSING TARIFFS

The societal loss from imposing tariffs is represented by the two triangles, *EGC* and *HFI.*

of resources resulting from the cost of domestic production exceeding the costs of purchasing the good abroad, as the economy expands production because of the tariff.

QUOTAS

Rather than setting tariffs, many countries impose **quotas**—limits on the amount of foreign goods that can be imported. For instance, in the 1950s, the United States imposed a quota on the amount of oil that could be imported, and until 2005 strict quotas controlled imports of textiles.

Producers often prefer quotas. Because the quantity imported is limited, the domestic price increases above the international price. Quotas enable domestic producers to know precisely the magnitude of the foreign supply. If foreign producers become more efficient or if exchange rates change in their favor, they still cannot sell any more. In that sense, quotas provide domestic producers with greater certainty than do tariffs, insulating them from the worst threats of competition.

Quotas and tariffs both succeed in raising the domestic price above the price at which the good could be obtained abroad. Both thus protect domestic producers. There is, however, one important difference: quotas enable those possessing permits to import to earn a profit by buying goods at the international price abroad and selling at the higher domestic price. The government is, in effect, giving away its tariff revenues. These profits are referred to as **quota rents.**

VOLUNTARY EXPORT RESTRAINTS

In recent years, international agreements have reduced the level of tariffs and restricted the use of quotas. Accordingly, countries have sought to protect themselves from the onslaught of foreign competition by other means. One approach that became popular in the 1980s was the use of *voluntary export restraints* (VERs). Rather than limiting imports of automobiles, for example, the United States persuaded Japan to limit its exports.

There are two interpretations of why Japan might have been willing to go along with this VER. One is that it worried the United States might take a stronger action, such as imposing quotas. From Japan's perspective, VERs are clearly preferable to quotas, because VERs allow the quota rents to accrue to Japanese firms. A second interpretation is that VERs enable Japanese car producers to act collectively in their self-interest to reduce production and raise prices, engaging in a kind of collusion otherwise illegal under American antitrust laws. The VER "imposed" output reductions on the Japanese car producers that they would have chosen themselves if they had been permitted to under law. No wonder, then, that they agreed to go along! The cost to the American consumer of the Japanese VER was enormous. American consumers paid more than $100,000 in higher prices for every American job created.

OTHER NONTARIFF BARRIERS

VERs and quotas are the clearest nontariff barriers, but today they are probably not the most important. A host of regulations have the same effect of imposing barriers to trade. For instance, health-related regulations have been abused in ways that restrict trade. When, in 1996, Russia threatened to halt U.S. exports of chickens on the grounds that its health regulations were not satisfied, U.S. chicken exporters were faced with a nontariff barrier. Various types of regulations have been used to establish nontariff barriers.

During the 1980s, as tariff barriers were being reduced, nontariff barriers increased. A study by the International Monetary Fund concluded that whereas about one-eighth of all U.S. imports were affected by protectionism in 1980, by the middle of the 1990s the figure had risen to one-fourth. It is estimated that trade barriers (including nontariff barriers) may prevent consumers and business from buying as much as $110 billion in imports they would otherwise have purchased. Japan was particularly harmed by these actions. By the early 1990s, about 40 percent of Japan's exports to the United States were limited by some form of U.S. protectionism.

Wrap-Up

COMPARISON OF QUOTAS AND TARIFFS

Both can be used to restrict imports by the same amount, with the same effect on consumers and domestic producers.

In the case of quotas, the difference between domestic price and international price accrues to the importer, who enjoys a quota rent.

In the case of tariffs, the difference accrues to government as tariff revenues.

VERs (voluntary export restraints) are equivalent to quotas, except that the quota rents are given to foreign producers.

"FAIR TRADE" LAWS

Most people believe competition should be fair. When someone can undersell them, they suspect foul play. The government has imposed a variety of laws to ensure that there is genuine and fair competition domestically. Laws have also been enacted by most countries to ensure "fair competition" in international trade. But most economists believe that in practice these are protectionist measures, reducing competition and restricting imports. To ensure fair competition, economists argue that the same laws that apply domestically should be extended internationally—that is, there should not be two standards of fairness, one applying domestically, the other internationally. The two most important "fair trade" laws that represent nontariff barriers are antidumping laws and countervailing duties.

International Perspective
SURROGATE COUNTRIES AND CANADIAN GOLF CARTS

Question: How, if Canada did not produce golf carts, could the cost of Canadian golf carts be used to accuse Poland of dumping? Answer: The United States sometimes achieves wonders when its markets are at stake.

The standard criterion for judging whether a country is dumping is whether it is selling commodities on the U.S. market at prices below those for which it sells them at home or elsewhere, or at prices below the costs of production. For nonmarket economies, the Department of Commerce formulated a special criterion: Is the price below what it would have cost to produce the good in a "comparable" (or "surrogate") country?

The Department of Commerce, which is responsible for implementing the law, knows no shame. In a famous case involving Polish golf carts, it decided that the country most like Poland was Canada—at a time when Poland's per capita income was a fraction of Canada's, and when Canada did not make comparable golf carts. Thus, the Commerce Department faced

the question: What would it have cost for Canada to produce these golf carts, had it chosen to do so? Not surprisingly, the resulting cost estimate was higher than the price the real golf carts were being sold for in the United States, and Poland was found guilty of dumping.

Similar charges have been made on similar grounds against Russian sales of natural resources. For years, Western countries had preached to the Soviet Union and the other socialist countries the virtues of the market. Beginning in 1989, with the demise of communism, former iron-curtain countries sought to transform their economies into market economies. Under the old regime, these countries had traded mainly with themselves, and generally engaged in barter. In the new era, they sought to enter international markets, like any other market economy.

Though the design and production quality of many of its manufactured goods made them unsuitable for Western markets, Russia had a wealth of natural resources—including uranium and aluminum—that it could produce on a competitive basis. Moreover, with the reduction of defense expenditures— good news from virtually every perspective—Russia's demand for many of these raw materials was greatly reduced.

American producers attempted to discourage Russian exports by filing, or threatening to file, dumping charges. Though Russia was probably not selling these commodities at prices below those prevailing at home or elsewhere, or at prices below the cost of production, the "surrogate" country criterion made the dumping charges a very real threat. Russia agreed to a cutback in aluminum production in 1994, to be matched by cutbacks in other countries.

To the Commerce and State Departments, this may have seemed a reasonable way to avoid trade conflict. But consumers paid dearly, in higher prices for aluminum and products using aluminum.

Antidumping Laws Dumping refers to the sale of products overseas at prices that are not only lower than those in the home country but below cost. Normally, consumers greet discounted sales with enthusiasm. If Russia is willing to sell aluminum to the United States at low prices, why should we complain? One possible concern is that by selling below cost, the foreign companies hope to drive American firms out of business. Once they have established a monopoly position, they can raise prices. In such a case, American consumers gain only in the short run. In competitive markets, however, this scenario simply cannot occur, for firms will have no power to raise prices. In almost all of the cases in which dumping has been found, markets are sufficiently competitive that foreign firms have no hope of establishing monopoly positions.

As administered, the antidumping laws are more frequently used as a protectionist tool. If dumping is discovered, a duty (tariff) is levied equal to the difference between the (calculated) cost of production and the price. Critics of the dumping laws worry that other countries will imitate American practices. If so, just as the international community has eliminated tariff barriers, a whole new set of trade barriers will have been erected.

Countervailing Duties A second trade practice widely viewed as unfair is for governments to subsidize domestic firms' production or exports. For example, the government may give certain domestic industries tax breaks or pay a portion of the firms' costs. These subsidies give the companies receiving them an unfair advantage. Trade is determined on the basis not of comparative advantage but of relative subsidy levels.

The usual logic of economics seems to be reversed. If some foreign government wants to subsidize American consumers, who benefit from the lower prices, why should they complain? Presumably, they would have a grievance only if the subsidies are part of a policy intended to drive American firms out of business and establish a monopoly position, after which prices will be raised. Most foreign subsidies do not fall into this category.

Opposition to these subsidies arises from the companies who see their businesses hurt. While the gains to consumers outweigh the losses to businesses, the gain to each consumer is small, and consumers are not well organized. Producers, being far better organized, are able and willing to bring their case to Washington. In response, Congress has passed laws allowing the U.S. government to impose **countervailing duties,** that is, taxes that offset any advantage provided by these subsidies.

But even governments that preach against other countries providing subsidies engage in the practice themselves, most commonly in agriculture. At various times, the U.S. government has subsidized the export and production of wheat, pork, peaches, and a host of other commodities.

Political and Economic Rationale for Protection

Free trade, by enabling each country to concentrate production where it has a comparative advantage, can make all countries better off. Why is protection nevertheless so popular? The basic reason is simple: protection raises prices. While the losses to consumers from higher prices exceed the gains to producers in higher profits, producers are well organized and consumers are not;

hence producers' voices are heard more clearly in the political process than are consumers'.

There is an important check on firms' ability to use the political process to advance their special interests: the interests of exporters, who realize that if the United States closes off its markets to imports, other countries will reciprocate. Thus, exporting firms like Boeing have forcefully advocated an international regime of freer and fairer trade through the kind of international agreements that will be described in the next section.

But before turning to a review of these international agreements, we need to take a closer look at some of the other economic aspects of protection. While free trade may make the country as a whole better off, certain groups may actually become worse off. Those especially affected include displaced firms and workers, low-wage workers, and those in industries that enjoyed limited competition without free trade.

DISPLACED FIRMS AND WORKERS

China has a comparative advantage in inexpensive textiles while the United States has a comparative advantage in manufacturing complex goods, like advanced telephone exchanges. If the United States starts to import textiles from China, U.S. textile manufacturers may be driven out of business, and their workers will have to find work elsewhere. More than offsetting these losses are the gains to the export industries. In principle, the gainers in those industries could more than compensate the losers, but such compensation is seldom made: hence, the losers oppose moves to open trade.

Typically, economists shed few tears for the lost profits of the businesses that are hurt when trade becomes open. After all, such a loss is just one of the risks that businesses face, and for which they are typically well compensated. New innovations destroy old businesses. But barring the door to new technologies or to cheaper products from abroad is bad economics—and bad economic policy.

Often, however, more sympathy is felt for workers affected by trade—though there is no reason why concern should be greater over displacements caused by open trade than by new innovations. When the economy is running at close to full employment, workers who lose their jobs typically do find new positions. But they often go through a transition period of unemployment, and when they eventually do find a new job, chances are good that their wages will be lower (in the United States, in recent years, a worker who succeeds in finding full-time employment experiences on average a 10 percent wage decline). While these particular laborers are worse off, workers as a whole benefit, because those who get newly created jobs in the export industries are paid far more (on average 13 to 15 percent more) than the average for the economy. Concern about the transitional costs borne by displaced workers has motivated Congress to pass laws to provide special assistance for these workers in finding new jobs and obtaining the requisite training.

BEGGAR-THY-NEIGHBOR POLICIES

Concerns about unemployment have provided the strongest motivation for protectionist policies. The argument is simple: if Americans do not buy foreign goods, they will spend the money at home, thereby creating more jobs for Americans. Deliberate attempts to increase national output and employment by reducing imports are called **beggar-thy-neighbor policies,** because the jobs gained in one country are at the expense of jobs lost in another. Such efforts ignore an important fact: if we do not buy goods from abroad, foreign purchasers will not buy our goods. As a result, U.S. exports to other countries will fall in tandem with our imports from other countries, causing jobs in our export industries to disappear. The benefits of specialization are denied to everyone, and national incomes fall.

The worst instances of these beggar-thy-neighbor policies occurred at the onset of the Great Depression. In 1930, the United States passed the Hawley-Smoot Tariff Act, raising tariffs on many products to a level that effectively prohibited many imports. Other countries retaliated. As U.S. imports declined, incomes in Europe and elsewhere in the world fell. As incomes declined and as these countries imposed retaliatory tariffs, they bought fewer goods from the United States. U.S. exports plummeted, contributing further to the economic downturn in the United States. The downturn in international trade that was set off by the Hawley-Smoot Tariff Act, charted in Figure 19.6, is often pointed to as a major factor contributing to the depth and severity of the Great Depression.

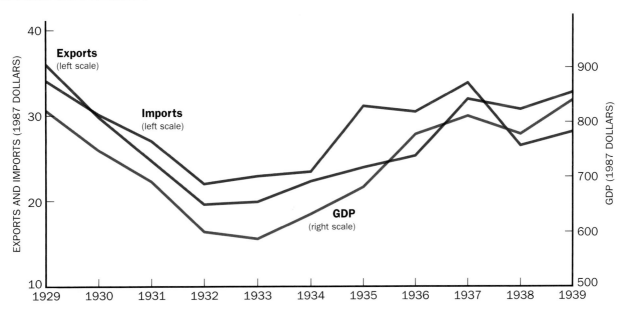

Figure 19.6

THE DECLINE IN INTERNATIONAL TRADE AND THE GREAT DEPRESSION

U.S. exports and imports fell dramatically during the Great Depression. One contributing factor in the decline in trade was the Hawley-Smoot Tariff Act, passed in 1930.

SOURCE: Bureau of Economic Analysis (www.bea.gov).

INTERNATIONAL TRADE AND JOBS

Restricting imports as a way of creating jobs tends to be counterproductive.

It is the responsibility of macroeconomic policy, not trade policy, to maintain the economy at full employment.

WAGES IN AFFECTED SECTORS

Beyond these short-run problems of transition and unemployment, long-run problems may face workers in affected sectors. The United States has a comparative advantage in producing goods such as airplanes and high-tech products that require highly skilled workers. As the United States exports more of these goods, its demand for these workers increases, driving up their wages. Similarly, the United States has a comparative disadvantage in producing goods that require much unskilled labor, such as lower-quality textiles. As imports compete against these U.S. industries and their production decreases, the demand for unskilled labor decreases. As a result, the wages of the unskilled workers are driven down.

This loss in income for unskilled workers is often blamed on imports from third world countries like China, where wages are but a fraction of those in the United States. The consensus among economists who have looked closely at the matter is that international trade explains a relatively small part of the decline in wages—perhaps 20 percent. Nonetheless, those who see their livelihood being threatened are among the most ardent advocates of trade restrictions. Again, economists argue that the appropriate response is not to restrict trade but to increase skills. The workers gaining the skills are better off, as their wages rise commensurately with the increase in their productivity. In addition, as more workers become skilled, the supply of workers still unskilled is reduced; and the smaller supply of unskilled workers leads to a rise in their real wages, offsetting the adverse effects of trade.

EFFECTS OF TRADE ON WAGES

International trade may lower wages of unskilled U.S. labor and those working in industries where competition is limited.

International trade raises wages of skilled U.S. workers.

INCREASED COMPETITION

International trade also has other adverse effects in industries in which competition is limited. Limited competition enables firms to enjoy monopoly or oligopoly profits.

DISTRIBUTION AND TRADE LIBERALIZATION

Trade liberalization may make a country as a whole better off, but it does not make everyone in the country better off. The gains to the winners are large enough that, in principle, any losers could be compensated, to everyone's benefit. But in practice, compensation is seldom made. Thus, trade liberalization often entails trade-offs to balance the gains of one group in the economy against the losses of another group. The problem is that often the losers are among the poorest in the country. For example, trade liberalization threatens to force low-paid textile workers in United States into unemployment. It is little comfort for the textile workers in South Carolina to know that new jobs are being created for aircraft engineers in Seattle or that all American consumers of textile products are now better off. In the United States, however, labor markets work reasonably well, and the laid-off textile worker can eventually get a new job, though often at markedly reduced wages.

While low-wage textile workers in the United States are hurt by trade liberalization, low-wage textile workers in developing economies gain. Trade liberalization increases the demand for the textiles they produce, and thus increases the demand for their labor. Unfortunately, matters can be far bleaker for those in developing countries to whom trade liberalization brings increased competition. In many developing countries, unemployment is 15 percent or more, so the loss of a job is likely to have severe consequences.

In Mexico, since the North American Free Trade Agreement was enacted wages have soared for those who produce goods for American car companies or other firms near the border of Texas. But in the south of Mexico, the poor have become even poorer. Highly subsidized American corn has depressed the already low incomes of Mexican farmers. To be sure, urban workers benefit, since they can buy corn for a lower price than would otherwise have been possible.

When diverse groups are affected so differently, it is not clear whether trade liberalization is a good thing *in the absence of policies to address its distributional effects.* But such assessments are not made by economists; in democracies, they are left to the political processes. Society as a whole does benefit from trade liberalization, and the role of the economist is to point out this potential for gain. Economists also have a role to play in explaining who will be affected, and to what degree.

Workers often receive some of these extra profits: particularly when the industries are unionized, they may earn wages far higher than workers of comparable skill employed elsewhere in the economy. After international trade introduces more competition, monopoly and oligopoly profits get competed away. Firms are forced to pay competitive wages—that is, the lowest wage that they can for workers with a given skill.

From the perspective of the overall economy, this competition that erodes market power and induces greater efficiency and responsiveness to consumers is one of the major virtues of free trade. From the perspective of those who see their higher wages and profits vanishing, it is one of free trade's major vices.

THE INFANT INDUSTRY ARGUMENT

While job loss and decreased wages and profits from international competition provide much of the political motivation behind protection, economists have asked if there are any *legitimate* arguments for protection. That is, are there circumstances where protection may be in the *national* interest, and not just in the interests of those being protected? Two arguments have been put forward.

The first is the **infant industry argument.** Costs in new industries are often high, dropping as experience is gained. The infant industry argument is that firms, particularly in less-developed countries, will never be able to get the experience required to produce efficiently unless they are protected from foreign competition.

Economists have traditionally responded to this argument skeptically. If it pays to enter the industry, eventually entrants will earn profits. Thus, the firm should be willing to initially charge a price below cost to gain the necessary experience, because today's losses will be more than offset by future profits. But more recently, the infant industry argument has found more favor. Firms can operate at a loss only if they can borrow funds. If capital markets do not work well, firms may not be able to borrow even if their eventual prospects are reasonable. Such market failures are a particular danger in less-developed countries.

This may be a legitimate argument. But it points to a need not for protection but for assistance, which can take the form of loans or direct subsidies. Economists argue for direct assistance rather than protection because the assistance is trans-

e-Insights

TRADE LIBERALIZATION IN INFORMATION TECHNOLOGY AND FINANCIAL SERVICES

In recent years, there have been important trade agreements in information technology (IT) and financial services. This is a distinct change from the past, when trade agreements focused on traded goods, such as cars, steel, and textiles. But the two areas draw markedly different reactions in many developing countries: while IT liberalization has been welcome, there is extensive opposition to liberalizations in financial services. Why the difference?

Economic theory says that unilateral liberalization—opening up one's market to the cheaper goods of foreigners—is a good thing. Even if domestic producers are worse off, their losses are more than offset by the gains of consumers. Unfortunately, producers often have a greater voice in the political process, and consumers cannot unite to compensate the producers for their losses. Countries therefore often resist trade liberalization. But IT is different. Most developing countries do not have a large IT sector that would be hurt by liberalization. Instead, both producers and consumers in developing countries are purchasers of IT products, and both gain by having access to IT at lower prices.

Financial service liberalization is quite a different matter. The existing domestic banks in developing countries fear greater competition from foreign banks. The greater efficiency of foreign banks is not their only worry; depositors may feel safer putting their money in a large American or European bank than in a small domestic bank. In addition, many firms in developing countries believe that the foreign banks are more likely to lend to Coca-Cola and IBM than to small domestic firms, and there are some grounds for these concerns. The government, too, may worry that the foreign banks will be less subject to pressure from the government. Sometimes such pressure is part of corruption—members of the government lean on the bank to lend to their friends. But it can also be part of economic policy—the government leans on the bank to increase lending in an economic downturn and to contract lending when the economy is overheated. In developing countries, this "guidance" from the government may be an important tool for macroeconomic stability.

Today, as many countries liberalize their financial markets, they are asking, "How can we gain the advantages of the new competition without suffering the disadvantages?" Until they find effective ways of ensuring a flow of capital to small domestic businesses, banks in developing countries will find powerful allies in resisting financial market liberalization.

parent: everyone can see that it is a subsidy to producers. Economists criticize protection because it is a hidden tax on consumers, with the proceeds transferred to producers. The lack of transparency encourages industries to spend resources on persuading government to impose these hidden taxes that benefit themselves.

STRATEGIC TRADE THEORY

Another argument for protection is that it can give a country a strategic trade advantage over rivals by helping to reduce domestic costs. There may be economies of scale: the larger the level of production, the lower the marginal costs. Protection ensures a large domestic sales base, and therefore a low marginal cost. The instances in which **strategic trade theory** might provide a rationale for protection appear relatively rare, however. Even then, it tends to be effective only when foreign governments do not retaliate by taking similar actions.

International Cooperation

Recognizing both the temptation of shortsighted trade policies and the potential gains from trade, nations large and small have engaged since World War II in a variety of efforts to reduce trade barriers.

GATT AND THE WTO

The **General Agreement on Tariffs and Trade (GATT),** an organization established after World War II, was replaced in 1995 by the **World Trade Organization (WTO).** GATT was founded on three guiding principles: *reciprocity*—if one country lowered its tariffs, it could expect other countries in GATT to lower theirs; *nondiscrimination*— no member of GATT could offer a special trade deal that favored only one or a few other countries; and *transparency*—import quotas and other nontariff barriers to trade should be converted into tariffs to allow their effective impact to be ascertained.

The lowering of trade barriers has proceeded in a number of stages, called *rounds* (the Kennedy Round, completed in 1967; the Tokyo Round, completed in 1979; the Uruguay Round, completed in 1994, and the Doha [Qatar] Round, currently slated to be completed by the end of 2005). Collectively, the rounds have reduced tariffs on industrial goods markedly, from an average of 40 percent in 1947 to less than 5 percent today.

The Uruguay Round produced agreements to reduce agricultural subsidies and to ensure that intellectual property rights—patents and copyrights—were respected. It also created the WTO to help enforce the trade agreements. Previously, a country that believed it was suffering from an unfair trade practice could bring a case to a GATT panel that would examine the evidence. However, there was little in the way of effective enforcement of subsequent decisions. Under the WTO, a country injured by an unfair trade practice will be authorized to engage in retaliatory actions. For example,

Brazil won a major WTO case in 2004 against U.S. cotton subsidies. That decision is under appeal; if the United States loses the appeal and then fails to remove its subsidies to cotton farmers, Brazil will be able to retaliate against U.S. exports to Brazil.

The Doha Round began in 2001 and almost collapsed in 2003 when delegates from developing nations walked out in protest over the subsidies that developed nations such as the United States and members of the European Union provide to their farmers. The European Union has agreed in principle to eliminate exports subsidies on farm products; the United States has not yet made a similar commitment.

THE GROWING PROTEST AGAINST THE WTO

In December 1999, the WTO held a meeting in Seattle to launch a new round of trade negotiations. But thousands of protesters—some violent—dominated the stage. What brought on such a vehement reaction? Old-fashioned protectionist sentiment played a role, but there were other important factors.

Some WTO critics believed that the agenda in previous rounds of trade negotiations had been set by the more advanced industrial countries—to further their interests—and that the outcomes reflected their economic power. Not only had they gained the lion's share of the benefits, but they had done so at the expense of some poorer countries. The World Bank estimated that after the round of trade negotiations concluded in 1994, the poorest region in the world, sub-Saharan Africa, was actually worse off. While poorer countries were forced to cut their tariffs against goods produced in the more advanced industrial countries, the more advanced industrial countries continued to protect their agricultural sectors. While financial services had been opened up, industries that relied more heavily on unskilled workers, such as the construction and maritime industries, remained closed.

Thousands of protesters converged in Seattle to protest the WTO conference held there in December 1999.

Environmental and human rights issues were two other prominent areas of intense debate. Environmentalists and human rights advocates wanted to use trade policy to help achieve their objectives. They worried that countries with inadequate protections of the environment or of labor rights would be able to undercut American firms, whose losses would increase pressure within the United States to erode those standards here. The insistence by some on including clauses in trade agreements concerning labor and the environment was met with an equally adamant resistance by others, threatening to stall all efforts at trade liberalization. There was consensus on a few issues—for example, countries should not be allowed to export goods produced by child or prison labor. But beyond that, the debate raged on and it is likely to continue in the foreseeable future.

Case in Point

THE BANANA WAR

How could a dispute over bananas lead to unemployment among Scottish cashmere workers? The explanation lies in the spillover effect of the banana war between the United States and the European Union (EU). This dispute revolved around the claim by the United States that the EU was following discriminatory trade practices.

Beginning in 1993, the EU imposed a banana import tariff that favored producers in former European colonies in the Caribbean, Africa, and the Pacific over those in Latin America. The United States and five Latin American countries complained to the WTO. The United States claimed that EU banana import tariffs were harming the country. Since the United States does not produce bananas, one might reasonably ask how it could be harmed by the EU's policy on banana imports. While not a producer itself, the United States is home to two food distributors, Chiquita Brands and Dole, that do grow bananas in Central America.

The WTO ruled that the EU regime was in violation of GATT and ordered the EU to change its policies. The EU did, instituting a new banana import regime on January 1, 1999. However, the United States and Latin America banana producers argued that the new policy still effectively discriminated against them, and the dispute was sent to the WTO Dispute Settlement Body. The United States claimed victory in the banana war when, in April 1999, the Dispute Settlement Body accepted the results of the WTO arbitrators, agreeing that the new EU policies harmed the United States. This decision paved the way for the United States to impose sanctions against EU products. The WTO ruled that the United States could impose $191 million in sanctions against the EU, an amount determined by estimating the economic damages to the United States resulting from the EU policies.

To retaliate against Europe, the United States imposed 100 percent tariffs on a range of European products, effectively doubling their prices in the United States. The list of goods hit by the punitive tariffs included Scottish cashmere, Italian cheese, and German coffee makers. The targeted products were chosen to bring maximum political pressures on the EU. The WTO ruling allowed the United States to impose these high tariffs until the EU revised its banana policy to eliminate discrimination against Latin American producers. The EU conceded defeat, and the banana war ended.

REGIONAL TRADING BLOCS

GATT and WTO have made some progress in reducing trade barriers among all countries. But the difficulties of reaching agreements involving so many parties have made progress slow. In the meantime, many countries have formed *regional trade blocs,* agreeing with their more immediate neighbors not only to eliminate trade barriers but also to facilitate the flow of capital and labor. Perhaps the most important of these is the **European Union,** the successor to the *Common Market,* which now embraces most of Europe. The **North American Free Trade Agreement, NAFTA,** creates a free trade zone within North America—that is, an area within which goods and services trade freely, without tariffs or other import restrictions. There are also many smaller free trade zones, such as those between New Zealand and Australia, and among groups of countries in Latin America and in Central America.

While the gains from internationally coordinated reductions in trade barriers are clear, the gains from regional trading blocs are more controversial. Reducing trade barriers within a region encourages trade by members of the trading bloc. Lowering barriers among the countries involved results in **trade creation.** But it also leads to **trade diversion.** Trade is diverted away from countries that are not members of the bloc but might, in fact, have a comparative advantage in a particular commodity. Under these conditions, the global net benefits will be positive if the trade creation exceeds the trade diversion. Typically, when trade blocs are formed, tariffs against outsiders are harmonized. If the external trade barriers are harmonized at the lowest common level (rather than at the average or highest levels) at the same time that internal trade barriers are lowered, the effects of trade creation are more likely to exceed those of trade diversion.

Expanding regional trading blocs to cover investment flows raises particular anxieties, especially when the bloc includes countries with very different standards of living. During the debates over NAFTA, some argued that Mexico would suck up huge amounts of investment that would otherwise have gone to businesses in the United States. According to this view, American firms would move to Mexico to take advantage of the low-wage labor and the capital that flowed to Mexico would not be available for investment in the United States.

Such arguments failed to take into account that capital markets were already global. Capital flows to good investment opportunities wherever they are. Good opportunities to invest in the United States will attract capital, regardless of how much Americans invest in Mexico. Investment barriers impede this flow of capital to its most productive use, thereby lowering world economic efficiency.

Often trade debates are based on a "zero-sum" view of the world, the belief that when one country (Mexico) gains, another (the United States) must lose. For example, many people argue that when a country imports, it loses jobs: the gains to foreign workers from their exports are at the expense of domestic firms to which those jobs somehow belonged. The debate over "outsourcing"—the move by U.S. firms to import goods and services that these same firms formerly produced in the United States—is of this sort. Earlier in this chapter we learned what was wrong with this argument. The theory of comparative advantage says that when countries specialize in what they produce best, *both* countries are better off. Workers enjoy higher

THE WORLD TRADE ORGANIZATION

The World Trade Organization (WTO) is the global organization that deals with the rules of trade between nations. The WTO's Web site, www.wto.org, contains material for a range of users, from the general public to students, academics, and trade specialists. It includes introductions to WTO activities and a large database of official documents. In recent years, the WTO has become a focus of protest by those opposed to globalization and free trade. One group that has actively campaigned against the WTO is Global Trade Watch, whose Web site (www.citizen.org/trade/) provides information on the views of those fighting what they identify as the WTO's model of globalization.

wages when they move into sectors where their productivity is highest, and consumers benefit from the lower prices. So too with investment. When investment flows to where its return is highest, world output (income) is increased.

But just as not everyone necessarily gains from trade according to comparative advantage, so too not everyone will necessarily gain from the free flow of capital. There will be some investment diversion from other countries to Mexico, as Mexico becomes more attractive to investors throughout the world because of its improved access to the huge American market. Most economists believe that the net effect on investment in the United States will be negligible, and could even be positive. Industries within the United States that see their opportunities expand by selling more to Mexico will increase their investment, more than offsetting the reduced investment from firms that decline in the face of competition from Mexican imports.

In fact, investment flows augment the gains from trade that would occur in their absence because there are important trade-investment links. American companies producing abroad tend to use more parts from America, just as French companies producing abroad tend to use more French parts. Thus, flows of investment often serve as a precursor to exports.

Wrap-Up

AREAS OF INTERNATIONAL COOPERATION

Multilateral trade agreements—WTO
   Based on principles of reciprocity, nondiscrimination, and transparency

Regional trade agreements—NAFTA, European Union
   Risk of trade diversion rather than trade creation
   May be better able to address complicated issues, such as those involving investment

Review and Practice

SUMMARY

1. The benefits of economic interdependence apply to individuals and firms within a country as well as to countries within the world. No individual and no country is self-sufficient.

2. The principle of comparative advantage asserts that countries should export the goods in which their production costs are relatively low.

3. Specialization tends to increase productivity for three reasons: specializing eliminates the time it takes a worker to switch from one production task to another, workers who repeat a task become more skilled at it, and specialization creates a fertile environment for invention.

4. A country's comparative advantage can arise from natural endowments, acquired endowments, superior knowledge, specialization, or interactions of these factors.

5. There is a basic difference between trade among individuals and trade among countries: trade among countries may actually leave some individuals within the country worse off. Though free trade enhances national income, fears about job loss and wage reductions among low-skilled workers have led to demands for protection.

6. Countries protect themselves in a variety of ways besides imposing tariffs. The most important nontariff barriers are quotas, voluntary export restraints, and regulatory barriers. Quotas and voluntary export restraints are now banned by international agreement.

7. While all countries benefit from free trade, some groups within a country may be harmed. In the United States, unskilled workers and those in industries where, without trade, there is limited competition may see their wages fall. Some workers may lose their jobs and may require assistance to find new ones.

8. Laws nominally intended to ensure fair trade—such as antidumping laws and countervailing duties—often are used as protectionist measures.

9. Beggar-thy-neighbor policies, which attempt to protect jobs by limiting imports, tend to be counterproductive.

10. The WTO, which replaced GATT, provides a framework within which trade barriers can be reduced. It is based on reciprocity, nondiscrimination, and transparency.

KEY TERMS

imports
exports
bilateral trade
multilateral trade
absolute advantage
comparative advantage
protectionism
free trade
commercial policies
tariffs
quotas
quota rents
dumping
countervailing duties
beggar-thy-neighbor policies
infant industry argument
strategic trade theory
General Agreement on Tariffs and Trade (GATT)
World Trade Organization (WTO)
European Union
North American Free Trade Agreement (NAFTA)
trade creation
trade diversion

REVIEW QUESTIONS

1. Why are all voluntary trades mutually beneficial?

2. Does a country with an absolute advantage in a product necessarily have a comparative advantage in that product? Can a country with an absolute disadvantage in a product have a comparative advantage in that product? Explain.

3. Why does specialization tend to increase productivity?

4. "A country's comparative advantage is dictated by its natural endowments." Discuss.

5. What are the various ways in which countries seek to protect their industries against foreign imports?

6. How do tariffs and quotas differ?

7. Why are consumers worse off as a result of the imposition of a tariff?

8. What are nontariff barriers to international trade?

9. How is it possible that while there are gains to free trade, some groups are harmed? Which are the groups in the United States that are most adversely affected?

10. What are beggar-thy-neighbor policies? What are their consequences?

11. What is meant by trade diversion versus trade creation?

PROBLEMS

1. David Ricardo illustrated the principle of comparative advantage in terms of the trade between England and Portugal in wine (port) and wool. Suppose in England it takes 120 laborers to produce a certainty quantity of wine, while in Portugal it takes only 80 laborers to produce the same quantity. Similarly, in England it takes 100 laborers to produce a certain quantity of wool, while in Portugal it takes only 90. Draw the opportunity set for each country, assuming each has 72,000 laborers. Assume each country commits half its labor to each product in the absence of trade, and designate that point in your graph. Now describe a new production plan, with trade, that can benefit both countries.

2. If you continue with the example of Problem 1, which country has an absolute advantage in wine? in wool? Which country has a comparative advantage in wine? in wool?

3. For many years, an international agreement called the Multifiber Agreement limited the amount of textiles that the developed economies of North America and Europe could buy from poor countries in Latin America and Asia. Textiles can be produced by relatively unskilled labor with a reasonably small amount of capital. Who benefited from the protectionism of the Multifiber Agreement? Who suffered? The Multifiber Agreement expired on January 1, 2005. Who should benefit from its end? Who will suffer?

4. Both the European Union and the United States produce cars and television shows. Assume the labor costs (in worker hours) required for the production of cars and programs is as follows:

LABOR COSTS OF PRODUCING CARS AND TV SHOWS (WORKER HOURS):

	European Union	United States
Labor required to make a car	100	80
Labor required to to produce a TV show	600	400

Assume each region has 240,000 worker hours to divide between producing cars and television shows. Initially, assume workers are divided equally between producing cars and television shows.

(a) What are the initial levels of production of cars and TV shows in each region? What is total production in the two regions?

(b) Draw the production possibilities curves for the two regions.

(c) Which region has an absolute advantage in producing cars? Which region has an absolute advantage in producing television shows?

(d) Which region has a comparative advantage in producing cars? Which region has a comparative advantage in producing television shows?

(e) Starting with the initial levels of production, demonstrate how comparative advantage can be exploited to raise joint production of cars by 10 while leaving television show output unchanged.

5. In 2002, President George W. Bush imposed tariffs on foreign-produced steel. Who gained from this policy? Who lost? (In 2003, the WTO ruled that the tariffs were illegal.)

6. Many Americans have objected to the importation of textiles and garments from poor countries because the conditions of production in those countries is much worse than it is for most American workers. If these imports from poor countries are reduced, who benefits? Who loses?

7. If Mexican workers receive a third of the wages that U.S. workers do, why don't all American firms move down to Mexico?

8. If Mexico becomes a more attractive place to invest, is the United States helped or hurt?

Learning Goals

In this chapter, you will learn

1 How technological change and imperfect competition are linked

2 About the role of patents in promoting innovation

3 Why basic research is a public good

4 How governments promote technological progress

Chapter 20

TECHNOLOGICAL CHANGE

For much of the twentieth century, the United States has led the world in discovering and applying new technologies. Alexander Graham Bell and the telephone, the Wright brothers and the airplane, Thomas Edison and a host of electrical devices, for example, are all familiar early success stories. This tradition of innovation and invention continued as Americans came up with products such as the transistor and the laser. U.S. companies such as IBM, Eastman Kodak, and Xerox grew to become household names. More recently, Intel, Microsoft, Google, and Genentech have experienced rapid growth and financial success based on their innovations.

The great strength of the market economy has been its ability to increase productivity, raise living standards, and innovate. Yet the basic competitive model on which we focused in Part Two simply *assumed* the state of technology as given. In fact, the huge changes in living standards that modern economies have experienced over the past two hundred years and the truly amazing differences between the economy in 1900 and the economy in 2000 are in large part due to technological change. We are not manufacturing more of the same goods as the economy in 1900. We are making goods that the people of 1900 never dreamed of. Instead of producing more horse-drawn carriages, we produce cars and airplanes. Instead of producing more horseshoes, we produce tires and jogging shoes. Key to the whole process of economic growth, then, is technological progress—thinking up new ways to do not just old things but also entirely new things. And for this reason, *ideas* are central to explaining economic growth. Indeed, economists estimate that as much as two-thirds of all increases in productivity prior to 1973 were attributable to technological progress.

We have become so accustomed to the current level of technological change that it is hard to believe how different the expectations of reputable economists were in the early 1800s. Real wages of workers were little higher than they had been more than four hundred years earlier, when they had increased after the deaths of a large part of the population of Europe in the bubonic plague created a scarcity of labor. After half a millennium of slow progress at best, Thomas Malthus, one of the greatest economists of that time, saw population expanding more rapidly than the capacity of the economy to support it. His prediction of declining living standards earned economics the nickname of "the dismal science." Today, many continue to predict that the world economy will be unable to grow faster than the population and that living standards must inevitably decline. Such forecasts have been proved wrong over and over again by technological advances.

If we are to understand what determines the pace of innovation, we must go beyond the basic competitive model by recognizing two important factors. First, industries in which technological change is important are almost always imperfectly competitive. Second, the basic competitive model of Part Two assumed that individuals and firms receive all the benefits and pay all the costs of their actions, yet the basic research that leads to technological change can produce important *positive externalities*.

Alexander Graham Bell, Henry Ford, the Wright brothers, and others were all rewarded for their inventions, some richly so. But these inventors reaped but a fraction of what society gained. Similarly, Tim Berners-Lee, Robert Cailliau, and their colleagues at the European particle physics center (CERN) in Geneva, Switzerland, invented the World Wide Web and hypertext markup language, or HTML, in 1990, and since then programmers from around the world have been able to use and benefit from their ideas.[1] The creation of these new products conferred benefits well beyond what consumers had to pay for them.

Links Between Technological Change and Imperfect Competition

In modern industrialized economies, competition often takes the form of trying to develop both new products and new ways of making existing products. In industries in which technological change is important, such as the computer and drug industries, firms devote considerable resources to R & D—research (discovering new ideas, products, and processes) and development (perfecting, for instance, a new product to the point at which it can be brought to the market).

Technological change and imperfect competition are inevitably linked for four major reasons. First, to make R & D expenditures pay, and therefore stimulate innovation, inventions are protected from competition by patents (which are specifically designed for that purpose). Second, industries in which technological change is important typically have high fixed costs—costs that do not change as output increases—and thus their average costs decrease over a wide range of output, another characteristic that limits competition. Third, industries characterized by rapid technological change are also industries in which the benefits of increasing experience in a new production technique can lead to rapidly decreasing costs. Finally, because

---

[1]For an interesting history of the Internet, see Janet Abbate's *Inventing the Internet* (Cambridge: MIT Press, 1999).

THE NEW ECONOMY AND INNOVATION

The new economy sometimes has been characterized as an innovation in the process of innovation. Just as the Industrial Revolution represented a marked change in the way that goods are produced, the new economy has strikingly changed how ideas are produced and disseminated.

A century ago, inventors like Edison, Westinghouse, and the Wright brothers, working alone or with a few assistants, created innovations that transformed the economy, but in the past hundred years the innovation process has been centered around large corporations, such as DuPont and AT&T, with vast laboratories and research budgets in the hundreds of millions of dollars. In the new economy, small firms once again seem to be playing a central role. Evidently, important innovations can occur on a far smaller scale—and then when they are successful, production can be quickly ramped up.

One of the reasons for this speed—and one of the reasons why the Internet has increased productivity—is that these innovations help markets work better. New firms can obtain from others much of what they previously had to provide for themselves, including a sizable portion of their accounting and personnel services. And, at least in some cases, the Internet has significantly lowered the costs of marketing.

Because of the new technologies, and especially the Internet, new ideas can be disseminated far more quickly today. It used to take years, sometimes decades, for discoveries to spread from one part of the economy to another.

The Internet has both increased productivity and enabled new ideas to spread more quickly.

banks are generally unwilling to lend funds to finance R & D, raising capital is difficult for new and small firms. All these factors make entry difficult, and reduce competition of the sort assumed by the basic competitive model.

PATENTS AND THE PRODUCTION OF IDEAS

Ideas appear to be important for technological change, but how are ideas produced? Can we use some of the basic concepts of economics to understand the process?

Most advances result from the deliberate allocation of resources to R & D. The typical large corporation may spend as much as 3 percent of its revenue on research. Though many discoveries have occurred almost by accident (such as Alexander Fleming's discovery of penicillin), in the modern economy these are more the exception than the rule. In order for firms and individuals to have an incentive to allocate their valuable time and resources to research, they must reap a return. They can profit from their work in one of two ways—either by using it themselves to make or sell a product or by licensing the right to use it to others. In either case, however, the inventor has to prevent others from freely using the idea. Otherwise, the inventing firm would have a hard time getting a return, because competition would drive the price down to the marginal cost of producing the product. And the expense of discovery is itself a fixed cost; once it is made and developed, it typically lowers the marginal cost of production. In short, for the inventor to obtain a return, she must be able to exclude users who do not pay for her invention. But some ideas are not very excludable. After Henry Ford had devised the modern assembly line, he might have kept it secret for a while by barring visitors to his factory, but certainly anyone who saw one could set up the same process in another factory. Most software companies keep their source code secret in order to exclude users who have not paid a licensing fee. To increase the incentive to invent, inventors must be given property rights to their work. If property rights are insecure—if a firm planning on undertaking research is

Thinking Like an Economist

INTELLECTUAL PROPERTY RIGHTS AND DISTRIBUTION

As the importance of innovation in the economy has grown, so too has the importance of intellectual property rights. Hence, it was no surprise that the United States pushed for stronger intellectual property protection in the so-called Uruguay Round of the World Trade Organization's trade negotiations, completed in 1994. Many developing countries objected to this initiative.

The key to understanding this dispute lies in the nature of intellectual property rights. How these rights are defined—for instance, the length of the patent—has significant distributional effects. Most inventions are produced in the developed world; stronger intellectual property rights increase the incomes of the patent holders but force consumers in the developing world to pay higher prices. In the past, businesses outside the more advanced countries often freely pirated books, copied CDs, and produced goods such as drugs that were covered by patents. Not surprisingly, many in these developing countries objected to stronger intellectual property rights protections. Two issues in particular grabbed popular attention.

The first concerned the patenting of drugs derived from plants and animals in the developing world. While the drug companies insisted that they should be rewarded for creating useful medicines, those in the developing countries maintained that the medicinal properties of the matter used were already well known and that the companies merely verified them. Moreover, they argued that local people deserved greater returns for preserving the biodiversity on which such drugs depend.

The second issue also concerned drugs. Previously, companies in countries like South Africa had manufactured knockoff drugs, selling them for a fraction of the prices charged by the drug companies from the advanced industrial countries. Under the Uruguay Round agreement, people in developing countries would have to pay whatever the drug companies in the developed countries decided. In the case of life-preserving AIDS drugs, this policy would condemn thousands to a premature death, as few could afford the prices the drug companies insisted on charging. At first, the U.S. government backed the American firms, threatening trade retaliation if South Africa refused to comply. But in the end, the international outrage was so great that the American government and the drug companies caved in and agreed to provide the drugs at cost.

uncertain about whether it will be allowed to capture the benefits of any new process, machine, or article of manufacture that it produces—then fewer resources will be invested in research and the production of these innovations.

Society has another consideration, however. Producing a new idea may be very costly, but it needs to be produced only once. Your laptop embodies thousands of new ideas, but these ideas do not have to be reproduced each time a new laptop is manufactured. The screen, memory chips, and case did have to be produced for each laptop; they are examples of **rivalrous goods**—the memory chips in your laptop cannot be in your roommate's laptop. But the same is not true of the machine's design. Goods whose consumption or use by one person does not exclude consumption by another are **nonrivalrous goods**—a concept we introduced in Chapter 11. If both you and your roommate are taking economics, both of you can use an idea like the law of supply and demand. If your roommate does her homework first, the idea is still available to you when you get around to studying. The marginal cost of *using* such a nonrivalrous good is zero: it costs nothing to use the idea one more time. So from society's perspective, the idea should be freely available to anyone who wants to use it.

Recall that in Chapter 11, a *pure public good* was defined as always available to others and as having a marginal cost of zero when provided to an additional person (it is nonrivalrous). Most types of knowledge come close to satisfying this definition, though it is rarely entirely *impossible* to exclude consumption by others. Thus, we can think of knowledge or an idea as a public good. And like other public goods, it is accompanied by a tension between providing incentives for its production, on the one hand, and ensuring it is widely used, on the other.

Societies address this tension through **patents.** The U.S. Constitution empowers Congress to grant "for limited Times to Authors and Inventors the exclusive Right to their respective Writings and Discoveries." Economists refer to this creative output as **intellectual property.** The limited time for most inventions is currently twenty years. During this period, other producers are precluded from making or using the invention in a product of their own, without the permission of the patent holder. A patent holder may allow others to use its patent (typically for a fee, called a **royalty**) or to sell its product.

THE TRADE-OFF BETWEEN SHORT-TERM EFFICIENCY AND INNOVATION

The patent system grants the inventor a temporary monopoly, enabling her to appropriate some part of the returns on her inventive activity. In Chapter 12, we saw that compared to a firm in a competitive market, a monopoly produces a lower level of output that sells at a higher price. In Chapter 10, we saw that competitive markets, in which price is equal to marginal cost, ensure economic efficiency. In our early analysis, we assumed the state of technology as given. We refer to this kind of economic efficiency as **static efficiency.**

But the overall efficiency of the economy requires harmonizing these short-term concerns with the long-term objectives of stimulating research and innovation. Firms will innovate only if they can reap a return on their investment, and that in

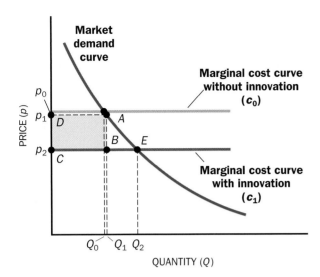

Figure 20.1

ECONOMIC EFFECT OF PATENTS

Here, an innovation has reduced the marginal cost of production from c_0 to c_1. Before the innovation, the equilibrium price is p_0, which equals c_0. However, an innovator with a patent will drop the price to p_1, just below p_0, and sell the quantity Q_1. Total profits are the shaded area $ABCD$. When the patent expires, competitors reenter the market; price falls to p_2, which equals c_1; and profits drop to zero.

turn requires that they possess some degree of monopoly power. An economy in which short- and long-term concerns are appropriately balanced is said to have the property of **dynamic efficiency.**

A key provision of the patent law that affects how static efficiency is weighed against the incentives for innovation necessary for dynamic efficiency is the *life of the patent*. If the life of a patent is short, then firms can appropriate the returns from their innovation only briefly. They thus have less incentive to innovate than if the patent protection (and monopoly) lasted longer. If the life of a patent is long, then they enjoy large incentives to innovate but the benefits of the innovation are reduced. Consumers, in particular, must wait a long time before prices fall. The twenty-year patent period is intended to strike a balance between benefits to consumers and return to investments in R & D.

An Example: The Sweet Melon Company Figure 20.1 illustrates the effect of a patent owned by the Sweet Melon Company on a new, cheaper process for producing frozen watermelon juice. To keep things simple, the marginal cost of production is constant in this example. Before the innovation, all producers face the same marginal cost of c_0. Sweet Melon's innovation reduces the marginal costs of production to c_1. Imagine that this industry is perfectly competitive before the innovation, so that price equals marginal cost, c_0. But now Sweet Melon is able to undercut its rivals. With patent protection, the firm sells the good for slightly less than p_0. Its rivals drop out of the market because at the new, lower price, they cannot break even. Sweet Melon now has the whole market. The company sells the quantity Q_1 at the price p_1, making a profit of AB on each sale. Total profits are shaded area $ABCD$ in the figure. The innovation pays off if the profits received exceed the cost of the research. (These profits may be thought of as "rents" associated with the firm's superior technology.)

When the patent expires, other firms using the less-expensive technology enter the industry. Competition forces the price down to the now lower marginal costs, c_1, and output expands to Q_2. The new equilibrium is at E. Consumers are clearly better off. Static economic efficiency is enhanced, because price is now equal to marginal cost. But Sweet Melon reaps no further return from its expenditures on R & D.

If no patent were available, competitors would immediately copy the new juice-making process, and the price would drop to c_1 as soon as the innovation became available. Sweet Melon would receive absolutely no returns. (In practice, of course, imitation takes time, during which the company would be able to obtain *some* returns from the innovation.) If the patent were made permanent, consumers would enjoy only a small benefit from the innovation, since other companies could not compete. Output would remain at Q_1, slightly greater than the original output, and the price would remain high.

Breadth of Patent Protection How broad a patent's coverage should be is as important as its duration. If an inventor comes up with a product quite similar to, but in some way distinct from, one that has already been patented, can this inventor also be granted a patent? Or does the original patent cover "minor" variants? This issue became critical in the early days of the American automobile industry.

Soon after Henry Ford's Model T had burst into the American marketplace—its sales rocketed from 58,000 in 1909 to 730,000 in 1916—Ford was taken to court for infringing upon the patent of George Baldwin Selden, who argued that his patent covered all self-propelled, gasoline-powered vehicles. Selden tried to force Ford and other pioneers of the automobile industry to pay royalties to him, but Ford successfully challenged the patent claim. Recently controversies have concerned patents in genetic engineering and superconductivity. Does a firm that decodes a fraction of a gene and establishes a use for that information, for example, get a patent? If so, does the patent cover the fraction in question or the whole gene?

The original innovators have every incentive to claim broad patent coverage, encompassing their own product and those that are in any way related. Later entrants argue for narrow coverage, so that they will be allowed to produce variants and applications without paying royalties. As usual in economics, there is a trade-off. Broad coverage ensures that the first inventor reaps more of the returns on her innovation. But excessively broad coverage inhibits follow-on innovation, as others see their returns to further developing the idea squeezed by the royalties they must pay to the original inventor.

Trade Secrets If patents protect the profits of innovation, why do many firms not bother to seek patent protection for their new products and processes? A major factor in this decision is the patent process itself, which requires applicants to disclose the details of the new product or process—information that may be extremely helpful to a firm's rivals in furthering their own R & D programs.

To prevent such disclosure, companies sometimes prefer to keep their own innovations a **trade secret.** A trade secret is simply an innovation or production process that a firm does not disclose to others. The secret formula for Coca-Cola, for example, is not protected by a patent. Trade secrets play an important role in metallurgy; new alloys usually are not patented. But trade secrets have one major disadvantage compared with patents. If a rival firm *independently* discovers the same new process—for making an alloy, say—it can use the process without paying royalties, even though it was second on the scene.

Some of the returns to an invention come simply from being first in the market. Typically, the firm that first introduces a new product has a decided advantage over rivals, as it builds up customer loyalty and a reputation. Latecomers often have a hard time breaking in, even if there is no *patent* or trade secret protection.

Limitations to Patents There are other limitations to the use of patents. Many of the most important ideas are not *patentable*—for instance, the basic mathematics behind the inner workings of computers, discovered by Alan Turing. Turing received no return on his innovation, which was of immense value. The *ideas* that led to the transistor or to the laser—the understandings of the underlying physics—similarly were not patentable.

What is considered patentable has changed over time. A recent new category of patents involves business applications. Thus, the *idea* of a mutual fund with certain distinctive characteristics, or a special type of auction provided by an Internet firm, might today be patentable. Some people believe that these new patents have provided much of the spur for the new economy. But many of these patents are being challenged on the grounds that they are not sufficiently *novel* and nonobvious to deserve protection.

Whitney's cotton gin

ELI WHITNEY AND THE COTTON GIN

Obtaining a patent does not necessarily guarantee the inventor a return on the discovery. Others may "infringe" on the patent—that is, use the idea without paying for it—forcing the inventor to go to court for redress. The story of Eli Whitney and the cotton gin provides a famous example.

Late in the eighteenth century, the textile mills of England and the northern American states were up and humming, but they seemed always to be short of cotton. The kind of cotton grown in the southern United States could have filled the need, but separating the seeds from the cotton was labor-intensive and hence costly. Eli Whitney invented the cotton gin to perform that task inexpensively, then did what an inventor is supposed to do. He applied for a patent and received one in 1794. After finding a partner to put up the money, he started a business to make machines that would clean the seeds out of cotton. The cotton gin turned out to be a wonder, bringing prosperity to the American South. But Whitney received little of the benefit.

The problem was that Whitney's machine was both very effective and very simple. Cotton planters found it easy to copy the cotton gin, and they were careful to make a few minor changes in their versions. When Whitney sued for patent infringement, courts in cotton-growing states tended to find that his patent had not been infringed. Eventually, the states of South Carolina, North Carolina, Tennessee, and Georgia agreed to pay a lump sum to Whitney to purchase the rights to his invention, though the amount paid was barely enough to enable Whitney and his partner to recoup their expenses.

Whitney continued his lifelong career as an inventor, but he never bothered to patent an invention again. As he once wrote: "An invention can be so valuable as to be worthless to the inventor." Whitney's experience was extreme. Today patent laws provide essential protection for scientific firms engaged in producing new and better products. They may choose to share their new technology by selling others the use of their patents in return for royalties, which represent a substantial fraction of the revenues of some firms.

R & D AS A FIXED COST

Patents and trade secrets are not the only reasons why industries in which technological change is important are generally not perfectly competitive. A second explanation is that R & D expenditures are fixed costs. That is, the cost of inventing something does not change with the frequency of its use in production.[2] The size of fixed costs helps determine how competitive an industry is. The larger the fixed costs relative to the size of the market, the greater the likelihood it will have few firms and limited competition.

---

[2]R & D expenditures can themselves be varied. Differences in the expenditure level will affect when new products will be brought to market and whether a firm will beat its rivals in the competition for new products.

Because expenditures on R & D are fixed costs, industries with large R & D expenditures face declining average cost curves up to relatively high levels of output. We saw in Chapter 6 that firms typically have U-shaped average cost curves. The presence of fixed costs means that average costs initially decline as firms produce more; but for all the reasons discussed in Chapter 6, there is some level of output beyond which average costs increase. When there are large fixed costs, large firms will have lower average costs than small firms and enjoy a competitive advantage (Figure 20.2). Industries with large fixed costs thus tend to have relatively few firms and limited competition. It is not surprising, therefore, that the chemical industry—in which R & D is tremendously important—is highly concentrated.

Increased size also provides firms with greater incentives to undertake research. Suppose a small firm produces 1 million pens a year. If it discovers a better production technology that reduces its costs by $1 per pen, it saves $1 million a year. A large firm that makes the same discovery and produces 10 million pens a year will save $10 million a year. Thus, large firms have more incentive to engage in R & D, and as they do, they grow more than their smaller rivals.

But while a large firm's R & D department may help the firm win a competitive advantage, it may also create managerial problems. Bright innovators can feel stifled in the bureaucratic environment of a large corporation, and they may also feel that they are inadequately compensated for their research efforts. In the computer industry, for example, many capable people have left the larger firms to start up new companies of their own.

Thus, size has both advantages and disadvantages when it comes to innovation. Important inventions and innovations—including nylon, transistors, and the laser—have been produced by major corporations; on the other hand, small enterprises and individual inventors have produced Apple computers, Polaroid cameras, and Kodak film, all of which sparked the growth of major corporations. One objective of antitrust policies is to maintain an economic environment in which small, innovative firms can compete effectively against established giants.

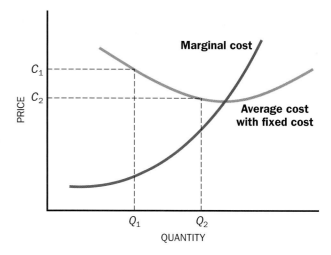

Figure 20.2

COSTS OF RESEARCH AND DEVELOPMENT

R & D costs are fixed costs—they do not vary with the scale of production. In industries that are R & D intensive, average costs will be declining over a wide range of outputs. Firms with low levels of output (Q_1) have higher average costs than those with higher output (Q_2).

LEARNING BY DOING

Some increases in productivity occur not as a result of explicit expenditures on R & D but as a by-product of actual production. As firms gain experience in manufacture, their costs fall. This kind of technological change is called **learning by doing.** The systematic relationship between cumulative production experience and costs—often called the **learning curve**—was first noticed in the aircraft industry; as more planes of a given type were produced, companies found that their costs of production fell dramatically. Such a learning curve is said to be *steep.*

This is the third reason why technological change and imperfect competition go together: the marginal cost falls as the scale of production (and the experience accumulated) increases. The first firm to enter an industry therefore has an advantage over other firms. Even if some of what the first company has learned spills over into other firms, not all of it does. Because of the knowledge the first firm has gained, its costs will be below those of potential rivals, and thus it can always undercut them. Since potential entrants know of this advantage, they are reluctant to enter industries in which learning by doing has a significant impact on costs. By the same token, companies realize that if they can find a product that provides significant benefits from learning by doing, the profits they earn will be relatively secure. Hence, just as firms race to be the first to obtain a patent, so too they race to be the first to enter a product market in which there is a steep learning curve. This behavior is commonly displayed in the computer chip industry.

When learning by doing is important, firms will produce beyond the point at which marginal revenue equals *current* marginal costs, because producing more today has an extra benefit. It reduces future costs of production. How much extra a firm produces depends on the rapidity with which experience pays off.

ACCESS TO CAPITAL MARKETS

Banks are generally unwilling to lend funds to finance R & D expenditures, because the ventures are often very risky and their risks cannot be insured. When a bank makes a loan for a building, the bank winds up with the building if the borrower defaults. If the bank lends for R & D and the research project fails, or a rival beats the firm to the patent office, the bank may wind up with nothing. Banks also often have a hard time judging the prospects of an R & D endeavor—inventors are always optimistic about their ideas. In addition, the inventor is often reluctant to disclose all the information about his idea, either to banks or to potential investors, fearful that someone will steal his idea and beat him either to the market or to the patent office.

Established firms in industries with limited competition and growing demand have little difficulty financing their research expenditures—they can pay for R & D out of their profits. For this reason, most R & D occurs in such firms. In contrast, raising capital *is* a problem for new and small firms, and also for firms in industries in which intense competition limits the profits that any one company can earn. Thus, a firm's dominant position in an industry may be self-perpetuating. Its greater output gives it more to gain from innovations that reduce the cost of production. And its greater profits give it more resources to expend on R & D.

Today much of the R & D in new and small companies is financed by venture capital firms. These firms raise capital, mainly from pension funds, insurance companies, and wealthy individuals, and then invest it in the most promising R & D ventures. Venture capital firms often demand, as compensation for their risk taking, a significant share of the new enterprise, and they usually keep close tabs on how their money is spent.

SCHUMPETERIAN COMPETITION

Although competition in markets in which innovation is important may not live up to the ideal of perfect competition discussed in Chapter 2, it still can be intense. Competition focuses on producing new products as much as on selling old products at lower prices. This kind of competition is often referred to as *Schumpeterian competition,* after a great economist of the early twentieth century, Joseph Schumpeter. Schumpeter began his career in Austria (serving from spring to October 1919 as minister of finance to the emperor of the Austro-Hungarian Empire), and ended it as a distinguished professor of economics at Harvard. His vision of the economy was markedly different from that of the competitive equilibrium model. That model focuses on equilibrium, a changeless condition. He questioned the very concept of equilibrium: to him the economy was always in flux, and the economist's role was to understand the forces driving its changes.

Schumpeter argued that the economy was characterized by a process of creative destruction. An innovator could, through a new product or lower costs of production, establish a dominant position in a market. But eventually, that dominant position would be destroyed, as another new product or process was invented.

He worried that the giant corporations he saw being formed during his lifetime would stifle innovation and end this process of creative destruction. His fears, so far, have been unfounded; indeed, many of the largest firms, like IBM, have not been able to manage the innovative process in a way that keeps up with upstart rivals.

Modern-day Schumpeterians often turn to biology to help them understand the process of change, describing changes as *evolutionary.* They see a slow process of change, with many random elements; firms that are the fittest—that, by luck or skill, manage to discover new products or new ways of doing business that are better, in a particular environment, than their rivals—survive, and their practices spread to other firms.

As respect for and understanding of the importance of innovation have grown, so too have the number of economists who think of themselves as Schumpeterians.

Wrap-Up

COMPETITION AND TECHNOLOGICAL CHANGE

HOW COMPETITION AFFECTS TECHNOLOGICAL CHANGE

Competition spurs R & D:	Competition impedes R & D:
A new innovation enables firms to enjoy profits (profits are driven to zero in standard markets).	Competitors may imitate, thus eroding returns from innovation.
Unless firms innovate, they will not survive.	Competition erodes the profits required to finance R & D.

HOW TECHNOLOGICAL CHANGE AFFECTS COMPETITION

R & D spurs competition:	R & D impedes competition:
R & D provides an alternative to prices as a way for firms to compete; it is one of the most important arenas for competition in modern economies.	Patents give a single firm a protected position for a number of years.
	The fixed costs of R & D give large firms an advantage; thus industries in which R & D is important may have few firms.
	Learning by doing gives a decided advantage to the first entrant into a market.
	Limited access to capital markets for financing R & D is a disadvantage to new and small firms.

Basic Research as a Public Good

R & D expenditures on inventions or innovations almost always give rise to externalities. Externalities arise, as we first noted in Chapter 11, whenever one individual's or firm's action produces costs or benefits to others. The total benefits produced by an R & D expenditure are referred to as its *social benefit*. Even when they have patents, inventors appropriate only a fraction of the social benefit of an invention. A firm that discovers a cheaper way of producing is likely to lower its price during the life of the patent to steal customers away from its rivals, a move that benefits consumers. After the patent expires, consumers benefit even more as rivals beat the price down further. And the benefits of an invention developed by researchers in one industry spill over to others. The transistor, which revolutionized electronics, was invented at AT&T's Bell Laboratories. AT&T reaped the benefits from its direct application to telephone equipment. But the benefits in better radios, television sets, and other products accrued to other firms and many more consumers.

From society's viewpoint, a particularly valuable kind of R & D is **basic research**—the kind of fundamental inquiry that produces a wide range of applications. Basic research in physics, for example, led to the ideas behind so many of the things we take for granted today—the laser, the transistor, atomic energy. The private returns to firms from any basic research they might undertake—which would dictate the amount of R & D spent on basic research in the absence of government intervention—are negligible in comparison with its social benefits. Indeed, the externalities flowing from basic research are so extreme that it can be considered a public good.

Recall the two defining properties of public goods. First, it is difficult to exclude anyone from their benefits. Basic research involves the discovery of underlying scientific principles or facts of nature. Such facts—for example, superconductivity, or even the existence of certain materials that exhibit superconductivity at temperatures considerably above absolute zero—cannot be patented.

Second, the marginal cost of an additional individual enjoying a public good is zero (i.e., consumption is nonrivalrous). Informing an additional person of a basic discovery does not detract from the knowledge that the original discoverer has, though doing so may reduce the potential profits she might earn from it. Indeed, sharing the fruits of basic research as soon as they are available can yield enormous benefits—as other researchers use this knowledge to seek further innovations.

As is true of all public goods, private markets yield an undersupply of basic research. Accordingly, the government supports basic research through the National Science Foundation, the National Institutes of Health, and other organizations. Some of the expenditures of the Department of Defense on R & D also go into basic research. Still, economists are voicing increasing concern that expenditures on basic research are inadequate. Support by the federal government for R & D, outside of defense, has fallen, as a percentage of the nation's output, over the past thirty years, and more than half of government R & D expenditures remain defense related. This emphasis explains why, while the United States devotes about the same proportion of its economy to R & D as do Japan and Germany (as shown in Figure 20.3), less of the total is spent in developing new products and processes to make American industry more competitive. And more is spent in developing better and more effective weapons.

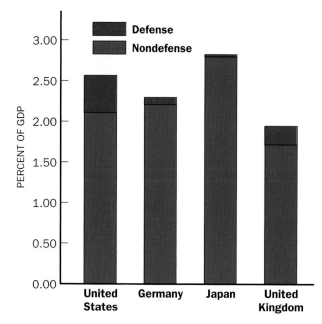

Figure 20.3

COMPARISON OF R & D EXPENDITURES ACROSS COUNTRIES

Total U.S. expenditures, as a percentage of the nation's output, are similar to those of other major industrialized countries. The difference lies in how these expenditures are allocated: U.S. expenditures are concentrated more heavily in defense than those of Germany or Japan.

SOURCE: National Science Foundation, *Science and Engineering Indicators* (2000).

Government Promotion of Technological Progress

Government's efforts to stimulate innovative activity enjoys widespread support, as long as that encouragement takes the form of protecting intellectual property rights and supporting basic R & D. But its other methods of promoting R & D have generated more criticism.

SUBSIDIES

One way in which government has sought to encourage new technologies is through subsidies. Critics of this approach argue that governments have a poor track record in choosing what to subsidize. As evidence, they note that the Concorde, the supersonic airplane developed with the support of the French and British governments that flew commercially from 1976 to 2003, was never able to pay for itself. Closer to home, the U.S. government has spent billions of dollars in an unsuccessful attempt to develop synthetic fuels. Broad-based subsidies, such as R & D tax credits, do not depend on government selection of particular projects, but their relatively high cost to the government makes them controversial. Critics claim that little additional research is generated per dollar of tax revenue lost.

In response, supporters of more active involvement of government in R & D claim that applied research has large positive externalities, implying that the private sector underinvests in it. Policies that support particular sectors of the economy are called **industrial policies** (a term applied to all sectors, including agriculture). They admit that government has not always picked winners. But advocates note that R & D is by its very nature risky. Moreover, they claim that government's successes have in fact been impressive. They point, for example, to the more than 1,000 percent increase in the productivity of agriculture over the past century. This improvement has resulted not only from research undertaken at state agricultural colleges (which the federal government has helped for more than a century) but also from government-supported diffusion of knowledge through agricultural extension services.

International Complications Subsidies have, however, raised the specter of unfair competition in the international arena. Countries facing competition from foreign firms that receive government subsidies often impose countervailing duties—that is, taxes on imports that are intended to offset the benefits of those subsidies. This outcome creates problems; if, for instance, Europe and the United States become engaged in a contest to support some industry, the industry will benefit, but at the expense of the taxpayers in both countries. Thus, international agreements have tried to reduce the extent of subsidization. Broad-based R & D subsidies (such as those provided through the tax system) are still permitted, but more narrowly focused subsidies are either prohibited or viewed as questionable practices.

PROTECTION

Firms in less-developed countries often argue that they need to be insulated from competition from abroad in order to develop the knowledge base required to compete effectively in world markets. This is the **infant industry argument** for protection. Most economists are skeptical. They see this argument mainly as an excuse by rent-seeking firms eager to insulate themselves from competition so they can raise prices and increase profits. The best way to learn to compete is to compete, not to withdraw from competition. If some help is needed to enable firms to catch up, it should be provided in the form of subsidies, whose costs—unlike the hidden costs of higher prices that result from protection—are explicit and obvious.

RELAXING ANTITRUST POLICIES

The antitrust policies explored in Chapter 13 were founded on the belief that government should push markets toward the model of perfect competition. But an increasing awareness of the importance of R & D in modern industrial economies has led some to reconsider this stance.

A major argument for change is that cooperation aimed at sharing knowledge and coordinating research among firms in an industry has the effect of internalizing the externalities of R & D, thereby providing firms with an incentive to invest. But antitrust authorities have long worried that cooperation in R & D could easily grow into cooperation in other areas, such as price setting, which would not serve the public interest. Public policy has tried to find an effective balance. In 1984, the National Cooperative Research Act was passed to allow some cooperative ventures. Enterprises registered under the act are shielded from the risk of paying triple damages in a private antitrust suit but are not shielded from all antitrust risk. By the end of the 1980s, more than a hundred such ventures had been registered. Among the best-known are the Electric Power Research Institute, formed by electric power companies; Bell Communications Research, formed by local telephone companies; and Sematech, a consortium of computer chip manufacturers.

Wrap-Up

TECHNOLOGICAL CHANGE AND THE BASIC COMPETITIVE MODEL

Basic competitive model	Industries in which technological change is important
Assumes fixed technology	The central question is what determines the pace of technological change. Related issues include what determines expenditure on R & D and how learning by doing affects the level of production.
Assumes perfect competition, with many firms in each industry	Competition is not perfect; industries where technological change is important tend to have relatively few firms.
Perfect capital markets	Firms find it difficult to borrow to finance R & D expenditures.
No externalities	R & D confers benefits to others besides the inventor; even with the protection afforded by patents, the inventor appropriates only a fraction of the social benefits of an invention.
No public goods	Basic research is a public good: the marginal cost of an additional person making use of a new idea is zero (nonrivalrous consumption), and it is often difficult to exclude others from enjoying the benefits of basic research.

Technological Change and Economic Growth

Living standards in the United States are far higher today than they were one hundred years ago. The reason is that productivity—the amount produced by the average worker per hour—has increased enormously. Underlying these increases is technological change. In the 1970s and 1980s the pace of growth in productivity in the United States slowed down markedly, from almost 3 percent to around 1 percent. In the latter half of the 1990s, it picked up again, by some measures surpassing even pre-1970 rates. Some of the change has to do with changes in levels of investment in capital, but much of it has to do with the pace of innovation, which has resulted largely from the deliberate allocation of resources to R & D. No wonder then that governments focus so much attention on the issue of how to create an economic environment that is conducive to innovation. While the *incentives* provided by intellectual property protection and government expenditures on basic research are important, several other features of the economy have played a vital role in helping the United States maintain a dominant position. These factors include financial markets (especially venture capital firms) that are willing to finance new ventures, a labor force that is willing to take the risks associated with working for an upstart firm likely to fail, a university system that has attracted the best scientists from around the world, and close ties between research universities and corporations.

Review and Practice

SUMMARY

1. Ideas are different from the goods envisioned in the basic competitive model—they are nonrivalrous.

2. Industries in which technological change is important are almost necessarily imperfectly competitive. Patents are one way the government makes it difficult and costly for firms to copy the technological innovations of others. A firm with a patent will have a government-enforced monopoly. The expenditures on R & D are fixed costs; when they are large, there are likely to be few firms in the industry, and price competition is more likely to be limited.

3. Long-lasting and broad patents reduce competition (at least in the short run), but provide greater incentives to innovate. Excessively broad patent coverage may discourage follow-on innovation.

4. Learning by doing, which provides companies (or countries) that begin making a product first an advantage over all later entrants in lowering costs of production, may be a source of technological advantage.

5. Research and development generally provides positive externalities to consumers and other firms. But since the innovating firm cannot capture all the social benefits from its invention, it will tend to invest less than a socially optimal amount.

6. Basic research has both of the main properties of a public good: it is difficult to exclude others from the benefits of the research, and the marginal cost of an additional person making use of the new idea is zero.

7. A number of governmental policies encourage technological advance: patents, direct spending on research, tax incentives to encourage corporate R & D, temporary protection from technologically advanced foreign competitors, and the relaxation of antitrust laws to allow potential competitors to work together on research projects.

KEY TERMS

rivalrous goods
nonrivalrous goods
patents
intellectual property

royalty
static efficiency
dynamic efficiency
trade secret
learning by doing
learning curve
basic research
industrial policies
infant industry argument

REVIEW QUESTIONS

1. In what ways do industries in which technological change is important not satisfy the assumptions of the basic competitive model?

2. Why do governments grant patents, thereby conferring temporary monopoly rights? Explain the trade-off society faces in choosing whether to offer patents for long or short terms, and whether to offer broad or narrow patents.

3. How do the effects of learning by doing provide an advantage to incumbent firms over prospective entrants?

4. Why might it be harder to raise capital for R & D than for other projects? How can established firms deal with this problem? What about start-up firms?

5. How do positive externalities arise from R & D? Why do externalities imply that there may be too little expenditure on research by private firms?

6. Explain how basic research can be thought of as a public good. Why is society likely to underinvest in basic research?

7. What are the arguments for and against industrial policies?

8. What possible trade-off does society face when it considers loosening its antitrust laws to encourage joint R & D ventures?

PROBLEMS

1. Imagine that Congress is considering a bill to reduce the current twenty-year life of most patents to eight years.

What negative effects might this change have on the rate of innovation? What positive effect might it have for the economy?

2. Suppose that many years ago, one inventor received a patent for orange juice, and then another came forward and requested a patent for lemonade. The first inventor maintained that the orange juice patent should be interpreted to cover all fruit juices, while the second inventor argued that the original patent included only one particular method of making one kind of juice. What are the trade-offs for society as it sets rules for deciding cases such as these?

3. Although a patent ensures a monopoly on that particular invention for some time, it also requires that the inventor disclose the details of the invention. Under what conditions might a company (like Coca-Cola) prefer to use trade secrets rather than patents to protect its formulas?

4. Why might a company invest in R & D even if it does not believe it will be able to patent its discovery?

5. Learning by doing seems to be important in the semiconductor industry, in which the United States and Japan are the main producers. Explain why U.S. and Japanese firms may race to try to bring out new generations of semiconductors. If learning by doing is important in the semiconductor industry, why might other nations try to use an infant industry strategy to develop their own semiconductor industry?

Learning Goals

In this chapter, you will learn

1 About the principal investment alternatives available for your savings

2 The important characteristics of each of these investment options

3 Why some assets yield higher rates of return than others

4 Whether it is possible to "beat the market"

5 Some of the basic rules for intelligent investing

Chapter 21

A STUDENT'S GUIDE TO INVESTING

The 1990s saw a tremendous rise in the value of the stock market—it seemed as if almost every day some new company was selling shares to the public and creating new billionaires overnight. This picture all changed abruptly in 2000 when the stock market collapsed, causing millions to see their paper wealth disappear. The ups and downs of the stock market are often taken as key signals of the economy's health, and the swings of the financial market that we have seen during the past ten years are nothing new. When Alexander Hamilton, as the first U.S. secretary of the treasury under President George Washington, set up the first market for the new government's bonds in 1791, prices skyrocketed by more than 1,000 percent in the first month of trading before collapsing in value.

But what can economics tell us about the stock market and how it behaves? And what can economics tell us about how you should invest your money? Every decision to save is accompanied by a decision about what to do with the savings. They might go under the mattress, but usually savings are invested—most often in bank accounts, the stock or bond market, or the real estate market. These financial opportunities can be thought of as enticements to defer consumption—to save. Broadly speaking, an **investment** is the purchase of an asset in the expectation of receiving a return. For the economy as a whole, **real investment** must be distinguished from **financial investment.** Real investment includes the purchase of new factories and machines. Financial investment is the purchase of financial assets such as stocks and bonds that are expected to generate income or to appreciate in value.

This chapter examines financial investment. It first takes up the major alternatives available to savers and discusses the characteristics of those that are important to investors. From these characteristics, we can establish a simple theory to explain how the prices of financial assets such as stocks and bonds are determined. We can use what we learn about the characteristics of investment alternatives and the theory of asset prices to develop some strategies for intelligent investing.

Investment Alternatives

Savers wishing to invest are offered a range of possibilities. The choices they make depend on the amount of money they have to invest, their motivations to save, their willingness to bear risk, and such personal characteristics as age and health. Of the seemingly endless array of destinations for one's money, five are most important: bank deposits, including certificates of deposit (CDs); housing; bonds; stocks; and mutual funds. In making choices among them, investors focus on four characteristics: return, risk, tax liability, and liquidity.

BANK DEPOSITS

A *bank savings account* (or a similar account) offers three advantages: it pays interest, it allows easy access to the money in it, and it offers security. Even if the bank goes bankrupt, the federal government, through the Federal Deposit Insurance Corporation (FDIC), insures its deposits of up to $100,000.

As savings increase, the value of a higher interest rate also increases. A **certificate of deposit (CD),** which specifies an interest rate on money deposited in a bank for a preset length of time, is as safe as an ordinary bank account and yields a slightly higher return. The drawback of a CD is that withdrawals of money before the preset time has expired are subject to a penalty. The ease with which an investment can be turned into cash is called its **liquidity.** Perfectly liquid investments can be converted into cash speedily and without any loss in value. CDs are less liquid than standard saving accounts.

HOUSING

Two-thirds of American households invest by owning their own homes. Making this investment is far riskier than putting money into a savings account or a CD. Home prices usually increase over time, but not always, and recently the rate of increase has varied widely in different parts of the country. For example, over the past ten years, house prices have gone up almost 530 percent in Massachusetts but only 75 percent in Oklahoma. Prices may rise rapidly in one year, then remain flat or even fall in other years. Most families borrow most of the funds needed to purchase a house, and the owner bears the risk, since she is responsible for paying back the loan regardless of the market price of the house.

Housing as an investment has two other attributes—one attractive and one unattractive. On the positive side, property taxes and the interest on the loan used to purchase the house are generally tax deductible, and for most homeowners the capital gains escape taxation altogether. On the negative side, housing is usually fairly illiquid. If you try to sell your house quickly, on average you will receive less than if you have more time to make the sale. Moreover, the costs of selling a house are substantial, often more than 5 percent of the value of the house—in any case, more than the costs of selling stocks and bonds.

CALCULATING INTEREST RATES

The Federal Reserve Banks of New York and Chicago have Web sites that explain how interest rates are calculated. Their addresses are www.ny.frb.org/education/calc.html#calc and www.chicagofed.org/consumer_information/abcs_of_figuring_interest.cfm.

BONDS

Bonds are a way for corporations and government to borrow. The borrower—whether a company, a state, a school district, or the U.S. government—promises to pay the lender (the purchaser of the bond, or investor) a fixed amount in a specified number of years. In addition, the borrower agrees to pay the lender each year a fixed return on the amount borrowed. Thus, if the interest rate on a ten-year bond is 10 percent, a $10,000 bond will pay the lender $1,000 every year, and $10,000 at the end of ten years. The date on which a loan or bond is to be paid in full is called its *maturity*. Bonds that mature within a few years are called *short-term bonds;* those that mature in more than ten years are called *long-term bonds*. A long-term government bond may have a maturity of twenty or even thirty years.

Bonds may seem relatively safe, because the investor knows what amounts will be paid. But consider a corporate bond that promises to pay $10,000 in ten years and pays $1,000 every year until then. Imagine that an investor buys the bond, collects interest for a couple of years, and then realizes that he needs cash and wants to sell the bond. There is no guarantee that he will get $10,000 for it. He may get more and he may get less. If the market interest rate has fallen to 5 percent since the original bond was issued, a new $10,000 bond now would pay only $500 a year. Clearly, the original bond, which pays $1,000 a year, is worth considerably more. Thus, a decline in the interest rate leads to a rise in the value of bonds; and by the same logic, a rise in the interest rate leads to a decline in the value of bonds. This uncertainty about market value is what makes long-term bonds risky.[1]

Even if the investor holds the bond to maturity, that is, until the date at which it pays the promised $10,000, there is still a risk, since he cannot know for sure what $10,000 will purchase ten years from now. If the general level of prices increases

---

[1]The market price of the bond will equal the present discounted value of what it pays. For instance, a 3-year bond that pays $10 per year each of 2 years and $110 at the end of the 3rd year has a value of

$$\frac{10}{1+r}+\frac{10}{(1+r)^2}+\frac{110}{(1+r)^3},$$

where r is the market rate of interest. We can see that as r goes up, the value of the bond goes down, and vice versa.

at a rate of 7 percent over those ten years, the real value of the $10,000 will be just one-half what it would have been had prices remained stable during that decade.[2]

Because of the higher risk caused by these uncertainties, long-term bonds must compensate investors by paying higher returns, on average, than comparable short-term bonds. And because every corporation has at least a slight chance of going bankrupt, corporate bonds must compensate investors for that higher risk by paying higher returns than government bonds. These higher returns more than compensate for the additional bankruptcy risk, according to economic research. That is, if an investor purchases a very large number of good-quality corporate bonds, the likelihood that more than one or two will default is very small, and the overall return will be considerably higher than the return from purchasing government bonds of the same maturity (the same length of time until they come due).

Some corporate bonds are riskier than others—that is, there is a higher probability of default. These bonds must pay extremely high returns to induce investors to take a chance on them. When Chrysler appeared to be on the verge of bankruptcy in 1980, Chrysler bonds were yielding returns of 23 percent. Obviously, the greater a firm's debt, the more likely it is to be unable to meet its commitments, and the riskier are its bonds. Especially risky bonds are called *junk bonds;* the yields on such bonds are much higher than those from a financially solid firm, but the investor must take into account the high probability of default.

SHARES OF STOCK

Those with savings might also choose to invest in shares of corporate stock. When people buy shares in a firm, they literally own a fraction (a share) of the total firm. Thus, if the firm issues 1 million shares, an individual who owns 100 shares owns 0.01 percent of the firm. Investors choose stocks as investments for two reasons.

First, firms pay some fraction of their earnings—their receipts after paying workers, suppliers of materials, and all interest due on bank and other loans—directly to shareholders. These payments are called **dividends.** On average, firms distribute one-third of earnings as dividends; the remainder, called **retained earnings,** is kept for investment in the company. The amount of a dividend, unlike the return on a bond, depends on a firm's earnings and on what proportion of those earnings it chooses to distribute to shareholders.

In addition to receiving dividends, those who invest in stocks hope to make money by choosing stocks that will appreciate in value and that can then be sold at the higher price. The increase in the realized price of a share (or any other asset) is called a **capital gain.** (If the asset is sold at a price below that at which it was purchased, the investor realizes a *capital loss.*)

Shares of stock are risky for a number of reasons. First, the earnings of firms vary greatly. Even if firms' dividends are the same, differences in profits will lead to differences in retained earnings, and these will be reflected in the value of the shares. In addition, the stock price of a company depends on the beliefs of investors

---

[2]If prices rise at 7 percent a year, with compounding, the price level in 10 years is $(1.07)^{10}$ times the level it is today; $(1.07)^{10}$ is approximately equal to 2—thus prices have doubled.

regarding the prospects of the economy, the industry, and that particular firm. Loss of faith in any one of these could lead to a drop in the stock price. Thus, an individual who has to sell all his shares because of some medical emergency might find they have declined significantly in value. Even if the investor believes that the shares will eventually return to a higher value, he may be unable to wait.

Shares of stock are riskier than corporate bonds. When a firm goes bankrupt and must pay off its investors, the law requires bondholders to be paid off as fully as possible before shareholders receive any money at all. As a result, a bondholder in a bankrupt company is likely to be paid some share of her original investment, while a shareholder may receive nothing. But over the long run, shares of stock have yielded very high returns. While corporate bonds yielded on average an annual real rate of return of 2 percent in the period from 1926 to 2003, shares of stock in the same period yielded a real return of nearly 10 percent.

MUTUAL FUNDS

A **mutual fund** gathers funds from many different investors into a single large pool of funds, with which it can then purchase a large number of assets. A *money market* mutual fund invests its funds in CDs and comparably safe assets.

The advantage of a money market mutual fund is that it offers both higher rates of interest than bank accounts and high liquidity. The fund managers know that most individuals will leave their money in the account, and some will be adding money to the account as others pull money out. They are thus able to put a large proportion of the fund in certificates of deposits and still not have to pay the penalties for early withdrawal. In this way, money market mutual funds give investors the easy access to their funds associated with banks, while providing them the higher return associated with CDs.

Money market mutual funds may also invest their customers' money in short-term government bonds, called **Treasury bills,** or **T-bills.** Treasury bills are available only in large denominations ($10,000 or more). They promise to repay a certain amount (their face value, say, $10,000) in a relatively short period, less than 90 or 180 days, and investors buy them at less than their face value. The difference between the amount paid and the face value becomes the return to the purchaser.

Internet Connection

INDEX FUNDS

Many mutual funds are designed to follow the return of a market index, such as the Standard and Poor's (S&P) 500 index. Standard and Poor's Web site at www.spglobal.com provides the latest information on the performance of their indexes. If you follow the links on the left side of the page, you will find a primer on the mathematics of calculating market indexes.

With most money market mutual funds, you can even write a limited number of checks a month against your account. The major disadvantages of mutual funds are that they may require that you maintain a high minimum balance in your account and they may not be insured by the federal government. However, some money market funds invest only in government securities or government-insured securities, making them virtually as safe as bank accounts.

Other mutual funds invest in stocks and bonds. Typically, they buy stock or bonds in dozens, sometimes hundreds, of different companies. Investors recognize the advantage of **diversification**—of not putting all their eggs in the same basket. If you put all your savings into a single stock and that firm has a bad year, you'll suffer a large loss. If you own stock in two companies, losses in one company may offset gains in the other. Mutual funds, in effect, allow much broader diversification. Of course, if the whole stock market does badly, a stock mutual fund will suffer too. When stocks go down, bonds often go up, so some mutual funds invest in both stocks and bonds. Others invest in risky ventures that, if successful, promise high returns; these are sometimes referred to as "growth" funds. There are many other specially designed mutual funds, and together they are enormously popular. For most investors, the first foray into the bond or stock market is through the purchase of a mutual fund.

Desirable Attributes of Investments

Table 21.1 sets forth the various investment opportunities we have described, with a list of their most important attributes. In surveying the broad range of investment opportunities available, individuals must balance their personal needs against what the different investment options have to offer. The ideal investment would have a high rate of return, be low risk, and be exempt from tax. Unfortunately, as economists always like to point out, investors face trade-offs. You can expect to get more of one desirable property—say a higher expected return—only at the expense of another, such as safety. To understand what is entailed in these trade-offs, we need to take a closer look at each of the principal attributes of investments.

EXPECTED RETURNS

First on the list of desirable properties are high returns. As we have noted, returns have two components: the interest (on a bond), dividend payment (on a stock), or rent (on real estate) and the capital gain. For instance, if you buy some stock for $1,000, receive $150 in dividends during the year, and at the end of the year sell the stock for $1,200, your total return is $150 + $200 = $350 (a rate of return of 35 percent). If you sell the stock for only $900, your total return is $150 − $100 = $50 (a rate of return of 5 percent). If you sell it for $800, your total return is a *negative* $50 (a rate of return of −5 percent).

Table 21.1

ALTERNATIVE INVESTMENTS AND HOW THEY FARE

Investment	Expected returns	Risk	Tax advantages	Liquidity
Banking savings accounts	Low	Low	None	High
CDs (certificates of deposit)	Slightly higher than savings accounts	Low	None	Slightly less than savings accounts
Houses	High returns from mid-1970s to mid-1980s; in many areas, negative returns in late 1980s, early 1990s, high returns since late 1990s	Used to be thought safe; viewed to be somewhat riskier now	Many special tax advantages	Relatively illiquid; may take long time to find "good buyer"
Federal government long-term bonds	Normally slightly higher than T-bills	Uncertain market value in short run; uncertain purchasing power in long run	Exempt from state income tax	Small charge for selling before maturity
Corporate Bonds	Higher return than federal bonds	Risks of long-term federal bonds plus risk of default	None	Slightly less liquid than federal bonds (depends on corporation issuing bond)
Stocks	High	High	Capital gains receive tax preference if stocks held for more than 1 year	Those listed on major exchange are highly liquid; others may be highly illiquid
Mutual Funds	Reflect assets in which funds are invested	Reflect assets in which funds are invested; reduced risk from diversification	Reflect assets in which funds are invested	High
T-bills	About same as CDs	Low	Exempt from state income tax	Small charge for selling before maturity

Few assets offer guaranteed returns. If the stock market booms, a stock share might yield 20 percent; but if the market drops, the total return might be zero or even negative. To compare two alternative investment options, we apply the concept of **expected returns.** The expected return on an asset is the single number that takes into account both the various possible returns per dollar invested and the chances that each of those possibilities will occur. If there is a one-in-four chance (a 25 percent probability) a stock will yield a 20 percent return over the next year, a one-in-two chance (a 50 percent probability) the return will be 5 percent, and a one-in-four chance (a 25 percent probability) the return will be zero, the expected return on the stock is 7.5 percent (.25 × 20 percent + .5 × 5 percent + .25 × 0 percent).

PG&E EMPLOYEES LEARN WHY DIVERSIFICATION IS IMPORTANT

In January 2001, Pacific Gas & Electric Company (PG&E), a major supplier of electricity to northern California, quite suddenly found itself facing bankruptcy. Under California's utility deregulation statutes, PG&E was prohibited from raising its prices to consumers but had to pay market prices for the electricity it purchased to deliver to them. When skyrocketing demand and energy shortages in the West led to record energy prices, PG&E quickly ran out of cash. Wall Street was equally quick to respond. PG&E's stock price plummeted from $31.64 on September 11, 2000, to $10.19 in January. The utility's bonds were downgraded to the lowest echelons of the

INVESTING IN THE NEW ECONOMY

Investors worry about risk. Risk can be reduced by *diversification,* that is, by not putting all your eggs in one basket. Dividing investments among a large number of securities lowers the risk because the value of some may go up when the value of others goes down. In spite of the distinct advantages of risk diversification, many individuals own relatively few securities. One of the reasons is that it is costly to buy and sell different stocks. As a result, individuals have increasingly turned to mutual funds. Mutual funds are financial intermediaries that buy large numbers of securities. Transactions costs are lowered because the securities are bought in bulk. But nothing is free in life. Mutual fund managers have to make a living, and they too charge transaction fees. These costs are substantially lower than if the individual tried to buy an equally diversified portfolio on her own, but they can be considerable nonetheless. Mutual funds have significant tax disadvantages as well. For instance, say you buy shares in a mutual fund in January 2000. In February 2000, the mutual fund sells some shares that it purchased ten years ago, and records a large capital gain.

Then the value of the fund decreases—perhaps because it was a high-technology fund, and technology shares plummeted in April 2000. At the end of the year you may think you have incurred a loss. But the IRS will still insist you pay a tax as if you had a capital gain, because you owned shares in the mutual fund at the time the capital gain was realized. This may seem grossly unfair—you are worse off, yet you have to pay a tax as if you were better off—but that is the way the tax law works.

The new economy has opened up new possibilities for individuals to diversify without large transaction costs. At least one new economy firm (FOLIO*fn*) is offering to allow investors to trade large numbers of stock for a single monthly fee, *with no marginal costs.* This arrangement enables individuals to obtain a highly diversified portfolio, to avoid the transaction costs of mutual funds, and to avoid the tax disadvantages of mutual funds. Like all innovations, it will take time for it to penetrate throughout the economy; but if successful, it may revolutionize how individuals—especially small investors—invest their money.

junk bond range, indicating that Wall Street thought there was little chance that bondholders would be repaid or receive interest. PG&E suspended dividends on its stock, laid off workers, and hired bankruptcy lawyers to assess its options.

For some PG&E employees, the energy crisis that put at risk the booming California economy carried a double threat. Workers were clearly in danger of losing jobs. But more than 80 percent of PG&E's workers were also shareholders who owned stock through the company's retirement plan. PG&E for years had contributed stock one-for-one when employees purchased company stock for their individual 401(k) retirement accounts. Employees had the option of selling the PG&E stock and replacing it with other assets, but not everyone took advantage of the chance to diversify. When PG&E stock lost two-thirds of its value, these workers' 401(k) retirement plans followed suit. Though their pensions and 401(k) could not be seized by a bankruptcy court, workers whose 401(k) plans were heavily invested in PG&E stock had no protection from the risk that stock prices would nosedive.

Longtime employees who failed to diversify out of PG&E stock to obtain a more balanced portfolio saw their dreams of early retirement and a secure old age vanish. When asked why so many employees were overinvested in PG&E stock, one employee replied that people believed in the company that had provided a good living for them (and in some cases, their parents) for most of their lives. The sudden collapse of PG&E underscores the importance of diversification to minimize (though not avoid entirely) the risk of holding individual stocks.[3]

A crowd protests rate hikes by the California utility PG&E, which were made in an effort to fend off bankruptcy.

An important first lesson in investment theory is as follows: *If there were no differences between assets other than the ways in which they produce returns (interest, dividends, etc.), then the expected returns to all assets would be the same.* Why? Suppose an asset offered an expected return of 10 percent while all others offered 6 percent. Investors, in trying to buy the higher-yielding asset, would bid more for it, thereby pushing up its price. As the price rose, the expected return would decline. The upward pressure would continue until the expected return declined to match the level of all other investments.

In fact, for different assets the expected returns per dollar invested differ markedly from one another, because return is affected by a number of other important attributes. These include risk, tax considerations, and liquidity (the ease with which an asset can be sold).

RISK

Most of us do not like the risk that accompanies most future-oriented economic activity. We might spend a few dollars on some lottery tickets or occasionally play the slot machines, but for the most part we try to avoid or minimize risks. Economists say that individuals are *risk averse* and their behavior displays **risk aversion.**

---

[3]Based on an article by Jennifer Bjorhus, "PG&E's 'Family' Falling Apart," *San Jose Mercury News,* January 22, 2001, p. 1.

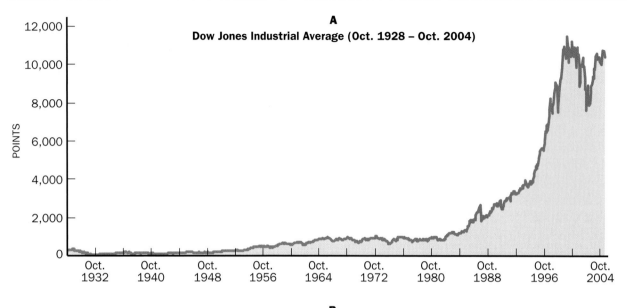

A
Dow Jones Industrial Average (Oct. 1928 – Oct. 2004)

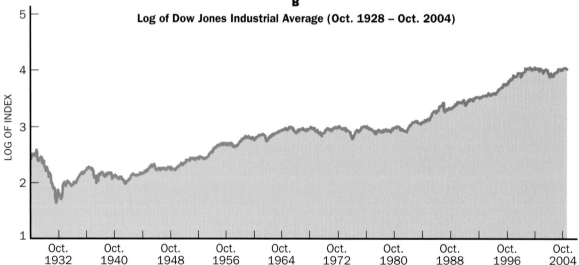

B
Log of Dow Jones Industrial Average (Oct. 1928 – Oct. 2004)

Figure 21.1

STOCK MARKET INDEXES

Panel A shows the closing monthly value of the Dow Jones industrial average, an index of stock prices that is based on the prices of shares in major companies. Panel B plots the natural log of the Dow Jones index so that percentage changes in the level of stock prices can be seen more clearly.

A prime consideration for any investor, therefore, is the riskiness of any investment alternative. Bank accounts, in this regard, are safe. Since government deposit insurance was instituted in the 1930s after the bank failures that occurred during the Great Depression, no one in the United States has lost money in an insured bank account. But investments in housing, stocks, and bonds and most other investments involve risk. The return may turn out to be substantially lower, or higher, than initially expected.

Historically, stocks have yielded a higher average return than bonds, but stocks are riskier—prices on the stock market fluctuate, and they can do so quite dramatically. On the single day of October 19, 1987, stock prices on the New York Stock Exchange fell by 508 points, a drop in value of 23 percent.

Panel A of Figure 21.1 shows the closing monthly value of the Dow Jones industrial average, an index of stock prices that is based on the prices of shares in major companies. Today, thirty companies are included in the index, which was revised in 1999 to include such firms as Microsoft and Intel. Because the index has grown so much since 1928, the 1929 stock market crash barely shows up in the figure. Though the index fell in value almost 13 percent on October 28, 1929, this was a decline of only 38 points—well within the typical range of daily fluctuations in the market today. The largest one-day drop occurred on October 27, 1997, when the Dow Jones index lost 554 points.

The percentage change in the level of stock prices can be seen more clearly by plotting the natural log of the Dow Jones index (panel B). Here, the magnitude of the 1929 crash clearly stands out. The 1929 crash was not simply a one-day drop—three of the five biggest percentage daily declines over the 1900–2000 period occurred in late October and early November of 1929. The record for the largest percentage drop on a single day is held by December 12, 1914, when the market lost 24 percent of its value. Second is October 19, 1987, when the market fell 23 percent. The stock market decline between August 2000 and March 2001 shows up clearly in panel A.

While the New York Stock Exchange is by far the largest stock market in the world, there are others, and in recent years the Nasdaq market has grown in importance. The Nasdaq stock market, created in 1971, is heavily weighted toward the new technology companies. The stocks of Microsoft and Intel, for example, are traded on the Nasdaq market, not the New York Stock Exchange. The addition of Microsoft and Intel to the Dow Jones index in 1999 marked the first time that companies traded on the Nasdaq market, and not the New York Stock Exchange, were included in the index.

Both the Dow Jones index and the Nasdaq index show a tendency to rise over time—leading to capital gains for those who hold stock—but both also show the ups and downs that occur over shorter periods. It is these fluctuations in value that make investing in stocks risky.

Risk can never be avoided completely, and it has been said that financial markets are the places where risk is bought and sold. We can see the effects of changes in risk in Figure 21.2. A reduction in the riskiness of an asset makes it more desirable, thereby shifting the demand curve for the asset to the right. In the short run, the supply of an asset is inelastic. Even in the longer run, supply is likely not to be perfectly elastic. Accordingly, as illustrated in the figure, the price of the asset goes up, from p_0 to p_1. Accompanying the increase in price is a reduction in the return per dollar invested.

An asset that is less risky will have a higher demand. The higher demand will lead to a higher price and lower return. Therefore, the expected return will be lower on assets that are safer. Economists say such desirable assets sell at a *premium,* while assets that are

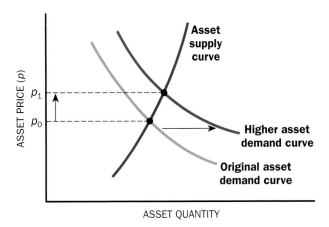

Figure 21.2

EFFECTS OF DIFFERENCES IN RISK

Lowering risk shifts the demand curve for the asset to the right, increasing the equilibrium price and lowering the average return.

riskier sell at a *discount*. Still, market forces ensure that assets of comparable risk must yield the same expected returns.

TAX CONSIDERATIONS

Since different assets are treated differently in the tax code, tax considerations are obviously important in choosing a portfolio. After all, individuals care about after-tax returns, not before-tax returns. Investments that face relatively low tax rates are said to be *tax-favored*.

State and municipal bonds illustrate this point. These bonds yield a lower return than do corporate bonds of comparable risk and liquidity. So why do people buy them? The answer is that the interest on bonds issued by states and municipalities is generally exempt from federal tax. The higher your income, the more valuable this tax exemption is, because your tax savings are greater the higher your tax *rate* (which tends to increase with income). The higher demand for these tax-exempt bonds from high-income investors drives up their price, thereby driving down the return received on the bonds. We can expect the return to decline to the point at which the after-tax return for high-income individuals is at most only slightly higher than for an ordinary taxable bond of comparable risk.

Investing in housing, particularly a house to live in, is another tax-favored form of investment enjoyed by most Americans. Most homeowners can deduct their real estate taxes and the interest payments on their mortgage when calculating their income for tax purposes. In addition, the capital gain from owning the house is not taxed until the house is sold. Even then, the capital gain (up to $500,000 for a married couple) from the sale is not taxed at all. If the tax advantages of home ownership were ever withdrawn, we could expect housing prices to decline precipitously in the short run (in which supply is inelastic), as illustrated in Figure 21.3. It is not likely that tax preferences for housing will be suddenly removed, however, because most voters own houses, and politicians are loathe to anger such a large number of their constituents.

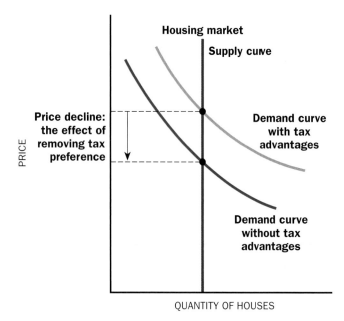

Figure 21.3

EFFECT OF REMOVING TAX PREFERENCES FOR HOUSING

Removing tax preferences for housing will shift the demand curve for housing down, and this will, in the short run (with an inelastic housing supply), cause marked decreases in the price of housing.

LIQUIDITY

The fourth important attribute to consider is liquidity. An asset is liquid if the costs of selling it are very low. A bank account is completely liquid (unless the bank goes bankrupt), because you can turn it into cash at virtually no charge by writing a check. Corporate stock in a major company is fairly liquid, because the costs of selling at a well-defined market price are relatively small.

In the basic competitive model, all assets are assumed to be perfectly liquid. There is a well-defined price at which anything can be bought and sold; any household or firm can buy or sell as much as it wants at that price; and the transaction is virtually without cost. But these assumptions are not always met: the costs of selling or buying an asset are often significant. As noted above, for instance, the costs of selling a house can be 5 percent or more of the house's value. At times, even municipal bonds have been fairly illiquid. The prices at which such bonds could be bought and sold have been known to differ by more than 20 percent.

Expectations and the Market for Assets

Gardeners today find shocking the price of tulip bulbs in early-seventeenth-century Holland, where one bulb sold for the equivalent of $16,000 in today's dollars. The golden age of tulips did not last long, however; and in 1637, prices of bulbs fell by more than 90 percent. Dramatic price swings for assets are not only curiosities of history. Between 1973 and 1980, the price of gold rose from $98 to $613, or by 525 percent; then, from 1980 to 1985, it fell to $318. Between 1977 and 1980, the price of farmland in Iowa increased by 40 percent, only to fall by more than 60 percent from 1980 to 1987. On October 19, 1987, stock values on the U.S. stock market fell by half a trillion dollars—almost 25 percent. Even a major war would be unlikely to destroy one-fourth of the U.S. capital stock in a single day. But there was no war or other external event to explain the 1987 drop.

How can the basic demand and supply model explain these huge price swings? If asset prices depend on the four basic attributes discussed above—expected return, risk, tax treatment, and liquidity—how can demand curves, or supply curves, shift so dramatically as to cause these large price movements?

The answer lies in the critical role that expectations play in the market for assets. Assets such as gold, land, or stocks are long-lived; they can be bought at one date and sold at another. For this reason, the price that individuals are willing to pay for them today depends not only on today's conditions—the immediate return or benefit—but also on some expectation of what tomorrow's conditions will be. In particular, the demand for an asset will depend on what the asset is expected to be worth in the future.

To see how expectations concerning future events affect *current* prices, consider a hypothetical example. People suddenly realize that new smog-control devices will, ten years from now, make certain parts of Los Angeles much more attractive places to live than they are today. As a result, future-oriented individuals will think that ten years from now the price of land in those areas will be much higher, say $1 million an acre. But, they also think, nine years from now it will already be widely recognized that in one short year an acre will be worth $1 million. Hence, nine years from now investors will be willing to pay almost $1 million for the land—even if, at that date (nine years from now), the smog has not yet been eliminated. In that case, these same individuals think, eight years from now investors will realize that in one short year the price will rise to almost $1 million and will pay close to that amount. Working backward like this makes it apparent that if people are confident land is going to be much more valuable in ten years, its price rises today.

Thinking Like an Economist

THE DISTRIBUTION OF WEALTH AND OWNERSHIP OF ASSETS

Although America is a very wealthy society, that wealth is distributed unevenly among American families. The chart shows median family net worth in 2001, classified by 2001 income percentiles. The median income of the 20 percent of families with the lowest incomes was $10,300, and the median net worth of these families was just $7,900. That means that half of the families in this income group had net worth less than $7,900. For families in the top 10 percent of income earners, median family income was $169,600, and median net worth was $833,600.

Not only is less wealth possessed by poor families than by high-income families, but the types of financial and nonfinancial assets held by families also differ by income. Wealthy families are more likely to own stocks and bonds, to hold mutual funds, and to have retirement accounts. The value of holdings of nonfinancial assets—cars, homes, nonresidential property, and businesses—varies widely by income as well. High-income families tend to have greater holdings in cars, residential property, and other property than do families with lower incomes, but the biggest difference across income categories is in the ownership of businesses. The median value of business equity held by the 10 percent of families with the highest 2001 income was $239,500, compared with holdings of $54,400 for the 10 percent of families with the next highest incomes.

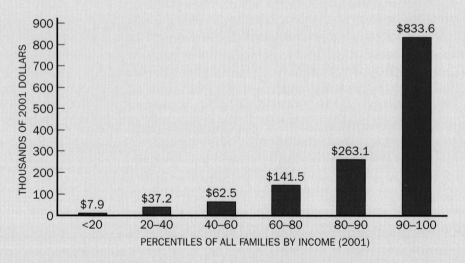

MEDIAN NET WORTH BY INCOME PERCENTILE

Thus, while changes in tastes or technology or incomes or the prices of other goods *today* could not account for some of the sharp changes in asset values described at the start of this section, changes in expectations concerning any of these variables in the future will have an effect *today* on the demand. Markets for assets are linked together over time. An event that is expected to happen in ten or fifteen or even fifty years can have a direct bearing on today's market.

To evaluate the effects of expected future prices on an asset's current price, the concept of present discounted value, introduced in Chapter 3, is important. By calculating the present discounted value, we can measure and compare returns anticipated in the future. Demand today for an asset will depend on the present discounted value that it is expected to fetch when sold in the future.

Present discounted values can change for two reasons. First, they can change because of a change in the expected price of an asset at the time one anticipates selling it. This type of change is illustrated in Figure 21.4. That such expectations of future prices can be quite volatile helps explain the volatility of asset prices. Investors in seventeenth-century Holland were willing to pay enormous prices for tulip bulbs because they expected to be able to sell the bulbs at even higher prices. Such price increases that are solely based on the expectation that prices will be higher in the future—and not based on increases in the actual returns yielded by the asset—are called **asset price bubbles.** Prices continue to rise as long as everyone expects them to rise. Once people believe that the rise will stop, the current price crashes. The tremendous increase in stock prices in the United States during the 1990s led many to worry that it was a bubble that would eventually crash. Others pointed to increased productivity that promised higher corporate profits in the future—an increase in the actual returns that stocks can pay.

Second, present discounted values can change because the interest rate changes. An increase in the interest rate reduces the present discounted value of the dollars that investors expect to receive in the future. This is one reason why increases in the interest rate are often accompanied by drops in share prices on the stock market, and vice versa. Smart investors therefore seek to forecast interest rates accurately. So-called Fed watchers try to anticipate changes in Federal Reserve policies that will affect the interest rate.

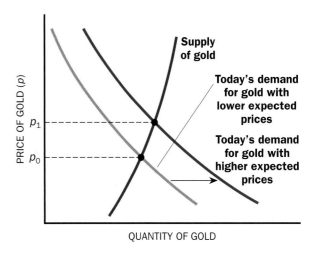

Figure 21.4

HOW EXPECTATIONS CAN SHIFT DEMAND

Expectations that the price of an asset like gold will rise in the future can cause the demand curve to shift to the right, thereby raising the current price.

FORMING EXPECTATIONS

Changes in expectations about future returns or interest rates thus can be reflected in large changes in asset prices today. In part, individuals and firms form expectations by looking at past experience. If a company has steadily grown more valuable, investors may come to expect that pattern to continue. If the Federal Reserve acts to slow the economy by raising interest rates every time inflation rates increase, people come to expect inflation to be followed by higher interest rates.

Psychologists and economists have studied how individuals form expectations. Sometimes people are *myopic,* or short-sighted. They expect what is true today to be true tomorrow. The price of gold today is what it will be tomorrow. Sometimes they are *adaptive,* extrapolating events of the recent past into the future. If the price of gold today is 5 percent higher than it was last year, they expect its price next year to be 5 percent higher than it is today.

When people make full use of all relevant available data to form their expectations, economists say that their expectations are *rational*. The price of gold rises during an inflationary period, but the price of gold also goes down when inflation subsides. Thus, if a person knows that economic analysts are predicting lower inflation, she will not expect the gold price increases to continue. Even when individuals form their expectations rationally, they will not be right all the time. Sometimes they will be overly optimistic, sometimes overly pessimistic (although in making their decisions, they are aware of these possibilities). But the assumption of rational expectations is that on average they will judge correctly.

The 1970s was a decade when adaptive expectations reigned. Many investors came to expect prices of assets such as land and housing to continue to rise rapidly. The more they invested, the more money they made. The idea that the price of a house or of land might fall seemed beyond belief—even though history is full of episodes (most recently in Japan during the 1990s) when such prices fell dramatically. The weak real estate markets of the 1980s in many regions reminded investors of the importance of incorporating historical data in forming expectations.

But in this, as in all types of fortune-telling, history never repeats itself exactly. Since the situation today is never precisely like past experience, it is never completely clear which facts will be the relevant ones. Even the best-informed experts are likely to disagree. When it comes to predicting the future, everyone's crystal ball is cloudy.

Efficient Market Theory

The demand for any asset depends on all four of its basic attributes—average return, risk, tax treatment, and liquidity. In a well-functioning market, there are no bargains to be had: you get what you pay for. If some asset yields a higher average return than most other investments, it does so because that asset has a higher risk, is less liquid, or receives less favorable tax treatment.

That there are no bargains does not mean the investor's life is easy. He still must decide what he wants, just as he does when he goes into a grocery store. Figure 21.5 shows the kind of choices he faces. For the sake of simplicity, we ignore liquidity and tax considerations and focus only on average returns and risk. The figure shows the opportunity set in the way that is usual for this case. Because "risk" is bad, to get less risk we have to give up some average returns. That is why the trade-off has a positive slope. We can see that assets with greater risk have a higher average return. Point *A* represents a government T-bill—no risk but low return. Point *B* might represent a stock or mix of stocks of average riskiness; point *C*, a stock or mix of high risk. A very risk-averse person might choose *A*; a less risk-averse person, *B*; a still less risk-averse person, *C*.

The theory that prices perfectly reflect the characteristics of assets—there are no bargains—is called the **efficient market theory.** Since much of the work on efficient market theory has been done on publicly traded

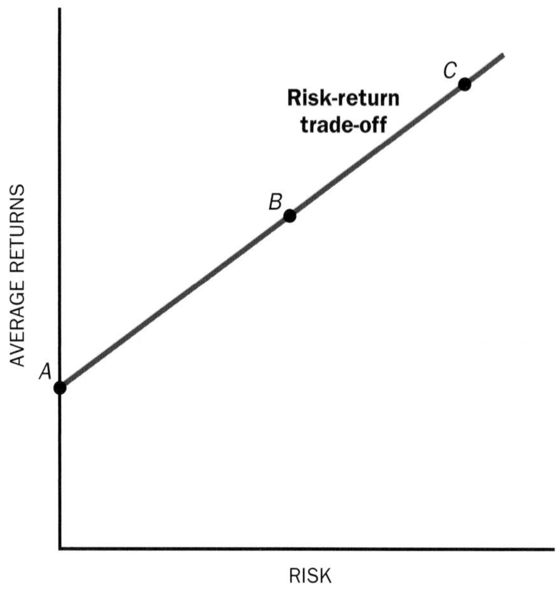

Figure 21.5

THE RISK-RETURN TRADE-OFF

To get a higher expected return, an investor must accept more risk.

stocks, our discussion centers on them. The lessons can be applied to all asset prices, however.

EFFICIENCY AND THE STOCK MARKET

Most people do not think they can wander over to the racetrack and make a fortune. They are not so skeptical about the stock market. They believe that even if they themselves cannot sit down with the *Wall Street Journal* or browse an online broker's site and pick out all the best stocks, someone who studies the stock market for a living could do so. But economists startled the investment community in the early 1960s by pointing out that choosing successful stocks is no easier—and no harder—than choosing the fastest horses.

The efficient market theory explains this discrepancy in views. When economists speak of an efficient market, they are referring to one in which relevant information is widely known and quickly distributed to all participants. To oversimplify a bit, they envision a stock market where all investors have access to *Barron's* and *Fortune* magazines or to one of the many Internet sites devoted to providing good information about businesses, and where government requires businesses to disclose certain information to the public. Thus, each stock's expected return, its risk, its tax treatment, and so on will be fully known by all investors. Because participants have all the relevant information, asset prices will reflect that knowledge.

But it turns out that this broad dissemination of information is not only unrealistic but also unnecessary for the stock market to be efficient. Economists have shown that efficient markets do not require that *all* participants have information. If enough participants have information, prices will move as if the whole market had the information. All it takes is a few people knowledgeable enough to recognize a good deal (bad deal), and prices will quickly be bid up (or down) to levels that reflect complete information. And if prices reflect complete information, then even uninformed investors, purchasing at current prices, will reap the benefit; while they cannot "beat the market," neither do they have to worry about being "cheated" by an overpriced security.

You cannot beat an efficient market anymore than you can beat the track. You can only get lucky in it. All the research done by the many big brokerage houses and individual investors adds up to a market that is in some respects like a casino. This is the irony of the view, held by most economists, that the stock market is an efficient one. If you are trying to make money in an efficient stock market, it is not enough to choose companies that you expect will be successful in the future. If you expect a company to be successful and everyone else also expects it to be successful, given the available information, then the price of the shares in that company will already be high. The only way to make abnormally high profits on stock purchases is to pick companies that will surprise the market by doing better than is generally expected. There are always such companies—the problem is to identify them before everyone else! When Microsoft shares first became available to the public in March 1968, they sold for 19 cents. By 2000, those shares were worth $58 dollars each. Early investors in technology stocks made enormous returns because technology firms did better than anyone had initially expected. Because of the success of many of these companies during the late 1990s, whenever a new one would "go public"—sell shares to the public for the first time—the price would often jump immediately to a very high level. The initial public offering of Google in 2004 exemplified this phenomenon. An investor buying the stock at high market prices can expect to earn only a normal level of profit. Of course, the trick is to know when to sell stocks before everyone else also decides it is time to sell. In 2000, the prices of technology stocks dropped dramatically. Today, shares of Microsoft trade for around $27 each.

The one exception is not really an exception because it involves trading with knowledge that other stock market participants do not have. *Inside traders* are individuals who buy and sell shares of companies for which they work. Studies show that their inside knowledge does in fact enable them to obtain above-average returns. Federal law requires inside traders to disclose when they buy and sell shares in their own company. People who may not have the inside knowledge but imitate the stock market behavior of the insiders also do slightly above average. The law also restricts the ability of insiders to share their information with outsiders and profit from their extra knowledge, and it exacts penalties for violations. After Ivan Boesky made untold millions trading on insider information in the 1980s, he paid large fines and even served time in jail. More recently, Martha Stewart spent five months in jail for obstructing an investigation into possible insider trading.

Because prices in an efficient market already reflect all available information, any price changes are a response to *unanticipated* news. If it was already known that something good was going to occur—for instance, that some new computer model better than all previous computers was going to be unveiled—the price of the firm's stock would reflect this knowledge (it would be high) before the computer actually hit the market. Investors might not know precisely how much better than its competitors the new computer was, and hence they could not predict precisely by how much future earnings were likely to rise. They would make an estimate. The market will reflect the average of these estimates. When the new computer is introduced, there is some chance that it will be better than this average, in which case the price will rise further. But there is also a chance that it will not be quite as good as this average estimate, in which case the price will fall, even though the computer is in fact better than anything else on the market. In the latter case, the "surprise" is that the computer is not as good as the market anticipated.

Since tomorrow's news is, by definition, unanticipated, no one can predict whether it will cause the stock price to rise or to fall. In an efficient stock market, prices will move unpredictably, depending on unexpected news. When a stock has an equal chance of rising or falling in value relative to the market as a whole, economists say that its price moves like a **random walk.** Figure 21.6 shows a computer-generated random walk, giving an idea of how unpredictable such a path is.

The phrase *random walk* conjures up the image of a drunk who rambles down the street with generally unstable—and unpredictable—movements. So too with the stock market. Although the level of all stock prices drifts upward, whether any particular stock will do better or worse than that average is unpredictable. If the stock market is indeed a random walk, it is virtually impossible for investors to beat the market. You can do just as well by throwing darts at the newspaper financial page as you can by carefully studying the prospects of each firm. The only way to do better than the market, on average, is to take greater risks; but taking greater risks also betters your chance of doing worse than the market.

The randomness of the market has one important consequence: *some* individuals are going to be successful. This is bad news for people who want to believe that their insights, rather than luck, are what has enabled them to beat the market.

EFFICIENT MARKETS OR RANDOM NOISE?

Although most economists agree there is little evidence that individuals can consistently beat the market, even when they spend considerable money on information, they disagree over how to interpret this finding. Some see it as evidence of the efficiency of the market, as we have seen. But other economists view it as evidence of nothing more than the market's randomness. Those in the latter group point out that large changes in stock market prices often seem to occur in the absence of any "news" of sufficient magnitude to account for these changes. For example, there are usually ten or fifteen days in the year when the stock market changes by more than 2 percent—a very large change for a single day—without any obvious news-related explanation.

The famous economist John Maynard Keynes compared predictions of the stock market to predictions of the winner of a beauty contest in which what one had to decide was not who was most beautiful, but who the judges would think was the most beautiful. If investors suddenly "lose confidence" in a particular stock or in the whole stock market, or if they believe others are losing confidence, share prices may fall dramatically.

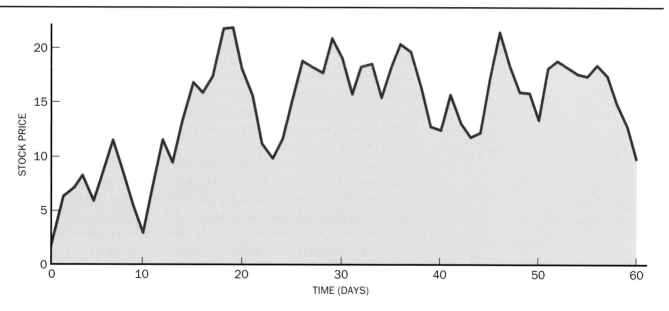

Figure 21.6

A COMPUTER-GENERATED RANDOM WALK

The series plotted here can be thought of as the closing price for a stock over 60 consecutive trading sessions. There is no predicting at the end of each day whether the stock will close higher or lower the next day.

Strategies for Intelligent Investing

So far, we have investigated major investment alternatives available to those who save, some of the important attributes of each, and the ways in which their prices reflect these attributes. If you are lucky enough (have enough money) to be considering some of these alternatives, keep in mind the following four simple rules. These rules will not tell you how to make a million by the time you are twenty-five, but they will enable you to avoid the worst pitfalls of investing.

1. *Know the attributes of each asset, and relate them to your personal situation.* Each asset has characteristic returns, risk, tax treatment, and liquidity. In making choices among different assets, your attitude toward each of these attributes should be *compared with the average attitudes reflected in the marketplace.* Most individuals prefer safer, tax-favored, more liquid assets. That is why those assets sell at a premium (and produce a correspondingly lower average return). Are you willing to pay the amount required by the market for the extra safety or extra liquidity? If you are less risk averse than average, you will find riskier assets attractive. You will not be willing to pay the higher price—and accept the lower return—for a safer asset. And if you are confident that you are unlikely to need to sell an asset quickly, you will not be willing to pay the premium that more liquid assets require. If you are putting aside money for tuition next year, on the other hand, you probably will want to choose a relatively liquid asset.

2. *Give your financial portfolio a broad base.* In choosing among financial assets, you need to look not only at each asset separately but also at all of your assets together. A person's entire collection of assets is called her **portfolio.** (The portfolio also includes liabilities—what she owes—but consideration of these would take us beyond the scope of this chapter.) This rule is seen most clearly in the case of risk. One of the ways you reduce risk is by diversifying your investment portfolio. When a portfolio is well-diversified, it is extremely unlikely that something will go wrong with all the assets simultaneously. An investor with a diversified portfolio must still worry about events such as recessions or changes in the interest rate, which will tend to make all stocks go up or down. But events that primarily affect one firm will have a small impact on the overall holdings.

   Many mutual funds claim more than just diversification: they claim that their research and insight into markets enable them to pick winners. Our discussion of efficient markets casts doubt on these claims. Many other mutual funds do no research, claim no insights, and do nothing more than provide portfolio diversification. These are called *index funds.* There are several measures of the average price of stocks in the market. For instance, the Standard & Poor's (S&P) 500 index is the average price of 500 stocks chosen to be representative of the market as a whole. Other indexes track prices of various categories of stocks, such as transportation, utilities, or high technology. Index funds link their portfolio to these stock market indexes. Thus, there are a number of index funds that buy exactly the same mix of stocks that constitute the S&P 500 index. Naturally, these index funds do about as well as—no better and no worse than—the S&P 500 index, after a small charge for managing the fund is taken into account.

Because the index funds have low expenses, particularly in comparison with funds that are trying to outguess the market, they yield higher average returns to their investors than other funds with comparable risk.

3. *Look at* all *the risks you face, not just those in your financial portfolio.* Many people may be far less diversified than they believe. For example, consider someone who works for the one big company in town. She owns a house, has a good job, and has stock in the company, money in the bank, and a pension plan. But if that single company goes broke, she will lose her job, the value of her stock will fall, the price of her house is likely to decline as the local economy suffers, and even the pension plan may not pay as much as expected.

4. *Think twice before you think you can beat the market!* Efficient market theory delivers an important message to the personal investor. If an investment adviser tells you of an opportunity that beats the others on all counts, don't believe him. The bond that will produce a higher than average return carries with it more risk. The bank account that has a higher interest rate has less liquidity. The dream house at an unbelievable price probably has a leaky roof. The tax-favored bond will have a lower return—and so on. Efficient market theory, as we have seen, says that information about these characteristics is built into the price of assets, and hence built into the returns. Basically, investors can adjust the return to their portfolios only by adjusting the risk they face. Burton Malkiel, author of the best-selling book *A Random Walk Down Wall Street,* applies this theory to personal investment: "Every investor must decide the trade-off he or she is willing to make between eating well and sleeping well. The decision is up to you. High investment returns can be achieved only at the cost of substantial risk taking."[4]

---

[4]7th ed. (New York: Norton, 1999, p. 281)

Review and Practice

SUMMARY

1. Investment options for individuals include putting savings in a bank account of some kind or using them to buy real estate, bonds, or shares of stock or mutual funds.
2. Returns on investment can be received in four ways: as interest, dividends, rent, and capital gains.
3. Assets can differ in four ways: in their average returns, their riskiness, their treatment under tax law, and their liquidity.
4. By holding assets that are widely diversified, individuals can avoid many of the risks associated with specific assets, but not the risks associated with the market as a whole.
5. Today's price of an asset is influenced by expectations of the asset's price in the future. Expectation of a higher price in the future will cause the asset's price to rise today.
6. Asset prices can be very volatile because expectations about future returns can shift quickly.
7. The efficient market theory holds that all available information is fully reflected in the price of an asset. Accordingly, changes in price reflect only unanticipated events and, therefore, are random and unpredictable.
8. There are four rules for intelligent investors: (1) evaluate the characteristics of each asset and relate them to your personal situation; (2) give your financial portfolio a broad base; (3) look at all the risks you face, not just those in your financial portfolio; and (4) think twice before believing you can beat the market.

KEY TERMS

investment
real investment
financial investment
certificate of deposit (CD)
liquidity
dividends
retained earnings
capital gain
mutual fund
Treasury bills (T-bills)
diversification
expected returns
risk aversion
asset price bubbles
efficient market theory
random walk
portfolio

REVIEW QUESTIONS

1. Suppose an investor is considering two assets with identical expected rates of return. What three characteristics of the assets might help differentiate the choice between them?
2. List the principal alternative forms of investment that are available. What are the returns on each called? Rate them in terms of the characteristics described in Question 1.
3. True or false: "Two assets must have equal expected returns." If we modify the statement to read "Two assets that are equally risky must have equal expected returns," is the statement true? Explain your answer.
4. If you found out that several company presidents were buying or selling stock in their own companies, would you want to copy their behavior? Why or why not?
5. What is the efficient market theory? What implications does it have for whether you can beat the market? Does it imply that all stocks must yield the same expected return?
6. Why do economists expect the market to be efficient?
7. What alternative interpretations are given to the observation that individuals cannot, even by spending considerable money on information, consistently beat the market?
8. List and explain the four rules for intelligent investing.
9. True or false: "A single mutual fund may be a more diversified investment than a portfolio of a dozen stocks." Explain.

PROBLEMS

1. Imagine a lottery in which 1 million tickets are sold at $1 apiece, and the winning ticket receives a prize of $700,000. What is the expected return to buying a ticket in this lottery? Will a risk-averse person buy a ticket in this lottery?

2. Would you expect the rate of return on bonds to change with their length of maturity? Why or why not?

3. Why might a risk-averse investor put some money in junk bonds?

4. Would you predict that
   (a) the before-tax return on housing would be higher or lower than the before-tax return on other assets?
   (b) investors would be willing to pay more or less for a stock that has a high return when the economy is booming and a low return when the economy is in a slump than they would pay for a stock whose returns follow just the opposite pattern?
   (c) an investment with low liquidity would sell at a premium or at a discount compared with a similar investment with higher liquidity?

5. Imagine a short-term corporate $1,000 bond that promises to pay 8 percent interest over three years. This bond will pay $80 at the end of the first year and the second year, and $1,080 at the end of the third year. After one year, however, the market interest rate has increased to 12 percent. What will the bond be worth to an investor who is not too concerned about risk at that time? If the firm appears likely to go bankrupt, how will the expected return on this bond change?

6. The golfer Lee Trevino once said: "After losing two fortunes, I've learned. Now, when someone comes to me with a deal that's going to make me a million dollars, I say, 'Tell it to your mother.' Why would a stranger want to make me a million?" Explain how Trevino's perspective fits the efficient market theory.

GLOSSARY

absolute advantage: a country has an absolute advantage over another country in the production of a good if it can produce that good more efficiently (with fewer inputs)

adverse selection: the phenomenon that, as an insurance company raises its price, the best risks (those least likely to make a claim) drop out, so the mix of applicants changes adversely; now used more generally to refer to effects on the mix of workers, borrowers, products being sold, and so forth that results from a change in wages (interest rates, prices) or other variables

affirmative action: actions by employers to seek out actively minorities and women for jobs and to provide them with training and other opportunities for promotion

aggregate saving: the sum of the savings of all individuals in society

antitrust laws: laws that discourage monopoly and restrictive practices and encourage greater competition

asymmetric information: a situation in which the parties to a transaction have different information, as when the seller of a used car has more information about its quality than the buyer

average cost: *total costs* divided by total output

average tax rate: the ratio of taxes to taxable income

average variable costs: total *variable costs* divided by total output

backward induction: approach of starting from the end of the game and working backward to determine the best strategy, often used for strategic interactions that occur a repeated but fixed number of times

basic competitive model: the model of the economy that pulls together the assumptions of self-interested consumers, profit-maximizing firms, and perfectly competitive markets

basic research: fundamental research; it often produces a wide range of applications, but the output of basic research itself usually is not of direct commercial value; the output is knowledge, rather than a product; it typically cannot be patented

beggar-thy-neighbor policies: restrictions on imports designed to increase a country's national output, so-called because they increase that country's output while simultaneously hurting the output of other countries

behavioral economics: a field of economics that rejects the basic model of consumer choice, arguing instead to draw upon the findings of psychologists and economists who conduct laboratory experiments to study the ways people actually make choices

benefit taxes: taxes that are levied on a particular product, the revenues of which go for benefits to those who purchase the product

bilateral trade: trade between two parties

block grants: grants to states, which are given considerable discretion in how the money is spent

budget constraints: the limitations on consumption of different goods imposed by the fact that households have only a limited amount of money to spend (their budget); the budget constraint *defines* the opportunity set of individuals when the only constraint that they face is money

capital gain: the increase in the value of an asset between the time it is purchased and the time it is sold

capital goods: the machines and buildings firms invest in with funds from the *capital market*

capital market: the various institutions concerned with raising funds and sharing and insuring risks, including banks, insurance markets, bond markets, and the stock market

cartel: a group of producers with an agreement to collude in setting prices and output

causation: the relationship that results when a change in one variable is not only correlated with but actually produces a change in another variable; the change in the second variable is a consequence of the change in the first variable, rather than both changes being a consequence of a change in a third variable

certificate of deposit (CD): an account in which money is deposited for a preset length of time and yields a slightly higher return to compensate for the reduced liquidity

Coase's theorem: the assertion that, if property rights are properly defined, then people will be forced to pay for any negative externalities they impose on others and market transactions will produce efficient outcomes

collusion: when firms act jointly (more nearly as they would if there were a monopolist) to increase overall profits

command-and-control approach: the approach to controlling environmental externalities in which the government provides detailed regulations about what firms can and cannot do, including what technologies they can employ

commercial policies: policies directed at affecting either imports or exports

comparative advantage: a country has a comparative advantage over another country in one good as opposed to another good if its *relative* efficiency in the production of the first good is higher than the other country's

compensating wage differentials: differences in wages that can be traced to nonpecuniary attributes of a job, such as the degree of autonomy and risk

competition: rivalry between producers for customers or between consumers for goods and services

complements: two goods are complements if an increase in the price of one will reduce the demand for the other

constant, diminishing, or increasing returns to scale (economies of scale): when all inputs are increased by a certain proportion, output increases in equal, smaller, or greater proportion, respectively; increasing returns to scale are also called *economies of scale*

consumer protection legislation: laws aimed at protecting consumers, for instance by assuring that consumers have more complete information about items they are considering buying

consumer sovereignty: the idea that individuals are the best judges of what is in their own interests and promotes their well-being

consumer surplus: the difference between what a person would be willing to pay and what he actually has to pay to buy a certain amount of a good

corporation income taxes: taxes based on the income, or *profit,* received by a corporation

correlation: the relationship that results when a change in one variable is consistently associated with a change in another variable

countervailing duties: duties (*tariffs*) that are imposed by a country to counteract subsidies provided to a foreign producer

cross subsidization: the practice of charging higher prices to one group of consumers in order to subsidize lower prices for another group

deadweight loss: the difference between what producers gain and (the monetary value of) what consumers lose when output is restricted under imperfect competition; also, the difference between what the government gains and what consumers lose when taxes are imposed

demand: the quantity of a good or service that a household or firm chooses to buy at a given price

demand curve: the relationship between the quantity demanded of a good and the price, whether for an individual or for the market (all individuals) as a whole

demographic effects: effects that arise from changes in characteristics of the population such as age, birthrates, and location

diminishing marginal utility: the principle that says that as an individual consumes more and more of a good, each successive unit increases her *utility,* or enjoyment, less and less

diminishing returns to scale: the principle that as one input increases, with other inputs fixed, the resulting increase in output tends to be smaller and smaller

distribution: the allocation of goods and services produced by the economy

diversification: spreading one's wealth among a large number of different assets

dividends: that portion of corporate *profits* paid out to shareholders

dominant strategy: strategy that works best no matter what the other player does in a game

dumping: the practice of selling a good abroad at a lower price than at home, or below costs of production

dynamic efficiency: an economy that appropriately balances short-run concerns (*static efficiency*) with long-run concerns (focusing on encouraging R & D)

earned income tax credit: a reduction in taxes provided to low-income workers based on the amount of income they earn and the size of their family

economic rent: payments made to a factor of production that are in excess of what is required to elicit the supply of that factor

economies of scope: the situation that exists when it is less expensive to produce two products together than it would be to produce each one separately

efficiency wage theory: the theory that paying higher wages (up to a point) lowers total production costs, for instance by leading to a more productive labor force

entitlement programs: programs that provide benefits automatically to individuals meeting certain criteria (such as age)

entry deterrence: the reduction of competition by preventing other firms from entering the market

entry-deterring practices: practices of incumbent firms designed to discourage the entry of rivals into the market

equilibrium: a condition in which there are no forces (reasons) for change

equilibrium price: the price at which *demand* equals *supply*

equilibrium quantity: the quantity demanded and supplied at the *equilibrium price,* where *demand* equals *supply*

European Union: an important regional trade bloc that now covers most of Europe

excess demand: the situation in which the quantity demanded at a given price exceeds the quantity supplied

excess supply: the situation in which the quantity supplied at a given price exceeds the quantity demanded

exchange: the act of trading that forms the basis for markets

exchange efficiency: the condition in which whatever the economy produces is distributed among people in such a way that there are no gains to further trade

excise taxes: taxes on a particular good or service

experimental economics: the branch of economics which analyzes certain aspects of economic behavior in a controlled, laboratory setting

exports: goods produced domestically but sold abroad

externality: a phenomenon that arises when an individual or firm takes an action but does not bear all the costs (negative externality) or receive all the benefits (positive externality)

factor demand: the amount of an input demanded by a firm, given the price of the input and the quantity of output being produced; in a competitive market, an input will be demanded up to the point where the value of the *marginal product* of that input equals the price of the input

financial investment: investment in stocks, bonds, or other financial instruments; these investments provide the funds that allow investments in *capital goods*

fixed costs: the costs resulting from fixed inputs, sometimes called overhead costs

four-firm concentration ratio: the fraction of output produced by the top four firms in an industry

free-rider: someone who enjoys the benefit of a (public) good without paying for it; because it is difficult to preclude anyone from using a pure *public good,* those who benefit from the goods have an incentive to avoid paying for them (that is, to be a free-rider)

free trade: trade among countries that occurs without barriers such as *tariffs* or *quotas*

fringe benefits: compensation that is not in the form of direct cash to a worker, such as health insurance, retirement pay, and life insurance

fully funded program: a pension program in which each worker pays into an individual retirement account that is invested until the worker retires

game table: table showing the payoffs to each player of a game

game theory: theory designed to understand strategic choices, that is, to understand how people or organizations behave when they expect their actions to influence the behavior of others

game tree: diagram used to represent *sequential games*

General Agreement on Tariffs and Trade (GATT): the agreement among the major trading countries of the world that created the framework for lowering barriers to trade and resolving trade disputes; established after World War II, it has been succeeded by the *World Trade Organization (WTO)*

general equilibrium: the full *equilibrium* of the economy, when all markets clear simultaneously

general equilibrium analysis: a simultaneous analysis of all *capital, product,* and *labor markets* throughout the economy; it shows, for instance, the impact on all prices and quantities of immigration or a change in taxes

gift and estate taxes: taxes imposed on the transfers of wealth from one generation to another

horizontal equity: the principle that says that those who are in identical or similar circumstances should pay identical or similar amounts in taxes

horizontal merger: a merger between two firms that produce the same goods

human capital: the stock of accumulated skills and experience that make workers more productive

imperfect competition: any market structure in which there is some competition but firms face downward-sloping *demand curves*

imperfect information: a situation in which market participants lack information (such as information about prices or characteristics of goods and services) important for their decision making

imperfect substitutes: goods that can substitute for each other, but imperfectly so

imports: goods produced abroad but bought domestically

incentives: benefits, or reduced costs, that motivate a decision maker in favor of a particular choice

income effect: the reduced consumption of a good whose price has increased that is due to the reduction in a person's buying power, or "real" income; when a person's real income is lower, normally she will consume less of all goods, including the higher-priced good

income elasticity of demand: the percentage change in quantity demanded of a good as the result of a 1 percent change in income (the percentage change in quantity demanded divided by the percentage change in income)

individual income taxes: taxes based on the income received by an individual or household

industrial policies: government policies designed to promote particular sectors of the economy

infant industry argument: the argument that industries must be protected from foreign competition while they are young, until they have a chance to acquire the skills to enable them to compete on equal terms

inferior good: a good the consumption of which falls as income rises

information: the basis of decision making that can affect the structure of markets and their ability to use society's scarce resources efficiently

intellectual property: proprietary knowledge, such as that protected by patents and copyright

interest: the return a saver receives in addition to the original amount she deposited (loaned) and the amount a borrower must pay in addition to the original amount he borrowed

investment: the purchase of an asset that will provide a return over a long period of time

job discrimination: discrimination in which disadvantaged groups have less access to better paying jobs

joint products: products that are naturally produced together, such as wool and mutton

labor force participation decision: the decision by an individual to seek work actively, that is, to participate in the *labor market*

labor market: the market in which services of workers are bought and sold

law of supply and demand: the law in economics that holds that, in *equilibrium,* prices are determined so that *demand* equals *supply*; changes in prices thus reflect shifts in the *demand* or *supply curves*

learning by doing: the increase in productivity that occurs as a firm gains experience from producing and that results in a decrease in the firm's production costs

learning curve: the curve describing how costs of production decline as cumulative output increases over time

life-cycle saving: saving that is motivated by a desire to smooth consumption over an individual's lifetime and to meet special needs that arise in various times of life; saving for retirement is the most important aspect of life-cycle saving

liquidity: the ease with which an investment can be turned into cash

loanable funds market: the market in which the *supply* of funds is allocated to those who wish to borrow; *equilibrium* requires that saving (the supply of funds) equals investment (the demand for funds)

luxury taxes: excise taxes imposed on luxuries, goods typically consumed disproportionately by the wealthy

macroeconomics: the top-down view of the economy, focusing on aggregate characteristics

managerial slack: the lack of managerial efficiency (for instance, in cutting costs) that occurs when firms are insulated from competition

marginal benefits: the extra benefits resulting, for instance, from the increased consumption of a commodity

marginal cost: the additional cost corresponding to an additional unit of output produced

marginal product: the amount output increases with the addition of one unit of an input

marginal rate of transformation: the amount of extra production of one good that one obtains from reducing the production of another good by one unit, moving along the *production possibilities curve*

marginal revenue: the extra *revenue* received by a firm for selling one additional unit of a good

marginal tax rate: the extra tax that will have to be paid as a result of an additional dollar of income

marginal utility: the extra *utility,* or enjoyment, a person receives from the consumption of one additional unit of a good

market clearing price: the price at which *supply* equals *demand,* so there is neither excess supply nor excess demand

market demand curve: the total amount of a particular good or service demanded in the economy at each price; it is calculated by "adding horizontally" the individual *demand curves* (that is, at any given price, it is the sum of the individual demands)

market economy: an economy that allocates resources primarily through the interaction of individuals (households) and private firms

market failures: situations in which a market economy fails to attain economic efficiency

market structure: term used to describe the organization of the market, such as whether there is a high degree of *competition,* a *monopoly,* an *oligopoly,* or *monopolistic competition*

market supply curve: the total amount of a particular good or service that all the firms in the economy together would like to supply at each price; it is calculated by "adding horizontally" the individual firm's *supply curves* (that is, it is the sum of the amounts each firm is willing to supply at any given price)

marketable permits: a permit issued by the government, which can be bought and sold, that allows a firm to emit a certain amount of pollution

matching programs: programs in which federal outlays depend on state expenditures

merit goods: goods that are determined by government to be good for people, regardless of whether people desire them for themselves or not

microeconomics: the bottom-up view of the economy, focusing on individual households and firms

monopolistic competition: the form of imperfect competition in which the market has sufficiently few firms that each one faces a downward-sloping *demand curve,* but enough that each can ignore the reactions of rivals to what it does

monopoly: a market consisting of only one firm

monopoly rents: see *pure profit*

moral hazard: the principle that says that those who purchase insurance have a reduced incentive to avoid what they are insured against

multilateral trade: trade between more than two parties

mutual fund: a fund that gathers money from different investors and purchases a range of assets; each investor then owns a portion of the entire fund

Nash equilibrium: game *equilibrium* when both players execute their *dominant strategies* (that is, neither player would change his strategy if offered the chance to do so at the end of the game)

natural monopoly: a *monopoly* that exists because average costs of production are declining beyond the level of output demanded in the market, thus making entry unprofitable and making it efficient for there to be a single firm

nominal rate of interest: the percentage return on a deposit, loan, or bond; the nominal rate of interest does not take into account the effects of inflation

nominal wage: the average wage not adjusted for changes in the prices of consumer goods

nonpecuniary attributes: aspects of a job other than the wage it pays

nonrivalrous goods: goods whose consumption or use by one person does not exclude consumption by another person

normal good: a good the consumption of which rises as income rises

normative economics: economics in which judgments about the desirability of various policies are made; the conclusions rest on value judgments as well as facts and theories

North American Free Trade Agreement (NAFTA): the agreement between Canada, the United States, and Mexico that lowered trade and other barriers among the countries

oligopoly: the form of *imperfect competition* in which the market has several firms, sufficiently few that each one must take into account the reactions of rivals to what it does

opportunity cost: the cost of a resource, measured by the value of the next-best alternative use of that resource

opportunity set: a summary of the choices available to individuals, as defined by *budget constraints* and *time constraints*

Pareto efficient: a resource allocation is said to be Pareto efficient if there is no rearrangement that can make anyone better off without making someone else worse off

partial equilibrium analysis: an analysis that focuses on only one or a few markets at a time

patent: a government decree giving an inventor the exclusive right to produce, use, or sell an invention for a period of time

pay-as-you-go program: pension programs, such as Social Security, in which the taxes paid by today's workers go to pay the benefits of today's retirees

payroll taxes: taxes based on payroll (wages) that are used to finance the Social Security and Medicare programs

perfect competition: a situation in which each firm is a *price taker*—it cannot influence the market *price*; at the market price, the firm can sell as much as it wishes, but if it raises its price, it loses all sales

piece-rate system: a compensation system in which workers are paid specifically for each item produced

positive economics: economics that describes how the economy behaves and predicts how it might change—for instance, in response to some policy change

positive externalities: phenomena that occur when an individual or firm takes an action but does not receive all the benefits

present discounted value: how much an amount of money to be received in the future is worth right now

price: the price of a good or service is what must be given in exchange for the good

price ceiling: a maximum *price* above which market prices are not legally allowed to rise

price discrimination: the practice of a firm charging different *prices* to different customers or in different markets

price dispersion: a situation that occurs when the same item is sold for different *prices* by different firms

price elasticity of demand: the percentage change in quantity demanded of a good as the result of a 1 percent change in *price* (the percentage change in quantity demanded divided by the percentage change in price)

price elasticity of supply: the percentage change in quantity supplied of a good as the result of a 1 percent change in *price* (the percentage change in quantity supplied divided by the percentage change in price)

price floor: a minimum *price* below which market prices are not legally allowed to fall

price system: the economic system in which *prices* are used to allocate scarce resources

price taker: firms that take the *price* for the good or service they sell as given; the price is unaffected by their level of production

principal: the original amount a saver deposits in a bank (lends) or a borrower borrows

prisoner's dilemma: a situation in which the noncooperative pursuit of self-interest by two parties makes them both worse off

private marginal cost: the *marginal cost* of production borne by the producer of a good; when there is a negative externality, such as air pollution, private marginal cost is less than social marginal cost

private property: ownership of property (or other assets) by individuals or corporations; under a system of private property, owners have certain *property rights*, but there may also be legal restrictions on the use of property

privatization: the process whereby functions that were formerly undertaken by government are delegated instead to the private sector

producer surplus: the difference between the *price* for which a producer would be willing to provide a good or service and the actual price at which the good or service is sold

product differentiation: the fact that similar products (like breakfast cereals or soft drinks) are perceived to differ from one another and thus are imperfect substitutes

product market: the market in which goods and services are bought and sold

production efficiency: the condition in which firms cannot produce more of some goods without producing less of other goods; the economy is on its *production possibilities curve*

production function: the relationship between the inputs used in production and the level of output

production possibilities: the combination of outputs of different goods that an economy can produce with given resources

production possibilities curve: a curve that defines the opportunity set for a firm or an entire economy and gives the possible combination of goods (outputs) that can be produced from a given level of inputs

product-mix efficiency: the condition in which the mix of goods produced by the economy reflects the preferences of consumers

profits: total *revenues* minus total costs

progressive tax system: describes a tax system in which the rich pay a larger fraction of their income than the poor

property rights: the rights of an owner of *private property*; these typically include the right to use the property as she sees fit (subject to certain restrictions, such as zoning) and the right to sell it when and to whom she sees fit

property taxes: taxes based on the value of property

protectionism: the policy of protecting domestic industries from the competition of foreign-made goods

public good: a good, such as national defense, that costs little or nothing for an extra individual to enjoy and the costs of preventing any individual from the enjoyment of which are high; public goods have the properties of nonrivalrous consumption and nonexcludability

pure profit: the profit earned by a monopolist that results from its reducing output and increasing the *price* from the level at which price equals *marginal cost*; also called *monopoly rents*

quotas: limits on the amount of foreign goods that can be imported

quota rents: *profits* that result from the artificially created scarcity of *quotas* and accrue to firms that are allocated the rights to import

rational choice: a process in which individuals weigh the costs and benefits of each possibility and in which the choices made are those within the opportunity set that maximize net benefits

rationing systems: any system of allocating scarce resources, applied particularly to systems other than the *price system*; rationing systems include rationing by coupons and rationing by queues

real investment: the investment that is part of aggregate expenditures, such as the purchase of new factories and machines

real product wage: the wage divided by the price of the good being produced

real rate of interest: the real return to saving, equal to the nominal rate of interest minus the rate of inflation

real wage: the average wage adjusted for changes in the prices of consumer goods

regressive tax system: describes a tax system in which the poor pay a larger fraction of their income than the rich

regulatory capture: a term used to describe a situation in which regulators serve the interests of the regulated rather than the interests of consumers

relative elasticity: a good is said to be **relatively elastic** when its *price elasticity of demand* is greater than unitary; a good is said to be **relatively inelastic** when the price elasticity of its demand is less than unitary

relative price: the ratio of any two prices; the relative price of CDs and DVDs is just the ratio of their prices

rent seeking: the name given to behavior that seeks to obtain benefits from favorable government decisions, such as protection from foreign competition

repeated games: games that are played many times over by the same players

reputation: the "good will" of a firm resulting from its past performance; maintaining one's reputation provides an incentive to maintain quality

reservation wage: the wage below which an individual chooses not to participate in the *labor market*

restrictive practices: practices of oligopolists designed to restrict competition, including vertical restrictions like exclusive territories

retained earnings: that part of the net earnings of the firm that are not paid out to shareholders, but kept by the firm

revenue curve: the relationship between a firm's total output and its *revenues*

revenues: the amount a firm receives for selling its products, equal to the *price* received multiplied by the quantity sold

right-to-work laws: laws that prevent union membership from being a condition of employment

rivalrous goods: goods whose consumption or use by one person excludes consumption by another person

royalty: a fee charged by a patent holder that allows others to use its patent

sales tax: a tax imposed on the purchase of goods and services

scarcity: term used to describe the limited availability of resources, so that if no *price* were charged for a good or service, the *demand* for it would exceed its *supply*

search: the process by which consumers gather information about what is available in the market, including *prices,* or by which workers gather information about the jobs that are available, including wages

sequential game: a game in which players take turns and each can observe what choices were made in earlier moves

shortage: a situation in which *demand* exceeds *supply* at the current *price*

signal: to convey information, for example a prospective worker's earning a college degree to persuade an employer that he has desirable characteristics that will enhance his productivity

sin taxes: *excise taxes* on alcohol and tobacco

slope: the amount by which the value along the vertical axis increases as the result of a change in one unit along the horizontal axis; the slope is calculated by dividing the change in the vertical axis (the "rise") by the change in horizontal axis (the "run")

social insurance: insurance provided by the government to individuals, for instance, against disabilities, unemployment, or health problems (for the aged)

social marginal cost: the *marginal cost* of production, including the cost of any negative externality, such as air pollution, borne by individuals in the economy other than the producer

static efficiency: the efficiency of the economy with given technology; taxes used to finance basic research and monopoly power resulting from patents cause a loss in static efficiency

statistical discrimination: differential treatment of individuals of different gender or race that is based on the use of observed *correlations* (statistics) between performance and some observable characteristics; it may even result from the use of variables like education in which there is a causal link to performance

strategic behavior: decision making that takes into account the possible reactions of others

strategic trade theory: the theory that protection can give a country a strategic advantage over rivals, for instance by helping reduce domestic costs as a result of economies of scale

substitutes: two goods are substitutes if the demand for one increases when the price of the other increases

substitution effect: the reduced consumption of a good whose *price* has increased that is due to the changed *trade-off,* the fact that one has to give up more of other goods to get one more unit of the high-priced good; the substitution effect is associated with a change in the *slope* of the *budget constraint*

sunk costs: costs that have been incurred and cannot be recovered

supply: the quantity of a good or service that a household or firm would like to sell at a particular *price*

supply curve: the relationship between the quantity supplied of a good and the *price,* whether for a single firm or the market (all firms) as a whole

surplus: the magnitude of the gain from trade, the difference between what an individual would have been willing to pay for a good and what she has to pay

tariffs: taxes imposed on imports

tax expenditure: the revenue lost from a *tax subsidy*

tax subsidies: subsidies provided through the tax system to particular industries or to particular expenditures, in the form of favorable tax treatment

theory: a set of assumptions and the conclusions derived from those assumptions put forward as an explanation for some phenomena

thin (or incomplete) markets: markets with relatively few buyers and sellers

time constraints: the limitations on consumption of different goods imposed by the fact that households have only a limited amount of time to spend (twenty-four hours a day); the time constraint defines the *opportunity set* of individuals if the only constraint that they face is time

time inconsistency: a phenomenon that occurs when it is not in the best interest of a player to carry out a threat or promise that was initially designed to influence the other player's actions

time value of money: the fact that a dollar today is worth more than a dollar in the future

total costs: the sum of all *fixed costs* and *variable costs*

trade creation: new trade that is generated as a result of lowered *tariff* barriers

trade diversion: trade that is diverted away from outside countries as a result of lowering *tariffs* between the members of a trading bloc

trade-offs: the amount of one good (or one desirable objective) that must be given up to get more of another good (or to attain more of another desirable objective)

trade secret: an innovation or knowledge of a production process that a firm does not disclose to others

tragedy of the commons: an analogy used to describe the deletion of a common resource when individual users fail to take into account the impact of their actions on the common resource

transfer programs: programs directly concerned with redistribution, such as AFDC, TANF, and Medicaid, that move money from one group in society to another

Treasury bills (T-bills): short-term government bonds that are available only in large denominations

trusts: organizations that attempted to control certain markets in the late nineteenth century; they were designed to allow an individual or group owning a small fraction of the total industry to exercise control

union shops: unionized firms in which all workers are required to join the union as a condition of employment

unitary elasticity: a *demand curve* has unitary elasticity if the demand for the commodity decreases by 1 percent when the *price* increases by 1 percent; if *demand* has unitary elasticity, then expenditures on the good do not depend at all on price; a *supply curve* has unitary elasticity if the supply of the commodity increases by 1 percent when the price increases by 1 percent

utility: the level of enjoyment an individual attains from choosing a certain combination of goods

value of the marginal product of labor: the value of the extra output produced by an extra unit of labor; it is calculated by multiplying the *marginal product* of labor times the *price* of the good which is being produced

variable costs: the costs resulting from variable inputs

vertical equity: the principle that people who are better off should pay more taxes

vertical merger: a merger between two firms, one of which is a supplier or distributor for the other

voting paradox: the fact that under some circumstances there may be no determinate outcome with majority voting: choice A wins a majority over B, B wins over C, and C wins over A

wage discrimination: paying lower wages to women or minorities

World Trade Organization (WTO): the organization established in 1995 as a result of the Uruguay round of trade negotiations; replacing *GATT*, it is designed to remove trade barriers and settle trade disputes

zero elasticity: the situation that exists when the quantity demanded (or supplied) will not change, regardless of changes in *price*

CREDITS

INDEX